DAY BY DAY IN
JEWISH SPORTS HISTORY

DAY BY DAY IN
JEWISH SPORTS HISTORY

by

Bob Wechsler

KTAV Publishing House, Inc.
in association with
The American Jewish Historical Society

Copyright © 2008 by Bob Wechsler

Library of Congress Cataloging-in-Publication Data

Wechsler, Robert.
Day by day in Jewish sports history / by Robert Wechsler.
p. cm.
ISBN – 13: 978-0-88125-969-8 (Paperback) ISBN – 978-1-60280-013-7 (Hardcover)
1. Jewish athletes – United States – History. 2. Jewish athletes – Israel – History. 3. Jewish athletes – History. 4. Jews – Sports – United States – History. 5. – Jews – Sports – Israel – History. 6. Jews – Sports – History. 7. Olympics – History. I. Title.
GV709.6.W43 2007
796.089'924073–dc22
                                                         2007020008

Published by:
KTAV Publishing House, Inc.
930 Newark Avenue
Jersey City, NJ 07306
e-mail: bernie@ktav.com
www.ktav.com
Tel: (201) 963-9524
Fax: (201) 963-0102

DEDICATION

This book in calendar form is published on the 75th anniversary of Hank Greenberg's 1933 rookie year in Major League Baseball. Greenberg emerged from his first season with the Detroit Tigers to become both a Hall of Fame baseball player and a beacon for Jewish Americans. At a time when the social standing of Jews in America, and especially in Europe, was not only difficult but perilous, the 6-foot-4 Greenberg demonstrated that a Jew can excel at the "national pastime," and do it with power, grace and dignity. I've always thought that the characterization by the great "Washington Post" sports-writer Shirley Povich said it beautifully: "Hank Greenberg was the perfect standard-bearer for Jews: He was smart, he was proud, and he was big!"

– Ira Berkow

Ira Berkow is a New York Times Pulitzer Prize winning sports columnist and author; his most recent book is "Full Swing – Hits, Runs and Errors in A Writer's Life."

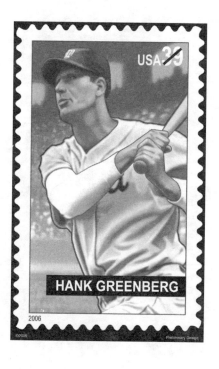

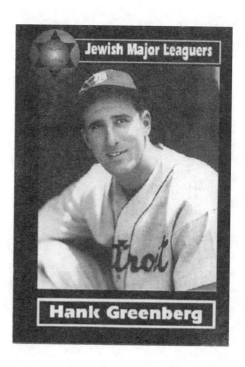

TABLE OF CONTENTS

  Jewish athletes featured on Wheaties boxes
  NBA first-round draft picks
  Jewish athletes on Time Magazine covers
  Jewish women on Sports Illustrated covers
  Winning jockeys in triple crown races
  Tallest Jews in the NBA
  Longest consecutive-game hitting streaks
  Final outs of Sandy Koufax's no-hitters
  Final outs of Ken Holtzman's no-hitters
  NFL first-round draft picks
  Foreign-born major-league players
  20-game winners
  Players on Stanley Cup-winning teams
  Major sports league teams' principal owners

ACKNOWLEDGMENTS

I would like to thank the staffs at public libraries in Easton (Pa.), Allentown, and Philadelphia, as well as at YIVO Institute for Jewish Research and the Dorot Jewish Division of the New York Public Library.

Also, thanks to college library staffs and volunteers at Pennsylvania State University, Rutgers University, West Virginia University, Syracuse University, Lafayette College, Lehigh University, Moravian College, New York University, and City College of New York.

Personal thanks to Shel Wallman of Jewish Sports Review, Martin Abramowitz of Jewish Major Leaguers, hockey maven Irv Osterer, Chad Reese of the Pro Football Hall of Fame, and Matt Zeysing of the Naismith Memorial Basketball Hall of Fame.

For their help in providing photographs, I thank Rosie Leutzinger of the Professional Bowlers Association, Steve Kirschner of the University of North Carolina, Greg Hotchkiss of the University of Pittsburgh, Mike Stagnitta of Lehigh University, Kevin Bonner of Temple University, Susan Cornelius Edson of Syracuse University, and Phil LaBella of Lafayette College.

The U.S. Olympic Committee gave permission to use a majority of the photos that appear in this book. Many others were file publicity photos sent by request over a three-decade period to The Express-Times by various professional sports teams and organizations.

Special thanks to the American Jewish Historical Society, Jeffrey Gurock for his preface, and Ira Berkow for writing the dedication to Hank Greenberg.

Suggestions and guidance from KTAV's Bernie Scharfstein and Adam Bengal were invaluable in bringing this "*meshugenah*" project to fruition.

Thanks to James Moening and Nina Lewis for technical help, to Scott and Jill Homiak for their encouragement, to Lynn and Evan Myers for their hospitality, and to Hope Hartman for continuous support while we simultaneously worked on our books.

And finally, thanks to commissioners Florence and Joe Wechsler, who on April 17, 1948, merged their leagues to form one superconference.

PREFACE

By Jeffrey S. Gurock

Like its parent discipline, American Jewish history, the serious study of Jews, Judaism and this country's sports has come a long way from the days when its defensive writers felt that they needed to prove that Jews were athletic, much like other amateur chroniclers were out to evidence that these loyal United States citizens could be pioneers and patriots. Today, scholars of the American Jewish athletic scene are instead concerned with understanding the dynamics of how a foreign cultural phenomenon - called sports - entered into the lives of immigrant Jewish men and women – and especially their children – and to comprehend the identity issues that arose in attempting to be Jews and athletes. Their findings have positioned this sub-field squarely within an increasingly-sophisticated American Jewish historiography.

Yet, as we continue to conceptualize the details of the Jewish encounter with American sports, essential spade-work still needs to be done to bring to the fore the primary source materials requisite to advance our inquiries. Day by Day in Jewish Sports History which provides a world perspective while focusing on the American scene does just that and is thus a welcome addition to our team. A discerning reader will, for example, run with the intriguing finding that in "1947 CCNY barred its teams from competing against any team coached by Everett Shelton because of anti-Semitic remarks he allegedly made during a December 28, 1946 loss in New York" and place that prideful response within the larger context of post-war Jewish activism to insure group status in America. Similarly, a student of black-Jewish relations will ponder the realities of the day that led Joe Choynski and Jack Johnson to "share a jail cell for 28 days after Texas Rangers arrest[ed] them for participating in a bout involving mixed races." By the way, the Jewish heavyweight beat the future champion. All told, Bob Wechsler's effort, chock full of sports trivia, will educate and entertain fans and scholars alike.

Jeffrey S. Gurock is Libby M. Klaperman Professor of Jewish History
at Yeshiva University where he also serves as assistant men's basketball coach.
He is the author of Judaism's Encounter with American Sports *(Indiana University Press).*

INTRODUCTION

While growing up in the 1950s, I was aware of only a handful of Jewish athletes.

I saw Dolph Schayes and the Syracuse Nationals play Philadelphia in an NBA game in Hershey, Pa., but I was more interested in watching Wilt Chamberlain and the Warriors.

I knew Joe Ginsberg, the Baltimore Orioles' catcher from 1956 to 1960, was Jewish. However, I also owned baseball cards of Barry Latman and Saul Rogovin without realizing they, too, were *landsmen*.

The announcement that former boxer Ruby Goldstein – a champion way before I was born – was going to speak at my Jewish Community Center's father-son banquet was kind of disappointing. The great Johnny Unitas had been the guest speaker the previous year.

Then in 1962 when I was studying for my bar mitzvah, the rabbi invited my family for seder. I quickly lost interest in searching for the *afikoman* when I found an even better prize in his study – a book on Jewish athletes.

"I knew you'd be interested in that one," Rabbi Kramer said smiling. I borrowed the book – probably *Jews in American Sports* by Harold and Meir Ribalow – and discovered the stories of Barney Ross, Benny Leonard, and Benny Friedman.

Since the publication of the Ribalow book in 1948, Jewish participation in sports has been well documented. Most volumes, however, are either sociological studies or synopses of the careers of just the greatest 100 or so Jewish athletes.

In daily journalism, retrospectives are saved for the ends of superstars' careers, inductions into Halls of Fame, and obituaries. Most athletes are fortunate to get their retirements announced in a line of tiny type in the "transactions" list.

In 36 years of producing newspaper sports sections, I've observed athletes' careers a day at a time. Tomorrow there's another regular-season college basketball game in Madison, Wis.; the second round of a tennis tournament in Bastad, Sweden; a six-round bout on the undercard of a boxing show in Bay St. Louis, Miss.

I take special interest in charting the careers of Jewish athletes – the pitching or batting lines of Steve Stone, Norm Miller, and Eddie Zosky; the point totals for Neal Walk, Ernie Grunfeld, and Anita Kaplan in basketball; the standings of Amy Alcott, Bruce Fleischer, and Jonathan Kaye on the golf leaderboards.

Day by Day in Jewish Sports History is the culmination of years of recording such information from newspapers and wire services. Library microfilm, almanacs, and Internet sites such as www.retrosheet.org for baseball boxscores and www.paperofrecord.com for *The Sporting News* archive helped fill in past performances.

Basketball and boxing, so important to early 20th Century immigrants in helping them assimilate into American culture, are well represented here. So are traditionally "non-Jewish" sports such as equestrian, speed skating, and even bullfighting.

The daily calendar format awards the same importance to winning an Olympic gold medal as scoring a hat trick in a minor-league hockey game. A game-winning goal by Sarah Whalen in soccer gets the same treatment as a Sandy Koufax no-hitter.

Day by Day in Jewish Sports History celebrates the wide participation and accomplishments of Jews in athletics – one event at a time.

Bob Wechsler

JANUARY 1

GAMEBREAKERS

1920 – **Arnold Horween** kicks the winning extra point as Harvard beats Oregon 7-6 in the Rose Bowl. The Crimson complete a 9-0-1 season and win their last of seven national football championships.

1930 – **Harry Edelson,** born in Tel Aviv, catches touchdown passes of 55 and 39 yards for Southern Cal as the Trojans beat Pitt 47-14 in the Rose Bowl.

1935 – **Barney Mintz** throws a 25-yard touchdown pass and kicks two extra points as Tulane rallies from a 14-0 halftime deficit to beat Temple 20-14 in the first Sugar Bowl game in New Orleans. **Dave Smukler** plays the entire 60 minutes for Temple and runs 25 yards for a touchdown.

1949 – **Sid Tanenbaum** scores 15 points as the New York Knicks defeat the Philadelphia Warriors 88-80.

1949 – **Joel Kaufman** scores 19 points to lead NYU past Connecticut 70-51.

2001 – **Hayden Epstein's** 41-yard field goal in the fourth quarter provides the margin of victory as Michigan defeats Auburn 31-28 in the Citrus Bowl in Orlando, Fla.

STRONG IN DEFEAT

1929 – California halfback/safety **Benny Lom** rushes for 121 yards and is named the Rose Bowl's outstanding player despite an 8-7 loss to Georgia Tech.

MAZEL TOUGH

1914 – **Waldemar Holberg** of Denmark wins a 20-round decision over Ray Bronson in Melbourne, Australia, to capture the vacant world welterweight title. Holberg will hold the crown for only 23 days.

1915 – Light-heavyweight **Battling Levinsky** fights three bouts – one each in New York City, Brooklyn, N.Y., and Waterbury, Conn. Two are 10-rounders and one goes 12 rounds. All are declared no-decisions, and Levinsky earns $400 for his day's work.

1929 – **Joey Sangor** beats junior-lightweight champion Tod Morgan in 10 rounds in Milwaukee, but is not declared the new champion because Wisconsin state law prohibits a bout to be decided by a referee or judge.

1937 – **Helen Bernhard** defeats Hope Knowles 6-0, 8-6 to win the National Junior Girls Indoor Tennis Championship in Brookline, Mass. A year later, she retains her title with a 3-6, 7-5, 6-3 victory over Cissy Madden.

1948 – Miami freshman **Sidney Schwartz** defeats **Grant Golden** 6-0, 6-2, 3-6, 6-2 to win the National Junior Indoor tennis title for the second time at the 7th Regiment Armory in N.Y.

1965 – **Julie Heldman** defeats Carmen Coronado 6-3, 1-6, 6-2 to win the Valencia Open clay-court tennis tournament in Spain.

RECORD SETTERS

1947 – **Al Hoisch** sets three Rose Bowl records in UCLA's 45-14 loss to Illinois. He returns a kickoff 103 yards for a touchdown, registers 170 yards total kick return yards (on four attempts), and averages 44.5 yards per return.

A STAR IS BORN

1885 – **Young Joseph Aschel** (British welterweight boxer)

1886 – **Jacob Livingston** (New York Giants pitcher)

1898 – **Young Montreal** (bantamweight boxer)

1907 – **Norman Armitage** (fencing)

1911 – **Hank Greenberg** (Detroit Tigers, Pittsburgh Pirates first baseman/outfielder)

1915 – **Andre Jesserun** (welterweight boxer)

1921 – **Bernard Kapitansky** (Long Island U., NFL Brooklyn Dodgers guard)

1921 – **Herbie Kronowitz** (middleweight boxer)

1977 – **Eyal Erlich** (Israeli tennis)

JANUARY 2

GAMEBREAKERS

1939 – **Sammy Kaplan** scores 12 points as the Kingston Colonials of the American Basketball League defeat the Troy Haymakers 43-27.

1954 – **Boris Nachamkin** scores 32 points and grabs a career-high 26 rebounds as NYU defeats Miami of Ohio 82-79.

1957 – Substitute **Rudy LaRusso** makes eight straight foul shots in overtime as Dartmouth defeats Connecticut 70-67.

1984 – Ohio State tight end **John Frank** catches four passes for 57 yards as the Buckeyes beat Pitt 28-23 in the Fiesta Bowl.

1999 – **Jay Fiedler** completes 28 of 39 passes for 317 yards including a 25-yard touchdown pass as the Jacksonville Jaguars beat the Cincinnati Bengals 24-7 to clinch the AFC Central title.

2001 – **Bubba Berenzweig** scores at 2:36 of overtime to give the Milwaukee Admirals a 2-1 victory over the Manitoba Moose in an International Hockey League game.

STRONG IN DEFEAT

2005 – Making his first start for the Miami Dolphins, third-string quarterback **Sage Rosenfels** throws for a 76-yard touchdown on his first pass of the game and finishes with 264 yards passing in a 30-23 loss to the Baltimore Ravens.

MAZEL TOUGH

1925 – In the final bout of an elimination tournament to crown a champion in the featherweight division, **Louis Kid Kaplan** beats **Danny Kramer** in New York. The fight is stopped in the ninth round when Kramer suffers a broken nose.

2006 – **David Hymovitz** of the Danbury Trashers is named United Hockey League Player of the Week after scoring five goals and adding eight assists in four games.

John Frank *(San Francisco 49ers)*

JEWS ON FIRST

1964 – **Mordechai Spiegler** scores his first of 25 official international soccer goals, connecting on a penalty kick in Israeli's 3-0 victory over Hong Kong.

2005 – **Chanoch Nissany** becomes the first Israeli to sign a testing contract with a Formula One racing team when the 41-year-old driver joins Minardi.

RECORD SETTERS

1985 – **Stu Mittleman** sets an American record of 577.75 miles in a six-day running race in Boulder, Colo.

TRANSITIONS

1947 – CCNY bars its athletic teams from competing against any team coached by Wyoming basketball coach Everett Shelton because of anti-Semitic remarks he allegedly made during a Dec. 28, 1946 loss in New York.

1965 – **Dan Goldstein** of Fairleigh Dickinson is named to the All-America soccer team.

A STAR IS BORN

1904 – **Irving Cohen** (boxing manager)
1910 – **Samuel Horwitz** (Univ. of Chicago football)

JANUARY 3

GAMEBREAKERS

1940 – **Bobby Lewis** scores 17 points to lead NYU to a 53-39 basketball victory over Syracuse.

1941 – **Ralph Kaplowitz** scores 14 points in NYU's 55-39 victory over Illinois Wesleyan.

1942 – **Red Holzman** scores 15 points as CCNY defeats Geneva 61-22. **Bob Davidoff** scores 17 points and **Morty Lazar** adds 13 as NYU defeats Fort Monmouth military base 46-43. **Mel Hirsch's** 15 points lead Brooklyn College to a 47-41 overtime win over Davis & Elkins.

1945 – **Paul Schmones** scores 12 points to lead CCNY past St. John's 42-41. **Sid Tanenbaum's** 16 points lead NYU to a 52-30 victory over Cornell.

1948 – **Hilty Shapiro** scores 13 points and **Lionel Malamed** adds 12 as CCNY defeats Moravian College 74-60.

1953 – **Boris Nachamkin** scores 27 points as NYU defeats West Virginia 78-75.

1963 – **Art Heyman** collects 36 points and 14 rebounds as Duke beats Penn State 95-55.

2006 – **Yotam Halperin** of Israel scores 26 points to lead Union Olimpija Ljubana of Slovenia to an 89-68 European Basketball League victory over HKK Siroki Eronet of Bosnia.

MAZEL TOUGH

1928 – **Newsboy Brown (Dave Montrose)** wins a 10-round decision over Johnny McCoy in Los Angeles to capture the California version of the world flyweight title.

1930 – **Maxie Rosenbloom** wins all 10 rounds against **Leo Lomski**, a 6-to-5 prefight favorite, in a light heavyweight fight in New York City.

TRANSITIONS

1959 – **Alan Seiden** of St. John's scores his 1,000th career point in an 81-76 victory over Temple.

2004 – **Larry Brown** earns his 900th NBA coaching victory as the Detroit Pistons defeat the Golden State Warriors 99-93.

A STAR IS BORN

1905 – **Bernard Kopkind** (Syracuse lacrosse)

1918 – **Harry Platt** (Brown University basketball)

1933 – **Sam Match** (tennis)

1978 – **Brian Natkin** (Texas-El Paso football, Tennessee Titans tight end)

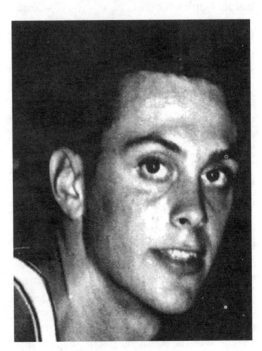

Larry Brown
(University of North Carolina Athletic Communications)

JANUARY 4

GAMEBREAKERS

1904 – **Jacob Mazer** scores 16 points – all on free throws – as the Detroit Athletic Club defeats Yale 24-23.

1939 – **John Bromberg** scores 12 points and **Ossie Schechtman** adds 11 as Long Island University beats Kentucky 52-34 at Madison Square Garden. **Bernie Opper** scores six points for the Wildcats.

1941 – **Jules Kasner** scores 22 points as Brooklyn College defeats the University of Newark 63-22.

1942 – **Sid Luckman** throws a 20-yard touchdown pass as the Chicago Bears beat the NFL All-Stars 35-24 in New York.

1947 – **Leo Gottlieb** scores 22 points and **Ralph Kaplowitz** adds 14 as the New York Knicks defeat the Detroit Falcons 62-50 in a Basketball Association of America game.

1947 – Led by **Sid Tanenbaum's** 20 points, NYU defeats SMU 76-63.

1949 – **Irwin Dambrot** scores 14 points as CCNY defeats St. John's 58-56 in overtime.

1958 – **Rudy LaRusso** scores 22 points and grabs 21 rebounds to lead Dartmouth past Yale 82-70 in the Ivy League opener.

MAZEL TOUGH

1921 – **Abe Friedman** wins a 10-round decision over **Young Montreal** to win the New England bantamweight title in Boston.

1958 – **Willie Harmatz** rides Seaneen to victory in the San Carlos Handicap at Santa Anita racetrack in Arcadia, Calif.

1975 – **Barry Asher** rallies from 23rd place, then beats Mickey Higham 236-186 in the final to win the Alameda (Calif.) Open, his eighth and final victory on the PBA pro bowling tour.

Red Auerbach *(Boston Celtics)*

TRANSITIONS

1928 – The New York Yankees purchase infielders **Jimmie Reese** and Lyn Lary from the Oakland Oaks of the Pacific Coast League for $125,000. The Yankees beat out a dozen other teams in the bidding, including the Chicago Cubs who offered $150,000. But the talent-stocked Yankees agreed to allow the infielders to play in Oakland for the 1929 season before calling them up to the major leagues.

1985 – The Boston Celtics retire uniform No. 2 in honor of long-time coach **Red Auerbach,** signifying the second-most influential person in the organization. No. 1 had been retired in honor of team founder Walter Brown.

A STAR IS BORN

1877 – **Otto Herschmann** (Austrian swimming, fencing)
1880 – **Dr. Arnold Goldwater** (cycling)
1943 – **Larry Yellen** (Houston Astros pitcher)

JANUARY 5

GAMEBREAKERS

1929 – **Louis Hayman** scores 17 points as Syracuse defeats Cornell 31-18.

1929 – **Moritz Haeusler** scores two goals as New York Hakoah defeats the Newark Skeeters 4-1 in the Eastern Soccer League.

1935 – **Sid Gross'** free throw in the final minute gives NYU a 23-22 victory over Kentucky in front of a record crowd of 16,500 at Madison Square Garden. **Willie Rubenstein** of NYU is the game's top scorer with six points, while Gross adds five.

1942 – **Harold Judenfriend** comes off the bench and hits a 35-foot shot that enables CCNY to send the game into overtime against St. John's. Judenfriend then hits a 30-footer as CCNY wins 38-36 and earns a bid to the NIT Tournament.

1968 – **Steve Chubin** of Anaheim goes 18-for-18 from the foul line and scores 38 points as the Amigos beat the Indiana Pacers 124-121 in an American Basketball Association game.

1968 – Columbia center **Dave Newmark** scores 40 points, including 26 in the second half of a 100-72 victory over Yale.

1993 – **Danny Schayes** of the Milwaukee Bucks scores 15 points and grabs a season-high 15 rebounds in a 114-110 victory over the Minnesota Timberwolves.

MAZEL TOUGH

1931 – **Benny Bass** wins a 10-round decision over Lew Massey in Philadelphia to retain his world super featherweight title. On the undercard, heavyweight **Jack Gross,** conceding 41 pounds to Roy "Ace" Clark, scores a sixth-round knockout. 1963 – The San Diego Chargers, coached by **Sid Gillman,** beat the Boston Patriots 51-10 for the American Football League championship.

2002 – **Anna Smashnova** of Israel beats Tatiana Panova of Russia 6-2, 6-2 to win her third WTA Tour tennis title, the hard-court ASB Bank Classic in Auckland, New Zealand.

TRANSITIONS

2006 – Former head coach **Marv Levy** is named general manager and vice president of football operations for the Buffalo Bills.

A STAR IS BORN

1898 – **Morris Holman** (CCNY basketball)

1904 – **Herman Silverberg** (featherweight boxer)

1961 – **Roger Samuels** (San Francisco Giants, Pittsburgh Pirates pitcher)

1968 – **Juan Espil** (Argentina basketball)

1975 – **Daniela Krukower** (Argentina judo)

Danny Schayes
(Syracuse University Athletics)

JANUARY 6

GAMEBREAKERS

1929 – **Bela Rosenberg** scores twice as the Brooklyn Wanderers take over first place in the American Soccer League with a 4-2 victory over the Providence Gold Bugs.

1943 – **Harry Boykoff** scores 45 points, breaking the Madison Square Garden record of 37, as St. John's beats St. Joseph's 76-46.

1947 – **Leo Gottlieb** scores 21 points and **Ossie Schechtman** adds 14 as the New York Knicks of the Basketball Association of America end the St. Louis Bombers' seven-game winning streak, 59-57. **Nathan Militzok** hits a field goal and Schechtman adds a free throw in the final minute to clinch the victory.

1948 – **Ivy Summer** scores a game-high 12 points to lead St. John's to a 38-34 win over CCNY.

1948 – **Max Zaslofsky** scores 18 points to lead the Chicago Stags to a 79-74 victory over the New York Knicks in a matchup between NBA division leaders at Madison Square Garden. Zaslofsky, a Brownsville native, is honored in a pregame ceremony and receives gifts including a TV set, a $500 savings bond, a wristwatch, and a plaque.

1968 – **Neal Walk** scores a career-high 39 points as Florida defeats LSU 97-80.

1975 – **Yehoshua Feigenbaum** scores his third hat trick in international soccer matches as Israel beats the United States 3-0.

1979 – **Nancy Lieberman** scores 33 points as Old Dominion defeats Queens 106-53.

MAZEL TOUGH

1974 – **Jonathan Lewis** wins the British Under-20 Fencing Championships saber title in London.

1980 – **Shlomo Glickstein** of Israel celebrates his 22nd birthday by beating Robert Van't Hof 7-6, 6-4 to win a hard-court tennis tournament in Hobart, Australia. **Brian Gottfried** teams with Raul Ramirez to beat

Tom Okker and Wojtek Fibak in a five-set final of the WCT Doubles Championship in London.

TRANSITIONS

2007 – Former head coach **Larry Brown** returns to the Philadelphia 76ers as executive vice president.

A STAR IS BORN

1877 – **Jacob Mazer** (basketball)
1915 – **Ibolya Csak** (Hungarian women's high jumper)
1958 – **Shlomo Glickstein** (Israeli tennis)
1959 – **Nancy Rubin** (golf)
1976 – **Jeff Pickler** (minor-league baseball)

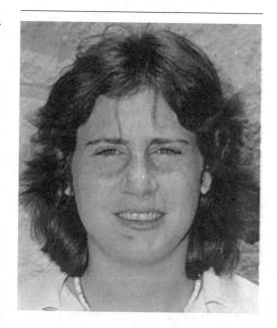

Nancy Lieberman
(U.S. Olympic Committee)

JANUARY 7

GAMEBREAKERS

1940 – **Mike Bloom** scores 17 points as the Washington Brewers defeat the Wilkes-Barre Barons 41-24 in the American Basketball League.

1948 – **Max Zaslofsky** scores 18 points as the Chicago Stags defeat the New York Knicks 79-74.

1978 – **Mark Roth** beats Lee Taylor 212-196 in the final of the PBA Lite Classic in Torrance, Calif.

2004 – **Liad Suez** scores 26 points, including Villanova's final four baskets, as the Wildcats defeat Miami 58-55 in women's basketball.

MAZEL TOUGH

1903 – **Young Otto (Arthur Susskind)** scores his first of a record 42 career first-round knockouts when he stops Paddy Dee in a lightweight fight in New York City.

JEWS ON FIRST

1990 – **Mathieu Schneider** of the Canadiens scores his first NHL goal against Vancouver Canucks goalie Kirk McLean in a 5-3 Montreal victory.

TRANSITIONS

1927 – **Abe Saperstein** takes his Savoy Ballroom basketball team of Chicago on its first road trip – 48 miles to Hinckley, Ill. The team will eventually be known as the Harlem Globetrotters.

1941 – Former Detroit Tigers shortstop **Lou Brower** is named manager at Waterloo of the Three-I League.

1957 – **Red Holzman** resigns as head coach of the St. Louis Hawks to take an assistant coaching job with the New York Knicks. Holzman, who will become the Knicks' head coach in 1967, has an 83-120 record in four seasons with the Hawks in Milwaukee and St. Louis.

1960 – Former Los Angeles Rams coach **Sid Gillman** signs a three-year contract as head coach of the Los Angeles Chargers of the new American Football League.

1995 – **Mickey Berkowitz**, Israeli basketball's all-time leading scorer, scores two points in his final game as Hapoel Tel Aviv loses to Benen Herzliya 107-88.

A STAR IS BORN

1875 – **Gustav Flatow** (German gymnast)

1897 – **Arthur Strauss** (Phillips College and pro football halfback)

1912 – **Jerry Nemer** (Southern Cal basketball)

Red Holzman
(New York Knicks)

JANUARY 8

GAMEBREAKERS

1936 – **Willie Rubenstein** scores nine points and **Len Maidman** adds eight as NYU beats Kentucky 41-28.

1939 – **Moe Goldman** scores 16 points as the Philadelphia Sphas defeat the Washington Brewers 48-36 in the ABL.

1944 – **Ivy Summer** scores 23 points as St. John's defeats Rhode Island State 58-48.

1948 – **Don Forman** scores a school-record 35 points as NYU beats Duke 77-56.

1949 – **Ira Kaplan** of NYU beats Olympic 100-meter champion Harrison Dillard two of three in the Great American Sprint Series at the Knights of Columbus Games in Brooklyn, N.Y. After narrowly losing in the 80 meters, Kaplan captures the 60 and 100 dashes.

1961 – **Howie Carl** scores 24 points to lead DePaul past Dayton 75-64.

1972 – One day after scoring 38 points in a 77-72 win over Columbia, **Arnie Berman** of Brown scores another 38 points in a 101-88 victory over Cornell.

1989 – San Francisco tight end **John Frank** catches a 5-yard touchdown pass as the 49ers beat the Chicago Bears 28-3 in the NFC championship game.

2005 – **Dan Grunfeld** scores a career-high 29 points as Stanford defeats 13th-ranked Arizona 87-76.

MAZEL TOUGH

1926 – **Sid Terris** wins a 10-round decision over European lightweight champion Lucien Vinez in New York.

1949 – **Ira Kaplan** of NYU wins the Great American Sprint Series at the Knights of Columbus track meet in Brooklyn, N.Y.

1960 – **Sylvia Wene** bowls her third career perfect game – and the first by a woman in U.S. All-Star Match-Play Tournament history – during qualifying in Omaha, Neb. She wins the tournament for the second time a week later.

1978 – **Eliot Teltscher** defeats Onny Parun 6-3, 7-5, 6-1 to win the Auckland Challenger tennis tournament in New Zealand.

2004 – Welterweight **Jackie Fields,** who compiled a 74-9-3 record with 30 knockouts, is elected to the International Boxing Hall of Fame in the old-timers category.

TRANSITIONS

1895 – The first Israel Gymnastic Club, exclusively for German and Austrian Jews, is established in Constantinople, Turkey.

1936 – **Rudi Ball** is selected to the German national hockey team that will compete in the Olympics in Garmisch-Partenkirchen, Germany.

1941 – The Baseball Writers Association of America names Detroit Tigers left fielder **Hank Greenberg** and New York Giants catcher **Harry Danning** to the 1940 major-league all-star team.

A STAR IS BORN

1899 – **Nat Krinsky** (CCNY basketball)

1936 – **Alan Goldstein** (North Carolina, Oakland Raiders running back)

1941 – **Eugene Zubrinsky** (San Jose State high jumper)

1966 – **Brent Novoselsky** (Penn, Chicago Bears, Minnesota Vikings tight end)

JANUARY 9

GAMEBREAKERS

1909 – **Ira Streusand** scores 14 points and **Jacob Goldman** adds 10 as CCNY defeats Lehigh 28-21.

1932 – **Hyman Ginsberg** scores 14 points to lead Geneva to a 46-27 victory over West Virginia.

1937 – **Moe Goldman** scores 15 points and **Inky Lautman** adds 12 as the Philadelphia Sphas defeat the Jersey Reds 49-41 in the American Basketball League.

1944 – **Moe Frankel** hits a shot from mid-court at the buzzer as the Wilmington Blue Bombers beat New York 46-45 to win the ABL first-half title.

1946 – **Harry Boykoff** scores 27 points and **Lennie Doctor** adds 15, and St. John's scores the game's first 14 points and defeats CCNY 27-15.

1951 – **Mel Seeman** scores 20 points and **Abe Becker** adds 18 as NYU defeats West Virginia 76-64.

2005 – **Shay Doron** scores 37 points and shoots 20-for-22 from the foul line as the 21st-ranked Maryland women defeat fifth-ranked North Carolina 92-77.

MAZEL TOUGH

1945 – Welterweight **Maxie Berger** of Montreal decisions Solomon Stewart in eight rounds at the Broadway Arena in Brooklyn, N.Y., for his 14th consecutive victory.

1965 – **Mark Lazarus** scores in the 62nd minute to give Brentford, a Third Division team, a 1-1 tie with Burnley of the First Division in the third round of England's FA Cup soccer tournament.

1968 – New Orleans Buccaneers guard **Larry Brown**, a late roster replacement when Bob Verga of Dallas is called away to military duty, is named MVP of the first American Basketball Association All-Star Game in Indianapolis.

1972 – **Esther Rot** runs 100 meters in 11.45 seconds to set an Israeli women's record and qualify for the Olympics in Munich.

1977 – **Jody Scheckter** of South Africa wins the Formula One Argentina Grand Prix in Buenos Aires as only four drivers are able to complete all 53 laps because of 120-degree heat.

TRANSITIONS

1999 – Long-time NFL referee **Jerry Markbreit** works his final game when the San Francisco 49ers visit the Atlanta Falcons.

2001 – **Barney Aaron,** European light heavyweight champion who fought between 1819 and 1834, is elected to the International Boxing Hall of Fame.

2003 – **Louis "Kid" Kaplan,** 108-17-13 lifetime as a featherweight and lightweight, is elected to the International Boxing Hall of Fame.

A STAR IS BORN

1891 – **Joe Welling** (lightweight boxer)

1907 – **Harry Richman** (Illinois football guard, Chicago Bears)

1921 – **Agnes Keleti** (Hungarian gymnast)

1937 – **Paul Haber** (handball)

1970 – **Jeff Kent** (Rhode Island basketball)

JANUARY 10

GAMEBREAKERS

1928 – **Nat Holman** scores 15 points and **Davey Banks** adds six as the Original Celtics beat the Fort Wayne Hoosiers 37-30 at Madison Square Garden for their 11th straight American Basketball League victory.

1932 – CCNY scores all 10 overtime points – including three by **Moe Goldman** – as the Beavers beat St. John's 28-18. It is CCNY's first victory over the Redmen since 1926.

1946 – **Harry Boykoff** scores 27 points and **Lenny Doctor** adds 15 as St. John's defeats CCNY 75-50. **Paul Schmones** leads CCNY with 14 points.

1948 – **Nelson Bobb** scores 26 points as Temple defeats Duke 58-54.

1962 – Sophomore **Barry Kramer** scores 30 points as NYU beats Fairleigh Dickinson 80-72.

1964 – **Jeff Neuman's** foul shot with three seconds left in overtime gives Penn a 70-69 victory over Yale.

1976 – **Ernie Grunfeld** scores a career-high 43 points, including 11-for-11 from the foul line, as Tennessee beats Kentucky 90-88 in overtime.

1977 – Washington Capitals goaltender **Bernie Wolfe** makes 26 saves and posts his only NHL shutout, beating the Detroit Red Wings 2-0. The shutout is only the second in franchise's three-year history.

2002 – **David Bluthenthal** scores 16 points and grabs 18 rebounds as Southern Cal upsets 11th-ranked UCLA 81-77. **Jordan Kardos** scores 25 points and grabs a career-high seven rebounds in Illinois-Chicago's 75-66 victory over Wisconsin-Green Bay.

2002 – **Steve Dubinsky** scores the winning goal as the Chicago Blackhawks defeat the Anaheim Mighty Ducks 2-1.

MAZEL TOUGH

1988 – **Amos Mansdorf** of Israel beats Ramesh Krishnan 6-3, 6-4 in the final of a Challenger tennis tournament in Auckland, New Zealand.

RECORD SETTERS

1957 – **Dolph Schayes** of the Syracuse Nationals sets an NBA record by making 18 consecutive free throws, and finishes with 40 points in a 118-110 loss to the Minneapolis Lakers.

TRANSITIONS

1954 – All-Star **Jack Molinas** of the Fort Wayne Pistons is banned for life from the NBA for betting on his team on many occasions. Molinas will later be cleared of the charges by a grand jury, but the lifetime ban is upheld.

1961 – **Allie Sherman** replaces Jim Lee Howell as head coach of the NFL's New York Giants.

2002 – Five Jews are elected to the International Boxing Hall of Fame – featherweight **Benny Bass** and bantamweight **Harry Harris** in the old-timers category, **Young Dutch Sam** in the pioneer category, and manager **Irving Cohen** and promoter **Sam Silverman** in the non-participants division.

2004 – **Jerry Greenbaum**, winner of 19 senior events and runner-up in the 1999 British Senior Amateur, is inducted into the Georgia Golf Hall of Fame.

A STAR IS BORN

1893 – **Sylvan King** (Princeton football fullback)

1897 – **Whitey Bimstein** (boxing trainer)

1915 – **Herman Neugass** (Tulane sprinter)

1917 – **Arthur Gold** (British high jumper)

1931 – **Gordon Polofsky** (Tennessee, Chicago Cardinals fullback/linebacker)

1931 – **Henry Myerson** (Harvard football lineman)

1972 – **Jonathan Ohayon** (Canadian archery)

JANUARY 11

GAMEBREAKERS

1930 – **Max Posnack** scores seven points to lead St. John's to a 28-23 victory over CCNY. **Lou Spindell** scores 11 points and **Milt Trupin** adds seven for CCNY. **Hy Lefft** scores nine points and **George Newblatt** adds seven as NYU defeats Rutgers 52-30.

1930 – **Moritz Haeusler** scores two goals as the Hakoah All-Stars defeat Bridgeport 4-0 in an Atlantic Coast Soccer League match in Brooklyn.

1936 – **Cy Kaselman** scores 17 points as the Philadelphia Sphas defeat the Brooklyn Visitations 43-40.

1938 – **Irv Torgoff** scores 14 points and **John Bromberg** adds 10 as LIU defeats Princeton Seminary 85-17.

1943 – **Harry Boykoff** of St. John's scores 30 points to break the Convention Hall record in a 62-40 win over Temple in Philadelphia.

1948 – **Max Zaslofsky** scores 31 points as the Chicago Stags beat the New York Knicks 99-86.

1949 – **Hilty Shapiro** scores 18 points to lead CCNY to a 64-50 victory over West Virginia.

1960 – **Sid Cohen** scores a career-high 26 points as Kentucky beats Tulane 68-42.

1972 – **Johan Neeskens** scores three of his team's first four goals as the Netherlands beats Norway 9-0 in a World Cup soccer qualifier.

2003 – **Michal Epstein** gets 25 points, seven rebounds, and five assists in Providence's 80-77 women's basketball victory over Pittsburgh.

STRONG IN DEFEAT

1966 – **Rudy LaRusso** of the Los Angeles Lakers scores 11 points, but the West loses the NBA All-Star Game in Cincinnati, 137-94.

MAZEL TOUGH

1902 – **Jewey Cooke** wins a seven-round decision over Dave Barry to win the English Gold & Silver Belt lightweight boxing competition in London.

1936 – **Maurice Holtzer** of France knocks out Georges LePerson in the 13th round in Paris to retain his European featherweight title.

1975 – **Tom Okker** beats Marty Riessen 7-6, 7-6 in the final of an indoor tennis tournament in Chattanooga, Tenn.

JEWS ON FIRST

1970 – Kansas City linebacker **Bob Stein** becomes the first Jewish player to participate in the Super Bowl as the Chiefs beat the Minnesota Vikings 23-7 in New Orleans.

TRANSITIONS

1966 – **Sandy Koufax** is named male Athlete of the Year for 1965 by the Associated Press.

2006 – Boxing historian **Hank Kaplan** and trainer **Whitey Bimstein** are elected to the International Boxing Hall of Fame.

A STAR IS BORN

1856 – **David Seligman** (Harvard rowing)

1967 – **Ronnie Stern** (NHL Vancouver Canucks, Calgary Flames, San Jose Sharks)

1971 – **Noah Cantor** (Canadian Football League defensive tackle)

JANUARY 12

GAMEBREAKERS

1938 – **Si Boardman** scores 19 points in NYU's 47-33 victory over Union. **Mike Bloom's** 12 points lead Temple to a 40-23 victory over Muhlenberg.

1944 – **Irv Rothenberg** scores 18 points to lead LIU to a 51-39 victory over West Virginia.

1964 – **Tal Brody** scores 28 points to lead Illinois to an 87-70 victory over Iowa.

2002 – **Eyal Berkovic** scores two goals as Manchester City defeats Norwich City 3-1 in England's Division One soccer.

2002 – **Jeff Halpern** scores at 2:18 of the first period as the Washington Capitals beat the Florida Panthers 1-0.

2002 – **Paul Vitelli** scores 20 points and grabs nine rebounds as Yale defeats Cornell 79-74.

MAZEL TOUGH

1974 – **Ilana Kloss** beats her doubles tennis partner, Linky Boshoff, 6-2, 7-5 to win a Sugar Tournament event in East London, South Africa.

1977 – **Ernie Grunfeld** scores 22 points as Tennessee beats Kentucky 71-67 in overtime.

1998 – **Andy Gabel** defeats **Dan Weinstein** in a U.S.-record time of 43.032 seconds to win the 500-meter final at the U.S. Olympic short-track speed skating trials in Lake Placid, N.Y.. A day earlier, Gabel won the 1,000-meter pursuit race.

2002 – **Sasha Cohen** wins the silver medal at the U.S. Figure Skating Championships in Los Angeles and earns a spot on the U.S. Olympic team.

2002 – **Anna Smashnova** of Israel beats top-seeded Tamarine Tanasugarn of Thailand 7-6, 7-6 (7-2) to win the Canberra Classic in Australia, her second WTA hard-court tournament victory in as many weeks.

RECORD SETTERS

1958 – **Dolph Schayes** of the Syracuse Nationals scores a third-period basket during a 135-109 victory over the Detroit Pistons and breaks George Mikan's all-time NBA scoring record. Schayes, who scored 18,438 career points, finishes the game with 23 points for a record 11,770 – six more than Mikan.

1960 – **Dolph Schayes** of the Syracuse Nationals becomes the first NBA player to surpass 15,000 career points, scoring 34 in a 127-120 victory over the Boston Celtics.

TRANSITIONS

1966 – **Red Auerbach** wins his 1,000th game as an NBA coach as the Boston Celtics beat the Los Angeles Lakers 114-102.

JEWS ON FIRST

1985 – Filling in while Albany head coach Phil Jackson is serving a one-game suspension, assistant coach **Charley Rosen** gets his first Continental Basketball Association victory as the Patroons defeat the Toronto Tornados 114-111 in overtime. Rosen will coach Rockford to the 1989 league championship.

A STAR IS BORN

1895 – **Henry Bostick** (Philadelphia A's third baseman)

1896 – **Umberto de Morpurgo** (Italian tennis)

1941 – **Nessim Max Cohen** (Moroccan middleweight boxer)

1943 – **Maurice Manasseh** (India cricket)

1960 – **Ken Kaplan** (New Hampshire guard, Tampa Bay Buccaneers)

JANUARY 13

GAMEBREAKERS

1931 – **Allie Schuckman** scores eight points and **Max Posnack** adds seven as St. John's beats LIU for the fourth year in a row, 38-27.

1934 – **Cy Kaselman** scores 14 points, **Shikey Gotthoffer** 13 and **Red Wolfe** 10 as the Philadelphia Sphas defeat the Union City Reds 80-43 in the American Basketball League.

1949 – **Nelson Bobb** scores 29 points as Temple beats St. John's 81-79 in overtime.

1950 – **Irv Rothenberg** scores 19 points as the Paterson Crescents defeat the Hartford Hurricanes 87-85 in the ABL. **Ralph Kaplowitz** scores 22 points for Hartford.

1968 – Florida center **Neal Walk** collects 28 points and 23 rebounds in a 96-78 win over fourth-ranked Kentucky.

1988 – Playing in just his second international soccer match, defenseman **Jeff Agoos** scores to give the United States a 1-0 victory over host Guatemala.

1988 – **Mike Kelfer** of Boston University collects two goals and four assists in a 10-6 hockey victory over Wisconsin.

2002 – **Eyal Berkovic** of Israel scores two goals as Manchester United beats Norwich 3-1 in English soccer.

MAZEL TOUGH

1933 – **Ben Jeby** knocks out Frankie Battaglia in the 12th round in New York to win the New York State version of the world middleweight title.

1996 – **Damon Keeve** wins the heavyweight division at the U.S. Olympic Judo Trials in Colorado Springs, Colo.

2004 – **Jason Lezak** wins the 100 freestyle at the FINA World Cup Short-Course Swimming Championships in Stockholm. He adds the 50 freestyle gold medal a day later.

2006 – **Larry Brown** becomes the fourth NBA coach to win 1,000 games when the New York Knicks defeat the Atlanta Hawks 105-94.

RECORD SETTERS

1935 – **Milton Green** of Harvard ties the world record of 5.8 seconds in the 45-yard high hurdles in a track meet against Yale and Princeton.

A STAR IS BORN

1902 – **Baroness Maud Levi** (tennis)
1910 – **Fay Gulack** (gymnastics)
1917 – **Moe Becker** (Duquesne basketball)
1929 – **Moe Savransky** (Cincinnati Reds pitcher)
1930 – **Sidney Cole** (jockey)

Jeff Agoos
(U.S. Olympic Committee)

JANUARY 14

GAMEBREAKERS

1930 – **Jack Grossman** scores 26 points to lead Rutgers to a 55-25 win over Drexel.

1939 – **Ralph Dolgoff's** game-high nine points lead St. John's to a 40-26 victory over Niagara.

1940 – **Ace Goldstein** scores 12 points as the Jersey Reds defeat the Wikes-Barre Barons 32-23 in the American Basketball League.

1956 – North Carolina's **Lenny Rosenbluth** scores 45 points in a 103-99 double-overtime victory over Clemson.

1974 – **Ernie Grunfeld** scores 20 points and grabs 10 rebounds as Tennessee beats Kentucky 67-54.

MAZEL TOUGH

1909 – **Abe Attell** knocks out Freddie Weeks in the 10th round in Goldfield, Nev., to retain his world featherweight title.

1921 – World lightweight champion **Benny Leonard** knocks out Richie Mitchell at Madison Square Garden in one of the first fights in which women are encouraged to attend as spectators. Leonard is knocked down in the first round, but gets up and floors Mitchell six times before the fight is stopped in the sixth round. The gate of $133,745 is the largest at the time for a non-heavyweight fight.

1959 – **Sylvia Wene** wins the All-Star Match-Play bowling tournament in Omaha, Neb.

1972 – **Felix Brami** of Tunisia knocks out Marius Cordier in the eighth round in Marseilles to win the French junior lightweight title.

1974 – **Brian Gottfried** beats Jean Chanfrau of France 6-3, 6-4 to win the Pacific Coast Indoor Tennis Tournament in Portland, Ore.

1978 – **Marshall Holman** rolls a strike in the 10th frame to beat Jimmy Certain 221-218 in the PBA Ford Open final in Alameda, Calif.

2006 – **Sasha Cohen** wins the U.S. Figure Skating Championship in St. Louis, finishing 28 points ahead of runner-up Kimmie Meissner. **Emily Hughes** finishes third.

Benny Leonard

RECORD SETTERS

1968 – **Steve Chubin** hands out a league-record 22 assists in the Anaheim Amigos' 130-123 loss to the Dallas Chaparrals in the American Basketball Association.

TRANSITIONS

1942 – The Boston Red Sox give catcher **Moe Berg** his unconditional release to enable him to accept a government appointment as goodwill ambassador to Latin America.

1989 – **Arnold Blum**, five-time winner of the state amateur championship, is inducted into the Georgia Golf Hall of Fame.

A STAR IS BORN

1915 – **Mike Bloom** (Temple basketball)
1920 – **Danny Bartfield** (featherweight boxer)
1934 – **Pierre Darmon** (French tennis player)

JANUARY 15

GAMEBREAKERS

1938 – **Moe Goldman** scores 15 points and **Inky Lautman** adds 10 as the Philadelphia Sphas defeat the Brooklyn Visitations 46-42 in the American Basketball League. **Nat Frankel** scores 20 for Brooklyn.

1938 – **Mike Bloom** scores 17 points as Temple defeats Manhattan 45-38. **John Bromberg's** 23 points lead LIU past DePaul 55-29.

1957 – **Lenny Rosenbluth** scores 29 points, including 17 of 19 from the foul line, and grabs 14 rebounds as North Carolina beats North Carolina State 83-57.

1959 – **Larry Zeidel** scores early in the second period to give Hershey a 1-0 lead and later adds an assist as the defending league champion Bears beat the American Hockey League All-Stars 5-2.

1969 – **Steve Bilski** hits a 25-foot shot at the buzzer to give Penn a 32-30 victory over ninth-ranked Villanova.

1994 – Dartmouth quarterback **Jay Fiedler** is named the outstanding player for the East team in the East-West Shrine Game at Stanford. Fiedler completes 8 of 13 passes for 150 yards, including a 13-yard touchdown pass.

1994 – **Lev Berdichevsky** scores four goals for the Roanoke Express in an East Coast Hockey League game against Columbus.

2000 – Backup quarterback **Jay Fiedler** throws touchdown passes of 70 and 38 yards in Jacksonville's first two possessions of the second half, and the Jaguars hand the Miami Dolphins their worst loss in history, 62-7 in the AFC playoffs. Fiedler completes 7 of 11 passes for 172 yards, and becomes the Dolphins' starting quarterback the next season.

2002 – **Vered Borochovski** of Israel wins the women's 400-meter individual medley at a FINA World Cup swim meet in Imperia, Italy, in 1:02.25.

STRONG IN DEFEAT

1975 – **Ernie Grunfeld** scores 26 points and grabs 13 rebounds, but Tennessee loses to Kentucky 88-82.

MAZEL TOUGH

1917 – **Willie Jackson** knocks out Johnny Dundee in the first round in Philadelphia, handing the future world lightweight champion his second loss in 40 fights.

1929 – **Herman Weiner** knocks down **Battling Levinsky** three times in the first 37 seconds of a heavyweight fight in Hagerstown, Md. Levinsky, a former light heavyweight champion, will fight one more time before retiring.

1931 – **Miklos Szabados** beats **Viktor Barna** 21-12, 24-22, 21-14 to win the world table tennis championship in Budapest. The two finalists combine to win the men's doubles title.

1989 – **Aaron Krickstein** beats Andrei Chesnokov 6-4, 6-2 in the final of a hard-court tennis tournament in Sydney, Australia.

TRANSITIONS

1925 – **Benny Leonard,** world lightweight champion since 1917, retires from boxing at the urging of his mother.

A STAR IS BORN

1905 – **Jackey Snyder** (boxing)
1945 – **David Pleat** (English soccer)
1948 – **Henry Nissen** (Australian flyweight boxer)
1970 – **Irena Palina** (Russian table tennis)
1976 – **Doug Gottlieb** (Notre Dame, Oklahoma State basketball)

JANUARY 16

GAMEBREAKERS

1937 – **Cy Kaselman** scores 16 points and **Shikey Gotthoffer** adds 12 as the Philadelphia Sphas defeat the New York Jewels 37-32 in the American Basketball League. **Mac Kinsbrunner** scores 12 for New York.

1938 – **Reds Rosan** scores 14 points to lead the Philadelphia Sphas to a 44-38 ABL victory over Newark. **Nat Frankel** scores 36 points as the Brooklyn Visitations defeat the New York Celtics.

1946 – NYU's **Sid Tanenbaum** scores 15 points and **Dolph Schayes** adds 13 in a 62-46 victory over Cornell.

1964 – **Neil Farber** scores 22 points as Columbia posts a 69-66 upset victory over Princeton, led by Bill Bradley.

1992 – **Limor Mizrachi** leads Maryland with 16 points as the Terrapins upset top-ranked Virginia 67-65 in women's basketball.

STRONG IN DEFEAT

2005 – **Shay Doron** ties a school record with 39 points in Maryland's 95-91 overtime loss to Florida State in women's basketball.

MAZEL TOUGH

2002 – After winning bronze medals five years in a row, **Sarah Abitbol** and her partner Stephane Bernadis of France win a silver medal in the pairs competition at the European Figure Skating Championships in Lausanne, Switzerland.

RECORD SETTERS

1932 – **Solomon Furth** runs an American-best 15 4/5 seconds in the 110-meter indoor hurdles in Brooklyn, N.Y.

TRANSITIONS

1946 – Toronto Argonauts coach **Lew Hayman** becomes owner of the Montreal Alouettes of the Canadian Football League.

1970 – The NCAA, in a battle with the AAU over control of college athletics, places Yale's basketball team on two years' probation after backup center **Jack Langer** participates in the Maccabiah Games in Israel despite NCAA objections. Yale also is prevented from competing in Eastern College Athletic Conference events.

1995 – Palm Beach, Fla., millionaire **Malcolm Glazer** purchases the Tampa Bay Buccaneers for $192 million.

A STAR IS BORN

1946 – **Lydia Lazarov** (Israeli sailing)
1977 – **Arik Ze'evi** (Israeli judo)

Solomon Furth
(U.S. Olympic Committee)

JANUARY 17

GAMEBREAKERS

1999 – **David Hymovitz** of the Indianapolis Ice scores two goals and adds two assists as the East beats the West 10-7 in the International Hockey League All-Star Game in Cincinnati. Hymovitz receives the game's Rising Star Award.

2004 – Goalie **Gabe Winer** makes 22 saves as Massachusetts hands Maine its first home ice hockey shutout in nearly four years with a 1-0 victory.

STRONG IN DEFEAT

1961 – **Dolph Schayes** of the Syracuse Nationals scores 21 points in the East's 153-131 loss to the West in the NBA All-Star Game in Syracuse.

MAZEL TOUGH

1930 – **Jackie "Kid" Berg** wins a 10-round decision over Tony Canzoneri in a highly publicized non-title bout in New York City.

1981 – **Mark Roth** leads qualifying by 349 pins and beats Earl Anthony 253-220 in the final to win the PBA Showboat Invitational bowling tournament in Las Vegas.

RECORD SETTERS

1965 – Shot put specialist **Gary Gubner** sets an American heavyweight record of 412 pounds in the press en route to a weight lifting total of 1,180 pounds.

1998 – **Missy Leopoldus** scores a Penn State gymnastics record of 39.625 in the all-around against Illinois.

A STAR IS BORN

1926 – **Don Forman** (NYU basketball, Minneapolis Lakers)
1957 – **Rami Meron** (Israeli wrestler)
1973 – **Danny Buxbaum** (minor-league baseball)

Gary Gubner
(U.S. Olympic Committee)

JANUARY 18

GAMEBREAKERS

1955 – **Dolph Schayes** of the Syracuse Nationals scores 15 points and grabs 13 rebounds as the East beats the West 100-91 in the NBA All-Star Game in New York.

1958 – **Dolph Schayes** scores 18 points in the East's 130-118 victory in the NBA All-Star Game in St. Louis.

1969 – **Neal Walk** scores 35 points as Florida beats Furman 110-65.

1976 – **Randy Grossman** catches a 7-yard pass for Pittsburgh's first touchdown in the Steelers' 21-17 victory over the Dallas Cowboys in Super Bowl X in Miami.

1988 – **John Frank** of the 49ers catches a 5-yard touchdown pass as San Francisco beats the Chicago Bears 28-3 in the NFC championship game.

MAZEL TOUGH

1907 – **Abe Attell** knocks out Harry Baker in the eighth round in Los Angeles to retain his world featherweight title.

1927 – **Pinky Silverberg** weighs in at 112½ pounds and is unable to make weight for a scheduled lightweight fight against 121-pound Sammy Tisch in New York. Silverberg's brother **Herman Silverberg** stands in and wins a 10-round decision.

1934 – **Harry Mizler** beats Johnny Cuthbert in 15 rounds in London to win the British lightweight title.

1936 – **Myer Rosenblum** wins his second straight gold medal in the hammer throw at the Australian Track and Field Championships in Hobart.

1964 – **Alain Calmat** of France wins his third straight European Figure Skating Championship title in Grenoble, France.

JEWS ON FIRST

1984 – **Steve Richmond**, just called up from Tulsa by the New York Rangers, scores in the third period of his NHL debut against the St. Louis Blues. New York wins 6-2. Richmond, a defenseman, will score four career goals in 159 games.

TRANSITIONS

1947 – The Pittsburgh Pirates purchase American League home run champion **Hank Greenberg's** contract from the Detroit Tigers for a reported $25,000 to $35,000.

1959 – **Henry Wittenberg** is named coach of the United States wrestling team that will compete in the Soviet Union.

A STAR IS BORN

1902 – **David Ziff** (Syracuse and pro football end)

1907 – **Irving Constantine** (Syracuse and pro football running back

1924 – **Max Labovitch** (New York Rangers hockey)

1928 – **Alex Gomelsky** (Soviet Union basketball coach)

1964 – **Andrea Leand** (tennis)

1969 – **Willie Simms** (Wisconsin basketball, Continental Basketball Association)

1972 – **Keith Glauber** (Cincinnati Reds pitcher)

JANUARY 19

GAMEBREAKERS

1909 – **Sam Melitzer** scores 20 points to lead Columbia to a 51-24 victory over Princeton.

1934 – **Ben Kramer** scores 17 points as Long Island U. beats Brooklyn Pharmacy 32-24 for its 17th straight victory.

1935 – Duquesne's **Ed Kweller** scores a team-high 10 points in a 35-27 victory over West Virginia.

1946 – **Max Zaslofsky** scores a game-high 14 points to lead St. John's to an 80-33 rout of Niagara. **Donny Forman** scores 15 points to lead NYU past Canisius 51-45.

1957 – **Alan Seiden** scores 29 points as St. John's defeats St. Francis (N.Y.) 68-66.

MAZEL TOUGH

1921 – **Nat Holman** plays in four basketball games, going 3-1 with three different teams – Detroit, Union City, and the Rochester Centrals.

2002 – One day after winning the 100-meter freestyle, **Jason Lezak** of the United States wins the gold medal in the 50-meter freestyle at a World Cup swimming meet in Paris.

TRANSITIONS

1958 – The Canadian Football Council withdraws from the Canadian Rugby Union and adopts the new name Canadian Football League. **Syd Halter** is named the CFL's first commissioner.

1963 – **Al Davis** signs a three-year contract to become coach and general manager of the Oakland Raiders.

1965 – Former Chicago Bears quarterback **Sid Luckman** is elected to the Pro Football Hall of Fame.

1972 – **Sandy Koufax**, at 36, becomes the youngest player elected to the baseball Hall of Fame. His 344-vote total, in his first year of eligibility, is the highest in the history of the Baseball Writers Association of America balloting.

A STAR IS BORN

1880 – **Baron Robert Philippe Gustave de Rothschild** (French bobsledding)

1881 – **John Levine** (Yale fullback)

1983 – **Ben Zeskind** (minor-league baseball)

1990 – **Logan Hansen** (tennis)

Jason Lezak
(U.S. Olympic Committee)

JANUARY 20

GAMEBREAKERS

1920 – **Hyman Levinson** scores 19 points to lead Pitt to a 37-27 victory over West Virginia.

1934 – **Cy Kaselman** scores 17 points to lead the Philadelphia Sphas to a 40-28 victory over the Newark Bears in the American Basketball League.

1968 – Columbia center **Dave Newmark** scores 22 points as the Lions beat Cornell 93-51 in a key Ivy League game. **Neal Walk** scores 28 points as Florida upsets Tennessee 59-46.

2000 – **David Bluthenthal** scores 18 points and ties a Southern Cal record with 28 rebounds in a 95-92 overtime victory over Arizona State.

2004 – In an 84-63 victory over Lafayette, Penn center **Jennifer Fleischer** scores 17 points, grabs 14 rebounds, and ties a school women's record with seven blocked shots.

2006 – **Dan Grunfeld** scores 25 points as Stanford defeats UCLA 75-64.

2007 – **Jonathan Bornstein** tallies the winning goal in his first game with the national soccer team as the United States defeats Denmark 3-1 in Carson, Calif.

MAZEL TOUGH

1929 – **Baron Umberto de Morpurgo** defeats Jacques Brugnon to win the Monte Carlo tennis tournament.

1973 – **Barry Asher** beats Don Johnson 258-228 to win the PBA Showboat Invitational in Las Vegas. The winning check is for $11,111.11.

1980 – **Harold Solomon** beats Tim Gullickson 7-6, 6-0 in the final to win an indoor tennis tournament in Baltimore for the second straight year.

TRANSITIONS

1929 – Binghamton second baseman **Jake Pitler** is named manager at Elmira of the New York-Penn League.

1964 – **Sandy Koufax** of the Los Angeles Dodgers wins the S. Rae Hickok Award as the professional athlete of the year. He is awarded a $10,000 diamond-studded belt.

A STAR IS BORN

1859 – **Lucius Nathan Littauer** (Harvard football coach)

1905 – **Ike Danning** (St. Louis Cardinals catcher)

1926 – **Irwin Alterson** (Cornell basketball)

1972 – **Oleg Veretelnikov** (Uzbekistan decathlete)

JANUARY 21

GAMEBREAKERS

1948 – **Al Friedman** of the Mohawk Redskins scores 14 points to help the New York State Professional League All-Stars defeat the Utica Olympians 68-61.

1951 – **Max Zaslofsky** scores 27 points as the New York Knicks defeat the Rochester Royals 88-83 in overtime. **Red Holzman** scores 14 points for Rochester.

1979 – Steelers tight end **Randy Grossman** catches three passes for 29 yards as Pittsburgh beats the Dallas Cowboys 35-31 in Super Bowl XIII in Miami.

1990 – **Robert Burakovsky** has five goals and an assist for IDK of the Swedish Hockey League in a game against Brynas.

1992 – **Limor Mizrachi** scores 12 of Maryland's final 14 points, including the game-winning basket with 15 seconds left in a 63-59 women's basketball victory over Clemson. The sophomore guard is also named Atlantic Coast Conference player of the week.

2005 – **Dan Grunfeld** scores 25 points as Stanford beats UCLA 75-64, the Cardinal's eighth straight win at Pauley Pavilion – the most by a Bruins opponent in 40 years.

MAZEL TOUGH

1949 – **Harriet Ella Beloff**, 15, of Philadelphia wins the Middle Atlantic Junior Women's Figure Skating Championship at Madison Square Garden.

1979 – **Harold Solomon** beats Marty Riessen 7-5, 6-4 in the final of a hard-court tennis tournament in Baltimore.

RECORD SETTERS

1914 – **Alvah Meyer** of the United States sets a world indoor record of 6.4 seconds in the 60-yard dash in Paterson, N.J.

JEWS ON FIRST

1989 – Defenseman **Ronnie Stern** of the Vancouver Canucks scores his first of 75 career NHL regular-season goals in a 5-4 overtime loss to the New York Rangers. Stern also finishes his career with seven playoff goals.

A STAR IS BORN

1905 – **David Skudin** (NYU football guard)

1906 – **Maurice Holtzer** (French featherweight boxer)

1921 – **Jackie Goldsmith** (St. John's basketball)

1964 – **Allan Silverstein** (minor-league baseball)

1972 – **H. Waldman** (UNLV and St. Louis University basketball)

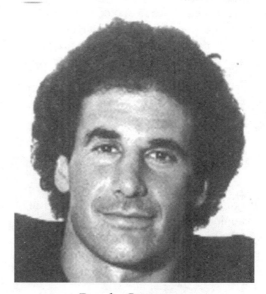

Randy Grossman
(Pittsburgh Steelers)

JANUARY 22

GAMEBREAKERS

1921 – **Jerry "Itch" Cohen** scores 12 points and **Max "Trixie" Messinger** adds eight as the Rochester Centrals professional basketball team defeats West Virginia University 36-14.

1922 – **Nat Holman** scores 12 points to lead the Original Celtics to a 33-21 victory over the Power Brothers team of Passaic, N.J., in the second game of a doubleheader. The Celtics beat Wilkes-Barre of the EPBL 38-18 in the first game at Madison Square Garden.

1947 – **Ossie Schechtman** scores 17 points and **Sonny Hertzberg** adds 15 as the New York Knicks defeat the Chicago Stags 74-64.

1960 – **Dolph Schayes** of the Syracuse Nationals collects 19 points and 10 rebounds as the East beats the West 125-115 in the NBA All-Star Game in Philadelphia.

1968 – **Neal Walk** scores 33 points as Florida beats Georgia 90-63.

1989 – **John Frank** of the 49ers catches two passes for 15 yards as San Francisco beats the Cincinnati Bengals 20-16 in Super Bowl XXIII in Miami.

2000 – **David Bluthenthal** of Southern Cal scores 26 points and grabs seven rebounds as the Trojans upset No. 2-ranked Arizona 80-72. Bluthenthal is named Pac-10 Conference Player of the Week.

2004 – **Mathieu Schneider** scores two goals as the Detroit Red Wings beat the Los Angeles Kings 5-4.

MAZEL TOUGH

1911 – **Lily Kronberger** of Hungary wins her fourth consecutive world figure skating championship in Vienna.

1949 – **Vic Hershkowitz** captures the National AAU four-wall handball championship.

1977 – **Mark Roth** wins the Showboat Invitational in Las Vegas by beating two Bowling Hall of Famers in the final two matches. Roth eliminates Dick Weber 237-211 in the semifinals, then knocks off Earl Anthony 237-211 in the final.

2002 – **Jason Lezak** wins the 100-meter freestyle at a FINA World Cup swim meet in Stockholm.

2007 – With an assist in a 3-1 victory over the Minnesota Wild, **Mathieu Schneider** runs his point-scoring streak to 12 games – one short of the Detroit Red Wings' franchise record.

TRANSITIONS

1963 – Fifteen-year veteran **Dolph Schayes** becomes the first professional basketball player to appear in 1,000 games as the Syracuse Nationals lose to the St. Louis Hawks 113-93.

A STAR IS BORN

1913 – **Harry Mizler** (British lightweight boxer)

1916 – **Michel Haguenauer** (French table tennis)

1933 – **Lenny Rosenbluth** (North Carolina basketball, Philadelphia Warriors)

1945 – **Neil Rosendorff** (South African cricket)

1948 – **Bob Stein** (Univ. of Minnesota, Kansas City Chiefs, Los Angeles Rams, San Diego Chargers and Minnesota Vikings linebacker)

1958 – **Marty Hogan** (racquetball)

JANUARY 23

GAMEBREAKERS

1937 – **Moe Frankel's** one-handed shot from the side with 10 seconds left gives the Jersey Reds a 35-33 American Basketball League victory over the Paterson Y Boosters. **Moe Spahn** scores 12 points to lead the Reds, while **Phil Rabin** tops Paterson with 16.

1938 – **Moe Spahn** tallies 15 points and **Moe Frankel** scores the winning basket with six seconds remaining as the Jersey Reds defeat the New York Celtics 34-32.

1942 – **Ash Resnick** scores nine points to lead the Original Celtics to a 45-40 victory over the world champion Detroit Eagles.

1946 – **Sid Tanenbaum** scores 21 points to lead the New York Knicks to a 74-58 victory over the Boston Celtics.

STRONG IN DEFEAT

1959 – **Dolph Schayes** of the Syracuse Nationals scores 13 points in the East's 124-108 loss to the West in the NBA All-Star Game in Detroit.

1975 – **Bob Fleischer** compiles 31 points and 16 rebounds, but Duke loses to Wake Forest 90-71.

MAZEL TOUGH

1908 – **Harry Lewis** knocks out Frank Mantell in the third round in New Haven, Conn., to claim the world welterweight title.

1946 – **Irving Mondschein** wins the high jump at the Philadelphia Inquirer Indoor Games.

1955 – **Sylvia Wene** rolls games of 193 and 165 on the final day to overtake five-time champion Marion Ladewig and win the U.S. All-Star Match Play Bowling Tournament in Chicago.

1977 – **Brian Gottfried** defeats Guillermo Vilas 6-3, 7-6, 8-6 to win the Baltimore International indoor tennis tournament.

1994 – The Buffalo Bills, coached by **Marv Levy**, beat the Kansas City Chiefs 30-13 for their record fourth straight AFC championship.

2003 – **Irina Slutskaya** of Russia wins her fifth European Figure Skating title in Malmo, Sweden.

RECORD SETTERS

1947 – **Harry Boykoff** of St. John's scores a Madison Square Garden-record 54 points in a 71-52 win over St. Francis. Boykoff breaks the record of 53 set by George Mikan of De-Paul.

TRANSITIONS

1950 – A Baltimore group headed by **Carroll Rosenbloom** is granted an NFL franchise. The Colts are awarded the holdings of the defunct Dallas Texans.

1973 – Swimmer **Mark Spitz** is named Male Athlete of the Year for 1972 by the Associated Press.

A STAR IS BORN

1916 – **Irwin Witty** (NYU basketball)
1971 – **Yuri Yevseychik** (Greco-Roman wrestler)
1981 – **Alyssa Beckerman** (gymnastics)

JANUARY 24

GAMEBREAKERS

1952 – **Larry Zeidel** scores the winning goal as the Indianapolis Capitals defeat Buffalo 8-4 in the American Hockey League.

1999 – Arizona State relief pitcher **Drew Friedberg**, making a rare start, pitches a one-hitter and strikes out seven as the Sun Devils defeat Hawaii-Hilo 10-0.

STRONG IN DEFEAT

1956 – **Dolph Schayes** of the Syracuse Nationals scores 14 points, but the East loses the NBA All-Star Game 108-94 in Rochester, N.Y.

MAZEL TOUGH

1909 – **Lily Kronberger** of Hungary wins the women's world figure skating championship for the second straight year in Budapest.

1935 – World champion **Viktor Barna** of Hungary defeats **Abe Berenbaum** 21-9, 21-19 and United States champion **Sol Schiff** 21-7, 21-5 in New York in the final match of a 21-city exhibition table tennis tour.

1953 – **Vic Hershkowitz** beats Sam Costa 21-13, 21-9 to win the New York State handball championship in Brooklyn.

JEWS ON FIRST

1934 – **Mike Jacobs** promotes his first of more than 500 fights with champion **Barney Ross** taking on Billy Petrolle in a non-title fight. Ross wins a 10-round decision in New York.

2002 – Israeli junior middleweight **Yuri Foreman** makes his pro boxing debut with a first-round knockout of Israel Felix at the Park Central Hotel in New York.

TRANSITIONS

1966 – Two weeks after being named Male Athlete of the Year by the Associated Press, **Sandy Koufax** wins the Hickok Pro Athlete of the Year Award.

1980 – **Fred Wilpon**, a high school teammate of **Sandy Koufax**, becomes president and CEO of the New York Mets.

2000 – Chicago Fire assistant **Mike Jeffries** is named head coach of the Dallas Burn of Major League Soccer.

A STAR IS BORN

1899 – **Bob Berman** (Washington Senators catcher)

1911 – **Albert Weiner** (Muhlenberg, Philadelphia Eagles running back)

1918 – **Bernie Weiner** (Kansas State and pro football)

1938 – **Gyula Torok** (Hungarian flyweight boxer)

1984 – **Yotam Halperin** (Israeli basketball)

JANUARY 25

GAMEBREAKERS

1936 – **Ben Kramer** scores 10 points to lead LIU to a 36-20 victory over St. John's, the Blackbirds' 23rd straight win. Temple's **Louis Dubin** scores 12 points and **Meyer Bloom** adds 11 in a 42-36 victory over Manhattan.

1950 – **Irv Rothenberg** scores 29 points as the Paterson Crescents defeat the Bridgeport Aer-A-Sols 87-78 in the ABL.

1968 – **Steve Chubin** scores a game-high 34 points as the Anaheim Amigos defeat the Oakland Oaks 124-115 in the American Basketball Association.

2003 – **Evan Wax** scores all of Yale's goals in a 4-3 hockey victory over Connecticut.

2003 – **Robert Gherson** makes 39 saves as the Sarnia Sting defeat the Guelph Storm 4-0 in the Ontario Hockey League.

2006 – Team captain **David Hymovitz** scores the game-winning goal as his team wins the United Hockey League All-Star Game 9-7 in St. Charles, Mo.

STRONG IN DEFEAT

2004 – **Skip Kendall** loses in a one-hole play-off with Phil Mickelson in the 90-hole Bob Hope Classic in LaQuinta, Calif., to finish second in a PGA event for the fourth time. Kendall pockets $486,000. **Jonathan Kaye**, the only other Jewish golfer on the tour, finishes two strokes back in fourth place and earns $216,000.

MAZEL TOUGH

1911 – **Harry Lewis** knocks out Johnny Summers in the fourth round in London to retain his world welterweight title.

1958 – **Willie Harmatz** rides Round Table to victory in the Santa Anita Maturity race in Arcadia, Calif.

1961 – **Ronald** and **Vivian Joseph** win the junior pairs title at the U.S. National Figure Skating Championships in Colorado Springs, Colo.

1975 – **Brian Gottfried** defeats Allan Stone 3-6, 6-2, 6-3 to win the Baltimore indoor tennis tournament.

1981 – **Eliot Teltscher** beats doubles partner Tim Gullickson 6-4, 6-2 in the San Juan hard-court tennis tournament final in Puerto Rico.

1993 – Long Beach State, coached by **Seth Greenberg**, upsets top-ranked Kansas 64-49. Twelve days earlier, then-No. 1-ranked Kentucky lost 101-86 to Vanderbilt, coached by **Eddie Fogler**.

RECORD SETTERS

1928 – American speed skater **Irving Jaffee** sets a world record of 2:30.6 in the mile in Oslo, Norway.

2003 – **Maxim Podoprigora** of Austria sets a European short-course swimming record of 2:06.95 in the 200 breaststroke in Berlin.

TRANSITIONS

1956 – **Hank Greenberg** is elected to the Baseball Hall of Fame.

1992 – Oakland Raiders owner and former coach **Al Davis** is elected to the Pro Football Hall of Fame.

MEMORY LANE

1906 – **Teddy Sandwina** (heavyweight boxer)

1920 – **Al Phillips** (British featherweight boxer)

1925 – **Artie Levine** (welterweight boxer)

1932 – **Martin Engel** (hammer throw)

1959 – **Larry Rubens** (Montana State, Green Bay Packers, Chicago Bears center)

JANUARY 26

GAMEBREAKERS

1934 – **Cy Kaselman** scores 17 points as the Philadelphia Sphas defeat the Trenton Moose 36-25 in the ABL.

1946 – **Harry Boykoff** scores 28 points and **Max Zaslofsky** adds 14 to lead St. John's to a 57-52 victory over Temple. **Stan Waxman** scores 17 points and **Jackie Goldsmith** adds 12 as LIU defeats Canisius 55-49.

1951 – **Abe Becker's** 24 points lead NYU to an 87-72 victory over Notre Dame.

1963 – **Art Heyman** scores 28 points as Duke defeats West Virginia 111-71.

1968 – **Art Heyman** scores eight of his 31 points in the final four minutes as the Pittsburgh Pipers beat the Minnesota Muskies 115-107 in the American Basketball Association. The victory allows the Pipers to tie the Muskies for first place in the East Division.

1999 – **Mathieu Schneider** scores his 100th NHL goal, breaking a 1-1 tie as the New York Rangers defeat the Washington Capitals 4-1.

MAZEL TOUGH

1936 – **Morris Davis** wins the AAU 15-kilometer walk in 1 hour, 15 minutes, 44.8 seconds.

1966 – **Valery Kaplan** of the Soviet Union wins the men's 500 meters at the European Speed Skating Championships in Deventer, Netherlands.

1997 – **Irina Slutskaya** of Russia wins the European Figure Skating championship for the third time in Paris.

2006 – A day after winning the 100 freestyle, **Jason Lezak** captures the 50 freestyle at the World Cup Short-Course Swimming Championships in Moscow.

2007 – **Ben Agosto** teams with Tanith Belbin to win their fourth straight dance title at the U.S. Figure Skating Championships in Spokane, Wash.

TRANSITION

1955 – University of Cincinnati coach **Sid Gillman** is named head coach of the NFL's Los Angeles Rams.

1976 – **Herb Brown** replaces Ray Scott as head coach of the Detroit Pistons.

2003 – One day after **Eli Hami** becomes the 23rd men's player in Yeshiva basketball history to score 1,000 career points, **Daniela Epstein** scores 16 points in a victory over SUNY-Maritime to become the school's first woman to reach the 1,000-point plateau.

2004 – The New Jersey Nets name 33-year-old assistant **Lawrence Frank** head coach after firing Byron Scott.

A STAR IS BORN

1908 – **Robert Halpern** (CCNY and pro football guard)

1913 – **Henry Kozloff** (Penn basketball)

1918 – **Al "Bummy" Davis** (welterweight boxer)

1918 – **Louis Jacobson** (Irish cricket)

1972 – **Dana Rosenblatt** (middleweight boxer)

1973 – **Steve Arffa** (minor-league baseball)

1977 – **Justin Gimelstob** (tennis)

Ben Agosto
(U.S. Olympic Committee)

JANUARY 27

GAMEBREAKERS

1939 – **Jules Bender** scores 17 points as the Wilkes-Barre Barons defeat the Washington Brewers 52-36 in the ABL.

1939 – **Irv Torgoff** scores 18 points to lead LIU past Toledo 46-39.

1949 – Player-coach **Lenny Rader** scores 21 points as the Montgomery Rebels defeat the Southern Basketball League All-Stars 110-83.

1968 – **Neal Walk** scores 36 points and grabs a school-record 31 rebounds as Florida defeats Alabama 88-75.

1969 – **Neal Walk** collects 30 points and 24 rebounds in Florida's 80-66 victory over Mississippi.

MAZEL TOUGH

1913 – **Alvah Meyer** runs a world-best time in the 100 meters at the Lyceum Games in New York, but the AAU later disallows the record because of a timing error.

1928 – **Joey Sangor** hands **Sammy Dorfman** his first loss in 43 fights with a 10-round decision in New York.

1930 – **Viktor Barna** of Hungary beats **Laszlo Bellak** of Hungary 21-14, 16-21, 21-16, 21-12 to win the world table tennis championship in Berlin.

1979 – **Marshall Holman** beats top seed **Mark Roth** 217-186 to win the PBA Quaker State Open in Grand Prairie, Texas.

RECORD SETTERS

1934 – **Irving Jaffee** of the United States breaks a 30-year-old world speed skating record by covering 25 miles in 1 hour, 26.1 seconds.

1935 – **Milton Green** of Harvard equals his world record of 5.8 seconds in the 45-yard high hurdles twice in the same meet in Boston – during a qualifying heat and again during the final.

1938 – **Cy Kaselman** scores an American Basketball League-record 27 points as the Philadelphia Sphas defeat the first-half champion Jersey Reds 65-47 in the league's second-half opener. Kaselman breaks **Phil Rabin's** record of 25 points set two years earlier. His 12 field goals also are a league record, as is the Sphas' team total. **Moe Spahn** leads the Reds with 17 points.

2001 – **David Bluthenthal** sets a Pac-10 Conference record by making his 42nd consecutive free throw as Southern Cal beats Oregon State 73-47.

TRANSITIONS

1970 – The New York Jets select Florida defensive back **Steve Tannen** with their first-round draft pick, the 20th overall selection.

A STAR IS BORN

1899 – **Bela Guttman** (Hungarian soccer)
1909 – **Lou Halper** (welterweight, middleweight boxer)
1952 – **Brian Gottfried** (tennis)

Steve Tannen *(New York Jets)*

JANUARY 28

GAMEBREAKERS

1939 – **Cy Kaselman** scores 22 points, **Petey Rosenberg** 13 and **Mike Bloom** 10 as the Philadelphia Sphas defeat the Washington Brewers 62-42.

1942 – **Stan Waxman** hits the winning shot in the fifth overtime period as LIU beats West Texas State 58-56.

1991 – Toronto Maple Leafs goalie **Peter Ing** makes 32 saves to notch his only career NHL shutout, 4-0 over the Minnesota North Stars. Ing posts a 20-37-9 career record over parts of four seasons.

1995 – **Anita Kaplan** scores 19 points and **Jamila Wideman** adds eight as Stanford routs Southern Cal 109-53 in women's basketball.

STRONG IN DEFEAT

2006 – **Mike Cammalleri** scores both goals for the Los Angeles Kings in a 6-2 loss to the Calgary Flames.

MAZEL TOUGH

1926 – **Louis "Kid" Kaplan** knocks out Bobby Garcia in the 10th round to retain his world featherweight title in Hartford, Conn.

1930 – The Illinois State Athletic Commission declares **Leo Lomski** the winner of a Jan. 17 fight against James J. Braddock that had originally been called a 10-round draw.

The referee said he "erred" on the original scorecard.

1932 – **Jackie Fields** decisions champion Lou Brouillard in 10 rounds in Chicago to regain the world welterweight title he lost a year and a half earlier.

1935 – **Barney Ross** wins a 10-round decision over Frankie Klick in Miami to retain his world junior welterweight title.

1965 – **Gary Gubner** wins the shot put for the second straight year at the Millrose Games in New York.

1978 – **Mark Roth** wins the PBA Quaker State Open in Grand Prairie, Texas, beating **Marshall Holman** 216-213 when Holman leaves the 6-7-10 on his final ball.

2000 – **Irina Slutskaya** wins her fourth European Figure Skating championship, taking the gold medal in Vienna.

A STAR IS BORN

1891 – **Barney Sedran** (basketball)
1915 – **Al Reid** (featherweight boxer)
1938 – **Leonid Zhabinskiy** (weight lifting)
1978 – **Vitaly Pisetsky** (Wisconsin football placekicker)

JANUARY 29

GAMEBREAKERS

1936 – **Jules Bender** scores a game-high 10 points to lead LIU past St. Francis (N.Y.) 31-23. **Java Gotkin** scores 11 points and **Rip Kaplinsky** adds eight as St. John's beats La Salle 40-26.

1938 – **Bernie Opper** scores 10 points in Kentucky's 42-19 victory over Vanderbilt.

1940 – **Inky Lautman** scores 14 points as the Philadelphia Sphas defeat the Wilkes-Barre Barons 44-32 in an ABL game in Norristown, Pa. **Jules Bender** scores 16 for the Barons.

MAZEL TOUGH

1934 – **Myer Rosenblum** wins the hammer throw with a toss of 43.29 meters at the Australian Track and Field Championships in Adelaide.

1961 – **Vivian** and **Ronald Joseph** win the junior pairs title at the U.S. Figure Skating Championships in Colorado Springs.

1967 – **Valery Kaplan** of the Soviet Union captures the 500-meter race in 41.9 seconds and wins the men's all-around silver medal at the European Speed Skating Championships in Lahti, Finland.

1984 – **Andrea Leand** beats Pascale Paradis-Mangon of France 0-6, 6-2, 6-4 for her only victory on the women's pro tennis tour at the indoor Ginny Tournament in Pittsburgh.

2004 – **Shraga Weinberg** and **Ham Lev** of Israel defeat a Dutch team 5-7, 7-6 (7-4), 6-1 to win the World Team Cup wheelchair tennis men's doubles championship in Christchurch, New Zealand.

2005 – **Irina Slutskaya** of Russia wins her sixth European Figure Skating championship in Turin, Italy, matching the record set by Katarina Witt and Sonja Henie.

2005 – **Paul Goldstein** defeats Cecil Mamiit 6-2, 6-2 to win the USTA Challenger Hilton Waikoloa tennis tournament.

RECORD SETTERS

1953 – **Jack Molinas** grabs a school-record 31 rebounds as Columbia beats Brown 70-60.

1983 – **Dara Torres** sets a world record of 25.69 seconds in the 50-meter freestyle in Amersfoort, Netherlands.

1995 – **Jerry Markbreit** referees his record fourth Super Bowl. **Ron Botchan**, one of only two active officials who played in the NFL, is the game's umpire.

JEWS ON FIRST

1991 – Goalie **David Littman** makes his NHL debut, stopping 15 of 18 shots afer replacing Darcy Wakaluk in the second period of the Buffalo Sabres' 8-3 loss to the St. Louis Blues. Littman will appear in only three NHL games over the next two years – one more for Buffalo and one for Tampa Bay.

TRANSITIONS

1981 – American League owners approve the sale of the Chicago White Sox to **Jerry Reinsdorf** and **Eddie Einhorn** for $20 million.

A STAR IS BORN

1931 – **Hy Cohen** (Chicago Cubs pitcher)

1950 – **Jody Scheckter** (South African auto racing).

1975 – **Galit Chait** (Israeli figure skater)

JANUARY 30

GAMEBREAKERS

1960 – **Jeff Cohen** collects 34 points and 20 rebounds as William & Mary defeats West Virginia 94-86.

2001 – **Gabe Frank** comes off the bench and scores 17 points in 31 minutes, including 5-for-5 from 3-point range, as the Rockford Lightning beat the Yakima Sun Kings 114-108 in a Continental Basketball Association game.

MAZEL TOUGH

1932 – **Viktor Barna** of Hungary beats doubles partner **Miklos Szabados** 21-19, 14-21, 16-21, 21-19, 21-18 for the men's table tennis world championship in Prague. **Anna Sipos** of Hungary wins the women's title, beating Maria Mednyanszky 21-17, 21-16, 21-19. Barna and Sipos also win their respective doubles titles and combine to win the mixed doubles crown.

1951 – **Dick Savitt** beats Ken McGregor of Australia 6-3, 2-6, 6-3, 6-1 to win the Australian Open singles tennis championship – his first of two grand slam titles for the year.

1964 – **Gary Gubner** wins the shot put with a toss of 62 feet, 6½ inches at the Millrose Games at Madison Square Garden.

1974 – **Ilana Kloss** beats doubles partner Linky Boshoff 7-5, 6-1 to win the East London Border Championship tennis tournament in South Africa.

1988 – **Fabrice Benichou** knocks out Thierry Jacob in the ninth round to win the European bantamweight championship in Calais, France.

2000 – **Paul Goldstein** defeats Andre Sa 6-2, 6-7, 7-6, 6-4 to win a USTA Challenger tennis tournament in Walkoloa, Hawaii.

JEWS ON FIRST

1999 – **Missy Leopoldus** registers the first perfect score in Penn State women's gymnastics history, scoring a 10 on the balance beam in a victory over Florida. She also ties the school record of 9.95 in the floor exercise.

RECORD SETTERS

1939 – **Sid Weinstein** shaves eight seconds off the national outdoor 2-mile speed skating record while winning the event in 6:10.6 at the St. Paul (Minn.) Silver Skates competition.

A STAR IS BORN

1808 – **Young Dutch Sam** (boxing)
1898 – **Bill Schwarz** (minor-league catcher)
1912 – **Jadwiga Wajsowna** (Polish discus thrower

Dick Savitt

JANUARY 31

GAMEBREAKERS

1938 – **Bernie Opper** scores a game-high 10 points to lead Kentucky past Alabama 57-31.
1953 – **Jerry Domershick** scores 23 points to lead CCNY past Franklin & Marshall 86-80.
1959 – Dartmouth's **Rudy LaRusso** scores 28 points in a 71-59 win over Brown.

STRONG IN DEFEAT

1959 – **Alan Seiden** scores a career-high 38 points, but St. John's loses to Loyola of Chicago 95-85 in double overtime.

MAZEL TOUGH

1891 – **Edward Lawrence Levy** wins the first British amateur weight lifting championship.
1908 – **Abe Attell** knocks out Frankie Neil in the 13th round to retain his world featherweight title in San Francisco.
1930 – **George Goldberg** wins a 12-round decision over Harry Sankey in Brooklyn to win the National Guard New York State featherweight title.
1959 – **Lew Stieglitz** of the U.S. Navy wins the 2-mile run in 8:55.1 at the Millrose Games in New York.
1981 – **Marshall Holman** beats Richard Martinez 209-203 to win his second PBA Quaker State Open in Grand Prairie, Texas.

A STAR IS BORN

1848 – **Nathan Straus** (harness racing)
1912 – **Ed Horowitz** (Yale basketball)
1915 – **Maurice Patt** (Carnegie Tech, Detroit Lions, Cleveland Rams end)

Marshall Holman
(Professional Bowlers Association)

FEBRUARY 1

GAMEBREAKERS

1921 – **Nat Holman** scores 16 points as the Camden Skeeters beat Coatesville 44-18 in an Eastern Basketball League game.

1935 – Long Island University's **Phil Rubinowitz** scores 14 points in a 60-29 rout of Holy Cross.

1939 – **Bobby Lewis** scores 14 points and **Ben Auerbach** adds 13 as NYU defeats St. John's 40-33. **Jack Garfinkel** leads St. John's with nine.

1954 – **Jerry Domershick** scores 24 points to lead CCNY to a 69-58 win over Rider.

1965 – **Ron Watts** scores a game-high 29 points and grabs 15 rebounds as Wake Forest defeats Clemson 82-75.

1991 – **Mike Kelfer** scores with 2:34 left in overtime as the Kansas City Blades rally from a four-goal deficit to defeat the Phoenix Roadrunners 6-5 in the International Hockey League.

1997 – **Danny Allouche** of Israel scores a career-high 20 points, including three 3-pointers, as Missouri beats Kansas State 85-63.

2006 – **Shay Doron** scores 26 points as Maryland defeats Miami 88-77 in women's basketball.

STRONG IN DEFEAT

1959 – **Dolph Schayes** scores a career-high 50 points, but the Syracuse Nationals lose in overtime to the Boston Celtics, 129-127.

MAZEL TOUGH

1890 – **Louis Rubenstein** of Montreal wins the unofficial world figure skating title in St. Petersburg, Russia.

1975 – **Mark Roth** beats hometown favorite Steve Jones 299-233 to win his first Pro Bowlers Association tournament, the King Louie Open in Overland Park, Kan.

1985 – **Judy Blomberg** and Michael Seibert win their fifth straight ice dancing title at the U.S. Figure Skating Championships in Kansas City.

1994 – **Gary Jacobs** earns a 12-round decision over Tek N'kalankete in Levallois, France, to retain his European welterweight title.

2004 – **Shahar Peer** of Israel defeats third-seeded Nicole Vaidisova of the Czech Republic 6-1 6-4 in the junior girls final at the Australian Open tennis tournament.

2004 – **Jonathan Kaye** finishes two strokes ahead of Chris DiMarco and wins the FBR Open in Scottsdale, Ariz. His second career PGA Tour title is worth $936,000.

TRANSITIONS

1964 – **Red Auerbach** wins his 800th game as an NBA coach as the Boston Celtics beat the Philadelphia 76ers 119-111.

1965 – **Walter Blum** wins the George Woolf Award as the top jockey of 1964.

1984 – **David Stern**, executive vice president of the NBA, is named the league's fourth commissioner.

1993 – **Gary Bettman**, the NBA's assistant general consul, takes office as NHL commissioner.

A STAR IS BORN

1878 – **Alfred Hajos-Guttmann** (Hungarian swimming, soccer)

1906 – **Hal-Alec Natan** (German sprinter)

1930 – **Marty Reisman** (table tennis)

1941 – **Jerry Greenbaum** (golf)

1964 – **Eli Ohana** (Israeli soccer)

FEBRUARY 2

GAMEBREAKERS

1935 – **Sam Winograd** scores a game-high 11 points as CCNY defeats Temple 38-28.

1938 – **Cy Kaselman** scores 16 points and **Inky Lautman** adds 15 as the Philadelphia Sphas defeat the Kingston Colonials 46-26 in the ABL.

1946 – Cornell's **Irwin Alterson** scores 24 points in a 70-58 victory over Penn.

1947 – **Ben Goldfaden** scores 24 points as the Trenton Tigers defeat the Philadelphia Sphas 96-86 in three overtimes. **Stanley Brown** scores 25, **Inky Lautman** 14, **Bernie Opper** 13, **Red Klotz** 12 and **Sol Schwartz** 11 for the Sphas.

1962 – **Barry Kramer** scores 27 points in NYU's 77-59 win over Mount St. Mary's.

1968 – **Art Heyman** scores 37 points, including 16 in the fourth quarter, as the Pittsburgh Pipers beat the Dallas Chapparels 112-105 in an American Basketball Association game.

2002 – Defender **Jeff Agoos**, playing in his 122nd international soccer match, scores his fourth career goal on a 25-yard free kick as the United States beats Costa Rica 2-0 in the final of the Gold Cup Tournament in Pasadena, Calif. America wins its first major soccer trophy in more than a decade.

2003 – **Mathieu Schneider** of the Los Angeles Kings assists on the game's first two goals as the Western Conference wins the NHL All-Star Game 6-5 in Sunrise, Fla.

MAZEL TOUGH

1914 – **Ted "Kid" Lewis** defeats Paul Til in 12 rounds in London to win the European featherweight championship.

1935 – **Arthur Rosenstein** of the 92nd Street YMHA wins the 1-mile walk in 6:30.6 in the Millrose Games at Madison Square Garden.

1946 – **Alf James** decisions Willie Miller in 12 rounds to win the vacant South African lightweight title in Johannesburg.

1947 – **Herb Flam** wins the Los Angeles Met tennis tournament.

1965 – **Bill Wishnick** drives his 28-foot boat to victory in the Sam Griffith Memorial Race, a round trip between Miami and Cat Cay in the Bahamas. His winning time is 3 hours, 18 minutes.

1996 – **Margie Goldstein-Engle** wins the Budweiser/America Grand Prix Association equestrian championship aboard Hidden Creek's Laurel.

RECORD SETTERS

1938 – **Harry Platt** scores a school-record 48 points as Brown defeats Northeastern 77-52.

1962 – **Gary Gubner** sets a world indoor record of 63 feet, 10¼ inches in the shot put at the Millrose Games in New York.

TRANSITIONS

1944 – Chicago Bears quarterback **Sid Luckman** is named National Football League MVP in a football writers' poll.

A STAR IS BORN

1910 – **Alex Levinsky** (Chicago Black Hawks, New York Rangers, Toronto Maple Leafs hockey)

1917 – **Maxie Berger** (Canadian lightweight boxing)

1918 – **Sid Schacht** (St. Louis Browns, Boston Braves pitcher)

1937 – **Boris Michail Gurevitch** (Soviet Greco-Roman wrestling)

FEBRUARY 3

GAMEBREAKERS

1934 – Behind 14 points by **Harry Litwack**, the Philadelphia Sphas defeat the Brooklyn Visitations 30-28 in the ABL.

1937 – **Phil Rabin** scores 26 points as the Kingston Colonials defeat the Brooklyn Jewels 39-30 in the ABL. **Mac Kinsbrunner** scores 14 for Brooklyn.

1939 – **Irv Resnick** scores 17 points, **Bobby Lewis** adds 14 and **Ben Auerbach** contributes 11 as NYU defeats Union 63-34.

1968 – **Neal Walk** scores 35 points in Florida's 91-85 victory over Vanderbilt.

2007 – **Mike Cammalleri** has two goals and two assists as the Los Angeles Kings beat the Florida Panthers 7-0.

MAZEL TOUGH

1952 – Temple, coached by **Pete Leaness**, defeats San Francisco 2-0 to capture the intercollegiate soccer championship at Kezar Stadium. USF came into Soccer Bowl 1952 with a 40-match winning streak.

1963 – **Herman Barron** becomes the first golfer in the 24-year history of the PGA Seniors Championship to shoot four sub-70 rounds while beating runner-up John Barnum by two strokes in Port St. Lucie, Fla. Barron finishes at 16-under-par 272.

1975 – **Victor Neiderhoffer** beats Sharif Khan 3-1 to win the North American Squash Racquets championship in Mexico City.

1983 – At the U.S. Figure Skating Championships in Pittsburgh, **Judy Blumberg** and Michael Seibert win their third of five consecutive ice dancing titles.

JEWS ON FIRST

1943 – **Max Kaminsky** of the Buffalo Bisons plays in the first American Hockey League All-Star Game in Cleveland. Kaminsky and the East Division beat the West Division 5-4.

TRANSITIONS

1928 – **Dolly Stark**, a former basketball coach at Dartmouth, is added to the National League umpiring staff.

1949 – **Motsy Handler** and Ray Parker are appointed co-head coaches of the Chicago Cardinals of the NFL.

1976 – Temple coach **Harry Litwack** is elected to the Basketball Hall of Fame.

1990 – **Larry Brown** posts his 500th career victory as a professional basketball coach as the San Antonio Spurs beat the Chicago Bulls 112-111.

A STAR IS BORN

1931 – **Lew Lazar** (British middleweight boxer)

1932 – **Maria Itkina** (Soviet Union sprinter)

1960 – **Ken "Zion Lion" Klingman** (middleweight boxer)

1964 – **Jill "Zion Lion" Matthews** (boxing)

Harry Litwack *(Temple University)*

FEBRUARY 4

GAMEBREAKERS

1936 – **Harry Bassin** scores a game-high 11 points as Georgetown upsets defending national champion NYU 36-34, ending the Violets' 20-game winning streak.

1939 – **Ralph Dolgoff** scores 13 points to lead St. John's to a 51-50 victory over West Virginia.

1968 – **Steve Chubin** scores 34 points to lead the Anaheim Amigos to a 132-120 victory over the Houston Monarchs in the American Basketball Association.

1989 – **Danny Schayes** of the Denver Nuggets scores an NBA career-high 37 points in a 127-126 victory over the Utah Jazz.

2001 – **Eric Himelfarb** collects three goals and one assist as the Sarnia Sting beat the London Knights 4-1 in an Ontario Hockey League game.

STRONG IN DEFEAT

1981 – **Danny Schayes** of Syracuse blocks eight shots in a 66-65 loss to Seton Hall.

MAZEL TOUGH

1909 – **Abe Attell** knocks out Eddie Kelly in the seventh round in New Orleans to retain his world featherweight title.

1927 – **Charley Phil Rosenberg** wins a 15-round decision over Bushy Graham in New York to retain his world bantamweight title. But the New York Athletic Commission strips Rosenberg of his title because the bout is fought despite his not making weight.

1932 – On the opening day of competition at the Winter Olympics in Lake Placid, N.Y., American speed skater **Irving Jaffee** dethrones world-record holder Ivar Ballangrud of Norway in the 5,000-meter race.

1968 – **James Prigoff** wins the National Open squash racquets title in New York.

1975 – **Brian Gottfried** defeats Geoff Masters 6-4, 4-6, 6-4 in the final of the Dayton Indoor tennis tournament.

1978 – **Mark Roth** rallies by striking out in the final frame to beat Joe Berardi 209-198 in the final of the PBA King Louie Open in Overland Park, Kan.

2001 – **Dan Weinstein** celebrates his birthday by winning his first World Cup short-track speed skating gold medal in the 1,000-meter event in Graz, Austria.

2001 – **Alex Averbukh** of Israel wins the pole vault by clearing 10 feet, ¼ inch at the European Athletic Association indoor meet in Donetsk, Ukraine.

RECORD SETTERS

1948 – **James Fuchs** sets a world indoor shot put record of 17.54 meters in Boston.

1972 – **Arnie Berman** of Brown shoots a school-record 25-for-26 from the foul line in an 89-73 victory over Cornell.

A STAR IS BORN

1906 – **Phil Tobias** (flyweight boxer)
1969 – **Leah Goldstein** (Canadian cycling)
1981 – **Dan Weinstein** (speed skating)

FEBRUARY 5

GAMEBREAKERS

1938 – **Shikey Gotthoffer** scores 16 points and **Inky Lautman** adds 12 as the Philadelphia Sphas defeat the New York Celtics 42-35 in the American Basketball League.

1957 – **Lenny Rosenbluth** scores eight of his team's 12 points in overtime, and finishes with 25 as unbeaten North Carolina defeats Maryland 65-61 in double overtime.

MAZEL TOUGH

1934 – **Maxie Rosenbloom** fights Joe Knight to a 15-round draw in Miami and retains his world light heavyweight title.

1939 – **Joseph Fishbach** of St. John's defeats Chauncey Steele of Columbia 6-1, 4-6, 6-4, 6-1 to repeat as Eastern Intercollegiate Indoor Tennis champion.

1950 – **Richard Bergmann** of Austria beats Ferenc Sido of Hungary 12-21, 15-18, 21-7, 21-14, 21-13 to win the world table tennis championship in Budapest. **Angelica Rozeanu** of Romania tops Gizella Farkas of Hungary for the women's title.

1978 – **Stu Goldstein** defeats Rainer Ratinac 15-10, 15-13, 15-8 in the final to win the World Pro Squash Championship in Minneapolis.

2000 – **Andy Bloom** wins the shot put at the Millrose Games in New York with a toss of 68 feet,½ inch.

TRANSITIONS

1960 – University of New Mexico coach **Marv Levy** is named head football coach at the University of California.

1998 – **Irena Kirszenstein-Szewinska** of Poland, winner of track and field medals in four consecutive Olympics, is named to the International Olympic Committee.

2005 – Seventy-three years after playing his final game, **Benny Friedman** is elected to the Pro Football Hall of Fame.

Andy Bloom
(U.S. Olympic Committee)

A STAR IS BORN

1942 – **Gary Wood** (Cornell, New York Giants quarterback)

1946 – **Norm Miller** (Houston Astros, Atlanta Braves outfielder)

1970 – **Michael Shmerkin** (Israeli figure skater)

FEBRUARY 6

GAMEBREAKERS

1937 – **Cy Kaselman** scores 15 points and **Reds Rosan** adds 10 as the Philadelphia Sphas defeat the New York Celtics 44-38 in the ABL.

1954 – **Boris Nachamkin** scores 31 points and matches his career high by pulling down 26 rebounds in NYU's 91-77 victory over Pitt.

1959 – **Howie Carl** of DePaul scores an Alumni Hall-record 37 points in an 80-70 victory over Western Kentucky.

1960 – **Sid Cohen** scores a game-high 20 points to lead Kentucky past Mississippi 61-43.

1963 – **Art Heyman** scores 22 points, grabs 10 rebounds and hands out 13 assists as third-ranked Duke beats defending Atlantic Coast Conference champion Wake Forest 92-66. **Steve Nisenson** scores 45 points as Hofstra defeats West Chester 75-68.

1964 – **Barry Kramer's** 27 points help NYU beat Holy Cross 103-83.

1999 – **Jamila Wideman** scores a season-high 24 points as Stanford defeats Southern Cal 103-69 in women's basketball.

2005 – **Josh Miller** punts seven times for 316 yards – a 45.1-yard average – as the New England Patriots defeat the Philadelphia Eagles 24-21 in the Super Bowl. Miller's final punt pins the Eagles on their 4-yard line with 46 seconds remaining.

STRONG IN DEFEAT

1958 – **Alan Seiden** scores 30 points but St. John's loses to West Virginia 87-78.

MAZEL TOUGH

1947 – **Herman Barron** and Ben Hogan both shoot 65 to tie for first place in an 18-hole pro-am golf tournament in San Antonio.

1977 – **Tom Okker** wins the United Virginia Bank tennis tournament in Richmond with a 3-6, 6-3, 6-4 victory over Vitas Gerulaitis.

1986 – **Gillian Wachsman** and her partner Todd Waggoner win the pairs title at the U.S. Figure Skating Championships in Uniondale, N.Y.

1988 – **Marshall Holman** wins four matches, including 275-211 over Ron Bell in the final, to capture the Bowlers Journal Florida Open in Venice, Fla.

1993 – **Gary Jacobs** knocks out Ludovic Proto in the ninth round in Paris to win the European welterweight title.

1994 – **Skip Kendall** shoots 19-under-par to win the Nike Tour's season-opening Inland Empire Open in Moreno Valley, Calif., by six strokes over Emlyn Aubrey.

2000 – **Bruce Fleisher** wins the PGA Senior Tour's Royal Caribbean Classic in Key Biscayne, Fla., for the second year in a row, finishing two strokes ahead of Vicente Fernandez.

TRANSITIONS

1968 – World figure skating champion **Alain Calmat** of France lights the Olympic flame to open the 10th Winter Olympics in Grenoble.

1992 – **Larry Brown** is named head coach of the NBA's Los Angeles Clippers.

A STAR IS BORN

1882 – **Harry Fisher** (basketball)

1906 – **Paul Winter** (French discus, shot put)

1952 – **Bruce "Mouse" Strauss** (middleweight boxer)

1969 – **Mike Zimmerman** (minor-league baseball)

1972 – **David Binn** (San Diego Chargers center)

FEBRUARY 7

GAMEBREAKERS

1931 – **Monty Banks** scores 13 points as NYU ends St. John's 24-game winning streak 27-23. **Louis Bender** scores 18 points in Columbia's 53-31 victory over Army. **Louis Hayman's** 11 points lead Syracuse past Colgate 39-24.

1938 – **Bernie Opper** scores a game-high 14 points – a career high – as Kentucky beats Michigan State 44-27.

1953 – **Boris Nachamkin** scores 27 points and grabs 15 rebounds, and **Mark Solomon** adds 21 points as NYU defeats North Carolina 82-78. **Al Lifson** leads the Tar Heels with 24 points. **Jack Molinas** scores 38 points, including a school-record 15 field goals, as Columbia defeats Army 83-57.

1956 – **Lenny Rosenbluth** of North Carolina scores 45 points in a 115-63 rout of William & Mary.

1962 – **Barry Kramer** scores 32 points, makes 14 straight foul shots and grabs nine rebounds as NYU defeats Furman 108-82.

1976 – **Ernie Grunfeld** scores a game-high 32 points as Tennessee beats Kentucky 92-85.

2004 – **David Hymovitz** scores three goals in a span of 3:58 of the second period as the Binghamton Senators defeat the Philadelphia Phantoms 6-5 in the American Hockey League. In his first minor-league hockey game, **Evan Wax** scores the winning goal as the Atlantic City Boardwalk Bullies defeat the Reading Royals 5-2 in the East Coast Hockey League.

STRONG IN DEFEAT

2007 – Duke freshman **Jon Scheyer** scores a career-high 26 points in the Blue Devils' 79-73 loss to fifth-ranked North Carolina.

MAZEL TOUGH

1934 – **Barney Ross** wins a 12-round decision over Polo Nebo in Kansas City, Mo., to retain his world junior welterweight title.

1937 – **Richard Bergmann** of Great Britain becomes the youngest man to win the world table tennis championship.

1949 – **Thelma Thal** teams with Mildred Shaihan to win the women's doubles title at the U.S. Table Tennis Championships.

1949 – **Myra Shapiro** wins the Middle States outdoor speed skating championship in Newburgh, N.Y.

1971 – **Kathy Harter** defeats Beverly Vercoe 6-2, 6-2 to win the singles and teams with Sue Blakely to capture the doubles at the Wellington Championships tennis tournament in New Zealand.

1981 – **Marshall Holman** beats **Mark Roth** 200-179 to win the BPAA U.S. Open bowling championship in Houston.

1999 – **Bruce Fleisher** wins the Royal Caribbean Classic in Key Biscayne, Fla., by two strokes over Isao Aoki. He leads all three rounds of his first tournament on the Senior PGA Tour.

RECORD-SETTERS

1952 – **Dolph Schayes** of the Syracuse Nationals begins an NBA-record 706-game consecutive-game streak which ends in December 1961.

A STAR IS BORN

1869 – **Edwin Hyneman** (Penn football)

1927 – **Al Richter (**Boston Red Sox outfielder)

1967 – **Mike Hartman** (Buffalo Sabres, New York Rangers)

1983 – **Scott Feldman** (Texas Rangers pitcher)

1984 – **Dan Grunfeld** (Stanford basketball)

FEBRUARY 8

GAMEBREAKERS

1937 – **Bernie Opper** scores 10 points as Kentucky defeats Mexico University 60-30.

1939 – **John Bromberg** scores 13 points as LIU runs its record to 14-0 with a 48-31 victory over Duquesne. **Lou Lefkowitz** scores 13 points to lead CCNY to a 51-35 victory over Fordham.

1960 – **Sid Cohen** scores 16 points as Kentucky routs Mississippi State 61-43.

1968 – **Steve Chubin** scores 31 points as the Anaheim Amigos beat the New Orleans Buccaneers 122-118 in the American Basketball Association.

MAZEL TOUGH

1806 – **Samuel Elias** ("**Dutch Sam**") beats London Prize Ring heavyweight champion Tom Belcher in a 57-round fight in Virginia Water, England.

1932 – **Irving Jaffee** wins the 10,000-meter speed skating event at the Olympics in Lake Placid, N.Y.

1942 – **Herman Barron** becomes the first Jewish golfer to win a significant national event when he captures the PGA Western Open in Phoenix. He shoots an 8-under-par 276 and defeats runner-up Henry Picard by two strokes.

1963 – **Alain Calmat** of France wins his second straight men's title at the European Figure Skating Championships in Budapest.

1970 – **Nancy Ornstein** defeats Janet Newberry 3-6, 6-4, 7-5 to win the March of Dimes tennis tournament in San Diego.

2004 – **Bruce Fleisher** becomes the first three-time winner of the Royal Caribbean Classic in Key Biscayne, Fla., by shooting 6-under-par 210, one stroke better than Dana Quigley. His 17th victory on the senior golf tour is worth $217,500.

2004 – Ending a two-year retirement, **Robert Dover** rides Rainier to victory in the USET Grand Prix freestyle Olympic qualifying equestrian event in Wellington, Fla.

RECORD SETTERS

1943 – **Harry Boykoff** of St. John's sets a Madison Square Garden record with 45 points in a 76-48 win over St. Joseph's. Boykoff breaks the record of 27 points set by Bob Gerber of Toledo in 1942.

1958 – **Rudy LaRusso** of Dartmouth ties an Ivy League record with 32 rebounds against Columbia.

1969 – **Steve Bilski** sets a Penn school record by making 17 free throws as the Quakers defeat Columbia 91-81. He will match that record one year later against Columbia.

A STAR IS BORN

1894 – **Joe Fox** (British bantamweight, featherweight boxer)

1901 – **Max Kadesky** (Iowa and pro football)

1945 – **Steve Goldman** (Ottawa Roughriders, college football coach)

1973 – **Eli Zuckerman** (Israeli yachting)

1987 – **Jessica Jerome** (ski jumping)

Herman Barron

FEBRUARY 9

GAMEBREAKERS

1933 – **Harold "Reds" Rosan** scores 17 points to lead Temple to a 42-28 victory over West Virginia.

1935 – **Ben Goldfaden** scores 11 points in George Washington's 29-26 victory over St. John's. **Len Maidman** scores 14 points and **Sid Gross** and **Milt Schulman** add 10 apiece as NYU defeats Navy 46-36.

2002 – **Maurice Rozenthal** scores two goals and adds one assist as France ties heavily favored Switzerland 3-3 in Olympic ice hockey pool play in West Valley City, Utah.

2006 – **Mathieu Schneider** scores his 18th goal of the season with 6:31 remaining to give the Detroit Red Wings a 3-2 victory over the Nashville Predators.

MAZEL TOUGH

1985 – **Marshall Holman** beats Wayne Webb 233-205 in the final and becomes the first two-time winner of the BPAA U.S. Open bowling championship in Venice, Fla.

1986 – **Brad Gilbert** defeats Stefan Edberg 7-5, 7-6 in the final of the U.S. Indoor Tennis Championships in Memphis.

RECORD SETTERS

1959 – **Howie Carl** makes a school-record 23 free throws as DePaul beats Marquette 89-80.

1963 – **Abigail Hoffman** of Canada sets a U.S. women's indoor record of 2:13.7 in the 800-meter run at the All-Eastern Indoor Track and Field Meet in Baltimore.

1974 – **Irina Kirszenstein-Szewinska** of Poland ties the women's world indoor 60-meter record of 7.1 seconds in Warsaw.

1981 – **Danny Schayes** ties a Syracuse school record by grabbing 23 rebounds in a 66-64 win over Georgetown.

2002 – **Amit Tamir** of Israel scores a University of California freshman-record 39 points and hits 5-of-6 shots from 3-point range in a 107-103 overtime victory over 15th-ranked Oregon. The Golden Bears' center is named national Player of the Week by ESPN.

JEWS ON FIRST

2002 – Junior guard **Laine Selwyn** posts the first triple-double in Pittsburgh women's basketball history with 12 points, 11 rebounds and 10 assists in a 77-45 victory over St. John's.

TRANSITIONS

1960 – **Willie Harmatz** is presented the Woolf Award as the nation's top jockey.

A STAR IS BORN

1812 – **Israel Lazarus** (English boxer)
1908 – **Jackie Fields** (welterweight boxer)
1934 – **Willie Harmatz** (jockey)
1979 – **Irina Slutskaya** (Russian figure skating)

FEBRUARY 10

GAMEBREAKERS

1987 – **Mike Kelfer's** overtime goal gives Boston University a 4-3 win over Northeastern in the championship game of the 35th annual Beanpot Hockey Tournament in Boston. Kelfer is named the tournament's MVP.
1993 – **Ronnie Stern** of the Calgary Flames scores three goals in a 13-1 rout of the San Jose Sharks.

STRONG IN DEFEAT

1968 – **Neal Walk** scores a career-high 38 points, but Florida loses 93-92 to LSU.

MAZEL TOUGH

1922 – **Benny Leonard** wins a 15-round decision over Rocky Kansas in New York to retain his world lightweight title.
1952 – **Angelica Rozeanu** of Romania wins the women's singles title at the World Table Tennis Championships in Bombay, India.
1954 – **Lawrence Demmy** and partner Jean Westwood of Great Britain win the ice dancing competition at the World Figure Skating Championships in Oslo, Norway. The title is the fifth in a row for Demmy.
1968 – **Willie Harmatz** rides Most Host to victory in the Charles H. Strub Stakes at Santa Anita in Arcadia, Calif.
1979 – **Mark Roth** opens the final with nine consecutive strikes and beats **Marshall Holman** 279-227 in the Rolaids Open bowling tournament in Florissant, Mo., for his 17th PBA title.
2002 – **Yulia Beygelzimer** defeats top-seeded Eszter Molnar 6-2, 6-1 to win an International Tennis Federation tournament in Leece, Italy.

Angelica Rozeanu

RECORD SETTERS

1951 – **James Fuchs** breaks his world indoor shot put record with a toss of 58 feet, 3½ inches at the Baxter Mile Meet in New York.

A STAR IS BORN

1895 – **Frankie Callahan** (lightweight boxer)
1917 – **Eddie Turchin** (Cleveland Indians shortstop)
1921 – **Sam Dietchman** (CCNY basketball)
1923 – **Allie Sherman** (Brooklyn College, Philadelphia Eagles quarterback, New York Giants football coach)
1930 – **Issy Bloomberg** (South African weightlifter)
1950 – **Mark Spitz** (swimming)
1968 – **Eddie Zosky** (Toronto Blue Jays, Florida Marlins, Milwaukee Brewers, Houston Astros infielder)
1975 – **Idan Tal** (Israeli soccer)

FEBRUARY 11

GAMEBREAKERS

1914 – **Barney Sedran** scores a career-high 34 points – mostly from what will eventually become 3-point range against a backboardless hoop – as the Utica Indians beat Cohoes 74-44 for the New York State League basketball title.

1927 – **Davey Banks** scores 17 points and **Nat Holman** adds 16 as the New York Celtics defeat the New York Rens 39-23.

1939 – **Shikey Gotthoffer** scores 16 points, **Petey Rosenberg** adds 15 and **Inky Lautman** contributes 10 as the Philadelphia Sphas defeat the Troy Haymakers 67-41 in the ABL.

1941 – **Solly Cohen** scores 16 points to lead LIU past Brooklyn College 64-47.

1950 – **George Feigenbaum** scores 23 points as the Hartford Hurricanes defeat the New York Harlem Yankees 108-92 in the ABL.

1952 – **Max Zaslofsky** of the New York Knicks scores 11 points as the East beats the West 108-91 in the NBA All-Star Game in Boston.

STRONG IN DEFEAT

1919 – University of Cincinnati center **Ferdinand Isserman** scores a game-high 14 points, but the Bearcats lose to Kentucky 34-20.

MAZEL TOUGH

1789 – **Solomon Sodicky** defeats Pardoe Wilson in a bareknuckle fight in Herts, England.

1926 – **Harry Mason** wins the British lightweight crown in London when Ernie Rice is disqualified in the fifth round for a low blow.

1948 – **Richard Bergmann** beats Bohumil Varna 21-12, 18-21, 21-19, 14-21, 21-10 to win the world table tennis championship in London. **Leah Thall** teams with **Dick Miles** to win mixed doubles.

1956 – In their first doubles pairing, **Angela** **Buxton** and Althea Gibson defeat Anne Silcock and Susan Chatrier in the French Indoors tennis tournament.

1990 – **Martin Jaite** beats Luiz Mattar 3-6, 6-4, 6-3 in the final of a hard-court tennis tournament in Guaruja, Brazil.

RECORD SETTERS

1992 – **Howie Rosenblatt** and Cincinnati teammate Martin St. Amour set an East Coast Hockey League record by scoring within three seconds of each other early in the third period against Raleigh.

A STAR IS BORN

1885 – **Sidney Abrahams** (British track)
1947 – **Abigail Hoffman** (Canadian middle distance runner)
1981 – **Mike Seidman** (UCLA, Carolina Panthers tight end)

Barney Sedran
(Naismith Memorial Basketball Hall of Fame)

FEBRUARY 12

GAMEBREAKERS

1924 – **Alexander Neufeld-Nemes** scores a hat trick as Hakoah Vienna defeats WR Association 3-1 in an Austrian soccer match.

1969 – **Neal Walk** scores 34 points as Florida defeats LSU 95-79.

1993 – **Scott Drevitch** scores in overtime to give the Dayton Bombers a 6-5 victory over the Birmingham Bulls in the East Coast Hockey League.

1998 – **Jeff Pickler** of Tennessee goes 6-for-6 with six RBI's as the Volunteers defeat the College of Charleston 19-4.

1998 – Goalie **Sara DeCosta** posts the shutout as the United States beats Japan 10-0 en route to the women's hockey gold medal at the Olympic Games in Nagano, Japan. DeCosta is in goal for three of Team USA's five victories in the tournament.

2003 – **Jinga Gosschalk** of Holland leads the Long Beach State women's basketball team with 20 points in a 75-70 victory over Cal-Riverside.

STRONG IN DEFEAT

1965 – **Steve Nisenson**, Hofstra's all-time leading scorer, totals a career-high 47 points in a 98-96 overtime loss to Wagner.

2005 – **Jordan Farmar** scores 27 points in UCLA's 83-73 loss to Arizona.

MAZEL TOUGH

1932 – **Emilia Rotter** and **Laszlo Szollas** of Hungary win a bronze medal in pairs figure skating at the Olympics in Lake Placid, N.Y.

1965 – Brother and sister **Ronald** and **Vivian Joseph** win the pairs title at the United States Figure Skating Championship in Lake Placid, N.Y.

2000 – **Sasha Cohen** wins a silver medal at the U.S. Figure Skating Championships in Cleveland. She is still three months shy of meeting the age eligibility requirement to qualify for the World Championships.

2006 – **Shahar Peer** of Israel wins her first WTA title, defeating Jelena Kostanic of Croatia 6-3, 6-1 in the Pattaya Women's Open hard-court tournament in Thailand.

Ronald Joseph
(U.S. Olympic Committee)

RECORD SETTERS

1949 – **Henry Laskau** sets a world record of 6:24.6 in the one-mile walk at the New York Athletic Club games.

A STAR IS BORN

1886 – **Leach Cross** (lightweight boxer)

1908 – **Miklos Sarkany** (Hungarian water polo)

1921 – **Albert Axelrod** (fencing)

1927 – **Henry Herscovici** (shooting)

1965 – **Ruben Amaro Jr.** (Cleveland Indians, Philadelphia Phillies, California Angels outfielder)

1971 – **Nathan Kahan** (Belgian middle-distance runner)

1980 – **Adam Stern** (Boston Red Sox, Baltimore Orioles outfielder)

FEBRUARY 13

GAMEBREAKERS

1932 – **Rudi Ball** scores a hat trick as Germany beats Poland 4-1 to win the bronze medal in ice hockey at the Olympics in Lake Placid, N.Y.

1937 – **Cy Kaselman** scores 15 points, **Shikey Gotthoffer** 13, and **Inky Lautman** 10 as the Philadelphia Sphas defeat the Kingston Colonials 48-34. **Phil Rabin** scores 12 for Kingston.

1941 – **Max Kaminsky** scores the winning goal as the Springfield Indians beat the Indianapolis Capitals 3-1 in an American Hockey League game.

MAZEL TOUGH

1928 – **Irving Jaffee** beats favorite Bernt Evensen of Norway in the 10,000-meter speed skating preliminaries at the Winter Olympics in St. Moritz, Switzerland. But the event is soon canceled because of thawing ice, and despite protests from other skaters that Jaffe should be awarded the gold medal, no official winner is recognized.

1936 – **Emilia Rotter** and **Laszlo Szollas** of Hungary win the Olympic pairs figure skating bronze medal in Garmisch-Partenkirchen, Germany.

1937 – **Viktor Barna** of Hungary beats Jimmy McClure of the United States 21-18 in the fourth game to win the English Open table tennis tournament.

1961 – Unranked **Dick Savitt** beats Whitney Reed, the top-ranked American, 6-2, 11-9, 6-3 to win the U.S. Indoor tennis championship in New York for the third time.

1998 – **Gordie Sheer** teams with Chris Thorpe to win the silver medal in the men's pairs luge event at the Olympics in Nagano, Japan, ending a 34-year medal dry spell for the United States in the event.

1999 – **Adam Goucher** wins the 4-kilometer race at the U.S. Winter Cross Country Championships in Tacoma, Wash., finishing 11 seconds ahead of second-place finisher Jason Stewart.

1999 – **Irina Slutskaya** of Russia wins the European Figure Skating championship in Vienna.

1999 – **Jamie Silverstein** and her partner Justin Pekarek win the ice dancing competition at the World Junior Figure Skating Championships in Salt Lake City.

2000 – **Dan Weinstein** wins the Short-Track Speed Skating National Championship in Walpole, Mass.

2000 – **Deena Drossin** captures the women's 4k, one day after winning the 8-kilometer race at the U.S. National Cross Country Championships in Greensboro, N.C.

RECORD SETTERS

1955 – **Sylvia Wene** of Philadelphia bowls a 727 series in Allentown, Pa., to break the women's world record for 30 frames. The series is her 11th over 700 for her career and sixth of the year, and raises her average for the year to a record 207.

TRANSITIONS

1951 – Quarterback **Sid Luckman** retires after 12 years as a player to become vice president of the Chicago Bears.

A STAR IS BORN

1887 – **Guy Zinn** (New York Highlanders, Boston Braves, Baltimore Terrapins outfielder)

1899 – **Spider Reinhardt** (Yale football)

1902 – **Louis Oshins** (CCNY football)

1918 – **Lew Hamity** (Univ. of Chicago football, Chicago Bears)

1971 – **Alon Harazi** (Israeli soccer)

FEBRUARY 14

GAMEBREAKERS

1947 – Columbia guard **Sherry Marshall** scores 17 points as the Lions defeat Cornell 41-27.

1979 – **Viki Peretz** scores a hat trick as Israel beats Greece 4-1 in soccer.

2001 – **Greg Gardner** makes 27 saves as the Dayton Bombers defeat Greensboro 6-0 in an East Coast Hockey League game.

2003 – **Brian Horwitz** goes 4 for 4 with two homers and a school-record eight RBI's as California defeats Texas-Pan American.

STRONG IN DEFEAT

1948 – **Nitzi Bobb** scores 29 points in Temple's 81-75 loss to West Virginia.

1991 – **Willie Simms** scores 14 points and hands out 10 assists in Wisconsin's 73-71 loss to second-ranked Ohio State.

MAZEL TOUGH

1927 – **Irving Jaffee** wins the 5-mile event in 14 minutes, 4.5 seconds at the National Outdoor Speed Skating Championships in Saranac Lake, N.Y.

1936 – **Felix Kasper** of Austria takes the bronze medal in figure skating at the Winter Olympics in Garmisch-Partenkirchen, Germany.

1937 – **Leonard Hartman** defeats Herbert Bowman 1-6, 6-4, 6-4, 7-5 to win the New Jersey Indoor tennis championship in East Orange.

1953 – **James Fuchs** wins his third straight national AAU indoor shot put championship.

1971 – **Kathy Harter** defeats Shelley Monds 6-1, 6-0 and also wins the women's doubles and mixed doubles at the Auckland Grass Court tournament in New Zealand.

1998 – **Alan Fried** wins the 63-kg. division at the FILA Wrestling Tournament in Colorado Springs.

1999 – **Bruce Fleisher** becomes the first golfer to win his first two tournaments on the Senior PGA Tour, beating Larry Nelson by three strokes in the American Express Invitational in Sarasota, Fla.

2004 – **Lenny Krayzelburg** swims the first leg and **Jason Lezak** competes in the third leg as the Irvine Novaquatics win the 400 medley relay in the Spring National Swimming Championships in Orlando, Fla.

RECORD SETTERS

1939 – **Dick Pinck** scores a Southern Conference-record 34 points as Washington & Lee defeats Richmond 49-26.

A STAR IS BORN

1913 – **Mel Allen** (broadcasting)
1922 – **Jerome Fleishman** (NYU basketball)
1969 – **Adriana Brandao Behar** (Brazilian beach volleyball)
1978 – **Deena Kastor** (distance runner)
1983 – **Eric Nystrom** (Michigan hockey, Calgary Flames)
1983 – **Sada Jacobson** (fencing)

Irving Jaffee
(U.S. Olympic Committee)

45

FEBRUARY 15

GAMEBREAKERS

1927 – **Nat Holman** scores 11 points and **Davey Banks** adds six as the New York Celtics defeat the Fort Wayne Hoosiers 25-20.
1936 – **Willie Schwartz** scores 12 points as LIU defeats St. Thomas 45-36 for its 30th straight victory.
1939 – **Nat Frankel** scores 18 points and **Sammy Kaplan** adds 11 as the Kingston Colonials defeat the Wilkes-Barre Barons 46-30.
1940 – **Al Goldstein** scores 12 points to lead CCNY past Manhattan 26-25.
1951 – **Harvey Babetch** of Von Steuben scores 87 points, including 35 in the fourth quarter of a high school basketball game against Taft in Chicago. Babetch makes 37 field goals and 13 free throws.
1975 – **Ernie Grunfeld** of Tennessee scores 29 points in a 103-98 victory over Kentucky.
1983 – **Zahi Armeli** scores three goals as Israel beats Belgium's Olympic soccer team 3-2.

MAZEL TOUGH

1975 – **Harold Solomon** beats Stan Smith 6-4, 6-1 for his first indoor WCT tournament victory in Toronto.
1977 – Maccabi Tel Aviv upsets the Red Army Team CSKA Moscow 91-79 in Virton, Belgium, during the European Cup basketball tournament.
2003 – **Deena Drossin** captures her sixth U.S. National Long-Course Cross-Country championship in Houston, completing the 8-kilometer course in 29 minutes, 6 seconds. Duke freshman **Clara Horowitz** wins the women's junior 6K championship in 23:34.

RECORD SETTERS

1913 – **Abel Kiviat** sets a 10-lap track world indoor mile record of 4:18.15 in New York.
2002 – **Cory Pecker** of the Erie Otters scores a team-record four goals – including the game-winner 3:17 into overtime – and adds an assist in a 5-4 victory over the Ottawa 67's in the Canadian Hockey League.

TRANSITIONS

1946 – **Hank Greenberg** signs a contract with the Detroit Tigers for $60,000.
1947 – **Harry Boykoff** becomes the first St. John's player to score 1,000 career points during a 46-36 victory over Niagara.
1973 – **Marv Levy** is named coach of the Montreal Alouettes of the Canadian Football League.
2001 – **Ilana Kloss** of South Africa is named CEO and commissioner of World Team Tennis.
2005 – **Donna Geils Orender,** a senior vice president for the PGA golf tour, is named president of the WNBA.

A STAR IS BORN

1892 – **Soldier Bartfield** (welterweight boxer)
1897 – **Gerrit Kleerekoper** (Dutch gymnastics coach)
1903 – **Harry Felix** (lightweight boxer)
1957 – **Gilles Elbilia** (French welterweight boxer)

FEBRUARY 16

GAMEBREAKERS

2002 – **David Bluthenthal** scores a career-high 31 points, including 23 in the second half, and grabs nine rebounds as Southern Cal beats ninth-ranked Arizona 94-89.

2002 – Goalie **Sara DeCosta** makes 21 saves as the United States beats Finland 5-0 in an Olympic women's hockey game in Salt Lake City.

2006 – **Dan Grunfeld** scores a career-high 31 points as Stanford defeats Arizona State 82-69.

STRONG IN DEFEAT

2000 – **Willie Simms** of the Grand Rapids Hoops scores 25 points and grabs 12 rebounds in a 110-106 loss to the Yakima Sun Kings in a Continental Basketball Association game.

MAZEL TOUGH

1935 – **Viktor Barna** of Hungary wins the world table tennis championship for the fourth year in a row, beating **Miklos Szabados** of Hungary 17-21, 21-17, 19-21, 21-11, 21-19 in London. Barna and Szabados team up to win the doubles.

1946 – **Joe Renick** rides Concordian to victory in the McLennan Handicap at Hialeah Park in Florida.

1952 – **Henry Laskau** wins the one-mile walk at the AAU indoor track championships in New York.

1968 – **Alain Calmat** of France wins a silver medal in men's figure skating at the Winter Olympics in Grenoble, France.

1975 – **Harold Solomon** wins the WCT Rothman's International tennis tournament in Toronto.

RECORD SETTERS

1952 – **Don Sheff** swims the third leg as Yale sets a world record of 8:29.4 in the 800 freestyle relay in New Haven, Conn.

1962 – NYU sophomore **Gary Gubner** tosses 64 feet, 11¾ inches in the shot put at the New York Athletic Club Games, breaking the world indoor record he set two weeks earlier.

TRANSITIONS

2001 – **Larry Brown** posts his 1,000th career victory as a professional basketball coach as the Philadelphia 76ers defeat the Los Angeles Clippers 108-93. Brown won 229 games in the American Basketball Association before switching to the NBA.

A STAR IS BORN

1858 – **Laurence "Lon" Myers** (sprinter and middle distance runner)

1983 – **Ben Benditson** (soccer)

Sara DeCosta *(U.S. Olympic Committee)*

FEBRUARY 17

GAMEBREAKERS

1923 – **Sig Edelstein** scores 22 points – 16 on free throws – as CCNY defeats Syracuse 30-22.

1929 – **Max Wortmann** scores three goals as the Hakoah All-Stars of the Eastern League defeat the Rochester Celtics 6-0 in the quarterfinals of the National Challenge Cup soccer tournament.

1960 – **Jon Feldman** scores 42 points, **Dick Markowitz** adds 22 and **Jeff Feldman** contributes 12 as George Washington defeats West Virginia 97-93.

1961 – **Sid Amira** scores a game-high 18 points as Penn defeats Cornell 65-58. **Ed Mazria** scores 30 points to lead Pratt to an 80-61 win over Brooklyn College.

2002 – **Joel Shanker** of the Philadelphia Kixx is named the Major Indoor Soccer League All-Star Game MVP after his two-point goal gives the East a 17-15 overtime victory over the West in Cleveland.

2006 – **Scott Greenman** ties a career high with 27 points and hits 3-point shots at the end of regulation and the first overtime period as Princeton defeats Cornell 76-68 in double overtime.

STRONG IN DEFEAT

1963 – **Jerry Greenspan** scores 30 points, but Maryland loses to Wake Forest 81-78.

MAZEL TOUGH

1931 – **Julia Jones** of NYU wins a three-way fenceoff to capture the women's national junior foils title.

1934 – Lightweight boxer **Abe Wasserman** runs his record to 28-0-4 with a six-round decision over Georgie Leone in Brooklyn.

1974 – **Tom Okker** beats top seed Ilie Nastase 6-3, 6-4 in the WCT Toronto International indoor final.

1975 – **Victor Niederhoffer** beats Peter Briggs 15-10, 15-3, 15-12 in New York to win his fourth straight U.S. National squash title and fifth overall.

1961 – **Eugene Glazer** wins the foil title at the first New York Athletic Club international fencing tournament.

1995 – **Dana Rosenblatt** knocks out Randy Williams in the fourth round in Atlantic City to win his first defense of his WBC Continental Americas middleweight title.

2001 – **Deena Drossin** wins her fourth United States 8-kilometer national title at the USA Winter Cross Country Championship in Vancouver, Wash. She defends her title in 26 minutes, 14 seconds.

RECORD SETTERS

1952 – **Herbert Klein** of Germany sets a world record of 1:05.8 in the 100 breaststroke in Hamburg, Germany.

1952 – **Dolph Schayes** begins a streak of 764 consecutive appearances in NBA games.

1963 – **Dolph Schayes** scores 12 points and sets an NBA career scoring record of 18,958 points as the Syracuse Nationals beat the Detroit Pistons 143-124.

JEWS ON FIRST

1994 – **Steve Dubinsky** scores his first of 25 career NHL goals in the Chicago Blackhawks' 4-2 loss to the Vancouver Canucks.

A STAR IS BORN

1887 – **Henry S. Frank** (Johns Hopkins lacrosse

1940 – **Denis Gamsy** (South African cricket)

1954 – **Mickey Berkowitz** (Israeli, UNLV basketball)

1970 – **Scott Kaplan** (Pitt football placekicker)

1978 – **Amir Hadad** (Israeli tennis)

1984 – **Jennifer Fleischer** (Penn women's basketball)

FEBRUARY 18

GAMEBREAKERS

1939 – **Bernie Opper** scores a team-high 11 points as Kentucky defeats Tennessee 36-34 in overtime.

1960 – **Charley Rosen** scores 16 points to lead Hunter to an 80-41 win over Lowell Tech.

1961 – **Sid Amira** breaks a 45-all tie and finishes with a game-high 21 points as Penn defeats Columbia 54-50.

2004 – **Shlomi Arbeitman** scores a hat trick as Israel defeats Azarbaijan 6-0 in soccer.

MAZEL TOUGH

1916 – **Elaine Rosenthal** wins a golf tournament in Palm Beach, Fla.

1928 – **Fritzi Burger** of Austria wins a silver medal in figure skating in St. Moritz, Switzerland, and becomes the first Jewish athlete to win a Winter Olympics medal.

1930 – **Kid Berg** knocks out **Mushy Callahan** in the 10th round to win the world junior welterweight title in London.

1932 – **Kingfish Levinsky** soundly defeats Jack Dempsey in a four-round exhibition fight in Chicago, convincing Dempsey to give up a comeback attempt at regaining the heavyweight title he lost to Gene Tunney in 1927. On the same card, **Barney Ross** wins a six-round decision over Billy Gladstone.

1944 – In a non-title fight in New York, **Al "Bummy" Davis** stops "Bobcat" Bob Montgomery with one punch, handing the lightweight champion his first knockout loss in 70 fights.

1979 – **Amy Alcott** beats Sandra Post in a three-hole playoff and wins the LPGA Elizabeth Arden Classic in Miami.

1984 – **Gilles Elbilia** of France knocks out Nino LaRocca in the sixth round to retain his European welterweight title in Capo d'Orlando, Italy. LaRocca came into the fight with a 56-0 record.

2002 – **Ilya Averbukh** and his partner Irina Lobacheva of Russia win a silver medal in ice dancing at the Winter Olympics in Salt Lake City.

RECORD SETTERS

1928 – **Lillian Copeland** sets a U.S. record of 115 feet, 6½ inches in the discus in Los Angeles.

1953 – **Jack Molinas** scores a Columbia school-record 41 points in an 81-58 victory over Princeton.

1967 – **Abigail Hoffman** of the University of Toronto sets a world indoor record of 2:08.4 in the 880 meters at the Achilles International track meet in Vancouver.

2004 – **Lawrence Frank** of the New Jersey Nets sets an NBA coaching record by winning his 10th game without a loss at the start of his career with a 98-92 victory over the Atlanta Hawks.

2006 – **Scot Mendelson** presses a world-record 1,008 pounds on his first attempt in the Fit Expo at the Iron Man Bodybuilding contest in Pasadena, Calif. He tops the previous record by three pounds.

A STAR IS BORN

1882 – **Benny Yanger** (lightweight boxer)

1904 – **Aubrey Goodman** (Univ. of Chicago and Baylor football, Chicago Cardinals)

1927 – **Marvin Schatzman** (basketball)

1931 – **Jimmy Jacobs** (handball, boxing manager)

1932 – **Alphonse Halimi** (Algerian bantamweight boxer)

1975 – **Adam Goucher** (cross country)

FEBRUARY 19

GAMEBREAKERS

1927 – **Izzy Zarakov** scores two goals as Harvard defeats Yale 6-2 in ice hockey.

1936 – **Mac Kinsbrunner** scores 12 points to lead the New York Jewels to a 24-15 victory over the Kingston Colonials in the ABL.

1936 – **Sol Kopito** scores a game-high 12 points to lead CCNY past Princeton 36-30.

1938 – **Inky Lautman** scores 16 points and **Shikey Gotthoffer** adds 12 as the Philadelphia Sphas defeat the Brooklyn Visitations 48-39 in the ABL.

1941 – NYU's **Ralph Kaplowitz** scores 15 points in a 41-35 victory over Fordham.

1946 – **Jackie Goldsmith** scores 41 points in LIU's 78-49 victory over the Camp Upton military team.

1950 – **Irv Rothenberg** scores 25 points as the Paterson Crescents defeat the Scranton Miners 74-62 in the ABL.

1992 – **Ronnie Stern** of the Calgary Flames scores his first of three NHL hat tricks with three goals in a 6-4 win over the Boston Bruins.

MAZEL TOUGH

1940 – **Sanford Goldberg** upsets prerace favorites Glenn Cunningham, Chuck Fenske, and Gene Venzke to win the 1,000-yard run in 2:12.9 at the Seton Hall Indoor Games at the Newark Armory.

1973 – **Vic Niederhoffer** defeats Bob Hetherington 15-7, 15-9, 15-11 to win the U.S. National Squash championship in Princeton, N.J.

1980 – **Gennadi Karponosov** of the Soviet Union teams with Natalia Linichuk to win the pairs ice dancing gold medal at the Olympics in Lake Placid, N.Y.

1989 – **Brad Gilbert** beats Johan Kriek 6-2, 6-2 in the final of an indoor tennis tournament in Memphis.

2006 – **Adam Goucher** wins the 4-kilometer race in 10 minutes, 50 seconds at the U.S. Cross Country Championships at Van Cortland Park in New York.

RECORD SETTERS

1961 – **Maria Itkina** of the Soviet Union ties the world indoor 60-meter record of 7.3 seconds in Brest-Litovsk, Belarus.

A STAR IS BORN

1900 – **Morris Glassman** (Columbus pro football)

1913 – **Solly Dukelsky** (middleweight boxer)

1921 – **Leonard "Butch" Levy** (University of Minnesota and pro football)

1932 – **Don Taussig** (Houston Colt .45s, San Francisco Giants, St. Louis Cardinals outfielder)

1965 – **Wayne Rosenthal** (Texas Rangers pitcher)

1973 – **Mark Mendelblatt** (yachting)

1980 – **Tal Burstein** (Israeli basketball)

Adam Goucher
(U.S. Olympic Committee)

FEBRUARY 20

GAMEBREAKERS

1937 – Behind **Inky Lautman's** 15 points, the Philadelphia Sphas beat the Brooklyn Jewels 33-23 in the ABL.

1944 – **Inky Lautman** scores with six seconds left as the Philadelphia Sphas defeat the Trenton Tigers 39-38 to win the American Basketball League second-half title.

1944 – **Max Labovitch** scores the winning goal as the New York Rovers score three times in the third period to beat the Brooklyn Crescents 3-1 in the Eastern Hockey League.

MAZEL TOUGH

1939 – **Al "Bummy" Davis** runs his lightweight record to 32-0 with an eight-round split decision over **Mickey Farber** before a record crowd of 6,000-plus at St. Nicholas Arena in New York.

1946 – Eighteen days after defeating him for the South African lightweight title, **Alf James** knocks out Willie Miller in the ninth round of a rematch.

1965 – **Gary Gubner** wins his third straight national AAU indoor shot put title. **Abigail Hoffman** of Canada wins the women's 800 meters in 2:11.8.

1992 – **Gary Jacobs** wins a 12-round decision over Del Bryan in Glasgow, Scotland, to capture the British welterweight title.

2000 – **Bruce Fleisher** wins the PGA Senior Tour GTE Classic in Tampa, Fla., by four strokes over Dana Quigley.

2005 – **Jonathan Erlich** and **Andy Ram** of Israel defeat Cyril Suk and Pavel Vilner of the Czech Republic 6-4, 4-6, 6-3 to win the doubles title at the ABN AMRO World tennis tournament in Rotterdam, Netherlands.

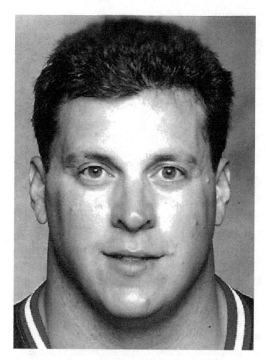

Adam Schreiber
(New York Giants)

RECORD SETTERS

1972 – **Larry Brown** of the Denver Rockets sets an American Basketball Association record with 23 assists in a 146-123 victory over the Pittsburgh Condors. He also sets records of 18 assists in one half and 10 in one quarter.

A STAR IS BORN

1876 – **Ike Samuls** (St. Louis Cardinals infielder)

1897 – **Danny Frush** (featherweight boxer)

1962 – **Adam Schreiber** (Texas football, Seattle Seahawks, New Orleans Saints, Philadelphia Eagles, New York Jets, Minnesota Vikings, New York Giants guard/center)

1982 – **Jason Hirsh** (Houston Astros, Colorado Rockies pitcher)

FEBRUARY 21

GAMEBREAKERS

1937 – **Nat Frankel** scores 11 points as the Brooklyn Visitations end the Jersey Reds' 16-game home winning streak with a 31-30 victory in the ABL.

1940 – **Ben Auerbach** scores with 28 seconds left to give NYU a 40-38 victory over St. John's for its 16th straight victory. **Bobby Lewis** scores 13 and Auerbach adds 12 for NYU, while **Jack Garfinkel** scores nine for St. John's. In the first game of the Madison Square Garden doubleheader, **Sol Schwartz** scores 10 and **Ossie Schechtman** adds eight as LIU defeats DePaul 44-33.

1965 – **Barry Kramer** scores an NBA-career high 13 points as the New York Knicks beat the Cincinnati Royals 109-104.

STRONG IN DEFEAT

1949 – **Marty Zippel** scores 13 points in a 61-37 loss at La Salle and becomes the first basketball player in modern Lafayette College history to score 1,000 career points.

MAZEL TOUGH

1906 – **Abe Attell** wins a 15-round decision over Jimmy Walsh in Chelsea, Mass., to recapture the world featherweight title.

1948 – **Norman Wasser** wins the national AAU indoor shot put title.

1948 – **Alf James** wins a 12-round decision over George Angelo in Johannesburg to win the South African welterweight title.

1959 – **Michael Herman** wins the long jump at the national AAU indoor track championships.

1965 – **Ronald** and **Vivian Joseph** win the pairs title at the North American Figure Skating Championships in Rochester, N.Y.

1972 – **Vic Niederhoffer** captures his second national squash racquets championship in Detroit.

2002 – **Sarah Hughes** of the United States rallies from fourth place after the short program to win the gold medal in ladies figure skating at the Olympics in Salt Lake City,

Utah. **Irina Slutskaya** of Russia wins the silver medal. American goalie **Sara DeCosta** earns a silver when Canada beats the U.S. 3-2 for the gold medal in women's hockey.

RECORD SETTERS

1936 – **S. Mortimer Auerbach** sets a competitive five-mile record of 39.079 mph for Class 91 cubic inch hydroplanes in Palm Beach, Fla.

TRANSITIONS

1976 – **Red Holzman** posts his 500th victory as an NBA coach as the New York Knicks beat the New Orleans Jazz 102-98.

A STAR IS BORN

1906 – **Jacob Friedman** (pro football end)
1968 – **Daniel Calichman** (soccer)
1969 – **Scot Mendelson** (weight lifting)
1981 – **Adam Greenberg** (Chicago Cubs outfielder)

Marty Zippel *(Lafayette College)*

FEBRUARY 22

GAMEBREAKERS

1958 – **Alan Seiden** scores 30 points as St. John's defeats Fordham 82-74.

2007 – **Jon Scheyer** scores a game-high 18 points, including two free throws with 5.7 seconds remaining to seal the victory, as Duke defeats Clemson for the 21st consecutive time, 71-66.

STRONG IN DEFEAT

1969 – **Steve Chubin** scores 34 points, but the New York Nets lose to the New Orleans Buccaneers 139-131 in the American Basketball Association.

MAZEL TOUGH

1915 – **Charles Pores** wins the Brooklyn-to-Sea Gate Marathon, a race shortened to 20 miles because of bad weather.

1917 – **William Rosenbaum** teams with F.B. Alexander to win the National Indoor Tennis doubles championship in New York.

1933 – **Maxie Rosenbloom** beats Al Stillman in 10 rounds in St. Louis to retain his world light heavyweight title.

1941 – For the third straight year, **Allen Tolmich** wins a national AAU indoor title when he captures the 70-yard high hurdles, tying the world record of 8.4 seconds at Madison Square Garden. **Nat Jaeger** wins the one-mile racewalking title.

1947 – **Irving Kintisch** wins the shot put at the AAU indoor track championships.

1981 – **Amy Alcott** wins the LPGA Bent Tree Ladies Classic in Sarasota, Fla., by one stroke over JoAnne Carner.

RECORD SETTERS

1964 – **Gary Gubner** of NYU breaks his National AAU indoor meet record in the shot put with a toss of 63 feet, 2½ inches at Madison Square Garden.

A STAR IS BORN

1884 – **Abe Attell** (featherweight boxer)
1902 – **Jacob Sack** (Pitt and pro football)
1902 – **Col. David Marcus** (Army boxing)
1915 – **Milton Kobrosky** (Trinity, Conn., and pro football)
1944 – **Tom Okker** (Dutch tennis)
1956 – **Amy Alcott** (golf)
1972 – **Haim Revivo** (Israeli soccer)

FEBRUARY 23

GAMEBREAKERS

1939 – **Sammy Kaplan** scores 12 points and **Nat Frankel** adds 10 as the Kingston Colonials defeat the Troy Haymakers 34-22 in the American Basketball League.

1947 – **Max Zaslofsky** scores 22 points as the Chicago Stags beat the New York Knicks 82-68.

1963 – In his final home game, **Art Heyman** of Duke scores 40 points and grabs 24 rebounds as the Blue Devils complete a perfect regular season with a 106-93 win over North Carolina.

1991 – **Danny Schayes** of the Milwaukee Bucks scores 31 points and grabs a team-high 12 rebounds in a 118-103 victory over the Cleveland Cavaliers.

MAZEL TOUGH

1908 – **Harry Lewis** knocks out Frank Mantell in the third round in New Haven, Conn., to win the world welterweight championship.

1931 – **Jackie "Kid" Berg** wins a 10-round decision over Goldie Hess in Chicago to retain his world super lightweight title.

1946 – **Bernard Mayer** wins his second national AAU indoor shot put title.

1957 – **Henry Laskau** wins for the 10th consecutive year in the 1-mile walk at the national AAU indoor track and field championships, finishing in 6 minutes, 39.7 seconds.

1958 – **Dick Savitt** defeats Budge Patty 6-1, 6-2, 3-6, 12-10 to win the U.S. Indoor tennis championship in New York.

1973 – **Irena Kirszenstein-Szewinska** of Poland wins the long jump at the national AAU indoor track championships.

1975 – **Amy Alcott**, competing in just her third tournament since turning pro, finishes one stroke ahead of Sandra Post in the Orange Blossom Classic in St. Petersburg, Fla., to secure her first of 29 career LPGA victories.

1980 – **Saoul Mamby** wins the WBA junior welterweight title with a 14th-round knockout of Sang-Hyun Kim in Seoul, South Korea.

1996 – **Leonid Zaslavsky** of Australia wins the 62-kg. freestyle wrestling title at the Oceania Championships in Footscray, Australia.

2003 – **Bruce Fleisher** makes up two strokes on the 17th hole of the final round and finishes one stroke ahead of Hale Irwin in capturing the Verizon Classic senior golf tournament in Lutz, Fla. In five appearances on the TPC of Tampa Bay course, Fleisher runs his record to two victories, two seconds, and one third.

2006 – **Sasha Cohen** wins the silver medal and **Irina Slutskaya** of Russia captures the bronze in women's figure skating at the Winter Olympics in Turin, Italy.

RECORD SETTERS

1909 – **Clair Jacobs** sets a world indoor record of 12 feet, 3 inches in the pole vault in Chicago.

TRANSITIONS

1996 – **Ernie Grunfeld** is named president and general manager of the New York Knicks.

A STAR IS BORN

1865 – **Barney Dreyfuss** (Pittsburgh Pirates executive)

1871 – **Digby Jephson** (British cricket)

1920 – **Richard Bergmann** (Austrian table tennis)

1969 – **Frank Charles** (Houston Astros catcher)

1977 – **Rami Zur** (canoeing)

FEBRUARY 24

GAMEBREAKERS

1924 – **Erno Schwarcz** scores two goals as Hakoah Vienna defeats Simmeringer Soccer Club 3-2.

1940 – **Ralph Kaplowitz** scores 11 of his game-high 13 points in the first half as NYU beats Rutgers 64-33. **Ben Auerbach** adds nine points and **Irving Dubinsky** contributes eight.

1947 – **Ben Goldfaden** scores 17 points to lead the Jersey City Atoms to a 75-64 victory over the Trenton Tigers in the ABL.

1956 – North Carolina's **Lenny Rosenbluth** gets 31 points and 14 rebounds in the Tar Heels' 73-65 victory over Duke.

1959 – **Rudy LaRusso** scores 29 points to lead Dartmouth to its 15th straight victory – 81-64 over Holy Cross.

1961 – **Ed Mazria** scores 42 points as Pratt defeats Lowell 92-58.

1984 – **Danny Schayes** of the Denver Nuggets has 17 points and 17 rebounds in a 117-110 victory over the Phoenix Suns.

1994 – Stanford center **Anita Kaplan** scores a career-high 34 points in an 80-50 victory over sixth-ranked Southern Cal.

2001 – **David Bluthenthal** scores 29 points, including seven in overtime, as Southern Cal beats Oregon 87-80.

MAZEL TOUGH

1927 – **Milton Baron** drops the first two games, then rallies to beat Dallas Haines to win the Class B National Squash Tournament title at Columbia University.

1934 – **Milton Sandler** wins his second of three straight titles in the 600 meters at the AAU Indoor Track and Field Championships.

1952 – **Dick Savitt** beats Billy Talbert 6-2, 6-3, 6-4 to win the U.S. National Indoor tennis championship in New York. Disappointed at being left off the U.S. Davis Cup team, Savitt announces his retirement after the tourna-ment, but he makes a comeback in 1958 and wins two more U.S. Indoor championships.

1962 – **Gary Gubner** wins the shot put at the AAU indoor track championships.

1985 – **Amy Alcott** beats runner-up Betsy King by one stroke to win the LPGA Circle K Tucson Open.

1991 – **Kenny Bernstein** clinches his first Top Fuel victory and the 31st triumph overall on the NHRA circuit at the Arizona Nationals in Phoenix. His previous victories were in the Funny Car division.

RECORD SETTERS

1940 – **Allen Tolmich** wins the national AAU indoor 60-yard hurdles title in 8.4 seconds at Madison Square Garden, breaking his world record by 0.1 second. **Stanford Braun** and **David Urbach** run on NYU's first-place distance medley relay team and **Howard Bogrow** runs the third leg of the Violets' victorious mile-relay team.

2004 – New Jersey Nets coach **Lawrence Frank** sets an American professional sports record by winning his 13th straight game at the start of his career with an 86-74 victory over the Toronto Raptors. The record of 12 was shared by Boston Red Sox manager Joe Morgan (1988) and New York Giants manager Jim Price (1884).

TRANSITIONS

1963 – **Dolph Schayes** of the Syracuse Nationals hits a foul shot in the first minute of the game to reach 19,000 career NBA points in a 143-126 victory over the New York Knicks.

A STAR IS BORN

1911 – **Fred Sington** (Brooklyn Dodgers, Washington Senators outfielder; Alabama football tackle)

1917 – **Moe Becker** (Duquesne basketball)

FEBRUARY 25

GAMEBREAKERS

1927 – **Davey Banks** scores 15 points to lead the New York Celtics to a 27-25 ABL victory over the Rochester Centrals.

1928 – **Max Rubenstein** scores a game-high eight points as CCNY defeats rival NYU 29-26 in the basketball season finale.

1939 – **Petey Rosenberg** scores 14 points and **Shikey Gotthoffer** adds 11 as the Philadelphia Sphas defeat the Brooklyn Visitations 61-43.

1984 – **Danny Schayes** scores 26 points as the Denver Nuggets defeat the Kansas City Kings 148-136.

STRONG IN DEFEAT

1920 – **Benny Valgar** outpoints featherweight champion Johnny Kilbane in an eight-round fight in Newark, N.J. However, Kilbane keeps his title because Valgar does not knock him out.

MAZEL TOUGH

1901 – **Joe Choynski** knocks out future heavyweight champion Jack Johnson in three rounds in Galveston, Texas. The two fighters then share a jail cell for 28 days after Texas Rangers arrest them for participating in a bout involving mixed races.

1925 – In the first outdoor match allowed in San Francisco since the city legalized boxing, **Joe Benjamin** decisions **Jack Silver** in 10 rounds to capture the Pacific Coast lightweight title.

1927 – Maccabi Tel Aviv defeats Hapoel-Allenby 3-0 in the first Soccer Derby in Tel Aviv.

1931 – **Ira Singer** wins the 60 yards and **William Werner** captures the standing long jump at the AAU indoor track and field championships in New York.

1933 – **Milton Sandler** wins the 600 at the AAU indoor track championships in New York.

1937 – **Joe Fishbach** beats John Nogrady 6-4, 6-2, 6-3 to win the Metro Indoors tennis championship.

1939 – **Allen Tolmich** wins the AAU national indoor 65-meter hurdles in 8.4 seconds.

1950 – **James Fuchs** of Yale wins his third straight IC4A indoor shot put title.

2002 – **Nicolas Massu** of Chile fights off two match points in the second set and rallies to defeat Agustin Calleri of Argentina 2-6, 7-6 (7-5), 6-2 to win the Copa AT&T Tournament in Buenos Aires, his first victory on the pro tennis tour. **Gaston Etlis** of Argentina wins his second straight doubles title.

2006 – **Nicolas Massu** of Chile defeats Alberto Martin of Spain 6-3, 6-2 to win the ATP Brasil Open in Salvador, Brazil.

TRANSITIONS

1954 – The CCNY Board of Higher Education, by a 2-1 vote, clears coach **Nat Holman** of all charges in the basketball betting scandals of 1951 and reinstates him as associate professor of hygiene.

RECORD SETTERS

1961 – **Jeff Cohen** scores a school-record 49 points for William & Mary against Richmond.

A STAR IS BORN

1913 – **Herman Bassman** (football)
1918 – **Stanley Rosen** (NYU football)
1924 – **Nelson "Nitzi" Bobb** (Temple basketball)
1944 – **Francois Cevert** (French auto racing)

FEBRUARY 26

GAMEBREAKERS

1926 – **Davey Banks** hits a shot from half-court in the final minute to give the Philadelphia Sphas a 26-25 victory over the New York Celtics.

1950 – **George Feigenbaum** scores 27 points as the Hartford Hurricanes defeat the Paterson Crescents 95-88 in the ABL. **Irv Rothenberg** scores 28 for Paterson.

1957 – **Lenny Rosenbluth** scores 30 points, including a three-point play in the final 46 seconds, as top-ranked North Carolina holds off 17th-ranked Wake Forest 69-64.

1961 – **Howie Carl's** 25 points lead DePaul past Notre Dame 78-57.

MAZEL TOUGH

1910 – **Max Himmelhock** of the Detroit YMHA wins a 15-minute decision over Frank Lust for the AAU 125-pound wrestling title in Chicago.

1933 – **Erich Seelig** wins a 12-round decision over Helmut Hartkopp in Berlin to win the German light-heavyweight title. Seelig will fight only one more time in Germany before he is thrown out of the German Boxing Association.

1949 – **James Fuchs** of Yale wins the shot put at the IC4A indoor meet.

1960 – **Carole Wright** wins the U.S. National Indoor Tennis championship with a 6-1, 6-2 victory over Lois Felix in Brookline, Mass.

1990 – **Rick Aronberg** of Clemson wins his fourth straight Atlantic Coast Conference championship in the 1,650-yard freestyle.

2000 – **Alex Averbukh** of Israel wins a gold medal in the pole vault at a height of 5.75 meters at the European Indoor Championships in Ghent, Belgium.

2006 – **Alex Averbukh** of Israel clears 19 feet, 3/8 inch to win the pole vault at the KBC Flanders Indoor Championships in Ghent, Belgium.

RECORD SETTERS

1927 – **Lillian Copeland** breaks her world record in the javelin, throwing 38.21 meters in Los Angeles.

TRANSITIONS

1998 – **Howard Milstein** and **Steven Gluckstern** purchase the New York Islanders for $195 million.

A STAR IS BORN

1900 – **Harry Herbert** (Syracuse and Boston U. football)

1907 – **Cy Malis (**Philadelphia Phillies pitcher)

1911 – **Bill "Chick" Starr** (Washington Senators catcher)

1943 – **Valery Kaplan** (Soviet speed skater)

1945 – **Steve Hertz** (Houston Colt .45s third baseman)

FEBRUARY 27

GAMEBREAKERS

1980 – **Neil Simons** of Clemson collects six hits in a 22-7 victory over Georgia.

1987 – **Bruce Lefkowitz** scores 31 points and grabs 20 rebounds as Penn defeats Brown 95-92 in overtime.

1999 – **Jeff Halpern** scores his third career hat trick as Princeton defeats Dartmouth 7-3 in an ECAC hockey game.

2000 – **Willie Simms** of the Grand Rapids Hoops scores 22 points in a 96-94 win over the La Crosse Bobcats in the Continental Basketball Association.

2001 – **Bubba Berenzweig** scores 1:05 into overtime – his fourth game-winning goal of the season – to give the Milwaukee Admirals a 6-5 victory over the Chicago Wolves in the American Hockey League.

STRONG IN DEFEAT

1945 – Rhode Island State overwhelms Yeshiva College 130-74. Total of 204 points sets a collegiate basketball record for most total points in a game. All-American Ernie Calverley of Rhode Island leads in scoring with 37 points. **Bernie Scharfstein** of Yeshiva College scores 10 points.

1959 – **Jeff Cohen** scores 30 points in William & Mary's 85-82 loss to West Virginia.

MAZEL TOUGH

1907 – Jockey **Walter Miller** rides winners in all five races at Oakland Race Course.

1911 – **Matt Wells** wins a 20-round decision over Freddie Welsh in London to capture the British lightweight title and Lord Lonsdale's Belt.

1937 – **Nat Jaeger** wins the 1,500-meter race-walking title at the National AAU indoor track championships.

1943 – **Bernard Mayer** wins the National AAU indoor shot put championship.

1951 – **Ingebord Mello de Preiss** of Argentina, who also won the women's javelin, throws the discus 126 feet, 5¾ inches to claim the gold medal at the Pan American Games in Buenos Aires. The United States men's foil team, which includes **Byron Krieger**, **Nathan Lubell**, and **Albert Wolff**, wins a fencing gold medal.

1954 – **Martin Engel** of NYU wins the IC4A indoor 35-pound weight toss.

1954 – **Robert Cohen** knocks out John Kelly in the third round in Belfast, Northern Ireland, to win the European bantamweight title.

1964 – **Alain Calmat** of France wins the silver medal at the World Figure Skating Championships in Dortmund, Germany.

1977 – **Brian Gottfried** defeats top-seeded Guillermo Vilas 2-6, 6-1, 6-3 in the final of the American Airlines hard-court tennis tournament in Palm Springs, Calif.

2005 – **Dudi Sela** of Israel defeats Sadik Kadir of Australia 6-1, 6-1 to win an ATP Challenger tennis tournament in Gosford, Australia.

FEBRUARY 28

GAMEBREAKERS

1931 – **Allie Schuckman** scores eight points to lead St. John's to a 27-20 win over Temple. **Milt Trupin** leads CCNY with 10 points in a 29-24 victory over NYU. **Sam Seigel** scores 10 for NYU. **Louis Hayman** scores 12 points in Syracuse's 47-29 victory over Pitt.

1998 – **Tony Schrager** of Stanford hits two home runs in a 15-3 victory over Arizona State.

2004 – **Liad Suez** of Israel scores 23 points, including two foul shots with 3.8 seconds remaining, as Villanova's women's basketball team upsets top-ranked Connecticut 59-56.

STRONG IN DEFEAT

1969 – **Steve Chubin** scores 37 points but the New York Nets lose to the Miami Floridians 124-120 in overtime in the American Basketball Association.

2007 – **Cory Pecker** scores both Binghamton goals, but the Senators lose 3-2 to the Wilkes-Barre/Scranton Penguins in the American Hockey League.

MAZEL TOUGH

1908 – **Abe Attell** knocks out Eddie Kelly in the seventh round in San Francisco to retain the world featherweight title.

1910 – In his 18th world featherweight title defense, **Abe Attell** knocks out Harry Forbes in the sixth round in New York.

1936 – **Maurice Holtzer** of France retains his European featherweight title with a 15-round decision over Joseph Parisis in Paris.

1948 – **James Fuchs** of Yale wins the shot put and **Irving Mondschein** of NYU captures the high jump at the IC4A indoor championships.

2002 – Hapoel Tel Aviv becomes the first Israeli soccer team to reach the quarterfinals of the UEFA Cup by beating Parma of Italy 2-1.

2004 – **Omri Holtzman** of Hunter College wins the 1,500 and 5,000 meter runs at the CUNY Athletic Conference indoor track championships at the 168th Street Armory.

RECORD SETTERS

1963 – **Larry Brown** hands out a school- and Atlantic Coast Conference tournament-record 13 assists as North Carolina beats South Carolina 93-76 in a first-round game. Brown also scores 12 points.

2004 – Auburn freshman **Adrienne Binder** wins the 1,650-yard freestyle in a meet- and pool-record 15:51.70 to win the Southeastern Conference championship in Athens, Ga.

TRANSITIONS

1932 – The Macabee Association of America holds final tryouts for selection of the team to represent the United States at the first World Maccabiah Games in Tel Aviv.

1963 – **Art Heyman** of Duke is named college basketball Player of the Year by the Associated Press. **Barry Kramer** of NYU joins him on AP's All-America team. Heyman then goes out and scores 21 points, grabs 18 rebounds and hands out 10 assists in an 89-70 victory over Virginia in the first round of the Atlantic Coast Conference tournament.

A STAR IS BORN

1888 – **Milton Erlanger** (Johns Hopkins lacrosse)
1919 – **Leo Cantor** (football)
1954 – **Arnie Mausser** (soccer goalie)
1968 – **Mike Milchin** (Minnesota Twins, Baltimore Orioles pitcher)

FEBRUARY 29

GAMEBREAKERS

2004 – Detroit Red Wings defenseman **Mathieu Schneider** notches a goal and an assist in a 4-2 victory over the Philadelphia Flyers.

MAZEL TOUGH

1932 – World welterweight champion **Jackie Fields** knocks out Jimmy Belmont in the ninth round of a non-title fight in Pittsburgh. **Benny Leonard**, in his most impressive performance on his comeback tour, wins a 10-round decision over welterweight Billy McMahon at St. Nicholas Arena in New York.
1936 – Harvard captain **Milton Green** wins the 45 high hurdles, the 50-yard sprint and the broad jump in the first Ivy Quads indoor track meet between Harvard, Yale, Cornell, and Dartmouth at Boston Garden. **Arthur Loeb** of Yale wins the 35-pound weight throw.
1940 – Lightweight boxer **Jackie "Kid" Berg** wins by a sixth-round disqualification over Eddie Ryan in London.
1952 – **Lawrence Demmy** and partner Jean Westwood of Great Britain win the ice dancing title at the World Figure Skating Championships in Paris.

TRANSITIONS

1972 – Swimmer **Mark Spitz** is awarded the James E. Sullivan Memorial Trophy as the top U.S. amateur athlete of 1971.

A STAR IS BORN

1872 – **Sigmund Hart** (bantamweight boxer)
1924 – **Al Rosen** (Cleveland Indians third baseman)
1976 – **Lior Mor** (Israeli tennis)

Mark Spitz
(U.S. Olympic Committee)

MARCH 1

GAMEBREAKERS

1926 – Center **Jacob Goldberg** scores nine points to lead Dickinson to a 38-36 overtime upset of Penn.

1941 – **Petey Rosenberg** scores 15 points, **Reds Rosan** 11, **Shikey Gotthoffer** 10, and **Irv Torgoff** eight as the Philadelphia Sphas of the American Basketball League beat the Harlem Rens 55-48 in the semifinals of the four-team Max Rosenblum Basketball Tournament in Cleveland

1957 – **Lenny Rosenbluth** scores 40 points as North Carolina beats Duke 86-72 and completes an unbeaten 24-game regular-season schedule.

1963 – **Ron Watts** scores 16 points as Wake Forest beats North Carolina 56-55 in the Atlantic Coast Conference semifinals.

1968 – **Art Heyman** scores 33 points as the Pittsburgh Pipers beat the New Jersey Americans 135-125 in the American Basketball Association.

1969 – **Neal Walk** of Florida scores 34 points and pulls down 25 rebounds as the Gators beat Georgia 96-78.

1972 – Substitute **Ronnie Rosenthal** of Israel scores twice within two minutes to tie the game, then completes a hat trick in extra time as the Tottenham Hotspurs beat the Southampton Saints 6-2 in an F.A. Cup British soccer match.

MAZEL TOUGH

1911 – **Matt Wells** beats Freddie Welsh in 20 rounds to capture the British lightweight title.

1916 – **Ted "Kid" Lewis** wins a 20-round decision over Harry Stone in New Orleans to retain the world welterweight title.

1947 – **Bernard Mayer** of NYU wins the shot put and teammate **Irving Mondschein** captures the high jump at the IC4A indoor meet.

1958 – **Michael Herman** of NYU wins his second straight long jump title at the IC4A indoor meet.

1962 – **Alain Calmat** of France wins his first of three straight European Figure Skating Championship titles in Geneva, Switzerland.

1984 – **Isabelle Carmichael** wins the Empire State Building Run-Up, setting a women's record of 13 minutes, 32 seconds for climbing 86 floors.

1986 – **Lennie Friedman** of North Carolina wins his first of two straight Atlantic Coast Conference 142-pound wrestling titles in Raleigh, N.C.

2003 – **Sasha Cohen** captures her first major international skating title, the ISO Grand Prix Final in St. Petersburg, Russia.

JEWS ON FIRST

1953 – Jockey **Willie Harmatz** posts his first of 1,771 career victories, riding Bueno Boy to victory at Agua Caliente.

RECORD SETTERS

1964 – **Steve Nisenson** ties the tournament record with 33 points as Hofstra defeats Muhlenberg 82-70 in the consolation game of the Middle Atlantic Conference tournament.

2003 – Israeli swimmer **Shilo Ayalon** of Georgia Tech sets a conference record of 14:47.99 in winning the 1,650 freestyle and adds second-place finishes in the 500 freestyle and 400 individual medley at the Atlanic Coast Conference championships at North Carolina. Ayalon is named the meet's most outstanding swimmer.

A STAR IS BORN

1913 – **Nathan Bor** (lightweight boxer)
1934 – **Abie Grossfeld** (gymnastics)
1967 – **Gilad Bloom** (Israeli tennis)

MARCH 2

GAMEBREAKERS

1935 – **Jules Bender** and **Leo Merson** score 12 points apiece to lead LIU to a 56-24 victory over Wagner. **Henry Kozloff** scores 14 points to lead Penn to a 34-22 victory over Columbia.

1941 – **Irv Torgoff** scores 17 points, **Petey Rosenberg** adds 12 and **Inky Lautman** contributes eight as the Philadelphia Sphas beat the Original Celtics 43-38 in the championship game of the Max Rosenblum Basketball Tournament in Cleveland. The loss ends the Original Celtics' 60-game winning streak.

1951 – **Dolph Schayes** has 15 points and a team-high 14 rebounds as the East beats the West 111-94 in the first NBA All-Star Game in Boston.

1963 – **Art Heyman** scores 15 of his 24 points in a 10-minute span of the second half to break the game open, and adds 11 rebounds as Duke defeats Wake Forest 68-57 for the Atlantic Coast Conference championship.

2000 – **Greg Gardner** makes 31 saves in posting his College Hockey America Conference-record 12th shutout of the season as Niagara blanks Nebraska-Omaha 6-0.

MAZEL TOUGH

1914 – **Alvah Meyer** wins the 75-yard dash in a record 7.35 seconds and also captures the 300, while **Abel Kiviat** takes the 1,000 at the AAU Indoor Track Championships in New York.

1926 – **Charley Phil Rosenberg** wins a 10-round decision over George Butch in St. Louis to retain his world bantamweight championship.

1930 – **Solomon Furth** of NYU wins the 70-yard hurdles at the IC4A indoor meet.

1931 – **Emilia Rotter** and **Laszlo Szollas** of Hungary win the pairs figure skating title in Berlin, their first of four world championships.

1947 – Led by first-place finishes by **Bernard Mayer** in the shot put and **Irving Mondschein** with a meet-record 6-7¼ in the high jump, NYU captures its fifth team title and retires the 25-year-old IC4A indoor track championships trophy.

1951 – One day after winning the discus, **James Fuchs** of the United States captures the gold medal in the shot put at the Pan American Games in Buenos Aires, Argentina.

1962 – **Carole Wright** wins her second U.S. National Indoor tennis championship.

1962 – NYU sophomore **Gary Gubner** wins the shot put with a meet-record 63 feet, 0 inches at the New York Knights of Columbus Invitational at Madison Square Garden.

1969 – **Julie Heldman** defeats Nancy Richey 5-7, 6-1, 10-8 to win the Curacao International tennis tournament.

1996 – **Kerri Strug** wins the all-around at the McDonald's American Cup gymnastics championships in Fort Worth, Texas.

RECORD SETTERS

1949 – **Henry Laskau** of the United States breaks his world indoor record with a time of 6:22.7 in the 1-mile racewalk at the New York Pioneer Club Games.

TRANSITIONS

1973 – Former San Diego Chargers coach **Sid Gillman** is named executive vice president and general manager of the Houston Oilers.

A STAR IS BORN

1902 – **Moe Berg** (Boston Red Sox, Brooklyn Dodgers, Washington Senators, Chicago White Sox, Cleveland Indians catcher)

1905 – **Pinky Sober** (track and field)

1910 – **Natie Brown** (heavyweight boxer)

1924 – **Cal Abrams** (Brooklyn Dodgers, Pittsburgh Pirates, Cincinnati Reds, Baltimore Orioles, Chicago White Sox outfielder)

MARCH 3

GAMEBREAKERS

1934 – **Willie Rubenstein** leads the way with 11 points as NYU finishes its season 16-0 with a 24-18 victory over previously unbeaten CCNY.

1957 – **Dolph Schayes** scores 47 points as the Syracuse Nationals beat the Philadelphia Warriors 112-86.

1961 – **Jeff Cohen** scores 38 points and grabs 19 rebounds as William & Mary defeats West Virginia 88-76 in the Southern Conference Tournament semifinals.

1962 – **Art Heyman** scores 32 points and pulls down 18 rebounds as Duke beats South Carolina 92-75 in the Atlantic Coast Conference tournament semifinals.

2000 – Clemson pitcher **Scott Berney** allows six hits over eight innings as the Tigers defeat UNLV 8-0. Berney runs his scoreless-innings streak to 30.

2002 – **Jordan Kardos** scores 24 points to lead Illinois-Chicago to a 79-68 victory over Detroit in the Horizon League tournament semifinals.

MAZEL TOUGH

1928 – **David Adelman** of Georgetown wins the shot put at the IC4A meet.

1929 – **Julius Seligson** of Lehigh defeats Ted MacDonald of Dartmouth 6-4, 6-4, 6-1 to win the intercollegiate indoor tennis championship at Cornell.

1929 – **Solomon Furth** wins the running broad jump and takes second in the 70 high hurdles to lead NYU to the IC4A indoor track and field championship at Madison Square Garden.

1931 – **"Newsboy" Brown** wins a 10-round decision over Speedy Dado in Los Angeles to win the California State bantamweight title.

1935 – **Lew Farber** wins a 12-round decision over Chris Pineda in Manila and claims the world junior featherweight title.

1951 – **Leon Genuth** of Argentina wins the gold medal in middleweight wrestling at the Pan American Games in Buenos Aires.

1962 – **Gerald Ashworth** of Dartmouth sets a meet record of 9.4 seconds in the 100-yard dash at the annual Ivy Heps.

1985 – **Martin Jaite** beats Diego Perez 6-4, 6-2 in the final of a clay-court tournament in Buenos Aires for his first of 12 victories on the men's tennis tour.

TRANSITIONS

1976 – The California Angels trade outfielder **Dick Sharon** to the Boston Red Sox – the third time Sharon has been traded in the off-season. On Oct. 20, 1975, the San Diego Padres sent him to the St. Louis Cardinals, who shipped him to the Angels on Jan. 12.

A STAR IS BORN

1910 – **Eddie "Kid" Wolfe** (lightweight boxer)

1917 – **Lou Labovitch** (minor-league hockey)

1944 – **Fred Goldsmith** (Rice, Duke, Lenoir-Rhyne football coach)

1947 – **Billy Evans** (Boston College basketball)

1968 – **Scott Radinsky** (Los Angeles Dodgers, Chicago White Sox, St. Louis Cardinals, Cleveland Indians pitcher)

1973 – **Romans Vainsteins** (Latvian cyclist)

1983 – **Sarah Poewe** (South African swimmer)

Dick Sharon *(San Diego Padres)*

MARCH 4

GAMEBREAKERS

1931 – **Lloyd Rosenbaum** scores nine points to pace Princeton to a 34-33 victory over Rutgers. **Jack Grossman** leads the Scarlet Knights with 13 points.

1939 – **Bernie Opper** leads all scorers with 13 points as Kentucky beats Tennessee 46-38 in the Southeastern Conference tournament championship game.

1944 – With four starters missing the final game of the season because of military duty, Cornell backup center **Irwin Alterson** scores 15 points in a 51-28 upset victory over Canisius.

1948 – **Lou Lipman** scores 23 points in LIU's 38-20 win over Muhlenberg.

1965 – **Ron Watts** scores 18 points and grabs 20 rebounds as Wake Forest defeats North Carolina 92-76 in the first round of the Atlantic Coast Conference tournament.

1967 – **Mark Lazarus** scores the winning goal as the Queens Park Rangers defeat West Bromwich Albion 3-2 in the League Cup final at Wembley Stadium. It is the first time a Third Division club wins a major soccer trophy in England.

1978 – **Bobby Gross** scores 26 points to lead the Portland Trail Blazers past the Cleveland Cavaliers 105-100.

2006 – **David Meckler** scores a short-handed goal in the fifth overtime to give Yale a victory over Union in the first round of the ECACHL playoffs, ending the longest hockey game in NCAA history.

MAZEL TOUGH

1933 – **Mort Reznick** of NYU wins the 35-pound weight toss at the IC4A indoor meet.

1967 – **Pierre Darmon** defeats Alexander Metrevell 4-6, 17-15, 6-2, 2-6, 9-7 in the four-hour final of the Moscow Indoor tennis tournament.

1990 – **Brad Gilbert** beats Jonas Svensson 6-1, 6-3 in the final of the indoor ABN World Tournament in Rotterdam, Netherlands.

1993 – **Aaron Krickstein** beats Grant Stafford 6-3, 7-6 (9-7) in the final of a hard-court tournament in Durban, South Africa.

1995 – **Valery Belenky**, representing Germany, wins a gold medal on men's still rings at the McDonald's American Cup gymnastics championships in Seattle.

2004 – **Shahar Peer** of Israel wins her first international tennis title by defeating Suchanan Viratprasert 6-4, 7-5 in the Bendigo Challenger in Australia. Peer has to survive three qualifying rounds to reach the main draw.

RECORD SETTERS

1931 – Syracuse swimmer **Joseph Wohl** sets world backstroke records of 6:48.4 in the 500 yards and 12:35.5 in the half mile.

1950 – **Henry Laskau** sets a world record of 6:19.23 in the mile walk at the Knights of Columbus Games in New York.

TRANSITIONS

1962 – The Boston Celtics beat the St. Louis Hawks 123-120 to give **Red Auerbach** his 700th coaching victory in the NBA.

A STAR IS BORN

1927 – **Dick Savitt** (tennis)
1947 – **Doug Beal** (Ohio State, U.S. national volleyball team coach)

MARCH 5

GAMEBREAKERS

1930 – **Louis Hayman** scores 22 points as Syracuse defeats Cornell 58-24.

1932 – **Moe Spahn** scores 14 points to lead CCNY to a 43-26 victory over Howard University in a charity basketball game at Rockland Palace in Manhattan.

1944 – **Hy Buller** scores the winning goal as the Indianapolis Capitals defeat Providence 6-2 in an American Hockey League game.

1964 – **Ron Watts** scores 18 points and grabs 14 rebounds as Wake Forest beats Virginia 79-60 in the first round of the Atlantic Coast Conference tournament.

1968 – **Barry Leibowitz** scores 28 points as the Dallas Chaparrals beat the Oakland Oaks 135-117 in the American Basketball Association.

2000 – **Aron Eizenman** scores 16 minutes into overtime as Penn State beats Eastern Michigan 3-2 for the American College Hockey Association Division I national championship in Minot, N.D.

2001 – Senior captain **Aron Eizenman** scores two goals and is named tournament MVP as Penn State beats Delaware 7-2 to win its second straight national club hockey championship in Tucson, Ariz.

2003 – **Jeff Halpern** registers his sixth career two-goal game as the Washington Capitals beat the Buffalo Sabres 2-1.

MAZEL TOUGH

1923 – **Yussel Pearlstein** of New York, who claims to be the heavyweight boxing champion of Palestine, knocks out Carmine Caggiano, who bills himself as the heavyweight champion of Italy. After the fight in Brooklyn, Pearlstein says he's now the Italian heavyweight champion.

1927 – **Alfred H. Miller** of Harvard wins the 70-yard dash at the IC4A indoor meet.

1932 – **George Weinstein** of NYU wins the 70-yard dash at the IC4A indoor meet.

1934 – **Barney Ross** fights Frankie Klick to a 10-round draw in San Francisco and retains his world junior welterweight title.

1966 – **Walter Blum** rides Boldnesia to victory in the Santa Anita Derby.

TRANSITIONS

1966 – Player representatives select United Steel Workers executive **Marvin Miller** as executive director of the Major League Players Association.

A STAR IS BORN

1903 – **Lou Rosenberg** (Chicago White Sox infielder)

1916 – **Harry Shuman** (Philadelphia Phillies, Pittsburgh Pirates pitcher)

1919 – **Grigori Novak** (Soviet Union weightlifter)

1962 – **Elise Burgin** (tennis)

Barney Ross

MARCH 6

GAMEBREAKERS

1920 – **Harry Levine** scores 25 points to lead Pitt to a 33-24 victory over West Virginia.

1937 – **Harry Danning's** inside-the-park homer off Luis Tiant Sr. highlights a seven-run fifth inning as the defending National League champion New York Giants beat Almandares 7-3 in a spring training game in Havana.

1937 – **Nat Frankel** scores 18 points as the Brooklyn Visitations defeat the Philadelphia Sphas 40-32.

2000 – Stanford junior **Justin Wayne** pitches a three-hitter, striking out 12 in a 1-0 victory over Santa Clara. The decision is Wayne's 15th straight victory. Wayne and Clemson pitcher **Scott Berney** are named two of the five national players of the week by Collegiate Baseball.

MAZEL TOUGH

1913 – **Abel Kiviat** wins the 600- and 1,000-yard runs at the AAU Indoor Track and Field Championships in New York.

1922 – **Augie Ratner** knocks out Jack Delaney in the first round of a middleweight fight in New York City.

1943 – **Bernard Mayer** of NYU wins the shot put at the IC4A indoor meet in New York.

1965 – **Alain Calmat** of France wins the men's world figure skating championship in Colorado Springs, Colo. **Ronald** and **Vivian Joseph** of the United States win a silver medal in pairs skating.

A STAR IS BORN

1917 – **Irving Torgoff** (LIU basketball, Washington Capitols, Baltimore Bullets, Philadelphia Warriors)

1978 – **Sage Rosenfels** (Iowa State, Washington Redskins, Miami Dolphins, Houston Texans quarterback)

Augie Ratner

MARCH 7

GAMEBREAKERS

1936 – **Shikey Gotthoffer** scores 16 points as the Philadelphia Sphas defeat the Kingston Colonials 40-18 in the ABL.

1946 – **Hilty Shapiro** scores 17 points as CCNY upsets once-beaten NYU 49-44 in the final game of the regular season.

1957 – **Lenny Rosenbluth** of North Carolina scores an Atlantic Coast Conference tournament-record 45 points in an 81-61 first-round win over Clemson.

1959 – **Rudy LaRusso** hits a last-second shot to give Dartmouth a 69-68 victory over Princeton in a playoff game at Yale to decide the Ivy League championship.

1960 – **Howie Carl** scores 24 points as DePaul beats Air Force 69-63 in an NCAA first-round game in Chicago.

1990 – **Danny Schayes** of the Denver Nuggets scores a season-high 28 points against the Minnesota Timberwolves.

2007 – **Matt Kamine** pitches a five-hit shutout as Lafayette defeats Davidson 1-0 in eight innings.

STRONG IN DEFEAT

1966 – **Steve Chubin** of Rhode Island scores 23 points in a 95-65 loss to Davidson in the first round of the NCAA tournament in Blacksburg, Va.

MAZEL TOUGH

1916 – **Joe Benjamin** wins a six-round decision over Jimmy Fox to win the Pacific Coast featherweight title in Portland, Ore.

1925 – **Alfred H. Miller** of Harvard wins the IC4A indoor 70-yard dash.

1936 – **Milton Green** of Harvard wins the 50-meter hurdles at the IC4A indoor meet.

1947 – Middleweight **Artie Levine** decisions **Herbie Kronowitz** in the final all-Jewish main event at Madison Square Garden.

1964 – **Gary Gubner** of NYU wins his third straight IC4A indoor shot put title.

TRANSITIONS

1968 – After one of the bloodiest hockey fights in NHL history, **Larry Zeidel** of the Philadelphia Flyers is suspended for four games and Eddie Shore of the Boston Bruins is suspended for three games. Anti-Semitic comments directed at Zeidel from the Boston bench triggered the stick-swinging mayhem. The game is played before a sparse crowd in Toronto, because the Flyers were forced to play their home games on the road because of roof damage at their home arena, the Spectrum.

A STAR IS BORN

1898 – **Mac Baker** (basketball)
1917 – **Herman Fishman** (minor-league baseball)
1920 – **Harry Kuniansky** (Georgia football)
1971 – **Tal Banin** (Israeli soccer)

MARCH 8

GAMEBREAKERS

1941 – **Moe Becker** scores 15 points to lead Duquesne past West Virginia 51-37.

1955 – **Harvey Babetch** scores 21 points as Bradley defeats Oklahoma City 69-65 in the first round of the NCAA basketball tournament.

1968 – **Dave Newmark** of Columbia scores 13 points and grabs 17 rebounds in an NCAA first-round 83-69 victory over La Salle.

1996 – **Joel Stransky** scores all of South Africa's points in a 25-19 rugby victory over Australia.

2006 – **Adam Stern** goes 3-for-4 with a two-run single, an RBI triple and an inside-the-park homer as Canada upsets the United States 8-6 in the World Baseball Classic in Scottsdale, Ariz. Stern also makes two spectacular catches in center field.

MAZEL TOUGH

1969 – **Ben Gurevitch** of the Soviet Union wins the 90-kg. freestyle wrestling title at the World Championships in Mar del Plata, Argentina.

1997 – **Adam Goucher** of Colorado wins the 3,000 meters at the NCAA indoor track championships in Indianapolis with a time of 7:54.20.

1998 – **Kenny Bernstein** beats Larry Dixon in the Top Fuel final at the NHRA Gatornationals.

1999 – **Antonio Garay**, a defensive end on the football team, becomes the first Boston College wrestler to capture an East Coast Wrestling Conference title when he pins Marc DeFrancesco of Rider in 1 minute, 43 seconds of the heavyweight final.

2004 – **Damion Hahn** of Minnesota defeats Ryan Fulsaas of Iowa 7-2 to win his second straight Big Ten Conference 197-pound wrestling championship.

2007 – **Adrienne Binder** of Auburn wins the 500 freestyle in 4 minutes, 36.96 seconds at the NCAA women's swimming championships in Minneapolis. Two days later, she wins a silver medal in the 1,650 freestyle.

TRANSITIONS

1951 – The International Table Tennis Federation bans Egypt for refusing to play Israel.

1956 – It is discovered that defenseman Ab Hoffman is really 9-year-old **Abigail Hoffman** when she is required to produce a birth certificate after being named to her pee wee hockey league all-star team. Hoffman, who cut her hair and posed as a boy because there were no girls' hockey teams in the Toronto area, went on to become a four-time Olympian in track and field.

1963 – The New York Titans of the American Football League are sold to a five-man syndicate headed by **David "Sonny" Werblin**.

A STAR IS BORN

1910 – **Louis Bender** (Columbia basketball)
1912 – **Seymour Stark** (Syracuse football)
1926 – **Marvin "Mendy" Rudolph** (basketball referee)
1927 – **Joel Kaufman** (NYU basketball)

MARCH 9

GAMEBREAKERS

1922 – **Alexander Neufeld-Nemes** scores a hat trick as Hakoah Vienna's soccer team defeats Floridsdorfer FG 3-1.

1937 – **Ralph Kaplowitz** scores 13 points to lead Long Island University to a 28-23 overtime victory over NYU in the Metropolitan AAU Tournament final. **Irv Torgoff** of LIU ties the game 21-21 with 17 seconds left in regulation.

1957 – **Dolph Schayes** shoots 18-for-18 from the foul line and helps the Syracuse Nationals clinch an NBA playoff berth with a 94-92 victory over the Boston Celtics.

1957 – **Lenny Rosenbluth** scores 29 points and grabs 19 rebounds as North Carolina wins the Atlantic Coast Conference tournament with a 95-75 victory over South Carolina.

1991 – **Dennis Goldstein** gets two goals and an assist as North Carolina upsets top-ranked Syracuse 10-3 in lacrosse.

2002 – **Mike Cammalleri** scores three goals as Michigan defeats Lake Superior State 4-1 to even their Central Collegiate Hockey Association best-of-three first-round playoff series at one game apiece. The next day, Cammalleri gets two goals and an assist in a 4-1 Wolverines victory.

MAZEL TOUGH

1935 – **Barney Ross** wins a 12-round decision over Henry Woods in Seattle to retain his world junior welterweight title.

1940 – **Lorraine Fischer** wins the 300 individual medley at the AAU Swimming Championships.

1969 – **Julie Heldman** defeats Virginia Wade 6-1, 6-4 in the finals of the WLOD tennis tournament in Fort Lauderdale, Fla.

1978 – **Gennadi Karponosov** of the Soviet Union and partner Natalia Linichuk win the ice dancing title at the World Figure Skating Championships in Ottawa.

2003 – **Damion Hahn** of Minnesota beats top-seeded Nik Fekete of Michigan State 5-2 to win the Big Ten Conference 197-pound wrestling title in Madison, Wis.

2007 – U.S. Army Capt. **Boyd Melson** defeats Andre Penn of the Air Force to win the 152-pound title at the Armed Forces Boxing Championships at Lackland Air Force Base in Texas.

Lenny Rosenbluth
(University of North Carolina Athletic Communications)

69

MARCH 10

GAMEBREAKERS

1946 – **Sonny Hertzberg** scores 12 points to lead the New York Gothams over the Paterson Crescents 49-47 in the final game of the American Basketball League season.

1946 – **Moe Roberts** posts the shutout in goal as the Washington Lions defeat the New York Rovers 1-0 in an Eastern Hockey League Boardwalk Cup playoff game.

1952 – **Norm Grekin** has 17 points and 16 rebounds to lead La Salle past St. John's 51-45 in the quarterfinals of the NIT tournament.

1953 – Led by **Howie Landa** and **Herb Finkelstein**, Lebanon Valley, the smallest school in the history of the NCAA Division 1 tournament, upsets Fordham 80-67 in the first round in Philadelphia. The Flying Dutchmen have no player taller than 6-foot-1.

1957 – **Lenny Rosenbluth** scores 38 points as North Carolina beats South Carolina 95-75 for the Atlantic Coast Conference championship.

MAZEL TOUGH

1929 – **Cy Yellin** wins the U.S. national amateur pocket billiards title.

1929 – **Michael Schmookler** wins the AAU one-wall handball title with a 14-21, 21-8, 21-15, 21-7 victory over **Sy Alexander**.

1933 – **Maxie Rosenbloom** wins a 15-round decision over Adolf Heuser in New York to retain his world light heavyweight title.

1962 – **Robert Mack** of Yale wins the 2-mile run and **Gary Gubner** of NYU finishes first in the shot put at the IC4A indoor meet.

1968 – **Tom Okker** defeats Marty Riessen 8-6, 6-3, 6-3, then teams with Riessen to win the men's doubles and combines with Nancy Richey to capture the mixed doubles at the Colombian International tournament in Barranquilla.

2002 – **Damion Hahn** of Minnesota upsets top-ranked Andy Hrovat of Michigan 8-4 to win the 184-pound title at the Big Ten Conference wrestling championships in Champaign, Ill.

RECORD SETTERS

1905 – **Harry Fisher** makes 13 field goals in a basketball game for Columbia, setting a school record that stands until 1953.

1974 – **Irena Kirszenstein-Szewinska** of Poland sets a world indoor 60-meter record of 7.24 seconds in Goteborg, Sweden.

2006 – **Clara Horowitz** breaks the Duke school record by 12 seconds in the 5,000 meters at the NCAA Indoor Track and Field Championships in Fayetteville, Ark. The 10th-seeded Horowitz finishes second in 15:52.47.

JEWS ON FIRST

1932 – **Moe Roberts**, on loan from the minor-league New Haven Eagles, replaces injured goalie Ray Worters and helps the New York Americans beat the New York Rangers 5-1 in his first NHL start.

TRANSITIONS

1926 – **Arnold Horween**, the captain of Harvard's 1920 team, is named football coach at his alma mater.

1990 – The New York Knicks retire No. 613 in honor of former coach **Red Holzman**, who posted 613 coaching victories with the franchise.

A STAR IS BORN

1880 – **Mike Jacobs** (boxing promoter)

1890 – **Ira Streusand** (CCNY basketball)

1927 – **Lou Limmer** (Philadelphia A's first baseman)

1938 – **Ron Mix** (Southern Cal, Los Angeles/San Diego Chargers, Oakland Raiders offensive lineman)

1959 – **Avital Selinger** (Dutch volleyball)

1961 – **Mitch Gaylord** (gymnastics)

1970 – **Sandra Wasserman** (Belgian tennis)

MARCH 11

GAME BREAKERS

1958 – **Rudy LaRusso** and **Chuck Kaufman** both score 24 points as Dartmouth beats Connecticut 75-64 in the first round of the NCAA tournament in New York.

1963 – **Barry Kramer** has 37 points, 9 rebounds, and 6 assists as NYU beats Pitt 93-83 in a first-round NCAA tournament game in Philadelphia. Kramer becomes the first NYU player to surpass 1,000 career points.

1994 – UConn freshman **Doron Sheffer** scores a season-high 25 points as the Huskies defeat St. John's 97-77 in the Big East Conference tournament semifinals.

STRONG IN DEFEAT

1942 – **Brooms Abramovic** scores 33 points in Salem College's 77-63 loss to West Virginia.

MAZEL TOUGH

1920 – **Ted "Kid" Lewis** knocks out Johnny Bee in the fourth round in London to win the British welterweight championship.

1929 – **Abie Bain** registers his third straight first-round knockout, stopping Billy Smith in a lightweight fight in Philadelphia.

1951 – **Angelica Rozeanu** beats Gizella Farkas of Hungary to win the world table tennis championship in Vienna.

1989 – **Fabrice Benichou** wins the IBF super bantamweight championship with a 12-round majority decision over Jose Sanabria in Limoges, France.

RECORD SETTERS

1947 – **Harry Boykoff** of St. John's scores 54 points, more than the entire St. Francis (N.Y.) team, in the Redmen's 71-52 victory. He breaks George Mikan's Madison Square Garden record of 53 points set in the 1945 NIT semifinals.

1967 – **Gary Gubner** sets a U.S. record of 430 pounds in the standing press at the New York State AAU weight lifting championships in Poughkeepsie.

2000 – **Dan Weinstein** sets an American record of 42.058 seconds in the 500-meter short-track speed skating event in Sheffield, England.

TRANSITIONS

1997 – Wyoming names Clemson assistant **Larry Shyatt** men's basketball coach. Shyatt will coach the Cowboys to a 19-9 record and NIT berth before returning to Clemson as the Tigers' head coach.

A STAR IS BORN

1890 – **Albert Loeb** (Georgia Tech football)
1943 – **Bob Plager** (St. Louis Blues hockey)

MARCH 12

GAMEBREAKERS

1926 – Track and basketball star **Bobbie Rosenfeld** plays center as the Toronto Pattersons beat London 3-0 for the Ontario Ladies Hockey Association championship.

1938 – Tulsa Ice Oilers goalie **Sam "Porky" Levine** posts his third consecutive shutout in a 1-0 victory over the St. Louis Flyers of the American Hockey Association. Levine, who previously blanked the Wichita Skyhawks 6-0 on March 5 and the St. Paul Saints 7-0 on March 10, runs his shutout streak to a franchise-record 195 minutes, 1 second.

1952 – **Hy Buller** and Wally Hergesheimer score hat tricks as the New York Rangers beat the Chicago Black Hawks 10-2.

1957 – **Lenny Rosenbluth** collects 29 points and 19 rebounds as North Carolina beats Yale 90-74 in the first round of the NCAA Tournament.

1959 – **Alan Seiden** scores 25 points as St. John's defeats Villanova 75-67 in the first round of the NIT Tournament.

1962 – **Barry Kramer** collects 15 points, 7 rebounds, and 3 assists as NYU beats Massachusetts 70-50 in the first round of the NCAA tournament.

1994 – **David Hymovitz** scores 17 seconds into Boston College's victory over New Hampshire in the quarterfinals of the Hockey East Tournament. The goal is the quickest in tournament history.

1995 – **Ronnie Stern** of the Calgary Flames scores three goals in a 4-4 tie with the Dallas Stars for his third career hat trick.

2005 – Quad City goaltender **Robert Gherson** stops 34 shots and picks up his first professional point when he assists on a second-period power-play goal as the Mallards defeat the Port Huron Beacons 7-0 in a United Hockey League game.

STRONG IN DEFEAT

1962 – **Rick Kaminsky** has 23 points and 10 rebounds, but Yale loses 92-82 in overtime to Wake Forest in the first round of the NCAA tournament in Philadelphia.

MAZEL TOUGH

1933 – **Jimmy Jacobson** beats Coleman Clark in the final of the U.S. National Table Tennis Championships in Chicago.

1960 – **Taffy Pergament** wins the Novice Ladies singles title at the Middle Atlantic Figure Skating Championships in Iceland.

TRANSITIONS

1970 – **Art Modell** resigns as president of the NFL.

2003 – In his first game with the Detroit Red Wings, **Mathieu Schneider** records an assist for his 500th career NHL point. He becomes the 44th defenseman to reach that plateau.

A STAR IS BORN

1895 – **Harry Fisher** (Columbia basketball)
1914 – **Irwin Klein** (NYU basketball/football)
1963 – **Scott Freedman** (paddle tennis)
1969 – **Dan Greenbaum** (U.S. volleyball)
1972 – **Doron Sheffer** (UConn basketball)
1974 – **Walid Badir** (soccer)

Dan Greenbaum
(U.S. Olympic Committee)

MARCH 13

GAMEBREAKERS

1937 – **Reds Rosan** scores 15 points and **Inky Lautman** adds 11 as the Philadelphia Sphas defeat the Jersey Reds 51-34 in the ABL.

1952 – **Norm Grekin** collects 21 points and 10 rebounds as La Salle defeats Duquesne 59-46 in the NIT semifinals.

1959 – **Al Buch** scores a team-high 15 points as California defeats Utah 71-53 in the NCAA West Region final in San Antonio.

1959 – **Don Goldstein** has 19 points and 13 rebounds – both game highs – as unranked Louisville upsets second-ranked Kentucky 76-61 in an NCAA Mideast Regional semifinal in Evanston, Ill. Louisville is invited to the tournament only because Southeastern Conference champion Mississippi State declines a bid because of the state legislature's unofficial policy prohibiting state-supported universities from competing against teams with black players.

1964 – **Jack Hirsch** scores 21 points as UCLA beats Seattle 95-90 in the second round of the NCAA tournament.

1991 – **Willie Simms** shoots 12-for-15 and scores 31 points as Wisconsin defeats Bowling Green 87-79 in overtime in the first round of the NIT.

STRONG IN DEFEAT

1953 – **Bill Schyman** scores a team-high 17 points, but DePaul loses to Indiana 82-80 in the second round of the NCAA basketball tournament.

1969 – **Neal Walk** has 27 points and 17 rebounds in Florida's first-ever postseason basketball game, but the Gators lose 82-66 to Temple in the first round of the NIT.

1976 – **Ernie Grunfeld** scores 36 points, a Tennessee record for an NCAA playoff game, but the Vols lose 81-75 to VMI in a first-round upset. A year later on the same date, Grunfeld has 26 points and 12 rebounds in a 93-88 overtime loss to Syracuse in another first-round game.

MAZEL TOUGH

1937 – **Dan Taylor** of Columbia wins the shot put at the IC4A indoor meet.

1937 – **Izzy Richter** of Penn State retains his heavyweight title at the Eastern Intercollegiate Boxing Championships in Syracuse, N.Y.

1961 – **Robert Mack** of Yale wins the 2-mile run at the IC4A indoor championships.

1995 – **Tamara Levinson** and **Jessica Davis** combine to give the United States the team title in the all-around at the Pan Am Games rhythmic gymnastics competition in Mar del Plata, Argentina. Levinson finishes second in the individual all-around and Davis takes third.

1996 – **Gary Jacobs** knocks out Edwin Murillo in the fifth round in London to win the IBF International welterweight title.

A STAR IS BORN

1929 – **Jack Laskin** (wrestling)

Ernie Grunfeld *(New York Knicks)*

MARCH 14

GAMEBREAKERS

1920 – **Mac Baker** leads NYU to a 49-24 victory over Rutgers in the National AAU Basketball Tournament final and is named to the All-America team.

1950 – **Irwin Dambrot** scores 20 points and **Eddie Roman** adds 17 as CCNY hands Kentucky its worst loss in history, 89-50 in the NIT quarterfinals.

1958 – **Chuck Kaufman** scores 22 points and **Rudy LaRusso** adds 13 points and 15 rebounds as Dartmouth beats Manhattan 79-62 in the NCAA East semifinals.

1962 – **Rudy LaRusso** scores 50 points – the most ever by a Jewish NBA player – to lead the Los Angeles Lakers to a 125-115 victory over the St. Louis Hawks in the final game of the regular season.

1973 – **Neal Walk** of the Phoenix Suns scores 29 points and grabs 26 rebounds, including a team-record 18 in the second half of a 120-114 win over the Philadelphia 76ers.

1996 – **Doron Sheffer** scores 19 points and adds six assists and three blocked shots as Connecticut beats Colgate 68-59 in the first round of the NCAA tournament in Indianapolis.

1998 – **Mathieu Schneider** scores both Toronto goals as the Maple Leafs defeat the Calgary Flames 2-1.

2003 – **Gili Kollan** of Israel ties an Arizona State school record with five goals and adds two assists as the Sun Devils defeat Wagner 12-5 in women's water polo.

STRONG IN DEFEAT

1961 – **Barry Multer** scores 23 points, but Rhode Island loses to St. Bonaventure 86-76 in the first round of the NCAA tournament. **Dick Markowitz** of George Washington collects 25 points and 11 rebounds and **Jon Feldman** adds 11 points and five rebounds in an 84-67 loss to Princeton.

MAZEL TOUGH

1923 – **Oakland Jimmy Duffy** knocks out Jack Josephs in the second round in Oakland to retain his Pacific Coast welterweight title.

1927 – **Mushy Callahan** knocks out Andy DiVodi in the second round in New York to retain the world junior welterweight title.

1957 – **Dorothy Watman Levine** wins both the singles and doubles at the U.S. National Indoor tennis championships.

1998 – **Adam Goucher** of Colorado wins the NCAA indoor track 3,000-meter title in 7:46.03 in Indianapolis.

2003 – **Zhanna Bloch** of Ukraine, competing in the World Indoor Track and Field Championships for the first time in 10 years, wins the 60-meter dash in 7.04 seconds in Birmingham, England.

RECORD SETTERS

1940 – **Harold Bogrow** runs the final leg as NYU sets a world indoor record of 3:15 in the mile relay at the Dartmouth Carnival. Bogrow then runs the second leg of a world-record time of 1:27.7 in the half-mile relay.

TRANSITIONS

1938 – The Hakoah Vienna soccer club disbands. Founded in 1901, the all-Jewish team wins Austrian national championships in 1924–26 and 1928–29 and sets attendance records on its tour of the United States in 1926–27.

2001 – **David Pleat** is appointed manager of the Tottenham Hot Spurs of English soccer.

A STAR IS BORN

1910 – **Harry Blitman** (featherweight boxer)
1936 – **Herb Brown** (basketball)

MARCH 15

GAMEBREAKERS

1927 – **Nat Holman** hits a shot from three-quarters court to tie the American Basketball League game at 35-35, and the Brooklyn Celtics go on to defeat the Philadelphia Warriors 45-38 in overtime. **Davey Banks** leads the Celtics with 17 points and Holman adds nine.

1937 – **Inky Lautman** scores 16 points, **Cy Kaselman** 12 and **Shikey Gotthoffer** 10 as the Philadelphia Sphas defeat the Kingston Colonials 55-29 in the ABL.

1952 – **Norm Grekin** scores 15 points, grabs 15 rebounds, and is named tournament co-MVP as La Salle beats Dayton 75-64 in the NIT championship game.

1957 – **Larry Friend** of California scores 25 points and grabs seven rebounds as the Golden Bears beat Brigham Young 86-59 in the NCAA West Region semifinals in Corvallis, Ore. **Lenny Rosenbluth** scores 39 points as North Carolina beats Canisius 87-75 in the East Region semifinals in Philadelphia.

1958 – **Mel Brodsky** has 16 points and eight rebounds as Temple beats Dartmouth 69-50 in the NCAA East Regional final. **Rudy LaRusso** of Dartmouth has game-highs of 19 points and 21 rebounds.

1963 – **Art Heyman** scores 22 points as Duke beats NYU 93-83 in the NCAA Eastern Regional semifinals in Philadelphia. **Barry Kramer** scores 34 points for NYU.

1990 – **Nadav Henefeld** scores 19 points to lead Connecticut over Boston University 76-52 in the first round of the NCAA Tournament in Hartford, Conn.

2007 – **Max Gornesh** goes 4 for 5, **David Dayan** drives in five runs with three hits, and **Danny Wajcman** adds three hits as Yeshiva posts its first varsity baseball victory, 13-11 over Philadelphia Biblical in the first game of a season-opening doubleheader. The Maccabees went 0-18 in 2006, their first varsity season.

STRONG IN DEFEAT

1984 – **Howard Levy** scores 24 points, but Princeton loses to UNLV 68-56 in the first round of the NCAA basketball tournament.

MAZEL TOUGH

1906 – **Abe Attell** retains his world featherweight title in Baltimore when Tony Moran is disqualified in the third round.

1952 – **Vic Hershkowitz** wins the U.S. and AAU championships combined four-wall handball tournament in Detroit with a 21-11, 21-16 victory over **Ken Schneider**.

1959 – **Bobby Gusikoff** wins the singles and teams with **Sol Schiff** to win the doubles at the U.S. Table Tennis National Open in Inglewood, Calif. Schiff also wins the mixed doubles and senior men's singles.

1965 – **Dan Millman** of the University of California wins three events at the NCAA Far Western Regional gymnastics competition.

1975 – **Victor Silberman** wins the 163-pound freestyle title at the Canadian National Wrestling Championships. **Len Gang** captures the 105-pound Greco-Roman title.

1980 – **Paul Friedberg** of Penn wins the NCAA fencing saber championship at Penn State.

A STAR IS BORN

1892 – **Soldier Bartfield** (welterweight, middleweight boxer)

1916 – **Sol Maggied** (Ohio State football)

1926 – **Hy Buller** (New York Rangers defenseman)

1959 – **Eliot Teltscher** (tennis)

1979 – **Kevin Youkilis** (Boston Red Sox infielder)

MARCH 16

GAMEBREAKERS

1929 – **Moritz Haeusler** scores two goals as New York Hakoah of the Eastern Soccer League defeats the touring Saberia team of Budapest, Hungary, 3-0.

1938 – Center **Meyer Bloom** scores six points and plays strong defense as Temple beats Colorado 60-36 for the first NIT championship at Madison Square Garden. Temple is declared national champion; the NCAA Tournament won't begin for another year.

1957 – **Lenny Rosenbluth** scores 23 points as North Carolina beats Syracuse 67-38 in the NCAA basketball regional final.

STRONG IN DEFEAT

1962 – **Barry Kramer** has 26 points and 10 rebounds, but NYU loses to Villanova 79-76 in the NCAA East semifinals.

1963 – **Barry Kramer** scores 29 points in NYU's 83-73 loss to West Virginia.

MAZEL TOUGH

1940 – **Richard Bergmann** defeats Alfred Liebster in the singles final, then teams with Liebster to defeat **Viktor Barna** and Steve Boros in the doubles final at the English Open table tennis championships in Wembley.

1952 – **Vic Hershkowitz** beats **Irving Kirzner** to win the National AAU and U.S. Championships in handball. Kirzner and George Andrews win the doubles title by defeating **Sam Bienstock** and **Morris Kravitz**.

1969 – **Julie Heldman** defeats Peaches Bartkowicz 5-7, 6-2, 6-3 to win the Colombian International in Barranquilla, her third straight tennis tournament title.

RECORD SETTERS

1941 – **Allen Tolmich** sets a world indoor record of 5.4 seconds in the 45 low hurdles, breaking a mark that has stood for 40 years. He also ties the 45 high hurdles record of 5.6 seconds at the Knights of Columbus meet in Cleveland.

1956 – **Fred Cohen** of Temple grabs an NCAA tournament-record 34 rebounds in a 65-59 victory over Connecticut in a regional semifinal.

1964 – **Ronald Krelstein** of Memphis sets an NRA civilian shooting record of 200 with 19 bulls-eyes out of 20 in the outdoor pistol from 25 yards.

TRANSITIONS

2000 – Former Chaminade and Cornell coach **Al Walker** is named men's basketball coach at SUNY-Binghamton.

A STAR IS BORN

1872 – **Phil King** (Princeton football)

1904 – **Buddy Myer** (Washington Senators, Boston Red Sox second baseman)

1909 – **Philip Erenberg** (gymnastics)

1915 – **Bernie Friedkin** (featherweight boxer)

1916 – **Lew Farber** (bantamweight boxer)

1921 – **Danny Kapilow** (welterweight boxer)

MARCH 17

GAMEBREAKERS

1921 – **Barney Sedran** scores six points and **Marty Friedman** adds five as the Trenton Bengals of the Eastern Basketball League beat the Wilkes-Barre Barons of the Pennsylvania State League 33-20.

1937 – **Ralph Kaplowitz** scores 22 points as LIU defeats New Mexico Normal School 43-39 in the first round of the National AAU Tournament in Denver.

1937 – **Phil Rabin** scores 18 points as the Kingston Colonials defeat the Jersey Reds 40-38, enabling the Philadelphia Sphas to clinch the ABL's second-half title.

1946 – **Mike Bloom** scores 19 points as the Baltimore Bullets beat the New York Gothams 70-59 in the first game of the American Basketball League semifinals.

1962 – **Dave Waxman** gets 12 points and five rebounds as UCLA beats Oregon State 88-69 in the NCAA West Region final in Provo, Utah, and qualifies for the Final Four for the first time.

1968 – **Mordechai Spiegler** scores a hat trick as Israel beats Ceylon 7-0 in an Olympic Games soccer qualifier.

2000 – **Jeff Halpern** of the Washington Capitals scores two goals for the first time in his NHL career in a 4-2 victory over the Carolina Hurricanes.

MAZEL TOUGH

1913 – **Harry Lewis**, in the final victory of his career, floors Jack Harrison for a 23-count with one punch in a welterweight fight in London. Harrison is knocked down for an eight-count, gets up, and falls to the floor for a seven-count, then drops for another eight-count before the referee stops the fight in the third round.

1922 – **Young Otto** (**Arthur Susskind**) stops Jack Miller in New York for his last of a record 42nd career first-round knockouts.

1933 – **Ben Jeby** fights Vince Dundee to a 15-round draw and retains his New York world middleweight title.

1934 – **Bernard Kaplan** of Western Maryland retains his Eastern Intercollegiate Boxing Association 175-pound title in Syracuse, N.Y. **Lou Wertheimer** of Syracuse wins the 135-pound championship.

1951 – **Daniel Chafetz** of Columbia wins the epee at the NCAA fencing championships.

1979 – **Mark Roth** beats Eddie Ressler 246-197 in the final of the King Louie Open bowling tournament in Overland Park, Kan.

1984 – **Mark Roth** rallies by finishing with four strikes and beats Guppy Troup 244-237 in the BPAA U.S. Open in Oak Lawn, Ill.

2005 – **Sarah Poewe** swims the second leg as Georgia retains its title in the 400 medley relay at the NCAA Women's Swimming and Diving Championships in West Lafayette, Ind. One night later, Poewe and Georgia win their first of two 200 medley relay titles.

JEWS ON FIRST

1908 – **Leach Cross** knocks out Irish hero Frankie Madden in the fifth round in New York on St. Patrick's Day. A write-up of the bout and a photo of Cross appear in the next day's Forward – the first time a boxing match is covered by the Jewish press.

1939 – **Harry Platt** of Brown scores seven points in the first-ever NCAA basketball tournament game. Brown loses 42-30 to Villanova.

TRANSITIONS

1949 – **Max Zaslofsky** is named to the Basketball Association of America all-star team for the third straight year.

A STAR IS BORN

1904 – **Alfred Henry Miller** (Harvard and pro football)

1905 – **Young Johnny Brown** (boxing)

1942 – **Meyer Feldberg** (South African swimmer)

MARCH 18

GAMEBREAKERS

1925 – **Nat Holman** scores 11 points to lead the Original Celtics to a 30-24 victory over Pulasky Post.

1950 – **Nat Holman's** CCNY basketball team rallies from an 11-point deficit to beat Bradley 69-61 for the NIT championship as **Irwin Dambrot** scores 23 points. CCNY will beat Bradley again in 10 days to win the NCAA championship.

2000 – **Michael Goldkind** scores in the second period to break a 1-1 tie, and Connecticut goes on to defeat Iona 6-1 in the MAAC Hockey League championship game

2007 – **Mike Cammalleri** scores two goals in the Los Angeles Kings' 5-3 victory over the Anaheim Ducks.

MAZEL TOUGH

1901 – **Harry Harris** wins a 15-round decision over British champion Thomas "Pedlar" Palmer in London to win the undisputed world bantamweight title. Harris never gets to defend his crown, which he vacates to move up a weight class.

1928 – **Allie Wolff** of Penn State wins his second of three straight Intercollegiate Boxing Association middleweight titles in Philadelphia.

1930 – **William Werner** wins the standing long jump at the AAU indoor track meet in New York.

1933 – **Bernard Kaplan** of Western Maryland wins the light heavyweight title at the Eastern Intercollegiate Boxing Championships in State College, Pa.

1935 – **Ruth Aarons** becomes the only American to win a women's world championship in table tennis.

1936 – **Traute Kleinova** of Czechoslovakia teams with Miloslav Harm to win the mixed doubles at the world table tennis championships.

1947 – **Al Phillips** wins a 15-round decision over Cliff Anderson in London to capture the British Empire and British featherweight titles.

1960 – **Stanley Tarshis** of Michigan State wins his second straight horizontal bar title at the NCAA gymnastics championships in University Park, Pa.

1978 – **Steve Krisiloff** comes in second behind Gordon Johncock in the season-opening Indy car race in Phoenix. It is Krisiloff's best finish in 104 career races.

1978 – **Brian Gottfried** defeats Raul Ramirez 7-5, 7-6 to win the Volvo Classic in Washington, D.C.

1982 – **Alexander Flom** of George Mason wins the foil and **Pete Schifrin** of San Jose State captures the epee title at the NCAA fencing championships.

2006 – **Roman Greenberg**, raised in Israel and living in England, stops Alex Vassiley at the end of the sixth round to capture the vacant IBO Intercontinental heavyweight title in Monte Carlo, Monaco.

TRANSITIONS

1933 – New York Giants manager John J. McGraw names International League shortstop **Andy Cohen** his starting second baseman, replacing future Hall of Famer Rogers Hornsby.

1981 – **Larry Brown**, who coached at UCLA the previous two seasons, is named head coach of the New Jersey Nets.

A STAR IS BORN

1905 – **Benny Friedman** (Michigan, New York Giants quarterback)

1920 – **Mickey Rutner** (Philadelphia A's infielder)

1983 – **Stephanie Cohen-Aloro** (French tennis)

MARCH 19

GAMEBREAKERS

1978 – **Nancy Lieberman** collects 20 points and eight rebounds as Old Dominion defeats Texas 70-60 for the NWIT women's basketball championship in Amarillo, Texas.

1995 – **Juan Espil** of Argentina scores 27 points, including 23 in the second half, in a 68-67 victory over the United States in the opening game of the Pan American Games basketball tournament in Mar del Plata, Argentina.

2005 – **Jon Scheyer** scores 27 points and **Sean Wallis** adds 15 as Glenbrook North High School of Northbrook defeats Carbondale 63-51 to win the Illinois Class AA state basketball championship in Decatur. All five starters and the first sub off the bench for the Spartans are Jewish.

MAZEL TOUGH

1932 – "**Newsboy" Brown** wins a 12-round decision over Chris Pineda in Manila to win the Orient bantamweight title. Governor General Theodore Roosevelt awards Brown the title belt.

1935 – **Jack Londin** defeats **Dave Margolis** in the final of the National AAU one-wall handball championships.

1935 – **Leonard Bennett** decisions Alvin Lewis in Seattle to win the Washington State welterweight boxing title.

1960 – **Jimmy Jacobs** wins the YMCA-AAU men's four-wall handball championship by beating defending champion John Sloan in Minneapolis.

1978 – **Brian Gottfried** defeats Raul Ramirez 7-5, 7-6 to win an indoor tennis tournament in Washington, D.C.

1972 – **Tom Okker** beats Arthur Ashe 4-6, 6-2, 6-3 to win the Kemper Open indoor tennis tournament in Evanston, Ill.

1984 – **Adam Feldman** of Penn State beats Israeli **Yehuda Kovacs** of Notre Dame in the foil final at the NCAA fencing championship.

1994 – **Alan Fried** of Oklahoma State and **David Hirsch** of Cornell both win NCAA wrestling titles in Chapel Hill, N.C. Hirsch beats Jody Straylor of Old Dominion 2-1 for the 126-pound title. Fried decisions Gery Abas of Fresno State 15-6 for the 142-pound crown.

2000 – **Sarah Poewe** of South Africa wins the 100-meter breaststroke in 1:06.21 at the World Short-Course Swimming Championships in Athens.

2002 – **Adrienne Binder** wins the 400 individual medley at the Phillips 66 Spring Nationals swim meet.

2004 – Dartmouth senior **Byron Friedman** wins the downhill at the U.S. Alpine Championships in Girdwood, Alaska, finishing nearly two seconds ahead of runner-up Jeremy Transue.

2005 – **Irina Slutskaya** of Russia edges **Sasha Cohen** to win her second World Figure Skating championship in Moscow.

TRANSITIONS

1969 – The Phoenix Suns lose a coin flip for the No. 1 pick in the NBA draft. After the Milwaukee Bucks choose Lew Alcindor (Kareem Abdul-Jabbar) of UCLA with the first pick, the Suns select Florida center **Neal Walk** with the second pick overall.

2003 – Figure skater **Sarah Hughes** becomes the second Jewish athlete to win the Sullivan Award as the United States' top amateur athlete. Swimmer **Mark Spitz** won in 1971.

A STAR IS BORN

1868 – **Senda Berenson Abbott** (basketball pioneer)

MARCH 20

GAMEBREAKERS

1934 – **Inky Lautman** scores 12 points to lead the Philadelphia Sphas to a 39-25 victory over New Britain in the ABL. **Moe Spahn** scores 12 points for New Britain, which began the season in Hoboken, moved to Camden after four games, and finally wound up in Connecticut.

1937 – **Cy Kaselman** scores 13 points and **Reds Rosan** adds 10 as the Philadelphia Sphas defeat the New York Celtics 46-33 in the ABL.

1947 – **Irwin Dambrot** scores 16 points as CCNY beats Wisconsin 70-56 in the first round of the NCAA tournament.

2005 – **Shay Doron** scores 18 of her 26 points in the second half as Maryland rallies to defeat Wisconsin-Green Bay 65-55 in the first round of the NCAA women's basketball tournament.

MAZEL TOUGH

1897 – **Dolly Lyons** knocks down Johnny Lavack three times to win a 20-round featherweight fight that is stopped by New York City police.

1925 – **Charley Phil Rosenberg** wins a 15-round decision over Eddie "Cannonball" Martin in New York to win the world bantamweight title.

1927 – **Harry Libenson** of New York wins the national AAU flyweight boxing championship.

1948 – **Samuel Steadman**, a forward at the University of Michigan, shares in the first NCAA ice hockey championship when the Wolverines score four times in the third period to defeat Dartmouth 8-4 in Colorado Springs.

1952 – **Leah Thal Neuberger** wins the U.S. Open table tennis tournament in Cleveland.

1955 – **Dick Miles** wins the men's singles and **Leah Thal Neuberger** the women's singles at the U.S. Open table tennis tournament in Rochester, N.Y. **Erwin Klein** and **Richard Bergmann** win the men's doubles.

1977 – **Brian Gottfried** wins the Volvo Classic tennis tournament with a 6-1, 6-2 victory over Bob Lutz in Washington, D.C.

1983 – **Brian Teacher** beats Mark Dickson 1-6, 6-4, 6-2, 6-3 in the final of the Munich Cup indoor tennis tournament.

2004 – **Damion Hahn** of Minnesota decisions Ryan Fulsaas of Iowa 7-2 to win his second straight NCAA 197-pound wrestling title in St. Louis.

2005 – **Emily Jacobson** of Columbia/Barnard wins the women's saber title at the NCAA fencing championships in Houston. **Boaz Ellis** of Ohio State defeats **Gabriel Sinkin** of NYU 15-8 to capture the men's foil title.

RECORD SETTERS

1992 – **Kenny Bernstein** earns the title "King of Speed" when he becomes the first NHRA drag racer to top 300 mph, clocking 301.70 during qualifying at the Gatornationals in Gainesville, Fla.

A STAR IS BORN

1906 – **Nikolaus "Mickey" Hirschl** (Austrian wrestling)

1909 – **Marchy Schwartz** (Notre Dame football)

1937 – **David Segal** (British sprinter)

1956 – **Bruce Manson** (tennis)

1985 – **Adrienne Binder** (Auburn swimming)

Emily Jacobson (*U.S. Olympic Committee*)

MARCH 21

GAMEBREAKERS

1929 – New York Hakoah gets goals from **Jozsef Eisenhoffer** and **Siegfried Wortmann** in a 2-0 victory over Madison Kennel of St. Louis in the first of two games to decide the U.S. National Challenge Cup soccer championship at Sportsman's Park in St. Louis.

1959 – **Alan Seiden,** playing with four fouls since midway through the second half, scores a game-high 22 points as St. John's rallies to beat Bradley 77-71 in double overtime to capture the NIT title.

1964 – **Jack Hirsch** scores 13 points and grabs six rebounds to help UCLA beat Duke 98-83 in Kansas City to finish 30-0 and win its first national championship.

1998 – **Jeff Halpern** scores two goals and is named tournament MVP as Princeton wins its first ECAC hockey championship with a 5-4 double-overtime victory over Clarkson.

MAZEL TOUGH

1910 – **Young Joseph Aschel** stops **Jack Goldswain** in the 11th round in Paris to retain his British welterweight title.

1914 – **Matt Wells** wins a 20-round decision over Tony McCormick in Sydney, Australia, to win the world and British Empire welterweight championships.

1924 – **Abe Goldstein** wins a 15-round decision over Joe Lynch in New York to win the world bantamweight title.

1942 – **Byron Krieger** of Wayne State wins a gold medal in foil at the NCAA fencing championships.

1964 – **Dan Millman** of the United States wins the first world trampoline gymnastics championship at the Royal Albert Hall in London.

1965 – **Erwin Klein** wins the men's singles and teams with **Bernard Bukiet** to capture the doubles at the U.S. Table Tennis Championships in Detroit.

1976 – **Harold Solomon** beats Onny Parun of New Zealand 6-3, 6-1 in the final of the Volvo Classic indoor tennis tournament in Washington, D.C. Solomon also teams with Eddie Dibbs to capture the doubles.

1981 – **Marshall Holman** beats Wayne Webb 181-168 to win the PBA King Louie Tournament in Overland Park, Kan.

1981 – **Paul Friedman** of Penn wins the saber title at the NCAA fencing championships.

1998 – **Jill "Zion Lion" Matthews** beats Anissa Zamarron in a 10-round decision to win the IFBA and IWAF junior flyweight boxing titles.

2002 – **Ben Weston** of Cal-Santa Cruz wins the 500 freestyle at the NCAA Division III swimming championships in Oxford, Ohio.

2004 – **Yulia Beygelzimer** defeats Eugenia Linetskaya 6-3, 2-6, 6-2 to win an ITF tennis tournament in Orange, Calif.

TRANSITIONS

1948 – The Chicago Stags lose their regular-season finale 82-70 to the St. Louis Bombers, but **Max Zaslofsky** wraps up the Basketball Association of America scoring title with 1,007 points in 48 games for a 20.9 average.

1961 – **Art Modell** purchases the Cleveland Browns for $4 million.

A STAR IS BORN

1909 – **Mac Kinsbrunner** (St. John's basketball)

1936 – **Larry Boardman** (lightweight boxer)

1964 – **Bruce Mesner** (Maryland football, Buffalo Bills defensive lineman)

MARCH 22

GAMEBREAKERS

1943 – **Hy Gotkin** scores with one second remaining to give St. John's a 51-49 win over Rice in the first round of the NIT tournament. **Harry Boykoff** leads St. John's with 21 points.

1945 – **Sid Tanenbaum** scores 17 points as NYU beats Tufts 59-44 in the first round of the NCAA basketball tournament.

1955 – **Max Zaslofsky** scores the only point in overtime as the Fort Wayne Pistons defeat the Minneapolis Lakers 98-97 in the NBA playoffs. Both teams miss seven field goals in the extra session.

1957 – **Lenny Rosenbluth** scores four of North Carolina's eight points in the third overtime period as the Tar Heels beat Michigan State 74-70 in the NCAA basketball semifinals.

1970 – **Yehoshua Feigenbaum** scores a hat trick as Israel beats Ethiopia 5-1 in soccer.

MAZEL TOUGH

1905 – **Abe Attell** retains his world featherweight title by fighting Kid Goodman to a 15-round draw in Boston.

1930 – **David Stoop** of Penn State defeats John C. Dempsey of Navy in the bantamweight final of the intercollegiate boxing championships in Philadelphia.

1941 – **Leonard "Butch" Levy** of Minnesota wins the NCAA wrestling heavyweight title in Bethlehem, Pa.

1957 – **John Davis** of Illinois wins the pommel horse, **Norman Marks** of Los Angeles State the free exercise and **Abie Grossfeld** of Illinois the horizontal bars at the NCAA Gymnastics Championships in Annapolis, Md.

1959 – **Arthur Shurlock** of California wins the pommel horse and **Stanley Tarshis** of Michigan State finishes first on the horizontal bar at the NCAA gymnastics championships in Berkeley, Calif.

1970 – **Paul Haber** wins the U.S. Handball Association singles championship.

1998 – Jewish fencers take the top three spots in the foil competition at the NCAA Championships. **Ayo Griffin** of Yale beats **Yaron Roth** of Penn 15-13 for first place, and **Cliff Bayer** of Penn beats Brian Stone of Notre Dame 15-8 for third place.

2002 – **Galit Chait** and **Sergei Sakhnovksy** win a bronze medal in ice dancing in Nagano, Japan, for Israel's first medal in the World Figure Skating Championships.

2002 – **Adrienne Binder** wins the 400 individual medley in 4:44.65 at the U.S. Spring National swimming championships in Minneapolis. Her time is the fastest ever for a non-collegian.

2003 – **Damion Hahn** of Minnesota scores a two-point takedown with three seconds remaining to beat top-seeded Jon Trenge of Lehigh 5-4 for the 197-pound title at the NCAA wrestling championships in Kansas City, Mo.

TRANSITIONS

1893 – After meeting with James Naismith, gymnastics instructor **Senda Berenson Abbott** organizes the first women's collegiate intramural basketball game at Smith College. With nine women on each side because the court is so large, the sophomore class of 1895 plays the freshman class of 1896. The game resumes after a short delay when the freshman center dislocates her shoulder on the opening tip.

A STAR IS BORN

1905 – **Nate Weinstock** (Western Maryland football)

1907 – **John Shapiro** (NYU football)

1974 – **Irena Olevsky** (synchronized swimming)

MARCH 23

GAMEBREAKERS

1926 – **Nat Holman** scores 18 points as the New York Celtics defeat Consumers Power 39-39 in Jackson, Mich.

1939 – **Irv Torgoff** scores 12 points as Long Island University beats Loyola of Chicago 44-32 in an NIT final matching two unbeaten teams. **Ralph Kaplowitz** and **Ossie Schechtman** each add nine points for LIU.

1957 – **Lenny Rosenbluth** of North Carolina scores 20 points as the Tar Heels beat Wilt Chamberlain and Kansas 54-53 in triple overtime in the NCAA basketball final.

1963 – **Art Heyman** scores 22 points as Duke beats Oregon State 85-63 in the NCAA championship consolation game in Louisville, Ky. Despite not playing in the final, Heyman is named MVP of the Final Four

MAZEL TOUGH

1912 – **Mortimer Lindsey** leads the Brunswick All-Stars to the American Bowling Congress team championship. Lindsey wins another team title with New Haven in 1914 and the individual all-events crown in 1919.

1929 – **Allie Wolff** of Penn State finishes off an undefeated college career by winning his third straight Intercollegiate Boxing Association middleweight (160-pound) championship. Teammate **Jules Epstein**, who later wins an Academy Award for the screenplay of Casablanca, captures the bantamweight (115-pound) title.

1935 – **Ralph "Ruffy" Silverstein** of Illinois beats Orville Nickerson of Oklahoma Southwest State Teachers College to capture the NCAA 175-pound wrestling title in Bethlehem, Pa.

1946 – **David Shapiro** of Illinois wins the NCAA 165-pound wrestling championship in Stillwater, Okla., with a 15-9 decision over George Walker of Oklahoma State.

1957 – **Bernie Balaban** of NYU wins the individual saber crown and **James Margolis** of Columbia wins the epee at the NCAA fencing championships in Detroit.

1969 – **Julie Heldman** defeats Virginia Wade 6-1, 6-4 in the final of a tennis tournament in Fort Lauderdale, Fla.

1974 – **Fred Lewis** captures the U.S. Handball Association singles championship in Knoxville, Tenn.

1975 – **Harold Solomon** wins the Memphis Classic indoor tennis tournament with a 2-6, 6-1, 6-4 victory over Jiri Hrebec.

1987 – Cornell fencer **William Mandell** wins the NCAA foil title.

1997 – **Carrie Sheinberg** wins the giant slalom at the U.S. Alpine Championships at Sugarloaf, Maine.

2002 – **Irina Slutskaya** of Russia wins her first world title, defeating four-time champion Michelle Kwan at the World Figure Skating Championships in Nagano, Japan.

RECORD SETTERS

1975 – **Wendy Weinberg** sets an American record of 2:18.2 in the 200 butterfly at the Bremen Swimfest in West Germany.

A STAR IS BORN

1896 – **Jake Friedman** (Hartford Blues football)

1912 – **Irwin Klein** (basketball)

1919 – **Marvin Rottner** (Loyola of Chicago basketball)

1926 – **Norm Mager** (CCNY basketball)

1933 – **Abraham Cohen** (Tenn.-Chattanooga, CFL Hamilton Tiger-Cats, AFL Boston Patriots guard)

1937 – **Boris Mendelovitch Gurevich** (wrestling)

1970 – **Justin Duberman** (Pittsburgh Penguins hockey)

MARCH 24

GAMEBREAKERS

1934 – **Inky Lautman** scores 12 points and **Moe Goldman** adds 11 as the Philadelphia Sphas defeat the Union City Reds 47-38. **Julius Bender** scores 12 in a losing cause.

1944 – Player-coach **Jules Rivlin** hits a 45-foot shot from midcourt in the final second to give the Fort Warren (Wyo.) Broncos a 45-43 victory over Twentieth Century Fox in the quarterfinals of the AAU National Basketball Championships in Denver.

1974 – Chicago Blackhawks rookie goalie **Mike Veisor** runs his record to 6-0 and makes 33 saves in a 6-0 victory over the Minnesota North Stars for his first NHL shutout.

2002 – **Stacey Britstone** scores with 6:43 left in the third overtime period to give Western Ontario a 4-3 victory over Quebec-Trois Riviere in Canada's University Cup national hockey championship game.

MAZEL TOUGH

1933 – **Maxie Rosenbloom** knocks out Bob Godwin in the fourth round in New York to retain his world light heavyweight title.

1954 – **Dorothy Watman Levine** captures the U.S. Women's Indoor tennis championship and teams with Barbara Ward to win the doubles in Brookline, Mass.

1954 – Apprentice jockey **Walter Blum** rides four winners, giving him seven in two days, including the featured Fort Meade Purse aboard Kim Jolie at Laurel Race Course in Maryland.

1956 – **Gerald Kaufman** of Columbia wins the epee title at the NCAA fencing championships in Annapolis, Md.

1957 – **Herb Flam** wins the Good Neighbor tennis tournament in Miami Beach for the second year in a row. **Suzy Kormoczy** of Hungary defeats Edda Buding 10-8, 1-6, 7-5 to win the Cairo Championship.

1973 – **Tom Okker** wins the Union Trust Co. tennis tournament in Merrifield, Va., by beating Arthur Ashe 6-3, 6-7, 7-6 in the final.

1979 – **Yuri Rabinovich** of Wayne State beats Mike Sullivan of Notre Dame 5-2 in a fence-off to win the NCAA saber title at Princeton.

2002 – **Sada Jacobson** of Yale defeats Louise Bond-Williams of Ohio State 15-9 to capture her second straight saber title at the NCAA fencing championships in Madison, N.J.

JEWS ON FIRST

1942 – **Bernie Fliegel** becomes the only player to defeat the Harlem Globetrotters in three consecutive games, scoring a game-high 17 points in the Glen Falls Lions' 46-44 victory. Two days earlier, Fliegel played for both the Wilmington Blue Bombers and the Newark Hebrews, combining for 13 points in the two victories.

1943 – **Sid Gordon** of the New York Giants hits his first of 202 career home runs off Jim Tobin in an 11-3 victory over the Boston Braves.

RECORD SETTERS

2000 – UCLA freshman **Anthony Ervin** sets a world record of 21.21 seconds in the 50-meter freestyle in the preliminaries of the NCAA swimming championships.

TRANSITIONS

1990 – **Marshall Holman** is elected to the Pro Bowlers Association Hall of Fame.

A STAR IS BORN

1907 – **Solomon "Happy" Furth** (track and field
1965 – **Angela Zuckerman** (speed skating)
1981 – **Ezra Poyas** (Australian rules football)

MARCH 25

GAMEBREAKERS

1923 – **Alexander Neufeld-Nemes** scores four goals as Hakoah Vienna's soccer team defeats Admira Vienna 6-1.

1928 – **Davey Banks** scores 11 points and **Nat Holman** adds six as the Original Celtics beat Fort Wayne 27-26 in Brooklyn to win the best-of-five World Championship series 3-1.

1941 – **Butch Schwartz** scores 19 points and **Ossie Schechtman** adds 12 as Long Island University beats Ohio University 25-21 for its second NIT championship.

1979 – **Nancy Lieberman's** 20 points and seven rebounds help Old Dominion defeat Louisiana Tech 75-65 for its first of two straight AIAW women's basketball titles in Greensboro, N.C.

MAZEL TOUGH

1929 – **Jackie Fields** wins eight of the 10 rounds against Young Jack Thompson to capture the vacant National Boxing Association welterweight title in Chicago. The NBA crown is recognized in 23 states.

1934 – **William Steiner** wins the AAU Metropolitan Marathon in New York.

1944 – **Charles Batterman** of Columbia captures both the 1-meter and 3-meter diving titles at the NCAA Championships.

1950 – **John Blum** of Yale wins the 220 freestyle in 2:10.0 at the NCAA swimming championships in Columbus, Ohio.

1967 – **Jim Kamman** of Michigan defeats Wayne Wells of Oklahoma 6-5 to win the 152-pound title at the NCAA Wrestling Championships at Kent State.

2001 – **Sada Jacobson** of Yale defeats Marisa Mustilli of St. John's 15-6 to win the women's saber title at the NCAA Fencing Championships in Kenosha, Wis.

2006 – **Hagar Shmoulefeld** of Israel decisions Svetla Taskova of Bulgaria to win the Women's International Boxing Federation Inter-Continental and WIBA European super flyweight titles in Tel Aviv.

2006 – **David Cohen** rides Proud Tower Two to a 1¼-length victory in the $2 million Dubai Golden Shaheen horse race.

2007 – Wayne State freshman **Slava Zingerman** of Israel wins the men's epee title in the NCAA Fencing Championships in Madison, Wis. Sophomore **Daria Schneider** of Columbia/Barnard captures the women's saber title.

RECORD SETTERS

2000 – **Anthony Ervin** of UCLA wins the NCAA 100 freestyle championship, setting a United States record of 47.36 seconds in College Station, Texas.

2007 – **Skip Kendall** sinks a 6-foot birdie putt on the third playoff hole to defeat Paul Claxton and win the Louisiana Open in Broussard, La. The victory is the third on the Nationwide golf tour for Kendall, who sets a record for the longest span between Tour victories – 12 years, eight months and 27 days.

TRANSITIONS

2004 – **Molly Wasserman** of Williams College is named women's ice hockey College Division Player of the Year after recording 26 goals and 20 assists in 27 games.

A STAR IS BORN

1891 – **Charley White** (lightweight boxer)
1918 – **Howard Cosell** (broadcasting)
1938 – **Alan Koch** (Washington Senators, Detroit Tigers pitcher)
1969 – **Eric Helfand** (Oakland A's catcher)
1971 – **Perry Klein** (C.W. Post, Atlanta Falcons quarterback)

MARCH 26

GAMEBREAKERS

1968 – **Art Heyman** scores 32 points as the Pittsburgh Pipers beat the Indiana Pacers 121-108 in Game 2 of the American Basketball Association Eastern Division semifinals.

1981 – **Mickey Berkowitz** scores 20 points as Maccabi Tel Aviv beats Cinudine Bologna 80-79 for its second European Cup basketball championship in four years.

2004 – **Mike Cammalleri** scores his first professional hat trick and adds an assist as the Manchester Monarchs defeat the Norfolk Admirals 5-3 in the American Hockey League.

MAZEL TOUGH

1908 – **Harry Lewis** wins a 15-round decision over Terry Martin in Baltimore to retain his world welterweight title.

1909 – **Abe Attell** knocks out Frankie White in the eighth round to retain his world featherweight title in Dayton, Ohio.

1914 – **Mortimer Lindsey** and his New Haven, Conn., team win the American Bowling Congress championship in Buffalo, N.Y.

1923 – **Jack Bloomfield** knocks out Horace "Soldier" Jones in the fifth round to win the British Empire light-heavyweight title.

1927 – **Allie Wolff** of Penn State wins the 160-pound title and **D.J. Weintraub** of Navy captures the 125-pound crown at the college boxing championships in Syracuse, N.Y.

1935 – **Maurice Holtzer** of France wins a 15-round decision over Vittorio Tamagnini in Paris to capture the vacant European featherweight title.

1938 – **Laszlo Bellak** of Hungary wins the U.S. table tennis championship in Philadelphia.

1949 – **Alex Treves** of Rutgers wins his second straight saber title at the NCAA fencing championships.

1949 – **Robert Weinberg** of Michigan wins the 50 freestyle in 23.1 seconds at the NCAA swimming championships.

1949 – **Martin Korik** of Tennessee, the 1948 and 1950 Southeastern Conference pole vault champion, clears a career-high 14 feet 1 5/8 inches in Gainesville, Fla.

1954 – **Morley Shapiro** of Ohio State wins the NCAA 3-meter diving title.

1955 – **Jimmy Jacobs** wins his first of six national four-wall handball championships, beating **Vic Hershkowitz** 21-20, 21-7 in Los Angeles.

1955 – **Barry Pariser** of Columbia wins the saber title at the NCAA fencing championships at Michigan State.

1961 – NYU wins the team championship and all three individual titles at the NCAA fencing championships at Princeton. **Herbert Cohen**, the national fencer of the year, wins his second straight foil title, while **Jerry Halpern** wins epee.

1983 – **John Friedman** of North Carolina wins the saber title at the NCAA fencing championships.

1992 – **Aaron Krickstein** beats Alexander Volkov 6-4, 6-4 in the final of a hard-court tournament in Johannesburg.

2005 – **Deena Kastor** wins the United States women's 8-kilometer cross-country title in 25 minutes, 5 seconds in New York.

A STAR IS BORN

1956 – **Ilana Kloss** (South African tennis)

MARCH 27

MAZEL TOUGH

1934 – **Barney Ross** wins a 10-round decision over Bobby Pacho in Los Angeles to retain his world super lightweight title.

1935 – **Dave Margolis** and **Danny Levinson** beat George Kronengold and **Harry Wasserspring** to win their second straight National AAU one-wall handball doubles championship.

1936 – **Barney Ross** beats Izzy Janazzo to end a streak of eight consecutive welterweight champions who lost in their first title defense.

1954 – **Robert Goldman** of Penn wins the epee and **Steve Sobel** of Columbia captures the saber at the NCAA fencing championships in Chicago.

1954 – **Vic Hershkowitz** beats Bob Bradley 21-15, 21-18 and wins the four-wall singles title at the National Handball Championships in Chicago. **Sam Haber** and **Ken Schneider** win the doubles title.

1955 – **Donald Faber** of UCLA wins the free exercise and **George Wikler** of Southern Cal wins gold on flying rings at the NCAA gymnastics championships.

1960 – **James Prigoff** wins the U.S. Squash title for the fifth time.

1976 – **Mark Roth** beats Larry Laub 235-202 in the final of the Rolaids Open bowling tournament in Florissant, Mo.

1977 – **Brian Gottfried** beats Marty Riessen 6-3, 6-2 to win a hard-court tournament in La Costa, Calif.

1995 – Skiier **Carrie Sheinberg** wins the U.S. Alpine Championships combined title after finishing second in the slalom and fourth in the giant slalom at Park City, Utah.

2004 – Earning her first international figure skating medal, **Sasha Cohen** wins the silver at the World Championships in Dortmund, Germany.

Vic Hershkowitz

TRANSITIONS

1979 – UCLA hires former Denver Nuggets coach **Larry Brown** to replace Gary Cunningham as men's basketball coach.

2004 – Massachusetts-Lowell senior forward **Ilad Inbar** is named National Association of Basketball Coaches Division II men's player of the year. The Israeli averages 19.7 points and 7.0 rebounds, and finishes his career as the River Hawks' all-time leading scorer with 2,099 points.

A STAR IS BORN

1903 – **Harry Mason** (British lightweight boxer)

1909 – **William Lazar** (Penn basketball)

1910 – **Rudi Ball** (German hockey)

1911 – **Paul Friesel** (swimming)

1958 – **Steve Shull** (William & Mary, Miami Dolphins linebacker)

MARCH 28

GAMEBREAKERS

1929 – One week after beating Madison Kennel of St. Louis 2-0 in the first game of the two-game series, New York Hakoah wins 3-0 in Dexter Park, Brooklyn, to wrap up the U.S. National Challenge Cup soccer championship. **Erno Schwarcz**, **Max Gruenwald**, and **Moritz Haeusler** score for Hakoah, the Eastern Soccer League champion.

1937 – **Cy Kaselman** scores 13 points and **Moe Goldman** and **Shikey Gotthoffer** add 10 apiece as the Philadelphia Sphas tie the ABL best-of-seven championship series at one game apiece with a 39-36 victory over the Jersey Reds in North Bergen, N.J.

1950 – CCNY, coached by **Nat Holman**, beats Bradley 71-68 at Madison Square Garden for the NCAA basketball championship. **Irwin Dambrot** blocks a last-second shot by Gene Melchiorre, and passes to **Norm Mager** for an easy basket to preserve the victory.

MAZEL TOUGH

1891 – **Edward Lawrence Levy** of England completes all eight lifts and wins the first World WeightliftingChampionship competition at Cafe Monica in Picadilly, London.

1931 – **Marcus Schussheim** defeats Ed Svigals 21-18 in the final to win the first U.S. National Table Tennis Championship at the Pennsylvania Hotel in New York.

1936 – **Isaac Richter** of Penn State wins the national collegiate heavyweight boxing championship.

1941 – **Earl Shanken** of the University of Chicago wins the long horse for the second year in a row at the NCAA gymnastics championships in Annapolis, Md.

1951 – **Sylvia Wene** rolls a 300 game in Philadelphia and becomes the first woman to bowl a sanctioned perfect game on the East Coast.

1957 – **James Margolis** of Columbia wins the epee and **Bernie Balaban** of NYU the saber at the NCAA fencing championships in Detroit.

1959 – **Andy Fitch** of Yale wins the NCAA wrestling 115-pound title with a 3-3, 5-4 overtime victory over Dick Wilson of Toledo in Iowa City.

1977 – **Brian Gottfried** beats Marty Riessen 6-2, 6-2 to win the LaCosta Classic tennis tournament.

1982 – **Amy Alcott** beats runner-up JoAnne Carner by one stroke to win the LPGA Women's Kemper Open in Miami.

1992 – **Paul Cohen** of Syracuse becomes the second goalie in American Hockey League history to score when he tallies against the Rochester Americans.

2002 – 15-year-old **Jessica Jerome** wins the "large hill" title at the U.S. ski jumping and Nordic combined championships in Steamboat Springs, Colo. A day earlier, she won the smaller "normal hill" title.

TRANSITIONS

1973 – **Neal Walk** finishes the season with a Phoenix Suns team-record 1,006 rebounds. He averages 20.2 points and 12.4 rebounds for the year.

2005 – **Bruce Pearl**, who coached Wisconsin-Milwaukee to a school-record 26 wins including two NCAA tournament games, is named men's basketball coach at Tennessee.

A STAR IS BORN

1906 – **Stanley Rosen** (Rutgers and pro football)

1909 – **Solly Krieger** (middleweight boxer)

1923 – **Joey Varoff** (lightweight boxer)

1936 – **Bobby Gusikoff** (table tennis)

1967 – **Lucy Wener** (Georgia gymnastics)

MARCH 29

GAMEBREAKERS

1943 – **Harry Boykoff** of St. John's scores 13 points in a 48-27 win over Toledo in the NIT final. Boykoff finishes with 56 points in three games and is named tournament MVP.

1944 – **Max Kaminsky** scores the winning goal as the Buffalo Bisons beat the Indianapolis Capitols 4-2 in Game 5 of the American Hockey League playoffs, enabling Buffalo to clinch the series 4-1. **Hy Buller,** a 17-year-old defenseman, scores twice for Indianapolis.

MAZEL TOUGH

1896 – **Alfred Flatow** of Germany beats 17 other gymnasts to win the gold medal in the parallel bars at the first modern Olympics in Athens.

1917 – **Elaine Rosenthal** defeats Dorothy Campbell Hurd in the match-play final to win the Women's North and South Amateur Golf Championship at Pinehurst, N.C.

1941 – **Henry Wittenberg** wins his second straight AAU wrestling 174-pound title in New York.

1945 – **Dick Miles** beats **Sol Schiff** in the finals to win the U.S. National Table Tennis championship in New York. Miles will win nine titles in the next 10 years.

1952 – **Harold Goldsmith** of CCNY captures the foil title at the NCAA fencing championships in New Haven, Conn. **Steve Sobel, Daniel Chafetz**, and **Alfred Rubin** combine to claim the team title for Columbia.

1953 – **Leah Thal Neuberger** beats Sally Prouty in the U.S. national table tennis championship final in Kansas City.

1964 – **Ron Barak** of Southern Cal wins the NCAA gymnastics all-around title in Los Angeles. He also places first on the horizontal bar and parallel bars.

1969 – Indiana freshman **Mark Spitz** wins the 100-meter butterfly, his third gold medal of the three-day NCAA swimming championships in Bloomington, Ind.

1993 – **Aaron Krickstein** beats Grant Stafford in the South African Open tennis final.

2002 – **Dan Weinstein** wins the 1,000-meter race at the World Team Speed Skating Championships for the second year in a row.

2006 – **Daniel Madwed** wins the 200 butterfly at the USA Spring Nationals swimming championships in Federal Way, Wash.

JEWS ON FIRST

1930 – **Albert Schwartz** of Northwestern becomes the first swimmer to win three events at the NCAA championships – the 50 freestyle in 24.0 seconds, the 100 freestyle in 55.0 seconds, and the 220 freestyle in 2:16.6 in Cambridge, Mass.

1932 – The first World Maccabiah Games open in Tel Aviv, with athletes from 22 countries.

TRANSITIONS

1979 – Old Dominion junior guard **Nancy Lieberman** wins the Wade Trophy as the top collegiate women's basketball player.

1989 – **Eddie Fogler** resigns as Wichita State basketball coach to take over the same position at Vanderbilt.

1998 – **Marty Glickman** is presented the United States Olympic Committee's first Douglas MacArthur Award in lieu of the Olympic track and field medal he likely would have won in 1936.

A STAR IS BORN

1921 – **Howie Rader** and **Lenny Rader** (NYU basketball)

1950 – **Harold Reitman** (heavyweight boxer)

MARCH 30

GAMEBREAKERS

1998 – **Tony Schrager** hits two home runs as Stanford defeats UCLA 15-3.

MAZEL TOUGH

1928 – **Phil Wolf** wins the all-events title at the American Bowling Congress championships.

1929 – **Albert Schwartz** of Northwestern wins the 100 freestyle in 53.2 seconds at the NCAA swimming championships.

1945 – **Seymour Schlanger** of Ohio State wins the 440 freestyle in 4:55.4 and the 1,500 freestyle in 20:11.4 at the NCAA swimming championships.

1947 – **Robert Weinberg** of Michigan wins the 50 freestyle in 23.3 seconds and the 100 freestyle in 52.2 seconds at the NCAA swimming championships in Seattle.

1963 – **Jay Lustig** of Columbia wins the foil title at the NCAA fencing championships at the Air Force Academy.

1992 – **Aaron Krickstein** beats Alexander Volkov 6-4, 6-4 in the South African Open hard-court final in Johannesburg.

2003 – **Stephanie Mogerman** of Claremont Mudd wins the women's 57kg division at the National Collegiate Judo Championships in Spokane, Wash.

JEWS ON FIRST

1896 – Jewish swimmers win three of the four aquatic events at the first moden Olympics in Athens. **Alfred Hajos-Guttman** of Hungary finishes first and **Otto Herschmann** of Austria wins the silver medal in the 100 meters. Though 29 swimmers enter the race, only three compete as **Dr. Paul Neumann** of Austria wins the 500 freestyle. **Hajos-Guttman** wins his second gold medal of the day by beating eight other swimmers in the 1,200 freestyle.

TRANSITIONS

1966 – **Sandy Koufax** and Don Drysdale end their 32-day contract holdout with the Los Angeles Dodgers. Both players had asked for $500,000 over three years. Koufax signs a one-year contract for $130,000 for what will become his final season.

1966 – **Dolph Schayes,** who leads the Philadelphia 76ers to the Eastern Division title, is named NBA Coach of the Year.

A STAR IS BORN

1901 – **Sydney Pierce** (Canadian hurdler)

1917 – **Allen Tolmich** (track and field)

1942 – **Randy Cardinal** (Houston Colt .45s pitcher)

Aaron Krickstein
(Association of Tennis Professionals)

MARCH 31

GAME BREAKERS

1979 – With **Arnie Mausser** in goal, the Fort Lauderdale Strikers beat the New England Tea Men 2-0 in the North American Soccer League.

STRONG IN DEFEAT

1962 – **Larry Yellen** of Hunter College strikes out 12 and pitches eight innings of no-hit ball, but yields two singles and two unearned runs in the ninth in a 2-0 loss to Bridgeport. Mike McLaughlin pitches a no-hitter for the winners with 14 strikeouts and six walks.

MAZEL TOUGH

1907 – **Marshall Levy** beats R.F. Matak 582-385 in a rolloff after they tie for first place in singles at the American Bowling Congress championships in St. Louis.

1921 – **Abe Schieman** of Rochester, N.Y., wins the individual all-events title with a score of 1,909 at the American Bowling Congress championships in Buffalo, N.Y. **Sam Schliman** is a member of the winning five-man Saunders team of Toronto.

1944 – **Charles Batterman** wins the 1-meter and 3-meter diving championships at the AAU National Indoor swimming meet.

1952 – **Leah Thal Neuberger** wins her fifth of nine U.S. Open table tennis championships in Cleveland.

1962 – **Herbert Cohen** of NYU wins the NCAA foil championship in Columbus, Ohio, and is named fencer of the year. **Barton Nisonson** of Columbia wins the saber title.

1962 – **Michael Aufrecht** of Illinois wins the NCAA gymnastics championship on the pommel horse.

1973 – **Walter Blum** rides Royal and Regal to victory in the Florida Derby at Gulfstream Park. In the next race on the day's card, he takes Mr. Prospector to a track-record 1:07 4/5 over six furlongs.

1974 – **Tom Okker** beats Tom Gorman 4-6, 7-6 (7-2), 6-1 in the final of the WCT Rotterdam indoor tournament.

1991 – **Amy Alcott** beats runner-up Dottie Pepper by eight strokes to win her third Nabisco Dinah Shore Invitational in Rancho Mirage, Calif. The victory is her 29th and last on the LPGA Tour.

2002 – **Anthony Ervin** of California wins the 100-meter freestyle in an American-record 41.62 seconds, and also swims on the Golden Bears' victorious 400 relay team at the NCAA swimming championships in Athens, Ga.

2002 – **Yulia Beygelzimer** defeats Amandine Dulon 7-5, 3-6, 6-3 to win an ITF tennis tournament in Amiens, France.

2007 – **Ben Wildman-Tobriner** swims the 50 freestyle in 21.88 seconds for his first world title at the World Swimming Championships in Melbourne, Australia.

RECORD SETTERS

1935 – **Herman Neugass** ties the 100-yard dash world record in a wind-aided 9.4 seconds in Austin, Texas.

1940 – **Allen Tolmich** of Detroit sets world indoor records of 6.0 seconds in the 50 low hurdles and 8.4 seconds in the 70 high hurdles at Madison Square Garden.

TRANSITIONS

1964 – **Dolph Schayes** is named head coach of the Buffalo Braves, an NBA expansion team. Schayes had been the NBA's supervisor of officials the last two seasons.

A STAR IS BORN

1958 – **Margie Goldstein-Engle** (equestrian)

APRIL 1

GAMEBREAKERS

1999 – **Todd Simon** gets two goals – including his 26th of the season – and an assist as the Cincinnati Cyclones beat the Fort Wayne Komets 4-2 in an International Hockey League game.

2001 – **Craig Breslow** strikes out 16 batters, allowing two runs in eight innings, as Yale defeats Cornell 6-4 in 10 innings.

MAZEL TOUGH

1919 – **Mortimer Lindsey** wins the all-events title with a 1,933 total at the American Bowling Congress championships in Toledo, Ohio.

1930 – **Ray Miller** knocks out Johnny Canzoneri 40 seconds into the first round of a lightweight fight in Allentown, Pa.

1931 – **Albert Schwartz** wins the 100 and 220 freestyle races at the AAU Indoor Swimming Championships.

1940 – **David Katzen** wins a 12-round decision over Alec Knight in Johannesburg to capture the South African bantamweight title.

1957 – **Alphonse Halimi** of Algeria wins the world bantamweight championship in Paris with a 15-round decision over Mario D'Agata of Italy.

1963 – Jockey **Walter Blum** learns he will be suspended 10 days for careless riding, then goes out and wins four races at Gulfstream Park.

1990 – **Tony Sills** rallies from six strokes back and wins a one-hole playoff with Gil Morgan at the Independent Insurance Agents Open in The Woodlands, Texas, for his only victory on the PGA Tour.

2001 – **Dan Weinstein** helps the United States edge Canada in the 5,000-meter relay at the World Short-Track Speed Skating Championships in South Korea. The gold medal is the first for the United States in the event since 1976.

RECORD SETTERS

2007 – At 18 years, 10 months, and 9 days, **Morgan Pressel** becomes the youngest golfer to win a major tournament on the LPGA Tour. She shoots a bogey-free final round and finishes at 3-under-par 285, one stroke ahead of three other players in the Kraft Nabisco Championship in Rancho Mirage, Calif.

JEWS ON FIRST

1960 – **Hirsch Jacobs** becomes the first trainer with 3,000 victories when Blue Water wins the second race at Aqueduct.

2007 – **Jordan Farmar** becomes the first player to appear in an NBA Developmental League game and an NBA game on the same day. Farmar has 18 points, six assists, and three steals in 41 minutes of play as the Los Angeles D-Fenders lose 109-101 to the Anaheim Arsenal in the afternoon. At night, Farmar scores four points and grabs four rebounds in the Los Angeles Lakers' 126-103 victory over the Sacramento Kings.

TRANSITIONS

1970 – An investment group headed by **Bud Selig** purchases baseball's Seattle Pilots for $10.8 million.

A STAR IS BORN

1894 – **Morrie Schlaiffer** (welterweight boxer)

1898 – **Joe Alexander** (Syracuse football, New York Giants lineman)

1905 – **Sammy Stein** (pro football)

1914 – **Murray Franklin** (Detroit Tigers first baseman)

1922 – **Emil "Bus" Mosbacher** (yachting)

1985 – **Shay Doron** (Maryland women's basketball)

APRIL 2

GAMEBREAKERS

1932 – **Red Wolfe** scores 11 points as the Philadelphia Sphas beat the Philadelphia Moose 29-22 to win the best-of-five Eastern Basketball League championship series 3-1. After winning their third straight EBL title, the Sphas will join the American Basketball League the following season.

1998 – Michigan defenseman **Bubba Berenzweig** scores the game's first two goals as the Wolverines defeat New Hampshire 4-0 in the NCAA Division I hockey semifinals in Boston. Two days later, Berenzweig has an assist and is named to the all-tournament team as Michigan beats Boston College 3-2 in the final.

2003 – **Shawn Green** goes 4 for 4 with a homer, two doubles, and three RBI's as the Los Angeles Dodgers shut out the Arizona Diamondbacks 5-0.

STRONG IN DEFEAT

2000 – Making his first start in goal in Augusta's East Coast Hockey League season finale, **Leeor Shtrom** makes 51 saves and stops nine of 10 shots in an overtime shootout as the Lynx lose to the South Carolina Stingrays 2-1.

MAZEL TOUGH

1910 – **Harry P. Cline** runs 129 consecutive billiards and beats Albert Cutler 500-42 to retain his world 18.2 balkline title in St. Louis.

1928 – **Phil Wolf** scores 1,937 to win the all-events title at the American Bowling Congress championships in Kansas City.

1938 – **Benjamin Alperstein** of Maryland wins the featherweight title and **David Bernstein** of Catholic University wins the bantamweight crown at the intercollegiate boxing championships in Charlottesville, Va.

JEWS ON FIRST

1949 – **Leah Thal Neuberger** wins the women's title and teams with **Thelma Thal** to win their second straight women's doubles crown at the U.S. Table Tennis Championships in New York.

1960 – **Eugene Glazer** of NYU wins the foil and teammate **Gilbert Eisner** captures the epee at the NCAA fencing championships in Urbana, Ill.

1966 – **Steve Cohen** of Penn State wins his first of two consecutive all-around titles at the NCAA gymnastics championships at University Park, Pa.

RECORD SETTERS

2006 – **Deena Kastor** breaks her American record by 19 seconds, finishing second in the Berlin Half Marathon in 1:07.34.

JEWS ON FIRST

1935 – **Mary Hirsch**, 22-year-old daughter of trainer **Max Hirsch,** becomes the first woman licensed by the Jockey Club to train racehorses.

1956 – **Harry Hirschkowitz** of New York wins his two matches, but the United States table tennis team loses to China 5-4 in Tokyo in the first athletic competition between the two countries.

TRANSITIONS

1973 – **Larry Brown**, who took over a Carolina Cougars team that finished 14 games under .500 and brought it to a division title, is named American Basketball Association Coach of the Year.

2007 – Longtime NBA referee **Mendy Rudolph** is elected to the Basketball Hall of Fame.

A STAR IS BORN

1972 – **Eyal Berkovic** (Israeli soccer)

APRIL 3

GAMEBREAKERS

1938 – Defenseman **Alex Levinsky** scores to break a 1-1 tie, and the Chicago Black Hawks upset the New York Americans 3-2 to win the Stanley Cup semifinal series two games to one.

1943 – **Sol Schwartz** scores 14 points as the Philadelphia Sphas beat the Trenton Tigers 44-42 to win the best-of-seven American Basketball League championship series 4-3. **Irv Torgoff** hits a 70-foot shot at the end of the first half to give the Sphas a 25-24 lead.

2002 – **Steve Dubinsky**, traded by Chicago to Nashville two months earlier, scores two goals as the Predators beat the Blackhawks 3-1. Dubinsky just misses a hat trick when he fails to make a shot from center ice into an empty net in the final seconds.

STRONG IN DEFEAT

2004 – **Jeff Halpern** scores his 18th and 19th goals of the season, but the Washington Capitals lose 3-2 in overtime to the New York Rangers. With four goals and four assists in four games, Halpern is named NHL Offensive Player of the Week.

2006 – UCLA guard **Jordan Farmar** scores a game-high 18 points, but the Bruins lose 73-57 to Florida in the NCAA championship game in Indianapolis.

MAZEL TOUGH

1937 – **Isaac Richter** of Penn State wins his second straight heavyweight title and **Benjamin Alperstein** of Maryland captures the lightweight title at the national collegiate boxing championships in Sacramento.

1948 – **Albert Axelrod** of CCNY wins the foil at the NCAA fencing championships in Annapolis, Md.

1948 – **Carol Pence** wins the 100 breaststroke at the AAU Swimming Championships.

1950 – **Reba Kirson Monness** wins the women's singles at the U.S. table tennis championships.

1965 – **Mike Jacobson** of Penn State wins the all-around as the Nittany Lions capture their eighth NCAA gymnastics championship at Southern Illinois. **Dan Millman** of California finishes first in the vault.

1977 – **Brian Gottfried** defeats Cliff Richey 6-1, 7-6 to win the Southwest Pacific Open in Los Angeles.

1983 – **Amy Alcott** beats Beth Daniel and Kathy Whitworth by two strokes in the Nabisco Dinah Shore Invitational in Rancho Mirage, Calif., the first of three times she will win the tournament.

TRANSITIONS

1993 – A day after being named national basketball coach of the year by the Associated Press, **Eddie Fogler** resigns at Vanderbilt to take over the coaching job at South Carolina.

1996 – Long Beach State coach **Seth Greenberg** is named men's basketball coach at the University of South Florida. Greenberg was 105-70 in six seasons at Long Beach.

2002 – **Jamie Sokolsky** of the Long Beach Ice Dogs is named defenseman of the year in the West Coast Hockey League after recording 14 goals and 38 assists in 65 games.

A STAR IS BORN

1917 – **Roy Ilowit** (CCNY, Brooklyn Dodgers football)

1921 – **Dick Conger** (Detroit Tigers, Pittsburgh Pirates, Philadelphia Phillies pitcher)

1924 – **Phil Farbman** (CCNY basketball)

1927 – **Eva Szekely** (Hungarian swimmer)

APRIL 4

GAMEBREAKERS

1936 – **Inky Lautman** scores 17 points to lead the Philadelphia Sphas to a 30-27 victory over the Brooklyn Visitations in the ABL.

1968 – **Art Heyman** scores 34 points as the Pittsburgh Pipers beat Minnesota 125-117 in Game 1 of the American Basketball Association Eastern Division finals.

1997 – **Danny Schayes** of the Orlando Magic collects 21 points, 11 rebounds, and a career-high six steals in a 93-84 victory over the New York Knicks.

2003 – Cal Lutheran pitcher **Jason Hirsch** tosses a one-hitter – a swinging bunt with one out in the eighth inning – and strikes out 18 batters in a 16-0 victory over Occidental.

2006 – Guard **Shay Doron** is one of three Maryland players with 16 points as the Terrapins defeat Duke 78-75 in overtime to win the NCAA women's championship in Boston.

MAZEL TOUGH

1916 – **Benny Valgar** wins a four-round decision over Tony Vatlan to win the AAU Boxing Championships 115-pound title in Boston.

1936 – **Viktor Barna** of Hungary wins the U.S. National men's table tennis tournament. **Ruth Aarons** of the United States wins her third women's national title.

1943 – **Norman Siegel** of Rutgers wins the 300 medley in 3:35.7 at the National AAU swimming championships in New York.

1984 – Coached by **Larry Brown**, Kansas beats Oklahoma 83-79 for the NCAA basketball championship.

2000 – **Cliff Bayer** wins the foil event at a World Cup fencing tournament in Bonn, Germany, and secures a spot on the U.S. Olympic roster.

2003 – **Lenny Krayzelburg** wins the 100 backstroke in 54.26 seconds at the U.S. National Spring Swimming Championships in Indianapolis.

2004 – **Sean Rosenthal** and Larry Witt defeat Matt Fuerbringer and Casey Jennings 21-17, 21-14 to capture the Fort Lauderdale Open on the pro beach volleyball tour.

RECORD SETTERS

1906 – Jockey **Walter Miller** rides winners in the first three races at Bennings Track near Washington, D.C., giving him a record eight consecutive victories over two days.

TRANSITIONS

1933 – The German Boxing Federation excludes Jewish boxers from participating in bouts and orders cancellation of all contracts involving Jewish promoters.

1957 – The NBA fines Boston Celtics coach **Red Auerbach** $300 for punching St. Louis Hawks owner **Ben Kerner** before Game 3 of the NBA finals.

2003 – **Seth Greenberg**, who went 108-100 at South Florida over the previous six seasons, is named men's basketball coach at Virginia Tech.

A STAR IS BORN

1775 – **Samuel Elias** (boxing)

1925 – **Victor Frank** (track and field)

1943 – **Mike Epstein** (Baltimore Orioles, Washington Senators/Texas Rangers, Oakland A's, California Angels first baseman)

1965 – **Fabrice Benichou** (junior featherweight boxer)

1982 – **Dmitry Salita** (junior welterweight boxer)

1985 – **Dudi Sela** (Israeli tennis)

APRIL 5

GAMEBREAKERS

1930 – **Cy Kaselman** scores 15 points as the Philadelphia Sphas beat the Philadelphia Elks 32-24 to win the best-of-five Eastern Basketball League championship series 3-2. The title is the first of 10 in two leagues by the Sphas.

1930 – **Moritz Haeusler** scores the first two goals, and the Hakoah All-Stars defeat the Newark Americans 6-2 in Atlantic Coast League soccer.

1931 – **Andy Cohen's** eighth-inning home run gives the Newark Bears of the International League a 2-1 exhibition victory over the Philadelphia Phillies.

2002 – In his first start of the season, **Scott Schoeneweis** allows five hits over 8 1/3 innings and **Alan Levine** gets the last two outs for the save as the Anaheim Angels beat Texas 3-1. **Gabe Kapler** has two hits for the Rangers.

2003 – **Cory Pecker** scores three goals as the Cincinnati Mighty Ducks skate to a 4-4 tie with the Cleveland Barons in the American Hockey League.

MAZEL TOUGH

1922 – **Sid Terris** of New York wins the national AAU bantamweight boxing championship.

1941 – **Frank Spellman** wins the Junior Middle Atlantic Weightlifting Championships 165-pound division in Wilmington, Del.

1952 – **Henry Wittenberg**, now a New York City police sergeant, ends his four-year retirement to beat Enzo Marinelli for his eighth AAU 191-pound wrestling title in Ithaca, N.Y.

1963 – **Pierre Darmon** defeats Jan-Erik Lundquist to win the Monaco tennis tournament.

1975 – **Yuri Rabinovich** of Wayne State wins the saber title at the NCAA Fencing Championships at Cal State-Fullerton.

1986 – **Brian Ginsberg** of UCLA wins the floor exercise at the NCAA gymnastics championships.

1989 – **Gary Jacobs** wins a 12-round decision over George Collins in London to win the WBC International and British Empire welterweight titles.

2001 – **Dmitry Salita** of Brooklyn wins the New York City Golden Gloves 139-pound title by beating Joseph Rios.

TRANSITIONS

1953 – San Diego Padres left fielder **Herb Gorman** hits a pair of doubles in two at-bats, then takes himself out of a Pacific Coast League game against the Hollywood Stars in the sixth inning. The 28-year-old dies of a massive heart attack on the way to the hospital. The second game of the scheduled doubleheader is postponed.

A STAR IS BORN

1904 – **Pinky Silverberg** (flyweight boxer)
1908 – **Harry Cornsweet** (Brown football)
1945 – **Rich Stotter** (Univ. of Houston, Houston Oilers linebacker)
1959 – **Stacy Margolin** (tennis)
1977 – **Jonathan Erlich** (Israeli tennis)

Henry Wittenberg

APRIL 6

GAMEBREAKERS

1919 – **Joszef "Cziby" Braun**, playing in his second international soccer match, scores the winning goal as Hungary defeats Austria 2-1.

1924 – **Gyorgy Molnar** scores three goals as Hungary defeats Italy 7-1 in a soccer match in Budapest.

1927 – **Nat Holman** scores 11 points to lead the Brooklyn Celtics to a 29-21 victory over the Cleveland Rosenblums in the first game of the best-of-five ABL championship series. Brooklyn scores 21 points on foul shots.

1940 – **Moe Goldman** scores 14 points and **Inky Lautman** adds 13 as the Philadelphia Sphas defeat the Washington Brewers 51-44 in the ABL final.

2007 – In his debut with the Colorado Rockies, **Jason Hirsch** allows five hits and one run while striking out a career-high eight batters and walking none in 6 2/3 innings of a 4-3 victory over the San Diego Padres.

STRONG IN DEFEAT

2006 – In his third major-league game, **Ian Kinsler** hits a home run and goes 3-for-3 in the Texas Rangers' 10-6 loss to the Detroit Tigers.

MAZEL TOUGH

1824 – English boxer **Barney Aaron** knocks out Peter Warren in 29 rounds in Colnbrook.

1920 – **Samuel Seeman** of Brooklyn wins the national AAU featherweight boxing championship in Boston.

1934 – **Harry Devine** stops Werther Arcelli in the eighth round in Worcester, Mass., to capture the New England welterweight title.

1939 – With **Moe Roberts** in goal, the Cleveland Barons defeat the Philadelphia Ramblers 2-0 in an International-American Hockey League playoff game. Cleveland wins the Calder Cup championship series 3-1.

1952 – **Henry Wittenberg** ends a four-year retirement and beats Enzo Marinelli in the 191-pound final for his eighth AAU national wrestling title.

1973 – **Marshall Avener** of Penn State ties for first place in the all-around in the NCAA gymnastics championships in Eugene, Ore.

1980 – **Sharon Shapiro** of UCLA wins the all-around and sweeps all four individual events at the AIAW national collegiate women's gymnastics championships.

RECORD SETTERS

1939 – **Harold "Bunny" Levitt** makes 499 consecutive shots in a 7½-hour basketball foul-shooting exhibition at Madison Street Armory in Chicago. The 5-foot-4 Levitt misses his next shot, then makes 371 in a row before quitting after midnight after most of the spectators have left. The Harlem Globetrotters offer $1,000 to anyone who can break his record.

JEWS ON FIRST

1973 – **Ron Blomberg** of the Yankees faces Luis Tiant of the Red Sox and becomes baseball's first official designated hitter. He walks with the bases loaded in his first at-bat and goes 1-for-3 in a 15-5 loss to Boston.

A STAR IS BORN

1925 – **Hal Schacker** (Boston Braves pitcher)

APRIL 7

GAMEBREAKERS

1927 – **Davey Banks** and **Nat Holman** score five points each as the Brooklyn Celtics take a 2-0 lead in the ABL championship series with a 28-20 win over the Cleveland Rosenblums.

1951 – **Red Holzman** scores 12 points to help the Rochester Royals defeat the New York Knicks 72-65 in Game 1 of the NBA Finals. Holzman will eventually coach the Knicks to their only two NBA titles.

1970 – **Norm Miller** hits a pinch-hit three-run homer off Gaylord Perry to give the Houston Astros an 8-5 victory over the San Francisco Giants on opening day.

1977 – Maccabi Tel Aviv defeats Varese, Italy, 78-77 to capture the European Championship Cup basketball tournament in Belgrade, Yugoslavia. Jim Boatwright scores 26 points and **Mickey Berkowitz** adds 17 for the winners.

1996 – **Scott Schoeneweis** of Duke allows three hits, including two infield singles, and strikes out eight in a 3-0 victory over Virginia.

2003 – **Tal Karp** scores her first two goals against international competition as Australia defeats Cook Islands 11-0 in the Oceanic Women's Soccer Tournament.

2007 – **Adam Greenberg's** three-run homer breaks a 1-1 tie in the fifth inning and sparks the Wichita Wranglers to a 5-1 victory over the Corpus Christi Hooks in the Texas League.

MAZEL TOUGH

1914 – **Al McCoy** knocks out champion George Chip in the first round in Brooklyn to win the world middleweight title.

1915 – **Augie Ratner** decisions J.H. Smith to capture the 145-pound title at the AAU Boxing Championships in Boston.

1935 – **Abe Berenbaum** wins a five-set final over Mark Schlude to capture the U.S. National Table Tennis championship in Chicago.

2002 – **Jason Lezak** swims the final leg as the United States sets a world record of 3:29.00 in the 400 medley relay at the World Short Course swimming championships in Moscow.

2002 – **Margie Goldstein-Engle** wins a jumpoff to capture the Budweiser American Grand Prix Association Show Jumping Championship in Wellington, Fla.

RECORD SETTERS

1979 – **Neil Simons** of Clemson has four hits, including three home runs, walks three times, scores six runs, and drives in an Atlantic Coast Conference-record 10 runs in a 41-9 victory over North Carolina State. The Tigers score 18 runs in the ninth inning.

TRANSITIONS

1969 – The Phoenix Suns lose a coin flip with the Milwaukee Bucks for the right to pick first in the NBA draft. The Suns pick Florida center **Neal Walk** after the Bucks select Kareem Abdul-Jabbar.

A STAR IS BORN

1892 – **Julius Hirsch** (German soccer)
1896 – **Benny Leonard** (lightweight boxer)
1917 – **Danny Kaplowitz** (LIU basketball)
1918 – **Alexander "Petey" Rosenberg** (St. Joseph's basketball, Philadelphia Warriors)

APRIL 8

GAMEBREAKERS

1937 – **Jimmie Reese** hits a game-winning RBI double in the 13th inning as the San Diego Padres beat the Mission Reds 4-1 in the Pacific Coast League.

1940 – **Moe Goldman** scores 14 points and **Petey Rosenberg** adds 10 as the Philadelphia Sphas defeat the Washington Brewers 48-30 in Coatesville, Pa., to clinch the ABL round-robin playoff championship with a 7-0 record.

MAZEL TOUGH

1903 – **Jewey Cooke** of England wins the South African middleweight title with a 19-round decision over Tom Duggan in Johannesburg.

1919 – **Dave Rosenberg** of New York wins the national AAU welterweight boxing championship. **David Kamins** of New York captures the flyweight crown.

1922 – **Fred J. Meyer** clinches the 190-pound and heavyweight titles for the second consecutive year at the AAU wrestling championships in Boston.

1926 – **Armand Emanuel** of San Francisco wins the national AAU heavyweight boxing title.

1956 – **Herb Flam** beats Vic Seixas 6-1, 7-5 to win the St. Andrews Invitational tennis tournament in Kingston, Jamaica.

1961 – **Stephen Friedman** wins the 160-pound AAU national wrestling championship.

1967 – **Kathy Harter** defeats Ingrid Lofdahl 6-3, 6-2 to win a clay-court tennis tournament in Cannes, France.

2007 – **Dudi Sela** and **Noam Okun** win singles matches, and **Jonathan Erlich** and **Andy Ram** win their doubles match as Israel defeats Italy 3-2 in a Davis Cup European Zone tie. The victory sends Israel into the World Group for the first time in nine years.

RECORD SETTERS

1950 – **Herman Barron** hits three tee shots into the water and finishes with a record 11 on the par-3 16th hole during the third round of The Masters. "That's a record you can keep," he says.

1967 – **Mark Spitz** sets his first world swimming record in the 100 butterfly (49.9 seconds) at the AAU indoor championships in Dallas. He also wins the 200 butterfly in an American record of 1:50.6, and swims on two relay teams for his first national titles.

2002 – **Deena Drossin** sets a world road-racing record of 14 minutes, 54 seconds in winning the Carlsbad 500 in Carlsbad, Calif. She is the first American woman to hold the world record since 1986.

JEWS ON FIRST

1992 – **Ruben Amaro Jr.** hits his first of 16 major-league homers and adds two doubles in the Philadelphia Phillies' 11-3 win over the Chicago Cubs.

TRANSITIONS

1966 – Oakland Raiders coach and general manager **Al Davis** reluctantly becomes the second commissioner of the American Football League, replacing Joe Foss. Davis will resign on July 25 to return to the Raiders.

A STAR IS BORN

1904 – **Hirsch Jacobs** (horse trainer)

1951 – **Larry Shyatt** (Wyoming, Clemson basketball coach)

1981 – **Matt Ford** (Milwaukee Brewers pitcher)

APRIL 9

GAMEBREAKERS

1927 – **Nat Holman** scores 12 points and **Davey Banks** adds eight as the Original Celtics beat the Cleveland Rosenblums 35-32 in Brooklyn to sweep the best-of-five American Basketball League championship series.

1955 – **Dolph Schayes** scores 28 points as the Syacuse Nationals beat the Fort Wayne Pistons 109-104 in Game 6 of the NBA Finals.

1963 – **Sandy Koufax** pitches a two-hitter and strikes out 14 as the Los Angeles Dodgers beat the Houston Astros 2-0. The shutout is Koufax's first of a league-leading 11 that season.

1974 – **Johan Neeskens** scores two goals as The Netherlands defeats Sweden 5-1 in soccer.

2007 – **Ian Kinsler** goes 4 for 4 with two RBI's, and his tiebreaking RBI single ignites a six-run sixth inning as the Texas Rangers defeat the Tampa Bay Devil Rays 8-4. Kinsler will later be named American League Player of the Week.

MAZEL TOUGH

1914 – **Augie Ratner** decisions **Joe Tiplitz** in the 145-pound final of the New York State Boxing Championships in Brooklyn.

1920 – **Phil Wolf** and the Brucks No. 1 team of Chicago win the American Bowling Congress team championship in Peoria, Ill.

1928 – **Corporal Izzy Schwartz** wins a 15-round decision over Routier Parra in New York to retain the New York State version of the world flyweight championship.

1930 – **Abraham Miller** defeats Frankie Wallace in the bantamweight final at the AAU boxing championships in Boston.

1931 – **Cy Yellin** beats defending champion Robert Cole 400-263 to win the U.S. Amateur billiards championship in Newark, N.J.

1932 – Jewish boxers capture three titles at the national collegiate championships in State College, Pa. – **Robert Goldstein** of Virginia, lightweight; **Al Wertheimer** of Syracuse, featherweight, and **David Stoop** of Penn State, bantamweight.

1932 – **William Steiner** wins the first Governor's Race, a 15-mile run from Schenectady to Albany, N.Y., in 1 hour, 24 minutes, 7 seconds.

1942 – **Frank Spellman** wins the Junior National Weightlifting Championships 165-pound class in Bristol, Conn.

1961 – **Suzy Kormoczy** of Hungary defeats Ann Haydon of Great Britain 6-2, 6-0 in the final of the Masters Invitational clay-court tournamenat in St. Petersburg, Fla.

1984 – **Bruce Manson** defeats **Shahar Perkiss** of Israel 6-7, 6-3, 7-6 to win a Challenger tennis tournament in Ashkelon, Israel.

1988 – **John Witchel** of Stanford wins the 500-yard freestyle at the NCAA Swimming Championships in 4:15.67.

2003 – **Sada Jacobson** defeats Alessandra Lucchino of Italy 15-12 to win the epee at the World Junior Fencing Championships in Trapani, Italy.

JEWS ON FIRST

1976 – **Al Clark** makes his debut as an American League umpire at third base in an 11-inning game between the Minnesota Twins and the Texas Rangers in Arlington, Texas.

A STAR IS BORN

1797 – **Aby Belasco** (British boxer)
1946 – **Mara Cohen-Mintz** (Israeli tennis)
1982 – **Yulia Raskina** (Belarus rhythmic gymnastics)

APRIL 10

GAMEBREAKERS

1926 – **Chick Passon** scores 23 points as the Paterson Legionaires defeat Metropolitan Basketball League champion Yonkers 41-24.

1955 – Led by **Dolph Schayes'** 13 points, the Syracuse Nationals rally to beat the Fort Wayne Pistons 92-91 in Game 7 to win their only NBA championship.

2001 – **Scott Schoeneweis** shuts out the Toronto Blue Jays on three hits in the Anaheim Angels' 6-0 victory.

2004 – **Mathieu Schneider** scores a power-play goal with 2:45 remaining to give the Detroit Red Wings a 2-1 victory over the Nashville Predators in a first-round NHL playoff game.

2006 – **Scott Feldman** allows two hits in 2 1/3 scoreless innings to earn his first major-league victory as the Texas Rangers defeat the Tampa Bay Devil Rays 12-9. **Ian Kinsler** hits a two-run homer for Texas.

STRONG IN DEFEAT

1985 – **Danny Schayes** of the Denver Nuggets has 23 points and 12 rebounds in a 129-127 loss to the Los Angeles Clippers.

MAZEL TOUGH

1919 – **Young Montreal (Morris Billingkoff)** wins a 12-round decision over **Johnny Rosner** in Providence, R.I., to claim the American flyweight title. However, he rejects the title in order to compete in the bantamweight division.

1923 – **Harry Marcus** (118 pounds) and **Al Bender** (112) win AAU boxing titles in Boston.

1931 – **Jackie "Kid" Berg** wins a 10-round decision over Billy Wallace in Detroit to retain his world super lightweight title.

1934 – **Ruth Aarons** defeats Jay Purves to win the National Table Tennis Championship in Cleveland.

1943 – **Henry Wittenberg** wins his third national AAU wrestling title and his first at 191 pounds in New York.

1954 – **Garry Garber** of Maryland beats Roy Kuboyama of Wisconsin in the final to capture the NCAA 119-pound boxing title in State College, Pa.

1967 – **Beverly Klass** wins the LPGA World International satellite golf tournament in North Myrtle Beach, S.C.

1977 – **Brian Teacher** defeats Bill Scanlon 6-3, 6-3 to win an indoor tennis tournament in Jackson, Miss.

1999 – **Margie Goldstein-Engle** rides Hidden Creek's Alvaretto to victory in the Budweiser American Invitational equestrian event.

2005 – **Oren Eisenman** scores nine goals in the tournament as Israel captures the gold medal in the International Ice Hockey Federation Division 2 Group B World Championships in Belgrade. Israel defeats Iceland 4-2 to finish with a 4-0-1 record.

2005 – **Logan Hansen** defeats Sanaz Marand 7-5, 6-2 to win the Girls 16 title at the Easter Bowl tennis tournament in Palm Springs, Calif.

TRANSITIONS

1991 – **Mark Roth** is elected to the Pro Bowling Hall of Fame.

A STAR IS BORN

1883 – **Benny Yanger** (featherweight boxer)
1951 – **Mark Roth** (bowling)
1978 – **Jessica Davis** (rhythmic gymnastics)
1980 – **Andy Ram** (Israeli tennis)

APRIL 11

GAMEBREAKERS

1921 – **Barney Sedran** scores a team-leading 10 points as the New York Whirlwinds beat the Original Celtics 40-24 in a matchup of two of the best basketball teams of their day before 11,000 fans at the New York Armory. **Marty Friedman** holds the Celtics' top scorer to two points.

1928 – **Andy Cohen**, in his first start at second base for New York, gets three hits, drives in two runs, and scores twice on opening day as the Giants beat the Boston Braves 5-2.

1931 – The Philadelphia Sphas beat Camden 36-33 to win the best-of-five Eastern Basketball League championship series 3-1. **Cy Kaselman** scores 12 points, **Harry Litwack** adds eight, and **Babe Liman** scores the winning basket.

1931 – **Jack Grossman** hits a pair of two-run homers as Rutgers defeats Lehigh 8-6.

1954 – **Dolph Schayes** scores 16 points to lead the Syracuse Nationals to a 65-63 victory over the Minneapolis Lakers, forcing a Game 7 of the NBA Finals.

MAZEL TOUGH

1942 – **Butch Levy** wins the AAU heavyweight wrestling title in New Orleans.

1946 – **Tiger Burns (Dan Levene)** wins a 12-round decision over Johnny Pieters in Johannesburg to capture the vacant South African middleweight title.

1956 – **Erwin Klein** and **Leah Neuberger** win the mixed doubles at the World Table Tennis championships in Tokyo.

1962 – Jockey **Walter Blum** rides four winners at Gulfstream Park.

1976 – **Harold Solomon** beats Ken Rosewall 6-4, 1-6, 6-1 in the final of an indoor tennis tournament in Houston.

1976 – **Izhak Shum** scores two goals as Israel defeats Japan 4-1 in a World Cup soccer qualifier.

1998 – **Sherman Greenfield** of Canada beats Dan Obremski of the United States 15-13, 15-3 to win the Pan American Games racquetball title in Winnipeg.

JEWS ON FIRST

1928 – **Dolly Stark** makes his debut as a National League umpire at third base in a game between the Chicago Cubs and the Reds in Cincinnati.

1961 – **Al Forman** makes his debut as a National League umpire at third base in a 10-inning game between the St. Louis Cardinals and the Braves in Milwaukee.

RECORD SETTERS

1953 – Hungarian swimmer **Eva Szekely** sets a world record of 5:50.4 in the 400 individual medley in Budapest.

TRANSITIONS

1947 – **Jules Rivlin** of the Toledo Jeeps is named MVP of the National Basketball League.

2001 – The Bridgeport Barrage of the National Lacrosse League make **Scott Hochstadt** of Maryland the No. 3 overall pick in the league's inaugural draft.

A STAR IS BORN
1982 – **Jordan Cila** (soccer)

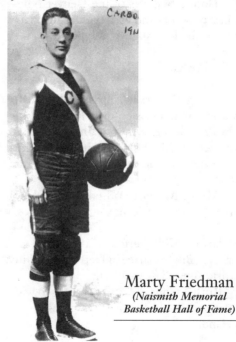

Marty Friedman
(Naismith Memorial Basketball Hall of Fame)

APRIL 12

GAMEBREAKERS

1965 – **Larry Sherry** pitches three perfect innings in relief, striking out two for his first save of the season as the Detroit Tigers defeat the Kansas City Athletics 6-2.

2005 – **Jason Marquis** hits a bases-loaded triple and allows five hits with six strikeouts in 6 1/3 innings as the St. Louis Cardinals defeat the Cincinnati Reds 5-4.

MAZEL TOUGH

1941 – **Courtney Shanken** of the University of Chicago wins the rope climb and all-around at the NCAA gymnastics championships. His brother **Earl Shanken** of Chicago wins the pommel horse.

1947 – **Abraham Balk** of NYU captures both the foil and epee titles at the NCAA fencing championships in Chicago.

1949 – **Dick Miles** wins the men's title and **Leah Thal Neuberger** captures the women's crown at the U.S. Table Tennis Championships in New York.

1958 – **Abie Grossfeld** of Illinois wins the NCAA gymnastics all-around title and also finishes first in free exercise and on the horizontal bar in East Lansing, Mich.

1992 – **Margie Goldstein-Engle** rides show horse Liquid Asset to victory in the Cadillac Grand Prix of Houston.

2003 – **Pavel Gofman** of Israel wins the all-around at the Romanian International gymnastics meet.

RECORD SETTERS

2006 – **Jeff Maier's** RBI double in the second inning gives him a school-record 169 career hits as Wesleyan defeats Bates 14-2. Ten years earlier, Maier was in the first row of the right-field stands at Yankee Stadium when he interfered with Baltimore Orioles outfielder Tony Tarasco on a fly ball that umpires ruled was a home run by Derek Jeter in an American League playoff game.

Abie Grossfeld
(U.S. Olympic Committee)

A STAR IS BORN

1911 – **Charles "Buckets" Goldenberg** (Wisconsin football, Green Bay Packers lineman)

1914 – **Gretel Bergmann** (German track and field)

1914 – **Maxie Shapiro** (lightweight boxer)

1984 – **Adam Rosen** (British luge)

APRIL 13

GAMEBREAKERS

1921 – **Barney Sedran** scores 19 points as the New York State League champion Albany Senators beat the Pennsylvania State League champion Scranton Miners 36-19 to win their best-of-three series 2-1

1971 – **Norm Miller's** three-run homer caps Houston's five-run rally in the ninth inning as the Astros beat the St. Louis Cardinals 8-4.

1975 – **Steve Stone** pitches a four-hitter as the Chicago Cubs beat the Montreal Expos 7-0.

2001 – **Craig Breslow** pitches a one-hitter and strikes out 11 Harvard batters in Yale's 7-0 victory.

2002 – **Ezra Poyas** scores two goals as the Richmond Tigers defeat Melbourne 96-76 in Australian Rules Football.

2004 – **Doron Scheffer** scores 15 points as Hapoel Jerusalem defeats Real Madrid 83-72 to win the ULEB Cup basketball tournament in Charleroi, Belgium.

MAZEL TOUGH

1908 – **Rudolph Schwartz** wins the AAU 105-pound wrestling championship in New York.

1947 – **Henry Wittenberg** wins the AAU 191-pound wrestling title in San Francisco.

1957 – **Jimmy Jacobs** beats **Vic Hershkowitz** in the national U.S. Handball Association championship match for the third straight year. Jacobs rallies from a 13-3 deficit in the final game to win 10-21, 21-15, 21-14 in Dallas.

1957 – **Red Auerbach's** Boston Celtics win their first of nine NBA titles, beating the Minneapolis Lakers 118-113 to complete a four-game sweep.

1980 – **Amy Alcott** posts her 10th victory on the LPGA Tour, winning the American Defender/WRAL Classic in Raleigh, N.C., by four strokes over runner-up Donna Caponi.

1985 – Brothers **Noah Riskin** and **Seth Riskin** of Ohio State tie for first place on the parallel bars at the NCAA gymnastics championships.

1994 – **Gary Jacobs** knocks out Alessandro Duran in the eighth round in Glasgow, Scotland, to retain his European welterweight title.

1996 – **Dana Rosenblatt** knocks out Howard Davis in the second round to capture the WBU middleweight title in Boston. He becomes the first Jewish middleweight champion since **Solly Krieger** in 1939.

1996 – **Damon Keeve** wins the heavyweight division at the U.S. Senior National Judo Championships.

RECORD SETTERS

2003 – While finishing third in the London Marathon, **Deena Drossin** sets an American marathon record of 2:21.15, surpassing by five seconds the mark set by Joan Benoit Samuelson in 1985 in Chicago.

JEWS ON FIRST

1955 – **Stanley Albert Landes** makes his debut as a National League umpire at third base of the Pirates-Dodgers game in Brooklyn. Landes will retire after the 1972 season.

TRANSITIONS

1969 – **Red Auerbach** is elected to the Basketball Hall of Fame.

1979 – **Red Holzman** of the New York Knicks is named NBA Coach of the Year.

APRIL 14

GAMEBREAKERS

1945 – **Art Hillhouse** scores 15 points as the Philadelphia Sphas rally from an 11-2 deficit and beat the Baltimore Bullets 46-40 to win the American Basketball League championship series. The Sphas clinch their final ABL title, and seventh in 12 years.

1962 – **Larry Sherry** pitches three innings of hitless relief and earns the win as the Los Angeles Dodgers beat the Milwaukee Braves 5-4.

1964 – **Sandy Koufax** pitches a complete game without issuing a walk for the ninth time, beating St. Louis 4-0 with six hits and 10 strikeouts in the only opening-day start of his career.

1969 – **Ken Holtzman** of the Chicago Cubs shuts out the Pittsburgh Pirates 4-0 on seven hits.

1977 – Larry Horn and **Steve Ratzer** combine on a five-hit shutout and **Larry Goldetsky** hits a two-run homer as the West Palm Beach Expos open their Florida State League season with a 10-0 victory over the Pompano Beach Cubs.

2007 – **Ryan Braun** hits three home runs and drives in five runs as the Nashville Sounds defeat the New Orleans Zephyrs 14-1 in the Pacific Coast League.

STRONG IN DEFEAT

2001 – Anaheim relief pitcher **Alan Levine** strikes out five of the six batters he faces in the Angels' 2-1 loss to the Seattle Mariners.

MAZEL TOUGH

1906 – **Myer Prinstein** of the United States is injured on his first try at the Olympic long jump competition and attempts only one more jump. But the first jump is good enough to win the gold medal in Athens. **Hugo Friend** of the United States captures the bronze.

1931 – **Cecil Hart** coaches the Canadiens to their second straight Stanley Cup as Montreal wraps up a 3-2 series victory with a 2-0 win over the Chicago Black Hawks.

1968 – **Mike Belkin** of Canada defeats Jaime Fillol 2-6, 6-0, 7-5, 6-4 to win the Masters Tennis Tournament in St. Petersburg, Fla.

2007 – **David Sender** of Stanford wins the vault at the NCAA gymnastics championships in State College, Pa.

RECORD SETTERS

1951 – **Carol Pence** improves her American record in the 200 breaststroke with a time of 2:45 at the AAU National Indoor Championships in Houston. One day later, she sets an American record in the 100 breaststroke.

JEWS ON FIRST

1908 – **Barney Pelty** of the Browns becomes the first Jewish pitcher to draw an opening-day starting assignment. St. Louis defeats the Cleveland Naps 2-1.

TRANSITIONS

1960 – The Phillies beat the Milwaukee Braves 5-4 in 10 innings in **Andy Cohen's** only game as Philadelphia's interim manager.

1993 – **James Bregman** becomes a charter member of the United States Judo Hall of Fame.

2001 – **Fred Lebow**, former director of the New York Marathon, is inducted into the Distance Runners Hall of Fame.

A STAR IS BORN

1935 – **Larry Friend** (University of California basketball, New York Knicks)

1964 – **Jim Grabb** (tennis)

1968 – **Jesse Levis** (Cleveland Indians, Milwaukee Brewers catcher)

1969 – **Brad Ausmus** (San Diego Padres, Houston Astros, Detroit Tigers catcher)

APRIL 15

GAMEBREAKERS

1928 – **Andy Cohen** hits a homer and two singles as the New York Giants beat the Philadelphia Phillies 8-1.

1947 – In his National League debut, **Hank Greenberg** hits an RBI double in the sixth inning as the Pittsburgh Pirates beat the Chicago Cubs 1-0.

1951 – **Max Zaslofsky** scores 24 points as the New York Knicks beat the Rochester Royals 92-89 in Game 5 of the NBA finals.

1968 – **Norm Miller** opens the bottom of the 24th inning with a single and scores on a bases-loaded error to give the Houston Astros a 1-0 victory over the New York Mets, ending the longest shutout in baseball history.

1988 – **Danny Schayes** scores 32 points, including 18 for 18 from the foul line, as the Denver Nuggets defeat the Houston Rockets 132-125.

1998 – **Haim Revivo** scores the winning goal in the 82nd minute as Israel shocks Argentina 2-1 in a friendly soccer match in Jerusalem.

STRONG IN DEFEAT

1927 – Playing his first game for Endler's All-Stars of Passaic, N.J., **Jammy Moscowitz** scores a team-high 10 points in a 32-27 loss to the world champion New York Celtics.

MAZEL TOUGH

1924 – One week after stopping **Mickey Diamond** in the first round of a featherweight fight in Philadelphia, **Benny Bass** knocks out George Wolgast in the first round in Boston.

1928 – **Siegfried Wortmann** scores as the New York Nationals of the American Soccer League defeat the Chicago Bricklayers 3-2 to capture the National Challenge Cup. A week earlier in the first game of the two-game series, Wortmann scored in a 2-2 tie.

1962 – **Bob Grossman** drives a Ferrari to first place in his division at the Sports Car Club of America Nationals at Marlboro Raceway in Maryland.

1962 – **Suzy Kormoczy** of Hungary defeats Rita Bentley of Great Britain 6-4, 6-4 in the final of a clay-court tennis tournament in Nice, France.

1978 – **Irwin Cohen** captures the under 209-pound title at the National AAU Judo Championships in Chicago.

1995 – Hall of Famer **Mark Roth** wins his first bowling title in seven years when he beats Walter Ray Williams Jr. 233-189 in the 10F Foresters Open in Markham, Ontario. It is his 34th career title.

2006 – **Lindsay Durlacher** decisions Spenser Mango 0-6, 4-2, 2-1 to win the 121-pound Greco-Roman wrestling title at the U.S. Nationals in Las Vegas.

JEWS ON FIRST

1928 – **Andy Cohen** of the New York Giants hits his first of 14 career home runs off Russ Miller in an 8-1 victory over the Philadelphia Phillies.

1931 – **Alta Cohen** gets two hits in one inning – one of them illegal – in his major-league debut with the Brooklyn Dodgers. Cohen bats cleanup out of turn and singles and eventually scores. The Boston Braves fail to notice the mistake, and Cohen comes up later in the inning in his proper place in the order and doubles. Boston wins 9-3.

A STAR IS BORN

1950 – **Dick Sharon** (Detroit Tigers, San Diego Padres outfielder)

1967 – **Dara Torres** (swimming)

APRIL 16

GAMEBREAKERS

1919 – **Jozsef Braun** scores the winning goal as Hungary defeats Austria 2-1 in soccer.

1921 – **Nat Holman** scores 22 points and **Barney Sedran** adds five field goals as the New York Whirlwinds beat the New York Celtics 40-20 at the New York Regent Armory. A few days later, the Celtics sign Holman away from the Whirlwinds.

1947 – **Al Rosen** of Oklahoma City smacks four doubles in four plate appearances against the Dallas Rebels of the American Association.

1976 – For the second time in his career in Japan, switch-hitter **Richie Scheinblum** of the Hiroshima Carp homers from both sides of the plate in a game against the Yomiuri Giants.

2005 – **Andy Rosenband** scores with eight seconds remaining to give the Chicago Storm a 6-5 victory over the Baltimore Blast in the Major Indoor Soccer League.

MAZEL TOUGH

1934 – Apprentice **Joe Jacobs** rides five winners in six races at Bowie Race Track.

1946 – **Henry Wittenberg** wins the AAU wrestling 191-pound title.

1950 – **Carol Pence** wins the 220 breaststroke at the National AAU Women's Indoor Swimming Championships in Palm Beach, Fla.

1956 – **Abe Segal** teams with Hugh Stewart to win the National Doubles tennis title.

1961 – **Steve Sandler** beats Carl Obert to win the National AAU one-wall handball title.

1983 – **Shlomo Glickstein** defeats **Amos Mansdorf** 6-3, 6-3 in the final of a hard-court tennis tournament in Glickstein's hometown of Ashkelon, Israel.

1999 – **Tamir Bloom** wins the Division 1 men's epee title at the National Fencing Championships in South Bend, Ind.

2004 – **Rami Zur** wins the men's 500-meter kayak sprint final at the U.S. Flatwater Canoe and Kayak Olympic Trials to qualify for the Athens Olympics. Zur will add firsts in the 1,000 and the two-man 1,000 during the weekend event at Lake Merritt, Calif.

RECORD SETTERS

1952 – **Grigori Novak** of the Soviet Union sets a world weight lifting record of 314.6 pounds in the two-handed snatch in Moscow.

JEWS ON FIRST

1989 – **Lucy Wener** of Georgia becomes the first gymnast to score a 10 in the NCAA championships with a perfect performance on the uneven bars. Her gold medal on the bars is her third in four years.

TRANSITIONS

1898 – Jewish Gymnastics and Athletics Club Attila Groningen, the oldest Jewish sports club in central Europe, is established in The Netherlands.

A STAR IS BORN

1936 – **Jerome Green** (Georgia Tech football, Boston Patriots)

1946 – **Edward Weitz** (weight lifting)

1952 – **Esther Rot** (Israeli track and field)

1976 – **Dan Kellner** (fencing)

1979 – **Justin Wayne** (Florida Marlins pitcher)

APRIL 17

GAMEBREAKERS

1914 – **Erskine Mayer** allows a fourth-inning home run, but the Philadelphia Phillies beat the New York Giants 3-1.

1924 – **Alexander Neufeld-Nemes** scores three goals as Hakoah Vienna defeats WR Association 6-2 in soccer.

1931 – **Andy Cohen** singles in the winning run in the ninth inning as the Newark Bears beat Rochester 3-2 in the International League.

1937 – **Reds Rosan** scores four of the Philadelphia Sphas' six points in overtime as Philadelphia defeats the Jersey Reds 44-43 to clinch its second straight ABL title. Rosan scores 13 points, **Shikey Gotthoffer** 11, and **Inky Lautman** 10 for the Sphas, who rally from a 3-1 deficit in the seven-game series.

1947 – **Jerome Fleishman** scores 16 points and **Ralph Kaplowitz** adds 14 as the Philadelphia Warriors beat the Chicago Staggs 85-74 in Game 2 of the Basketball Association of America finals.

1954 – **Angela Buxton** of England defeats J.W. Cawthorne 6-4, 6-0 in the final of the Cumberland Club Hard Courts tennis tournament in England.

1958 – **Marty Stabiner** makes his debut with St. Paul of the American Association, allowing only a bunt single through eight innings and finishing up with a 4-3 victory over Omaha.

1988 – **Danny Schayes** of the Denver Nuggets scores 32 points in a 132-125 victory over the Houston Rockets.

1994 – **Todd Simon**, Buffalo's fourth-line center, scores his only career NHL goal on a 4-on-3 power play with 11 seconds left in the first period, and the Sabres defeat the New Jersey Devils 2-0 in the first game of their best-of-seven first-round playoff series.

2002 – **Juan Pablo Sorin** scores in the 47th minute to give Argentina a 1-0 soccer victory over Germany.

MAZEL TOUGH

1787 – **Danny Mendoza** makes his boxing debut in Barnet, England, beating Sam Martin the Bath Butcher in 10 rounds.

1788 – In his boxing debut, **Elijah Crabbe** of England knocks out Stephen Oliver in 35 minutes.

1916 – **Joe Fox** wins a 20-round decision over Tommy Harrison in London to retain his British bantamweight title.

1948 – **Henry Wittenberg** wins his third straight AAU wrestling title at 191 pounds.

1953 – **Boris Gurevich** of the Soviet Union wins the 52-kg. title in Greco-Roman wrestling at the World Championships in Napoli, Italy.

1976 – Twenty-one-year-old **Marshall Holman** beats Billy Hardwick 203-198 in the Firestone Tournament of Champions bowling final in Fairlawn, Ohio.

RECORD SETTERS

1951 – **Henry Wittenberg** loses to Dale Thomas in the 191.5-pound final at the National AAU Wrestling Championships in Tampa, Fla. The defeat ends Wittenberg's record streak of more than 300 consecutive victories.

TRANSITIONS

1957 – **Lenny Rosenbluth** of North Carolina is selected by the Philadelphia Warriors with the seventh pick of the NBA draft. **Larry Friend** of California goes to the New York Knicks with the fifth pick in the second round.

A STAR IS BORN

1919 – **Milt Aron** (lightweight boxer)

1951 – **Alan Globensky** (Quebec Nordiques hockey)

1962 – **John Frank** (Ohio State, San Francisco 49ers tight end)

APRIL 18

GAMEBREAKERS

1964 – **Sandy Koufax** strikes out the side on nine pitches in the third inning against Cincinnati, becoming the first pitcher to accomplish the feat twice.

1997 – **Steve Dubinsky** scores a hat trick as Indianapolis defeats Cleveland 6-3 in an International Hockey League Turner Cup finals playoff game.

1998 – **Scott Hochstadt** scores seven goals and is named tournament MVP as Maryland beats Virginia 14-11 for its first Atlantic Coast Conference lacrosse title.

2001 – **Jeff Halpern** scores 4:01 into overtime to give the Washington Capitals a 4-3 win over the Pittsburgh Penguins, evening their first-round NHL playoff series at 2 games apiece.

MAZEL TOUGH

1913 – **Edward Lindenbaum** wins his first of two consecutive rope climb titles at the National AAU Gymnastics championships.

1914 – **Max Woldman** wins a referee's decision over Patrick McCarthy for the AAU welterweight boxing title in Boston.

1922 – **Sid Terris** wins a three-round judge's decision over Louis Raddy to capture the AAU 118-pound boxing title in Boston.

1941 – **Mike Kaplan** of Boston decisions world welterweight champion Fritzie Zivic in a 10-round non-title fight in Boston.

1950 – **Vic Hershkowitz** beats **Marty Rosenfeld** to win the AAU one-wall handball title. **Sandy Blank** and **Artie Schwartz** combine for the doubles title.

1960 – **Suzy Kormoczy** of Hungary defeats Yola Ramirez 6-3, 6-2 in the final of a tennis tournament in Monte Carlo and finishes unbeaten in five events on the Riviera Tour.

1991 – **Leonard Friedman** stops Freddie Rafferty in the 10th round to win the South African cruiserweight title in Mabopane, South Africa.

1998 – Oklahoma senior **Dan Fink** wins the still rings at the NCAA gymnastics championships at Penn State.

2003 – **Dustin Greenhill** of Army wins the parallel bars and adds bronze medals in the high bar and vault at the USA Gymnastics Collegiate Nationals in Denton, Texas

2004 – **Jeff Salzenstein** defeats Wesley Moodie 6-3, 3-6, 7-5 in the final of a Challenger tennis tournament in Leon, Mexico

JEWS ON FIRST

1931 – **Jim Levey** of the St. Louis Browns hits his first of 11 career home runs off Tommy Bridges in a 7-3 victory over the Detroit Tigers.

1950 – **Al Rosen** of the Cleveland Indians hits his first of 192 career home runs off Fred Hutchinson in a 7-6 loss to the Detroit Tigers.

TRANSITIONS

1947 – Former world lightweight champion **Benny Leonard** dies of a stroke at age 51 while refereeing a bout between Eddie Giosa and Julio Jiminez at St. Nicholas Arena in New York.

1956 – **Al Rosen** of the Cleveland Indians becomes the first Jewish athlete to be featured on the cover of Sports Illustrated, which began publication in 1954.

A STAR IS BORN

1905 – **Syd Halter** (Canadian Football League commissioner)

1956 – **Seth Greenberg** (Long Beach State, South Florida and Virginia Tech basketball coach)

1964 – **Maria Mazina** (Russian fencing)

APRIL 19

GAMEBREAKERS

1920 – In his first start of the season, Washington's **Al Schacht** pitches his only career shutout as the Senators beat the Philadelphia A's 7-0.

1925 – **Si Rosenthal** of the San Antonio Bears hits three home runs in a Texas League game.

1941 – **Harry Danning** hits a grand slam homer as the New York Giants beat the Philadelphia Phillies 7-0.

1947 – **Ralph Kaplowitz** and **Jerome Fleishman** both score 11 points as the Philadelphia Warriors defeat the Chicago Staggs 75-72 in Game 3 of the Basketball Association of America finals. **Max Zaslofsky** scores 15 points to lead Chicago.

1950 – **Sid Gordon** of the Boston Braves hits the first of a National League-record 35 grand slam homers that season. The Braves beat the Giants 10-6.

1963 – **Sandy Koufax** pitches a two-hitter and strikes out 14 as the Los Angeles Dodgers beat the Houston Colt .45s 2-0.

2004 – **Gabe Kapler's** second RBI of the day, a run-scoring single in the eighth inning, gives Boston a 5-4 victory over the New York Yankees after the Red Sox trailed 4-1.

MAZEL TOUGH

1904 – **Michael Spring**, a 21-year-old clerk from New York who finished third a year earlier, wins the eighth Boston Marathon in 2 hours, 38 minutes, 4.4 seconds. Spring overcomes a four-minute lead by Sammy Mellor at the 20-mile mark and finishes almost 1½ minutes ahead of runner-up Thomas Hicks.

1947 – **Estelle Osher** of Hunter College wins the Women's Intercollegiate Fencing Championship at NYU.

1976 – **Harold Solomon** wins the WCT Marlboro Classic tennis tournament in Monte Carlo.

1986 – **Lucy Wener** of Georgia wins her first of three NCAA gymnastics titles on the uneven bars.

1988 – **Gary Jacobs** earns a 12-round decision over Wilf Gentzen in Glasgow, Scotland, to capture the British Commonwealth welterweight title.

TRANSITIONS

1944 – The Green Bay Packers select Michigan guard **Mervin Pregulman** in the first round of the NFL draft, the seventh player taken overall.

A STAR IS BORN

1902 – **Phil Kaplan** (lightweight boxer)
1913 – **Max Kaminsky** (St. Louis Eagles, Boston Bruins, and Montreal Maroons hockey)
1964 – **Harris Barton** (North Carolina football, San Francisco 49ers lineman)
1973 – **Tzipi Obziler** (Israeli tennis)

Harold Solomon
(Association of Tennis Professionals)

APRIL 20

GAMEBREAKERS

1926 – The all-Jewish Hakoah Vienna soccer team begins an 11-game tour of the United States by beating the Brooklyn Wanderers 3-1 as **Max Wortmann** scores two goals. Hakoah will post a 7-2-2 record on its first of two tours of the U.S.

1939 – **Hank Greenberg** hits a walk-off homer in the 14th inning to give the Detroit Tigers an 8-7 win over the Chicago White Sox in the second game of the season.

1941 – **Harry Feldman** of the Jersey City Giants allows eight hits, but shuts out the Montreal Royals 2-0 in the International League.

1952 – **Al Rosen** ends a 25-game homerless streak by hitting a pair of solo shots as the Cleveland Indians defeat the Detroit Tigers 7-2 in the second game of a doubleheader.

1957 – Rochester Red Wings pitcher **Duke Markell** blanks the Columbus Jets 7-0 in the International League.

1968 – **Larry Brown** scores 28 points as the New Orleans Buccaneers beat the Pittsburgh Pipers 109-100 in Game 2 of the American Basketball Association championship finals.

2000 – **Shawn Green** drives in three runs with two home runs as the Los Angeles Dodgers beat the Florida Marlins 7-1.

MAZEL TOUGH

1908 – **Harry Lewis** knocks out Billy "Honey" Mellody in the fourth round in Boston to retain his world welterweight title.

1929 – **Ben Sherman** and **Al Cornsweet** finish 1-2 in the 160-pound division at the National AAU freestyle wrestling championships in New York.

1933 – **Irving Jacobs** defeats **Jack Londin** in the finals of the National AAU one-wall handball championships.

1974 – **Veronica Burton** of England defeats **Paulina Peled** of Israel 4-6, 9-8, 6-1 to win the Cumberland Tennis Tournament in London.

1985 – **Shlomo Glickstein** beats Brad Drewett 6-4, 6-3 in the final of a hard-court tennis tournament in Jerusalem.

2001 – **Rebekah Green** of Kansas State wins the shot put at the Kansas Relays with a meet-record 56 feet, 0 inches. **Andy Bloom** wins the men's shot put a day later.

JEWS ON FIRST

1912 – Fenway Park opens in Boston. **Guy Zinn** of the New York Highlanders is the first batter in the first official major-league game, won by the Red Sox 7-6 in 11 innings. Zinn walks and also scores the first run in stadium history.

TRANSITIONS

1971 – **Abe Saperstein**, founder of the Harlem Globetrotters, is elected to the Basketball Hall of Fame.

1972 – **Marty Friedman** and **Eddie Gottlieb** are elected to the Basketball Hall of Fame.

1998 – Clemson names Wyoming head coach **Larry Shyatt** men's basketball coach. Shyatt will lead the Tigers to a 70-84 record in five seasons.

2006 – **Fran Wolf Deken**, a pro bowler and president of the Bowling Writers Association, is inducted into the United States Bowling Congress Hall of Fame.

A STAR IS BORN

1899 – **Willie Harmon** (welterweight boxer)

1950 – **Paulina Peled** (Israeli tennis)

APRIL 21

GAMEBREAKERS

1936 – **Jake Levy** allows six hits as the Savannah Indians beat the Jacksonville Tars 7-1 in the first South Atlantic League game played in Savannah in eight years.

1951 – Buffalo Bisons pitcher **Moe Savransky** collects four hits in a 9-1 victory over Springfield in the International League. Savransky pitches a six-hitter.

1954 – **Al Rosen** singles with one out in the ninth to break up Bob Turley's no-hit bid and scores on Larry Doby's homer as the Cleveland Indians beat the Orioles 2-1 in the first night game played at Memorial Stadium in Baltimore.

2002 – **Cory Pecker** has three goals and an assist as the Erie Otters beat the Windsor Spitfires 7-4 in the Ontario Hockey League Western Conference finals.

MAZEL TOUGH

1922 – **Lou Weissman** wins his second 25-foot rope climb title at the AAU National Gymnastics championships in New York with a time of 7 3/5 seconds. He also won the event in 1918 and 1923.

1950 – **Ken Schneider** wins the national 4-wall handball championship.

1951 – The Rochester Royals, coached by **Lester Harrison**, beat the New York Knicks 79-75 to win the NBA championship series 4-3. Future Knicks coach **Red Holzman** is a member of the championship team.

1959 – **Walter Blum** rides four winners to clinch the Gulfstream Park season riding championship.

1963 – **Eleazar Davidman** and **Gavriel Dubitsky** give Israel its first Davis Cup tennis victory, 4-1 over Turkey in the European Zone competition in Istanbul.

1968 – **Tom Okker** downs Marty Riessen 12-10, 6-1, 6-4 to win the South African Lawn Tennis championship in Johannesburg.

Pierre Darmon defeats Daniel Contet 7-5, 6-1, 8-6 to win the Aux-En-Provence tennis championship in France.

1991 – **Martin Jaite** beats Goran Prpic 3-6, 7-6 (7-1), 6-3 in the final of a clay-court tennis tournament in Nice, France.

1995 – **Ian Bachrach** of Stanford scores 9.7125 to win the NCAA gymnastics title in the vault at Columbus, Ohio.

RECORD SETTERS

1934 – **Moe Berg** of the Washington Senators sets an American League record for catchers by playing in his 117th consecutive game over a three-year period without commiting an error.

1935 – **Paul Friesel** ties the American record of 29 seconds in winning the 50-yard breaststroke at the AAU Metropolitan championships in New York.

TRANSITIONS

1972 – Denver Rockets guard **Larry Brown** is named coach of the Carolina Cougars of the American Basketball Association.

1996 – **Danny Schayes** of the Miami Heat appears in his 1,000th regular-season NBA game in the season finale against Atlanta.

A STAR IS BORN

1902 – **Phil "Lefty" Weinert** (Philadelphia Phillies, Chicago Cubs, New York Yankees pitcher)

1916 – **Leroy Monsky** (Alabama football)

1922 – **Arnold Blum** (golf)

1958 – **Steve Meister** (tennis)

1972 – **Todd Simon** (Buffalo Sabres hockey)

APRIL 22

GAMEBREAKERS

1930 – **Buddy Myer's** RBI single in the 12th inning gives the Washington Senators a 4-3 win over the Boston Red Sox.

1940 – **Dick Conger** pitches three innings of relief and earns his first of three major-league victories when the Detroit Tigers beat the Chicago White Sox 6-5 in 11 innings.

1952 – **Saul Rogovin** pitches a six-hitter as the Chicago White Sox hand the Detroit Tigers their eighth straight loss to open the season, 2-0.

1970 – **Mike Epstein's** sacrifice fly in the 18th inning gives the Washington Senators a 2-1 victory over the New York Yankees.

1999 – Detroit Tigers catcher **Brad Ausmus** hits a home run in the bottom of the eighth to beat the Boston Red Sox 1-0.

2004 – **Cody Haerther** goes 5-for-5 as Peoria defeats Kane County 10-7 in the Class A Midwest League.

MAZEL TOUGH

1937 – **Janice Lifson** wins the Metropolitan AAU 10-foot springboard diving championship for the fifth consecutive year.

1947 – Coached by **Eddie Gottlieb**, the Philadelphia Warriors beat the Chicago Stags 83-80 to win the first-ever NBA Finals series 4-1. **Ralph Kaplowitz** scores eight points for the Warriors, while **Max Zaslofsky** scores five for Chicago.

1972 – **Fred Lewis** wins the U.S. Handball Association four-wall singles title in Seattle.

1973 – **Brian Gottfried** wins the Clows Classic tennis tournament in Johannesburg, South Africa, when Jaime Fillol defaults in the final.

2001 – **Bruce Fleisher** wins the Las Vegas Senior Classic by three strokes. It's his 12th victory on the Senior golf tour but his first in nearly nine months.

2004 – **Dan Kellner** defeats **Jon Tiomkin** 15-6 to win the U.S. men's foil title at the fencing championships in Atlanta.

Mike Epstein *(California Angels)*

A STAR IS BORN

1887 – **Harold Bohr** (Danish soccer)

1894 – **Jake Pitler** (Pittsburgh Pirates second baseman, Brooklyn Dodgers coach)

1934 – **Peter Neft** (Pitt and Canadian Football League quarterback)

1973 – **Anita Kaplan** (Stanford basketball)

APRIL 23

GAMEBREAKERS

1927 – **Sol Mishkin** hits three two-run homers as Occidental College defeats Whittier 12-2.

1941 – In his first start for St. Louis, **Sam Nahem** pitches a three-hitter as the Cardinals defeat the Pittsburgh Pirates 3-1.

1952 – **Max Zaslofsky** scores 23 points to lead the New York Knicks past the Minneapolis Lakers 76-68, forcing a Game 7 in the NBA Finals.

1971 – In just his fourth major-league game, **Steve Stone** pitches a five-hitter as the San Francisco Giants beat the Pittsburgh Pirates 2-0.

MAZEL TOUGH

1925 – **Sydney Lee** defeats George Cooper in the finals of the English Under-16 Billiards Championships. Lee will win four straight British Amateur championships from 1931-34 and the world title in 1933.

1955 – **Angelica Rozeanu** of Romania beats Linde Wertl-Rumpler of Austria to win the women's singles, and also teams with Ella Zeller for the doubles title at the World Table Tennis championships in Utrecht, Netherlands.

1937 – **Claire Isicson** wins the AAU women's indoor long jump title.

1966 – **Paul Haber** wins the U.S. singles handball championship.

1978 – **Amy Alcott** beats Hollis Stacy in a one-hole playoff to win the LPGA American Defender Classic in Raleigh, N.C.

1978 – **Brian Gottfried** beats Ilie Nastase 3-6, 6-2, 6-1 to win the WCT Houston International clay-court tennis tournament.

2000 – **Alyssa Beckerman** of the United States wins the all-around with a score of 33.75 at the Spieth Sogipan International Cup gymnastics meet in Porte Alegre, Brazil.

RECORD SETTERS

1954 – Apprentice jockey **Willie Harmatz** rides six consecutive winners in races two through seven at Bay Meadows in San Mateo, Calif., to tie a 47-year-old United States record.

1960 – **Lew Stieglitz** of UConn sets an American record of 30:19.2 in the 10,000 meters at the Mount San Antonio College Relays in California.

2006 – **Deena Kastor** wins the London Marathon in 2 hours, 19 minutes, 35 seconds, improving her American record at the distance.

JEWS ON FIRST

1932 – **Moe Berg** of the Washington Senators hits his first of six career home runs off Bob Weiland in a 5-0 victory over the Boston Red Sox.

1951 – **Joe Ginsberg** of the Detroit Tigers and **Lou Limmer** of the Philadelphia Athletics both hit their first major-league home runs. Ginsberg hits his first of 20 career homers off Don Johnson in the Tigers' 7-4 victory over the St. Louis Browns. The Bronx-born Limmer's first of 19 homers – a two-run shot – comes off Vic Raschi as a pinch hitter in the ninth inning of a 5-4 loss at Yankee Stadium.

1997 – **David Nemirovsky** scores his first of 16 career NHL goals, but the Florida Panthers lose to the New York Rangers 3-2.

A STAR IS BORN

1886 – **Sam Karpf** (bowling)

1904 – **Ivor Goldsmid Montagu** (table tennis)

1944 – **Marty Fleckman** (golf)

APRIL 24

GAMEBREAKERS

1906 – **Barney Pelty** of the St. Louis Browns shuts out the Detroit Tigers 2-0.

1935 – **Sam Winograd** hits two doubles and a triple as CCNY routs Panzer College 21-5.

1947 – **Goody Rosen** drives in three runs with a homer and a single as Toronto beats Newark 3-1 in an International League game.

1951 – **Sid Gordon's** home run in the eighth inning gives the Boston Braves a 7-4 victory over the Brooklyn Dodgers.

1962 – **Don Taussig** hits a game-winning home run off Larry Jackson in the sixth inning as the Houston Colt .45s beat the St. Louis Cardinals 4-3. The homer is Taussig's last of four in the majors.

1965 – **Mike Epstein** hits his first professional home run and adds four singles and four RBI's as Stockton defeats San Jose 14-4 in the California League.

1999 – **Scott Drevitch** scores 14 minutes, 26 seconds into overtime as the Tacoma Sabercats beat the San Diego Gulls 3-2 in Game 2 of the West Coast Hockey League's Taylor Cup finals. Tacoma goes on to win the series 4-2.

2002 – **Nate Fish** of Cincinnati ties a Conference USA record by going 6 for 6 including a home run and three RBI's in an 18-3 victory over Miami of Ohio

2005 – **Shari Maslin** scores a team-high five goals as Penn State defeats Ohio U. 17-8 in lacrosse.

MAZEL TOUGH

1906 – **Otto Scheff** of Austria wins a bronze medal in the 1,500 freestyle swimming event at the Athens Olympics.

1943 – **Bernard Mayer** of NYU wins the shot put at the Penn Relays.

1948 – **Victor Frank** of Yale wins the Penn Relays discus title.

1954 – **Martin Engel** wins the hammer throw at the IC4A outdoor track championships in New York.

1955 – **Boris Mendelovitch Gurevich** of the Soviet Union wins the Greco-Roman flyweight title at the World Wrestling Championships, his second title in three years.

1964 – **Mike Berkowitz** wins the shot put at the Penn Relays in Philadelphia.

2004 – **Sada Jacobson** beats younger sister **Emily Jacobson** 15-13 to win the saber title at the U.S. Fencing Championships in Atlanta.

RECORD SETTERS

1915 – **Frank Kaufman** runs the first leg of Penn's mile relay team that sets a world record of 3:18.0. The record will stand for 13 years.

1937 – **Morrie Arnovich** hits a club-record three doubles as the Philadelphia Phillies defeat the Brooklyn Dodgers 7-3.

1962 – **Sandy Koufax** strikes out 18 Cubs batters in a 10-2 win in Chicago – the second time he has tied the major-league single-game record.

1976 – **Faina Melnik** of the Soviet Union sets her 11th and final world record in the discus, with a toss of 231 feet, 3 inches.

TRANSITIONS

2004 – Oregon defensive tackle **Igor Olshansky** is drafted by the San Diego Chargers as the third player selected in the second round – 35th overall. Olshansky, a native of Ukraine, will become the first native of the former Soviet Union to play in the NFL.

A STAR IS BORN

1907 – **Abraham Glantz** (South African cricket)

1914 – **Pedro Montanez** (Puerto Rican lightweight boxer)

1955 – **Ernie Grunfeld** (Tennessee basketball, New York Knicks, Kansas City Kings)

1957 – **Bernard Rajzman** (Brazil volleyball)

1971 – **Max Geller** (Israeli freestyle wrestler)

APRIL 25

GAMEBREAKERS

1921 – **"Lefty" Weinert** pitches three innings of hitless relief for his second career victory as the Philadelphia Phillies beat the Boston Braves 7-6.

1941 – Pinch hitter **Morrie Arnovich** hits a bases-loaded triple in the ninth inning to rally the New York Giants to a 7-4 win over the Philadelphia Phillies.

1948 – Buffalo pitcher **Saul Rogovin** shuts out Jersey City 10-0 in the International League.

STRONG IN DEFEAT

1997 – **Shawn Green** goes 3 for 4 and has his first two-homer game in the major leagues, but Toronto loses 13-8 to the Seattle Mariners.

MAZEL TOUGH

1928 – **Hy Miller** captures the 112-pound crown and **Harry Devine** wins the 126-pound title at the AAU Boxing Championships in Boston.

1933 – **Jack Londin** and **Sy Alexander** beat **Solly Goldman** and **Harry Grossman** to win the national AAU senior one-wall handball doubles title.

1954 – **Dick Savitt** beats Hamilton Richardson 4-6, 6-3, 6-4, 7-5 to become the first unseeded player to win the River Oaks International tennis tournament in Houston.

1959 – **Carl Shine** of Penn wins his second straight Penn Relays shot put title in Philadelphia.

1959 – **Arthur Shurlock** of California finishes first on the horizontal bar at the AAU Gymnastics Championships in Amherst, Mass.

1963 – **Albert Axelrod**, **Herbert Cohen**, and **Martin Jay Davis** win gold medals in team foil at the Pan American Games fencing competition in Sao Paulo, Brazil.

1999 – **Bruce Fleisher** wins the Senior PGA Home Depot Invitational in Charlotte, N.C., by one stroke over Terry Dill and Jim Holt.

JEWS ON FIRST

1926 – **Si Rosenthal** of the Boston Red Sox hits his first of four career home runs off Firpo Mayberry in a 6-2 loss to the Washington Senators.

1926 – Hakoah Vienna plays its first official soccer match in the United States, defeating New York of the Southern New York State Association before 25,000 fans at the Polo Grounds. **Alexander Nemes Neufeld**, **Moritz Haeusler**, **Max Gruenwald**, and **Max Wortmann** score for Hakoah.

RECORD SETTERS

1928 – Canadian lightweight **Al Foreman** stops **Ruby Levine** in 11.5 seconds of the first round at the Montreal Forum. The knockout is the fastest ever in any weight class.

TRANSITIONS

1950 – The New York Knicks select **Irwin Dambrot** of CCNY with the seventh pick in the first round of the NBA draft.

1974 – Former NBA President **Maurice Podoloff** and former Columbia and Army coach **Harry Fisher** are elected to the Basketball Hall of Fame.

2002 – **Cory Pecker** of the Erie Otters is named Ontario Hockey League player of the year. Pecker finishes with 53 goals and 46 assists in 56 games despite missing six weeks because of a broken arm.

APRIL 26

GAMEBREAKERS

1945 – **Harry Feldman** pitches a five-hitter as the New York Giants beat the Philadelphia Phillies 2-0.

1953 – **Al Rosen** hits his eighth career grand slam homer as the Cleveland Indians beat the Detroit Tigers 12-2 in the second game of a doubleheader.

MAZEL TOUGH

1906 – Fencer **Edgar Seligman** of Great Britain wins a silver medal in team epee in the unofficial Olympics in Athens.

1927 – **Harry Liebenson** wins a three-round decision over Joseph Lazarus to capture the 112-pound AAU boxing title.

1930 – **Lawrence Levy** of Cornell wins the shot put, **Sol Furth** of NYU the triple jump, and **Leonard Friedman** of Geneva sets a meet record of 197 feet, 0.25 inches in the javelin at the Penn Relays in Philadelphia.

1947 – **Irv Mondschein** captures the high jump and long jump and **Bernard Mayer** wins the discus at the Penn Relays.

1948 – **Seymour Greenberg** wins both the singles and doubles titles at the LaPlata Tennis Tournament in Buenos Aires, Argentina.

1959 – **Arthur Shurlock** finishes first on the horizontal bars at the AAU National Gymnastics Championships.

1964 – **Erwin Klein** wins the singles title and teams with **Bernard Bukiet** for the doubles title at the U.S. Open table tennis tournament in Inglewood, Calif.

1965 – **Julie Heldman** defeats Madonna Schacht 6-3, 4-6, 6-0 to win a clay-court tennis tournament in Naples, Italy.

1986 – **Marshall Holman** beats Mark Baker 233-211 to win his second Firestone Tournament of Champions title in Akron, Ohio. He becomes the sixth bowler to post 20 career victories, and the $50,000 first prize makes him the third bowler to earn $1 million in career earnings.

1987 – Doubles specialist **Jim Grabb** wins his first of two singles tennis tournaments, beating Andre Agassi 1-6, 6-4, 6-2 in the final of a hard-court event in Seoul, South Korea.

1998 – **Paul Goldstein** of Stanford beats teammate Ryan Wolters 6-1, 6-2 in the final to win the Pac-10 Conference tennis championship.

2002 – **Igor Praporshchikov** of Australia wins the 96-kg. freestyle wrestling title at the Oceania Championships in Koror, Palau.

TRANSITIONS

1933 – The German Boxing Commission rules that heavyweight Max Schmelling will be able to retain his Jewish manager, **Joe Jacobs**, but only in bouts outside of Germany. Schmelling had not fought in Germany in nearly four years.

1966 – **Red Auerbach** retires as coach of the Boston Celtics after 1,037 career wins and nine NBA titles in 20 seasons.

1966 – **Aaron Rosenberg**, an offensive guard at Southern Cal from 1931 to 1933, is elected to the National Football Foundation College Hall of Fame.

1973 – **Dolph Schayes** is elected to the Basketball Hall of Fame.

2006 – Former LSU coach **Skip Bertman** is among the inaugural class of 10 members selected to the College Baseball Hall of Fame in Lubbock, Texas.

A STAR IS BORN

1900 – **Victor Frank Sr.** (Penn football)
1972 – **Avi Nimni** (Israeli soccer)

APRIL 27

GAMEBREAKERS

1933 – **Jim Levey** drives in all three St. Louis runs as the Browns beat the Cleveland Indians 3-2.

1938 – **Sid Luckman's** two-run triple caps a six-run rally in the ninth inning as Columbia beats Fordham 8-7.

1940 – **Werner Kaspi** scores two goals and **Herbert Meitner** scores in the game's first minute as Israel (Palestine) wins its first international soccer match, beating Lebanon 5-1. Its first four international matches were all losses (twice to Egypt in 1934 and twice to Greece in 1938 in World Cup qualifiers).

1979 – **Ross Baumgarten** of the Chicago White Sox allows six hits in an 11-0 victory over the Texas Rangers.

1979 – **Joel Kramer** scores six points and pulls down a game-high 11 rebounds as the Phoenix Suns defeat the Kansas City Kings 120-99 and clinch their Western Conference best-of-seven semifinal series 4-1.

1997 – **Jon Saffer** hits a seventh-inning grand slam homer to break a 2-2 tie and give the Ottawa Lynx a 6-2 win over the Pawtucket Pawsox in the first game of an International League doubleheader.

2003 – **Shawn Green** hits a tie-breaking homer with two out in the eighth inning to give the Los Angeles Dodgers a 4-3 win over the Pittsburgh Pirates.

STRONG IN DEFEAT

1980 – Oakland catcher **Jeff Newman** goes 4-for-5 with two RBI's in a 20-11 loss to the Minnesota Twins.

MAZEL TOUGH

1906 – Sixteen-year-old **Otto Scheff** of Austria beats Henry Taylor of Great Britain by two seconds to win the 400 freestyle, the closest swimming competition of the Athens Olympics.

1929 – **David Adelman** of Georgetown wins his first of two consecutive titles in the shot put at the Penn Relays in Philadelphia.

1946 – **Bernard Mayer** wins the Penn Relays discus title.

1963 – **Gary Gubner** wins his second straight shot put title and **Stu Levitt** of Haverford win the javelin at the Penn Relays.

1986 – **Elise Burgin** wins her only tournament on the women's tennis tour, beating Tine Scheuer-Larsen of Denmark 6-1, 6-3 on clay at the Wild Dunes Classic in Charleston, S.C.

1996 – **Ian Bachrach** of Stanford scores 9.913 to win the NCAA gymnastics championship in the floor exercise.

2006 – **Matt Rosenfeld** of Texas finishes at even-par 210 to win the Big 12 Conference golf championship in Tulsa, Okla., by two strokes.

RECORD SETTERS

1937 – **Max Stein** wins the all-events title with a championship-record 2,070 at the ABC Bowling Tournament in New York.

1952 – **Eva Szekely** swims the third leg as Hungary sets a world record of 4:27.2 in the 4×100 freestyle relay in Moscow.

1962 – **Gary Gubner** wins the shot put at the Penn Relays with a meet-record 61 feet, 4.25 inches.

TRANSITIONS

1950 – The Boston Celtics name **Red Auerbach** their head coach. Auerbach coached the NBA's Tri-City Blackhawks to a 28-29 record the previous season.

APRIL 28

GAMEBREAKERS

1915 – **Erskine Mayer** of the Philadelphia Phillies shuts out the Brooklyn Dodgers 3-0.

1930 – **Max Greunwald** scores with 15 minutes remaining to give New York Hakoah a 3-2 victory over Bethlehem (Pa.) Steel in the championship game of the Atlantic Coast Soccer League.

1946 – Two days after the Dodgers trade him to the Giants, **Goody Rosen** is the hitting star as New York sweeps Brooklyn 7-3 and 10-4. He has three hits and scores two runs in the first game and adds two hits including a homer, three RBI's, and two runs in the nightcap.

1948 – Elmira catcher **Stu Komer's** solo home run gives the Pioneers a 6-5 victory over the Williamsport Tigers on the Eastern League's opening day.

1949 – **Sid Gordon** collects four hits including two home runs as the New York Giants beat the Boston Braves 10-9 in 10 innings.

1970 – With one out in the sixth inning and a Jacksonville runner on third, **Sheldon Andrens** goes in as a defensive replacement in left field for Asheville. Andrens makes a diving catch on a ball hit by Terry Humphreys and then throws out runner Pete Koegel at home to preserve the Tourists' 3-2 Southern League victory.

1974 – **Ron Blomberg** hits a double, a three-run homer, and a sacrifice fly as the New York Yankees beat the Texas Rangers 11-2 in the first game of a doubleheader. He also hits a double and a solo homer in the second game, won by Texas 8-5.

1981 – **Steve Ratzer** pitches a perfect fifth inning in relief and gets his only major-league victory as the Montreal Expos beat the Philadelphia Phillies 6-3.

MAZEL TOUGH

1906 – **Henrik Hajos Guttmann** of Hungary swims the second leg of the Olympic gold-medal winning 800 freestyle relay, held in an open bay near Athens.

1945 – **Milt Padway** wins the pole vault and **Seymour Cohen** captures the javelin at the Penn Relays.

1957 – **Abe Segal** scores his first of 24 Davis Cup tennis victories for South Africa when he beats Emilio Martinez 6-2, 0-6, 6-4, 6-3. South Africa beats Spain 5-0.

1962 – **Jeffrey Lerner** wins the National Open Paddle Tennis singles championship.

1969 – **Julie Heldman** beats Kerry Melville of Australia 7-5, 6-3 to become the first American woman in 13 years to win the Italian Open tennis tournament in Rome.

RECORD SETTERS

1900 – **Myer Prinstein** sets a world record of 24-7¼ in the broad jump in Philadelphia. The mark will stand as a Penn Relays record for 30 years.

JEWS ON FIRST

1932 – **Max Rosenfeld** of the Brooklyn Dodgers hits his first of two career homers, a three-run shot off Hal "Jumbo" Elliott in the eighth inning of an 11-5 victory over the Philadelphia Phillies.

TRANSITIONS

1987 – The San Francisco 49ers pick North Carolina tackle **Harris Barton** in the first round of the NFL draft. Barton is the 22nd player selected.

A STAR IS BORN

1969 – **Peter Ing** (Toronto Maple Leafs, Edmonton Oilers, Detroit Red Wings goalie)

1970 – **Bill Hurst** (Florida Marlins pitcher)

1976 – **Sara Whalen** (UConn soccer)

APRIL 29

GAMEBREAKERS

1935 – **Hank Greenberg** hits a grand slam home run in the Detroit Tigers' 18-0 rout of the St. Louis Browns.

1943 – Six days after pitching 18 innings of an International League-record 21-inning, 2-2 tie with Baltimore, **Dick Conger** tosses a four-hitter as Toronto defeats Newark 8-1.

1952 – **Al Rosen** of the Cleveland Indians hits three homers for the first time in his career and drives in seven runs in a 21-9 win over the Philadelphia Athletics.

1953 – **Cal Abrams's** home run starts a three-run rally in the eighth inning as the Pittsburgh Pirates beat the Chicago Cubs 4-3.

1955 – **Duke Markell** of the Rochester Red Wings pitches a no-hitter in a 9-0 win over the Columbus Jets in the International League.

1973 – **Ron Blomberg** goes 4 for 4 with three RBI's as the New York Yankees beat the Minnesota Twins 11-1 in the second game of a doubleheader.

2004 – **Tony Schrager** hits two home runs as the Pawtucket PawSox defeat the Ottawa Lynx 16-7 in an International League game.

MAZEL TOUGH

1944 – **Norman Wasser** of NYU wins the Penn Relays shot put title.

1950 – **Martin Korik** of Tennessee wins the pole vault and **Stanley Lampert** of NYU captures the shot put at the Penn Relays.

1955 – **Martin Engel** wins the hammer throw with a Penn Relays meet record of 183 feet, 4 inches.

2002 – **Charlee Minkin** wins the women's 52-kg. class and older sister **Davina Minkin** wins the 57-kg. gold medal at the U.S. Judo National Championships in Houston.

2006 – **Brian Mondschein** of Virginia Tech wins the pole vault by clearing 17 feet, 10½ inches at the Penn Relays. Mondschein becomes the Relays' first three-generation winner. His grandfather Irv won the high jump in 1947 and his father Mark won the pole vault in 1979.

RECORD SETTERS

1950 – **James Fuchs** improves his world shot put record to 17.82 meters in Los Angeles.

TRANSITIONS

1936 – After playing just 12 games, Detroit Tigers first baseman **Hank Greenberg** breaks his left wrist in a baseline collision with Jake Powell of the Washington Senators and misses the rest of the season.

1985 – **Norman Braman**, in partnership with **Edward Leibowitz**, purchases the Philadelphia Eagles from **Leonard Tose**.

A STAR IS BORN

1940 – **Barry Multer** (Rhode Island basketball)

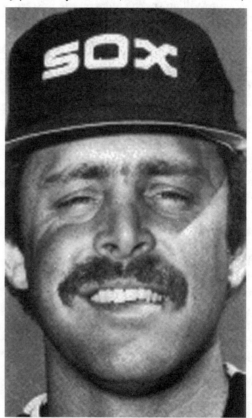

Ron Blomberg *(Chicago White Sox)*

APRIL 30

1922 – **Gyorgy Molnar** scores his first goal in international soccer play as Hungary ties Austria 1-1.

1927 – **Jonah Goldman** hits two triples and a double as Syracuse beats Michigan 10-2 in college baseball.

1932 – **Moe Berg's** RBI double in the eighth inning propels the Washington Senators to a 2-1 victory over the Philadelphia Athletics.

1944 – **Phil Weintraub** goes 4-for-5 with two doubles, a triple, and a homer with 11 RBI's and scores five runs as the New York Giants beat the Brooklyn Dodgers 26-8 in the first game of a doubleheader at the Polo Grounds. Weintraub also walks twice and lines out in his final at-bat with two runners on base. **Harry Feldman** pitches 5 2/3 innings of relief and is the winning pitcher in the most lopsided victory in Giants franchise history.

1947 – **Sid Gordon's** two-run single in the ninth inning gives the New York Giants a 4-3 win over the St. Louis Cardinals.

1997 – **Eli Ohana** scores two goals as Israel defeats Cyprus 2-0 in a World Cup soccer qualifier.

2001 – **Shawn Green** of the Dodgers hits two homers as Los Angeles beats the Florida Marlins 7-1.

STRONG IN DEFEAT

1948 – **Sid Gordon** hits two home runs in the New York Giants' 7-2 loss to the Boston Braves.

MAZEL TOUGH

1908 – **Abe Attell** knocks out Tommy Sullivan in the fourth round in San Francisco to retain his world featherweight title.

1949 – **Martin Korik** of Tennessee wins the pole vault, **James Fuchs** of Yale the shot put, and **Victor Frank** of Yale the discus at the Penn Relays in Philadelphia. Frank sets a meet record of 170 feet, 7.75 inches.

1955 – **Abie Grossfeld** wins his first of three straight horizontal bar titles at the AAU Gymnastics Championships in Rochester, N.Y.

1960 – **Jimmy Jacobs** and Dick Weisman beat **Vic Hershkowitz** and **Morris Singer** to win the national doubles handball championship in San Francisco.

1963 – **Robert Halperin** teams with Richard Stearns to win a yachting gold medal in the star class at the Pan American Games in Sao Paulo, Brazil.

1978 – **Harold Solomon** wins the indoor Alan King Classic tennis tournament in Las Vegas when Corrado Barazzutti withdraws with stomach pains while trailing 6-1, 3-0.

RECORD SETTERS

1948 – **Marv Rotblatt** strikes out a Big Ten Conference-record 18 batters as Illinois beats Purdue 9-2.

2005 – **Matt Kutler** of Brown sets an Ivy League career hits record of 260 despite missing the 2004 season with a broken thumb. He will be named Ivy League Player of the Year.

TRANSITIONS

1963 – The New York Knicks make **Art Heyman** of Duke the No. 1 overall pick in the NBA draft.

A STAR IS BORN

1879 – **Richard Weisz** (Hungarian wrestler)

1882 – **John Raphael** (British cricket, rugby)

1915 – **Leo Merson** (LIU basketball)

1919 – **Ossie Schechtman** (LIU basketball, New York Knicks)

1946 – **Rick Weitzman** (Northeastern basketball, Boston Celtics)

MAY 1

GAMEBREAKERS

1910 – **Barney Pelty** of the St. Louis Browns shuts out the Chicago White Sox 2-0 in the first game played at White Sox Park, later renamed Comiskey Park.

1927 – **Josef Nickolsburger** scores two goals as Hakoah Vienna plays the New York Giants of the American Soccer League to a 2-2 tie at the Polo Grounds. **Moritz Haeusler**, who played for Hakoah on its U.S. tour a year earlier, scores the tying goal for the Giants.

1948 – **Sol Israel** hits a two-run homer in the ninth inning to give Augusta a 3-1 win over Jacksonville in the Sally League.

1954 – **Al Rosen** drives in three runs with two homers and a double as the Cleveland Indians beat the Boston Red Sox 6-3.

2003 – **Aaron Rifkin** hits a grand slam homer as the Trenton Thunder defeat the Norwich Navigators 16-3 in the Eastern League.

2004 – Anthony Parker scores 21 points and **David Bluthenthal** adds 20 as Maccabi Tel Aviv defeats Skipper Bologna of Italy 118-74 for its fourth Euroleague Cup basketball championship in Tel Aviv.

MAZEL TOUGH

1922 – **Jack Bloomfield** knocks out Harry Drake in the ninth round in London to win the British light-heavyweight title.

1943 – **Pearl Perkins Nightingale** wins her third National AAU gymnastics all-around title in New York. She also places first on flying rings, vault, and parallel bars.

1954 – **Donald Faber** of UCLA wins the floor exercises at the AAU gymnastics championships in San Fernando, Calif.

1993 – **Yael Arad** of Israel defeats Gella van de Caveye of Belgium to win the under-61kg. class at the European Judo Championships in Athens.

2004 – **David Zilberman** of Concordia decisions defending champion Randeep Sodhi 6-1 to win the 96-kg. title at the Canadian Senior National Wrestling Tournament in Fredericton, New Brunswick.

JEWS ON FIRST

1942 – New York Giants pitcher **Harry Feldman** hits his first of two career home runs off Jake Mooty in a 13-9 loss to the Chicago Cubs.

1953 – Jockey **Ronald Behrens** rides his first career winner at Jamaica Racetrack in New York.

TRANSITIONS

1926 – An exhibition match between the all-Jewish Hakoah Vienna soccer club, the 1925 Austrian national champion, and players from the New York Giants and Indiana Flooring teams of the American Soccer League draws 46,000 fans in the Polo Grounds, an American soccer attendance record that will stand for 40 years. Although Hakoah loses 3-0, the team has considerable influence on soccer in the United States, as numerous teams adopt the name Hakoah.

1963 – **Maurice Podoloff** retires after 17 years as president of the NBA.

1992 – **Bob Plager** is named head coach of the St. Louis Blues of the NHL. Plager will coach only 11 games (4-6-1) before being replaced in late October.

A STAR IS BORN

1898 – **David "Pep" Tobey** (basketball coach and referee)
1909 – **Cy Kaselman** (basketball)
1942 – **Gerald Ashworth** (track and field)
1967 – **Yael Arad** (Israeli judo)
1987 – **Shahar Peer** (Israeli tennis)

MAY 2

GAMEBREAKERS

1925 – **Izzy Zarakov** hits a grand slam homer to lead Harvard to a 9-1 victory over Amherst.

1948 – **Herb Gorman** hits a grand slam homer in the second inning to lead Pueblo to a 7-6 victory over Sioux City in the Western League.

1951 – **Lou Limmer's** three-run double ignites an eight-run 11th inning as the Philadelphia Athletics snap a 10-game losing streak with a 3-1 win over the Detroit Tigers.

1954 – **Cal Abrams** of the Pirates hits two singles, a double, and an RBI triple, and scores four runs as Pittsburgh routs the Chicago Cubs 18-10.

2007 – **Mathieu Schneider** scores unassisted 16 minutes, 4 seconds into overtime to give the Detroit Red Wings a 3-2 victory over the San Jose Sharks in the NHL playoffs. Detroit's victory tied the second-round series at two games apiece.

STRONG IN DEFEAT

2000 – University of Cincinnati third baseman **Kevin Youkilis** goes 4 for 4, including a school-record three home runs in the Bearcats' 19-11 loss to Toledo.

MAZEL TOUGH

1963 – **Abie Grossfeld** of the United States wins on the horizontal bar and finishes second on rings at the Pan American Games gymnastics competition in Sao Paulo, Brazil. **James Margolis** and **Gilbert Eisner** of the United States win a fencing gold medal in team epee.

1982 – **Brian Gottfried** beats Mark Estep 6-7 (6-8), 6-2, 6-4 in the final of the hardcourt Robinson's Open tennis tournament in Oldsmar, Fla.

RECORD SETTERS

2004 – **Bruce Fleisher** wins the Bruno's Memorial Classic in Hoover, Ala., by a tour-record seven strokes over runners-up D.A. Weibring and Bruce Lietzke. The victory is Fleischer's 18th on the Senior golf tour.

JEWS ON FIRST

1951 – **Lou Limmer** of the Philadelphia A's hits a two-run pinch-hit homer in the ninth inning, tying the game against the Detroit Tigers 3-3. With **Saul Rogovin** on the mound and **Joe Ginsberg** behind the plate for the Tigers, it is the first meeting of a Jewish pitcher, catcher, and batter in major-league history. Detroit wins 5-4 in 10 innings.

1965 – **Art Shamsky** of the Cincinnati Reds hits his first of 68 career home runs, a two-run shot off Tom Parsons in a 9-4 victory over the New York Mets. Shamsky was pinch-hitting for Frank Robinson, who finished his career with 586 home runs.

A STAR IS BORN

1968 – **Jeff Agoos** (soccer)
1985 – **Sarah Hughes** (figure skating)

Sarah Hughes *(U.S. Olympic Committee)*

MAY 3

GAMEBREAKERS

1937 – **Hank Greenberg's** grand slam home run helps the Detroit Tigers beat the Chicago White Sox 12-9.

1947 – **Goody Rosen** collects four singles and four walks in eight trips to the plate as the Toronto Maple Leafs beat Baltimore 3-1 and 5-4 in an International League doubleheader.

1997 – **Jenny Schoen** hits a two-run homer in the first inning to give Purdue a 2-0 softball victory over Minnesota.

2000 – **David Hymovitz** scores the winning goal as the Houston Aeros defeat the Utah Grizzlies 3-2 to wrap up their American Hockey League playoff first-round series four games to one.

MAZEL TOUGH

1920 – **Battling Levinsky** wins a 12-round decision over Clay Turner in Portland, Ore., to retain his world light heavyweight title.

1935 – **Hirsch Demsitz** knocks out Kaj Olsen in the third round to win the Danish featherweight championship in Copenhagen.

1964 – **James Bregman** wins the 165-pound title at the AAU Judo Championships at the World's Fair in New York.

1998 – **Kenny Bernstein** beats Gary Scelzi in the finals to win the Top Fuel title at the NHRA Fram Route 66 Nationals.

JEWS ON FIRST

1899 – **Leo Fishel** of the New York Giants becomes the first Jewish pitcher in the major leagues, going all nine innings and allowing nine hits and striking out six in a 7-3 loss to the Philadelphia Phillies. He gets one hit in four at-bats in his only major-league appearance.

2004 – **Jason Marquis** of the St. Louis Cardinals and Greg Maddux of the Chicago Cubs both steal a base. They are the first opposing starting pitchers to steal a base in the same game since Warren Spahn of the Boston Braves and Bob Rush of the Cubs in the second game of a doubleheader on June 11, 1950.

James Bregman
(U.S. Olympic Committee)

A STAR IS BORN

1912 – **Moe Spahn** (CCNY basketball)

1923 – **Nathan Militzok** (Hofstra and Cornell basketball)

1925 – **Hal Saltzman** (minor-league baseball)

1932 – **Maria Itkina** (Soviet track and field)

1976 – **Jeff Halpern** (Washington Capitals, Dallas Stars hockey)

1982 – **Igor Olshansky** (Oregon, San Diego Chargers defensive lineman)

MAY 4

GAMEBREAKERS

1939 – **Phil Weintraub** of the Minneapolis Millers hits a double, triple, and two homers in an American Association game. Weintraub begins the day batting .647 over his last 10 games.

1951 – **Marv Rotblatt** is the winning pitcher in relief, picking up his third win of the season for the Chicago White Sox in a 6-5 victory over the Washington Senators. Rotblatt wins only one more game in the majors before being called for military service.

1952 – Cal-Berkeley junior **Ed Mayer** collects two hits and pitches a one-hitter with seven strikeouts in a 1-0 victory over Santa Clara.

1965 – **Neil Rubinstein** pitches the second no-hitter in University of Cincinnati history in a 3-0, seven-inning victory over Hanover in the second game of a doubleheader. Rubinstein strikes out 13, but commits an error, walks five batters, and hits four others with pitches.

1968 – **Art Heyman** scores 18 points for Pittsburgh as the Pipers defeat the New Orleans Buccaneers 122-113 to win the first American Basketball Association championship, 4 games to 3. **Larry Brown** scores 18 for New Orleans.

2002 – **Eyal Zimet** of Israel registers 13 kills and 13 defensive digs as Hawaii wins its first-ever NCAA title by beating top-ranked Pepperdine 29-31, 31-29, 30-21, 30-24 in the men's volleyball final.

MAZEL TOUGH

1910 – **Harry Lewis** knocks out Peter Brown in the third round in Paris to retain his world welterweight title.

1912 – **Tibor Fischer** of Hungary wins the 85-kg. Greco-Roman title, **Jozsef Pongracz-Pollak** of Hungary captures the 60-kg. crown, and **Oedoen Radvany** of Hungary takes his first of two straight 67.5-kg. titles at the European Wrestling Championships in Budapest.

1915 – **Charley White** knocks out Eddie Murphy in the first round of a lightweight fight in Boston.

1936 – **George Gulack** finishes first on flying rings at the AAU National Gymnastics Championships in New York.

1957 – **Abie Grossfeld** captures his third straight horizontal bar crown and **Arthur Shurlock** wins the pommel horse at the AAU National Gymnastics Championships in Chicago.

2003 – **Stephanie Cohen-Aloro** of France defeats **Yulia Beygelzimer** 6-4, 6-3 in an ITF clay-court tennis tournament final in Cagnew-Sur-Mar, France.

RECORD SETTERS

1937 – **Max Stein** scores a record 2,070 to win the all-events title at the American Bowling Congress championships in New York. He rolls 68 strikes – 20 in team, 23 in doubles and 25 in singles.

JEWS ON FIRST

2000 – Niagara University goalie **Greg Gardner** becomes the first player to sign a contract with the NHL's expansion Columbus Blue Jackets. Gardner set an NCAA Division I record by posting 12 shutouts in his senior season, four more than the previous record.

TRANSITIONS

1964 – **Barry Kramer** of NYU is selected with the seventh pick overall in the NBA draft by the San Francisco Warriors.

A STAR IS BORN

1903 – **Joey Sangor** (lightweight boxer)
1907 – **Milt Galatzer** (Cleveland Indians, Cincinnati Reds outfielder)
1919 – **Cy Block** (Chicago Cubs infielder)
1924 – **Sam Fox** (Ohio State football, New York Giants)
1970 – **Joanna Zeiger** (triathlete)

MAY 5

GAMEBREAKERS

2004 – **Woody Cliffords'** RBI single in the bottom of the ninth gives the Bowie Baysox a 1-0 victory over the Erie Sea Wolves in the second game of an Eastern League doubleheader. **Phil Avlas** hits three doubles as the Lancaster JetHawks defeat the Rancho Cucamonga Quakes 10-5 in the California League.

MAZEL TOUGH

1911 – **Young Joseph Aschel** of England wins a 15-round decision over Robert Eustache in Paris to capture the European welterweight title.
1925 – **Sid Terris** wins a 15-round decision over Johnny Dundee in the final boxing match at the original Madison Square Garden.
1928 – **George Gulack** finishes first on flying rings at the AAU Gymnastics Championships in Union City, N.J.
1941 – **Miltie Kessler** knocks out Jack Leves just 30 seconds into the first round of a welterweight fight in New York.
1973 – After finishing first on pommel horse and parallel bars, **Marshall Avener** wins the U.S. Gymnastics Championships all-around title at Penn State.
1974 – **Alexandra Meyerzon** wins the 100-meter butterfly in a Soviet-record 1:05.7 at the USSR National Swimming Championships.
1985 – **Amy Alcott** finishes four strokes ahead of four other golfers to win the LPGA Moss Creek Women's Invitational in Hilton Head Island, S.C.
2000 – **Michelle Feldman** beats Carolyn Dorin-Ballard 218-214 in the Greater San Diego Open bowling tournament.
2002 – **Joanna Zeiger** wins the St. Croix Half-Ironman Triathlon in the Virgin Islands for the third straight year. She finishes the 2K swim, 90K bike ride, and 21K run in 4 hours, 43 minutes, 2 seconds.

Marshall Avener
(U.S. Olympic Committee)

JEWS ON FIRST

1930 – Cleveland Indians shortstop **Jonah Goldman** hits a solo homer off Milt Gaston in an 18-3 loss to the Boston Red Sox – his only home run in 148 major-league games.
1951 – Brooklyn Dodgers outfielder **Cal Abrams** hits his first of 32 career home runs off John Blackburn in a 12-8 victory over the Cincinnati Reds.

TRANSITIONS

1997 – The Philadelphia 76ers hire **Larry Brown** as the 17th head coach in franchise history.

A STAR IS BORN

1886 – **Edward Siskind** (Fordham football)
1976 – **Juan Pablo Sorin** (Argentine soccer)
1980 – **Yossi Benayoun** (Israeli soccer)

MAY 6

GAMEBREAKERS

1939 – **Harry Danning** drives in three runs with a homer, double, and two singles as the New York Giants beat the St. Louis Cardinals 6-2.

1940 – **Hank Greenberg** hits a homer and two doubles – the second breaking a ninth-inning tie and giving the Detroit Tigers a 6-4 win over the New York Yankees.

1941 – **Phil Weintraub** smacks two home runs as the Los Angeles Angels beat the Hollywood Stars 8-6 in the Pacific Coast League.

1945 – **Phil Weintraub** and Ernie Lombardi hit back-to-back homers in the ninth inning to give the New York Giants a 4-3 victory over the Milwaukee Braves.

2000 – **Mark Williams** records 10 kills, including the championship clincher, as UCLA beats Ohio State 15-8, 15-10, 17-15 in the NCAA volleyball final.

2004 – **Shawn Green** hits a pair of home runs, including a three-run shot in the first inning, as the Los Angeles Dodgers defeat the Florida Marlins 9-3.

MAZEL TOUGH

1789 – **Daniel Mendoza** beats Richard Humphries in a fight that lasts 52 minutes in Stilton, England.

1823 – **Barney Aaron** of England beats Ned Stockton in a 40-round fight in Blindlow Heath.

1962 – **Willie Harmatz** rides Cadiz to victory in the Californian Handicap at Hollywood Park.

1969 – After giving up a run in the third inning of a 7-1, six-hit victory over the Los Angeles Dodgers, Chicago Cubs pitcher **Ken Holtzman** begins a streak of 33 2/3 scoreless innings.

1973 – **Jody Scheckter** of South Africa wins his first of four consecutive Formula 5000 races at Laguna Seca Raceway in Monterrey, Calif., part of a nine-race series sponsored by the Sports Car Club of America.

1978 – **Sharon Shapiro** wins the vault at the U.S. Gymnastics Federation Women's Championships in Uniondale, N.Y.

1995 – **Dana Rosenblatt** knocks out Chad Parker in the first round to retain his WBC Continental Americas middleweight title in Las Vegas.

2001 – **Bruce Fleisher** beats runner-up John Bland by three strokes to win his third straight Home Depot Invitational senior golf tournament title in Charlotte, N.C.

JEWS ON FIRST

1933 – **Hank Greenberg** makes his first start for Detroit and hits an eighth-inning homer off Earl Whitehill – his first of 331 career round-trippers – in the Tigers' 6-2 loss to the Washington Senators. Earlier in the game, Washington second baseman **Buddy Myer** is carried off the field after being hit by a pitch from Whit Wyatt.

TRANSITIONS

1986 – **Red Holzman** is elected to the Basketball Hall of Fame.

1994 – The NFL approves the transfer of the Philadelphia Eagles from **Norman Braman** to **Jeffrey Lurie.**

1996 – **Nancy Lieberman** is enshrined in the Basketball Hall of Fame.

A STAR IS BORN

1912 – **Ellen Preiss** (Austrian fencer)

MAY 7

GAMEBREAKERS

1927 – Goals by **Max Gold** and **Reszo Nickolsburger** give Hakoah Vienna a 2-0 victory over the Peel Cup All-Stars at Soldiers Field in Chicago, the first win on the team's second soccer tour of the United States.

1960 – Pitcher **Larry Sherry** and catcher **Norm Sherry** of the Dodgers become the 10th brothers' battery in major-league history. Larry is the winning pitcher in relief when Norm hits an 11th-inning home run – his first of 18 career round-trippers – off Ruben Gomez to beat Philadelphia 3-2 in Los Angeles.

1979 – **Jeff Stember** allows four singles as the Cedar Rapids Giants beat the Waterloo Indians 6-0 in a Midwest League game.

STRONG IN DEFEAT

1940 – **Harry Danning** hits two homers and a single, but the New York Giants lose to the Cincinnati Reds 7-6.

MAZEL TOUGH

1949 – **Vic Hershkowitz** of Brooklyn defeats Walter Plekan of Buffalo 21-18, 16-21, 21-12 to win the four-wall title at the national AAU handball championships in New York. Hershkowitz becomes the first to win both one-wall and four-wall titles in the same year. **Fred Lewis** and **Sam Haber** win the doubles title with a 21-13, 21-9 victory over Henry Herz and **Marshall Lehrer**.

1978 – **Tom Okker** teams with Wojtek Fibak to defeat Bob Lutz and Stan Smith 6-7, 6-4, 6-0, 6-3 in the finals of the WCT Doubles tennis tournament in Kansas City.

2000 – **Bruce Fleisher** wins the PGA Seniors Home Depot Invitational for the second year in a row in Charlotte, N.C., sinking a birdie putt on the third playoff hole against Hubert Green.

2000 – **Tomas Scheckter** wins from the pole position, edging series points leader Antonio Pizzonia of Brazil by 0.2 seconds at Donington Park for his second straight British Formula 3 victory.

2004 – **Jo Ankier** wins the 2,000 steeplechase in a meet-record 6 minutes, 52 seconds at the British Universities Outdoors Track and Field Championships at Gateshead.

2005 – **Jillian Schwartz** clears 14 feet, 11 inches to win the pole vault at the Modesto Relays.

2006 – Connecticut freshman **Jessica Foreman** wins the 100-meter dash in 11.63 seconds at the Big East Conference outdoor track and field championships.

TRANSITIONS

1923 – Phillies pitcher **Phil "Lefty" Weinert** knocks down Giants batter Casey Stengel in the fourth inning – two innings after hitting him with a pitch. Stengel throws his bat at Weinert and attacks the pitcher. Police escort Stengel from the field and the National League suspends him for 10 days.

1941 – **Hank Greenberg** hits two homers in his final game before entering the army and becoming the first active player to join the military in World War II. He is discharged on Dec. 5, two days before the attack on Pearl Harbor, and then re-enlists in the Army Air Corps.

A STAR IS BORN

1898 – **Mac Baker** (NYU basketball)
1908 – **Syd Cohen** (Washington Senators pitcher)

MAY 8

GAMEBREAKERS

1930 – **Andy Cohen** hits two homers and a triple and drives in five runs as the Newark Bears beat the Buffalo Bison in the International League.

1941 – **Sid Gordon** hits back-to-back triples – one driving in two runs in the 14th inning – as the Jersey City Giants beat Toronto 5-4 in the International League.

1951 – **Sid Gordon's** home run in the bottom of the ninth gives the Boston Braves a 2-1 win over the Cincinnati Reds.

1954 – **Marv Rotblatt** of Charleston blanks the Indianapolis Indians 6-0 on five hits in an American Association game.

1998 – **Sara Whalen** scores her first international goal as the United States beats Iceland 6-0 in soccer.

MAZEL TOUGH

1886 – **Lon Myers** beats W.G. George of England by six yards in a 1,160-yard match race at Madison Square Garden. Each athlete had previously won once in a series of three head-to-head races to determine the world's best middle-distance runner.

1919 – **Sam Seeman** (108 pounds), **David Rosenberg** (145), and **Al Silverstein** (158) win New York State Amateur boxing titles. Seeman and Silverstein win on second-round knockouts.

1930 – **Karoly Karpati** of Hungary wins the 66-kg. freestyle wrestling title at the European Championships in Brussels.

1934 – **William Steiner** wins the AAU Metropolitan Marathon in New York for the second time in three years.

1949 – **Vic Hershkowitz** beats Walter Plekan 21-18, 16-21, 21-12 to win the national four-wall handball title in New York.

1954 – The second Asian Games end in Manila, Phillipines. **Yoab Raanan** of Israel wins a gold medal in men's 3-meter springboard diving and a silver in 10-meter platform div

ing. **Ahuna Kraus** of Israel wins the women's high jump.

1954 – **Martin Engel** of NYU wins the hammer throw at 172 feet, 4 inches at the Metropolitan Intercollegiate Track and Field Association meet. All other events are rained out.

1970 – **Red Holzman** coaches the New York Knicks to his first of two NBA championships. The Knicks beat the Los Angeles Lakers 113-99 in the seventh and deciding game.

1998 – **Kenny Bernstein** beats Larry Dixon in the Top Fuel final at the NHRA Gatornationals.

2003 – **Joe Mendel** of Connecticut wins the 400-meter run in 46.10 seconds at the IC4A Championships at Princeton.

2005 – Maccabi Tel Aviv defeats Tau Ceramica of Spain 90-78 in Moscow to win its second straight Euroleague basketball championship and fifth overall.

RECORD SETTERS

1926 – **Lillian Copeland** sets a world record of 35.26 meters in the javelin.

1932 – **Jadwiga Wajsowna** of Poland breaks the world discus record with a toss of 39.76 meters in Lodz, Poland. She will improve her record nine more times.

TRANSITIONS

2003 – Goalie **Arnie Mausser**, who played for eight North American Soccer League teams, is elected to the National Soccer Hall of Fame.

A STAR IS BORN

1950 – **Lloyd Allen** (Texas Rangers, California Angels, Chicago White Sox pitcher)
1968 – **Mickael Madar** (French soccer)

MAY 9

GAMEBREAKERS

1926 – **Max Gruenwald** scores three goals as Hakoah Vienna's soccer team defeats the Sparta Club of Chicago 6-1 at White Sox Park.

1943 – In his first major-league game, **Eddie Turchin** enters as a defensive replacement at shortstop in the ninth inning and goes 2 for 2, including a game-winning single in the 13th inning as the Cleveland Indians beat the St. Louis Browns 6-5. Turchin's RBI is his only one in 11 major-league games.

1945 – Third baseman **Saul Rogovin**, a future major-league pitcher, drives in five runs with a triple and two singles as Chattanooga beats Little Rock 15-6 in the Southern Association.

1949 – **Hilty Shapiro's** 400-foot, two-run homer in the bottom of the ninth gives CCNY a 10-8 win over Fordham.

1997 – **Jordan Cila** scores a hat trick as the United States defeats El Salvador 6-1 in the first round of the U-17 CONCACAF soccer tournament.

2007 – **Jason Marquis** pitches his second career shutout and fourth complete game, allowing three hits in the Chicago Cubs' 1-0 victory over the Pittsburgh Pirates. He retires the first 16 batters he faces and wins his fifth straight decision.

MAZEL TOUGH

1936 – **Milton Green** of Harvard wins the 110 high hurdles in regional pre-Olympic qualifying, but chooses to boycott the national trials to protest the 1936 Games scheduled to be held in Germany. His roommate, **Norman Cahners**, also qualifies for the Olympics and decides to boycott the event.

1948 – **Herman Barron** finishes at plus-38, six points ahead of runner-up Bobby Locke, to win the Goodell Round Robin Invitational Golf Tournament in New Rochelle, N.Y.

1964 – **Ron Barak** wins the horizontal bars at the AAU Gymnastics Championships in Kings Point, N.Y.

1969 – **Tom Okker** wins the first pro tennis tournament in Japan.

2002 – **Deena Drossin** becomes the first female runner to win three straight national 15-kilometer titles at the Gate River Run in Jacksonville, Fla.

2006 – Yale junior first baseman **Marc Sawyer**, who batted .378, is named Ivy League baseball Player of the Year. Harvard freshman pitcher **Adam Cole** is named co-Rookie of the Year.

JEWS ON FIRST

1871 – A 25-year-old **Lipman Pike** becomes the first Jewish major-league baseball player when he debuts with the Troy Haymakers in a 9-5 loss to the Boston Red Stockings.

1908 – **Albert Rosenfeld** plays wing for Australia in the first Rugby League international test ever played in his country – an 11-10 loss to New Zealand.

1927 – Light-hitting White Sox shortstop **Moe Berg** volunteers to catch for the first time when two Chicago backstops are injured. Chicago beats the New York Yankees 2-1 in 10 innings, and Berg extends his major-league career for 12 years as a backup catcher.

RECORD SETTERS

1951 – Hungarian swimmer **Eva Szekely** sets a world record of 1:16.9 in the 100 breaststroke in Moscow.

A STAR IS BORN

1908 – **Art Dorfman** (Boston U. and pro football)

1909 – **Julia Jones** (fencing)

1919 – **Julius Heldman** (tennis)

MAY 10

GAMEBREAKERS

1958 – **Don Taussig's** two-run single in the ninth inning gives the San Francisco Giants a 3-2 victory over the Los Angeles Dodgers.

1965 – **Mike Epstein** hits two home runs and drives in five runs as Stockton defeats Fresno 15-8 in the California League.

MAZEL TOUGH

1927 – **George Fields** returns from a broken collarbone and rides Princess Tina to a five-length victory in the Rosedale Stakes at Jamaica Downs.

1931 – **Sy Alexander** defeats Ben Yedlin to win the National AAU one-wall handball championship.

1936 – **Joseph Goldenburg** finishes first on the flying rings at the AAU National Gymnastics Championships. He also wins the event in 1939 and 1941.

1941 – **Pearl Perkins Nightingale** wins her second of three National AAU women's gymnastics all-around titles in Union City, N.J. She also finishes first in vault and parallel bars.

1956 – **Pierre Darmon** scores his first of a French-record 47 victories in Davis Cup tennis competition, beating Martin Froesch of Switzerland 11-9, 1-6, 6-2, 6-8, 6-2 in the second round of European Zone play.

1958 – **Arthur Shurlock** finishes first on the pommel horse at the AAU gymnastics championships in San Fernando, Calif.

1960 – **Suzy Kormoczy** of Hungary defeats Ann Haydon of Great Britain 6-3, 4-6, 6-1 in the final of the Italian Championships clay-court tennis tournament in Rome.

1973 – **Red Holzman's** New York Knicks win their second NBA title in four years, beating the Los Angeles Lakers 102-93 for a 4-1 series win.

1981 – **Amy Alcott** finishes one stroke ahead of Sally Little to win the LPGA Lady Michelob Classic in Roswell, Ga.

1997 – **George Weissfisch** wins the heavyweight gold medal at the U.S. National Taekwondo Championships in Oakland.

RECORD SETTERS

1960 – Baltimore Orioles catcher **Joe Ginsberg**, struggling to handle Hoyt Wilhelm's knuckleball, allows three passed balls in one inning to tie the record set six days earlier by teammate Gus Triandos.

TRANSITIONS

1948 – The New York Knicks of the BAA draft **Dolph Schayes** with the fourth pick overall, then send his rights to the Syracuse Nationals. Schayes also is drafted by the Tri-City Blackhawks of the NBL. **Phil Farbman** of CCNY is selected in the first round by the Philadelphia Warriors.

2001 – Former major-leaguer **Steve Hertz** posts his 600th career coaching victory as Miami-Dade Community College beats Daytona Beach CC 9-0 in the NJCAA Gulf District baseball championship game.

A STAR IS BORN

1924 – **William Stein** (Georgia Tech football)

1959 – **Danny Schayes** (Syracuse basketball, Utah Jazz, Denver Nuggets, Milwaukee Bucks, Los Angeles Lakers, Phoenix Suns, Miami Heat, and Orlando Magic)

MAY 11

GAMEBREAKERS

1952 – **Saul Rogovin** makes his first relief appearance for the Chicago White Sox, entering in the seventh inning to preserve a 6-5 victory over the Detroit Tigers, his former team. Rogovin works out of a no-out, bases-loaded situation in the eighth.

1952 – **Lou Limmer** homers in both games as the Ottawa A's sweep Rochester 9-5 and 7-3 in the International League.

1963 – **Sandy Koufax** pitches his second career no-hitter, beating the San Francisco Giants 8-0. He retires the first 25 batters before walking Ed Bailey on a 3-2 pitch with one out in the ninth inning, then gets Harvey Kuenn to bounce back to the mound for the start of a game-ending double play.

1969 – **Ken Holtzman** of the Chicago Cubs pitches his first of three consecutive shutouts, blanking the San Francisco Giants 8-0 on nine hits.

1988 – **Eli Ohana** of Israel assists on the only goal as KV Mechelen of Belgium upsets defending champion AFC Ajax of The Netherlands 1-0 in the final of the Cup Winners Cup soccer tournament in Strasbourg.

MAZEL TOUGH

1906 – **Abe Attell** fights Kid Herman to a 20-round draw in Los Angeles to retain his world featherweight title.

1958 – New York Hakoah clinches the American Soccer League title.

RECORD SETTERS

1986 – In a race that began April 26, **Stu Mittleman** sets an unofficial world record of 11 days, 20 hours, 36 minutes, 50 seconds in a 1,000-mile run in Queens, N.Y. The record is not recognized because the length of the course cannot be verified.

JEWS ON FIRST

2002 – Atlanta Braves pitcher **Jason Marquis**, in his first game back from the disabled list, hits his first career home run off Brian Lawrence in a 5-1 victory over the San Diego Padres. Marquis allows three hits and strikes out five batters.

A STAR IS BORN

1922 – **Thelma "Tiby" Eisen** (baseball)
1937 – **Ildiko Rejto** (Hungarian fencer)

MAY 12

GAMEBREAKERS

1938 – **Buddy Myer** drives in four runs with a homer and two singles as the Washington Senators defeat the Detroit Tigers 7-6. **Hank Greenberg** hits a three-run homer for Detroit.

1946 – **Emil Moscowitz** and winning pitcher **Sam Nahem** combine on the shutout as the semi-pro Bushwicks of Brooklyn defeat the Freeport (L.I.) Gulls 2-0.

1950 – **Al Rosen's** three-run homer in the first inning sparks the Cleveland Indians to a 5-1 victory over the Chicago White Sox.

1975 – **Ken Holtzman** pitches a six-hitter and goes 3-for-4 at the plate as the Chicago Cubs beat the Houston Astros 2-0.

STRONG IN DEFEAT

1937 – **Hank Greenberg** homers over the center-field wall at Fenway Park, but the Tigers lose to the Red Sox 11-9.

MAZEL TOUGH

1934 – **Harry Goldstein** wins the singles title and **Dave Margolis** and **Danny Levinson** defeat **Sy Alexander** and **Jack Londin** to win the doubles crown at the National AAU one-wall handball championships.

1956 – **Arnold Blum** defeats Doug Sanders 1-up over 36 holes in the final of the 50th annual Southern Amateur golf championship in Atlanta. Blum also won the title in 1951.

1957 – **Vic Hershkowitz** retains his AAU one-wall handball title in Brooklyn, N.Y.

1984 – **Mitch Gaylord** wins the U.S. Gymnastics Federation all-around championship in Evanston, Ill.

2006 – **Clara Horowitz** of Duke wins the 10,000-meter run at the IC4A-ECAC outdoor meet at Princeton in 34 minutes, 26.98 seconds.

RECORD SETTERS

1934 – **Gerda Gottlieb** of Austria sets a women's world record of 4 feet, 4 inches in the standing high jump.

JEWS ON FIRST

1963 – **Art Shamsky** becomes the first player to hit a home run completely out of Westgate Park in San Diego in a Pacific Coast League game against Portland.

TRANSITIONS

1939 – Minneapolis Millers second baseman **Andy Cohen** gets his first full-time managing job when the Brooklyn Dodgers name him skipper of the last-place Pine Bluff Judges in the Cotton States League.

1998 – Tennessee second baseman **Jeff Pickler** is named Southeastern Conference baseball player of the year. He leads the conference in hitting (.445), hits (109), and doubles (30), and hits safely in 50 of 56 games.

A STAR IS BORN

1905 – **George Gulack** (gymnastics)

Mitch Gaylord
(U.S. Olympic Committee)

MAY 13

GAMEBREAKERS

1951 – **Al Rosen** hits a grand slam home run to help the Cleveland Indians beat the Chicago White Sox 11-2 in the first game of a doubleheader. Chicago's **Marv Rotblatt** pitches two scoreless innings of relief and starts a ninth-inning triple play by snaring a pop-fly bunt by Jim Hegan a few inches off the ground.

1965 – **Sandy Koufax** allows three hits and strikes out 13 as the Dodgers beat the Houston Astros 3-0.

1978 – **Larry Goldetsky,** the No. 9 hitter in Memphis' lineup, hits a grand slam homer and a two-run double in the Chicks' 12-7 victory over Knoxville in the Southern League.

2004 – **Tony Schrager** goes 3 for 3 with two home runs including a grand slam and five RBI's as the Pawtucket Red Sox defeat the Charlotte Knights 7-4 in the International League.

STRONG IN DEFEAT

1979 – **Joel Kramer** comes off the bench to replace Phoenix's injured starting center and scores 19 points in Game 6 of the Western Conference finals, but the Suns lose to the Seattle SuperSonics 106-105.

MAZEL TOUGH

1974 – **Steve Lieberman** of Arizona State captures the U.S. Intercollegiate Archery Championship for the third time in four years.

1979 – **Jody Scheckter** outraces Jacques Laffite and wins the Formula One Belgian Grand Prix in Zolder, Belgium.

1984 – **Amy Alcott** beats Cathy Marino by two strokes to win the LPGA United Virginia Bank Classic in Portsmouth, Va., for the second time.

1990 – **Riccardo Patrese** ends a seven-year victory drought on the Formula One racing circuit, beating Gerhard Berger in the San Marino Grand Prix at Imola.

2000 – **Igor Praporshchikov** of Australia wins the 85-kg. freestyle wrestling title at the Oceania Championships in Melbourne.

2001 – Maccabi Tel Aviv beats Panathinakos of Athens 81-67 in Paris to win its third European basketball championship, and first in 20 years.

2004 – Michigan freshman **Eric Tannenbaum** defeats Ron Tarquinnio of Pittsburgh 7-4 in the final bout to finish 5-0 and capture the 145.5-pound title at the University National Freestyle Wrestling Championships in Evanston, Ill.

RECORD SETTERS

1950 – **Frank Spellman** sets a national AAU middleweight lifting record of 261.75 pounds in the clean and press in Philadelphia.

A STAR IS BORN

1903 – **George Abramson** (Minnesota football, Green Bay Packers)

1922 – **Gladys Heldman** (tennis)

1972 – **Josh Taves** (Northeastern football, Oakland Raiders, Carolina Panthers defensive lineman)

1977 – **Sara DeCosta** (hockey goalie)

Frank Spellman (*U.S. Olympic Committee*)

MAY 14

GAMEBREAKERS

1972 – **Richie Scheinblum's** three-run homer in the fifth inning helps the Kansas City Royals end a five-game losing streak with an 8-4 win over the Cleveland Indians in the second game of a doubleheader.

1989 – **Steve Rosenberg** allows one hit in three innings of relief and earns his first of six career victories as the Chicago White Sox beat the Baltimore Orioles 8-5.

MAZEL TOUGH

1792 – **Danny Mendoza** defeats former sparring partner Bill Warr in 12 rounds in Croydon, England, and gains recognition as undisputed champion of the London Prize Ring.

1930 – **Max Shimon** defeats Joseph Hall to win the National Amateur Three-Cushion billiards championship.

1936 – **Izzy Richter** of Penn State wins the heavyweight title at the Intercollegiate Boxing Championships.

1961 – **Paul Cranis** beats defending champion Bobby Riggs 6-4, 6-8, 6-4 to win the National Paddle Tennis championship.

1975 – **Arnie Mausser** stops three penalty shots in overtime as the Hartford Bicentennials beat the New York Cosmos 2-1 in the North American Soccer League.

1984 – **Martin Jaite** defeats Ivan Kley 6-2, 6-4 to win a Challenger tennis tournament in Curitiba, Brazil.

1989 – **Jay Berger** beats Lawson Duncan 6-4, 6-3 in the final of a clay-court tennis tournament in Charleston, s.c.

2002 – **Kenny Bernstein**, in his final season of NHRA competition, beats Tony Schumacher in the Top Fuel final of the O'Reilly Nationals in Baytown, Texas.

2006 – **Shahar Peer** of Israel defeats Samantha Stosur of Australia 4-6, 6-2, 6-1 to win the ECM Prague Open tennis tournament, her second victory on the WTA tour and first on clay. Peer also teams with Marion Bartoli of France to win the doubles.

RECORD SETTERS

1948 – **Frank Spellman** sets an American record of 260 pounds in the press en route to a first-place finish in the 165-pound division at the AAU WeightliftingChampionships in Los Angeles.

JEWS ON FIRST

1995 – **Shawn Green** hits his first major-league homer off Cal Eldred as the Toronto Blue Jays beat the Milwaukee Brewers 8-3.

A STAR IS BORN

1913 – **Sam Renick** (jockey)
1915 – **Sammy Luftspring** (Canadian welterweight boxer)

Richie Scheinblum *(California Angels)*

MAY 15

GAMEBREAKERS

1945 – **Phil Weintraub's** sixth-inning homer breaks a 4-4 tie as the New York Giants earn a 5-4 win over the Chicago Cubs.

1953 – **Sid Gordon's** two-run homer in the eighth inning gives the Milwaukee Braves a 4-3 win over the Pittsburgh Pirates.

2002 – **Gabe Kapler** goes 4-for-4 as the Texas Rangers beat the Chicago White Sox 5-2.

STRONG IN DEFEAT

1942 – Despite scoring the only knockdown and winning 11 of the 15 rounds on the referee's scorecard, **Allie Stolz** loses a split decision to Sammy Angott in a lightweight title fight. There is post-fight speculation that the two judges who picked Angott were bribed by organized crime.

MAZEL TOUGH

1908 – **Phillip Schlossberg** of the USS New Jersey knocks out Beany Stauffner in the second round of a scheduled six-round fight to win the United States Navy heavyweight boxing title in San Francisco.

1955 – **Henry Laskau** wins the AAU 10-kilometer racewalking title in Staten Island, N.Y.

1971 – **Felix Brami** of Tunisia wins a 12-round decision over Kouider Meftah in Blois, France, to win the French featherweight boxing title.

RECORD SETTERS

1926 – **Lillian Copeland** sets an American record of 103-5½ in the discus.

JEWS ON FIRST

2004 – **Kevin Youkilis** becomes the seventh player in Boston Red Sox history to hit a home run in his first major-league game, going deep against Pat Hentgen in the fourth inning of a 4-0 victory over the Toronto Blue Jays. Youkilis also singles in the sixth.

TRANSITIONS

1995 – **Alex Gomelsky**, former coach of the Soviet Union national team, and NBA referee **Earl Strom** are elected to the Basketball Hall of Fame.

A STAR IS BORN

1879 – **William Bacharach** (swimming)

1893 – **Sam Fishburn** (St. Louis Cardinals infielder)

1901 – **Dave Rosenberg** (middleweight boxer)

1918 – **Johnny Siegal** (Columbia football, Chicago Bears end)

1954 – **Andrea Gyarmati** (swimming)

MAY 16

GAMEBREAKERS

1957 – **Larry Sherry** pitches a four-hitter as Fort Worth beats the Austin Senators 3-0 in a Texas League game.

1957 – **Sandy Koufax** allows four hits and strikes out 13 as the Los Angeles Dodgers beat the Chicago Cubs 3-2.

1969 – Chicago Cubs pitcher **Ken Holtzman** pitches his second straight shutout, blanking the Houston Astros 11-0 on three hits.

2006 – **Shawn Green's** third hit of the game, a two-out RBI single in the 15th inning, gives the Arizona Diamondbacks a 6-5 victory over the San Diego Padres.

STRONG IN DEFEAT

1969 – **Mike Epstein** of the Washington Senators hits three home runs in a 7-6 loss to the Chicago White Sox.

MAZEL TOUGH

1931 – **Julius Seligson** defeats Herbert Bowman in the finals of the Old Dominion tennis tournament in Richmond, Va.

1959 – **Willie Harmatz** rides Royal Orbit to a four-length victory over favorite Sword Dancer in the 85th Preakness in Baltimore, becoming the second Jewish jockey to win the Triple Crown race (**Walter Miller** rode Whimsical to victory in 1906).

1964 – In his first outdoor meet since recovering from a torn elbow muscle, **Gary Gubner** wins his third straight shot put title at the Metropolitan Intercollegiate track championships on Randall Island.

1971 – **Dave Hilton** knocks out Luigi Aprile in the second round to win the Canadian light middleweight title in Quebec City.

1982 – **Shlomo Glickstein** of Israel beats John Sadri 7-6 (7-2), 7-6 (8-6) in the final of the eight-man Bank of Oklahoma Tennis Classic in Tulsa.

1999 – **Sebastian Rothmann** knocks out Earl Morais in the 10th round in Johannesburg to win the vacant South African cruiserweight title.

2001 – Israel beats Bulgaria 5-1 to win the silver medal in its division at the IIHF World Senior Hockey Championships.

2004 – **Ariel Ze'evi** of Israel defeats Anatal Kovacs of Hungary to win his third 100-kg. title in four years at the European Judo Championships in Bucharest, Romania.

TRANSITIONS

1913 – Pittsburgh Pirates outfielder **Eddie Mensor**, who draws only eight walks all year, draws a free pass in the third inning to end Christy Mathewson's streak of 47 innings without issuing a base on balls.

A STAR IS BORN

1941 – **Debra Turner-Marcus** (Israeli track and field)

1978 – **Noam Okun** (Israeli tennis)

Shawn Green *(Toronto Blue Jays)*

MAY 17

GAMEBREAKERS

1909 – **Barney Pelty** of the St. Louis Browns shuts out the Washington Senators 4-0.

1935 – **Buddy Myer** goes 3 for 3 with four RBI's as the Washington Senators beat the Detroit Tigers 10-8.

1939 – **Morrie Arnovich** collects five hits in the Philadelphia Phillies' 7-3 win over the Pittsburgh Pirates.

1954 – **Dave Oliphant** strikes out 16 Johnson City batters as Bristol wins 5-2 in the Appalachian League.

1960 – **Larry Sherry** hits a solo homer in a five-run eighth inning and gets the win in relief as the Los Angeles Dodgers beat the Milwaukee Braves 6-4.

1981 – **Ross Baumgarten** pitches a four-hitter with no walks and four strikeouts as the Chicago White Sox beat the Pittsburgh Pirates 9-0.

STRONG IN DEFEAT

1988 – **Danny Schayes** of the Denver Nuggets scores 33 points in a 110-106 NBA playoff loss to the Dallas Mavericks.

MAZEL TOUGH

1918 – **Ted "Kid" Lewis** wins a 20-round decision over Johnny Tillman in Denver to retain the world welterweight title.

1923 – **Jack Bloomfield** stops Dave Magill in the 13th round in London to retain his British Empire light heavyweight title. **Harry Mason** wins by disqualification over "Seaman" Nobby Hall to win the British lightweight title.

1941 – **Myron Piker** of Northwestern wins the 100 and 220 at the Western Conference track championships in Minneapolis.

1947 – **Bernard Mayer**, **Stanley Lampert**, and **Irv Mondschein** sweep the top three places in the shot put at the Metropolitan Intercollegiate track championships at Triborough Stadium in New York.

1947 – **Hank Greenberg** hits his first home run into "Greenberg Gardens," a wire-enclosed left-field section of Forbes Field, as the Pittsburgh Pirates defeat the Brooklyn Dodgers 4-0.

1970 – **Julie Heldman** defeats Peaches Bartkowicz 6-1, 6-2 to win the Brussels Open tennis tournament in Belgium. **Tom Okker** beats Ilie Nastase 6-3, 6-4, 0-6, 4-6, 6-4 to win the men's title.

1992 – **Kerry Strug** wins the vault at the U.S. Gymnastics Championships in Chicago.

RECORD SETTERS

1958 – **Joel Landau** sets a Harvard school outdoor record of 14.44 seconds in the 110-meter hurdles at the Ivy League Heps meet.

1981 – **James Espir** becomes the first British runner to break 8 minutes in the 3,000 meters, finishing in 7:59.22 in Cwmbran, Wales.

JEWS ON FIRST

1939 – **Bill Stern** does the play-by-play in the first televised baseball game. W2XBS, an experimental station in New York, broadcasts Princeton's 2-1 victory over Columbia in 10 innings.

1975 – In a game against the Taiyo Whales, switch-hitter **Richie Scheinblum** of the Hiroshima Toyo Carp becomes the first player in Japanese League baseball history to hit home runs from both sides of the plate in the same game.

1977 – **Skip Jutze** hits the first grand slam homer in Seattle Mariners history off pitcher Rudy May in the third inning of a 10-2 win over Baltimore at the Kingdome.

A STAR IS BORN

1900 – **Frederick Meyer** (wrestling)

MAY 18

GAMEBREAKERS

1912 – **Harry Kane** pitches a no-hitter as the Marshall Athletics beat the Longview Cannibals 4-0 in the South Central League.

1931 – **Andy Cohen's** two-run homer in the eighth inning helps the Newark Bears beat the Buffalo Bison 4-1 in the International League.

1935 – **Buddy Myer** hits a tie-breaking three-run double in the eighth inning to give the Washington Senators a 10-8 win over the Detroit Tigers.

1940 – **Harry Danning's** bases-loaded single – his third hit of the game – gives the New York Giants a 6-4 win over the Chicago Cubs.

2003 – **Amy Rosson** pitches a four-hitter as Cal-Davis wins the NCAA Division II softball championship with a 4-0 victory over Georgia College & State in Salem, Ore.

MAZEL TOUGH

1910 – Welterweight boxer **Harry Lewis** takes on three opponents in Paris, knocking out Bert Roper in one round and Bob Davis in two rounds, and winning in the second round by disqualification over Bob Scanlon.

1952 – **Vic Hershkowitz** defeats **Irving Kirzner** 21-9, 21-20 to capture the AAU one-wall handball championship in Brooklyn, N.Y.

1959 – **Dave Hilton** wins a 12-round decision over Gerry Simpson in Quebec City to win the Canadian featherweight title.

1980 – **Harold Solomon** beats Guillermo Vilas 6-7, 6-2, 6-4, 2-6, 6-3 in the final of the German Open clay-court tennis tournament in Hamburg.

2000 – **Michelle Feldman** beats Kim Adler 242-230 in the final of the Bowl the Rouge Open in Grants Pass, Ore.

2001 – **Arik Ze'evi** beats Ghislain Lemaire of France in the final to win the European judo championship in the men's under-100 kilo division in Paris. He is the first Israeli male to win a title.

2003 – **Joe Mendel** of Connecticut wins the men's 400 meters and **Julie Siebert-Johnson** of Penn captures the women's javelin at the IC4A outdoor track championships in Princeton, N.J.

RECORD SETTERS

1935 – **Herman Neugass** of Tulane sets a Southeastern Conference record of 20.9 seconds in the 220-yard dash and ties the SEC mark of 9.6 seconds in the 100 at the conference championship meet in Birmingham, Ala.

1957 – **David Reisbord** and the Occidental College four-mile relay team set an American record of 16:53.6.

A STAR IS BORN

1917 – **Ralph Kaplowitz** (basketball)

1982 – **Roman Greenberg** (Israeli heavyweight boxer)

MAY 19

GAMEBREAKERS

1925 – **Moe Berg** collects five hits, including a game-winning triple, as the Reading (Pa.) Keys beat Jersey City in an International League game.

1954 – **Al Rosen** of Cleveland homers in his fifth straight game for the second time in his career as the Indians beat the Boston Red Sox 5-3.

1963 – **Sandy Koufax** pitches a two-hitter as the Los Angeles Dodgers beat the New York Mets 1-0.

1966 – **Sandy Koufax** pitches a three-hitter with 10 strikeouts in the Dodgers' 4-0 victory over the San Francisco Giants.

1985 – Goalie **Arnie Mausser** posts the shutout as the United States men's soccer team defeats Trinidad & Tobago 1-0 in a World Cup qualifier in Torrance, Calif.

STRONG IN DEFEAT

1951 – **Al Rosen's** second grand slam homer in six days gives Cleveland all its runs in a 9-4 loss to the Boston Red Sox.

MAZEL TOUGH

1957 – **Herb Flam** wins the Count of Godo tennis tournament in Barcelona, Spain.

1957 – **Henry Laskau** wins the 10-kilometer AAU racewalking title in New York.

1968 – **Tom Okker** defeats Bob Hewitt 10-8, 6-8, 6-1 to win the Italian National tennis tournament in Rome.

1963 – **Kenny Davidoff** beats Oscar Obert 21-9, 21-6 to win the National AAU one-wall handball championship in Brooklyn, N.Y.

2002 – **Kenny Bernstein** beats Larry Dixon in the Top Fuel final at the NHRA Matco Tools SuperNationals in Englishtown, N.J. The victory, his 63rd overall, raises his career record to 7-0 in finals at Old Bridge Township Raceway Park.

2002 – **Yulia Beygelzimer** defeats Alena Vaskova 2-6, 6-3, 6-3 to win an ITF tennis tournament in Szczecin, Poland.

2007 – Second-seeded **Paul Goldstein** wins a USTA clay-court tennis tournament in Forest Hills, N.Y., when fifth seed Adrian Garcia of Chile is unable to compete in the final.

RECORD SETTERS

1939 – **Eddie Feinberg** of the Phillies ties a major-league record for shortstops with no fielding chances in a 12-inning game against Cincinnati. But the career .184 hitter does get two hits in Philadelphia's 4-3 victory.

A STAR IS BORN

1928 – **Dolph Schayes** (NYU basketball, Syracuse Nationals)

MAY 20

GAMEBREAKERS

1930 – **Mort Wilner's** RBI single in the 10th inning gives Penn a 7-6 win over Lafayette.

1948 – Miami Beach player-manager **Harry Chozen** hits a grand slam home run as the Flamingos defeat the Havana Cubans 7-6 in the Florida International League.

1969 – **Ken Holtzman** of the Chicago Cubs stops the Los Angeles Dodgers 7-0 on five hits for his third straight shutout. He pitches 27 consecutive scoreless innings over four games before the San Diego Padres score in the first inning of his next start.

MAZEL TOUGH

1939 – **Myron Piker** of Northwestern wins his first of three straight 100-yard dash titles at the Western (Big Ten) Conference track and field championships in Ann Arbor, Mich.

1944 – **Norman Wasser** of NYU wins the shot put and **Arthur Greenberg** of Rhode Island State captures the hammer throw at the IC4A outdoor championships in Philadelphia.

1973 – **Brian Gottfried** beats Arthur Ashe 6-1, 6-3 to win the Alan King Classic hardcourt tournament in Las Vegas, his first of 16 singles titles on the men's tennis tour.

1973 – **Jody Scheckter** wins a Formula 5000 auto race at Michigan International Speedway.

2000 – **Danny Chocron** of Venezuela wins the 5-kilometer Open Water National Swimming Championship for the second time, covering the 4-mile distance from Pensacola to Gulf Breeze in 1 hour, 2 minutes, 11 seconds.

2001 – **Danielle Sanderson** of England wins the National 100-kilometer championship run in 8 hours, 17 minutes.

2004 – **Arik Ze'evi** of Israel defends his under-100 kg title at the European Judo Championships in Bucharest, Romania. Ze'evi also won the title in 2001 and 2003. **Yoel Rozbozov** wins the silver medal in under-73 kg.

JEWS ON FIRST

1956 – UCLA sophomore **Jimmy Jacobs** becomes the first to win three major four-wall handball titles in one year when he defeats John Sloan of Chicago 21-14, 21-7 in the national AAU tournament in New York. Jacobs previously captured the national YMCA and U.S. Handball Association championships.

1965 – Nine-year-old **Beverly Klass** becomes the youngest pro on the LPGA Tour when she plays in the Dallas Civitan Open.

TRANSITIONS

1973 – In the only instance in which one Jewish major-league baseball player is traded for another, the Texas Rangers send **Mike Epstein**, Rich Hand, and Rick Stelmaszek to the California Angels for **Lloyd Allen** and Jim Spencer.

2004 – **Mathieu Schneider** of the Detroit Red Wings and **Jeff Halpern** of the Washington Capitals are selected for the 26-player Team USA which will compete in the World Cup of Hockey in September.

A STAR IS BORN

1894 – **Augie Ratner** (middleweight boxer)

MAY 21

GAMEBREAKERS

1924 – **Max Gruenwald** scores two goals as Austria's national soccer team defeats Bulgaria 6-0 in Vienna.

1960 – Goalie **Howard Krongard** scores an unassisted goal to start the scoring, and Princeton wins its fourth straight Ivy League lacrosse championship with a 6-5 victory over Cornell.

1973 – **Zvi Rozen** scores two goals as Israel defeats Thailand 6-0 in a World Cup soccer qualifier in South Korea.

2000 – **Shawn Green** of the Dodgers hits a grand slam homer with two out in the ninth inning – one of a record six grand slams hit in the major leagues that day – as Los Angeles beats the Florida Marlins 12-3.

2004 – **Jeff Pickler** hits a leadoff single in the bottom of the 12th and **Dave Newhan** follows with an RBI double to give the Oklahoma City Redhawks a 4-3 victory over the Salt Lake Stingers in the Pacific Coast League.

STRONG IN DEFEAT

2002 – **Shawn Green** hits two solo homers for the Dodgers, but the Milwaukee Brewers score eight runs in the eighth inning to beat Los Angeles 8-6.

MAZEL TOUGH

1806 – In his final fight, 43-year-old English heavyweight **Daniel Mendoza** stops Harry Lee in the 53rd round in Farnsborough.

1925 – **Jackie "Kid" Berg** knocks out **Ted "Kid" Lewis** in the 10th round of a non-title fight in London.

1926 – **Charley Phil Rosenberg** knocks out Canadian bantamweight champion Bobby Ebber in the fifth round in Toronto.

1930 – **Al Foreman** of Canada knocks out Fred Webster in the first round in London to capture the British and British Empire lightweight titles.

1967 – **Pierre Darmon** scores his 47th and final Davis Cup tennis victory, 6-2, 6-2, 6-2 over Istvan Gulgas as France defeats Hungary 5-0 in the European Zone semifinals.

2000 – Stanford graduate **Nicole Freedman** wins the 64-mile U.S. National Cycling Road Race championship and Olympic qualifier with a time of 2 hours, 36 minutes, 56 seconds in Jackson, Miss.

RECORD SETTERS

1955 – **Alvin Frieden** and the University of Texas 4×100 relay team set a world record of 40.2 at the California Relays in Modesto, breaking the mark of 40.5 it tied a year earlier.

JEWS ON FIRST

1912 – **Guy Zinn** of the New York Highlanders hits his first of 15 career home runs off George Mogridge in a 9-8 win over the Chicago White Sox.

1976 – **Alfred Cohen** makes his debut as the home-plate umpire in a game between the Reds and Pirates as an emergency backup. Cohen umpires his second and final National League game the next day.

TRANSITIONS

1992 – **Ron Rothstein** is named head coach of the Detroit Pistons.

A STAR IS BORN

1921 – **Ruth Langer** (Austrian swimmer)
1936 – **Barry Latman** (Chicago White Sox, Cleveland Indians, Houston Astros, and Los Angeles/California Angels pitcher)
1943 – **Ronny Watts** (Wake Forest basketball)
1960 – **Sid Abramowitz** (Air Force and Tulsa football, Baltimore Colts, Seattle Seahawks, New York Jets, Indianapolis Colts tackle)
1972 – **Nicole Freedman** (cycling)

MAY 22

GAMEBREAKERS

1926 – **Heinrich Schoenfeld** scores three goals and **Erno Schwarcz** adds two as Hakoah Vienna beats the Brooklyn Wanderers of the American Soccer League 6-4 at Ebbets Field

1939 – After hitting a three-run homer in the eighth inning, **Jim Levey** steals home in the 11th, and Dallas goes on to defeat Fort Worth 13-11 in the Texas League.

1968 – **Lloyd Allen** pitches a seven-inning no-hitter for Idaho Falls, striking out 13 and walking two in a 1-0 victory over Magic Valley in the Pioneer League.

1980 – **Jeff Stember** pitches a three-hitter as the Shreveport Captains defeat the San Antonio Dodgers 1-0 in the first game of a Texas League doubleheader.

1995 – **Brian Kowitz** hits a 1-2 pitch into right field for a single with two out and the bases loaded in the 10th inning, giving the Richmond Braves a 2-1 victory over the Norfolk Tides in the International League.

2002 – **Shawn Green** hits an RBI triple as the Los Angeles Dodgers beat the Milwaukee Brewers 1-0. Green also throws out a Brewers runner at home to complete a double play.

STRONG IN DEFEAT

1937 – **Hank Greenberg**, batting against Boston pitcher Wes Ferrell, hits the longest home run in Fenway Park history over the center-field wall, just to the right of the flagpole. The Tigers lose 11-9 to the Red Sox.

MAZEL TOUGH

1906 – **Walter Miller** rides Whimsical to victory in the Preakness, held at Gravesend Racetrack in Brooklyn, N.Y. Whimsical is one of only four fillies to ever win the Triple Crown race traditionally held in Baltimore.

1933 – **Al Foreman** of Canada beats Jimmy Kelso on a third-round disqualification in Sydney, Australia, to recapture the British Empire lightweight title.

1937 – **Sam Stoller** of Michigan wins the 100-yard dash in 9.8 seconds at the Western Conference track and field championships in Ann Arbor, Mich.

1938 – **Milton Padway** of Wisconsin wins the pole vault at the Western Conference championships in Columbus, Ohio.

1977 – **Jody Scheckter** beats runner-up Niki Lauda and wins his first of two Formula One Grands Prix of Monaco.

2002 – **Josh Lefkowitz** of Williams College beats Kevin Whipple of Gustavus Adolphus 6-3, 2-6, 6-1 to win the NCAA Division III tennis championship in Santa Cruz, Calif.

2004 – **Anna Smashnova** of Israel defeats Alicia Molik of Australia 6-2, 3-6, 6-3 to win the Vienna Grand Prix clay-court tennis tournament for the second time in three years.

RECORD SETTERS

1980 – **Neil Simons** ties a College World Series record by scoring five runs in Clemson's 22-4 first-round victory over East Tennessee State.

TRANSITIONS

1980 – The Israeli Olympic Committee votes to join the boycott of the Olympic Games in Moscow.

A STAR IS BORN

1968 – **Alan Levine** (Texas Rangers, Chicago White Sox, Anaheim Angels, Detroit Tigers, Kansas City Royals, Tampa Bay Devil Rays, San Francisco Giants pitcher)

MAY 23

GAMEBREAKERS

1907 – **Barney Pelty** of the St. Louis Browns shuts out the Boston Red Sox 6-0.

1911 – **Erskine Mayer** pitches a South Atlantic League no-hitter as the Albany Babies beat the Augusta Tourists 2-0.

1951 – **Hy Cohen** pitches a shutout and executes a successful squeeze bunt as the Des Moines Bruins beat Wichita 2-0 in a Western League game.

1960 – **Sandy Koufax** pitches a one-hitter with 10 strikeouts and six walks as the Dodgers beat the first-place Pittsburgh Pirates 1-0. Pittsburgh's lone hit is a second-inning single by .187 hitter Benny Daniels, who plays in just 10 games that season for the World Champion Pirates.

1969 – Pitching for Fresno of the California League, **Steve Stone** strikes out 19 Lodi batters.

2002 – **Shawn Green** of the Dodgers has one of the best offensive days in baseball history with a single, double, and four home runs in six at-bats as Los Angeles beats the Milwaukee Brewers 16-3. He drives in seven runs, ties a modern major-league record by scoring six times, and sets a record with 19 total bases – one more than Joe Adcock of the Milwaukee Braves had against the Brooklyn Dodgers in 1954. His 450-foot homer with two out in the top of the ninth makes him the 14th player to hit four homers in a game.

MAZEL TOUGH

1936 – **Eddy Litzenberger** rides White Cockade to victory in The Withers Stakes at Aqueduct.

1976 – **Amy Alcott** wins the LPGA Classic in Jamesburg, N.J., by one stroke over runner-up Jane Blalock.

1982 – **Riccardo Patrese** of Italy wins his first of six Formula One races, beating runner-up Didier Pironi in the Grand Prix of Monaco.

1983 – With **Alan Mayer** in goal, the San Diego Sockers beat the Baltimore Blast 3-1 in the fifth and deciding game to win their first Major Indoor Soccer League title.

1997 – **Dawn Buth** and Stephanie Nickitas of Florida defeat Marissa Catlin and Michelle Anderson of Georgia 6-3, 3-6, 6-2 to win the doubles title in Palo Alto, Calif. They are the first two-time champions in NCAA women's tennis history.

2004 – **Adrienne Binder** wins the 800 freestyle in 8:34.53 at the Santa Clara International swimming championships.

RECORD SETTERS

1941 – **Howard Bogrow** and NYU's 2,400-yard relay team set a world track and field record.

1975 – **Boris "Dov" Djerassi** of Northeastern sets an IC4A meet record of 226 feet, 6 inches in the hammer throw.

TRANSITIONS

2001 – **Larry Brown** is named NBA Coach of the Year after leading the Philadelphia 76ers to their best record in 16 seasons. It is the first NBA award for Brown, who was named Coach of the Year in three of his four ABA seasons.

2001 – **Brian Teacher** of UCLA and **Brad Gilbert** of Pepperdine are elected to the Intercollegiate Tennis Association Hall of Fame in Athens, Ga.

2005 – Miami junior third baseman **Ryan Braun** is named Atlantic Coast Conference baseball Player of the Year after hitting .412 with 16 homers, 70 RBI's, and 21 stolen bases during the regular season.

A STAR IS BORN

1911 – **Fred Oberlander** (wrestling)

1969 – **Yelena Shushonova** (Ukraine gymnastics)

MAY 24

GAMEBREAKERS

1911 – **Barney Pelty** of the St. Louis Browns pitches his 21st and final career shutout, blanking the Boston Red Sox 1-0.

1964 – **Bennie Muller** scores his first international soccer goal in The Netherlands' 2-0 victory over Albania.

1971 – **Jerry Feldman** ends a 0-for-22 slump with two doubles and a triple as the Salt Lake City Angels defeat the Spokane Indians 4-1 in the Pacific Coast League.

1972 – **Steve Stone** scatters seven hits as the San Francisco Giants beat the Los Angeles Dodgers 1-0.

1980 – **Jeff Newman** goes 3 for 5 with four RBI's in the Oakland A's 15-7 victory over the Texas Rangers.

STRONG IN DEFEAT

1962 – In his first game with Greenville of the Sally League, **Shelly Brodsky** hits a single, double, and homer in a 7-5 loss to Knoxville.

MAZEL TOUGH

1907 – **Abe Attell** wins a 20-round decision over Kid Solomon in Los Angeles to retain his world featherweight title.

1930 – **Samuel Behr** of Wisconsin wins the shot put for the second straight year at the Western Conference track and field championships in Evanston, Ill.

1942 – **Frank Kay** captures the 181.25-pound title at the U.S. Weightlifting Championships in Cincinnati.

2000 – **Jamie Cohen** of Amherst beats Selinda Geyer of Agnes Scott College 6-3, 6-3, to win the NCAA Division III women's tennis championship.

2003 – **Nicolas Massu** teams with Fernando Gonzalez to win the deciding doubles match 6-4, 6-2 and give Chile a 2-1 victory over the Czech Republic for its first World Team Cup tennis title in Duesseldorf, Germany.

RECORD SETTERS

1957 – **David Reisbord** runs a leg of an Occidental College two-mile relay team that establishes a world record of 7:22.7.

2002 – **Shawn Green** hits his fifth home run in two games, tying a major-league record, in the Dodgers' 14-3 loss to the Arizona Diamondbacks. His 25 total bases in two games also ties a record shared by Ty Cobb (1925) and Joe Adcock (1954).

TRANSITIONS

1933 – The German Gymnastic Society rules that Aryan ancestry is mandatory for organization membership.

A STAR IS BORN

1933 – **Harry Kane** (track and field)
1940 – **Andrea Cohn** (golf)
1942 – **Ali Bacher** (South African cricket)
1946 – **Irena Kirszenstein-Szewinska** (Polish sprinter)

MAY 25

GAMEBREAKERS

1871 – Troy Haymakers second baseman **Lipman Pike** gets six hits in a 25-10 victory over the Brooklyn Mutuals.

1929 – **Jozsef Eisenhoffer's** goal 28 minutes into the second half gives the Hakoah All-Stars a 1-0 victory over the New York Giants in the Eastern Soccer League championship game at Dexter Park in Brooklyn.

1938 – **Hank Greenberg** hits two home runs in a game for the first of a major-league record 11 times that season. Rudy York and Greenberg hit back-to-back homers twice in Detroit's 7-3 win over the New York Yankees, becoming the fifth set of teammates to accomplish the feat.

1961 – **Sandy Koufax** allows three hits as the Dodgers beat the St. Louis Cardinals 1-0 on Tommy Davis's seventh-inning home run off Bob Gibson.

1962 – **Shelly Brodsky** hits a grand slam homer and a two-run double as Greenville beats Augusta 12-3 in the Sally League.

1969 – **Norm Miller** of the Houston Astros goes 4 for 5 in a 6-3 victory over the New York Mets.

1979 – **Ross Baumgarten** of the White Sox pitches his first of two one-hitters against the California Angels. Bobby Grich's leadoff double in the seventh spoils the no-hitter as Chicago wins 6-1.

1995 – **Joel Stransky** of Springboks scores 22 points as South Africa beats defending champion Australia 27-18 in the first round of the World Cup rugby tournament in Cape Town. He becomes the 12th player in history and first South African to score all four possible ways in a match – a try, a conversion, four penalty goals, and a dropped goal.

2002 – **Jake Wald's** two-run homer in the bottom of the eighth gives George Washington a 6-4 victory over Richmond in the Atlantic 10 Conference championship game. Wald also contributes an RBI single in the second inning.

STRONG IN DEFEAT

2003 – For the second year in a row, **Tomas Scheckter** leads the most laps (63) at the Indianapolis 500 before settling for a fourth-place finish.

MAZEL TOUGH

1946 – **Bernard Mayer** of NYU finishes first in the shot put at the IC4A outdoor championships in Annapolis, Md.

1975 – **Dror Polak** of Israel wins the Boys U17 division at the U.S. National Table Tennis Championships in Houston.

1987 – **Najib Daho**, a Moroccan boxer living in England, knocks out Pat Cowdell in the first round to win the British super featherweight title in Manchester, England.

1991 – **Fabrice Benichou** wins a 12-round majority decision over John Davison in Brest, France, to win the vacant European featherweight title.

RECORD SETTERS

2002 – **Shawn Green** hits two more homers and drives in six runs – his seventh home run in three games while going 11 for 13 with 14 RBI's in that span – as the Dodgers beat the Arizona Diamondbacks 10-5. His nine home runs in one calendar week set a National League record.

A STAR IS BORN

1845 – **Lipman Pike** (baseball)
1908 – **Al Friedman** (heavyweight boxer)
1945 – **Mike Stromberg** (Temple football, New York Jets linebacker)
1967 – **Andrew Sznajder** (Canadian tennis player)

MAY 26

GAMEBREAKERS

1940 – **Harry Danning** hits two home runs and drives in four runs as the New York Giants beat the Boston Bees 10-8.

1962 – For the second time in fewer than three years, **Sandy Koufax** strikes out 16 Philadelphia Phillies batters in the Los Angeles Dodgers' 6-3 victory.

1985 – **Jose Bautista** pitches a Carolina League no-hitter as the Lynchburg Mets beat the Prince William Pirates 6-0.

1997 – **Craig Katz** scores three goals for Princeton as the Tigers defeat Maryland 19-7 for the NCAA men's lacrosse title.

2001 – **Aaron Feldman's** two-run pinch-hit single in the top of the ninth inning gives Tulane a 13-10 victory over Oklahoma State in the NCAA regional tournament. **Jon Kaplan** drives in four runs for the Green Wave.

STRONG IN DEFEAT

2002 – Rookie **Tomas Scheckter** leads 85 laps of the Indianapolis 500 until he hits the wall with 27 laps remaining.

MAZEL TOUGH

1914 – **Charley White** wins a 10-round decision over lightweight champion Willie Ritchie in Milwaukee, but Ritchie retains his crown because the fighters agreed beforehand that White needed a knockout to take Ritchie's title.

1934 – **Samuel Klopstock** of Stanford wins the 200 low hurdles at the IC4A track and field championships in Philadelphia.

1962 – **Gary Gubner** of NYU wins his first of three straight IC4A outdoor shot put titles and his first of two discus crowns in Villanova, Pa.

1968 – **Tom Okker** defeats Bob Hewitt 10-8, 6-8, 6-1, 3-6, 6-0 to win the Italian Tennis Championship in Rome.

1996 – **Dawn Buth** and Stephanie Nickitas of Florida win their first of two NCAA women's tennis doubles titles, beating Cristina Moros and Farley Taylor of Texas 6-1, 6-2 in Tallahassee, Fla.

RECORD SETTERS

1912 – 19-year-old **Abel Kiviat** sets a world record of 3:59.2 in the 1,500 meters at the New York Post Office Clerks' Association Games at Celtic Park, Long Island. He will break the record two more times in the next two weeks.

1988 – **Brian Bark** of North Carolina State gets six hits to tie a College World Series record in a 13-3 win over Florida.

JEWS ON FIRST

2007 – In his second major-league game, **Ryan Braun** hits his first home run off Justin Germano in the Milwaukee Brewers' 6-3 loss to the San Diego Padres.

TRANSITIONS

2003 – **Larry Brown** resigns as coach of the Philadelphia 76ers. He compiled a 255-205 record in six seasons – his longest tenure in 31 years of coaching.

2004 – **Larry Nagler**, NCAA singles and doubles champion in 1960 while at UCLA, is inducted into the Intercollegiate Tennis Association Hall of Fame. Nagler was the only three-time Pac-10 Conference champion.

A STAR IS BORN

1906 – **Mauri Rose** (auto racing)
1915 – **Leon Efrati** (Italian featherweight boxer)
1981 – **Anthony Ervin** (swimming)

MAY 27

GAMEBREAKERS

1934 – **Buddy Myer** hits a two-run home run, a double, and two singles as the Washington Senators beat the Chicago White Sox 9-6.

1944 – **Mike Schemer** steals home in the ninth inning as Jersey City rallies from a 7-1 deficit to beat Syracuse 9-8 in the International League.

1952 – **Saul Rogovin** allows six hits as the Chicago White Sox blank the St. Louis Browns 3-0.

MAZEL TOUGH

1933 – **Mort Reznick** of NYU wins the 35-pound weight throw at the IC4A track and field championships.

1933 – **Baroness Maud Levi** beats Norma Taubele 6-2, 4-6, 6-2 to win the Eastern Clay Court tennis championship in Montclair, N.J.

1947 – **Al Phillips** of England wins by disqualification over Ray Famechon in the eighth round to capture the vacant European featherweight title.

1950 – **James Fuchs** of Yale wins the shot put and teammate **Victor Frank** captures his fourth straight discus title at the IC4A outdoor championships.

1956 – **Angela Buxton** of England teams with Althea Gibson to beat Darlene Hard and Dorothy Head Knode 6-8, 8-6, 6-1 to win the women's doubles title at the French Open.

1956 – **Henry Laskau** wins the AAU 25-kilometer racewalking title at Lake Hopatcong, N.J.

1979 – **Jody Scheckter** outraces Clay Ragazzoni of Switzerland and wins his second straight Formula One race at the Grand Prix of Monaco.

2000 – **Joanna Zeiger** finishes second among 28 triathletes in the U.S. Olympic Trials in Irving, Texas. She will finish fourth when the event is run for the first time in the Sydney Olympics.

2000 – **Alexander Jeltkov** wins the all-around title at the Canadian National Gymnastics Championships in Montreal.

2005 – **Philip Horowitz** defeats Dan Mayer 208-200 to win the National Senior Bowling Association championship.

2006 – **Shahar Peer** of Israel beats top-seeded Anastasia Myskina of Russia 1-6, 6-3, 7-6 (3) to win the Istanbul Cup, her third WTA tennis title of the year.

JEWS ON FIRST

1938 – **Hank Greenberg**, facing White Sox pitcher Frank Gabler, becomes the first batter to homer into the center-field bleachers at Comiskey Park as the Tigers beat Chicago 5-2.

TRANSITIONS

1939 – **Murray Franklin** is presented the Louisville Slugger Trophy for having the top batting average in organized baseball the previous year. Franklin batted .439 for Beckley (W.Va.) of the Mountain State League.

1945 – **Harry Chozen** of Mobile (Southern League) begins a 49-game hitting streak – the sixth-longest in baseball history.

1969 – The California Angels name **Harold "Lefty" Phillips** manager, replacing Bill Rigney.

1989 – **Brian Kowitz** of Clemson begins a 37-game hitting streak over two seasons during which he bats .430 and drives in 43 runs.

A STAR IS BORN

1955 – **Ross Baumgarten** (Chicago White Sox, Pittsburgh Pirates pitcher)

MAY 28

GAMEBREAKERS

1914 – **Erskine Mayer** of the Philadelphia Phillies shuts out the Pittsburgh Pirates 2-0.

1927 – **Max Gruenwald** scores two goals, including the tie-breaker on a penalty kick, as Hakoah Vienna's soccer team defeats Indiana Flooring 2-1 at the Polo Grounds in New York.

1934 – **Hank Greenberg** hits two home runs and drives in four runs as the Detroit Tigers beat the Boston Red Sox 12-6.

1951 – **Saul Rogovin**, just acquired by the Chicago White Sox from the Detroit Tigers, pitches a two-hitter and beats the St. Louis Browns 4-2.

1955 – **Jack Cohen** pitches a four-hitter as the Spartanburg Peaches beat the Asheville Tourists 7-0 in the Tri-State League.

1963 – **Sandy Koufax** allows six hits in the Dodgers' 7-0 win over the Milwaukee Braves.

1966 – **Mickey Abarbanel** of the Fox Cities Foxes pitches a no-hitter and strikes out 12 in a 9-1 victory over the Wisconsin Rapids Twins in the Midwest League.

2006 – **Aly Josephs** scores four goals as Northwestern defeats Dartmouth 7-4 to win its second consecutive NCAA women's lacrosse championship.

MAZEL TOUGH

1917 – **Benny Leonard** knocks out champion Freddie Welsh in the ninth round in New York to win the world lightweight boxing title.

1929 – **Mushy Callahan** retains his world junior welterweight title with a third-round knockout of Fred Mahan in Los Angeles.

1934 – **Barney Ross**, who already holds world titles in the lightweight and junior welterweight divisions, wins a 15-round decision over Jimmy McLarnin in New York to capture the world welterweight championship.

After the fight, Ross gives up his junior welterweight title.

1949 – **James Fuchs** of Yale wins the shot put, teammate **Victor Frank** wins the discus and **Irving Mondschein** of NYU captures the high jump at the IC4A outdoor championships in New York.

2001 – **Deena Drossin** wins the Bolder Boulder, a 10-kilometer road race in Boulder, Colo., in 33 minutes, 25 seconds. She finishes 17 seconds ahead of runner-up Ejagayou Dibaba of Ethiopia and is only the second American in 17 years to win the event. Drossin also wins the race in 2002 and 2003.

2006 – **Lindsey Durlacher** defeats Sam Hazewinkel twice in the 121-pound final to win the Challenge Tournament in Sioux City, Iowa, and qualify for the U.S. World Greco-Roman wrestling team.

2007 – **Audra Cohen** of Miami wins the NCAA tennis championship with a 7-5, 6-2 victory over Lindsey Nelson of Southern Cal.

JEWS ON FIRST

1921 – **Sammy Bohne** of the Cincinnati Reds hits his first of 16 career home runs off Whitney Glazner to help give the Reds a 3-2 lead over Pittsburgh. The game is suspended in the eighth inning, and the Pirates rally to win 4-3 when the game is resumed on June 30.

A STAR IS BORN

1914 – **Dave Smukler** (Temple football, Philadelphia Eagles fullback/linebacker)
1921 – **Aaron "Okey" Geffin** (rugby)
1946 – **Skip Jutze** (Houston Astros, St. Louis Cardinals, Seattle Pilots catcher)
1971 – **Nick Bravin** (fencing)

MAY 29

GAMEBREAKERS

1961 – **Sandy Koufax** pitches his second three-hitter against St. Louis in four days, striking out 13 as Los Angeles beats the Cardinals 2-1.

2001 – **Shawn Green** hits his second grand slam homer in eight days, connecting in the sixth inning of the Dodgers' 4-1 victory over the New York Mets.

2005 – Sophomore goaltender **Jesse Schwartzman** makes 12 saves, and allows just one second-half goal as Johns Hopkins rallies to defeat Duke 9-8 in Philadelphia for its first NCAA Division 1 men's lacrosse title in 18 years. Schwartzman is named Most Outstanding Player of the tournament.

2007 – **Kevin Youkilis** doubles and homers in the Red Sox's 4-2 victory over the Cleveland Indians, extending his hitting streak to 21 games. His ninth consecutive multi-hit game is the most by a Boston player since Jim Rice in 1978.

MAZEL TOUGH

1892 – **Joe Choynski** beats **Jack Hart** in a three-round light heavyweight bout in London for his third victory in five days.

1920 – **Max Gold** defeats George Klawiter to win the AAU four-wall handball singles championship in Los Angeles.

1937 – **Dan Taylor** of Columbia wins the shot put at the IC4A outdoor championships in New York.

1940 – **Phil Fox** wins the discus at the AAU Outdoor track meet in Fresno, Calif.

1948 – **Stanley Lampert** of NYU wins the shot put, **Victor Frank** of Yale captures the discus, and **Irving Mondschein** of NYU wins the high jump at the IC4A outdoor championships at Triborough Stadium in New York.

1949 – **Henry Laskau** wins the AAU 10,000-meter racewalking championship in New York.

1954 – **Martin Engel** of NYU wins his second straight hammer throw title at the IC4A outdoor championships in New York.

1964 – **Roger Ginsberg** wins the inaugural Bergen Open golf tournament in New Jersey.

1992 – **Fabrice Benichou** retains his European featherweight title with a 12-round decision over John Davison in Amneville, France.

JEWS ON FIRST

1942 – **Murray Franklin** of the Detroit Tigers hits his first of two career home runs off Al Smith in a 14-3 victory over the Cleveland Indians.

A STAR IS BORN

1883 – **Waldemar Holberg** (Danish boxer)
1899 – **Sidney Brews** (South African golfer)
1921 – **Howie Rader** (basketball)

Irv Mondschein *(U.S. Olympic Committee)*

MAY 30

1927 – The Hakoah All-Stars of Vienna beat the Philadelphia Stars 7-1 for their most lopsided victory on their second American soccer tour. **Max Gruenwald** scores three goals and **Moritz Haeusler** scores twice.

1937 – **Hank Greenberg** goes 5 for 5 with two homers as Detroit beats the St. Louis Browns 18-3.

1942 – A year to the day after hitting three home runs in a Memorial Day doubleheader, Buffalo Bisons infielder **Jim Levey** hits two homers, a single, a double, draws a walk, and drives in five runs in a 15-1 victory over Toronto in the first game of a twin bill.

1952 – **Al Rosen** hits two doubles and a single and drives in four runs as the Cleveland Indians beat the Detroit Tigers 11-4.

1959 – **Ed Mayer** of the Chicago Cubs earns his second and final major-league victory when he retires the only two batters he faces in the ninth inning of the second game of a doubleheader against the Los Angeles Dodges. **Sandy Koufax**, also pitching in relief, is the losing pitcher as the Cubs win 10-8.

2000 – Montclair State sweeps St. Thomas 13-3 and 6-2 to win the NCAA Division III championship in Grand Chute, Wis. **Greg Belson** is the winning pitcher in the first game, yielding seven hits in seven innings.

2003 – **Ryan Braun** goes 4 for 5 with a homer and three RBI's as Miami defeats Bethune-Cookman 10-5 in the first game of the College World Series regional tournament.

MAZEL TOUGH

1913 – On the verge of being knocked out, Jack Ortega kicks **Abe "The Newsboy" Hollandersky** below the belt and is disqualified, giving Hollandersky the Panamanian heavyweight title.

1920 – In the second year of championship competition, **Max Gold** wins the National AAU one-wall handball title.

1923 – **Jack Bernstein** wins a 15-round decision over champion Johnny Dundee to claim the world junior lightweight championship.

1925 – **Alfred Miller** of Harvard wins the 70-yard dash at the IC4A track meet in Philadelphia.

1936 – **Milton Green** of Harvard wins the long jump at the IC4A outdoor championships in Berkeley, Calif.

1941 – Driving in relief of Floyd Davis on lap 72, **Mauri Rose** goes on to win the Indianapolis 500. Rose will win the race on his own in 1947 and 1948.

1953 – **Martin Engel** of NYU wins the hammer throw at the IC4A outdoor championships in New York.

1964 – **Bob Grossman** wins his division of the Sports Car Club of America Double 400 at Bridgehampton, N.Y.

1964 – **Gary Gubner** of NYU wins his third straight IC4A outdoor shot put title in New York.

1965 – **Julie Heldman** defeats Gail Sherriff 9-7, 6-1 to win the Brussels Open clay-court tennis tournament.

2001 – Southern Cal senior **Dennis Kholev**, a Ukrainian immigrant to Israel, wins the NCAA pole vault championship with a school-record 18 feet, 6 inches.

JEWS ON FIRST

1930 – New York Yankees second baseman **Jimmie Reese** hits his first of eight career major-league homers off Hal Lisenbee in a 6-5 win over the Boston Red Sox.

A STAR IS BORN

1908 – **John Slade** (field hockey)
1913 – **Moe Goldman** (CCNY basketball)
1913 – **Abe Simon** (heavyweight boxer)

MAY 31

GAMEBREAKERS

1945 – **Goody Rosen's** two-run triple in the 13th inning gives the Brooklyn Dodgers a 6-4 win over the Pittsburgh Pirates.

1948 – **Sid Gordon** goes 4-for-4 in the second game of a doubleheader as the New York Giants beat the Brooklyn Dodgers 10-1 and move into first place.

1960 – **Norm Sherry's** grand slam home run breaks a 3-3 tie, and the Los Angeles Dodgers beat the St. Louis Cardinals 8-3.

1982 – **Stacy Winsberg** knocks the ball away from the Fresno State catcher and scores the winning run on a short fly ball as UCLA wins the first NCAA Division I softball championship 2-0 in eight innings.

2004 – Winning pitcher **Jason Marquis** goes 3-for-4 with a double – his first three-hit game since high school – as the St. Louis Cardinals defeat the Pittsburgh Pirates 8-3.

MAZEL TOUGH

1911 – **Georges Stern** rides Sunstar to victory in the Epsom Derby in England.

1926 – The Hakoah All-Stars of Vienna beat the Philadelphia Field Club 3-0 to complete their first American soccer tour with a 7-2-2 record.

1927 – **Mushy Callahan** wins a 10-round decision over Spug Myers in Chicago to retain his world junior welterweight title.

1941 – **Seymour Greenberg** of Northwestern beats defending champion John Tubin of Michigan to win the Big Ten Conference tennis championship in Chicago.

1947 – **Bernard Mayer** of NYU wins his second straight IC4A outdoor shot put title and **Victor Frank** of Yale wins his first of four straight discus titles in Philadelphia.

1952 – **Henry Laskau** wins the AAU 10-kilometer racewalking championship in the Bronx.

1958 – **Carl Shine** of Penn wins his first of two straight IC4A outdoor shot put championships, while **Joel Landau** of Harvard wns the 120-yard high hurdles and 220 low hurdles at Villanova, Pa.

1965 – **Walter Blum** rides Gun Bow to victory in the Metropolitan Mile at Aqueduct.

1968 – **Jackie Mekler** beats 437 other runners to win his fifth Comrades Marathon, a 54-mile race run on the same date every year in South Africa. His time of 6 hours, 1 minute, 11 seconds is nearly 2½ minutes ahead of the second-place finisher.

1998 – **Kenny Bernstein** beats Gary Scelzi in the Top Fuel final of the NHRA Fram Route 66 Nationals in Chicago. The victory is Bernstein's 20th in Top Fuel and 50th overall.

RECORD SETTERS

1889 – **Lon Myers** sets an American record of 4:29.5 in the mile – after winning a 300-yard race.

TRANSITIONS

1810 – After beating Ben Medley in a 49-round fight, **Samuel Elias** announces his retirement from boxing.

2006 – Arizona State freshman outfielder **Ike Davis** is named Pac-10 Conference baseball Rookie of the Year after hitting .339 with nine homers and a conference-leading 65 RBI's.

A STAR IS BORN

1935 – **Edward Pressman** (rowing)

JUNE 1

GAMEBREAKERS

1950 – **Sid Gordon** hits two home runs, including a grand slam, and collects seven RBI's as the Boston Braves beat the Pittsburgh Pirates 10-6.

1963 – **Larry Yellen**, making his first start for San Antonio of the Texas League, allows three hits in four scoreless innings before he leaves with tightness in his shoulder. But Yellen's RBI single beats El Paso 1-0.

1966 – **Sandy Koufax** allows seven hits as the Dodgers beat the St. Louis Cardinals 1-0.

MAZEL TOUGH

1935 – **Sidney Brews** of South Africa shoots a final-round 71 to win the PGA Philadelphia Open with a 54-hole score of 213.

1946 – Trained by **Max Hirsch**, Assault wins the Belmont Stakes to complete horse racing's Triple Crown.

1957 – **Lew Stieglitz** of Connecticut wins the two-mile run and **Michael Herman** of NYU wins the long jump at the IC4A outdoor championships in New York.

1958 – Third-seeded **Suzy Kormoczy** of Hungary becomes the only Jewish woman to win a Grand Slam tennis singles title when she defeats top-seeded Shirley Bloomer 6-4, 1-6, 6-2 in the French Open final.

1967 – **Marty Fleckman** shoots an eagle-2 on the 18th hole and goes on to defeat Michael Attenborough in a one-hole playoff in the British Amateur golf final in Formby, England.

1963 – **Gerald Ashworth** of Dartmouth wins the 100-yard dash and **Gary Gubner** of NYU wins the shot put and discus at the IC4A outdoor championships in New York.

1996 – **Jessica Davis** wins the Senior Rhythmic Gymnastics national championship all-around title in Athens, Ga.

1996 – Two days after winning the NCAA discus title with a toss of 211 feet, 1 inch, **Andy Bloom** of Wake Forest captures the shot put crown at 65 feet½ inch in Eugene, Ore. He is only the fifth competitor to win both events in the same meet.

2001 – Future Bowling Hall of Famer **Mark Roth** defeats Steve Neff 234-202 to win the Seattle Open for his first victory on the PBA Senior Tour.

JEWS ON FIRST

1881 – Iroquois, trained by **Jacob Pincus**, becomes the first American horse to win the English Derby. Another American horse will not win the race until 1954.

1939 – **Sam Taub** announces the first boxing match ever televised – Lou Nova's 11th-round knockout of former heavyweight champion Max Baer at Yankee Stadium.

2003 – A day after hitting two home runs and driving in seven runs in a 22-14 victory over Florida Atlantic, catcher **Brian Rose** becomes the first University of Florida player to hit grand slams in two consecutive games as the Gators defeat Miami 15-5 in the NCAA Regional Tournament.

RECORD SETTERS

1919 – **Charles Pores** knocks nearly two minutes off the 15-year-old American record for the 15-mile run and also exceeds the American 1-hour run record set in 1889 by more than 300 yards at Macombs Dam Park in New York.

A STAR IS BORN

1905 – **Saul Mielziner** (Carnegie Tech and pro football)

1928 – **Larry Zeidel** (Chicago Black Hawks, Detroit Red Wings, Philadelphia Flyers)

JUNE 2

GAMEBREAKERS

1902 – **Bill Cristall** of Oakland pitches a no-hitter as the Clamdiggers beat the Sacramento Gilt Edges 4-0 in the Carolina League.

1953 – **Al Rosen** hits a three-run homer in the eighth inning as the Cleveland Indians beat the Boston Red Sox 7-3.

2001 – Senior first baseman **Aaron Rifkin** goes 4 for 5 with three home runs and six RBI's as Cal State-Fullerton beats Mississippi State 9-3 to earn a trip to the College World Series.

2001 – **Jeff Agoos** scores the winning goal as the first-place San Jose Earthquakes beat the Colorado Rapids 2-1 in Major League Soccer.

2006 – **Kevin Youkilis** hits a two-run homer with two out in the top of the ninth to give the Boston Red Sox a 3-2 win over the Detroit Tigers.

MAZEL TOUGH

1901 – At 17 years, 8 months, and 5 days, **Georges Stern** becomes the youngest jockey to win the Prix du Jockey Club's French Derby when he rides Saxon to victory.

1956 – **Isaac Berger** wins the 132-pound title at the U.S. Weightlifting Championships in Philadelphia.

1973 – **Cary Feldman** wins the javelin title at the National AAU outdoor track championships.

1974 – **Ron Wayne** wins the Yonkers Marathon in 2 hours, 18 minutes, 53 seconds.

1974 – **Ken Lindner** and **Jeffrey Lerner** defeat Mike Wooden and Chuck Fonarow 4-6, 7-5, 6-4 to win the National Paddle Tennis Championship in Brooklyn.

2000 – **Michelle Feldman** beats Lynda Barnes 238-212 in the final of the Omaha Open pro bowling tournament.

2001 – **Sarah Poewe** of South Africa wins the 50-meter breaststroke in 32.10 seconds and the 100 breaststroke in 2:29.25 at the world swimming championships in Barcelona, Spain.

RECORD SETTERS

1912 – **Abel Kiviat** improves his world record in the 1,500 to 3:56.8 at the Celtic Park meet in New York.

1946 – At the Senior National Weightlifting Championships in Detroit, **Frank Spellman** sets an American record of 257.75 pounds in the press en route to winning the 165-pound title.

2001 – **Jillian Schwartz** of Duke sets an Atlantic Coast Conference and school record of 13 feet, 5½ inches in finishing third in the NCAA women's pole vault.

JEWS ON FIRST

1926 – **Buddy Myer** of the Washington Senators hits his first of 38 career home runs, connecting off Urban Shocker in a 9-5 loss to the New York Yankees.

TRANSITIONS

1943 – Trainer **Hirsch Jacobs** claims 2-year-old Stymie for $1,500. By the end of 1947, Stymie will become the world's leading money-winning thoroughbred, winning $816,060 for 22 stakes victories.

2003 – Former Philadelphia 76ers coach **Larry Brown** takes over as coach of the Detroit Pistons – the team that just eliminated the 76ers in the second round of the NBA playoffs.

A STAR IS BORN

1917 – **Milt Aron** (welterweight boxer)
1952 – **Gary Bettman** (NHL commissioner)

JUNE 3

GAMEBREAKERS

1925 – Harvard shortstop **Izzy Zarakov's** grand slam homer in the sixth inning rallies the Crimson to a 9-4 victory over Bates.

1950 – After a brushback from the Pirates' Bill Werle, **Sid Gordon** of the Boston Braves hits his third grand slam homer of the season – and second in three days. He also hits a two-run homer in the ninth and drives in seven runs in an 8-6 win over Pittsburgh.

1967 – **Mickey Abarbanel** of Evansville strikes out 15 Knoxville batters – one short of the Southern League record.

1971 – **Ken Holtzman** of the Cubs pitches his second career no-hitter, beating Cincinnati 1-0. Holtzman walks four batters, scores the game's only run in the third inning, and strikes out Tommy Helms and Lee May for the final two outs.

1977 – **Bobby Gross** scores 25 points as the Portland Trail Blazers defeat the Philadelphia 76ers 110-104 in Game 5 of the NBA Finals. The Blazers go on to win the title in six games.

1997 – **Mike Saipe** pitches a one-hitter as the New Haven Ravens beat New Britain 1-0 in the first game of an Eastern League doubleheader. **Eric Helfand** goes 5 for 5 with a homer, three doubles, and five RBI's as the Las Vegas Stars defeat the Tacoma Rainiers 11-4 in the Pacific Coast League.

MAZEL TOUGH

1950 – **Maurice Herzog** of France becomes the first person to climb a peak higher than 8,000 meters when he and Louis Lachenal summit on Annapurna, the world's 10th-highest mountain.

1967 – **Willie Harmatz** rides Biggs to victory in the Californian Stakes at Hollywood Park.

1973 – **Jody Scheckter** wins a Formula 5000 race at Mid-Ohio Speedway.

1975 – **Boris "Dov" Djerassi** of Northeast-

ern upsets defending champion Pete Farmer of UCLA and wins the NCAA hammer throw title with a toss of 225 feet, 5 inches in Provo, Utah.

1979 – **Mark Roth** and **Marshall Holman** beat **Larry Laub** and Palmer Fallgren 406-376 to win their second straight Columbia PBA Doubles Classic title in San Jose, Calif.

RECORD SETTERS

2001 – One day after setting a quarter-mile speed record of 4.477 seconds in the preliminaries, **Kenny Bernstein** wins his third straight NHRA Top Fuel final at the Lucas Oil Nationals in Joliet, Ill.

JEWS ON FIRST

2000 – **Gabe Kapler** becomes the first Texas player to hit home runs in his first two at-bats as a Ranger as Texas beats the Chicago White Sox 10-4.

TRANSITIONS

1949 – **Red Auerbach** resigns as coach of the Washington Capitals of the Basketball Association of America.

1974 – **Larry Brown**, former coach of the defunct Carolina Cougars, is named coach of the Denver Rockets of the American Basketball Association.

2002 – **Yaron Peters** of South Carolina is named national baseball player of the week after collecting six homers and eight RBI's in four NCAA regional tournament games. He hits two home runs as the Gamecocks beat North Carolina 3-1 for the regional championship.

2004 – Boston Red Sox third baseman **Kevin Youkilis** is named American League Rookie of the Month. In only 13 games since being called up from the minor leagues in mid-May, Youkilis hits .318 with four doubles, a homer and seven RBI's.

JUNE 4

GAMEBREAKERS

1924 – **Jozsef Eisenhoffer's** goal gives Hungary a 1-0 soccer victory over France.

1927 – **Reszo Nickolsburger** scores twice as Hakoah Vienna defeats the Irish All-Stars 4-2 at Dexter Park in Brooklyn, N.Y.

1951 – **Saul Rogovin** allows seven hits as the Chicago White Sox beat the Boston Red Sox 2-0. Rookie **Lou Limmer** hits a grand slam homer to give the Philadelphia A's a 7-6 victory over the St. Louis Browns.

1964 – **Sandy Koufax** pitches his third career no-hitter, beating the Philadelphia Phillies 3-0. He strikes out 12 and walks just one batter, Richie Allen on a 3-2 count in the fourth inning. He sets a major-league record with his 54th game of 10 or more strikeouts.

1968 – Just recalled from Triple-A Buffalo, **Mike Epstein** hits a two-run homer in the sixth inning to give the Washington Senators a 4-2 victory over the Oakland A's. The D.C. Stadium organist plays "Hava Nagila" as Epstein rounds the bases.

1969 – **Ron Blomberg** hits two home runs as the Manchester Yankees defeat the Elmira Pioneers 7-4 in the Eastern League.

2000 – **Frank Charles's** RBI single with one out in the bottom of the 15th inning gives the New Orleans Zephyrs a 2-1 victory over Memphis in the Pacific Coast League.

STRONG IN DEFEAT

1995 – In his first major-league at-bat, pinch-hitter **Brian Kowitz** hits an RBI double in the fifth inning, but the Atlanta Braves lose 6-2 to the Houston Astros.

MAZEL TOUGH

1906 – **Walter Miller** rides four winners and finishes second in the other two races at Belmont Park.

1931 – **Victor "Young" Perez** of Tunisia wins a 15-round decision over Valentin Angelmann to win the French flyweight title in Paris.

1938 – **Howard Brill** of NYU wins the shot put at the IC4A outdoor championships at Randall's Island, N.Y.

1966 – **Willie Harmatz** rides Travel Orb to victory in the Californian Stakes at Hollywood Park.

1971 – **Nessim Max Cohen** of Morocco wins a 12-round decision over Fabio Bettini to win the French middleweight title in Marseilles, France.

A STAR IS BORN

1947 – **Saoul Mamby** (junior welterweight boxer)

1951 – **Ed Newman** (Duke football, Miami Dolphins guard)

JUNE 5

GAMEBREAKERS

1927 – **Joe "Pete" Laszlo** scores three goals and **Teno Stern** adds two as Palestine Maccabi opens its United States soccer tour with a 6-4 win over the New York Stars at Ebbets Field in Brooklyn.

1978 – **Steve Stone** of the Chicago White Sox pitches a three-hitter with six strikeouts in a 2-0 victory over the Cleveland Indians.

2002 – **Scott Schoeneweis** allows four hits and strikes out four over 8 2/3 innings as the Anaheim Angels beat the Texas Rangers 3-0.

MAZEL TOUGH

1869 – Fenian, owned by **August Belmont** and trained by **Jacob Pincus**, wins the third Belmont Stakes at Jerome Park in New York. A silver figure of Fenian adorns the Belmont Trophy presented annually to the winner of the third Triple Crown race.

1955 – **Isaac Berger** wins the 132-pound division and **Richard Giller** captures the 165 title at the U.S. Weightlifting Championships in Cleveland.

1971 – **Walter Blum** rides Pass Catcher, a 34-1 underdog, to a half-length victory over Jim French in the Belmont Stakes in New York. Canonero 11, winner of both the Kentucky Derby and Preakness, finishes fourth.

1976 – **Dick Siderowf** sinks a six-foot birdie putt on the first playoff hole to defeat John Davies in St. Andrews, Scotland, to become the third American golfer to win the British Amateur twice.

1983 – **Mike Yellen** defeats Rubin Gonzales 11-6, 11-10, 11-3 to win the national racquetball title.

2005 – **Leah Goldstein** of Canada wins the 56-mile women's pro division of the Cooper Spur Circuit cycling race at Hood River, Ore.

RECORD SETTERS

1976 – **Irena Kirszenstein-Szewinska** of Poland breaks her world record in the 400 meters, going the distance in 49.75 seconds.

1999 – **Tony Schrager** of the Lansing Lugnuts hits a team-record three home runs in a Midwest League game.

TRANSITIONS

1939 – **Jimmie Reese** gets his first minor-league managing job, replacing Ken Penner at Bellingham (Wash.) of the Western International League. Unable to get Bellingham out of last place, he will hold the job only until mid-August.

1949 – Eighteen players – including **Harry Feldman** of the New York Giants and **Murray Franklin** of the Detroit Tigers – who had jumped to the outlaw Mexican League have their major-league eligibility reinstated by Commissioner A.B. Chandler.

1960 – **Nat Holman,** basketball coach at CCNY since 1919, announces his retirement.

JEWS ON FIRST

1967 – **Mike Epstein**, playing his first game for the Washington Senators, hits his first of 130 career home runs off Thad Tillotson in a 4-2 loss to the New York Yankees. Epstein's hit is a 200-foot drive down the left-field line that rolls for an inside-the-park homer.

JUNE 6

GAMEBREAKERS

1939 – With the Giants leading Cincinnati 6-0, **Harry Danning** hits a home run into the upper deck in right field at the Polo Grounds with two out in the bottom of the fourth. Danning is the first of five consecutive New York batters to homer. Danning adds an RBI single and the Giants go on to beat the Reds 17-3.

1948 – **Sid Gordon** hits a grand slam home run in the New York Giants' 16-4 victory over the Pittsburgh Pirates.

1957 – **Larry Sherry** allows five singles and strikes out six as Fort Worth defeats the Dallas Eagles 5-0 in the Texas League.

1969 – **Art Shamsky** goes 4-for-4 with two homers and three RBI's as the New York Mets beat the Philadelphia Phillies 6-5.

MAZEL TOUGH

1948 – **Henry Laskau** wins the AAU 10-kilometer racewalking championship in New York.

1970 – College freshman **Mark Levine** beats defending champion **Steve Sandler** 21-5, 21-11 to win the National AAU one-wall handball championship in Brooklyn, N.Y.

1986 – **Margie Goldstein** captures her first Grand Prix horse show, riding Daydream to victory in Cincinnati.

2004 – **Noam Okun** of Israel teams with Matias Boecker of the United States to defeat Mark Hlawaty and Brad Weston of Australia 6-7, 6-3, 6-4 in the doubles final at the Tallahassee Challenger tennis tournament.

RECORD SETTERS

1976 – Although he loses to Adriano Panatta 1-6, 4-6, 6-4, 6-7 in the French Open final, **Harold Solomon** sets a Grand Slam record by playing 30 sets in the tournament. Solomon won three matches in five sets, two in four sets, and one in straight sets.

1982 – **Stuart Mittleman** sets an American record of 12 hours, 56 minutes, 34 seconds in a 100-mile run.

JEWS ON FIRST

1958 – **Don Taussig** of the San Francisco Giants hits his first of four career home runs, connecting off Harvey Haddix in a 5-4 loss to the Cincinnati Reds.

TRANSITIONS

1946 – **Maurice Podoloff,** president of the American Hockey League, is named the first commissioner of the newly formed Basketball Association of America, forerunner of the NBA. Podoloff becomes the first person to lead two professional leagues simultaneously.

2002 – Long-time college and pro coach **Larry Brown** is elected to the Basketball Hall of Fame.

A STAR IS BORN

1908 – **Izzy Goldstein** (Detroit Tigers pitcher)

1932 – **Fred Lebow** (running)

1950 – **Bob Winograd** (WHA hockey)

JUNE 7

GAMEBREAKERS

1913 – Erskine Mayer of the Philadelphia Phillies shuts out the Pittsburgh Pirates 6-0.

1970 – Israel plays Sweden to a 1-1 tie in its second World Cup soccer match in Mexico. **Mordecai Spiegler** scores for the Israelis.

2003 – Ryan Braun hits two home runs, including the game-winner in the bottom of the ninth, as Miami defeats North Carolina State 10-9 in the NCAA baseball super regional. Braun collects four RBI's and his 12th game-winning hit of the season.

2006 – Brad Ausmus leads off the third inning with his first homer of the season to give the Houston Astros a 1-0 victory over the Chicago Cubs.

MAZEL TOUGH

1787 – Solomon Sodicky beats Bill Treadway in a 37-minute bare-knuckle fight in London's Hyde Park.

1999 – Anna Smashnova of Israel beats Laurence Courtois 6-3, 6-3 in Tashkent, Uzbekistan, for her first victory on the WTA tennis tour.

2003 – Dudi Sela of Israel teams with Gyorgy Balazs of Hungary to capture the boys doubles championship at the French Open tennis tournament.

2007 – Andy Ram of Israel wins his second Grand Slam tennis championship, teaming with Nathalie Dechy of France to defeat Katarina Srebotnik of Slovenia and Nenad Zimonjic of Serbia 7-5, 6-3 in the French Open mixed doubles final.

RECORD SETTERS

1924 – Harold Abrahams sets an English record of 24 feet, 2½ inches in the long jump, a mark that stands for 32 years. He also ties the world record of 9.6 seconds in the 100-yard dash, but the mark is never submitted for recognition because the track is not flat.

1986 – Ken Flax of Oregon wins the NCAA hammer throw championship in Indianapolis with a toss of 257 feet, 0 inches – breaking the American collegiate record by one foot.

TRANSITIONS

1967 – The last-place New York Yankees select high school player **Ron Blomberg** as the first overall pick in the free-agent baseball draft.

1969 – For the second time in a week, **Steve Sandler** defeats Carl Obert 21-16, 21-17 in Brooklyn to win the National AAU one-wall handball championship. The final match was replayed after Obert protested a referee's ruling on June 1 in a three-set loss.

1993 – Larry Brown is hired as the Indiana Pacers' head coach.

2005 – The Milwaukee Brewers select Miami third baseman **Ryan Braun** as the fifth overall pick in the free-agent baseball draft.

A STAR IS BORN

1938 – Howard Carl (DePaul basketball)
1940 – Herbert Cohen (fencing)
1956 – Robert Dover (equestrian)
1979 – Max Heyman
(super middleweight boxer)

Robert Dover *(U.S. Olympic Committee)*

159

JUNE 8

GAMEBREAKERS

1943 – In his debut with Buffalo, **Eddie Turchin** gets the game-winning RBI in the first game and scores the winning run in the nightcap as the Bison sweep the Syracuse Chiefs 2-1, 2-1 in the International League.

1970 – **Art Shamsky** hits a two-run homer to lead the New York Mets to a 2-0 victory over the Houston Astros.

1975 – **Ken Holtzman** of Oakland pitches 8 2/3 innings of no-hit ball before Detroit's Tom Veryzer hits a fly ball that Athletics center fielder Bill North misjudges. Holtzman just misses his third career no-hitter as the A's beat the Tigers 4-0.

1999 – Second baseman **Dave Newhan** goes 3 for 4 in his first major-league start in a 5-3 victory over Oakland and becomes the first San Diego Padres player in 19 years to collect hits in his first two at-bats.

STRONG IN DEFEAT

1950 – **Al Rosen** hits a grand slam homer, but the Cleveland Indians lose 7-6 to the Washington Senators.

MAZEL TOUGH

1924 – **Jackie "Kid" Berg** makes his pro boxing debut with an eighth-round knockout of John Gordon in England. The future junior welterweight champion posts a 162-26-9 record with 59 knockouts.

1927 – Hapoel Vienna plays a combined American Soccer League team (New York Giants, Bethlehem Steel) to a scoreless tie before 20,000 fans at the Polo Grounds. For the first major nighttime outdoor sports event in New York, the ball is painted white so it is easier to follow.

1970 – **Red Holzman** coaches the Knicks to their first NBA title as New York beats the Los Angeles Lakers 113-99.

1974 – **Paulina Peled** of Israel captures the Chichester tennis tournament in Sussex, England, beating British junior champion Susan Barker 6-2, 6-2.

1987 – **Gary Jacobs** knocks out Tommy McCallum in the fifth round in Glasgow to win the Scottish welterweight title.

1998 – **Adam Goucher** of Colorado wins the NCAA outdoor track 5,000-meter championship in 13:31.64 in Buffalo, N.Y.

2003 – **Paul Goldstein** defeats Alex Kim 2-6, 6-2, 4-0 (retired) to win the Tallahassee tennis tournament, his fifth title on the USTA Challenger circuit.

RECORD SETTERS

1912 – **Abel Kiviat** breaks the world record in the 1,500 he set a week earlier, running 3:55.8 in Cambridge, Mass. It is the first officially recognized world record at that distance, and it is a mark that will stand for five years.

1957 – **Maria Itkina** of the Soviet Union sets a world record of 53.6 seconds in the 400 meters in a track meet in Moscow.

A STAR IS BORN

1891 – **Manfred Suskind** (South African cricket)

1913 – **Bernard Kaplan** (Western Maryland and pro football)

1975 – **Sarah Abitbol** (French figure skating)

JUNE 9

GAMEBREAKERS

1914 – **Erskine Mayer** of the Philadelphia Phillies blanks the Pittsburgh Pirates for eight innings, then gives up a ninth-inning double to Honus Wagner before settling for a 3-1 victory. The hit is Wagner's 3,000th of his career.

1937 – **Harry Danning** hits a pinch-hit two-run homer in the ninth inning to give the New York Giants a 3-2 win over the St. Louis Cardinals.

1941 – **Sid Gordon's** bases-loaded triple in the sixth inning gives Jersey City a 3-1 victory over Buffalo in the International League.

1945 – **Mike Schemer** bangs out four hits as the Jersey City Giants beat Toronto in the International League.

1971 – **Dick Sharon** hits a home run in the bottom of the seventh and final inning to give Waterbury a 1-0 victory over Manchester in the second game of an Eastern League doubleheader.

2004 – **Cody Haerther's** game-ending two-run homer gives the Peoria Chiefs a 10-9 victory over Battle Creek in the Class A Midwest League.

MAZEL TOUGH

1920 – **Ted "Kid" Lewis** stops Johnny Basham in the ninth round in London to win the European welterweight title

1941 – **Abe Simon** knocks out Pete Tamalonis 56 seconds into the second round of a heavyweight fight in New York. It is Simon's first fight since losing to champion Joe Louis in March.

1965 – **Dick Siderowf** shoots a 1-under-par 139 to finish eight strokes ahead of runner-up Bill Bogle and win the Hochster Memorial amateur golf tournament in Scarsdale, N.Y.

1970 – **Ben Gurevitch** of the Soviet Union wins the 90-kg. freestyle title at the European Wrestling Championships in Berlin.

1974 – **Jody Scheckter** of South Africa earns his first of 10 Formula One auto racing victories, leading from start to finish at the Grand Prix of Sweden.

1978 – **Mark Roth** beats Earl Anthony 188-169 in the final of the City of Roses Open bowling tournament in Portland.

1996 – **Dick Siderowf** shoots 145 over two rounds to win the Metropolitan Golf Association Senior Amateur tournament in Paramus, N.J.

2002 – **Charlee Minkin** wins the women's 52-kg. division at the Benito Juarez Judo Championships in Mexico City.

RECORD SETTERS

1888 – **Victor Schifferstein** of the United States equals the world record of 10.0 seconds in the 100-yard dash. He also misses matching the long jump world record of 23 feet, 2 ¾ inches by one-quarter of an inch.

1951 – **Herbert Klein** of Germany sets a world record of 2:27.3 in the 200 breaststroke in Munich.

TRANSITIONS

1981 – The Utah Jazz select **Danny Schayes** of Syracuse with the 13th overall pick in the NBA draft.

A STAR IS BORN

1945 – **Faina Melnik** (Ukraine track and field)

1970 – **Steve Dubinsky** (Chicago Blackhawks, Nashville Predators, Calgary Flames)

1971 – **Gordie Sheer** (luge)

JUNE 10

GAMEBREAKERS

1947 – On **Herb Karpel** Night in Newark, Karpel earns his 100th career minor-league victory as the Bears beat the Rochester Red Wings 8-2 in the International League.

1953 – **Sid Gordon's** three-run homer in the eighth inning rallies the Milwaukee Braves to a 6-5 victory over the New York Giants.

1966 – **Steve Kolinsky's** squeeze bunt single in the 11th inning – his fifth hit of the game – gives Macon a 6-5 victory over Columbus in the Southern League.

2006 – **Adam Stern** hits an RBI single and a three-run homer in the seventh inning to give Pawtucket an 8-5 win over Richmond in the International League.

2007 – **Jason Hirsh** allows five hits in his first career complete game as the Colorado Rockies defeat the Baltimore Orioles 6-1.

1973 – **Red Holzman** coaches the Knicks to their second NBA title as New York beats the Los Angeles Lakers 102-93.

1973 – Los Angeles Macabee beats Cleveland Inter 5-3 to win its first of five United States Open Cup soccer titles in the next nine years.

1989 – **Fabrice Benichou** knocks out Frans Badenhurst in the fifth round to retain his IBF super bantamweight title in Frosinone, France.

1995 – **Jessica Davis** wins the Senior Rhythmic Gymnastics national championship all-around title in Jacksonville, Fla.

2000 – **George Weissfisch** wins the gold medal in the heavyweight division at the U.S. National Taekwondo team trials in Colorado Springs, Colo.

STRONG IN DEFEAT

1960 – **Norm Sherry** goes 3 for 4 with a pair of home runs and three RBI's in the Los Angeles Dodgers' 4-3 loss to the Cincinnati Reds.

1970 – **Mike Epstein** drives in eight runs, but the Washington Senators lose 12-10 to the Baltimore Orioles.

JEWS ON FIRST

1986 – **Nancy Lieberman** becomes the first woman to play for a men's professional basketball team in a regular-season game when she suits up with the Springfield Fame of the United States Basketball League in a 122-107 victory over Staten Island.

MAZEL TOUGH

1928 – **Clara Greenspan** defeats Florence Sheldon 6-2, 9-7 to win the Eastern Clay Court tennis title in Montclair, N.J.

1944 – **Norman Wasser** of NYU wins the NCAA shot put title with a toss of 49-1 in Milwaukee.

1946 – **Herman Barron** defeats Lew Worsham by three strokes in an 18-hole playoff to win the PGA Philadelphia Inquirer Invitational.

1973 – **Dick Siderowf** of Westport, Conn., beats P.H. Moody 5-and-3 in Porthcawl, Wales, to win his first of two British Amateur Golf Championships.

TRANSITIONS

1977 – **Ernie Grunfeld** of Tennessee is picked in the first round of the NBA draft – 11th overall – by the Milwaukee Bucks.

A STAR IS BORN

1891 – **Battling Levinsky** (light heavyweight boxer)

1977 – **Mike Rosenthal** (Notre Dame, New York Giants, Minnesota Vikings lineman)

JUNE 11

GAMEBREAKERS

1907 – **Barney Pelty** of the St. Louis Browns pitches his first of three consecutive shutouts, blanking the Philadelphia Athletics 3-0.

1944 – **Phil Weintraub's** 12th-inning homer gives the New York Giants a 6-5 win over the Philadelphia Phillies in the second game of a doubleheader.

1966 – **Mickey Abarbanel** allows three hits and strikes out 15 as the Fox Cities Foxes defeat Quad Cities 2-0 in the Midwest League.

MAZEL TOUGH

1934 – **Harry Mason** wins in the 14th round by disqualification over Len "Tiger" Smith to capture the vacant British welterweight title in Birmingham, England.

1966 – **Steve Sandler** defeats **Howie Eisenberg** to win the National AAU one-wall handball championship.

1975 – **Hank Greenberg** teams with Los Angeles Rams football player Bob Klein to win the Dewars Celebrity Tennis Tournament in Las Vegas.

1996 – **Nick Bravin** defeats **Cliff Bayer** to win the foil title at the U.S. National Fencing Championships in Cincinnati.

2005 – **Tomas Scheckter** leads 119 of the 200 laps to win the Bombardier 500 in Fort Worth, Texas, his second career Indy Racing League victory. He wins by less than a car length over Sam Hornish.

RECORD SETTERS

1898 – **Myer Prinstein** sets a world record of 23-8 7/8 in the long jump at the New York Athletic Club Games on Travers Island.

1932 – **Sol Furth** sets a Metropolitan AAU meet record in the triple jump with a leap of 48 feet, 3 inches.

2004 – **Jason Lezak** betters the meet record he set two years earlier, swimming the 100 freestyle in 49.20 seconds at the Janet Evans Invitational in Long Beach, Calif. Lezak outswims Ian Thorpe in the final major meet before the U.S. Olympic Trials.

A STAR IS BORN

1895 – **Jackie "Kid" Wolfe** (junior featherweight boxer)

1903 – **Sidney Franklin** (bullfighting)

1903 – **Moise Bouquillon** (French heavyweight boxer)

JUNE 12

GAMEBREAKERS

1915 – **Erskine Mayer** of the Philadelphia Phillies shuts out the Chicago Cubs 13-0.

1921 – **Sammy Bohne** goes 3 for 4 with an RBI and scores three runs as the Cincinnati Reds beat the Brooklyn Robins 7-1.

1944 – **Phil Weintraub** hits two home runs as the New York Giants outslug the Brooklyn Dodgers 15-9.

1951 – Two days after breaking his nose for the eleventh time, **Al Rosen** returns to the Cleveland Indians' lineup and bangs out three hits, including a home run and four RBI's, in an 8-4 victory over the Philadelphia Athletics. Two of the breaks occurred while boxing, six while playing football, and three while playing baseball.

1964 – **Sandy Koufax** stops the St. Louis Cardinals 3-0 on four hits.

1965 – **Sandy Koufax** blanks the New York Mets 5-0.

1980 – **Jeff Stember** allows two hits as the Shreveport Captains defeat Jackson 2-0 in the Texas League.

STRONG IN DEFEAT

1951 – Four days after hitting for the cycle in a Western International League game, **Sol Israel** does it again in Tacoma's 9-5 loss to Wenatchee.

MAZEL TOUGH

1922 – Jockey **Georges Stern** rides Ramus to his third French Derby victory.

1959 – **Carl Shine** of Penn wins the NCAA shot put title with a toss of 57 feet, 11¾ inches.

1971 – **Julie Heldman** defeats Barbara Hawcroft 6-4, 7-9, 6-3 to win the Players Tournament in Nottingham, England. She also teams with Francois Durr to win the doubles.

1981 – **Saoul Mamby** wins a 15-round decision over Jo Kimpuani in Detroit to retain his WBC junior welterweight title.

2004 – **Justin Gimelstob** defeats Dusan Vemic 7-6 (7), 6-2 to win the Forest Hills (N.Y.) Grass Court Challenger tennis tournament. Gimelstob also teams with Brandon Coupe to win the doubles title.

RECORD SETTERS

1889 – **N.M. Cohen** sets an English record for the 50-yard straightaway swim with a time of 25.4 seconds on the River Cam.

1926 – **Lillian Copeland** is the seventh of 10 Pasadena Athletic and Country Club runners who set a U.S. record of 58.5 seconds in the 500-yard (10x50) relay in Pasadena, Calif.

1967 – **Mike Epstein** of Washington records a record 32 putouts at first base in a 14-inning game against the Chicago White Sox. The Senators win 6-5.

A STAR IS BORN

1925 – **Dick Miles** (table tennis)

1943 – **Marv Albert** (broadcasting)

1948 – **Eddie Fogler** (North Carolina basketball, Vanderbilt and South Carolina coach)

1969 – **Mathieu Schneider** (Montreal Canadiens, New York Islanders, Toronto Maple Leafs, New York Rangers, Los Angeles Kings, Detroit Red Wings)

JUNE 13

GAMEBREAKERS

1962 – **Sandy Koufax** pitches a three-hitter as Los Angeles defeats the Milwaukee Braves 2-1.
1963 – **Sandy Koufax** allows three hits and strikes out 10 as the Los Angeles Dodgers defeat Houston 3-0.

MAZEL TOUGH

1867 – **Young Barney Aaron** regains his American lightweight title by beating Sam Collyer in 66 rounds in Aqua Creek, W.Va.
1922 – **Oakland Jimmy Duffy** wins a six-round decision over champion Travie Davis to capture the Pacific Coast welterweight title in Seattle.
1934 – **Baroness Maud Levi** retains her New York State singles tennis title.
1936 – Jockey **Eddy Litzenberger** rides Clang to victory in the Carter Handicap at Belmont Park.
1937 – **Leonard Hartman** defeats Frank Bowden in five sets to retain his Brooklyn tennis tournament title.
1941 – **Norman Armitage** retains his national saber title by beating all five opponents in the final round of the Amateur Fencers League of America championships in New York.
1960 – **Isaac Berger** wins the featherweight title at the AAU Weightlifting Championships in Cleveland.
1976 – **Jody Scheckter** outraces Patrick Depailler of France to win the Formula One Grand Prix of Sweden in Anderstorp.
1981 – **Marty Hogan** beats Craig McCoy 21-9, 21-12 in Tempe, Ariz., to become the first person to win four straight National Pro-Am Racquetball titles.
1999 – **Bruce Fleisher** wins the PGA Senior BellSouth Classic in Nashville, Tenn., by one stroke over Al Geiberger.
2004 – **Lenny Krayzelburg** wins the 100 backstroke in 55.28 seconds at the Janet Evans Invitational swim meet in Long Beach, Calif.

RECORD SETTERS

1974 – **Irena Kirszenstein-Szewinska** of Poland breaks her world record in the 200 meters with a time of 22.21 seconds in Potsdam, Germany.

JEWS ON FIRST

1962 – **Sandy Koufax** hits his first of two career home runs, connecting off Warren Spahn as the Los Angeles Dodgers beat the Milwaukee Braves 2-1.
2003 – **Sada Jacobson** wins the epee at the New York City World Cup and becomes the first American woman to achieve a No. 1 world ranking in fencing.

TRANSITIONS

1975 – **Elliott Maddox**, the Yankees' .305 hitter, tears cartilage in his knee when he slips on the Shea Stadium turf and misses the rest of the season.
1988 – **Larry Brown** is named coach of the San Antonio Spurs.
1998 – Barcelona Dragons defensive end **Josh Taves** is named Defensive Player of the Year in NFL Europe.

A STAR IS BORN

1875 – **Paul Neumann** (Austrian swimmer)
1918 – **Jack Garfinkel** (St. John's basketball, Rochester Royals, Boston Celtics)
1929 – **Bud Swartz** (St. Louis Browns pitcher)
1967 – **David Littman** (Buffalo Sabers, Tampa Bay Lightning goalie)

JUNE 14

GAMEBREAKERS

1912 – **Guy Zinn's** 10th-inning homer gives the New York Highlanders a 7-5 victory over the St. Louis Browns.

1925 – **Max Gruenwald** scores two goals as Hakoah Vienna ties Simmeringer sc 3-3 and clinches first place in Austria's national soccer league.

1930 – **Harry Rosenberg** hits two home runs and a single as the Mission Reds defeat the Hollywood Stars 9-5 in the Pacific Coast League.

STRONG IN DEFEAT

2002 – **Shawn Green** hits a pair of solo home runs, but the Los Angeles Dodgers lose 8-4 to the Anaheim Angels.

MAZEL TOUGH

1915 – **Charley White** knocks out **Young Abe Brown** in the first round of a lightweight fight in New York.

1924 – **Umberto de Morpurgo** of Italy defeats Axel Petersen of Denmark for his first of 54 career Davis Cup tennis victories. Denmark completes a 3-2 victory two days later, with Morpurgo accounting for both Italian points.

1937 – **Baby Yack (Benjamin Yakubowitz)** wins a 10-round decision over Frankie Martin in Toronto to capture the Canadian bantamweight title.

1947 – **Ladislav Hecht** of Czechoslovakia defeats Enrique Buse of Peru 6-3, 6-3, 6-3 in the final of the Brooklyn Tennis Tournament.

1953 – **Anita Kanter** wins the women's U.S. National hard-court tennis championship.

1955 – **Albert Axelrod** wins the foil and **Abram Dreyer Cohen** the epee at the AAU national fencing championships.

1957 – **Daniel Bukantz** wins the foil title at the U.S. Fencing Championships in Milwaukee.

1992 – **Yael Arad** of Israel wins the 61-kg. class at the Austrian Open judo championships.

1997 – **Max Heyman** makes his pro boxing debut with a first-round knockout of super middleweight Luis Medina in Albuquerque, N.M.

1998 – **Kenny Bernstein** beats Bob Vandergriff in the Top Fuel final at the NHRA Pontiac Nationals.

Daniel Bukantz
(U.S. Olympic Committee)

TRANSITIONS

2000 – USA Hockey names Providence senior goalie **Sara DeCosta** the college women's player of the year. DeCosta led the nation with a .943 save percentage, posting seven shutouts among 17 victories.

A STAR IS BORN

1896 – **Samuel Mosberg** (lightweight boxer)
1916 – **Al Hessberg** (Yale football)
1921 – **Charlie Furchgott** (Georgia football)

JUNE 15

GAMEBREAKERS

1907 – **Moxie Manuel** pitches both ends of a doubleheader as the New Orleans Pelicans beat the Birmingham Barons 1-0 in both nine-inning games. He allows two hits in the first game and six in the second, and does not give up a walk in either game while striking out 11. The feat comes in the middle of Manuel's Southern Association-record 58 consecutive shutout innings.

1907 – **Barney Pelty** of the St. Louis Browns pitches his second of three straight shutouts, stopping the Boston Red Sox 4-0.

1932 – **Jim Levey** is hit by a pitch with the bases loaded in the bottom of the ninth, forcing in the winning run as the St. Louis Browns beat the Philadelphia Athletics 9-8.

1934 – Playing his first game in two weeks, **Al Rosen** delivers a pinch-hit three-run double in the eighth inning to ignite a six-run rally, and the Cleveland Indians beat the Washington Senators 9-3.

1940 – **Harry Danning** hits for the cycle, including an inside-the-park homer that lands on the fly 460 feet in front of the Giants' clubhouse at the Polo Grounds as New York beats the Pittsburgh Pirates 11-1.

2002 – **Shawn Green** hits home runs off Angels pitcher **Scott Schoeneweis** his first two times at-bat, giving him four consecutive homers over two games. He is the 24th player to accomplish the feat, including **Hank Greenberg**, **Art Shamsky**, and **Mike Epstein**. The Dodgers beat Anaheim 10-5.

MAZEL TOUGH

1913 – **Georges Stern** rides Dagur to victory in the French Derby.

1926 – **Leo Lomski** retains his Pacific Coast middleweight title with a six-round decision over Jock Malone in Seattle.

1929 – **Clara Greenspan** wins the Metropolitan Clay Court tennis title with a 6-3, 9-7 win over Mrs. Bernard Stenz.

1930 – **Julius Seligson** defeats Edward Tarangioli 6-0, 6-1, 10-8 for his second Metropolitan Clay Court tennis title.

1956 – **Abe Cohen** wins the epee title at the U.S. Fencing Championships in the Bronx, New York.

1963 – **Gary Gubner** of NYU wins his first of two NCAA shot put titles with a toss of 62 feet, 5 inches in Albuquerque, N.M.

1974 – **Paulina Peled** of Israel wins her second straight tennis tournament in Great Britain, beating Kate Latham 5-7, 6-3, 6-4 in the Kent Championships final.

1974 – **Steve Sandler** beats Al Torres to win the AAU national one-wall handball championship in Brooklyn, N.Y.

1975 – Los Angeles Macabee beats New York Inter-Giuliana 1-0 to win the United States Open Cup soccer championship.

1986 – **Martin Jaite** defeats Paolo Cane 6-2, 4-6, 6-4 in the final of a clay-court tennis tournament in Bologna, Italy.

1990 – **Ken Flax** wins his second hammer throw title at the National AAU outdoor track championships.

1998 – **Tamir Bloom** finishes first out of 58 competitors in the epee at the National Fencing Championships in New York.

JEWS ON FIRST

2004 – **Larry Brown** becomes the first coach to win both an NCAA and NBA title when the Detroit Pistons defeat the Los Angeles Lakers 100-87 to complete a 4-1 series.

A STAR IS BORN

1915 – **Marty Pomerantz** (lightweight boxer)

1923 – **Solomon Israel** (minor-league baseball)

1975 – **Rachel Wacholder** (beach volleyball)

JUNE 16

GAMEBREAKERS

1927 – **Sol Mishkin** collects three hits in his professional baseball debut as the San Francisco Seals defeat the Los Angeles Angels 7-6 in the Pacific Coast League.

1956 – **Al Federoff's** RBI triple gives the San Diego Padres a 1-0 victory over the Vancouver Mounties in a Pacific Coast League game.

1971 – **Mike Epstein**, recently acquired by Oakland from Washington, hits homers in his first two times at bat, giving him four in a row over two games. The A's beat the Senators 5-1.

2002 – **Yaron Peters** hits a tie-breaking two-run homer in the ninth inning as South Carolina eliminates Nebraska from the College World Series, 10-8. The homer is his 29th of the season.

2006 – **Jason Marquis** allows five hits over eight innings as the St. Louis Cardinals defeat the Colorado Rockies 8-1.

MAZEL TOUGH

1923 – **Louis A. Clark** of Johns Hopkins wins the NCAA 100-yard dash in 9.9 seconds in Chicago.

1942 – **Norman Armitage** wins seven of eight bouts in the saber finals to win his fourth straight national fencing title in New York.

1950 – **Herb Flam** of UCLA wins the singles title and teams with Gene Garrett to win doubles at the NCAA tennis championships in Austin, Texas.

1991 – **Riccardo Patrese** of Italy outraces teammate Nigel Mansell to win the Formula One Mexican Grand Prix.

2002 – **Anna Smashnova** beats defending champion Iroda Tulyaganova of Uzbekistan 6-4, 6-1 to win the Wien Energie Grand Prix tournament in Vienna, her third victory of the season. The victory pushes her to 17th in the WTA rankings – the highest ever for an Israeli tennis player.

JEWS ON FIRST

1939 – **Milton Padway** becomes the first Jewish pole-vaulter – and 11th American – to clear 14 feet, reaching 14-2 in Los Angeles.

TRANSITIONS

1936 – The German Olympic Committee drops national high jump record-holder **Gretel Bergmann** from the national team, offering her a standing-room-only ticket to the Berlin Games instead.

1972 – **Roy Rubin** resigns as basketball coach and athletic director at Long Island University to become head coach of the Philadelphia 76ers. He will be replaced by Kevin Loughery at the All-Star break after posting a 4-47 record. The Sixers finish 9-73, the worst mark in the history of the NBA.

A STAR IS BORN

1919 – **Harold "Lefty" Phillips** (California Angels manager)

1979 – **Sergio Roitman** (Argentine tennis)

Norm Armitage *(U.S. Olympic Committee)*

JUNE 17

GAMEBREAKERS

1941 – **Harry Danning** hits two singles, a double, and drives in three runs as the New York Giants beat the Pittsburgh Pirates 8-3.

1963 – **Sandy Koufax** pitches his second straight shutout, allowing four hits and striking out nine as the Dodgers beat the San Francisco Giants 2-0.

1964 – **Sandy Koufax** pitches his second straight shutout, stopping the Milwaukee Braves 5-0 on three hits.

1980 – **Steve Stone** strikes out a career-high 11 batters as the Baltimore Orioles beat the California Angels 5-3.

1998 – **Brad Ausmus** singles in the winning run in the bottom of the ninth as the Houston Astros beat the St. Louis Cardinals 6-5.

STRONG IN DEFEAT

1923 – **Sammy Bohne** of the Cincinnati Reds singles with two out in the ninth inning, spoiling a no-hit bid by Dazzy Vance of the Dodgers. Brooklyn wins 9-0.

1997 – **Shawn Green** goes 3 for 4 with two homers in Toronto's 8-7 loss to the Atlanta Braves.

MAZEL TOUGH

1894 – Light heavyweight **Joe Choynski** wins a five-round decision over Bob Fitzsimmons in Boston.

1934 – **Maud Levi** retains her New York State singles tennis title and **Grace Sorber** teams with Norma Taubele to win the doubles championship.

1945 – **Norman Armitage** wins his last of 10 national saber titles in AAU fencing.

1948 – **Nathan Lubell** wins the foil and **Norman Lewis** the epee at the AAU national fencing championships.

1949 – **Norman Lewis** retains his epee title and **Daniel Bukantz** wins the foil at the AAU national fencing championships in New York.

1950 – **James Fuchs** of Yale wins his second straight NCAA shot put title with a toss of 56 feet, 11/16 inches.

1990 – **Amos Mansdorf** of Israel beats Alexander Volkov 6-3, 7-6 in the final of the Continental Grasscourt tennis tournament in Rosmalen, Netherlands.

2000 – LSU beats Stanford 6-5 to hand coach **Skip Bertman** his fifth NCAA baseball championship in 10 years. Losing pitcher **Justin Wayne**, who struck out seven of the first nine batters he faced, yields a game-winning single in the bottom of the ninth.

RECORD SETTERS

1973 – **Jody Scheckter** sets a Watkins Glen one-lap record of 120.09 mph in the time trials, then wins his fourth consecutive Formula 5000 race en route to the season championship.

Norm Lewis *(U.S. Olympic Committee)*

JUNE 18

GAMEBREAKERS

1933 – **Buddy Myer** of Washington homers in each game of a doubleheader with New York. The Senators win the first game 14-1, but the Yankees win the nightcap 3-2.

1962 – **Sandy Koufax** pitches a five-hitter, and the Dodgers beat the St. Louis Cardinals 1-0 when Tommy Davis hits a ninth-inning homer.

STRONG IN DEFEAT

1947 – **Hank Greenberg** hits two home runs in the Pittsburgh Pirates' 12-5 loss to the New York Giants.

1967 – Amateur golfer **Marty Fleckman,** the 23-year-old surprise leader after three rounds of the U.S. Open in Springfield, N.J., shoots an 80 on the final day to fall into a tie for 18th place behind winner Jack Nicklaus.

MAZEL TOUGH

1928 – **Woolf Bernato** of Great Britain teams with driver **Bernard Rubin** to win his first of three straight 24 Hours of Le Mans races.

1940 – **Benny Goldberg** knocks out Charley Parham in the 10th round to win the Michigan state bantamweight title in Detroit.

1949 – **James Fuchs** of Yale wins his first of two NCAA shot put titles with a toss of 56 feet, 1½ inches in Los Angeles. **Victor Frank** of Yale wins the discus at 168 feet, 9½ inches.

1964 – **Gary Gubner** of NYU wins his second straight NCAA shot put title with a toss of 61 feet, 8 inches.

1988 – **Ken Flax** wins the hammer throw at the National AAU outdoor track championships.

1994 – **Margie Goldstein-Engle** rides Sebastian to victory in the Town & Country Grand Prix equestrian event.

RECORD SETTERS

1931 – Newark second baseman **Andy Cohen** handles eight chances to set an International League record of 240 consecutive chances without an error.

A STAR IS BORN

1869 – **Samuel Liebgold** (racewalking)
1895 – **Johnny Rosner** (flyweight boxer)
1899 – **Sailor Friedman** (welterweight boxer)
1902 – **Johnny Brown** (British bantamweight boxer)
1931 – **Ed Miller** (Syracuse basketball, Baltimore Bullets)
1931 – **Wilf Rosenberg** (rugby)

Ken Flax
(U.S. Olympic Committee)

JUNE 19

GAMEBREAKERS

1907 – **Barney Pelty** of the St. Louis Browns beats the New York Highlanders 9-0 for his third consecutive shutout.

1948 – **Sid Gordon** hits two home runs in the New York Giants' 10-1 win over the St. Louis Cardinals.

1951 – **Herb Gorman's** sacrifice fly in the 16th inning gives the Hollywood Stars a 4-3 victory over Portland in the Pacific Coast League.

1969 – **Art Shamsky** hits two homers and two singles as the New York Mets beat the Philadelphia Phillies 6-5.

MAZEL TOUGH

1909 – **Monte Attell** knocks out Frankie Neil in the 18th round in Colma, Calif., to win the vacant American bantamweight title.

1915 – **Alvah Meyer** wins the 100-yard dash at the Metropolitan Track and Field Championships on Travers Island, N.Y.

1922 – **Ted "Kid" Lewis** knocks out Frankie Burns in the 11th round in London to retain the British Empire middleweight title.

1937 – **Sam Stoller** of Michigan, who threatened to retire from track after he was prevented from competing in the 1936 Olympics in Berlin, wins the NCAA 100-yard dash in 9.7 seconds in Berkeley, Calif.

1947 – **Herbie Kronowitz** decisions **Harold Green** in a 10-round middleweight fight at Ebbets Field to claim the Brooklyn middleweight championship.

1948 – **Irving Mondschein** of NYU wins his second straight NCAA high jump championship, clearing 6 feet 7 inches in Minneapolis.

1961 – Jockey **Walter Blum** rides six winners in eight races at Monmouth Park in New Jersey.

1966 – **Gary Gubner,** already an AAU shot put and discus champion, adds the AAU heavyweight wrestling title in York, Pa.

1971 – **Cary Feldmann** of Washington wins the NCAA javelin title with a throw of 259 feet in Seattle.

1971 – **Steve Sandler** defeats **Mark Levine** to win the National AAU one-wall handball championship. **Kenny Davidoff** and **Howie Eisenberg** beat Sandler and Don Weber for the doubles title.

1971 – **Pam Richmond** beats Arizona State teammate Peggy Michel 6-1, 6-2 to win the national collegiate women's tennis championship in Las Cruces, N.M. Richmond and Michel go on to beat Margie Cooper and Mona Schallau of Rollins 6-2, 6-4 for the doubles title.

1977 – Los Angeles Macabee beats Philadelphia German-Hungarian 5-1 to win the United States Open Cup soccer championship.

2003 – **Deena Drossin** wins the 10,000 meters at the U.S. Track and Field Championships in Stanford, Calif.

TRANSITIONS

2000 – **Skip Bertman** of LSU is named national college baseball coach of the year for the fifth time. He will retire in 2001 with 865 wins, seven Southeastern Conference championships, and five NCAA titles in 18 years.

A STAR IS BORN

1903 – **Joey Silvers** (lightweight boxer)
1923 – **Bernard Mayer** (track and field)
1968 – **Nadiv Henefeld** (Israeli, UConn basketball)

JUNE 20

GAMEBREAKERS

1941 – **Herb Karpel** pitches the 11th no-hitter in Eastern League history as the Binghamton Triplets beat the Elmira Pioneers 2-0.

1948 – Pitcher **Saul Rogovin** hits two of an International League-record 10 home runs in the first game of a doubleheader as the Buffalo Bison beat the Syracuse Chiefs 28-11.

1948 – **Al Rosen** of Kansas City goes 3 for 3 in the first game of an American Association doubleheader against Minneapolis, giving him eight consecutive hits – including five home runs – over the last 17 innings. The previous day, Rosen went 5 for 5 with four homers in a twinight doubleheader that did not end until after midnight.

1948 – **Sid Gordon** goes 4 for 4 with two homers and three RBI's as the New York Giants beat the St. Louis Cardinals 10-1.

1961 – **Sandy Koufax** loses his no-hitter when Ernie Banks singles with two out in the seventh. He settles for a two-hitter with 14 strikeouts as the Dodgers beat the Chicago Cubs 3-0.

1962 – **Barry Latman** allows five hits as the Cleveland Indians beat the Boston Red Sox 3-0.

1965 – **Sandy Koufax** allows one hit – Jim Hickman's fifth-inning homer – as the Dodgers beat the Mets 2-1.

1971 – **Steve Stone** allows three hits and strikes out 11 as the San Francisco Giants beat the San Diego Padres 2-0.

MAZEL TOUGH

1936 – **Joseph Goldenburg** captures first place on the flying rings at the AAU Gymnastics Championships in New York.

1943 – **Seymour Greenberg** wins his second straight U.S. National Clay Court tennis championship with a 6-1, 4-6, 6-3, 6-3 victory over Billy Talbert in Detroit.

1943 – **Norman Armitage** wins the U.S. National saber title in New York for the fifth time.

1944 – **Irving Mondschein** wins his first of three national decathlon championships at the AAU outdoor track championships.

1954 – **Henry Laskau** wins the 2-mile walk at the AAU outdoor track and field championships in St. Louis.

1959 – **Elliott Denman** wins the 3,000-meter walk at the AAU outdoor track and field championships in Boulder, Colo.

1961 – **Walter Blum** rides six winners at Monmouth Park in New Jersey.

1964 – **Carole Wright** wins her fifth straight New York State tennis title – and sixth in seven years – in Mamaroneck, N.Y.

2005 – Israeli tennis player **Jonathan Erlich** and **Andy Ram** win in Nottingham, England, for their second ATP doubles title of the year.

JEWS ON FIRST

1922 – **Mikhail Stern** of Romania becomes the first Jewish tennis player to compete in the Davis Cup. Stern loses 6-0, 6-1, 6-1 to Hassan Ali Fyzee of India, and Romania falls 3-0 in the first round of the World Group in Beckenham, England.

RECORD SETTERS

1952 – **Henry Laskau** sets an American record of 12 minutes, 52.7 seconds in the 3,000-meter walk in Long Beach, Calif.

A STAR IS BORN

1970 – **Oren Smadja** (Israeli judo)
1971 – **Josh Kronfeld** (New Zealand rugby)
1975 – **Maurice Rozenthal** and **Francois Rozenthal** (French hockey)

JUNE 21

GAMEBREAKERS

1980 – **Steve Stone** pitches a five-hitter with seven strikeouts as the Baltimore Orioles beat the Seattle Mariners 9-0.

1999 – **Shawn Green** has three hits, including a three-run homer and two-run homer, as the Toronto Blue Jays beat the Kansas City Royals 11-4.

MAZEL TOUGH

1930 – Lehigh senior **Julius Seligson** defeats Clifford Sutter of Tulane in straight sets to win his 60th straight collegiate tennis match and capture the Eastern Intercollegiate championship. Seligson will run his unbeaten record to 66 before losing to Sutter in the national finals a week later.

1941 – **Joe Fishbach** wins the Middle States tennis championship.

1947 – **Irving Mondschein** of NYU wins the NCAA high jump title at 6 feet, 6 13/16 inches in Salt Lake City.

1958 – **Stan Levenson** wins the 200 meters at the Canadian national track and field championships in Saskatoon, Saskatchewan.

1958 – **Isaac Berger** wins the featherweight title at the AAU weightlifting championships in Los Angeles.

1964 – **Bob Grossman** teams with Fernand Tavano and finishes ninth in the 24 Hours of Le Mans, a record sixth-straight top 10 finish for the American driver.

1974 – Southern Cal's **Bruce Manson** teams with Butch Walts to win the NCAA men's doubles tennis championship in Corpus Christie, Texas.

1998 – **Margie Goldstein-Engle** wins the Rolex/USET Show Jumping Championship at the U.S. Equestrian team headquarters in Gladstone, N.J.

2001 – **Michael Kalganov** of Israel wins the 500-meter race at the World Cup kayaking championships in France.

2002 – **Amir Hadad** of Israel and Martin Vassallo Arguello of Argentina beat Americans Brandon Hawk and Brandon Coupe 6-4, 6-4 to win the doubles title at the Seascape Challenger tennis tournament in Aptos, Calif.

TRANSITIONS

2002 – **Agnes Keleti**, winner of five Olympic gold medals for Hungary, is inducted into the International Gymnastics Hall of Fame in Oklahoma City.

Julius Seligson *(Lehigh University Athletics)*

JUNE 22

GAMEBREAKERS

1927 – In the final at-bat of his college career, Harvard three-sport athlete **Izzy Zarakov** hits a two-run homer with two out in the bottom of the ninth to give the Crimson a 6-5 victory over Yale.

1998 – **Dave Newhan** of Mobile has two hits including a home run and three RBI's in the Southern League All-Star Game.

STRONG IN DEFEAT

1952 – **Sid Gordon** of Boston hits a two-run homer in the first inning and wins a 100-pound bear cub for being the first Braves player to homer on "State of Maine Day." The Braves lose to the St. Louis Cardinals 7-2.

MAZEL TOUGH

1925 – **Harry Mason** knocks out Ernie Izzard in the ninth round to retain his British and European lightweight titles.

1930 – **Woolf Bernato** of Great Britain teams with Glen Kidston and becomes the first driver to win three straight 24 Hours of Le Mans races.

1942 – **Seymour Greenberg** defeats Harris Everett in five sets to capture the National Clay Court tennis championship.

1946 – **Bernard Mayer** of NYU wins the NCAA shot put title with a toss of 52 feet, 10½ inches in Minneapolis.

1956 – **Henry Laskau** wins the 3,000-meter racewalking title at the AAU championships in Bakersfield, Calif.

1975 – **Tom Okker** defeats Tony Roche 6-1, 3-6, 6-3 to win the John Player grass-court tennis tournament in Nottingham, England.

1980 – **Brian Gottfried** beats Sandy Mayer 6-3, 6-3 in the final of a grass-court tennis tournament in Great Britain.

1997 – **Igor Praporshchikov** of Australia wins the 76-kg. freestyle wrestling gold medal at the Oceania Championships in New Zealand.

2003 – **Jonathan Kaye**, a five-time runner-up on the PGA Tour, wins his first tournament in 194 career starts in a one-hole playoff with John Rollins at the Buick Classic in Harrison, N.Y. Kaye birdies the par-5 18th to force a playoff, then eagles the first playoff hole with a 15-foot putt.

RECORD SETTERS

1931 – **Leo De Korn** plays 246 holes of golf at Purchase (N.Y.) Country Club, but falls short of his attempt at 300 because of blisters on his feet. Later in the year, he sets a world record by playing 590 holes in 42½ hours.

1959 – **Sandy Koufax** strikes out 16 in a 6-2 win over the Phillies, setting a major-league record for a night game.

1974 – **Irena Kirszenstein-Szewinska** of Poland sets a world record of 49.9 seconds in the 400 meters in Rome.

TRANSITIONS

1943 – Former minor-league player **Sol Mishkin** is named manager of the Wellsville Yankees of the Class D New York-Penn League.

2002 – The Calgary Flames select Michigan freshman left wing **Eric Nystrom** with the No. 10 pick in the first round of the NHL Entry Draft.

A STAR IS BORN

1909 – **Harry Rosenberg** (New York Giants outfielder)

1930 – **Norm Greckin** (La Salle basketball)

1982 – **Ian Kinsler** (Texas Rangers second baseman)

JUNE 23

GAMEBREAKERS

1942 – **Sid Gordon** has four hits in Jersey City's 5-0 International League victory over Newark.

1963 – **Barry Latman** allows five hits and strikes out eight as the Cleveland Indians beat the Chicago White Sox 2-0.

1974 – **Johan Neeskens** scores twice on penalty kicks as The Netherlands takes a 2-0 lead and beats Bulgaria 4-1 in World Cup soccer.

2000 – **Sara Whalen** scores two goals as the United States beats Trinidad and Tobago 11-0 in a Gold Cup soccer match.

STRONG IN DEFEAT

1935 – **Hank Greenberg** hits a grand-slam home run in the ninth inning, but the Detroit Tigers lose 12-7 to the Washington Senators. Two years later to the day, Greenberg hits a grand slam in a 6-5 loss to the Boston Red Sox.

2000 – Dodgers outfielder **Shawn Green** hits a three-run homer and reaches base via base hit or walk for the 53rd consecutive game since beginning the streak on April 25. St. Louis beats Los Angeles 9-6 in 12 innings.

MAZEL TOUGH

1904 – **Abe Attell** wins a 15-round decision over Johnny Reagan in St. Louis to retain his world featherweight title.

1934 – **Sam Klopstock** of Stanford wins the 120 high hurdles at the NCAA track and field championships in Los Angeles.

1935 – **Baroness Maud Levi** defeats Norma Taubele 6-3, 9-7 to win the Eastern Clay Courts tennis championship in Montclair, N.J.

1939 – **Morrie Arnovich** of the last-place Philadelphia Phillies raises his National League-leading batting average to .399. He will finish the season at .324, third-best in the league.

1941 – **Abe Denner** wins a 15-round decision over Snooks Lacy in Providence, R.I., to retain his New England featherweight title.

RECORD SETTERS

1957 – **Isaac Berger** wins the 125-pound title at the National Weightlifting Championships in Daytona Beach, Fla.

1962 – **Gary Gubner** wins the shot put at the National AAU outdoor track championships with a meet-record 63-6½ in Walnut, Calif.

1979 – **Mark Roth** beats Dennis Lane 257-195 in the City of Roses Tournament in Portland, Ore., and becomes the fifth pro bowler to surpass a half million dollars in earnings.

RECORD SETTERS

1968 – **Mark Spitz** improves his world record in the 400 freestyle to 4:07.7 in Hayward, Calif.

2003 – **Sam Fuld** hits an RBI single in the eighth inning to set a College World Series record with his 24th career hit, but Stanford loses 14-2 to Rice in the championship game.

JEWS ON FIRST

1933 – **Barney Ross** beats Tony Canzoneri in 10 rounds in Chicago to capture both the world lightweight and junior welterweight titles. Ross becomes the first boxer to capture two titles simultaneously since the beginning of the Queensbury Rules era.

TRANSITIONS

1960 – Coach **Jimmie Reese** is named manager of the Pacific Coast League's San Diego Padres.

A STAR IS BORN

1892 – **Abel Kiviat** (track and field)

1900 – **Heinie Scheer** (Philadelphia A's infielder)

1935 – **Gyorgi Karpati** (Hungarian water polo)

1975 – **Tatiana Lysenko** (Ukrainian gymnast)

JUNE 24

GAMEBREAKERS

1914 – **Erskine Mayer** of the Philadelphia Phillies shuts out the Brooklyn Dodgers 2-0.

1938 – **Hank Greenberg** hits two homers as the Detroit Tigers beat the New York Yankees 12-8.

1950 – **Marv Rotblatt** becomes the Southern Association's first 10-game winner with a two-hitter in Memphis' 9-1 victory over Chattanooga.

1956 – **Al Rosen** collects his 1,000th career hit, a home run in the Cleveland Indians' 7-2, six-inning win over the Washington Senators.

1965 – On B'nai Brith Night in Williamsport, Pa., **Sherwin Minster** hits a two-run double to give the Mets a 2-1 victory over Springfield in the Eastern League.

1967 – **Mike Epstein** hits a grand slam homer in the first inning, and the Washington Senators go on to beat the Baltimore Orioles 8-3.

1995 – **Joel Stransky** scores all 15 points for Springboks of South Africa, including a dropkick that beats the New Zealand All Blacks 15-12 with seven minutes remaining in the second extra period to win the World Cup rugby championship in Johannesburg. Later, a permanent mark is placed at the "Joel Spot," 30 meters from the goal from where Stransky kicked the game-winner at Ellis Park Stadium.

MAZEL TOUGH

1934 – **Leonard Hartman** defeats Alfred Law 2-6, 7-5, 2-6, 6-1, 6-2 to win the Metropolitan Claycourt tennis title.

1942 – **Seymour Greenberg** wins the U.S. National Claycourt tennis championship.

1950 – **Herb Flam** of UCLA wins the NCAA tennis championship with a 6-3, 1-6, 6-1, 9-7 victory over Ricardo Barbieri of Rollins College.

1950 – **Jim Fuchs** wins his second straight National AAU outdoor shot put championship, and **Steve Seymour** wins his third javelin title in College Park, Md.

1961 – In his final competition, **Frank Spellman** wins the Senior National Weightlifting Championships 165-pound division in Santa Monica, Calif. **Isaac Berger** wins the 132-pound title and **Paul Goldberg** captures the 148-pound crown.

1967 – **Marty Fleckman** shoots a record-tying 209 to win the Northeast Amateur golf tournament in East Providence, R.I.

1980 – **Leonid Dervbinsky** wins the United States national epee fencing title.

JEWS ON FIRST

1955 – **Sandy Koufax** makes his major-league debut with Brooklyn, pitching two scoreless innings of relief against the Milwaukee Braves despite loading the bases before getting his first out.

2000 – **Max Birbraer** becomes the first Israeli player drafted by a National Hockey League team when the New Jersey Devils select him in the sixth round.

2003 – Florida batting coach **John Cohen** is named head baseball coach at Kentucky.

2007 – **Andre Sternberg** pitches one inning of hitless relief with two strikeouts to earn the victory as the Modi'in Miracle defeat the Petach Tikva Pioneers 9-1 in the inaugural Israel Baseball League game. Each of the league's six teams will play a 45-game schedule.

A STAR IS BORN

1942 – **Art Heyman** (Duke basketball, New York Knicks, Cincinnati Royals, Philadelphia 76ers, ABA New Jersey Americans, Pittsburgh/Minnesota Pipers, Miami Floridians)

1970 – **Limor Mizrachi** (Maryland. women's pro basketball)

1977 – **Cliff Bayer** (fencing)

JUNE 25

GAMEBREAKERS

1922 – **Heinie Scheer** collects his first major-league hit, an RBI single in the ninth inning that gives the Philadelphia Athletics a 2-1 victory over the Washington Senators.

1948 – **Ernie Silverman** pitches 4 2/3 innings of hitless relief as the Buffalo Bison defeat Jersey City 5-3 in the International League.

1954 – Memphis pitcher **Marv Rotblatt's** squeeze-bunt single in the second inning drives in both runs as the Chicks beat Chattanooga 2-1 in a Southern Association game.

1960 – **Joe Ginsberg** leads off the bottom of the 12th with a double and scores on a wild pitch to give the Chicago White Sox a 7-6 victory over the Boston Red Sox. Ginsberg goes 3 for 3 with two RBI's.

1969 – After pitching 18 consecutive scoreless innings, **Barry Latman** hurls a five-hitter as the Chicago White Sox beat the Washington Senators 4-1.

MAZEL TOUGH

1900 – **Siegfried Flesch** of Austria wins a fencing bronze medal for the individual saber at the Paris Olympics.

1917 – **Ted "Kid" Lewis** beats Jack Britton in 20 rounds in Dayton, Ohio, to regain the world welterweight title he lost to Britton a year earlier.

1917 – **Joe Fox** knocks out Joe Symonds in the 18th round to retain his British bantamweight title in London.

1930 – **Maxie Rosenbloom** wins a 15-round decision over champion Jimmy Slattery in Buffalo, N.Y., to capture the New York version of the world light heavyweight title.

1949 – **James Fuchs** wins the shot put at the AAU outdoor track championships in Fresno, Calif.

1960 – **Larry Nagler** of UCLA wins the NCAA singles tennis championship with a 3-6, 8-6, 6-4, 3-6, 6-4 victory over Whitney Reed of San Jose State. Nagler also teams with **Allen Fox** for the doubles title.

1961 – **Allen Fox** of UCLA beats Ray Senkowski of Michigan 6-1, 6-2, 6-4 for the NCAA tennis championship.

1965 – University of Houston junior **Marty Fleckman** sinks a 12-foot birdie putt on the final hole to win the NCAA golf championship by one stroke over Jim Wiechers of Santa Clara.

1978 – **Mark Roth** beats runner-up Jay Robinson by 200 pins to win the San Jose Open. He becomes the second bowler in history to earn more than $100,000 two years in a row.

RECORD SETTERS

1933 – In his first major-league game, Cleveland outfielder **Milt Galatzer** ties a record by drawing walks in all four plate appearances in the Indians' 9-0 loss to the Washington Senators. Galatzer gets his first two hits in a 10-1 loss in the nightcap.

1967 – **Mark Spitz** sets a world record of 4:10.6 in the 400 freestyle in Heywood, Calif.

JEWS ON FIRST

1878 – **Jake Goodman** hits the first home run in the history of the Milwaukee Grays franchise of the National League in an 11-4 loss to the Providence Grays. It was Goodman's only career home run.

1971 – **Ron Blomberg** of the New York Yankees hits his first of 52 career home runs off Pete Broberg in a 12-2 victory over the Washington Senators.

A STAR IS BORN

1908 – **Harry Rosen** (softball pitcher)
1939 – **Allen Fox** (UCLA tennis)

JUNE 26

GAMEBREAKERS

1996 – **Sandy Koufax** ties his National League record by striking out seven consecutive batters as the Dodgers beat the Atlanta Braves 2-1.

STRONG IN DEFEAT

1933 – Shortstop **Moe Berg** goes 2 for 4 in his final game for Princeton, but the Tigers lose 5-1 to Yale in the Big Three championship game at Yankee Stadium. The next day, Berg receives a $5,000 signing bonus from the Brooklyn Robins of the National League.

2005 – Amateur **Morgan Pressel**, 17, ties for second place in the U.S. Women's Open golf tournament at Cherry Valley in Colorado when Birdie Kim of South Korea holes a 30-foot bunker shot on 18.

MAZEL TOUGH

1916 – **Al McCoy** wins a 15-round decision over Hugh Ross in Bridgeport, Conn., to retain his world middleweight title.

1937 – **Phil Fox**, who also competed under the name **Phil Levy**, wins his first of three discus titles at the National AAU outdoor track championships. **Allen Tolmich** wins the 110-meter high hurdles and 200 hurdles and **Max Beutel** wins the 3,000-meter walk.

1948 – **Harry Likas** of the University of San Francisco defeats Vic Seixas to win the NCAA tennis championship in Los Angeles.

1948 – **Alf James** wins a 12-round decision over Gillie van der Westhuizen to retain his South African welterweight title in Johannesburg.

1962 – **Alphonse Halimi** decisions Piero Rollo in a 15-round fight in Tel Aviv to regain the European bantamweight title in the first pro boxing match held in Israel.

1965 – **Walter Blum** rides Affectionately to victory in the Vagrancy Handicap at Aqueduct. The horse carries 137 pounds, 17 more than the rest of the field and the highest total for an American female since Pan Zareta in 1916.

1982 – **Marty Hogan** defeats Dave Peck 11-9, 6-11, 11-5, 11-4 to win his fifth straight National Pro-Am Racquetball title in Palatine, Ill.

1994 – **Skip Kendall** shoots 12-under-par to win the Nike Tour Carolina Classic golf tournament in Cary, N.C., by two strokes over Pat Bates.

2004 – **Doug Heir** wins gold in the discus, javelin, and shot put at the National Sports Fest for Disabled Athletes in New London, Conn. The three golds bring his total to 302 in his 25-year career.

2004 – **Morgan Pressel** rallies over the last five holes to defeat Lisa Ferrero 1-up in the 36-hole final of the North and South Amateur golf tournament in Pinehurst, N.C. At 16, Pressel becomes the youngest winner in the 102-year history of the event.

RECORD SETTERS

1926 – **Lillian Copeland** sets an American record of 116-7½ in the javelin.

TRANSITIONS

1993 – **Samuel Berger**, president of the Canadian Football League in 1964 and 1971, is elected posthumously to the CFL Hall of Fame. Berger's Ottawa teams win four CFL championships before he purchases the Montreal Alouettes and wins three more titles.

1996 – The Los Angeles Clippers select Connecticut guard **Doron Sheffer** in the second round, making him the first Israeli to be drafted by an NBA team. Sheffer decides to play pro ball in Israel instead.

JUNE 27

GAMEBREAKERS

1959 – **Sandy Koufax** beats the Pittsburgh Pirates 3-0 for his first shutout since 1955, his rookie season.

1967 – **Mike Epstein** hits two homers as the Washington Senators beat the California Angels 9-4.

1980 – **Jeff Stember** shuts out the Jackson Mets for the third time this season as the Shreveport Captains win the Texas League game 4-0.

1991 – **Wayne Rosenthal** gives up three hits in 2 1/3 innings of relief, but Texas scores four runs in the seventh inning and beats Oakland 9-6 for Rosenthal's only major-league victory.

STRONG IN DEFEAT

1954 – San Diego shortstop **Al Federoff** and coach **Jimmie Reese** are both ejected in the eighth inning of a Pacific Coast League game after Federoff protests two strike calls by umpire Frank Walsh. Several fans threaten to come on the field to join the dispute. Federoff collects three of the Padres' four hits in a 1-0 loss to the San Francisco Seals.

MAZEL TOUGH

1910 – **Harry Lewis** knocks out **Young Joseph Aschel** in the seventh round after flooring him nine times to win the English welterweight title in London.

1921 – **Ted "Kid" Lewis** wins a 20-round decision over **Jack Bloomfield** in London to win the British middleweight title.

1928 – **Harry Blitman** decisions world featherweight champion Tony Canzoneri in a 10-round non-title fight in Philadelphia.

1953 – **Martin Engel** captures the hammer throw title at the National AAU outdoor track championships in Dayton, Ohio.

1977 – **Mark Roth** and **Marshall Holman** team up to win the BPAA Doubles Classic bowling tournament in San Jose. They finish 451 pins ahead of runners-up Don Johnson and Paul Colwell.

RECORD SETTERS

1934 – Speed skater **Irving Jaffee**, attempting the marathon distance of 25 miles for the first time, sets a world record of 1 hour, 26 minutes, 0.1 seconds at Grossinger's Resort in the Catskills. He breaks the old record by five minutes.

JEWS ON FIRST

1933 – **Milt Galatzer** of the Cleveland Indians hits his only career home run off Tommy Thomas in a 7-6 victory over the Washington Senators.

TRANSITIONS

1998 – Right wing **Michael Henrich** of the Ontario Hockey League's Barrie Colts is picked by the Edmonton Oilers in the first round of the NHL entry draft. He is the 13th player selected overall.

A STAR IS BORN

1910 – **Jack Portney** (lightweight boxer)
1913 – **Izzy Weinstock** (Pitt football, Philadelphia Eagles, Pittsburgh Steelers back)

JUNE 28

GAME BREAKERS

1928 – **Andy Cohen's** home run helps the New York Giants beat the Philadelphia Phillies 2-1.

1962 – **Shelly Brodsky** hits two doubles and three singles, driving in four runs as Greenville defeats Norfolk-Portsmouth 11-5 in the Sally League. His two-run single in the 11th inning breaks the game open.

STRONG IN DEFEAT

1998 – **Shawn Green** goes 3 for 4 with two homers in the Toronto Blue Jays' 10-3 loss to the Atlanta Braves.

MAZEL TOUGH

1913 – Jockey **Georges Stern** rides Bruleur to victory in the Cup de Paris.

1947 – **Bernard Mayer** wins the shot put and **Irv Mondschein** captures the long jump and triple jump at the Metropolitan AAU track meet at Triborough Stadium.

1952 – **Ed Rubinoff** wins the National Interscholastic tennis championship.

1968 – **Walter Blum** rides Jean-Pierre to victory in the Yankee Gold Cup Handicap at Suffolk Downs.

1981 – Los Angeles Macabee beats the Brooklyn Dodgers 5-1 to win the United States Open Cup soccer title.

RECORD SETTERS

1953 – **Valeria Gyengi** of Hungary sets a world record of 10:42.4 in the women's 800 freestyle in Budapest.

TRANSITIONS

1986 – Oakland fires Jackie Moore and replaces him with **Jeff Newman** as interim manager. Newman goes 2-8 in 10 games before the A's hire Tony LaRussa.

2006 – Two Israelis are selected in the second round of the NBA draft. **Lior Eliyahu**, a forward with Hapoel Galil Elyon, is chosen by the Orlando Magic and then traded to the Houston Rockets. The Seattle SuperSonics pick **Yotam Halperin**, a guard who plays for Union Olimpija Ljubana of Slovenia. In the first round, the Los Angeles Lakers pick UCLA guard **Jordan Farmar.**

A STAR IS BORN

1898 – **Joe Ironstone** (Ottawa Senators, Toronto Maple Leafs goalie)

1909 – **Jackie "Kid" Berg** (welterweight boxer)

1917 – **Sol Schiff** (table tennis)

JUNE 29

GAMEBREAKERS

1948 – **Sid Gordon's** two home runs, including his third grand slam of the season, help the New York Giants beat the Boston Braves 11-3.

1999 – **Shawn Green** of the Toronto Blue Jays goes 2 for 5 in a 6-5 victory over the Baltimore Orioles and begins a 28-game hitting streak.

2003 – **Gabe Kapler** collects three hits including two home runs and drives in four runs as the Boston Red Sox beat the Florida Marlins 11-7. One day earlier, in his first game with Boston, Kapler goes 4 for 5 with two doubles, a triple, and three RBI's in a 10-9 loss to the Marlins.

MAZEL TOUGH

1911 – **Tibor Fisher** of Hungary wins the 85-kg. Greco-Roman wrestling title at the European Championships in Vienna, Austria.

1935 – **Baroness Maud Levi** defeats Norma Taubele 4-6, 6-1, 6-2 to win the New Jersey State tennis championship in Hackensack, N.J.

1946 – **William Steiner** wins the 30-kilometer run at the AAU championship in San Antonio.

1958 – **Gerald Moss** defeats **Sidney Schwartz** 6-1, 6-2, 6-4 to win the Eastern Clay Court tennis championship in Hackensack, N.J.

2003 – **Joanna Zeiger** wins the Buffalo Springs Half-Ironman Triathlon in Lubbock, Texas.

2003 – **Irina Lenskiy** of Israel wins the 200 meters at a Grand Prix track and field meet in Prague.

JEWS ON FIRST

1938 – **Goody Rosen** of the Brooklyn Dodgers hits his first of 22 career home runs off Lou Felte in a 7-6 loss to the Boston Braves.

TRANSITIONS

1967 – At age 10 years, seven months, and 21 days, **Beverly Klass** becomes the youngest golfer ever to compete in the USGA Women's Open when she tees off in Hot Springs, Va. But Klass makes the cut in her three LPGA events, finishes 44th in one, and earns $131. She rejoins the Tour in 1976 after the LPGA passes a rule barring players under age 18 from full-time membership.

A STAR IS BORN

1906 – **Benny Lom** (Cal football)
1945 – **Michael Belkin** (Canadian tennis)
1952 – **Barry Silkman** (British soccer)

JUNE 30

GAMEBREAKERS

1922 – **Sammy Bohne's** three-run homer helps the Cincinnati Reds beat the Chicago Cubs 9-5.

1930 – **Jimmie Reese** hits a grand slam homer to help the New York Yankees defeat the Cleveland Indians 7-6.

1938 – Phillies outfielder **Phil Weintraub** gets the final hit in the last game played at the Baker Bowl in Philadelphia. Giants catcher **Harry Danning** collects three hits and three RBI's as New York wins 14-1.

1962 – **Sandy Koufax** pitches his first career no-hitter, beating the New York Mets 6-0. He becomes the first pitcher to strike out the side on nine pitches in the first inning, and he finishes with 13 strikeouts.

1974 – **Johan Neeskens** scores in the eighth minute, and The Netherlands beats East Germany 2-0 in World Cup soccer.

2004 – **Jordan Cila** scores two goals, including the game-winner, as the Colorado Rapids defeat the New York-New Jersey MetroStars 3-2 in Major League Soccer.

MAZEL TOUGH

1915 – **Elaine Rosenthal** defeats H.D. Hammond 4 and 3 to win the Western Open golf tournament in Midlothian, Ill.

1928 – Lehigh sophomore **Julius Seligson** defeats **Ben Gorchakoff** of Occidental 11-9, 6-0, 9-7 to win the intercollegiate tennis championship in Haverford, Pa.

1931 – **Lt. Morton Solomon** wins the National Rifle Association small-bore free rifle shooting championship.

1932 – **Baroness Maud Levi** wins the singles and teams with P.B. Hawk to capture the doubles in the clay-court Metropolitan Championship tennis tournament.

1940 – **Phil Fox** wins the National AAU discus championship for the third time.

1960 – **Dick Siderowf** defeats Bill Kufta 7-and-6 in a 36-hole final to win the Connecticut Amateur Golf Championship in East Norwalk, Conn.

1979 – **Marshall Holman** rallies to beat Jeff Mattingly 205-195 in the Seattle Open and becomes the youngest bowler to win 10 PBA titles.

1998 – **Jill Matthews** knocks out Lisa Houghton in the fourth round to retain the IFBA junior flyweight title.

2002 – **Kenny Bernstein** beats Andrew Cowin in the Top Fuel final at the NHRA Sears Craftsman Nationals at Gateway International Raceway in Madison, Ill.

RECORD SETTERS

1936 – **Gretel Bergmann** ties the German and European high jump record of 5 feet, 3 inches.

TRANSITIONS

1939 – **Hank Greenberg** of the Detroit Tigers, **Harry Danning** of the New York Giants, and **Morrie Arnovich** of the Philadelphia Phillies are selected to play in the All-Star Game. Although he is a unanimous pick and leads the National League in batting average, Arnovich does not get a chance to play in the game.

2003 – **Ernie Grunfeld** is hired as president of basketball operations of the Washington Wizards, one day after he is released from his contract as general manager of the Milwaukee Bucks.

A STAR IS BORN

1908 – **Morris Beckman** (lacrosse)

1931 – **Allan Jay** (British fencing)

1969 – **Tim Puller** (heavyweight boxer)

1979 – **Patrick Fleming** (Bowling Green, Canadian Football League punter)

JULY 1

GAMEBREAKERS

1910 – **Barney Pelty** of the St. Louis Browns pitches a 2-0 shutout in the first game played at White Sox (Comiskey) Park in Chicago. The victory comes three days after Pelty shuts out the Philadelphia A's 2-0.

1914 – **Erskine Mayer** of the Philadelphia Phillies pitches a six-hitter and hits his first of two career home runs in a 7-2 victory over the Boston Braves.

1930 – **Andy Cohen's** 10th-inning RBI single gives the Newark Bears a 12-11 victory over the Reading Keys in the International League.

1939 – **Buddy Myer** goes 4 for 4 as the Washington Senators beat the Philadelphia Athletics 9-4.

1942 – Pinch-hitter **Cy Block** delivers a bases-loaded single in the 11th inning to give Tulsa a 1-0 victory over Dallas in the Texas League.

1945 – **Hank Greenberg** homers off Charlie Gassaway of the Philadelphia Athletics in his first major-league game after four years in the military. Detroit wins the first game of a doubleheader 9-5.

MAZEL TOUGH

1928 – **Bobbie Rosenfeld** wins the long jump and discus events at the Canadian National track and field championships in Hamilton, Ontario.

1947 – **Al Phillips** stops Cliff Anderson in the eighth round to retain his British Empire featherweight title.

1984 – **Amy Alcott** beats Julie Inkster and Martha Nause by one stroke to win the Lady Keystone Open in Hershey, Pa.

2000 – In his first professional fight, **Nikolay Melandovich** of Israel stops Isaac Sebaduuka just 37 seconds into the first round in London to win the WBF Intercontinental feather-weight title. Melandovich earns the title shot based on an outstanding amateur record.

2001 – **Bruce Fleisher** shoots a final-round 2-under-par 68 to rally to a one-stroke victory over Gil Morgan and Isao Aoki in the U.S. Senior Open in Peabody, Mass. The victory, worth $430,000, is the first in a Grand Slam event by a Jewish male golfer since **Herman Barron** won the same event in 1963 in Port St. Lucie, Fla.

RECORD SETTERS

1882 – **Lon Myers** sets a U.S. record of 1:11.4 in the 600-yard run at the American AC Games at the Polo Grounds in New York.

1911 – **Abel Kiviat** sets an AAU record of 4:19.6 in the mile at an outdoor track meet in Pittsburgh.

1912 – **Gottfried Fuchs** scores an international-record 10 goals as Germany beats Russia 16-0 in the consolation round of the Stockholm Olympics soccer tournament.

JEWS ON FIRST

1987 – **Suzyn Waldman** signs on at 3 p.m. as WHN in New York becomes WFAN, the nation's first all-sports radio station.

TRANSITIONS

1985 – **Senda Berenson Abbott**, who organized the first-ever women's collegiate game between freshmen and sophomores at Smith College in 1893, is elected to the Basketball Hall of Fame.

A STAR IS BORN

1900 – **Lou Brower** (Detroit Tigers shortstop)
1945 – **Marc Savage** (pole-vaulter)
1957 – **Dave Jacobs** (Syracuse, New York Jets, Cleveland Browns, Philadelphia Eagles placekicker)
1958 – **Nancy Lieberman** (basketball)
1961 – **Doron Jamchi** (Israeli basketball)
1986 – **Olga Karmansky** (rhythmic gymnastics)

JULY 2

GAMEBREAKERS

1979 – **Steve Yeager** goes 4 for 5 with two homers and five RBI's, including a three-run homer with two out in the top of the 12th inning as the Los Angeles Dodgers beat the San Diego Padres 6-3.

1980 – **Ross Baumgarten** of the White Sox allows a seventh-inning single by Rod Carew and finishes with a one-hit, 1-0 shutout of the California Angels. Baumgarten, who walks one and strikes out five, will finish the season with a 2-12 record.

1996 – Modesto infielder **Dave Newhan** collects five hits and hits for the cycle in a Class A game against San Jose.

2004 – **David Stern** goes 4 for 4 with a home run and three RBI's as the Greenville Braves beat the Jacksonville Suns 9-6 in the Southern League.

MAZEL TOUGH

1932 – **Grace Surber** defeats **Carolyn Swartz Hirsch** in the final of the Metropolitan Clay Court tennis tournament.

1933 – **Baroness Maud Levi** beats **Grace Surber** 6-2, 6-2 to win the Women's Metropolitan Clay Court tennis tournament in New York.

1937 – At the AAU Outdoor Track and Field Championships in Milwaukee, **Allen Tolmich** wins the 110 high hurdles and 220 low hurdles, **Phil Levy** captures the discus, **Max Beutel** the 3,000-meter walk, and **Morris Fleischer** the 30k walk.

1938 – **Henry Cieman** of Canada wins the AAU outdoor 3-mile walk in Buffalo, N.Y.

1938 – **S. Mortimer Auerbach** of the United States wins the Duke of York Trophy by capturing a three-day speedboat race at Torquay, England.

1950 – **Herb Flam** defeats two-time defending champion **Sam Match** 6-8, 6-3, 6-0, 3-6, 6-2 to win the Utah State tennis tournament in Salt Lake City. Flam also teams with Ted Schroeder to win doubles

1950 – **Dick Savitt** captures the Eastern Clay Court championship by defeating Donald McNeill 6-4, 3-6, 6-3, 6-3 in Rye, N.Y. Savitt and **Sidney Schwartz** team to defeat **Seymour Greenberg** and Ricardo Balbieri 6-3, 6-2, 6-3 in the doubles final.

2000 – **Ivan Alexandrov** of Israel captures the gold medal in the 58.0-kg. Greco-Roman division at the World Junior Wrestling Championships in France.

2005 – **Rachel Wacholder** teams with Elaine Young to end the 50-match winning streak of Misty May and Kerri Walsh, 17-21, 27-20, 15-13 in the Cincinnati Open beach volleyball championships.

TRANSITIONS

1970 – Pitching coach **Larry Sherry** is named manager of the Mobile White Sox of the Southern League.

A STAR IS BORN

1883 – **Sigmund Harris** (Minnesota football)

1900 – **Joe Bennett** (Philadelphia Phillies third baseman)

1906 – **Karoly Karpati** (Hungarian wrestler)

1908 – **Gyorgy Brody** (Hungarian water polo goaltender)

JULY 3

GAMEBREAKERS

1903 – **John Raphael** of Oxford scores 103 runs in a cricket match against Cambridge. Oxford wins the three-day event by 268 runs.

1944 – **Dick Conger** pitches a three-hitter as the Los Angeles Angels defeat the Hollywood Stars 3-0 in the Pacific Coast League. More than $1 million is raised for War Bonds before the game.

1948 – **Steve Seymour** wins the National AAU outdoor javelin championship for the second straight year.

1951 – **Sid Gordon's** bases-loaded single in the ninth inning gives the Boston Braves a 4-3 win over the Brooklyn Dodgers.

1953 – **Al Rosen** of Cleveland homers in his fifth consecutive game as the Indians beat the Detroit Tigers 8-1.

1963 – **Sandy Koufax** ties a Dodgers team record with his seventh shutout of the season, allowing three hits and striking out nine as Los Angeles beats the St. Louis Cardinals 5-0.

1974 – **Johan Neeskens** scores the first goal in the 50th minute, and The Netherlands goes on to beat Brazil 2-0 in World Cup soccer.

1979 – **Steve Ratzer** pitches a four-hitter as the Denver Bears beat the Omaha Royals 6-0 in the American Association. In his next start, Ratzer allows four hits in a 2-0 victory over Iowa. He finishes the season 15-4 with a 3.59 ERA and is named the league's Pitcher of the Year.

1989 – **Eddie Zosky**, the Toronto Blue Jays' No. 1 draft pick out of Fresno State, hits an RBI single in his pro debut at Knoxville of the Southern League. Zosky begins at the Double-A level because Knoxville's two shortstops had combined for 33 errors.

STRONG IN DEFEAT

1948 – Brooklyn-born New York Giants third baseman **Sid Gordon** is given a special day at Ebbets Field. He homers twice, but the Dodgers win 7-5.

MAZEL TOUGH

1924 – **Ted "Kid" Lewis** wins a 20-round decision over **Johnny Brown** in London to win the European and British Empire welterweight titles.

RECORD SETTERS

1937 – **Allen Tolmich** of Wayne State twice breaks the world indoor record in the 200-meter hurdles at the AAU championships in Milwaukee. He runs 23.4 seconds in the first heat and 23.3 seconds in the final.

TRANSITIONS

1943 – **Phil "Motsy" Handler**, the team's line coach, is named head coach of the NFL's Chicago Cardinals. His teams will win two games in three years.

A STAR IS BORN

1911 – **Samuel Behr** (Wisconsin football)
1937 – **Dick Siderowf** (golf)
1952 – **Alan Mayer** (soccer goaltender)

JULY 4

GAMEBREAKERS

1906 – **Barney Pelty** of the St. Louis Browns allows one hit in a 3-0 victory over the Chicago White Sox. He loses the no-hitter in the ninth inning on an infield single by Edgar Hahn. Some accounts of the game indicate that the Browns' shortstop should have been charged with an error on the play.

1950 – Charleston left-hander **Moe Savransky** pitches a seven-inning no-hitter in a 7-0 Sally League victory over Savannah.

1952 – **Saul Rogovin** pitches the Chicago White Sox to a 2-0 victory over St. Louis, stopping the Browns on eight hits.

1954 – **Sid Gordon** hits a three-run homer in the eighth inning to give the Pittsburgh Pirates a 7-6 win over the New York Giants.

1959 – Macon outfielder **Shelly Brodsky** goes 6 for 7 in a Sally League doubleheader with Columbus. In his previous game, Brodsky went 4 for 4. He has nine singles and a homer during the streak.

1999 – **Shawn Green** hits two solo home runs as the Toronto Blue Jays beat the Tampa Bay Devil Rays 6-3.

STRONG IN DEFEAT

1905 – **Moxie Manuel** of the Baton Rouge Cajuns pitches a no-hitter but loses 4-0 to the Vicksburg Hill Billies in the second game of a Cotton States League doubleheader. Manuel is the winning pitcher in the first game.

MAZEL TOUGH

1903 – **Jewey Cooke** of England retains his South African middleweight title with a 20-round decision over Jim Holloway in Johannesburg.

1906 – **Abe Attell** wins a 20-round decision over Frankie Neal in Los Angeles to retain his world featherweight title.

1913 – **Sidney S. Abrahams** wins the long jump at the English AAA Track and Field National Championships in London.

1922 – **Benny Leonard** knocks out Rocky Kansas in the eighth round in Michigan City, Mich., to retain his world lightweight title.

1928 – **Lilian Copeland** wins her fourth straight AAU shot put title in Newark, N.J.

1935 – **Morris Davis** captures the 15-kilometer walk at the AAU Outdoor track championships in Lincoln, Neb.

1936 – **Irv Horowitz** wins the 15-kilometer walk at the AAU outdoor track championships.

1939 – **Phil Fox** wins the discus title at the National AAU outdoor track championships in Lincoln, Neb.

1951 – **Dick Savitt** beats **Herb Flam** 1-6, 15-13, 6-3, 6-2 in the Wimbledon semifinals.

1964 – **Julius Heldman** defeats William Milliken 7-5, 10-8 to win the U.S. Senior Clay Court tennis title in Cynwyd, Pa.

RECORD SETTERS

1950 – **Sid Gordon** of the Boston Braves ties a major-league record set in 1911 with his fourth grand slam of the season in a 12-9 win over the Philadelphia Phillies.

2004 – **Philip Rabinowitz** of South Africa becomes the world's fastest 100-year-old, knocking more than five seconds off the world record for the 100-meter run in Cape Town. Rabinowitz is timed in 30.86 seconds, breaking the previous mark of 36.19

A STAR IS BORN

1880 – **Paul "Twister" Steinberg** (pro basketball, pro football, minor-league baseball)

1896 – **John Alexander** (Rutgers, New York Giants football)

1903 – **Abe Saperstein** (basketball)

1903 – **Joey Sangor** (featherweight boxer)

1908 – **Bob Olin** (light heavyweight boxer)

1929 – **Al Davis** (Oakland/Los Angeles Raiders coach and owner)

JULY 5

GAMEBREAKERS

1951 – For the second time in three days, **Sid Gordon** delivers a game-winning hit with the bases loaded as the Boston Braves beat the Philadelphia Phillies 7-6 in 11 innings.

1964 – **Sandy Koufax** pitches a six-hitter as the Los Angeles Dodgers beat the New York Mets 5-0.

1966 – **Sandy Koufax** scatters 10 hits and strikes out eight in a 1-0 victory over the Cincinnati Reds. Koufax's 38th career shutout ties the club record held by Nap Rucker.

1988 – **Jose Bautista** allows five hits and strikes out six as the Baltimore Orioles beat the Chicago White Sox 5-1.

2006 – **Jason Hirsh** allows one hit – a single by the Albuquerque pitcher with two out in the third inning – as Round Rock (Texas) wins 4-0 in the Pacific Coast League.

MAZEL TOUGH

1914 – Jockey **Georges Stern** rides Sardanapale to victory in the Cup de Paris.

1920 – Lightweight champion **Benny Leonard** knocks out **Charley White** in the ninth round in Benton Harbor, Mich. White had knocked Leonard out of the ring with a left hook in the sixth round, but Leonard was able to return to the ring in time.

1921 – **Kaufman Geist** wins the triple jump at the AAU Outdoor track championships in Pasadena, Calif.

1926 – **Jack Silver** wins a 10-round decision over **Mushy Callahan** to capture the Pacific Coast lightweight title in San Francisco.

1948 – **Morris Fleischer** wins the 20-kilometer racewalking championship in Philadelphia.

1958 – **Albert Axelrod** wins the foil title at the U.S. National Fencing Championships in New York.

1963 – **Abigail Hoffman** wins the 400- and 800-meter runs at the Canadian National track and field championships in Saskatoon, Saskatchewan.

1968 – **Julie Heldman** wins the Swedish Open tennis tournament in Bastad by walkover in the final against **Kathy Harter.**

RECORD SETTERS

1947 – **Steve Seymour** sets an American record of 248 feet, 10 inches in the javelin at the National AAU meet in Lincoln, Neb.

TRANSITIONS

1967 – The LPGA lifts its ban on 10-year-old **Beverly Klass** from playing in the Lady Carling Open after her father threatens to sue.

2001 – Maccabi Tel Aviv basketball coach **Pini Gershon** resigns and is replaced by **Dennis Blatt**, who led Princeton to the Ivy League championship in 1981.

A STAR IS BORN

1764 – **Daniel Mendoza** (English boxer)
1977 – **Jonathan Erlich** (Israeli tennis)

Albert Axelrod
(U.S. Olympic Committee)

JULY 6

GAMEBREAKERS

1866 – **Lipman Pike** of the Philadelphia Athletics hits six home runs, including five in a row, in a 67-25 victory over the Alert Club of Philadelphia.

1917 – Omaha Rourkes second baseman **Phil Cooney** completes an unassisted triple play in a Western League game against the Denver Bears.

MAZEL TOUGH

1919 – The United States beats France 93-8 to win the basketball competition at the Inter-Allied Games in Paris. U.S. captain **Marty Friedman** accepts the championship trophy from General John J. Pershing.

1940 – **Sybil Koff Cooper** wins the 80 hurdles at the AAU Outdoor women's track championships in Ocean City, Md.

1951 – **Dick Savitt** of the United States beats Ken McGregor 6-4, 6-4, 6-4 to become the only Jewish tennis player to win a Wimbledon singles championship.

1958 – **Allen Rosenberg** is a member of the winning crew for the second straight year in the 8-oared shell competition at the U.S. Rowing Championships in Philadelphia.

1980 – **Amy Alcott** finishes three strokes ahead of JoAnne Carner and Sally Little to win the LPGA Mayflower Classic in Noblesville, Ind.

1984 – **Ken Chertow** of the United States wins the 56-kg. division of the World Junior Freestyle Wrestling Championships in Washington, D.C.

1986 – **Amy Alcott** birdies the first hole of a playoff with Lauren Howe to win the LPGA Mazda Hall of Fame Classic in Sugar Land, Texas.

2000 – **Jonathan Erlich** and **Harel Levy** beat Kyle Spencer of Britain and Mitch Sprengelmeyer of the United States 7-6 (7-2), 7-5 to win the doubles title at the Hall of Fame tennis championships in Newport, R.I.

It is the first ATP doubles title for an Israeli team since **Gilad Bloom** and **Shahar Perkiss** won in Tel Aviv in 1987.

2003 – **Ilana Kloss** teams with Kathi Rinaldi to defeat Jo Durie and Gretchen Magers 6-4, 4-6, 7-5 to win the women's Over-35 doubles championship at Wimbledon. **Andy Ram** of Israel reaches the mixed doubles final before he and partner Anastasia Rodionova lose 6-3, 6-3 to Martina Navratilova and Leander Paes.

RECORD SETTERS

1906 – **Jabez Wolffe** swims 18 miles from Dover to Ramsgate, England, in 6 hours, 6 minutes, 35 seconds, breaking the record of 8:30.0 set by Capt. Webb in 1875.

1941 – **Alfred Nakeche** of France sets a world record of 2:36.8 in the 200-meter breaststroke in Marseilles.

1952 – **Henry Laskau** walks one-half mile in 2 minutes, 48.2 seconds, or 10.70 mph, at Randall's Island in New York. Some officials regard the time as "physically impossible," but the AAU recognizes the feat as a record.

TRANSITIONS

1926 – **Louis "Kid" Kaplan** renounces his world featherweight title, admitting that he can no longer reduce to 126 pounds without endangering his health.

A STAR IS BORN

1905 – **David Mishel** (Brown and pro football)

1972 – **Zhanna Bloch** (Ukrainian sprinter)

JULY 7

GAMEBREAKERS

1962 – **Art Shamsky**, back in the lineup after missing two months with a hand injury, hits a 10th-inning home run to give Macon a 2-1 victory over Charlotte in the Sally League.

1963 – **Sandy Koufax** pitches a three-hitter for his second straight shutout as the Dodgers beat the Cincinnati Reds 4-0.

1979 – **Ken Holtzman** pitches a three-hitter and hits an RBI double as the Chicago Cubs beat the Houston Astros 6-0 in the first game of a doubleheader.

STRONG IN DEFEAT

1974 – **Johan Neeskens** of the Netherlands scores 90 seconds into the World Cup soccer final against West Germany. The goal is the quickest in finals history and is the first ever scored on a penalty shot. West Germany rallies to win 2-1.

MAZEL TOUGH

1912 – After seven false starts, **Alvah Miller** of the United States wins a silver medal in the 100 meters at the Olympics in Stockholm.

1924 – **Harold Abrahams** of Great Britain equals the Olympic record of 10.6 seconds – set by Abrahams in the preliminary heats – in the 100-meter dash in Paris. He becomes the first non-American to win the event, defeating favorites Jackson Scholz and Charles Paddock of the United States. His story is the basis for the 1981 film *Chariots of Fire*. Meanwhile, **Elias Katz** of Finland wins silver in the 3,000 steeplechase.

1941 – **Harold Bogrow** of NYU wins the 440 in 49.4 seconds at the New York Athletic Club track and field games.

1946 – **Irv Dorfman** of Yale rallies past Mark Brown of Miami 3-6, 3-6, 6-4, 9-7, 6-3 to win the Eastern Intercollegiate tennis title in Montclair, N.J.

1956 – **Angela Buxton** of Great Britain loses to Shirley Fry 6-3, 6-1 in the Wimbledon final, but teams with Althea Gibson to beat Fay Muller and Daphne Seeny of Australia 6-1, 8-6 for the women's doubles championship.

1962 – **Gilbert Eisner** wins the epee title at the U.S. Fencing Championships in New York.

1963 – **Herman Barron** of the United States defeats George Evans of England 3-and-2 over 36 holes to win the World Senior Golf Championship in Lytham St. Anne's, England.

1967 – **Ben Gurevitch** of the Soviet Union wins the 87-kg. freestyle wrestling title at the European Championships in Istanbul, Turkey.

1974 – **Mike Dikman** and **Artie Reyer** defeat top-seeded **Joel Wisotsky** and Rudy Obert 21-13, 21-16 to win the National AAU One-Wall Handball doubles title in New York.

1975 – **Marshall Holman** beats Carmen Salvaggio 279-213 in the final of the Fresno Open for his first career PBA title.

1980 – **Saoul Mamby** knocks out Esteban DeJesus in the 13th round in Bloomington, Minn., to retain his WBC super lightweight title.

RECORD SETTERS

1884 – American **Lon Myers** runs the 880 in a world-record 1:55.4 in Birmingham, England.

1968 – **Mark Spitz** sets a world record in the 400 freestyle of 4:08.8 in Santa Clara, Calif. – 0.4 seconds faster than the world mark set a few days earlier by French swimmer Alain Mosconi.

A STAR IS BORN

1898 – **Arnold Horween** (Harvard football, Chicago Cardinals back)

1921 – **Helen Bernhard** (tennis)

JULY 8

GAMEBREAKERS

1922 – **Sammy Bohne** hits a three-run homer off **Lefty Weinert** as the Cincinnati Reds beat the Philadelphia Phillies 7-1 in the first game of a doubleheader.

1951 – **Murray Franklin's** ninth homer of the season gives the Hollywood Stars a 1-0 victory over Portland in the Pacific Coast League.

1957 – Mike Lutz's looping single to right field with two out in the ninth spoils **Larry Sherry's** no-hitter as Fort Worth beats the San Antonio Missions 3-0 in the Texas League. Sherry strikes out 11 batters.

1973 – **Richie Scheinblum** hits a two-run homer in the 10th inning to give the California Angels a 5-3 victory over the Cleveland Indians and a sweep of a doubleheader.

1995 – **Mike Saipe** retires the first 16 batters and finishes with a nine-inning one-hitter with 13 strikeouts, but gets no decision as the Salem Avalanche beat the Wilmington Blue Rocks 1-0 in a 14-inning Carolina League game.

STRONG IN DEFEAT

1980 – **Steve Stone** of the Baltimore Orioles is the American League's starting pitcher and retires all nine batters he faces in the All-Star Game at Dodger Stadium. The National League wins 4-2.

MAZEL TOUGH

1944 – **Irv Mondschein** wins his first of three AAU decathlon titles, scoring 5,743 points in Elizabeth, N.J.

1959 – **Alphonse Halimi** is knocked out in the eighth round and loses his world bantamweight title to Joe Becerra in the first event ever held in the Los Angeles Memorial Sports Arena.

1966 – **Donald Spero** wins the single sculls world rowing title, covering 2,000 meters in 7:05.9 in Bled, Yugoslavia.

2000 – Penn senior **Cliff Bayer** wins the Division I men's foil title at the Summer National Fencing Championships in Austin, Texas.

2001 – **Margie Goldstein-Engle** rides Reggae to victory in the I Love New York Grand Prix equestrian event.

2006 – **Andy Ram** becomes the first Israeli to win a Grand Slam tennis event at the pro level when he teams with Vera Zvonareva of Russia to beat Bob Bryan and Venus Williams 6-3, 6-2 in the Wimbledon mixed doubles final. Ram and Zvonareva defeated Wayne and Cara Black 6-3, 7-6 (5) in the semifinals earlier in the day.

RECORD SETTERS

1922 – **Lilli Henoch** of Germany improves her world record in the discus, getting off a toss of 26.62 meters in Berlin.

TRANSITIONS

1948 – The struggling All American Football Conference holds a secret two-round draft for players who will be college seniors that year in order to get a jump on the NFL. The Los Angeles Dons select Michigan center **Dan Dworsky** with their first pick.

A STAR IS BORN

1883 – **Oszkar Gerde** (fencing)
1937 – **Joel Landau** (track and field)

JULY 9

GAMEBREAKERS

1938 – Two home runs by **Hank Greenberg** help the Detroit Tigers beat the Chicago White Sox 4-0.

1938 – **Morrie Arnovich's** RBI single in the 16th inning gives the Philadelphia Phillies a 4-3 win over the Brooklyn Dodgers.

1947 – **Al Rosen** of Oklahoma City hits his first pitch for a home run as the Texas League All-Stars defeat the first-place Houston Buffs 4-2.

MAZEL TOUGH

1923 – **Benny Valgar** decisions future world lightweight champion Jimmy Goodrich in a 10-round fight in Scranton, Pa.

1924 – **Alexandre Lippmann** of France wins an Olympic fencing gold medal in team epee.

1944 – **Irv Mondschein** finishes first in the pole vault and high jump en route to scoring 5,748 points for the AAU decathlon title at Elizabeth, N.J.

1950 – Down 5-1 and 15-40 in the third set, **Dick Savitt** rallies to defeat Donald McNeill 11-13, 4-6, 9-7, 6-1, 6-4 to win the New York State tennis championship in Forest Hills.

1950 – **Herb Flam** defeats **Sam Match** 6-3, 6-2, 5-7, 4-6, 9-7 to win the Colorado Men's Open tennis tournament in Denver for the second year in a row.

1950 – **Albert Yvel** of France wins on a 10th-round disqualification over Renato Tontini in Algiers to capture the European light heavyweight title.

1958 – **Walter Blum** rides Backbone to victory in the Providence Stakes at Narragansett Park in Pawtucket, R.I.

1960 – **Albert Axelrod** wins the foil and **David Micahnik** captures the epee at the U.S. Fencing Championships in New York.

1988 – **Eliot Teltscher** defeats Deon Joubert 6-1, 7-5 to win a Challenger tennis tournament in Asheville, N.C.

1992 – **Gary Jacobs** knocks out Robert Wright in the sixth round in Glasgow, Scotland, to retain his British welterweight title.

2000 – **Tanya Dubnicoff** wins the flying 200 meters and match sprints cycling titles at the Canadian National Track Championships in Bromont, Quebec.

RECORD SETTERS

1926 – **Lillian Copeland** sets American records of 101-1 in the discus and 38-¾ in the shot put at the National AAU track and field meet in Philadelphia.

1965 – **Irena Kirszenstein-Szewinska** of Poland sets a world record of 11.1 seconds in the 100 meters in Prague.

1967 – Seventeen-year-old **Mark Spitz** sets a world record of 56.3 seconds in the 100-meter butterfly at the Santa Clara International Invitational swim meet.

TRANSITIONS

1960 – **Sid Gillman** assumes the role of coach and general manager of the Los Angeles Chargers of the American Football League.

1998 – Milwaukee Brewers owner **Bud Selig** is elected the ninth commissioner of baseball by a unanimous vote of the league owners.

JEWS ON FIRST

2005 – In his first major-league at-bat, Chicago Cubs pinch hitter **Adam Greenberg** is hit in the head by the first pitch he faces from Valerio De los Santos of the Florida Marlins. Greenberg suffers a concussion and misses the remainder of the season.

A STAR IS BORN

1978 – **Sarah Solomon** (Maryland swimmer)
1987 – **Aleksandra Wozniak** (Canadian tennis)

JULY 10

GAMEBREAKERS

1960 – **Norm Sherry** goes 4 for 5 with a home run as the Los Angeles Dodgers beat the St. Louis Cardinals 11-7.

1973 – **Dick Sharon** goes 4 for 4 including two solo homers and a double as the Detroit Tigers beat the Texas Rangers 5-4.

MAZEL TOUGH

1912 – **Abel Kiviat** of the United States wins the Olympic silver medal in the 1,500 in Stockholm. Kiviat is awarded the silver in a photo finish for second and third place, one of the first instances of the technology's use. **Jacques Ochs** and **Gaston Salmon** of Belgium win team fencing gold medals and **Edgar Seligman** of Great Britain wins a silver in team epee.

1932 – **Baroness Maud Levi** wins the New York State clay-court tennis singles and doubles championships.

1933 – **Ben Jeby** wins a 15-round decision over Young Terry in Newark, N.J., to retain his National Boxing Association world middleweight title.

1964 – **Herbert Cohen**, **Albert Axelrod**, and **Eugene Glazer** sweep the medals in the foil at the U.S. National Fencing Championships in Atlantic City, N.J.

1966 – **Barry Asher**, a 19-year-old freshman at Santa Ana Junior College, beats Jim St. John 192-185 in the final of the Southern California Open in Encino for his first of eight career pro bowling victories.

1973 – **Barry Asher** beats Dennis Swayda 237-232 to win the PBA HBO Open in Tucson, Ariz.

1997 – **Larry Bulman** skippers the sloop Javelin to victory in Class B in the Marblehead-to-Halifax ocean race, finishing in 44 hours, 15 minutes, 33 seconds.

2002 – **Yogev Yosef** and **Shahaf Amir** of Israel win the double-handed 470 class gold medal at the World Sailing Games in Marseilles, France.

RECORD SETTERS

1926 – **Lilliian Copeland** sets a world record of 112-5½ in the javelin, breaking the old mark by more than six feet while earning her third gold medal at the National AAU meet in Philadelphia.

JEWS ON FIRST

1997 – **Michelle Feldman** beats Carolyn Dorin-Ballard in the final of the South Virginia Open in Danville after becoming the first woman to bowl a 300 game on national television.

A STAR IS BORN

1856 – **Isaac Seligman** (rowing)
1908 – **Robert "Buck" Halpern** (CCNY and pro football)

Norm Sherry *(California Angels)*

192

JULY 11

GAMEBREAKERS

1937 – New York Giants catcher **Harry Danning** hits a home run in both games of a doubleheader. New York sweeps the Brooklyn Dodgers 10-4 and 5-1.

1959 – **Barry Latman** of the Chicago White Sox pitches a four-hitter in an 8-3 win over the Kansas City Athletics and goes 3 for 4 at the plate.

MAZEL TOUGH

1906 – **Harry Simon** of the United States wins a silver medal in the London Olympics three-position free rifle shooting event.

1912 – **Imre Gellert** and **Samu Foti** of Hungary win Olympic gold medals in Stockholm in team combined gymnastics.

1925 – **Lillian Copeland** wins the 8-pound shot put at the first national AAU track meet for women in Pasadena, Calif., with a distance of 32 feet, 10¼ inches.

1964 – **Donald Spero** defeats Seymour Cromwell III in the single sculls final at the U.S. Olympic rowing trials in Pelham Manor, N.Y., to earn a trip to the Tokyo Games.

1967 – **Mark Rakita** of the Soviet Union captures the gold medal in saber at the World Fencing Championships in Montreal.

1970 – **Jerry Phillip Cohen** allows four hits and strikes out 14 as the Dallas-Fort Worth Spurs defeat the Memphis Blues 6-2 in a Texas League game.

1971 – **Harold Solomon** defeats Charles Owens 6-2, 2-6, 6-2, 6-4 to win the National Amateur Clay Court tennis championship in Chattanooga, Tenn.

1977 – **Mark Roth** beats local favorite Bobby Fliegman by 25 pins to win the Southern California Open in Norwalk, Calif. Roth becomes the third bowler to win three consecutive tournaments.

1993 – **Tarieli Melelashvili** of Georgia wins the 63-kg. Greco-Roman division at the Eu

ropean Junior Wrestling Championships in Goetzis, Austria.

2003 – **Mark Mendelblatt** sails to victory at the Laser Pacific Coast Championships on the Columbia River in Oregon.

RECORD SETTERS

1953 – **Martin Engel** sets an American mark of 195 feet, 4½ inches in the hammer throw, breaking a 40-year-old record.

1964 – **Marilyn Ramenofsky** sets an American and world record of 4:42.0 in the 400 freestyle in Los Altos, Calif.

2004 – One day after setting an American record of 48.17 seconds in the 100-meter freestyle semifinals, **Jason Lezak** wins the event at the U.S. Olympic Trials in Long Beach, Calif.

TRANSITIONS

1961 – Jockey **Sidney Cole** is killed during an accident during a workout between the first and second races at Aqueduct.

1977 – **Norm Sherry** is fired as manager of the injury-plagued California Angels after going 76-71 over parts of two seasons.

JEWS ON FIRST

1983 – **Julie Ridge** becomes the first swimmer to circle Manhattan Island twice, covering the 57-mile distance in 17 hours.

A STAR IS BORN

1897 – **Willie Jackson** (lightweight boxer)
1907 – **Harry Edelson** (Southern Cal football)
1924 – **Al Federoff** (Detroit Tigers second baseman)

JULY 12

GAMEBREAKERS

1962 – **Sandy Koufax** allows three hits over seven innings before injuring his throwing hand, and **Larry Sherry** pitches hitless ball over the final two innings as the Dodgers beat the New York Mets 3-0. The victory comes four days after Koufax and Don Drysdale combine on a three-hitter in a 2-0 victory over the San Francisco Giants.

1963 – **Sandy Koufax** pitches his third straight shutout, allowing three hits and striking out 13 as the Los Angeles Dodgers beat the New York Mets 6-0.

1970 – **Sheldon Andrens** hits an RBI double in the third, a home run in the fifth and a game-winning RBI single in the ninth as Asheville defeats Birmingham 4-3 in the Southern League.

STRONG IN DEFEAT

1951 – **Saul Rogovin** of the Chicago White Sox pitches all 17 innings of a 5-4 loss to the Boston Red Sox in the first game of a doubleheader.

MAZEL TOUGH

1912 – **Ivan Osiier** of Denmark wins a silver medal in individual epee at the Stockholm Olympics fencing competition.

1964 – **Julie Heldman** defeats Jean Danilovich 6-4, 0-6, 7-5 to win the Western tennis tournament in Indianapolis.

1969 – **Mike Belkin** defeats Peter Van Lingen 6-3, 9-11, 6-3 to win the Alabama Championships tennis tournament.

1971 – **Grigori Kriss** of the Soviet Union wins the epee title at the World Fencing Championships in Vienna, his first title since 1964.

1984 – **Aaron Krickstein** beats Jose-Luis Clerc 7-6, 3-6, 6-4 in the final of a clay-court tennis tournament in Boston.

1994 – **Tamara Levinson** finishes first and **Jessica Davis** takes second in the National Senior Rhythmic Gymnastics Championships.

2003 – **Clint Wattenberg** of Cornell defeats Pat Popolizio 7-2 to win the 185-pound division at the Canada Cup wrestling competition in Guelph, Ontario.

Ron Rothstein *(Detroit Pistons)*

RECORD SETTERS

1924 – **Harold Abrahams** runs the first leg of Great Britain's 4×100 relay team that sets a world record of 42.0 in a preliminary race at the Olympics in Paris.

1926 – **Elias Katz** runs the second leg as a club team from Finland sets a world record of 16:26.2 in the 1,500-meter relay.

1969 – **Mark Spitz** equals the world record of 1:54.3 in the 200-meter freestyle in Santa Clara, Calif.

TRANSITIONS

1988 – Detroit Pistons assistant coach **Ron Rothstein** is named the first head coach of the Miami Heat's NBA expansion franchise.

A STAR IS BORN

1889 – **Max "Marty" Friedman** (basketball)
1979 – **Scott Goldblat** (swimming)

JULY 13

GAMEBREAKERS

1952 – **Al Rosen's** two-run homer gives the Cleveland Indians a 2-1 win over the Washington Senators in the second game of a doubleheader.

1954 – **Al Rosen** of the Indians hits two home runs and drives in five runs in the All-Star Game in Cleveland. The American League wins 11-9.

1959 – **Stan Charnofsky** has four hits including two triples as the Edmonton Elks defeat the Regina Senators 9-5 in the Western Canada Baseball League.

1967 – **Mike Epstein** hits two homers and a triple and drives in four runs as the Washington Senators beat the Detroit Tigers 8-3.

STRONG IN DEFEAT

1952 – Detroit Tigers catcher **Joe Ginsberg** hits a home run with one out in the ninth inning to spoil Vic Raschi's no-hit bid in an 11-1 Yankees victory.

MAZEL TOUGH

1924 – **Elias Katz** finishes fifth, and combined with first- and second-place finishes by Paavo Nurmi and Ville Ritola, Finland earns eight points to capture the gold medal in the 3,000-meter team cross-country race at the Paris Olympics. In the 400-meter relay, **Louis Clarke** and the United States win a gold medal while **Harold Abrahams** and Great Britain win the silver.

1930 – **Umberto de Morpurgo** defeats Yoshiro Ota 6-0, 6-2, 6-1 to clinch Italy's 3-2 victory over Japan in the Davis Cup tennis European Zone final in Genoa.

1941 – **Artie Wolfe** defeats Nick Shinkarik to win the National AAU one-wall handball championship. **Morty Alexander** and Marvin Hecht beat **Joe Garber** and Wolfe for the doubles title.

1941 – **Seymour Greenberg** of Northwestern defeats Ronald Edwards of San Jose State 6-3, 6-1, 6-2 to capture the Eastern Intercollegiate tennis title in Montclair, N.J.

1947 – **Irving Mondschein** wins his third decathlon championship in four years, scoring 6,715 points, and **Steve Seymour** wins his first of three National AAU outdoor javelin titles in Bloomfield, N.J.

1952 – **Herb Flam** defeats **Irv Dorfman** in three sets to win the International Lawn Tennis Championship of Switzerland in Gstaad. **Anita Kanter** wins the U.S. National Clay Court tennis championship.

1968 – **Tom Okker** defeats Lew Hoad 6-1, 6-2 to win the Irish Open in Dublin.

1980 – **Amy Alcott** wins her second LPGA tournament in two weeks at the U.S. Women's Open in Nashville, Tenn. Her tournament-record score of 4-under-par 280 is nine strokes better than runner-up Hollis Stacy.

2003 – **David Mansour** wins the foil title at the British Fencing Association Championships in Cosford, England.

RECORD SETTERS

1955 – **Eva Szekely** of Hungary recaptures the world record in the 400 individual medley with a time of 5:40.8 at a swim meet in Budapest.

JEWS ON FIRST

1876 – **Lipman Pike** of the St. Louis Brown Stockings, who had hit 16 home runs during five seasons in the National Association, hits his first of four National League (major-league) home runs in a 3-0 win over the Hartford Dark Blues.

JULY 14

GAMEBREAKERS

1968 – Evansville left-hander **Mickey Abarbanel** throws his second consecutive shutout against Asheville, beating the Tourists 3-0 on three hits in the Southern League.

MAZEL TOUGH

1913 – **Leo Friede** defeats Ralph Britton of Canada by two minutes, 12 seconds to win the International Challenge Cup canoe race. Friede also beats Britton on the same date a year later to defend his title.

1929 – **Daniel Prenn** defeats Bunny Austin in five sets to give Germany a 3-2 victory over Great Britain in the Davis Cup tennis European final.

1932 – **Slapsy Maxie Rosenbloom** wins a 15-round decision over Lou Scozza in Buffalo, N.Y., to retain his world light heavyweight title.

1950 – **Victor Frank** of the United States wins the shot put and discus at the Canadian National track and field championships in Halifax, Nova Scotia.

1974 – Future Olympic swimmer **Wendy Weinberg** wins the 200 freestyle, 400 freestyle, and 200 butterfly at the Philadelphia Open.

1991 – **Bruce Fleisher** beats Ian Baker-Finch with a birdie on the seventh extra hole to win the New England Classic, his only victory on the PGA Tour.

2003 – **Michelle Feldman** wins her 12th career professional women's bowling title by defeating Kendra Gaines 250-170 in the final of the PWBA Dallas Open.

JEWS ON FIRST

1865 – **Lipman Pike** appears in his first baseball game as the Brooklyn Atlantics play the Gothams in Hoboken, N.J.

TRANSITIONS

1978 – **Red Auerbach** announces he has turned down an offer to become the New York Knicks' president and elects to remain in the Boston Celtics' front office.

A STAR IS BORN

1946 – **Barry Asher** (bowling)
1947 – **Steve Stone** (San Francisco Giants, Chicago White Sox, Chicago Cubs, Baltimore Orioles pitcher)
1970 – **Josh Miller** (Arizona football, CFL Baltimore Stallions, Pittsburgh Steelers, New England Patriots, Tennessee Titans punter)

Wendy Weinberg
(U.S. Olympic Committee)

JULY 15

GAMEBREAKERS

1922 – **Lefty Weinert** pitches a five-hitter and goes 2 for 4 with a game-winning RBI double as the Philadelphia Phillies beat the Chicago Cubs 2-1.

1952 – **Al Rosen** slides home with the winning run on the front end of a triple steal as Cleveland beats the New York Yankees 4-3.

1961 – **Don Taussig** hits a two-run double and a two-run triple as the St. Louis Cardinals defeat the Milwaukee Braves 12-4.

MAZEL TOUGH

1900 – World-record holder **Myer Prinstein** is awarded the silver medal in the long jump at the Paris Olympics without competing in the final. Prinstein's Syracuse University teammates prevented him from competing in the event, held on a Sunday, because it was their Sabbath. Alvin Kraenzlein of Penn won the gold by surpassing Prinstein's Friday qualifying distance by one centimeter.

1912 – **Jeno Fuchs, Dezso Foldes, Lajos Werkner,** and **Oszkar Gerde** of Hungary win fencing gold medals in team saber at the Stockholm Olympics. **Albert Bogen** and **Dr. Otto Herschmann** of Austria win silver medals. **Margareta Adler, Klara Milch**, and **Josephine Stricker** swim the first three legs for Austria's bronze-medal winning 4×100 freestyle relay team.

1924 – **Janos Gabay** of Hungary wins an Olympic fencing silver medal in team saber.

1940 – **Helen Bernhard** defeats Helen Jacobs 7-5, 8-6 in New York to retain her Middle States tennis championship.

1956 – **Angela Buxton** of England wins the Swedish International tennis tournament in Bastad.

1957 – **Herb Flam** wins the singles and teams with **Dick Savitt** to capture the doubles at the Nassau Bowl Invitational tennis tournament in Glen Cove, N.Y.

1959 – **Allan Jay** of Great Britain wins the foil at the World Fencing Championships in Budapest, and finishes second in epee. He is the last fencer to win two individual medals in the same year.

1977 – **Julie Heldman** defeats Diane Fromholtz 1-6, 6-1, 11-9 to win the GreenShield Welsh tennis championship in Newport, R.I.

1979 – **Brian Teacher** beats Stan Smith 1-6, 6-3, 6-4 to win a grass-court tennis tournament in Newport, R.I.

1990 – **Martin Jaite** of Argentina defeats Sergi Brugera 6-3, 6-7, 6-2, 6-2 in the final of the Swiss Open clay-court tennis tournament in Gstaad, Switzerland.

1990 – **Sherman Bergman** defeats Carlos Andino for his 21st consecutive first-round victory in kickboxing.

2001 – **Yulia Beygelzimer** defeats top seed Romana Tedjakusuma 6-2, 6-3 to win an ITF tennis tournament in Sezze, Italy.

2003 – **Philippe Kahn** and his crew sail Barn Door to their second straight victory in the Transpacific Yacht Race between Los Angeles and Honolulu in 7 days, 16 hours, 31 minutes, and 17 seconds.

TRANSITIONS

1963 – **Dolph Schayes** signs a two-year contact to become the first head coach of the Philadelphia 76ers, formerly the Syracuse Nationals.

2006 – The United States Postal Service issues 39-cent stamps commemorating baseball sluggers **Hank Greenberg**, Roy Campanella, Mickey Mantle, and Mel Ott.

A STAR IS BORN

1908 – **Louis Gordon** (Illinois football, Chicago Bears, Green Bay Packers, Chicago Cardinals)

1909 – **Erich Seelig** (German light heavyweight boxer)

JULY 16

GAMEBREAKERS

1938 – The Philadelphia Phillies beat the St. Louis Cardinals 2-1 on **Phil Weintraub's** seventh-inning homer.

1945 – Jersey City first baseman **Mike Schemer** turns two unassisted double plays in a 6-0 victory over Baltimore in the International League.

1953 – **Al Rosen's** grand slam homer gives the Cleveland Indians a 5-3 victory over the Philadelphia A's.

1965 – **Sandy Koufax** wins his 10th straight game, allowing four hits and striking out nine in a 3-0 victory over the Chicago Cubs. The light-hitting Koufax also delivers two key singles that lead to Dodgers runs.

MAZEL TOUGH

1804 – British boxer **Isaac Bitton** beats Bill Wood in 36 rounds.

1900 – **Myer Prinstein** wins the triple jump at the Paris Olympics with a leap of 47 feet, 5¾ inches. He becomes the only person to win gold medals in both the long jump and triple jump.

1908 – **Otto Scheff** of Austria wins a bronze medal in the 400 freestyle swimming at the Athens Olympics.

1924 – **Abe Goldstein** wins a 15-round decision over Charles Ledoux in the Bronx to retain his world bantamweight title.

1932 – **Dorothy Nussbaum** wins the 50-yard dash in 6.3 seconds at the AAU Outdoor track and field championships in Evanston, Ill.

1955 – **Allen Rosenberg** is a member of the winning crew for 8-oared shells at the U.S. Rowing Championships.

1960 – One day after teaming with Ann Haydon of Great Britain to win the doubles title, **Suzy Kormoczy** of Hungary defeats Haydon 1-6, 8-6, 8-6 to win the Budapest International tennis tournament.

1967 – **Mike Belkin** defeats Pancho Guzman of Ecuador 3-6, 6-3, 6-1, 6-2 to win the Western Tennis Tournament in Indianapolis.

1977 – **Johan Harmenberg** of Sweden wins the individual epee to go along with his team epee title at the World Fencing Championships in Buenos Aires.

RECORD SETTERS

1881 – American runner **Lon Myers** becomes the first foreigner to win a British national track and field title when he captures the 440 in a world-record 48.6 seconds at the Aston Lower Grounds in Birmingham.

1949 – With the Springboks trailing New Zealand 11-0, **Okey Geffen** kicks five straight penalties in five attempts for 15 points, and South Africa's national team rallies for a 15-11 rugby victory. Competing in his first test match, Geffen breaks the world test record of 14 set in 1928.

A STAR IS BORN

1906 – **Albert Cornsweet** (Brown, Cleveland Indians football)

1931 – **Norm Sherry** (Los Angeles Dodgers, New York Mets catcher, California Angels manager)

1967 – **Joel Stransky** (South African rugby)

1968 – **Ariel Solomon** (Colorado football, Pittsburgh Steelers, Minnesota Vikings offensive lineman)

1976 – **Anna Smashnova** (Israeli tennis)

JULY 17

GAMEBREAKERS

1917 – **Barney Pelty** of the St. Louis Browns shuts out the Philadelphia A's 2-0.

1943 – **Dick Conger** pitches a two-hitter as the Philadelphia Phillies beat the New York Giants 2-1 in the first game of a double-header.

1998 – **Shawn Green** of Toronto goes 3 for 5 with a solo homer and his first career grand slam as the Blue Jays beat the New York Yankees 9-6.

RECORD SETTERS

1880 – **Lon Myers** sets a world record of 1:56.5 in the 880.

MAZEL TOUGH

1924 – Brothers **Gerard** and **Maurice Blitz** of Belgium capture silver medals in water polo at the Paris Olympics. **Sidney Jelinek** of the United States wins a bronze medal in rowing for the coxed-fours event.

1930 – **Al Singer** knocks out Sammy Mandell at 1:32 of the first round in the Bronx to win the world lightweight championship.

1931 – **Eva Bein** wins the long-distance swim at the AAU Championships in New York.

1932 – **Daniel Prenn** defeats Giorgio DeStefani 6-1, 6-4, 1-6, 6-2 in reverse singles as Germany defeats Italy 5-0 in the Davis Cup European final. Prenn also won at singles and doubles.

1977 – **Harold Solomon** beats Mark Cox 6-2, 6-3 in the final of a clay-court tennis tournament in Cincinnati.

1977 – With **Shep Messing** in goal, the Cosmos defeat the Portland Timbers 2-0 in the North American Soccer League.

2005 – **Anna Smashnova** of Israel wins a WTA tournament in Modena, Italy, when Tathiana Garbin retires during the first set.

2005 – **Aleksandra Wozniak** of Canada defeats top-seeded Maria Jose Argeri of Argentina 6-1, 6-2 to win a USTA Challenger tennis tournament in Hamilton, Ontario.

RECORD-SETTERS

2000 – Texas Rangers outfielder **Gabe Kapler** begins a club-record 28-game hitting streak with a single during a 10-8 loss to the San Francisco Giants.

TRANSITIONS

1962 – **Sandy Koufax** leaves after pitching one inning of a 7-5 loss to Cincinnati. Circulatory problems will keep him out of the lineup until late September.

A STAR IS BORN

1936 – **James Margolis** (fencing)
1943 – **Roger Nathan** (British race car driver)

Shep Messing
(U.S. Olympic Committee)

199

JULY 18

GAMEBREAKERS

1944 – **Phil Weintraub** hits a grand slam home run in the third inning as the New York Giants beat the Pittsburgh Pirates 5-2.

2006 – San Diego Surf Dogs second baseman **Adam Mandel** goes 5 for 5 – all doubles – to lead the North to a 7-6 victory in the independent Golden Baseball League all-star game in Chico, Calif.

STRONG IN DEFEAT

1968 – **Marty Fleckman** leads the first round of the 50th PGA Championship by shooting a 66 in San Antonio. Fleckman will share the second- and third-round leads with Frank Beard before shooting a final-round 73 to finish in a tie for fourth place, two shots behind winner Julius Boros.

1972 – **Mike Epstein** goes 3 for 4 with two homers in the Washington Senators' 7-4 loss to the Milwaukee Brewers.

JEWS ON FIRST

1906 – **Jabez Wolffe,** a world-record-holding distance swimmer from Great Britain, makes his first of a record 22 unsuccessful attempts to swim the English Channel. He comes within sight of the French coast on three of his tries, once getting within 300 yards.

MAZEL TOUGH

1924 – **Janos Gabay** of Hungary wins a fencing bronze medal in individual saber at the Paris Olympics.

1998 – **Adam Karp** and partner Bill Sel defeat a team from Mexico 15-9, 15-7 to win the World Racquetball Championship doubles title in Cochabamba, Bolivia.

1998 – **Amit Inbar** of Israel wins the European windsurfing championship in Attica, Greece.

1998 – **Margie Goldstein-Engle** rides Caribe Du Moulin to first place in the Turfway Park Grand Prix equestrian event.

Sidney Franklin

TRANSITIONS

1945 – Brooklyn-born **Sidney Franklin** becomes a full matador in Madrid.

A STAR IS BORN

1882 – **Harry Baum** (basketball)
1888 – **Alvah Meyer** (track and field)
1899 – **Gyula Mandl** (soccer)
1980 – **David Bluthenthal** (Southern Cal basketball)

JULY 19

GAMEBREAKERS

1937 – **Harry Eisenstat** allows eight hits and strikes out 12 as the Louisville Colonels defeat the Toledo Mud Hens 9-2 to end a 15-game losing streak in the American Association.

1956 – Hornell Dodgers pitcher **Marty Stabiner** earns his 11th win of the season with a 16-0 shutout of Olean in the Class D Pony League.

1999 – **Shawn Green's** grand slam in the third inning helps the Toronto Blue Jays beat the Atlanta Braves 8-7.

STRONG IN DEFEAT

1979 – **Jeff Newman** of the Athletics goes 3 for 4 and hits two solo homers in Oakland's 10-2 loss to the New York Yankees.

MAZEL TOUGH

1909 – **Abel Kiviat** of the United States wins his first of four consecutive Canadian National track and field titles in the 1,500 meters in Winnipeg.

1952 – **Mikhail Perelman** of the Soviet Union wins a gymnastics gold medal in team combined exercises at the Olympics in Helsinki. Israel competes in its first Games, as women's high jumper **Tamar Matal** carries the flag during opening ceremonies.

1964 – **Carole Wright** and Justina Bricka defeat **Kathy Harter** and Kathy Blake 7-5, 6-1 to win the Middle States Women's Grass Court tennis tournament doubles in Philadelphia.

2001 – **Jerry Greenbaum** of Atlanta wins his second straight Northern Amateur senior golf championship in Chesterton, Ind., beating two-time champion Bob Hullender by three strokes.

2003 – **Alexander Averbukh** of Israel clears 19 feet, 5½ inches to win the pole vault at the Madrid Super Grand Prix track and field meet.

RECORD SETTERS

1966 – **Art Shamsky** of Cincinnati ties a major-league record for outfielders when he handles no fielding chances in an 18-inning game. The Reds beat the Chicago Cubs 3-2.

A STAR IS BORN

1919 – **Alf James** (South African lightweight, welterweight boxer)

Art Shamsky

(New York Mets)

JULY 20

GAMEBREAKERS

1918 – **Erskine Mayer** of the Pittsburgh Pirates blanks his former Philadelphia Phillies teammates 1-0 for his 12th and final career shutout.

1955 – **Saul Rogovin** hits a two-run double and pitches a five-hitter as the Philadelphia Phillies win their ninth straight game, 6-0 over the Cincinnati Reds.

MAZEL TOUGH

1924 – **Jackie Fields** of the United States decisions countryman Joe Salas to win the boxing gold medal in the featherweight class at the Paris Olympics. At 16 years, 162 days, he is the youngest-ever Olympic boxing champion.

1924 – **Umberto de Morpurgo** of Italy beats Jean Borotra in the third-place match to win the bronze medal in tennis at the Olympics in Stockholm.

1928 – **Corporal Izzy Schwartz** beats Frisco Grande in four rounds in Rockaway, N.Y., to retain his world flyweight title.

1962 – **Mark Midler** of the Soviet Union wins the foil title at the World Fencing Championships in Buenos Aires, his last of four world titles.

1974 – **Julie Heldman** beats Sue Mappin of Great Britain 6-3, 6-4 to retain her title in the Welsh grass-court tennis championships in Newport, R.I. **David Schneider** of South Africa wins the East of England tennis tournament by beating William Prinsloo 3-6, 6-1, 6-4.

1974 – Formula One rookie **Jody Scheckter** of South Africa takes the lead with five laps remaining and outraces Emerson Fittipaldi to win the British Grand Prix in Brands Hatch, England.

1976 – **Barry Asher** beats Dave Soutar 265-184 in the final of the PBA HBO Open in Tucson, Ariz.

2003 – **Nicolas Massu** of Chile defeats Raemon Sluiter of the Netherlands 6-4, 7-6 (3), 6-2 to win the Dutch Open clay-court tennis tournament in Amersfoort. It is Massu's second career title.

Jody Scheckter
(Formula One publicity photo)

JEWS ON FIRST

1969 – On the same day Neil Armstrong and Buzz Aldren walk on the moon, Cleveland Indians pinch hitter **Richie Scheinblum** hits his first of 13 career major-league home runs in a 5-4 win over the Detroit Tigers.

TRANSITIONS

2006 – After leading Kentucky to a school-record 44 victories and its first Southeastern Conference championship, **John Cohen** is named national coach of the year by collegebaseballinsider.com. The College Baseball Foundation previously named him coach of the year.

A STAR IS BORN

1897 – **Happy Foreman** (Chicago White Sox, Boston Red Sox pitcher)

JULY 21

GAMEBREAKERS

1949 – **Harry Feldman** goes 4 for 4 and pitches a shutout as the San Francisco Missions beat the San Diego Padres 13-0 in the Pacific Coast League.

1950 – **Murray Franklin's** bases-loaded single in the ninth inning gives the Hollywood Stars a Pacific Coast League victory over the Seattle Rainiers.

1978 – **Bob Tufts** tosses a four-hitter for his 13th victory as the Waterbury Giants defeat the Jersey City Indians 2-1 in the Eastern League.

MAZEL TOUGH

1957 – **Allen Rosenberg** wins his second of three gold medals for 8-oared shells at the U.S. Rowing Championships in Philadelphia.

1963 – **Donald Spero** wins the national single sculls rowing title on the Schuylkill River in Philadelphia.

1985 – **Doug Shapiro** becomes only the third American ever to finish the Tour de France cycling race. He places 74th – one hour, 39 minutes, 34 seconds behind winner Bernard Hinault of France.

2002 – Led by **Hershell Gutman** (82 runs) and **Isaac Massil** (67), Israel defeats Austria by 135 runs – its largest margin of victory in history – at the Euro Cricket Championships in Northern Ireland.

RECORD SETTERS

1934 – One day after setting a five-mile record of 45.226 mph, **S. Mortimer Auerbach** drives Emancipator III to a one-mile record of 50.571 mph for Class 125 cubic inch hydroplanes in Havre de Grace, Md.

1968 – **Lazar Naroditskiy** sets a Russian record of 8:26.6 in the 3,000-meter steeplechase at a track and field meet in Leningrad.

1984 – **Dara Torres** improves her world record in the 50 freestyle to 25.61 seconds in Mission Viejo, Calif.

1996 – **Shawn Green** of the Blue Jays ties a major-league record for outfielders with two assists in the same inning. Toronto beats the Detroit Tigers 5-4 in 12 innings.

TRANSITIONS

2001 – Fencer **Ildiko Rejto** of Hungary is named the top deaf female Olympic athlete of the century in a ceremony in Rome. Rejto competed in five Olympic Games between 1960 and 1976 and won seven medals.

A STAR IS BORN

1882 – **Hugo Friend** (track and field)
1908 – **Motsy Handler** (TCU football, Chicago Cardinals)

Doug Shapiro
(U.S. Olympic Committee)

JULY 22

GAMEBREAKERS

1914 – **Al Schacht** pitches a four-hitter as Newark defeats Providence 5-0 in an International League game.

1934 – **Hank Greenberg** scores four runs and drives in four runs as the Detroit Tigers beat the Cleveland Indians 17-8.

1953 – **Cal Abrams** hits his ninth and 10th homers of the season as the Pittsburgh Pirates beat the Cincinnati Reds 3-2.

1956 – In Montgomery's first game since the Southern Association team moved in midseason from Little Rock, the Rebels are blanked 2-0 by New Orleans Pelicans pitcher **Hy Cohen**. In another Southern Association game, **Barry Latman** allows two hits – one a misjudged fly ball that falls for a triple – as Memphis defeats Mobile 6-1.

1962 – **Suzy Kormoczy** of Hungary defeats Anna Dmitrieva of the Soviet Union 6-1, 4-6, 6-4 in the Hungarian Championships clay-court tennis tournament.

1964 – **Sandy Koufax** allows four hits and strikes out 12 as the Dodgers beat Houston 1-0. The victory is Koufax's 11th straight since a 1-0 loss to Cincinnati on May 27.

2001 – Outfielder **Joe Apotheker** goes 3 for 3 and is named MVP of the New England Collegiate Baseball League All-Star Game in Manchester, Conn.

2004 – Cardinals starter **Jason Marquis** pitches eight shutout innings as St. Louis defeats the Milwaukee Brewers 4-0. Marquis also hits a double, giving him 11 hits in his last 22 at-bats.

MAZEL TOUGH

1951 – **Dick Savitt** wins his second singles match of the tournament as the United States beats Japan 5-0 in Davis Cup preliminary-round play in Louisville, Ky. **Herb Flam** also wins a singles match.

1952 – **Claude Netter** wins an Olympic fencing gold medal in Helsinki when France beats Italy 8-6 in the final of the team foil competition.

1960 – **Peter Fugarasy** of Hungary wins the 200 breaststroke title at the AAU Swimming Championships in Toledo, Ohio.

1973 – **Tom Okker** beats Andres Gimeno 2-6, 6-4, 6-4, 6-7, 6-3 to win the Dutch Open tennis tournament.

1984 – **Aaron Krickstein** becomes the youngest winner of the U.S. Pro Tennis Championship when he beats defending champion Jose-Luis Clerc 7-6, 3-6, 6-4 in the final in Brookline, Mass.

2000 – **Adam Goucher**, who missed the entire spring running season with an Achilles injury, wins the 5,000-meter Olympic trials in 13:27.06

2001 – **Jeff Salzenstein** defeats Jeff Morrison 7-6 (7-3), 6-4 in the Seascape Challenger tennis final in Aptos, Calif., for his third career singles victory.

RECORD SETTERS

1939 – German sprinter **Hal-Alec Natan** helps the Charlottenburg SC 4×100 relay team set a world record of 40.8 seconds.

1945 – Mobile catcher **Harry Chozen's** second-inning home run off New Orleans pitcher Trader Horn extends his hitting streak to 47 games, breaking the Southern Association record set 20 years earlier by Johnny Bates. Chozen's streak reaches 49 games before he goes 0-for-5 in a 13-inning game against Nashville on July 29 – a game in which he lays down a sacrifice bunt in the 11th inning.

A STAR IS BORN

1904 – **Pincus Match** (CCNY basketball)
1934 – **Leon Rottman** (canoeing)
1938 – **Mark Rakita** (fencing)

JULY 23

GAMEBREAKERS

1950 – Tigers pitcher **Saul Rogovin** hits a grand slam homer off Eddie Lopat as Detroit beats the Yankees 6-5.

1954 – **Sid Gordon's** two-run pinch-hit home run in the seventh inning breaks a 4-4 tie and gives the Pittsburgh Pirates a 7-4 win over the Cincinnati Redlegs.

2001 – **Shawn Green** hits two home runs as the Dodgers beat the San Francisco Giants 5-0.

2006 – **Jason Marquis** pitches eight shutout innings of four-hit ball to become the National League's first 12-game winner, and the St. Louis Cardinals defeat the Los Angeles Dodgers 6-1.

MAZEL TOUGH

1925 – **Charley Phil Rosenberg** knocks out Eddie Shea in four rounds in the Bronx to retain his world bantamweight title.

1948 – **Steve Seymour** wins the javelin at the AAU outdoor track championships in Milwaukee.

1948 – **Dorothy Watman Levine** wins her second consecutive United States Western Junior girls singles tennis title.

1952 – **Maria Gorokhovskaya** of the Soviet Union wins a gold in the all-around and silver medals in vault, bars, balance beam, and floor exercises at the Olympics in Helsinki. **Agnes Keleti** of Hungary wins the gold in floor exercises and a bronze on bars. **Henry Wittenberg** of the United States wins a silver medal in light heavyweight freestyle wrestling. **Boris Gurevitch** of the Soviet Union takes gold in Greco-Roman wrestling's flyweight division. **Leonid Gissen** of the Soviet Union wins silver in rowing for eight-oared shell with coxswain.

1956 – **Herb Flam** wins the U.S. Clay Court tennis championship in New York.

1989 – **Amy Alcott** wins the LPGA Boston Five Classic in Danvers, Mass., by three strokes over runner-up Cathy Marino.

1989 – **Andrew Sznajder** of Canada defeats Karsten Braasch 7-6, 1-6, 6-1 in the final of a clay-court tennis tournament in Quebec.

1995 – **Robbie Weiss** defeats Sargis Sargsian 6-2, 6-2 in the final of a hard-court tennis tournament in Granby, Quebec.

1996 – **Kerry Strug**, the final competitor for the United States in Atlanta, completes her second vault to preserve the Americans' victory over Russia for their first Olympic gold medal in women's gymnastics team events. Strugg fell on her first attempt and suffered a third-degree lateral ankle sprain.

2000 – **Anna Smashnova** of Israel beats Dominique Van Roost 6-2, 7-5 in Knokke-Hist, Belgium, for her second victory on the WTA tennis tour.

2001 – **Anthony Ervin** wins the 50 freestyle at the World Swimming Championships in Fukuoka, Japan, in 22.09 seconds.

JEWS ON FIRST

2005 – **Adam Stern** of the Boston Red Sox hits his first career home run off Dustin Hermanson of Chicago in an 8-4 White Sox victory.

TRANSITIONS

1960 – Coach **Jimmie Reese** is appointed to replace George Metkovich as manager of the Pacific Coast League's San Diego Padres.

1968 – Club president **Abe Pollin** becomes sole owner of the NBA's Baltimore Bullets.

A STAR IS BORN

1903 – **Bob Barrabee** (NYU and pro football)

1948 – **Steve Tannen** (Florida, New York Jets safety)

JULY 24

GAMEBREAKERS

1955 – In a game stopped after six innings because of rain, Philadelphia pitcher **Saul Rogovin** runs his consecutive-inning scoreless streak to 15 as the Phillies beat the St. Louis Cardinals 3-0.

1957 – **Lou Limmer** hits a two-run homer in the final inning to give the Omaha Cardinals a 3-1 victory over the St. Paul Saints in the first game of an American Association doubleheader. Limmer adds two doubles and an RBI in the second game, but four hits and three RBI's by Saints catcher **Norm Sherry** help St. Paul win 6-4.

1960 – **Alan Koch** pitches a five-hitter for his second consecutive shutout of the Chattanooga Lookouts, leading the Birmingham Barons to an 8-0 victory in the Southern Association.

1974 – Playing his first game for the New York Stars, **Moses Lajterman** of Argentina kicks a 40-yard field goal in the fourth quarter to beat the Philadelphia Bell 17-15 before a World Football League record crowd of 64,719 at JFK Stadium in Philadelphia.

MAZEL TOUGH

1908 – At the Olympics in London, fencers **Alexandre Lippmann** and **Jen Stern** of France win gold medals and **Edgar Seligman** of Britain wins silver in team epee. **Jeno Fuchs** of Hungary wins an individual gold in saber, and teams with **Oszkar Gerde**, **Dezso Foldes**, and **Lajos Werkner** to win a gold in team saber. Lippmann wins a silver in individual epee.

1908 – **Richard Weisz** of Hungary beats Aleksandr Petrov of Russia 2-0 in the Greco-Roman heavyweight wrestling final at the London Olympics. **Jozsef Munk** and **Imre Zachar** of Hungary win silver in 4×200 freestyle relay swimming and **Clair Jacobs** of the United States wins a bronze in pole vault.

1923 – Champion **Benny Leonard** decisions **Lew Tendler** in 15 rounds before a crowd of 58,519 in New York to retain his lightweight title.

1950 – Collegiate champion **Herb Flam** beats top-ranked amateur Ted Schroeder in straight sets to win the singles, and teams with Art Larsen to capture the doubles title at the National Clay Courts tennis championships in River Forest, Ill.

1952 – **Maria Gorokhovskaya** of the Soviet Union wins the gold and **Agnes Keleti** of Hungary captures a silver in gymnastics team combined exercises at the Olympics in Helsinki. Gorokhovskaya also wins a silver and Keleti a bronze in team exercises with portable apparatus. **James Fuchs** of the United States wins bronze in the shot put.

1958 – **Boris Gurevich** of the Soviet Union wins the 52-kg. Greco-Roman title at the World Wrestling Championships in Budapest, Hungary.

1994 – **Daniel Kanner** of the United States wins the 200-meter freestyle at the Goodwill Games in St. Petersburg, Russia. The competition is delayed several days after competitors complain of a green substance in the water.

1999 – **Adriana Brandao Behar** of Brazil and teammate Shelda Bede win the women's world beach volleyball championship in Marseille, France.

RECORD SETTERS

1953 – **Eva Szekely** and **Valeria Gyengi** swim the final two legs as Hungary sets a world record of 5:10.8 in the 4×100 women's medley relay in Budapest.

A STAR IS BORN

1906 – **Morris Raskin** and **Julius Raskin** (CCNY football)

1922 – **Harry Boykoff** (St. John's basketball)

1963 – **Alan Veingrad** (East Texas State football, Green Bay Packers, Dallas Cowboys offensive lineman)

JULY 25

GAMEBREAKERS

1948 – **Saul Rogovin** pirches a three-hitter as the Buffalo Bison defeat Rochester 10-0 in the International League.

1953 – **Al Rosen** hits his 26th homer of the season with two out in the 10th inning to give the Cleveland Indians a 6-4 win over the Washington Senators.

1966 – Fox Cities left-hander **Mickey Abarbanel** allows a sixth-inning single, preventing him from becoming the first Midwest League pitcher to throw two no-hitters in one season. Abarbanel strikes out 11 in improving his record to 11-3 as the Foxes beat the Clinton Pilots 1-0.

1971 – With **Shep Messing** in goal, the United States men's soccer team defeats Barbados 3-0 in an Olympic qualifying match in Miami.

MAZEL TOUGH

1900 – **Siegfried Flesch** of Austria wins an Olympic bronze medal in the individual saber fencing event in Paris.

1906 – **Odon Bodor** runs the final leg of the 1,600 relay team to give Hungary a bronze medal at the London Olympics. The first-ever Olympic relay event requires a transfer by touch rather than handing off a baton.

1917 – **Benny Leonard** knocks out Johnny Kilbane in the third round to retain his world lightweight title.

1929 – **Jackie Fields** wins the unified world welterweight boxing championship in Detroit when Joe Dundee is disqualified in the second round because of a foul.

1931 – **Lillian Copeland** wins the javelin and shot put at the AAU Outdoor Track and Field meet in Jersey City.

1948 – **Sam Match** defeats **Harry Likas** in three sets to win the Pennsylvania Grass Courts tennis title.

1951 – **Carol Pence** wins the 200-meter breaststroke at the AAU Outdoor Swimming Championships in Detroit.

1953 – **Gerald Moss** defeats defending champion Jon Douglas in the Western Junior tennis final in Champaign, Ill.

1964 – **Walter Blum** rides Gun Bow to a 12-length victory in the Brooklyn Handicap at Aqueduct and sets a New York track record of 1:59 3/5 for 1¼ miles.

1976 – **Wendy Weinberg** of Baltimore wins a bronze medal in the 800-meter freestyle at the Montreal Olympics.

1993 – **Amos Mansdorf** of Israel beats Todd Martin 7-6 (7-3), 7-5 in the Newsweek Classic tennis final in Washington, D.C.

2004 – After beating the tournament's top seed in a rain-delayed morning semifinal, **Nicolas Massu** defeats French Open champion Gaston Gaudio 7-6 (7-3), 6-4 to win the Generali Open in Kitzbuehel, Austria.

A STAR IS BORN

1919 – **Mortimer Landsberg** (Cornell and pro football)

1935 – **Larry Sherry** (Los Angeles Dodgers, Detroit Tigers, Houston Astros, California Angels pitcher)

1964 – **Jose Bautista** (Baltimore Orioles, Detroit Tigers, St. Louis Cardinals, Chicago Cubs, San Francisco Giants pitcher)

JULY 26

GAMEBREAKERS

1938 – **Hank Greenberg** smacks two home runs – his 30th and 31st of the season – and **Harry Eisenstat** is the winning pitcher in relief as the Detroit Tigers beat the Washington Senators 6-5.

1962 – **Randy Cardinal** allows only a second-inning single as Jamestown defeats Geneva 2-0 in the New York-Penn League.

1980 – **Steve Stone** allows eight hits in 7 1/3 innings as the Baltimore Orioles beat the Milwaukee Brewers 4-1 for Stone's 14th consecutive victory, two short of the major-league record.

1997 – **Shawn Green's** three-run homer with two out in the eighth inning gives the Toronto Blue Jays a 6-5 victory over the Kansas City Royals.

STRONG IN DEFEAT

1939 – National League batting leader **Morrie Arnovich** of the Phillies goes 5 for 5 with two doubles and three singles in Philadelphia's 3-1 loss to the Pittsburgh Pirates. Arnovich will hold the batting lead until Aug. 11 and will eventually finish third with a .324 average.

MAZEL TOUGH

1924 – **Laurie Cohen** wins the men's 100- and 200-meter races at the Canadian National track championships in Winnipeg.

1933 – **Barney Ross** knocks out Johnny Farr in six rounds in Kansas City to win the world super lightweight title.

1937 – For the second time in five weeks, **Baby Yack (Benjamin Yakubowitz)** wins a 10-round decision over Frankie Martin in Toronto to retain his Canadian bantamweight title.

1947 – **Ladislav Hecht** of Czechoslovakia defeats **Dick Savitt** in four sets to win the Eastern Clay Court tennis championships in Jackson Heights, N.Y.

1952 – **Herbert Klein** of Germany wins an Olympic bronze medal in the 200 breaststroke in Helsinki.

1958 – **Abraham "Pinky" Danilowitz** of South Africa wins the gold medal in lawn bowls while claiming the world championship at the Commonwealth Games in Cardiff, Wales.

1976 – **Valentin Mankin** earns a silver medal in yachting at the Montreal Olympics as the Soviet Union finishes second to Sweden in the tempest division.

1987 – **Margie Goldstein** rides Daydream to victory in the Grand Prix of New Hampshire.

1992 – **Tatiana Lysenko** wins an Olympic gold medal when Russia captures the women's team gymnastics title in Barcelona. **Kerri Strug** and Team USA win the bronze.

RECORD SETTERS

1926 – **Lillian Copeland** sets a world record of 35.55 meters in the javelin in Potsdam, Germany.

1952 – **Judit Temes** of Hungary sets an Olympic record of 1:05.5 in the semifinals of the 100 freestyle in Helsinki.

1967 – **Mark Spitz** sets a world record of 2:06.4 in winning the 200 butterfly at the Pan American Games in Winnipeg.

A STAR IS BORN

1979 – **Sarah Shapiro** (speed skating)

Kerry Strug
(U.S. Olympic Committee)

JULY 27

GAMEBREAKERS

1914 – **Erskine Mayer** of the Philadelphia Phillies allows one hit and hits a double in a 2-0 victory over the St. Louis Cardinals.

1919 – **Al Schacht** pitches a two-hitter as the Rochester Skeeters shut out the Newark Bears in the International League.

1934 – **Hank Greenberg** hits two home runs and knocks in five runs as the Detroit Tigers take over first place with a 16-15 victory over the Chicago White Sox.

1937 – **Buddy Myer's** bases-loaded single in the ninth inning gives the Washington Senators a 6-5 win over the Chicago White Sox.

1938 – **Hank Greenberg** hits home runs in his first two times at bat, giving him four consecutive homers over two days. Detroit beats Washington 9-4.

1948 – **Al Rosen** hits five consecutive home runs over a two-day period for Kansas City of the American Association.

1957 – In the first home game ever televised by the Memphis Chicks, only 809 fans pay to see **Hy Cohen** pitch a six-hitter in a 7-1 victory over Atlanta in the Southern Association.

1966 – For the third time in his career, **Sandy Koufax** strikes out 16 Philadelphia Phillies, pitching 11 innings in the Dodgers' 2-1, 12-inning victory. Jim Bunning of the Phillies strikes out 12 Dodgers.

2004 – **Jason Marquis** allows three hits in seven innings and smacks a two-run double – his major league-leading 13th hit of the season among pitchers – as the St. Louis Cardinals defeat the Cincinnati Reds 6-0. The victory is Marquis' eighth straight.

MAZEL TOUGH

1923 – **Andre Jesserun** wins a 10-round decision over Joe Lynch in Vancouver, British Columbia, and claims the Pacific Coast bantamweight title.

1952 – **Grigori Novak** of the Soviet Union wins a silver medal in middle-heavyweight weight lifting at the Olympics in Helsinki.

Lev Vainschtein of the Soviet Union wins a bronze in free rifle.

1952 – **Dick Savitt** wins the Middle Atlantic National Indoors tennis title.

1973 – **Walter Blum**, nearly 20 years to the day after winning his first race, becomes the sixth jockey to ride 4,000 winners when his mount finishes first in the seventh race at Monmouth Park in Oceanport, N.J.

1980 – **Brian Gottfried** beats Jose-Luis Clerc of Argentina 7-5, 4-6, 6-4 in the final of a clay-court tennis tournament in Washington, D.C.

1986 – **Brad Gilbert** beats Mike Leach 6-2, 6-2 in the final of a hard-court tennis tournament in Livingston, N.J.

2000 – **Alyssa Beckerman** finishes first on the balance beam at the U.S. Gymnastics Championships in St. Louis.

2003 – **Andy Ram** of Israel teams with Marlo Ancic of Croatia to win the men's doubles title at the ATP RCA Tennis Championships in Indianapolis.

2003 – **Sean Rosenthal** teams with Larry Witt to beat Casey Jennings and Matt Fuerbringer 21-16, 18-21, 15-12 for their first AVP beach volleyball title at Belmar Beach, N.J.

RECORD SETTERS

1922 – World lightweight champion **Benny Leonard** fights **Lew Tendler** to a 12-round no-decision in a non-title fight before 60,000 fans in Jersey City, N.J. The gate of $400,000 is a record for a non-heavyweight fight.

2003 – **Jason Lezak** swims the final leg as the United States' 400-medley relay team sets a world record of 3:31.54 at the World Championships in Barcelona, Spain.

A STAR IS BORN

1883 – **Harry "Klondike" Kane** (Philadelphia A's, Philadelphia Phillies, Detroit Tigers pitcher)

JULY 28

GAMEBREAKERS

1950 – **Al Rosen** hits his 28th and 29th homers of the season in the Cleveland Indians' 13-1 win over the Boston Red Sox.

1973 – **Richie Scheinblum** goes 5 for 5, draws an intentional walk, and knocks in two runs as the California Angels beat the Kansas City Royals 19-8.

1996 – **Jesse Levis's** RBI single with two out in the 13th inning gives the Milwaukee Brewers a 4-3 victory over the Anaheim Angels.

MAZEL TOUGH

1906 – **Walter Miller** rides winners in all five races at Brighton Beach racetrack in Brooklyn.

1942 – **Joe Garber** defeats **Morty Alexander** to win the National AAU one-wall handball title. In the doubles final, **Vic Hershkowitz** and **Moe Orenstein** beat Alexander and Marvin Hecht.

1946 – **Herman Barron** leads all four rounds and wins the All-American Pro Golf Championship at the Tam O'Shanter Country Club in Chicago. He earns $10,500 in golf's richest tournament with a one-stroke victory over Ellsworth Vines.

1963 – **Ildiko Rejto** of Hungary wins the women's title at the World Fencing Championships in Gdansk, Poland.

1965 – **Brad Gilbert** beats **Brian Teacher** 7-6, 6-4 in the final of a hard-court tennis tournament in Livingston, N.J.

1996 – **Miryam Fox-Jerusalmi** of France wins a bronze medal in the Olympic whitewater canoe K-1 slalom event on the Ocoee River in Tennessee.

2001 – **Anthony Ervin** wins the 100 freestyle at the World Swimming Championships in Fukuoka, Japan.

2002 – Rookie **Tomas Scheckter** of South Africa becomes the first Jewish driver to win an Indy car race, finishing 1.703 seconds ahead of teammate Buddy Rice in the Indy Racing League's inaugural Michigan Indy 400 in Brooklyn, Mich. Scheckter started the race on the pole.

2002 – **Nicole Freedman** wins the 63.2-mile Snelling Road Race cycling event in Merced, Calif.

RECORD SETTERS

1949 – **James Fuchs** of the United States breaks Charles Fonville's world shot put record with a toss of 58-4 3/8 in Oslo, Norway.

TRANSITIONS

1948 – **Sol Mishkin** replaces Robert Dill as manager of the Newark (Ohio) Yankees during their first season in the Ohio-Indiana League.

1979 – Former San Diego Chargers tackle **Ron Mix** becomes just the second former AFL player to be inducted in the Pro Football Hall of Fame.

A STAR IS BORN

1870 – **Harry P. Cline** (billiards)

1885 – **Monte Attell** (bantamweight boxer)

1891 – **Maurice Blitz** (Belgian water polo)

1902 – **Sammy Vogel** (featherweight boxer)

1907 – **Julius Yablok** (Colgate and pro football)

1925 – **Harry "Herschel" Haft** (Austrian light heavyweight boxer)

JULY 29

GAMEBREAKERS

1938 – For the third time in four days, **Hank Greenberg** hits two home runs in a game, giving him 35 for the season. Detroit beats the Philadelphia A's 9-2.

1945 – **Goody Rosen** gets six hits in a double-header as the Brooklyn Dodgers beat the Milwaukee Braves 5-2 and 15-4.

1951 – Buffalo Bisons pitcher **Ernie Silverman** tosses a shutout as Syracuse walks in the International League game's only run with two out in the ninth inning.

1961 – **Alan Koch** allows one hit over seven innings and posts his fourth straight victory in the Birmingham Barons' 4-0 triumph over Little Rock in the Southern Association.

MAZEL TOUGH

1934 – **Doris Shiman** wins the 100 breast-stroke at the AAU Swimming Championships in Detroit.

1953 – **Walter Blum** rides his first of 4,382 career winning mounts, the **Hirsch Jacobs**-trained filly Tuscania, at Saratoga Race-course.

1961 – **Mark Midler** of the Soviet Union wins his third of four foil titles at the World Fencing Championships.

1962 – **Roger Ginsberg** wins the Westchester Amateur Golf Tournament.

1979 – **Amy Alcott** finishes three strokes ahead of Nancy Lopez to win the LPGA Peter Jackson Classic in Montreal.

1980 – **Johan Harmenberg** of Sweden wins the individual epee fencing gold medal at the Olympics in Moscow. **Valentine Mankin** of the Soviet Union wins a gold for yachting when he teams with Alexander Muzychenko in the Star class.

1992 – **Valery Belenky** of Azerbaijan wins a gold medal in Barcelona when the CIS captures the men's gymnastics team combined.

RECORD SETTERS

1939 – **Ruth Langer,** an Austrian swimmer living in England, wins the final Thames long-distance swim, setting a British record of 74 minutes, 4 seconds for the 5-mile event.

1949 – **James Fuchs** throws the shot put 58 feet, 4 27/64 inches to beat the established world record in the "Little Olympics," which matches the United States against Scandinavian countries in Oslo, Norway.

1976 – **Irena Kirszenstein-Szewinska** of Poland sets a world record of 49.29 in winning the gold medal in the 400 meters in Montreal.

JEWS ON FIRST

1984 – **Mitch Gaylord** scores the first 10 for an American gymnast in Olympic competition en route to a bronze medal in the parallel bars at Los Angeles. He also wins a bronze on the rings and a silver in the vault.

A STAR IS BORN

1913 – **Meyer Pincus** (CCNY basketball)
1922 – **Sonny Hertzberg** (CCNY basketball)
1948 – **Neal Walk** (Florida basketball, Phoenix Suns, New York Knicks, New Orleans Jazz center)

Hank Greenberg *(Jewish Major Leaguers)*

JULY 30

GAMEBREAKERS

1938 – **Harry Eisenstat** is the winning pitcher in both ends of a doubleheader, pitching five innings of shutout relief in the first game and four scoreless innings of relief in the nightcap. **Hank Greenberg** smacks three home runs in the twin bill, tying Babe Ruth's record of nine in a week, as the Detroit Tigers beat the Philadelphia A's 9-2 and 10-7.

1943 – **Sid Gordon** collects four hits including a double and triple as the New York Giants beat the Pittsburgh Pirates 13-7.

1948 – **Ernie Silverman** allows one hit in seven innings in relief of starter **Saul Rogovin** as Buffalo defeats Syracuse 5-4 in the International League.

1964 – Oklahoma City pitcher **Larry Yellen** hits a routine single to right field with the bases loaded in a Pacific Coast League game. The ball caroms off a sprinkler cover and winds up as a three-run double as the 89ers defeat Dallas 5-3.

1969 – **Greg Goosen** hits two homers and drives in three runs as the Seattle Pilots beat the Washington Senators 4-3. **Mike Epstein** hits a two-run homer for Washington.

1979 – **Steve Stone** allows one hit – Charlie Moore's third-inning home run – in 8 2/3 innings as the Baltimore Orioles beat the Milwaukee Brewers 2-1. Stone gets last-out relief help from Tippy Martinez after he issues his second walk of the game.

MAZEL TOUGH

1941 – **Georgie Abrams** scores his third straight victory over New York State world middleweight champion Billy Soose in a 10-round non-title fight at Madison Square Garden.

1948 – **Vic Hershkowitz** beats **Marty Rosenfeld** to win his second straight National AAU one-wall handball championship. Hershkowitz also teams with **Artie Wolfe** for the doubles title.

1951 – **Dick Savitt** wins the Middle Atlantic men's tennis singles title.

1974 – **Harold Solomon** beats Guillermo Vilas 1-6, 6-3, 6-4 to win the Washington Stars clay-court tennis tournament.

1976 – Japan beats the Soviet Union in the women's volleyball final at the Montreal Olympics. **Natalia Kushnir** and **Efim Chulak** earn silver medals for Russia

1978 – **Harold Solomon** defeats John Alexander 6-2, 6-2 to win the Louisville International tennis tournament.

1989 – **Martin Jaite** beats Goran Prpic 6-3, 6-2 in the final of a clay-court tennis tournament in Stuttgart, Germany.

1992 – **Yael Arad** becomes the first Israeli to win an Olympic medal when she finishes second in the 61-kg. (light middleweight) judo division in Barcelona.

2000 – **Bruce Fleisher** leads all three rounds and wins the Senior PGA Long Island Classic in Jericho, N.Y., for the second year in a row, finishing at 18 under par, two strokes ahead of Dana Quigley.

2006 – **Anna Smashnova** of Israel becomes the first tennis player to win back-to-back Budapest Grand Prix titles with a 6-1, 6-3 victory over Lourdes Dominguez Luno of Spain. **Shahar Peer** of Israel teams with Anna-Lena Groenefeld of Germany to win the doubles title at the Bank of the West Classic in Stanford, Calif.

TRANSITIONS

1936 – **Cecil Hart**, who led the Montreal Canadiens to two Stanley Cup championships before retiring as coach after the 1931–32 season, is rehired by the Canadiens to replace coach Sylvio Mantha.

1983 – **Sid Gillman**, who won 123 games in 18 years as an AFL and NFL coach, is inducted into the Pro Football Hall of Fame. He also will be inducted into the College Football Hall of Fame in 1989.

JULY 31

GAMEBREAKERS

1949 – **Sid Gordon** of the Giants hits home runs off Ken Raffensberger and Johnny Vander Meer in a nine-run second inning of the second game of a doubleheader against Cincinnati. New York sweeps the Reds 10-0 and 9-0.

1963 – **Barry Latman** pitches a four-hitter with 10 strikeouts as the Cleveland Indians beat the Los Angeles Angels 1-0.

2002 – Houston Astros catcher **Brad Ausmus** goes 4 for 6 with a homer and three RBI's in a 16-3 victory over the New York Mets.

2004 – **Brad Ausmus** goes 4 for 4 in the Houston Astros' 8-0 victory over the Cincinnati Reds.

2004 – **Brian Horwitz** ties a Salem Volcanoes franchise record with three doubles among his four hits in an 11-6 victory over Tri-City in the Northwest League.

MAZEL TOUGH

1801 – **Isaac Bittoon** wins his first boxing match, beating Tom Jones at Wimbledon, Surrey, England.

1928 – **Lillian Copeland** wins the silver medal in the discus with a toss of 121-7 7/8 – her best throw of the year – at the Olympics in Amsterdam. **Bobbie Rosenfeld** of Canada wins the silver medal in the 100 meters.

1932 – **Hans Haas** of Austria wins an Olympic silver medal in weight lifting's lightweight division in Los Angeles.

1949 – **Henry Laskau** wins the 38-mile marathon racewalk in 5 hours, 58 minutes, 1 second in Saratoga Springs, N.Y.

1964 – **Donald Spero** wins the national single sculls and quadruple rowing championships.

1982 – **Ken Klingman** knocks out Max Hord in the first round in West Palm Beach, Fla., then announces his retirement as a middleweight fighter with a 20-0 record – all knockouts within the first three rounds.

1984 – **Mitch Gaylord** wraps up the men's team gymnastics gold medal for the United States in Los Angeles with a 9.95 on the horizontal bar. **Abie Grossfeld** coaches the team.

1992 – **Oren Smadja** of Israel captures the judo bronze medal in the men's 70-kg. (lightweight) class at the Olympics in Barcelona. **Valery Belenky** of Azerbaijan wins a bronze in gymnastics all-around.

1998 – **Lenny Krayzelburg** wins the 200 breaststroke in 1:59.90 at the Goodwill Games in New York.

2005 – Unseeded **Dudi Sela** of Israel defeats fourth-seeded Bobby Reynolds 6-3, 3-6, 6-4 to win an ATP Challenger tennis tournament in Lexington, Ky.

RECORD SETTERS

1967 – **Mark Spitz** sets a world record of 56.3 seconds in the 100 butterfly at the Pan American Games in Winnipeg. He also anchors the United States' 800 freestyle relay team in capturing his fourth of five gold medals at the meet.

TRANSITIONS

1980 – The Texas Rangers beat Baltimore 7-4, snapping Orioles pitcher **Steve Stone's** 14-game winning streak, two shy of the American League record.

A STAR IS BORN

1909 – **Morris Bodenger** (Tulane football, Detroit Lions)

1912 – **Irv Kupcinet** (North Dakota football, Philadelphia Eagles)

AUGUST 1

GAMEBREAKERS

1918 – Starting pitcher **Erskine Mayer** of the Pittsburgh Pirates throws 15 1/3 scoreless innings against the Boston Braves. Pittsburgh wins 2-0 in 21 innings.

1939 – **Harry Danning** collects three hits, including a two-run triple in the sixth and a game-winning single in the 10th as the New York Giants end the Cincinnati Reds' 10-game winning streak with a 5-4 victory.

1951 – **Ernie Silverman** of Buffalo pitches his second straight International League shutout, beating Ottawa 8-0 on five hits.

1958 – Spokane pitcher **Larry Sherry** goes 4 for 4 with a homer, double, and four RBI's in a 12-2 Pacific Coast League victory over Salt Lake City.

STRONG IN DEFEAT

1971 – **Ron Blomberg** hits two homers and drives in three runs in the New York Yankees' 10-7 loss to the Minnesota Twins.

MAZEL TOUGH

1959 – **Isaac Berger** (132 pounds) and **Paul Goldberg** (148), both representing the York Barbell Company, win AAU weight lifting championships in York, Pa.

1971 – **Abigail Hoffman** of Canada wins the 800 meters at the Pan American Games in Cali, Colombia.

1971 – **Tom Okker** beats Rod Laver 6-3, 7-6, 6-7, 6-1 to win the Quebec International Open indoor tennis tournament.

1981 – **Keith Peache** of Great Britain wins the 100-kg. freestyle division at the European Market Wrestling Championships in Kelheim, Germany.

1992 – **Tatiana Lysenko** of Ukraine wins a gold medal on the balance beam and a bronze in vault at the Olympics in Barcelona.

2003 – **Dan Kellner** defeats American teammate **Jon Tiomkin** 15-13 in fencing to win the foil gold medal at the Pan American Games in the Dominican Republic.

2007 - Twenty-five years after winning her first national title, 40-year-old **Dara Torres** wins the 100 freestyle at the U.S. Nationals Swimming Championships in Indianapolis. Three days later, Torres sets an American record of 24.53 seconds in winning the 50 freestyle.

RECORD SETTERS

1952 – **Eva Szekely** of Hungary ties the Olympic record of 2:54.0 in the 200 breaststroke in the semifinals, then sets a record of 2:51.7 to win the gold medal in Helsinki.

1964 – **Marilyn Ramenofsky** improves her world record in the 400 freestyle, swimming the distance in 4:41.7 at the National AAU meet in Los Altos, Calif.

TRANSITIONS

1992 – Oakland Raiders coach and owner **Al Davis** is enshrined in the Pro Football Hall of Fame.

1998 – **Marilyn Fierro**, a seventh-degree black belt, becomes the first woman to be inducted into the Isshinryu Karate Hall of Fame in Knoxville, Tenn.

A STAR IS BORN

1901 – **Gerard Blitz** (Belgian water polo, swimming)

1903 – **Lea Kloot-Nordheim** (Dutch gymnast)

1908 – **Pinky Danilowitz** (South African bowls)

1976 – **David Nemirovsky** (Florida Panthers hockey)

Marilyn Ramenofsky
(U.S. Olympic Committee)

AUGUST 2

GAMEBREAKERS

1959 – **Marty Stabiner** pitches 7 2/3 innings of two-hit relief as Montreal defeats Miami 5-3 in the first game of an International League doubleheader. Sixteen hours earlier, Stabiner earned the victory with two scoreless innings of relief in Montreal's 5-4 win over Miami.

1998 – **Shawn Green** goes 4 for 5 with a homer as the Toronto Blue Jays beat the Minnesota Twins 6-4.

MAZEL TOUGH

1791 – Heavyweight champion **Daniel Mendoza** defeats Squire Fitzgerald in 26 minutes in a boxing match in England.

1928 – **Samuel Rabin** of Great Britain wins a bronze medal in middleweight freestyle wrestling at the Olympics in Amsterdam.

1932 – **Nickolaus Hirschl** of Austria wins an Olympic bronze medal in freestyle wrestling's heavyweight division in Los Angeles.

1936 – **Robert Fein** of Austria wins a weight lifting gold medal in the lightweight class at the Olympics in Berlin.

1946 – **Herb Flam** beats Herbert Behrens to retain his U.S. National Junior Tennis title in Kalamazoo, Mich.

1948 – **Henry Wittenberg** of the United States wins an Olympic gold medal in freestyle wrestling's light heavyweight division in London.

1952 – **Robert Antal** and **Sandor Geller** of Hungary win gold medals for water polo and soccer, respectively, at the Olympics in Helsinki. **Valeria Gyengi** of Hungary wins gold in the women's 400-meter freestyle with an Olympic-record time of 5:12.1.

1964 – **Donald Spero** finishes first in single sculls at the National Rowing Championships at Orchard Beach Lagoon in the Bronx, N.Y.

1970 – **Tom Okker** beats Roger Taylor 4-6, 6-0, 6-1 6-3 to win the Dutch Open hard-court tennis tournament.

1970 – **Dick Siderowf** defeats Rick Spears 2-up to win his third straight Metropolitan Amateur golf championship in Clifton, N.J.

1983 – **Marshall Holman** beats Del Ballard Jr. 234-194 to win the PBA AquaFest/Mr. Gattis Open in Austin, Texas. The victory is Holman's first in 2½ years.

1992 – **Joe Jacobi** of the United States teams with Scott Strausbaugh to win the Canadian slalom pairs canoeing gold medal at the Barcelona Olympics.

2003 – **Anna Smashnova** of Israel defeats Klara Koukalova of the Czech Republic 6-2, 6-0 to win the clay-court tennis Idea Prokom Open in Sopot, Poland.

2003 – **Sada Jacobson** defeats Alejandra Benitez of Venezuela 15-4 to win the saber gold medal in fencing at the Pan American Games in Santo Domingo, Dominican Republic. **Emily Jacobson**, Sada's younger sister, wins the bronze medal.

RECORD SETTERS

1932 – **Lilian Copeland** of the United States sets a world record of 133-1 5/8 to win the gold medal in the discus at the Olympics in Los Angeles.

1972 – **Mark Spitz** improves his world record in the 200 butterfly to 2:01.87, then 2:01.53 in Chicago.

TRANSITIONS

2007 - Milwaukee Brewers rookie third baseman **Ryan Braun** is named National League Player of the Month after hitting .345 with 11 homers and 25 RBIs in July.

A STAR IS BORN

1887 – **Aaron Kallet** (Syracuse football)
1967 – **Aaron Krickstein** (tennis)
1970 – **Jonathan Kaye** (golf)

AUGUST 3

GAMEBREAKERS

1949 – **Sid Gordon's** bases-loaded single in the seventh inning sparks the New York Giants to a 4-1 win over the Chicago Cubs.
1961 – **Art Shamsky** hits his second homer of the game in the 10th inning to give Topeka an 8-7 victory over Cedar Rapids in the Three-I League.
1963 – **Sandy Koufax** pitches a three-hitter as the Los Angeles Dodgers beat the Houston Colt .45s 2-0.

STRONG IN DEFEAT

1947 – **Hank Greenberg** hits a grand-slam homer in the first game and two solo homers in the nightcap, but the Pittsburgh Pirates lose 11-8 to the New York Giants in the opener before playing to a 6-6, 8-inning tie in the second game.
2001 – **Jason Marquis** allows two hits in eight innings and strikes out 13 batters, but the Atlanta Braves lose to the Milwaukee Brewers 3-2 in 11 innings.

MAZEL TOUGH

1928 – **Izzy Schwartz** knocks out Little Jeff in four rounds to retain his New York world flyweight title in Rockaway, N.Y.
1932 – **Karoly Karpati** of Hungary wins a silver medal in freestyle wrestling's lightweight division at the Olympics in Los Angeles.
1981 – **Shlomo Glickstein** of Israel beats Dick Stockton 6-3, 5-7, 6-4 in the final of a clay-court tennis tournament in South Orange, N.J.
1986 – **Amy Alcott** wins the LPGA National Pro-Am in Denver by one stroke over Pat Bradley and Chris Johnson.
1987 – **Andrew Sznajder** of Canada defeats Lloyd Bourne 6-4, 4-6, 6-3 in the final of the Seattle Challenger tennis tournament.

1997 – **Tanya Dubnicoff** wins the women's match sprint and 500-meter cycling titles at the Canadian National Track Championships in Calgary.
2000 – **Michelle Feldman** beats Leanne Barrette 188-173 in the final of the Lady Ebonite Classic women's pro bowling event.

RECORD SETTERS

1885 – American runner **Lon Myers** ties his world record of 1:55.4 in the half mile in Blackley, England.
1948 – **Eva Szekely** of Hungary sets an Olympic record of 3:01.2 in one of the heats of the 200 breaststroke in London. She finishes fourth in the finals. **James Fuchs** of Yale tops the old Olympic record in the shot put, but settles for a bronze medal behind two U.S. teammates.
1954 – **Judit Temes** swims the first leg of Hungary's world-record setting 4×100 medley relay team which finishes in 5:07.8 in Budapest.

TRANSITIONS

1949 – Six teams from the National Basketball League join with the Basketball Association of America to form the 17-team NBA. **Maurice Podoloff** is named league president.
1996 – **Ralph Horween,** who played for the Chicago Cardinals from 1921-23, is honored by the NFL as the first former player to turn 100.

A STAR IS BORN

1896 – **Ralph Horween** (Harvard football, Chicago Cardinals back)
1928 – **Marv Levy** (football coach)
1953 – **Bobby Gross** (Long Beach State basketball, Portland Trail Blazers, San Diego Clippers)

AUGUST 4

GAMEBREAKERS

1933 – **Hank Greenberg** drives in all three Detroit runs in the Tigers' 3-2, 11-inning victory over the Chicago White Sox.

1963 – **Larry Sherry** pitches the ninth inning and combines with Johnny Podres on a one-hitter as the Houston Astros beat the Los Angeles Dodgers 4-0.

2002 – **Shawn Green** of the Dodgers goes 4 for 6 with two home runs, including a game-tying, two-out homer in the ninth, as Los Angeles beats the Philadelphia Phillies 8-6 in 12 innings.

STRONG IN DEFEAT

1948 – **Lou Limmer** of the Omaha A's hits his Western League-leading 26th and 27th homers of the season in a doubleheader loss to first-place Lincoln.

1960 – **Alan Koch** strikes out six consecutive batters and 13 in all, but Birmingham loses to the Little Rock Travelers 3-2 in the Southern Association.

MAZEL TOUGH

1873 – **Lipman Pike**, considered by some to be the first professional baseball player, wins the Maryland state 100-yard dash.

1934 – **Harry Mizler** decisions Billy Quinlan in 15 rounds in Swansea, Wales, to retain his British lightweight title.

1936 – **Karoly Karpati** of Hungary wins the Olympic gold medal in the lightweight class for freestyle wrestling. **Jadwiga Wajsowna** of Poland wins a silver in the women's discus.

1948 – **Steve Seymour** of the Los Angeles Athletic Club captures a silver medal in the javelin at the Olympics in London.

1974 – **Dick Siderowf**, one of the United States' top amateur golfers, wins the New York Met title for the fourth time.

2002 – **Joanna Zeiger** wins the Vineman Half-Ironman Triathlon in Santa Rosa, Calif., in 4 hours, 23 minutes, 10 seconds.

2006 – **Jason Lezak** wins the 100 freestyle in 48.63 seconds at the U.S. Summer National championships in Irvine, Calif.

RECORD SETTERS

1972 – **Mark Spitz** twice improves his world-record time in the 100 butterfly in Chicago – to 54.72 and 54.56 seconds.

2003 – **Kevin Youkilis** of Pawtucket hits a two-run double in the third inning to tie the all-time minor-league record of reaching base in 71 consecutive games. The Red Sox beat the Buffalo Bisons 5-0 in an International League game. The streak ends with an 0-for-4 night a day later in a 9-0 loss to Syracuse.

JEWS ON FIRST

1993 – **Brad Ausmus** of the San Diego Padres hits his first career home run, connecting off Greg Brummert in an 11-10 victory over the San Francisco Giants.

TRANSITIONS

1999 – Major League Soccer fires commissioner Doug Logan and replaces him with NFL marketing executive **Don Garber.**

1999 – **Daniel Perlsweig**, a former jockey and trainer of 1980 Eclipse Award winner Lord Avie, receives the Dogwood Dominion Award, presented annually to the "unsung hero" of the thoroughbred industry.

2001 – Former Kansas City Chiefs and Buffalo Bills coach **Marv Levy** is inducted into the Pro Football Hall of Fame.

A STAR IS BORN

1976 – **Paul Goldstein** (tennis)

AUGUST 5

GAMEBREAKERS

1914 – **Erskine Mayer** of the Philadelphia Phillies pitches his fourth shutout of the season, stopping the Cincinnati Reds 5-0.

1951 – Detroit catcher **Joe Ginsberg** breaks a 2-2 tie in the first game with an RBI triple and snaps a 5-5 tie in the nightcap with a two-run double as the Tigers sweep the Boston Red Sox 3-1 and 8-5.

1959 – **Barry Latman** of the White Sox pitches a three-hitter with six strikeouts in a 2-0 shutout of Baltimore.

1999 – **Ben Gorewich** scores a hat trick as the St. Louis Vipers beat the Chicago Bluesmen 10-5 and clinch the Roller Hockey International Eastern Division title.

STRONG IN DEFEAT

1937 – **Eddie Feinberg** hits a grand-slam homer in the top of the ninth inning, but Centerville loses 5-4 when Federalsburg scores in the bottom of the 10th of an Eastern Shore (Md.) League game.

MAZEL TOUGH

1922 – **Benny Leonard** retains his world lightweight title with a 10-round no-decision against Ever Hammer in Michigan City, Mich.

1928 – **Bobbie Rosenfeld** runs the second leg of Canada's gold medal-winning women's 400-meter relay team at the Olympics in Amsterdam, while setting a world record of 48.4 seconds. **Ellis Smouha** of Great Britain wins a bronze in the men's 400-meter relay.

1931 – **Maxie Rosenbloom** wins a 15-round decision over Jimmy Slattery in Brooklyn to retain his world light heavyweight title.

1968 – **Julie Heldman** defeats Helga Niessen 4-6, 6-3, 6-3 to win the Bavarian Open tennis tournament in Munich, Germany.

1979 – **Harold Solomon** beats Jose Higueras 5-7, 6-4, 7-6 in the final of a clay-court tennis tournament in North Conway, N.H.

1987 – **Mark Roth** rolls a 299 game against George Brabham III en route to his 33rd career PBA title. He beats Chris Warren 259-215 in the final of the Buffalo Open in Cheektowaga, N.Y.

1998 – **Michelle Feldman** beats Kim Adler 205-192 in the final of the Lady Ebonite Classic bowling tournament in Louisville, Ky.

1999 – **Paul Goldstein** beats Cecil Mamiit 4-6, 6-0, 6-3 to win the tennis gold medal at the Pan American Games in Winnipeg. He is the first American male to win gold since 1983.

2000 – **Matt Rosenfeld** of Plano, Texas, beats Ryan Moore 3-and-2 to win the U.S. Junior Amateur golf championship in North Plaines, Ore.

RECORD SETTERS

1972 – **Mark Spitz** improves his world record in the 100-meter freestyle to 51.47 seconds in Chicago.

1983 – **Dara Torres** recaptures the world record in the women's 50-meter freestyle, attaining 25.62 seconds in Clovis, N.M.

TRANSITIONS

1927 – With the Chicago White Sox out of healthy catchers, backup infielder **Moe Berg** is called upon in the third inning of a 4-1 loss to the Boston Red Sox. "If the worst happens, kindly deliver the body to Newark," says Berg, who spends the next 12 seasons behind the plate.

A STAR IS BORN

1976 – **Gavin Fingleson** (Australian baseball)
1978 – **Harel Levy** (Israeli tennis)
1980 – **Yuri Foreman** (Israeli junior welterweight boxer)
1982 – **Jo Ankier** (British track)

AUGUST 6

GAMEBREAKERS

1948 – **Marv Rotblatt** of the Waterloo White Hawks pitches a no-hitter in a 3-2 victory over the Terre Haute Phillies in the Three-I League. He strikes out 11 but walks two and hits two batters. Both Terre Haute runs score on errors.

1954 – **Sid Gordon** drives in the winning run with a squeeze bunt with two out in the ninth inning as the Pittsburgh Pirates beat the St. Louis Cardinals 6-5. The hit is Gordon's fourth of the game.

1999 – Hours after arriving in Chicago after being called up from Triple-A Iowa, **Andrew Lorraine** pitches a three-hitter in the Cubs' 6-0 victory over the Houston Astros at Wrigley Field.

2000 – **Tony Schrager** hits a homer in the bottom of the ninth to give Daytona Beach a 5-4 victory over St. Petersburg in the Class A Florida State League.

MAZEL TOUGH

1942 – Lightweight contender **Allie Stolz** wins a 10-round decision over world featherweight champion Chalky Wright in an over-the-weight non-title fight in New York.

1950 – **Herb Flam** wins the Eastern Grass-court tennis championship.

1971 – **Henry Nissen** of Australia knocks out John McCloskey in the eighth round to win the British Empire flyweight title in Melbourne.

1989 – **Brad Gilbert** beats Jim Pugh 7-5, 6-0 in the final of a hard-court tennis tournament in Stratton Mountain, Vt.

1994 – **Margie Goldstein-Engle** rides Lacosta to first place in the Turfway Park Grand Prix equestrian event.

2001 – **Zhanna Bloch** of Ukraine defeats Marion Jones by .03 seconds to win the 100 meters at the World Track and Field Championships in Edmonton, ending Jones' streak of 42 consecutive victories in a 100 final. Bloch also beats Jones in an earlier semifinal heat.

2003 – **Dan Kellner**, **Jon Tiomkin**, and Jed Dupree give the United States a come-from-behind 45-44 victory over Cuba for the team foil gold medal at the Pan American Games in the Dominican Republic. Kellner outscores Cuban star Reiner Suarez in the final match after the U.S. trailed 30-40. The victory for the U.S. was the first in foil fencing against Cuba since 1971.

2006 – **Tzipi Obziler** of Israel wins the USTA Legg Mason Women's Pro Circuit tennis tournament when third-seeded Camille Pin of France retires while trailing 7-5, 2-5.

A STAR IS BORN

1932 – **Rafail Grach** (Soviet speed skater)

Brad Gilbert
(U.S. Olympic Committee)

AUGUST 7

GAMEBREAKERS

1961 – **Barry Latman** scatters 10 hits and runs his season record to 8-0 as the Cleveland Indians blank the Chicago White Sox 9-0.

1999 – **Chad Levitt** caps a 70-yard scoring drive with a 1-yard touchdown as the Oakland Raiders beat the St. Louis Rams 18-17 in an NFL preseason game.

MAZEL TOUGH

1927 – Maccabi Football Club of Tel Aviv beats the Brooklyn Wanderers 2-1 and completes its first American soccer tour with a 5-4-1 record.

1930 – World junior welterweight champion **Jackie "Kid" Berg** wins a 10-round decision in New York to end Kid Chocolate's 160-fight unbeaten streak as an amateur and pro.

1932 – **Albert Schwartz** of the United States wins an Olympic bronze medal in 100-meter freestyle swimming in Los Angeles.

1938 – **George Baskin** and **Harry Goldstein** defeat **Morty Alexander** and **Sy Alexander** to win their second straight National AAU one-wall handball doubles title. **Joe Garber** wins the singles title.

1938 – **Claire Isicson** wins her second straight National AAU outdoor track 50-meters championship in an American-record 6.4 seconds in Naugatuck, Conn. **Gretel Bergmann**, the former German national champion now living in the United States, wins the high jump and **Rose Auerbach** takes her second straight javelin title.

1950 – **Herb Flam** wins the Eastern Grass Courts tennis championship in South Orange, N.J.

1964 – **Abigail Hoffman** wins the 400- and 800-meter events for the second straight year at the Canadian National track and field championships in St. Lambert, Quebec.

1972 – **Barry Asher** rallies from 12th place at the start of the final round and beats Gary Dickinson by 172 pins to win the PBA Columbia 300 Open in Cranston, R.I.

1981 – **Brian Teacher** beats Bill Scanlon 7-6, 6-4 in the final of a hard-court tennis tournament in Columbus, Ohio.

1994 – Stanford center **Anita Kaplan** and the United States women's basketball team defeat France 87-63 to win the gold medal at the Goodwill Games in St. Petersburg, Russia. Kaplan scores 14 points in four tournament games.

2005 – **Dudi Sela** of Israel defeats Paul Baccanello of Australia 6-2, 6-3 to win an ATP Challenger tennis tournament in Vancouver.

2005 – **Ben Wildman-Tobriner** wins the 50-meter freestyle in 22.13 seconds to edge world champion Roland Schoeman at the U.S. National Swimming Championships in Irvine, Calif.

RECORD SETTERS

1909 – **Abel Kiviat** sets a world record of 2:47.2 for the two-thirds mile run.

A STAR IS BORN

1897 – **Leonard Sachs** (basketball, football)

AUGUST 8

GAMEBREAKERS

2004 – **Kevin Youkilis** and **Gabe Kapler** both go 3 for 4 as the Boston Red Sox outslug the Detroit Tigers 11-9. Youkilis hits two of the game's 10 home runs and drives in four runs, and Kapler hits two doubles and drives in a run.

MAZEL TOUGH

1928 – **Janos Garay, Attila Petschauer**, and **Sandor Gombos** help Hungary win a fencing gold medal in team saber at the Amsterdam Olympics.

1932 – **Abraham Kurland** of Denmark wins a silver medal in Greco-Roman wrestling's lightweight division at the Olympics in Los Angeles. **Nickolaus Hirschl** of Austria wins a bronze in the heavyweight division – five days after winning the bronze in freestyle wrestling.

1959 – **Willie Harmatz** rides Sky Clipper to victory in the Sapling Stakes at Monmouth Park in New Jersey and wins a track-record purse of $82,617.

1964 – **Walter Blum** rides Gun Bow to a 10-length victory over runner-up Mongo in the Whitney Stakes at Saratoga.

1967 – **Kathy Harter** wins the Canadian National grass-court tennis tournament in Montreal.

1976 – **Harold Solomon** beats Wojtek Fibak of Poland 6-2, 7-5 in the final of a clay-court tennis tournament in Louisville, Ky.

1983 – **Brian Teacher** beats Bill Scanlon 7-6, 6-2 in the final of the Buckeye Classic tennis tournament in Grove City, Ohio.

1984 – Two months after almost losing his right leg because of a staph infection in his knee, **Robert Breland** becomes the first American to win an Olympic silver medal in judo, finishing second in the middleweight division. **Daniel Adler** of Brazil wins a silver for yachting in the sailing class.

1997 – **Zhanna Bloch** of Ukraine wins the 200-meter women's title at the World Track and Field Championships in Athens.

1998 – **Paul Goldstein** defeats Hyung-Taik Lee 6-1, 6-4 in Lexington, Ky., to win his first USTA Challenger tennis tournament.

1999 – **Bruce Fleisher** leads all three rounds to win the PGA Senior Long Island Classic in Jericho, N.Y., by two strokes over Allen Doyle.

RECORD SETTERS

1965 – **Irena Kirszenstein-Szewinska** of Poland sets a world record of 22.7 seconds in the 200 meters at the European Championships in Warsaw.

1971 – **Faina Melnik** of the Soviet Union sets the first of her 11 world records in the discus with a toss of 64.22 meters in Helsinki.

1972 – Dodgers catcher **Steve Yeager** ties a National League record with 22 putouts and sets a major-league record for handling 24 chances in a 19-inning game. Los Angeles loses 3-2 to the Cincinnati Reds.

TRANSITIONS

1936 – Just before qualifying trials are scheduled, U.S. coaches remove **Marty Glickman** and **Sam Stoller** from the United States' 400-meter relay team at the Olympic Games in Berlin.

1946 – The Dreyfuss family, owner of the Pittsburgh Pirates since 1900, sells the franchise for $2.5 million.

A STAR IS BORN

1915 – **Alex Schoenbaum** (Ohio State football)
1915 – **Sam Stoller** (Michigan sprinter)
1977 – **Andy "Bubba" Berenzweig** (Michigan hockey, Nashville Predators)
1980 – **Craig Breslow** (San Diego Padres, Boston Red Sox pitcher)

AUGUST 9

GAMEBREAKERS

1934 – **Phil Weintraub**, recently called up from Nashville of the Southern Association where he batted .401, collects four hits as the New York Giants beat the Brooklyn Dodgers 16-5.

1978 – **Elliott Maddox** goes 4 for 6 as the New York Mets beat the Montreal Expos 10-3.

MAZEL TOUGH

1930 – **Henry Cieman** wins the 1-mile walk at the Canadian National Track and Field Championships in Toronto.

1932 – **Philip Erenberg** of the United States wins an Olympic gymnastics silver medal for Indian clubs at the Los Angeles Games.

1936 – **Ibolya Csak** of Hungary wins the gold medal in the high jump at the Olympic Games in Berlin. Her winning height is equal to the German national record held by **Gretel Bergmann**, who was prevented from competing by the Nazis.

1937 – **Benny Caplan** wins a 15-round decision over Dick Corbett in London to capture the British featherweight title.

1981 – **Brian Teacher** beats John Austin 6-3, 6-2 in the final of a hard-court tennis tournament in Columbus, Ohio.

1983 – **Marshall Holman** beats Kent Wagner 290-224 in the Venice (Fla.) Open for his second consecutive PBA bowling tournament victory and the 16th of his career. Holman leaves the 8-pin in the first frame, then strikes out in the final game.

1991 – **Fabrice Benichou** knocks out Salvatore Bottiglieri in the eighth round in Antibes, France, to retain his European featherweight title.

1992 – **Avital Selinger** and his Netherlands teammates win a silver medal in men's volleyball at the Olympics in Barcelona. **Ben Greenbaum** and the United States defeat Cuba 2-15, 15-13, 15-7, 15-11 for the bronze medal.

2001 – **Alex Averbukh** of Israel finishes second in the pole vault at the World Track and Field Championships in Edmonton by clearing 19 feet, 2¼ inches. It is the highest finish ever by an Israeli athlete.

RECORD SETTERS

2000 – **Dara Torres** sets American long-course swimming records in the 50-meter butterfly (26.5 seconds) and 100 butterfly (57.58 seconds).

A STAR IS BORN

1938 – **Donald Spero** (rowing)
1961 – **Brad Gilbert** (tennis)

Phil Weintraub (*Jewish Major Leaguers*)

AUGUST 10

GAMEBREAKERS

1916 – **Erskine Mayer** of the Philadelphia Phillies shuts out the Cincinnati Reds 1-0.

1933 – Light-hitting shortstop **Jonah Goldman** goes 4 for 4 for the Montreal Royals in an International League game against the Baltimore Orioles.

1951 – **Al Rosen's** two-run homer in the eighth inning gives the Cleveland Indians a 6-4 victory over the Chicago White Sox.

1965 – Salisbury third baseman **Steve Hertz** hits two home runs and a double and scores all three Astros runs in a 3-2 victory over the Thomasville Hi-Toms in a Western Carolinas League game.

2001 – **Haim Revivo** of Israel scores all three goals as Fenerbahce beats Samsunpor 3-0 in a Turkish League First Division soccer match.

STRONG IN DEFEAT

1968 – **Norm Miller** of the Houston Astros hits a grand slam homer in the ninth inning off Pirates reliever Elroy Face, but Pittsburgh wins the second game of a doubleheader 7-4. Miller drives in five runs as the Astros win the first game 16-3.

MAZEL TOUGH

1928 – The Netherlands wins the team combined exercises title in the first Olympic gymnastics competition for women in Amsterdam. Jewish members of the team are **Estella Agsteribbe**, **Elka de Levie**, **Helena Nordheim**, **Annie Polak,** and alternate **Judike Simons**.

1928 – **Jack Silver** knocks out "Rough House" Nelson in the first round of a lightweight fight in Aberdeen, Wash., breaking two of Nelson's ribs in the process. Silver donates a share of his purse to help pay Nelson's medical bills.

1932 – **Peter Jaffe** of Great Britain wins an Olympic silver medal for yachting in the Star class in Los Angeles.

1948 – **Frank Spellman** of the United States wins a gold medal in the 165-pound (middleweight) class in weight lifting at the Olympics in London. He sets Olympic records of 336.25 in the clean and jerk and 859.5 total.

1963 – **Laszlo Fabian** of Hungary teams with Istvan Timer to win the K-2 10,000-meter race at the World Kayaking Championships in Spittal, Austria.

1984 – **Carina Benninga** and the Netherlands field hockey team wrap up the Olympic gold medal in Los Angeles with a 2-0 victory over Australia. **Mark Berger** of the United States wins bronze in the judo heavyweight division.

2002 – **Alex Averbukh** captures Israel's first medal of any kind at a major track meet when he wins the pole vault at the European Track and Field Championships in Munich, Germany.

2003 – **Anna Smashnova** wins her second straight tennis title, beating Jelena Kostanic of Russia 4-6, 6-4, 6-0 in the final of the Nordea Nordic Light Open in Espoo, Finland. Smashnova runs her record in WTA finals to 8-0.

RECORD SETTERS

1953 – **Eva Szekely** and **Valeria Gyengi** swim the final two legs as Hungary improves its world record in the 4×100 women's medley relay to 5:09.2 in Bucarest.

2003 – **Amy Weisberger** sets a world powerlifting record of 515 squat, 305 bench, and 460 dead lift to win the 132-pound pro division at the IPA world championships in Harrisburg, Pa.

A STAR IS BORN

1906 – **Ed Wineapple** (Providence basketball, Washington Senators pitcher)

1920 – **Red Holzman** (basketball, Rochester Royals, Milwaukee/St. Louis Hawks player-coach, New York Knicks coach)

AUGUST 11

GAMEBREAKERS

1921 – **Sammy Bohne** goes 4 for 4 with two RBI's as the Cincinnati Reds beat the St. Louis Cardinals 6-1.

1945 – Making his second minor-league start, **Duke Markell** of the Hickory Rebels pitches a 4-0 no-hitter against the Thomasville Tommies in a North Carolina State League game.

1958 – **Joe Ginsberg's** seventh-inning homer gives Baltimore a 3-0 lead, and the Orioles hold on to beat the New York Yankees 3-2.

1960 – **Sandy Koufax** pitches a two-hitter and strikes out 13 as the Dodgers beat the Cincinnati Reds 3-0.

MAZEL TOUGH

1913 – **Abe "The Newsboy" Hollandersky** knocks out Jack Ortega in the 19th round of a scheduled 45-round fight to retain his Panamanian heavyweight title.

1928 – **Harry Isaacs** of South Africa wins a bronze medal in the boxing bantamweight division and **Harold Devine** of the United States takes a bronze in the featherweight division at the Olympics in Amsterdam. **Attila Petschauer** of Hungary wins a fencing silver medal in individual saber. **Istvan Barta** wins a silver in water polo when Hungary loses to Germany 5-2 in the final.

1932 – **Endre Kabos** of Hungary wins an Olympic fencing gold medal for team saber at the Los Angeles Games.

1948 – **George Worth** of the United States wins an Olympic fencing bronze medal in team saber in London.

1957 – In a match that is credited with popularizing beach volleyball, **Gene Selznick** and **Bernie Holtzman** defeat Mike O'Hara and Don McMahon to win the 26-team State Beach Open in Santa Monica, Calif.

1969 – **Julie Heldman's** second tournament victory in singles – 6-3, 6-4 over Winnie Shaw – gives the United States a 4-3 victory over Great Britain in the Wightman Cup tennis event in Cleveland.

1973 – Seventeen-year-old **Amy Alcott** birdies the 13th hole to beat Mary Lawrence 6-and-5 in the final of the USGA Junior Girls Golf Championship in Bernardsville, N.J.

1974 – **Ricky Meyer** of Long Island beats **Dr. Richard Raskind** of New York 3-6, 7-6, 6-3 to capture the Eastern Clay Court Championship. Raskind will later compete on the women's tennis tour as **Renee Richards**.

1984 – The U.S. men's volleyball team, coached by **Doug Beal**, beats Brazil 15-6, 15-6, 15-7 for the Olympic gold medal in Los Angeles. **Bernard Rajzman** wins a silver for Brazil.

2005 – **Olga Karmansky** wins the all-around after finishing second the previous four years at the USA Rhythmic Gymnastics Championships in Indianapolis.

JEWS ON FIRST

1951 – **Sid Gordon** hits a home run as the Boston Braves beat the Brooklyn Dodgers 8-4 in the first game to be televised in color. The Dodgers' loss is their first after building a 13½-game cushion in the National League, a lead they will eventually lose to force a playoff with the New York Giants.

A STAR IS BORN

1917 – **Lou Possner** (DePaul basketball)

1972 – **Andrew Lorraine** (California Angels, Cleveland Indians, Chicago White Sox, Chicago Cubs, Seattle Mariners, Oakland A's pitcher)

1973 – **Andy Bloom** (shot put, discus)

1983 – **Adam Podlesh** (Jacksonville Jaguars punter)

AUGUST 12

GAMEBREAKERS

1938 – **Buddy Myer** hits a grand slam homer as the Washington Senators rout the Boston Red Sox 13-1.

1961 – **Art Shamsky** hits a two-run homer to tie the game with two out in the ninth inning, and Macon goes on to defeat Asheville 4-3 in the Sally League.

1979 – **Ross Baumgarten** allows two hits, walks three, and strikes out five as the Chicago White Sox beat the Toronto Blue Jays 7-0 in the first game of a doubleheader.

STRONG IN DEFEAT

1966 – **Art Shamsky** of Cincinnati enters the game in the eighth inning as a defensive replacement with Pittsburgh leading the Reds 7-6 and hits three consecutive home runs in the Pirates' 14-11 victory in 13 innings. His two-run homer in the eighth puts the Reds ahead 8-7. His solo homer in the 10th ties the game 9-9, and another two-run homer in the 11th ties the score again at 11-11. He is the first National League player and third in major-league history to homer twice in extra innings.

MAZEL TOUGH

1900 – **Otto Wahle** of Austria wins a silver medal in the 1,000 freestyle at the Olympics in Paris, finishing more than a minute behind winner John Jarvis of Great Britain. Wahle also wins a silver in the 200 obstacle course swim, comprised of climbing over a pole, traversing a row of boats, and swimming under another row of boats. **Henri Cohen** of Belgium wins a silver medal in water polo as the Brussels Swimming and Water Polo Club loses to Great Britain 7-2 in the final.

1932 – **George Gulack** of the United States scores 56.9 on the flying rings to win a gymnastics gold medal at the Olympics in Los Angeles.

1957 – **Dick Savitt** wins the Eastern Grass Court tennis championship.

1966 – **Allen Fox** defeats Roy Emerson 6-3, 6-3 in the final of the Pacific Sun Southwest tennis tournament.

1979 – **Brian Gottfried** beats Eddie Dibbs 6-3, 6-0 to win a clay-court tennis tournament in Columbus, Ohio.

RECORD SETTERS

1967 – **Mark Spitz** equals his world record of 2:06.4 in the 200 butterfly at the AAU outdoor championships in Oak Park, Ill. Swimming for the Santa Clara Swimming Club, his 4×200 freestyle relay team also equals a world record of 7:52.1.

1974 – **Faina Melnik** of the Soviet Union sets a meet record of 64.22 meters in winning the discus at the European Track and Field Championships in Helsinki.

1998 – **Lenny Krayzelburg** breaks his American record with a time of 1:57.38 in winning the 200 backstroke at the U.S. National Swimming Championships in Fresno, Calif. Krayzelburg also wins the 100 backstroke in 54:64 and **Jason Lezak** wins the 100 freestyle in 49.94 seconds.

A STAR IS BORN

1912 – **Davey Day** (lightweight boxer)

AUGUST 13

GAMEBREAKERS

1956 – Omaha left-hander **Ed Mayer** pitches a five-hitter in a 5-1 American Association victory over the Louisville Colonials. Mayer (5-2) lowers his ERA to 2.51 and pitches his third complete game since joining the Cardinals.

1966 – **Sandy Koufax** of the Los Angeles Dodgers pitches a two-hit shutout through eight innings, striking out 11, and settles for a 6-1, five-hit victory over the Chicago Cubs.

1974 – **Ken Holtzman** allows seven hits as the Oakland Athletics defeat the New York Yankees 6-1.

MAZEL TOUGH

1915 – **Leo Friede** retains his title in the American Canoe Sailing Championship in Clayton, N.Y. Friede will win the title nine times through 1926.

1932 – **Istvan Barta**, **Miklos Sarkany**, and **Gyorgy Brody** of Hungary win gold medals in water polo at the Los Angeles Olympics. **Nathan Bor** of the U.S. takes a bronze in lightweight boxing and **Endre Kabos** of Hungary wins a bronze for fencing in individual saber.

1936 – **Endre Kabos** wins his first of two Olympic fencing gold medals as Hungary wins the team saber.

1978 – **Dana Gilbert** beats Viviana Segal of Argentina 6-2, 6-3 to win the U.S. Clay Court tennis championship in Indianapolis.

1989 – Winning his second of three tennis titles in consecutive weeks, **Brad Gilbert** beats Jason Stoltenberg 6-4, 6-4 in the final of a hard-court tournament in Livingston, N.J.

2005 – **Olga Karmansky** wins the rope, ball, and ribbon competitions, two days after capturing the all-around at the Visa Rhythmic Gymnastics Championships in Indianapolis.

2006 – **Alex Averbukh** of Israel clears 18 feet, 8½ inches to win the pole vault at the European Championships in Goteborg, Sweden.

A STAR IS BORN

1918 – **Sid Gordon** (New York Giants, Boston/Milwaukee Braves, Pittsburgh Pirates third baseman/outfielder)

1918 – **Traute Kleinova** (Czech table tennis)

AUGUST 14

GAMEBREAKERS

1907 – **Barney Pelty** of the St. Louis Browns pitches his fifth shutout of the season, out-dueling Walter Johnson of the Washington Senators for a 1-0 victory.

1937 – **Hank Greenberg** scores six runs as the Detroit Tigers sweep a doubleheader from the St. Louis Browns, 16-1 and 20-7.

1948 – **Ernie Silverman** pitches a two-hitter as the Buffalo Bisons defeat the Baltimore Orioles 2-0 in an International League game.

1950 – **Al Rosen's** two-run homer with two out in the ninth ties the game, and the Cleveland Indians go on to beat the first-place Detroit Tigers 3-2 in 10 innings.

1955 – **Sid Gordon** hits a ninth-inning homer in the first game and adds another shot in the nightcap as the New York Giants sweep the Pittsburgh Pirates 4-2 and 3-1.

1965 – **Sandy Koufax** pitches a 10-inning five-hitter, striking out 12 and walking none, as the Dodgers beat the Pittsburgh Pirates 1-0.

1980 – **Steve Stone** allows two hits as the Baltimore Orioles beat the New York Yankees 6-1.

MAZEL TOUGH

1922 – **Dave Rosenberg** wins a 15-round decision over Phil Krug in the Bronx to win the vacant New York world middleweight title.

1926 – At the first Canadian National track and field championship meet for women in Toronto, **Bobbie Rosenfeld** wins the shot put, javelin, and discus.

1936 – The United States defeats Canada 19-8 in the Olympic basketball gold-medal game played on a wet clay tennis court. **Sam Balter** of UCLA, who scores 17 points in two games including 10 in a 25-10 victory over Mexico, wins a gold medal for the United States, while **Irving Maretzky** earns a silver for Canada.

1965 – **Julie Heldman** defeats Faye Urban in the Toronto tennis final.

1978 – **Mark Roth** beats runner-up Palmer Fallgren by 174 pins to win the New England Open in Cranston, R.I., his seventh PBA Tour victory of the season.

2002 – **Jason Lezak** wins the 50-meter freestyle in 22.34 seconds – .01 seconds faster than runner-up **Anthony Ervin** at the U.S. National Swimming Championships in Fort Lauderdale, Fla. He adds the 100 freestyle title the next day.

RECORD SETTERS

1966 – **Art Shamsky** hits his fourth consecutive home run over two games, a two-run pinch-hit homer, to tie a major-league record in the Cincinnati Reds' 4-2 loss to the Pittsburgh Pirates.

TRANSITIONS

1927 – Representatives of Maccabi Hapoel and an Arab team from Jerusalem establish the Palestine Soccer Association.

A STAR IS BORN

1917 – **Marty Glickman** (Syracuse sprinter and football, broadcasting)
1971 – **Joel Shanker** (soccer)
1981 – **Scott Lipsky** (tennis)

Bobbie Rosenfeld

AUGUST 15

GAMEBREAKERS

1912 – Four days after Joe Jackson becomes the first American League player to accomplish the feat, **Guy Zinn** of the New York Highlanders steals home twice in a 5-4 win over Detroit.

1951 – **Al Rosen** of Cleveland becomes the ninth major-leaguer to hit four grand-slam homers in one season, and the Indians score seven times in the first inning of a 9-4 victory over the St. Louis Browns. **Sid Gordon** accomplished the feat a year earlier. **Saul Rogovin** pitches his second shutout of the season as the Chicago White Sox beat the Detroit Tigers 2-0.

1959 – **Larry Sherry** pitches 8 2/3 innings of scoreless relief as the Dodgers beat the St. Louis Cardinals 4-3. Sherry also hits a home run off Ernie Broglio and two singles.

2001 – **Shawn Green** of the Dodgers smacks three home runs and drives in a career-high seven runs in a 13-1 rout of the Montreal Expos. Green hits a three-run homer in the second inning and two-run shots in the fourth and seventh innings.

STRONG IN DEFEAT

1905 – **Harry Kane** of Savannah pitches a 13-inning no-hitter in the South Atlantic League, but loses 1-0 to the Jacksonville Jays.

1978 – **Steve Stone** of the White Sox pitches a two-hitter, but the Texas Rangers beat Chicago 1-0 on a seventh-inning homer by Richie Zisk.

MAZEL TOUGH

1936 – Hungary, with **Gyorgy Brody** in goal and **Miklos Sarkany** also on the team, earns its second straight Olympic gold medal in water polo with a victory over France. **Gerard Blitz** of Belgium wins a bronze in water polo. **Endre Kabos** of Hungary wins a fencing gold medal in individual saber after winning seven matches.

1965 – **Julie Heldman** wins the Canadian National grass-court tennis tournament in Toronto with a 6-3, 8-6 victory over Faye Urban in the final.

2003 – **Scott Freedman** defeats Vince Van Patten 6-0, 7-6 and also wins the men's doubles and mixed doubles at the U.S. Paddle Tennis Open National Championships in Venice Beach, Calif.

2004 – **Jason Lezak** swims the anchor leg as the United States wins a bronze medal in the 4×100 freestyle relay at the Olympics in Athens.

2004 – **Noam Okun** of Israel defeats Danai Udomchoke of Thailand 6-3, 4-6, 6-1 to win a USTA Challenger tennis tournament in Binghamton, N.Y.

RECORD SETTERS

1934 – **Jadwiga Wajsowna** of Poland sets her 10th and final world record in the discus, throwing 44.19 meters in Brussels.

JEWS ON FIRST

1981 – **James Espir** of Great Britain becomes the first Jewish runner to break the 4-minute mile mark with a time of 3:56.7 in Cwmbran, Wales.

TRANSITIONS

1924 – World lightweight champion **Benny Leonard** announces his retirement. He will return to the ring in six years after losing most of his money in the stock market crash of 1929.

A STAR IS BORN

1902 – **Charley Phil Rosenberg** (bantamweight boxer)

1912 – **Max Padlow** (Ohio State football, Philadelphia Eagles end)

AUGUST 16

GAMEBREAKERS

1917 – **Erskine Mayer** of the Philadelphia Phillies shuts out the Pittsburgh Pirates 3-0.

1924 – **Manfred Susskind** scores a career-high 64 runs as South Africa plays to a draw with England in an international cricket test match.

1947 – Ralph Kiner hits three home runs and **Hank Greenberg** and Billy Cox hit two apiece as the Pittsburgh Pirates beat the St. Louis Cardinals 12-7. Both teams combine to hit a major-league record 10 homers.

1958 – **Al Silvera's** three-run homer gives the Albany Senators a 10-8 victory over Williamsport in the Eastern League.

MAZEL TOUGH

1873 – At Newington Park in Baltimore, professional baseball player **Lipman Pike** races against a horse named Clarence. Given a head start, Pike wins.

1906 – Jockey **Walter Miller** rides four winners and one second-place finisher at Saratoga.

1981 – **Brian Gottfried** beats Tony Graham 6-3, 6-3 in the final of a hard-court tennis tournament in Stowe, Vt.

1992 – **Margie Goldstein-Engle** rides Daydream to victory in the Grand Prix of New Hampshire equestrian event.

RECORD SETTERS

1925 – **Lilli Henoch** of Germany sets a world record of 11.57 meters in the shot put in Leipzig.

TRANSITIONS

1964 – **Sandy Koufax** injures his elbow sliding into second base against St. Louis and misses the rest of the season. Despite the injury, he finishes with a four-hitter and 13 strikeouts in a 3-0 victory.

2000 – **Gabe Kapler** goes hitless in a Texas Rangers' victory over the Yankees, ending his 28-game hitting streak.

A STAR IS BORN

1901 – **Red Chapman** (featherweight boxer)

1903 – **Jack Silver** (lightweight, welterweight boxer)

1928 – **Victor "Chick" Zamick** (British hockey)

1934 – **Angela Buxton** (English tennis)

Margie Goldstein-Engel
(U.S. Olympic Committee)

AUGUST 17

GAMEBREAKERS

1937 – **Phil Weintraub's** eighth-inning homer gives Jersey City a 3-2 victory over Rochester in the International League.

1947 – Former major-league pitcher **Sam Nahem** posts his 21st consecutive victory, tossing a three-hitter in the semi-pro Brooklyn Bushwicks' 7-2 victory over the Bristol Bees.

2002 – **Sage Rosenfels** throws three fourth-quarter touchdown passes as the Washington Redskins rally from a 20-point deficit to beat the Pittsburgh Steelers 35-34 in a preseason game.

MAZEL TOUGH

1952 – **Bus Mosbacher** sails "Susan" to a six-second victory in the International Class at the Manhasset Bay Regatta on Long Island Sound.

1970 – **Tom Okker** defeats Ilie Nastase 4-6, 6-3, 6-3, 6-4 in the final of the West German Open clay-court tennis tournament in Hamburg.

1973 – Rollins College sophomore **Rayni Fox** of North Miami Beach beats Barbara Hallquist 4-6, 6-4, 6-3 to win the 57th U.S. Girls 18 and Under Grass Court tennis championship in Philadelphia.

1976 – **Shep Messing** posts the shutout as the Cosmos defeat the Washington Diplomats 2-0 in the North American Soccer League.

1997 – **Tanya Dubnicoff** of Winnipeg defeats Lori-Ann Muenzer of Toronto in the best-of-three sprint final to win the gold medal at the World Cup track cycling championships in Adelaide, Australia.

2002 – Top-seeded **Joshua Cohen** beats Jose Muguruza of Aruba 6-2, 6-0 to win the Boys 18 USTA Junior Grasscourts tennis tournament in Philadelphia.

2002 – **Kenny Bernstein** beats Larry Dixon in the finals of the Rugged Liner NHRA Nationals in Brainard, Minn., for his fourth Top Fuel title of the season and 65th of his career.

2003 – **Leah Goldstein** wins the British Columbia Time Trial Championship cycling race with a time of 51 minutes, 54 seconds.

RECORD SETTERS

2002 – **Adam Greenberg** of the Daytona Cubs sets a professional baseball record when he needs only four innings to hit for the cycle in a 17-1 Florida State League victory over the St. Lucie Mets. He leads off the bottom of the first with a homer, hits a two-run triple in the second, and adds a bunt single and a double in the fourth. Greenberg finishes 5 for 6 with five runs and four RBI's in just his seventh game with Daytona.

A STAR IS BORN

1923 – **Duke Markell** (St. Louis Browns pitcher)

1957 – **Pamela Glaser** (karate)

1969 – **Brian Kowitz** (Atlanta Braves outfielder)

AUGUST 18

GAMEBREAKERS

1959 – Winning pitcher **Larry Sherry** hurls 2 2/3 innings of hitless relief as the Los Angeles Dodgers beat the San Francisco Giants 7-0.

STRONG IN DEFEAT

1999 – **Gabe Kapler's** triple is the only Detroit Tigers hit off Tampa Bay pitchers Wilson Alvarez and Albie Lopez in a 4-0 loss to the Devil Rays.

2001 – **Shawn Green** hits his 36th homer of the season against the Mets and becomes the first Dodgers left-handed batter to drive in 100 runs in a season since Duke Snider in 1956. New York wins 5-4.

MAZEL TOUGH

1969 – **Julie Heldman** wins a tennis tournament in Moscow.

1980 – **Bruce Manson** and **Eliot Teltscher** defeat Sandy Mayer and Heinz Gunthardt 6-3, 3-6, 6-4 to win the doubles title at the Masters Canada hard-court tennis tournament in Toronto.

1985 – **Amy Alcott** beats Patty Sheehan in a two-hole playoff and wins the Nestle World Championship of Women's Golf in Buford, Ga.

1985 – **Brad Gilbert** beats Brad Drewett 6-3, 6-2 in the final of a hard-court tennis tournament in Cleveland.

1996 – **Margie Goldstein-Engle** rides Alvaretto to victory in the U.S. Open Jumper Championship.

2004 – U.S. fencer **Sada Jacobson** wins the bronze medal in women's individual saber, and swimmer **Jason Lezak** helps the U.S. men's 4×100 freestyle relay team also earn a bronze in the Athens Olympics.

2006 – **David Sender** of Stanford wins the vault at the U.S. Gymnastics Championships in St. Paul, Minn.

RECORD SETTERS

1913 – **Erskine Mayer** of the Phillies sets a National League record by yielding nine consecutive hits to the Chicago Cubs in the ninth inning of a 10-4 loss.

1935 – **S. Mortimer Auerbach** sets a five-mile record of 56.426 mph for Class 225 cubic inch hydroplanes in Red Bank, N.J.

1960 – **Howie Kitt** of Oceanside, N.Y., strikes out a Hearst Sandlot Classic–record seven batters in three innings as the New York Journal-American All-Stars lose 6-5 to the United States All-Stars at Yankee Stadium. Kitt wins the Lou Gehrig Award as the game MVP.

TRANSITIONS

1941 – The Cleveland Rams of the NFL purchase the Jersey City Giants of the American Football Association and name **Benny Friedman** the team's head coach.

A STAR IS BORN

1890 – **Maurice Podoloff** (basketball, hockey executive)

1962 – **Carina Benninga** (Dutch field hockey)

Sada Jacobson *(U.S. Olympic Committee)*

AUGUST 19

GAMEBREAKERS

1938 – **Hank Greenberg** hits three home runs, including a grand slam, and drives in eight runs in an 8-7, 7-4 doubleheader sweep of the St. Louis Browns.

1939 – **Hank Greenberg** hits a grand slam homer as the Detroit Tigers beat the St. Louis Browns 9-3.

1969 – **Ken Holtzman** of the Cubs beats the California Angels 3-0 and becomes the first pitcher since Sam Jones in 1923 to toss a no-hitter without recording any strikeouts. He walks three and forces Hank Aaron to ground out to second baseman Glenn Beckert for the final out. Ron Santo's three-run homer in the first inning gives Holtzman all the run support he needs.

1980 – Baltimore's **Steve Stone** wins his 20th game, holding the Angels hitless for 7⅓ innings in a 5-2 victory.

1998 – **Shawn Green** hits two of Toronto's seven home runs in a 16-2 win over Seattle.

MAZEL TOUGH

1900 – **Abe Attell** makes his pro boxing debut with a second-round knockout of Kid Lennett in San Francisco. The future world featherweight champion posts a 92-10-17 career record with 48 knockouts.

1973 – **Andrea Gyarmati** of Hungary wins the 200 backstroke and finishes third in the 100 backstroke at the European Cup swimming championships in Utrecht, the Netherlands. **Brent Zarnowiecki** of Sweden finishes second in the 400 individual medley.

1984 – **Brad Gilbert** beats Hank Pfister 6-3, 3-6, 6-3 in the final of a hard-court tennis tournament in Columbus, Ohio.

1984 – **Doug Shapiro** wins the five-day Coors Classic cycling race in Colorado, the most prestigious American road race of its time.

2001 – **Nicole Freedman** wins the Elite Women's National Criterium Champion cycling race in Downers Grove, Ill.

RECORD SETTERS

2006 – **Jason Lezak** swims the final leg as the United States sets a world record of 3:12.46 in the 400 freestyle relay at the Pan Pacific Championships in Victoria, British Columbia.

TRANSITIONS

1995 – **Max Patkin**, "The Clown Prince of Baseball," makes his final performance before a sellout crowd in Reading, Pa. Patkin appeared at more than 4,000 minor-league baseball games in more than 50 years.

A STAR IS BORN

1934 – **Renee Richards** (tennis)
1938 – **Valentin Mankin** (sailing)
1944 – **Mordechai Spiegler** (Israeli soccer)

Nicole Freedman (*U.S. Olympic Committee*)

AUGUST 20

GAMEBREAKERS

1921 – **Sammy Bohne** goes 4 for 5 with a triple and scores three runs as the Cincinnati Reds beat the Brooklyn Robins 12-5.

1937 – **Harry Danning** of the New York Giants collects five hits – four singles and a triple – in a 13-6 win over the Philadelphia Phillies.

1938 – **Morrie Arnovich** drives in four runs, including two with a home run, as the Philadelphia Phillies beat the New York Giants 8-7. **Phil Weintraub** also homers for the Phillies, while **Harry Danning** homers for the Giants.

1945 – **Mike Schemer** of the New York Giants hits his only major-league homer, a three-run shot off Hank Wyse in a 9-3 victory over the Chicago Cubs.

1961 – Yankees farmhand **Howie Kitt** allows one hit – a third-inning single – as Modesto beats Reno 7-1 in a California League game.

1965 – **Jerry Bark** pitches a two-hitter with 17 strikeouts as the Marion Mets of the Appalachian League defeat the Bluefield Orioles 7-0.

STRONG IN DEFEAT

1978 – **Elliott Maddox** of the Mets goes 4 for 5 in New York's 5-4 loss to the Los Angeles Dodgers.

MAZEL TOUGH

1904 – **Daniel Frank** beats **Myer Prinstein** in the long jump at the New York Metropolitan AAU Championships with a personal-best 23 feet, 11½ inches.

1949 – **Carol Pence** wins the 110 breaststroke at the AAU Outdoor Swimming Championships in San Antonio.

1966 – **Laszlo Fabian** of Hungary teams with Imre Szollosi to win the 10,000-meter kayak doubles event at the World Kayak Championships in Berlin.

1976 – **Nancy Rubin** of New Kensington, Pa., wins the inaugural PGA Junior Girls Championship in Lake Buena Vista, Fla., by one stroke over Michelle Jordan.

1989 – **Brad Gilbert** beats Stefan Edberg 6-4, 2-6, 7-6 in the final of a hard-court tournament in Cincinnati for his third tennis title in as many weeks.

2004 – **Arik Ze'evi** of Israel defeats Elco van der Geest of The Netherlands to win the bronze medal for judo in the men's 100-kilogram event at the Olympics in Athens. **Sergei Charikov** of Russia wins a fencing bronze medal in team saber.

2006 – **Harel Levy** of Israel teams with Martin Lee to defeat **Scott Lipsky** and David Martin 6-4, 7-5 and win the USTA GHI Bronx Classic doubles title.

RECORD SETTERS

1911 – **Odon Toldi** of Hungary sets a world record of 2:23.6 in the 200-yard breaststroke in Budapest.

1950 – **James Fuchs** improves his world shot put record to 58-8¾ in Visby, Sweden.

2002 – **Phil Avlas** of the Missoula Ospreys ties a Pioneer League record with four doubles in a game against the Ogden Raptors.

A STAR IS BORN

1904 – **Lester Harrison** (Rochester Royals basketball coach)

1904 – **Judikje Themans-Simons** (Dutch gymnast)

1920 – **Melvin Bleeker** (football)

1946 – **Marilyn Ramenofsky** (swimming)

AUGUST 21

GAMEBREAKERS

1945 – New York first baseman **Mike Schemer** goes 4 for 4 including a two-run triple in the ninth inning to rally the Giants to a 4-3 victory over the Chicago Cubs. Schemer runs his two-game streak to six consecutive hits.

1953 – **Al Rosen** hits three home runs and drives in seven runs as the Cleveland Indians sweep the St. Louis Browns 7-3, 3-2 in a doubleheader.

1967 – **Norm Miller** smacks three doubles and drives in two runs as the Houston Astros beat the St. Louis Cardinals 11-4.

2004 – **Shawn Green** hits two homers – including his eighth career grand slam – as the Los Angeles Dodgers beat the Atlanta Braves 7-4.

MAZEL TOUGH

1910 – **Abe Attell** knocks out Eddie Marino in the third round in Calgary to retain his world featherweight title.

1920 – **Samuel Gerson** of the United States captures the featherweight silver medal and **Frederick Meyer** of the U.S. takes the heavyweight bronze in freestyle wrestling at the Olympics in Antwerp.

1937 – **Arthur J. Thorner** wins the National Lefthanded Golfers Association championship.

1950 – **Irv Dorfman** defeats Fred Kovaleski to win the Yugoslav Tennis Tournament in Belgrade.

1976 – **Barbara Weinstein** wins the 10-meter platform diving at the AAU Swimming Championships in Philadelphia.

2004 – **Jason Lezak** swims the anchor leg as the United States wins the 400 medley relay at the Olympics in Athens in a world-record 3:30.68. **Lenny Krayzelburg** also earns gold for swimming in preliminary heats. **Sarah Poewe** swims the second leg of Germany's 4×100 medley relay to win a bronze medal. **Nicolas Massu** teams with Fernando Gon-

zalez of Chile to win the gold medal in tennis doubles. **Robert Dover** helps the United States equestrian team capture a bronze in team dressage.

RECORD SETTERS

1958 – **Maria Itkina** of the Soviet Union sets a European Championships record of 53.7 seconds in winning the 400 meters in Stockholm

1960 – Four days before the start of the Olympics in Rome, **Isaac Berger** breaks four world featherweight weight lifting records with 264 pounds in the press, 255 snatch, 336 clean and jerk, and 853 total.

JEWS ON FIRST

1922 – In the first international track and field meet for women in which the United States competed, **Maud Rosenbaum** of Chicago finishes third in the shot put with a toss of 57 feet at Pershing Stadium in Paris. Rosenbaum will later earn a national ranking in tennis as Baroness Maud Levi.

TRANSITIONS

1931 – A foot race between **Jim Levey** of the St. Louis Browns and Ben Chapman of the New York Yankees is canceled when Browns management objects. Rival players had wagered large amounts of money on the outcome.

A STAR IS BORN

1920 – **Leonard Pill** (minor-league baseball)
1921 – **Grant Golden** (tennis)
1955 – **Shaun Tomson** (surfing)
1978 – **Jason Marquis** (Atlanta Braves, St. Louis Cardinals, Chicago Cubs pitcher)

AUGUST 22

GAMEBREAKERS

1903 – **Barney Pelty** makes his major-league debut, allowing eight hits in the St. Louis Browns' 2-1 victory over the Boston Red Sox.

1933 – Detroit rookie **Hank Greenberg** hits a two-run homer with two out in the ninth inning as the Tigers end first-place Washington's 13-game winning streak, 10-8.

1950 – **Sid Gordon** smacks three doubles as the Boston Braves beat the St. Louis Browns 5-1.

1958 – **Al Silvera** hits a pinch-hit home run in the 10th inning to give the Albany Senators a 3-2 victory over the Allentown Red Sox in the Eastern League.

1959 – **Barry Latman** pitches a five-hitter and strikes out eight as the Chicago White Sox beat the Washington Senators 1-0.

1968 – **Lloyd Allen** of Idaho Falls pitches a seven-inning no-hitter with 13 strikeouts in a Pioneer League game against Magic Valley.

1968 – **Randy Phillip Cohen** of the Stockton Ports allows just a fourth-inning single by Steve McMillan and strikes out 16 in a 3-0 California League victory over the Visalia Mets.

1970 – **Ken Holtzman** allows one hit – a one-out single by Hal Lanier in the eighth inning – as the Chicago Cubs beat the San Francisco Giants 15-0.

MAZEL TOUGH

1920 – **Alexandre Lippmann** of France wins a silver medal in fencing for individual epee in Antwerp. **Gerard Blitz** of Belgium, who will later win a silver medal in water polo, captures the bronze in the 100-meter backstroke.

1964 – Gun Bow, ridden by **Walter Blum**, wins the Washington Handicap by two lengths over Lemon Twist at Arlington Park in Chicago.

1966 – **Laszlo Fabian** of Hungary teams with Imre Szollosi to win the K-2 10,000-meter race at the World Kayaking Championships in Berlin.

1999 – **Ildiko Rejto** of Hungary places first in foil in the women's 60-and-over division at the Veterans World Fencing Championship in Siofok, Hungary.

2004 – Less than 24 hours after winning the men's doubles, **Nicolas Massu** of Chile defeats Mardy Fish of the United States 6-3, 3-6, 2-6, 6-3, 6-4 to win the men's tennis gold medal at the Olympics in Athens. Massu, winning on hard courts for the first time, plays 10 sets over 7 hours, 43 minutes to earn the first two gold medals in Chile's history. **Deena Kastor** overtakes Elfenish Alemu of Ethiopia with less than a mile to go and wins the bronze medal in the women's marathon in 2:27:19.

RECORD SETTERS

1917 – **Jake Pitler** of the Pittsburgh Pirates sets a National League record for second basemen with 15 putouts in a 22-inning game against the Dodgers. Brooklyn wins 6-5.

1925 – **Bobbie Rosenfeld** of Canada sets a world record of 26.0 seconds in the 220-yard run in Toronto.

1950 – **James Fuchs** of the United States breaks his world shot put record for the third time, throwing 58 feet, 10¾ inches in Eskilstuna, Sweden.

1970 – **Mark Spitz** improves his world record in the 200 butterfly to 2:05.4 in Los Angeles.

A STAR IS BORN

1893 – **Frank Glick** (Princeton football)
1947 – **Ian Scheckter** (South African auto racing)
1956 – **Mark Gilbert** (Chicago White Sox outfielder)

AUGUST 23

GAMEBREAKERS

1934 – **Fred Sington's** home run gives Albany a 4-3 win over Newark in the International League.

1938 – **Buddy Myer** hits a bases-loaded single with none out in the 12th inning to give the Washington Senators a 6-5 win over the St. Louis Browns.

1956 – 12-year-old **Fred Shapiro** pitches the first perfect game in Little League World Series history, striking out 14 in six innings as Delaware Township, N.J., beats Colton, Calif., 2-0 in the semifinals.

1966 – **Mickey Abarbanel** allows a leadoff single by Dick Littlejohn in the top of the ninth and settles for a one-hitter with 14 strikeouts as the Fox Cities Foxes beat the Wisconsin Rapids Twins 3-0. Abarbanel, who earlier in the season pitched a no-hitter and a one-hitter, sets the Chicago White Sox's Midwestern League farm team's single-season record of 206 strikeouts.

1997 – **Gabe Kapler** goes 5 for 5 for Lakeland of the Florida State League against Sarasota.

1998 – Houston Astros catcher **Brad Ausmus** has four hits and five RBI's in a 13-3 win over the San Francisco Giants.

2002 – Freshman fullback **Matt Bernstein** scores two touchdowns in his first game as Wisconsin defeats Fresno State 23-21.

2003 – **Aaron Rifkin** ties a Trenton Thunder franchise record with seven RBI's in a 20-4 victory over Binghamton in the Eastern League. Among his four hits are a three-run homer and a two-run double.

MAZEL TOUGH

1912 – **Dr. Jeno Fuchs** of Hungary wins an Olympic fencing gold medal in saber in Stockholm.

1919 – **Charles Pores** wins the 5-mile run at the Metropolitan AAU meet in Jersey City. Only two runners finish the race on Pershing Field's newly resurfaced track.

1920 – Fencer **Alexandre Lippmann** of France wins a bronze medal in team epee at the Olympics.

1922 – **Dave Rosenberg** decisions Phil Krug for the second time in nine days and wins the New York State middleweight title.

1969 – **Julie Heldman** defeats Peaches Bartkowicz 6-3, 2-6, 6-2 to win the Moscow International tennis tournament.

1997 – **Margie Goldstein-Engle** rides Hidden Creek's Alvarado to first place in the North Fork Grand Prix equestrian event.

RECORD SETTERS

1970 – **Mark Spitz** sets a world record of 51.9 seconds in the 100-meter freestyle in Los Angeles.

JEWS ON FIRST

1934 – New York Giants catcher **Harry Danning** hits his first of 57 career home runs off Paul "Daffy" Dean in a 5-3 victory over the St. Louis Cardinals.

TRANSITIONS

1994 – New York Roadrunners Club President **Fred Lebow** is inducted into the USA Track and Field Hall of Fame.

A STAR IS BORN

1948 – **Ron Blomberg** (New York Yankees, Chicago White Sox infielder/designated hitter)
1951 – **Barbara Mizrahie** (golf)

AUGUST 24

GAMEBREAKERS

1909 – **Barney Pelty** of the St. Louis Browns pitches his fifth shutout of the season, blanking the New York Highlanders 3-0.

1932 – **Jim Levey** hits a two-run homer in the 11th inning to give the St. Louis Browns a 5-3 victory over the Philadelphia Athletics.

1950 – Columbia left-hander **Moe Savransky** pitches a two-hitter in a 4-0 South Atlantic League victory over Columbus. Four days later, Savransky tosses another two-hitter in a 6-0 triumph over Savannah.

1954 – **Sid Gordon** hits a game-winning homer as the Pittsburgh Pirates beat the St. Louis Cardinals 8-7.

2000 – **Eyal Berkovic** of Israel scores a hat trick as Glasgow Celtic of the Scottish League beats Jeunesse Esch of Luxembourg 7-0 in a UEFA Cup soccer qualifier.

STRONG IN DEFEAT

1968 – **Art Shamsky** hits his sixth pinch-hit homer in the New York Mets' 10-7 loss to the Cincinnati Reds.

MAZEL TOUGH

1920 – **Samuel Mosberg** of the United States beats Gotfred Johanssen of Denmark to win the Olympic boxing gold medal in the lightweight division in Antwerp. **Albert Schneider**, a U.S. citizen competing for Canada, wins the welterweight division. **Moe Herscovitch** of Canada wins bronze in the middleweight division.

1925 – **Elaine V. Rosenthal** wins the Women's Western Golf Association amateur championship at White Bear Yacht Club in St. Paul, Minn. She also won the event in 1915 and 1918.

1930 – **Harry Cieman** of Canada wins the 7-mile walk at the AAU Outdoor Track and Field Championships in Pittsburgh.

1952 – **Dick Savitt** wins the single title and teams with Kurt Nielsen of Denmark to win the doubles at the Canadian tennis championships in Toronto.

1958 – **Maria Itkina** of the Soviet Union wins the 400 meters in 53.7 seconds at the European Track and Field Championships in Stockholm.

1980 – **Eliot Teltscher** beats Terry Moor 6-2, 6-2 in the final of the Atlanta Open hard-court tennis tournament, while **Harold Solomon** tops Francisco Gonzalez 7-6, 6-3 in the final of a hard-court event in Cincinnati.

2004 – **Adriana Behar** and Shelda Bede of Brazil win the silver medal in women's beach volleyball at the Olympics in Athens, losing 21-17, 21-11 to Misty May and Kerri Walsh of the United States in the finals.

RECORD SETTERS

1999 – **Lenny Krayzelburg** sets a world record of 53.60 seconds in the 100-meter backstroke at the Pan-Pacific Championships in Sydney, Australia.

TRANSITIONS

1949 – **Philip Brownstein** is named coach of the NBA's Chicago Stags, a position he holds for one season.

A STAR IS BORN

1911 – **Viktor Barna** (table tennis)

AUGUST 25

GAMEBREAKERS

1937 – **Buddy Myer** drives in four runs with three singles, including the winning run in the ninth inning, as the Washington Senators beat the St. Louis Browns 7-6. **Harry Danning's** RBI single in the 11th inning gives the New York Giants an 8-7 win over the Chicago Cubs in the first game of a doubleheader.

1939 – **Harry Eisenstat** pitches a six-hit shutout as the Cleveland Indians beat the Philadelphia A's 6-0.

1970 – **Jerry Feldman** bangs out four hits as the El Paso Sun Kings rout the Shreveport Braves 15-2 in the Texas League.

1997 – **Brad Ausmus** singles in the winning run in the bottom of the ninth as the Houston Astros beat the San Francisco Giants 5-4.

STRONG IN DEFEAT

2005 – **Shawn Green** hits his 300th career homer, but the Arizona Diamondbacks lose 18-4 to the New York Mets.

MAZEL TOUGH

1925 – **Leo Lomski** knocks out Bert Colima in the second round in Seattle to win the Pacific Coast middleweight title.

1940 – **Suzy Kormoczy** defeats Klara Somogyi to win the Budapest International tennis tournament on her 16th birthday.

1951 – **Anita Kanter** of Santa Monica, Calif., wins the U.S. Girls National Outdoor Tennis Championship in Philadelphia.

1956 – **Stu Levenson** wins the 100- and 200-meter titles at the Canadian National track and field championships in Hamilton, Ontario.

1962 – **Dave Hilton** knocks out Rocky Clark in the fourth round to retain his Canadian featherweight title in St. John, New Brunswick.

1994 – **Andrew Borodow** of Canada wins the 130-kg. freestyle wrestling division at the Commonwealth Games in Victoria, British Columbia.

2000 – **Adriana Behar** and teammate Sheld Bede give Brazil a silver medal in women's beach volleyball at the Olympics in Sydney.

2003 – **Daniel Elkowitz** defeats Dolas Kadir of Turkey 8-6 to win the 54-kg. division in Taekwondo at the World University Games in South Korea.

2005 – **Dmitriy Salita** stops Shawn Gallegos in the ninth round to capture the NABA light welterweight title in New York.

RECORD SETTERS

1940 – **Herbert Mendelsohn** sets a one-lap record of 76.923 mph in capturing the National Sweepstakes powerboat race in Red Bank, N.J.

1971 – **Mark Spitz** improves his world record in the 100 butterfly to 55.0 seconds in Houston.

JEWS ON FIRST

2004 – Windsurfer **Gal Fridman** places second in the 11th and final race to capture Israel's first Olympic gold medal. Fridman finishes no lower than eighth in any preliminary race

A STAR IS BORN

1924 – **Suzy Kormoczy** (Hungarian tennis)
1952 – **Mike Veisor** (Chicago Blackhawks, Hartford Whalers goalie)

AUGUST 26

GAMEBREAKERS

1923 – **Max Gruenwald** scores twice as Hakoah Vienna opens its soccer season with a 4-0 victory over FC Ostmark.

1957 – Dallas outfielder **Don Taussig** homers in his fourth straight game – giving him 21 for the season in the Texas League. Taussig goes 10-for-18 with 10 RBI's in the four-game span.

1963 – Pitching in front of a Texas League regular-season record crowd of 7,091 in Tulsa, **Larry Yellen** tosses a four-hitter as San Antonio wins 10-0.

1966 – **Sandy Koufax** pitches a four-hitter as the Dodgers beat the San Francisco Giants 4-0.

2000 – **Zack Silverman** throws six touchdown passes as the Okanagan Sun defeats Abbottsford Air Force 64-31 in a Canadian Junior Football League game.

1994 – **Tanya Dubnicoff** of Canada wins the match-sprint cycling gold medal at the Commonwealth Games in Victoria, British Columbia.

2001 – **Joanna Zeiger** captures the Mrs. T's Triathlon in Chicago.

2002 – **Jason Lezak** (22.22 seconds) and **Anthony Ervin** (22.28) finish first and second in the 50 freestyle at the Pan Pacific Swimming Championships in Yokohama, Japan.

2004 – **Gavin Fingleson** of Australia wins an Olympic silver medal when the Aussies lose 6-2 to Cuba in the baseball final.

2006 – Tennis players **Jonathan Erlich** and **Andy Ram** of Israel defeat Mariusz Fyrstenberg and Marcin Matkowski of Poland 6-3, 6-3 to win the doubles title at the Pilot Pen Championships in New Haven, Conn.

MAZEL TOUGH

1925 – **Young Montreal** wins a decisive 10-round decision over Harry Martin to win the New England bantamweight title in Providence, R.I.

1962 – **Jackie Mekler** of South Africa wins his second of three Jackie Gibson Marathons in Johannesburg with a time of 2 hours, 37 minutes, 57 seconds.

1969 – **Don Aronow** wins the Hennessey Cup powerboat race in Long Beach, Calif.

1973 – **Tom Okker** beats Manuel Orantes 6-3, 6-2, 6-1 to win the Canadian Open tennis tournament.

1987 – **Mark Roth** beats Amleto Monacelli 258-202 in the first Number Seven PBA Invitational in Toronto.

JEWS ON FIRST

1999 – **Alex Averbukh** wins Israel's first-ever medal in the World Athletics Championships in Seville, Spain, taking third in the pole vault. He sets an Israeli national record of 5.80 meters.

A STAR IS BORN

1912 – **Aaron Rosenberg** (Southern Cal football)

1935 – **Al Silvera** (Cincinnati Reds outfielder)

1968 – **Brian Bark** (Boston Red Sox pitcher)

AUGUST 27

GAMEBREAKERS

1877 – Left fielder **Jay Pike** goes 1 for 4 in his only major-league game, helping the Hartford Dark Blues defeat the Cincinnati Reds 5-1.

1929 – **Buddy Myer's** RBI single in the 14th inning gives the Washington Senators a 5-4 win over the Boston Red Sox.

1942 – **Harry Feldman** allows six hits and singles home a run in the 11th inning as the New York Giants beat the Cincinnati Reds 2-0.

1949 – Former major leaguer **Goody Rosen** hits a grand-slam homer with two out in the eighth inning to give the Galt Terriers a 7-5 victory over the Brantford Red Sox in an Ontario Baseball Association playoff game.

1952 – **Al Rosen** hits an inside-the-park grand-slam homer in the Cleveland Indians' 6-5 loss to the Philadelphia A's.

1955 – **Sandy Koufax** strikes out 14 in a 7-0 win over Cincinnati, his first of 165 major-league victories.

1966 – **Tal Brody** of the University of Illinois leads Pittsburgh Oil to a 79-75 victory over Prague in the championship game of the Palm Trophy International Basketball Tournament in Loano, Italy.

1978 – **Ross Baumgarten** of the Chicago White Sox, making his second career start, shuts out the Cleveland Indians 6-0 on five hits.

2005 – In his 99th career start, St. Louis Cardinals pitcher **Jason Marquis** tosses his first major-league shutout, stopping the Washington Nationals 6-0 on three hits and no walks with three strikeouts.

MAZEL TOUGH

1915 – **Elaine V. Rosenthal** wins the Women's Western Golf Championship.

1925 – Despite fracturing his right big finger in the eighth round, **Louis "Kid" Kaplan** fights to a 15-round draw with Babe Herman in Waterbury, Conn., to retain his world featherweight title.

1960 – **Imre Farkas** of Hungary wins a bronze medal in 1,000-meter Canadian pairs and **Leon Rottman** of Romania captures a bronze in the 1,000-meter Canadian singles canoe races at the Olympics in Rome. **Klara Fried-Bonfalvi** of Hungary wins a bronze in 500-meter pairs kayaking.

RECORD SETTERS

1971 – **Mark Spitz** improves his world record in the 200 butterfly to 2:03.9 in the heats, then equals it in the finals of a swim meet in Houston.

1999 – **Lenny Krayzelburg** sets his second world record at the Pan-Pacific Championships in Sydney, Australia, with a time of 1:55.87 in the 200-meter backstroke.

TRANSITIONS

1951 – Wimbledon champion **Dick Savitt** becomes the first of three Jewish athletes to appear on the cover of Time magazine. The others are swimmer **Mark Spitz** (1972) and figure skater **Sarah Hughes** (2000).

1959 – The New York State education commissioner orders that former basketball coach **Nat Holman** be reinstated to the CCNY faculty with full back pay. Holman was cleared of negligence in the 1951 college basketball scandals.

1976 – **Renee Richards**, who was born Richard Raskind, is barred from competing at the U.S. Open tennis championships after refusing to submit to a chromosome qualification test.

A STAR IS BORN

1937 – **Michael Herman** (track and field)

AUGUST 28

GAMEBREAKERS

1935 – Former major-league outfielder **Alta Cohen** makes his debut on the mound, pitching the Toledo Mud Hens to a 5-3 victory over the St. Paul Saints in the American Association. Cohen strikes out seven, including a pinch hitter with the bases loaded and two out in the ninth.

1941 – **Sid Luckman** throws touchdown passes of 34 and 25 yards as the Chicago Bears beat the College All-Stars 37-13 before 98,200 fans at Soldier Field.

1948 – **Aaron Osofsky** of Smithfield-Selma pitches a no-hitter as the Indians beat the Lumberton Cubs 1-0 in the Tobacco State League.

1956 – **Harvey Cohen** pitches a four-hitter as the Peoria Chiefs beat the Waterloo White Hawks 7-0 in the Three-I League.

1977 – With **Shep Messing** making 11 saves in goal, the Cosmos beat the Seattle Sounders 2-1 in Portland, Ore., to win the NASL championship in Pele's final game with New York.

1998 – **Shawn Green** hits two homers, including a game-winning two-run shot in the seventh inning as the Toronto Blue Jays beat the Minnesota Twins 7-6.

2005 – **Shawn Green** collects three hits including his ninth career grand-slam homer as the Arizona Diamondbacks defeat the Philadelphia Phillies 10-5.

STRONG IN DEFEAT

1971 – **Ron Blomberg** hits two home runs and drives in all three Yankees runs in a 4-3 loss to the Kansas City Royals.

MAZEL TOUGH

1920 – **Gerard** and **Maurice Blitz** capture silver medals in water polo at the Olympics in Antwerp when Great Britain beats Belgium 3-2 in the final.

1954 – **Barbara Breit** wins the U.S. Girls Grass Court Tennis Championship in Philadelphia by defeating Darlene Hard 2-6, 6-2, 6-4.

1966 – **Marty Fleckman** shoots 277 to win the Eastern Amateur golf tournament.

2000 – **Joanna Zeiger,** tuning up for the Olympics, wins the triathlon at the U.S. Pro Women's Nationals in Chicago.

2005 – **Gaston Etlis** and Martin Rodriguez of Argentina win the doubles title at the Pilot Pen Tennis Classic in Hartford, Conn.

RECORD SETTERS

1955 – **Butch Rosenberg** sets a world water ski jumping record of 125 feet at the national championships in Winter Haven, Fla.

1972 – **Mark Spitz** wins the first two of his seven gold medals at the Olympics in Munich, winning the 200-meter butterfly in a world-record 2:00.7 and swimming the final leg on the 400 freestyle relay team that sets a world record of 3:26.42.

1999 – **Lenny Krayzelburg** swims 24.99 seconds in the 50-meter backstroke, his third world record at the Pan-Pacific Championships in Sydney, Australia.

JEWS ON FIRST

1922 – **Heinie Scheer** of the Philadelphia A's hits his first of six career home runs, a two-run shot off Frank Mack in a 7-2 victory over the Chicago White Sox.

1982 – **Julie Ridge** becomes the first Jewish swimmer to cross the English Channel from England to France, completing the swim in 17 hours, 55 minutes.

A STAR IS BORN

1913 – **Goody Rosen** (Brooklyn Dodgers, New York Giants outfielder)

AUGUST 29

GAMEBREAKERS

1944 – **Goody Rosen** hits a pinch-hit RBI single in the bottom of the ninth to give the Brookyn Dodgers a 2-1 victory over the Philadelphia Phillies.

1961 – **Sandy Koufax** pitches a two-hitter with 12 strikeouts as the Los Angeles Dodgers beat the Chicago Cubs 2-1.

1999 – **Eyal Berkovic** of Israel scores two goals as Celtic beats Hearts 4-0 in the Scottish Premier soccer league.

2004 – **Jason Marquis** allows four hits in 7 1/3 innings as the St. Louis Cardinals beat the Pittsburgh Pirates 4-0 for his 10th consecutive victory.

MAZEL TOUGH

1899 – In a bout promoted by newspapermen for the vacant world light-heavyweight title, **Joe Choynski** wins a 20-round decision over Jimmy Ryan in Dubuque, Iowa.

1918 – **Joseph Schwartz** of Philadelphia wins the national one-mile run in 4:17 in the Chicago Great Lakes AAU meet.

1937 – **Charles Zibelman** completes a seven-day, 147-mile swim down the Hudson River from Albany to New York. Zibelman, 46, who made a living giving swimming exhibitions under the name Charles Zimmy, lost both legs in a trolley accident when he was nine.

1959 – **Isaac Berger** of the United States wins a weight lifting gold medal in the featherweight division at the Pan American Games in Chicago. **Harold Goldsmith**, **Larry Silverman**, **Eugene Glazer**, and **Albert Axelrod** are members of the U.S.' gold-medal winning foil team in fencing.

1960 – Rome Olympics bronze medals are won by **Leon Rottman** of Romania in 1,000-meter Canadian canoe singles, **Imre Farkas** of Hungary in 1,000-meter Canadian canoe pairs, and **Klara Fried-Bonfalvi** of Hungary in women's 500-meter kayak.

1981 – **Saoul Mamby** wins a 15-round decision over Thomas Americo to retain his WBC super lightweight title in Djakarta.

2005 – **Rachel Wacholder** and Elaine Youngs upset top-seeded Misty May-Treanor and Kerri Walsh 19-21, 21-19, 15-11 to win the Boulder Open beach volleyball tournament in Boulder, Colo.

RECORD SETTERS

1964 – **Maria Itkina** breaks her world record in the 400 meters, running the distance in 53.0 seconds at the Russian National Championships in Kiev.

1972 – **Mark Spitz** wins the 200 freestyle in a world-record 1:52.78 at the Olympics in Munich.

2002 – **Jason Lezak** swims the anchor leg as the United States sets a world mark of 3:33.48 in the 4×100 medley relay at the Pan Pacific Games in Yokohama, Japan.

A STAR IS BOR

1906 – **Jonah Goldman** (Cleveland Indians shortstop)

1940 – **Dave Hilton** (Canadian featherweight boxer)

Eugene Glazer *(U.S. Olympic Committee)*

AUGUST 30

GAMEBREAKERS

1961 – **Larry Sherry** earns his 15th save of the season, pitching three innings of hitless relief with seven strikeouts, as the Los Angeles Dodgers defeat the Chicago Cubs 5-2.

1968 – **Art Shamsky** hits a grand-slam homer as the New York Mets beat the St. Louis Cardinals 8-2.

1995 – **Steve Arffa** of the St. Lucie Mets pitches a three-hit shutout against Vero Beach in a Florida State League game.

1998 – **Doron Sheffer** scores 15 points and **Nadav Henefeld** adds 12 against their former teammates as Maccabi Tel Aviv beats the University of Connecticut 90-73 in the championship game of the Bendel Basketball Tournament in Tiberius, Israel.

2005 – **Michael Schlact** allows just two infield singles as the Clinton Lumber Kings defeat the Burlington Bees 7-0 in the Midwest League.

STRONG IN DEFEAT

1997 – **Shawn Green** collects all three Toronto Blue Jays hits in a 4-1 loss to the Florida Marlins.

MAZEL TOUGH

1929 – **Dr. William Rosenbaum** teams with Frederick Baggs to win the National Doubles tennis title in Brookline, Mass.

1954 – **Maria Itkina** wins the 200 meters in 24.3 seconds and runs a leg of the Soviet Union's winning 4×100 relay team at the European Track and Field Championships in Bern, Switzerland.

RECORD SETTERS

1959 – **Harold Goldsmith** of the United States wins a fencing gold medal and **Albert Axelrod** takes the silver in individual foil at the Pan American Games in Chicago.

1960 – **Albert Axelrod** of the United States wins an Olympic bronze medal in fencing for individual foil – the first fencing medal for an American since 1932.

RECORD SETTERS

1968 – **Mark Spitz** improves his world record in the 100 butterfly to 55.6 seconds in Long Beach, Calif.

1971 – **Barry Asher** finishes 133 pins ahead of runner-up Mike Orlovsky and wins the South Bend Open in Indiana. He sets PBA records with 1,586 pins in his first six games, 10,380 actual pinfall in 42 games, and a gross pinfall of 10,756.

JEWS ON FIRST

2000 – **Sebastian Rozental** becomes the first soccer player from Chile to play for Independiente of Argentina, which acquires him on loan from the Glasgow Rangers of Scotland. Rozental scores in a 2-1 loss to Palmeiras.

A STAR IS BORN

1877 – **Joseph Knefler Taussig** (Navy football)

1899 – **Ray Arcel** (boxing trainer)

1943 – **Tal Brody** (Illinois, Israeli basketball)

AUGUST 31

GAMEBREAKERS

1938 – **Hank Greenberg** hits his 46th home run of the season and smacks two doubles as the Detroit Tigers beat the New York Yankees 12-6.

1948 – **Marv Rotblatt** earns his seventh straight victory as Waterloo defeats Terre Haute 14-1 in the Three-I League. He allows five hits and strikes out 13 before a league season-high attendance of 8,501 in Waterloo.

1951 – For the second time in two weeks, Chicago White Sox pitcher **Saul Rogovin** pitches a 2-0 shutout against Detroit, stopping the Tigers on seven hits.

1953 – **Al Rosen's** grand slam homer gives the Cleveland Indians a 5-3 win over the Philadelphia Athletics.

1966 – **Art Shamsky** pinch hits for Tony Perez – who was pinch-hitting for Gordy Coleman – and hits a three-run homer in the eighth inning as the Cincinnati Reds beat the Chicago Cubs 7-5.

1969 – Chicago Cubs pitcher **Ken Holtzman** goes 2 for 3 with a two-run homer and drives in three runs in an 8-4 victory over the Atlanta Braves.

1998 – **Brad Ausmus** drives in the winning run in the top of the ninth as the Houston Astros beat the Atlanta Braves 4-3.

MAZEL TOUGH

1915 – **Ted "Kid" Lewis** wins a 12-round decision over Jack Britton in Boston to win the world welterweight championship and become the first English boxer to win a world title in the United States.

1918 – **Elaine V. Rosenthal** wins her second Women's Western Golf Association amateur championship in Winnetka, Ill.

RECORD SETTERS

1959 – **Sandy Koufax** strikes out 18 Giants, including 15 of the last 17 batters he faces, to tie Bob Feller's 21-year-old major-league record for a nine-inning game, and Wally Moon's three-run homer in the ninth gives the Dodgers a 5-2 victory. Koufax also breaks Dizzy Dean's National League record of 17 strikeouts set in 1933 and surpasses Koufax's own major-league record of 16 strikeouts in a night game set a year earlier against the Phillies.

1964 – **Marilyn Ramenofsky** breaks her world record in the 400 freestyle, lowering it to 4:39.5 at the U.S. Olympic Trials in New York.

1972 – **Andrea Gyarmati** of Hungary sets an Olympic record of 1:04.01 during a heat of the 100 butterfly in Munich, then improves it to 1:03.8 in the semifinals. **Mark Spitz** wins the 100 butterfly in a world-record 54.27 seconds and helps break a world record with 7:35.78 in the 4×200 freestyle relay.

2005 – **Anna Smashnova** of Israel defeats Catalina Castano of Colombia 6-2, 6-2 to win a WTA tennis tournament in Budapest.

A STAR IS BORN

1909 – **Ladislav Hecht** (Czech tennis)

1940 – **Alain Calmat** (French figure skating)

1975 – **Gabe Kapler** (Detroit Tigers, Texas Rangers, Colorado Rockies, Boston Red Sox outfielder)

SEPTEMBER 1

GAMEBREAKERS

1929 – **Lou Grenfeld** scores the game-winning goal with five minutes remaining as New York Hakoah defeats Bethlehem (Pa.) Steel 5-4 in the first Eastern Soccer League game.

1931 – Bridgeport Bears catcher **Ike Danning** hits two homers and a single in an 11-9 victory over Norfolk of the Eastern League.

1969 – **Mike Epstein** goes 4 for 4 with a three-run homer as the Washington Senators defeat the California Angels 4-0.

2007 – **Julian Rauch** kicks a 24-yard field goal with 26 seconds remaining as Division I-AA Appalachian State stuns fifth-ranked Michigan 34-32 in one of college football's biggest upsets.

MAZEL TOUGH

1904 – **Myer Prinstein** wins the long jump at the Olympics in St. Louis with a leap of 24 feet, 1 inch. **Daniel Frank** of the United States wins the silver at 22-7¼.

1929 – **Barney Ross** makes his pro boxing debut with a six-round decision over Ramon Lugo in Los Angeles.

1950 – Jockey **Sidney Cole** rides his first of 436 career victories, bringing home Cassina first at the Fair Grounds in New Orleans.

1960 – **Morrie Oppenheim** of Chicago earns $3,000 for winning the Southern California Open bowling tournament in Los Angeles, his only victory on the PBA Tour.

1968 – **Bruce Fleisher,** a 19-year-old student at Miami Dade Junior College, becomes the fourth-youngest winner of the U.S. Amateur Golf Championship. He shoots a record 284 to defeat Marvin Giles III by one stroke in Columbus, Ohio.

1972 – **Mark Spitz** wins the 100 butterfly and 800 freestyle relay, bringing his gold-medal count at the Olympics in Munich to five. **Andrea Gyarmati** of Hungary wins a bronze medal in the women's 100 butterfly.

2001 – **Bob Litwin** beats Zan Guerry 7-5, 6-1 to win the USTA National 50 Grass Court Tennis Championship in Philadelphia. Litwin previously won national titles in 1991 (over 35s) and 1992 (over 40s).

2002 – **Margie Goldstein-Engle** rides Hidden Creek's Perin to her third straight equestrian championship in the Prudential Grand Prix Hampton Classic in Bridgehampton, N.Y.

TRANSITIONS

1950 – St. Paul first baseman **Lou Limmer** is named Rookie of the Year in the American Association after leading the league with 29 homers and 111 RBI's.

A STAR IS BORN

1924 – **Saul Mariaschin** (Harvard basketball)

1971 – **Doug Friedman** (Edmonton Oilers, Nashville Predators)

1976 – **Sebastian Rozental** (Chile soccer)

SEPTEMBER 2

GAMEBREAKERS

1906 – **Barney Pelty** of the St. Louis Browns shuts out the Detroit Tigers 1-0.

1925 – Making his first start in a professional game, **Ike Danning** hits a game-winning RBI double as the Vernon Tigers beat the Sacramento Solons 5-4 in the Pacific Coast League.

1937 – **Hank Greenberg** hits two homers, including the game-winner in the 10th inning, as the Detroit Tigers beat the Washington Senators 9-8.

2000 – Washington linebacker **Ben Mahdavi** returns a fumble 35 yards for a touchdown, blocks a punt that is recovered on the 1-yard line, and makes seven tackles in the Huskies' 44-20 victory over Idaho.

2004 – **Brian Horwitz** of Salem-Keizer goes 3 for 4 in a 10-2 victory over Everett on the final day of the season – and 11 for 23 in his final six games – to win the Northwest League batting title with a .347 average.

STRONG IN DEFEAT

1957 – **Hy Cohen** pitches a five-hitter, but gives up three unearned runs as the Memphis Chicks lose 3-2 to the Mobile Bears in the Southern Association. The loss ends Cohen's nine-game winning streak dating to June 9.

1960 – **Art Shamsky** drives in seven runs with a homer, double, and two singles, but Geneva loses to Wellsville 12-10 in a New York-Penn League game.

MAZEL TOUGH

1939 – **Frank Kay** of the United States wins a silver medal in the 181-pound class at the North American AAU weight lifting championships in Toronto.

1959 – **Paul Levy** and **Howard Fried** win gold medals as members of the U.S. epee team at the Pan American Games fencing competition in Chicago.

1960 – **Mark Midler** of the Soviet Union wins a fencing gold medal for team foil at the Olympics in Rome.

1966 – **Irena Kirszenstein-Szewinska** of Poland wins the 400 meters at the European Track and Field Championships in Budapest. A day later, she adds gold medals in the 200 and long jump.

1972 – **Peter Asch**, **Barry Weitzenberg**, and the United States win a bronze medal in water polo at the Munich Olympics. **Neal Shapiro** of the United States wins bronze in equestrian individual jumping.

RECORD SETTERS

1974 – **T.C. Yohannan** of India sets an Asian Games record of 26 feet, 5¾ inches in winning the long jump in Tehran, Iran.

TRANSITIONS

1989 – **Kenny Bernstein** announces he will switch from driving Funny Cars to Top Fuel, the top division for the National Hot Rod Association.

A STAR IS BORN

1918 – **Allie Stolz** (lightweight boxer)

SEPTEMBER 3

GAMEBREAKERS

1906 – Ty Cobb, in his first game back in Detroit's lineup in six weeks, misplays a fly ball into a home run, and **Barney Pelty** pitches the St. Louis Browns to a 1-0 victory over the Tigers.

1923 – **Alexander Nemes Neufeld** scores two goals and **Moritz Haeusler, Lajos Hess**, and **Norbert Katz** add one each as Hapoel Vienna beats West Ham United 5-0 and becomes the first non-British Isles soccer team to beat an English team on its home soil.

1955 – Six days after pitching a shutout for his first major-league victory, **Sandy Koufax** of the Brooklyn Dodgers blanks the Pittsburgh Pirates 4-0. They are his only two victories in his rookie season.

1999 – **Brian Kopka** kicks two field goals as Maryland beats Temple 6-0.

MAZEL TOUGH

1903 – **Abe Attell** beats Johnny Reagan in 20 rounds in St. Louis to win the vacant world featherweight title.

1940 – **Carl Earn** of Los Angeles defeats **Arthur Marx** of Beverly Hills in the final before teaming up with his opponent to win the doubles crown at the Santa Monica tennis tournament.

1955 – **Robert Cohen**, recognized in Europe as the world bantamweight champion, fights to a 15-round draw with Willie Toweel in Johannesburg to retain his title.

1960 – After a 10-hour battle with Yevgeny Minayev of the Soviet Union that ends at 4 a.m., **Isaac Berger** of the United States settles for a silver medal in the featherweight final of the Olympic weight lifting competition. **Jean Klein** and **Guy Nosbaum** of France win silver medals in rowing for coxed-fours. **Boris Goikhman** of the Soviet Union wins silver in water polo.

RECORD SETTERS

1927 – **Lillian Copeland** sets an American record of 39-6 3/8 in the shot put and also wins the discus at the AAU National Track and Field Meet in Eureka, Calif.

1972 – **Mark Spitz** completes his record-setting performance at the Munich Olympics, winning the 100 freestyle in a world-record 51.22 seconds and swimming the butterfly leg of the 400 medley relay for his sixth and seventh gold medals. **Andrea Gyarmati** of Hungary wins silver in the women's 100-meter backstroke.

2006 – **Yael Averbuch** of North Carolina registers the fastest goal in NCAA women's soccer history when she scores from 55 yards away just four seconds into a match against Yale. Averbuch has two goals and an assist as the Tar Heels win 4-0.

JEWS ON FIRST

1901 – **Bill Cristall** of the Cleveland Blues becomes the first American League pitcher to toss a shutout in his major-league debut, stopping the Boston Americans 4-0 on five hits in the second game of a doubleheader. It is Cristall's only major-league victory in six decisions.

TRANSITIONS

1921 – Henry Ford publishes his first of two diatribes in the Dearborn Independent blaming Jews for everything that is wrong with baseball. Part 2 appears a week later.

A STAR IS BORN

1910 – **Harry Dublinsky** (lightweight boxer)
1960 – **Brad Edelman** (Missouri football, New Orleans Saints guard)

SEPTEMBER 4

GAMEBREAKERS

1931 – **Buddy Myer** hits a two-run double to tie the game in the eighth inning, then delivers a game-winning RBI single in the 10th as the Washington Senators beat the New York Yankees 5-4.

1933 – **Hank Greenberg** hits a homer, triple and single, and drives in seven runs as the Detroit Tigers sweep a doubleheader from the Chicago White Sox, 8-0 and 5-4.

1953 – **Murray Franklin's** RBI triple in the 10th inning gives the Los Angeles Angels a 4-3 victory over the Oakland Oaks in the Pacific Coast League.

1955 – **Lou Limmer** hits his 17th homer of the year, a two-run shot in the ninth inning, to give Toronto a 2-0 victory over Buffalo in the International League.

1972 – **Steve Yeager** of the Los Angeles Dodgers hits his first of 102 career home runs off Jim McGlothlin in a 6-5 victory over the Cincinnati Reds.

1974 – **Johan Neeskens** scores two goals as The Netherlands defeats Sweden 2-1 in soccer.

1988 – San Francisco tight end **John Frank** catches touchdown passes of 11 and nine yards in the third quarter to rally the 49ers to a 34-33 victory over the New Orleans Saints.

1998 – **Shawn Green** goes 4 for 4 with a single, two doubles, and a homer in Toronto's 12-1 win over the Boston Red Sox. Green becomes the first player in Blue Jays history to record 30 homers and 30 stolen bases in the same season.

1999 – **Todd Braverman** kicks a 50-yard field goal with 27 seconds remaining to give Virginia a 20-17 victory over North Carolina.

2004 – **Jason Marquis** pitches seven shutout innings for his 11th straight victory as the St. Louis Cardinals defeat the Los Angeles Dodgers 5-1.

MAZEL TOUGH

1920 – **Oedoen Radvany** of Hungary wins the 67.5-kg. Greco-Roman wrestling title at the World Championships in Vienna, Austria.

1960 – **Vladimir Portnoi** of the Soviet Union wins an Olympic gymnastics silver medal in team combined exercises in Rome.

1972 – **Mark Rakita** of the Soviet Union wins a fencing silver medal in team saber at the Olympics in Munich, Germany.

1977 – A day after winning the 200 meters, **Irena Kirszenstein-Szewinska** of Poland wins the 400 at the first IAAF World Cup track meet in Dusseldorf, West Germany.

1983 – **Aaron Krickstein** rallies from two sets down to beat 15th-seeded Vitas Gerulaitis 3-6, 3-6, 6-4, 6-3, 6-4 in the third round of the U.S. Open tennis tournament. The 16-year-old Krickstein, the reigning USTA boys' 18 champion, loses to Yannick Noah in the next round.

RECORD SETTERS

1971 – **Mark Spitz** improves his world record in the 200 freestyle to 1:54.2 in Leipzig, Germany.

A STAR IS BORN

1858 – **Louis Stein** (bowling)

SEPTEMBER 5

GAMEBREAKERS

1905 – **Barney Pelty** of the St. Louis Browns shuts out the Cleveland Indians 5-0.

1944 – **Sam Nahem** hits two homers, drives in seven runs, and allows two runs and five hits in six innings on the mound as soldiers at Fort Toten, N.Y., defeat the Philadelphia Athletics 9-5 in an exhibition game.

1948 – **Cy Block** drives in four runs – including all three in the second game – as Buffalo sweeps an International League doubleheader from Montreal 2-1 and 3-1.

1953 – **Saul Rogovin** allows four hits as the Chicago White Sox beat the Cleveland Indians 2-0.

2005 – **Hayden Epstein** kicks three field goals, including a 45-yarder, and averages 40.6 yards for 10 punts as the Edmonton Eskimos defeat the Calgary Stampeders 25-23 in a Canadian Football League game.

STRONG IN DEFEAT

1954 – **Sid Gordon** goes 3-for-4 including a pair of two-run homers in the Pittsburgh Pirates' 12-5 loss to the Philadelphia Phillies.

1970 – Despite getting the loss, **Ken Holtzman** of the Chicago Cubs strikes out the first five batters he faces – Tommy Agee, Wayne Garrett, Cleon Jones, Donn Clendenon, and Ken Singleton – in a 5-3 defeat to the New York Mets. Holtzman finishes with 10 strikeouts.

MAZEL TOUGH

1910 – **Abe Attell** knocks out Billy Lauder in 17 rounds in Calgary to retain his world featherweight title.

1922 – **Joe Benjamin** knocks Eddie Mahoney down five times and scores a first-round TKO in a lightweight fight in Vernon, Calif.

1935 – **Karoly Karpati** of Hungary wins the 66-kg. freestyle wrestling title at the European Championships in Brussels, Belgium.

1938 – **Ibolya Csak** of Hungary wins the women's high jump, clearing 5 feet 4½ inches at the European Track and Field Championships in Paris.

1954 – **Judit Temes** swims on Hungary's gold-medal 4×100 freestyle relay team, and **Roman Brenner** of the Soviet Union wins the springboard and high diving competitions at the European Swimming Championships in Turin, Italy.

1959 – **Walter Farber** and **Allen Kwartler** win fencing gold medals as members of the U.S. saber team at the Pan American Games in Chicago.

1960 – **Gyula Torok** of Hungary wins the Olympic gold medal in boxing's flyweight class in Rome.

1964 – **Larry Mintz** wins the (148-pound) middleweight title at the first official U.S. Powerlifting Championships in York, Pa., with a total lift of 1,225 pounds.

1972 – **Valentin Mankin** of the Soviet Union wins the Olympic yachting gold medal in the Tempest class.

TRANSITIONS

1972 – Palestinian terrorists attack the Olympic village in Munich. By the end of the day, 11 Israeli athletes and coaches are killed.

A STAR IS BORN

1909 – **Harry Newman** (Michigan football, New York Giants quarterback)

1965 – **Imach Marcelo Salomon** (sumo wrestling)

1969 – **Valery Belenky** (Soviet Union, Germany gymnastics)

1982 – **Kimi Hirschovits** (Finland hockey)

SEPTEMBER 6

GAMEBREAKERS

1903 – **Barney Pelty** pitches a three-hitter as the St. Louis Browns beat the Detroit Tigers 1-0.

1921 – **Sammy Bohne** walks, steals second and advances on two errors to score the winning run in the 13th inning to give the Cincinnati Reds a 2-1 win over the Pittsburgh Pirates.

1941 – **Goody Rosen's** RBI single in the ninth inning gives Syracuse a 6-5 win over Newark in the International League.

1947 – Third baseman **Al Rosen** is presented the Texas League MVP Award before the game, then hits a double and a homer in the Oklahoma City Chiefs' 8-5 victory over the Dallas Rebels. Rosen, who is called up by the Cleveland Indians the next day, wins the league batting title with a .349 average.

1959 – **Sandy Koufax** strikes out 10 Chicago Cubs batters, giving him a Dodgers team-record 41 over three consecutive games.

1992 – **Tamir Linhart** scores all four goals as George Mason defeats Penn State 4-1 in soccer.

2002 – **Scott Schoeneweis** allows two hits over eight innings and gets ninth-inning relief help from closer Troy Percival as the Anaheim Angels beat the Detroit Tigers 1-0.

2006 – **Shawn Green** has three hits and a home run in each game – his first homers as a Met – as New York sweeps the Atlanta Braves 4-1 and 8-0.

STRONG IN DEFEAT

1952 – **Sid Gordon** collects five hits in the Boston Braves' 7-6, 17-inning loss to the Philadelphia Phillies in the first game of a doubleheader.

MAZEL TOUGH

1960 – **Allan Jay** of Great Britain wins a silver medal in fencing for team epee at the Olympics in Rome. Then he loses to six-time world champion Giuseppe Delfinio of Italy 5-2 in the individual epee final. **Robert Halperin** of the United States wins a bronze in yachting in the Star class. **David Segal** of Great Britain wins a track and field bronze in the 400-meter relay.

1959 – **Allen Kwartler** wins the individual saber title and **Walter Farber** finishes second at the Pan American Games fencing competition in Chicago.

1974 – **Faina Melnik** of the Soviet Union wins the discus at the European Track and Field Championships in Rome with a meet-record toss of 69.00 meters.

2005 – Blind Israeli golfer **Zohar Sharon** wins the Ontario Visually Impaired Golfer provincial championship at Cambridge Golf Club.

RECORD SETTERS

1953 – **Al Rosen** hits his 38th homer of the season in Cleveland's 4-2 win over the Chicago White Sox. Rosen's homer breaks his American League record of 37 homers by a third baseman set in 1950. He will finish the season with 43.

A STAR IS BORN

1904 – **Maxie Rosenbloom** (light heavyweight boxer)

1907 – **Al Singer** (lightweight boxer)

1911 – **Harry Danning** (New York Giants catcher

1928 – **Rudolph Plyukfelder** (Soviet weight lifting)

1944 – **Kenny Bernstein** (drag racing)

SEPTEMBER 7

GAMEBREAKERS

1916 – **Erskine Mayer** of the Philadelphia Phillies shuts out the Boston Braves 2-0.

1942 – **Herb Karpel** shuts out the Milwaukee Brewers over the final seven innings as the Kansas City Blues capture the American Association pennant with a 9-2 victory.

1948 – **Sid Gordon** ties the game with an RBI single in the ninth and wins it with his 30th homer of the season in the 11th inning as the New York Giants beat the Philadelphia Phillies 8-6 in the second game of a doubleheader.

1986 – **John Frank** catches a 10-yard touchdown pass as the San Francisco 49ers defeat the Tampa Bay Buccaneers 31-7.

2002 – Boston College defensive end **Antonio Garay** records two quarterback sacks for a loss of 19 yards and forces two fumbles in a 34-27 victory over Stanford.

MAZEL TOUGH

1904 – **Otto Wahle** of Austria, one of only four competitors, wins a bronze medal in the 400 freestyle swimming event at the Olympics in St. Louis.

1914 – **Charley White** scores a first-round TKO over Danny O'Brien in a lightweight fight in Denver.

1959 – Jockey **Louis Margolin** rides Turn Out to his first career victory at Belmont Park.

1970 – **Walter Blum** rides Distinctive to victory in the Governor Nicholls Stakes at Belmont Park.

1972 – **Irena Kirszenstein-Szewinska** of Poland wins a bronze medal in the 200-meter dash at the Olympics in Munich.

1976 – **Mark Roth** beats Tom Baker 264-193 in the final of the PBA Columbia 300 Open in Pittsburgh.

RECORD SETTERS

1935 – **S. Mortimer Auerbach** of the United States sets a one-mile record of 63.548 mph for Class 225 cubic inch hydroplanes at the Canadian National Exposition in Toronto.

1973 – **Faina Melnik** of the Soviet Union sets a world record of 227 feet, 11 inches in the discus in Edinburgh, Scotland.

1994 – **Tamas Deutsch** sets a Hungarian national record of 1:59.31 in the 200-meter backstroke at the World Swimming Championships in Rome. Three days later he sets a national record of 55.69 in the 100 backstroke.

2001 – **Shawn Green** hits a solo homer in the first inning to set a Dodgers franchise record of 44 home runs in a season, then adds a two-run homer in the sixth and two singles as Los Angeles beats St. Louis 7-1.

JEWS ON FIRST

1933 – **Phil Weintraub** of the New York Giants gets his first major-league hit – his first of 32 career home runs – off Heinie Meine in a 14-2 loss to the Pittsburgh Pirates.

1936 – **Morrie Arnovich** of the New York Giants hits his first of 22 career home runs off Ben Cantwell in a victory over the Philadelphia Phillies.

A STAR IS BORN

1875 – **Jewey Cooke** (English lightweight boxer)

1899 – **Joe Benjamin** (lightweight boxer)

1904 – **Daniel Prenn** (German tennis)

SEPTEMBER 8

GAMEBREAKERS

1908 – **Barney Pelty** of the St. Louis Browns shuts out the Cleveland Indians 2-0.

1945 – **Harry Feldman** of the New York Giants shuts out first-place Chicago, beating the Cubs 3-0 while allowing eight hits.

1985 – **Eli Ohana** scores a hat trick as Israel beats Taiwan 5-0 in a World Cup soccer qualifier.

1992 – **Scott Radinsky** pitches a scoreless eighth inning and earns his career-high 15th save as the Chicago White Sox beat the Detroit Tigers 4-3.

1999 – **Yossi Benayoun** scores three goals and **Haim Revivo** adds two as Israel beats San Marino 8-0 in a Euro 2000 soccer qualifying match.

2002 – **Jay Fiedler** passes for 207 yards and three touchdowns as the Miami Dolphins beat the Detroit Lions 49-21 in the season opener.

2003 – **Shawn Green** hits his sixth career grand-slam homer in the ninth inning to seal the Los Angeles Dodgers' 10-3 victory over the Arizona Diamondbacks

STRONG IN DEFEAT

1952 – **Sid Gordon** of the Boston Braves goes 5 for 8 in a 17-inning first game of a doubleheader with the Phillies. Philadelphia wins 7-6.

MAZEL TOUGH

1923 – **Bobbie Rosenfeld** beats world-record holder Helen Filkey and Canadian national champion Rosa Grosse in the 100 meters at the Canadian National Exhibition track championships in Toronto. Later that evening, Rosenfeld leads Hinde & Dauche to the city softball championship.

1924 – **Abe Goldstein** wins a 15-round decision over Tommy Ryan in Long Island City, N.Y., to retain his world bantamweight title.

1931 – **Louis "Kid" Kaplan** wins a 10-round decision over Jackie Pilkington in Hartford, Conn., to capture the New England lightweight championship.

1960 – **David Segal** runs the third leg as Great Britain earns a track and field bronze medal in the 400-meter relay at the Olympics in Rome.

1974 – **Ilona Kloss** of South Africa beats Mimi Jaisavec of Czechoslovakia 6-4, 6-3 to capture the Forest Hills Junior International Tennis Tournament.

1974 – The United States, with **David Weinberg** of West Newton, Mass., as coxswain, wins the eight-oared heavyweight crew title at the World Rowing Championships.

1996 – **Adriana Behar** of Brazil teams with Shelda Bede to win her first tournament on the FIVB beach volleyball world tour at Carolina Beach, Puerto Rico.

RECORD SETTERS

1964 – Columbus left-hander **Howie Kitt** sets a Southern League record by striking out five consecutive Knoxville batters.

A STAR IS BORN

1954 – **Johan Harmenberg** (Swedish fencing)
1976 – **Art Shurlock** (sailing)

Art Shurlock *(U.S. Olympic Committee)*

SEPTEMBER 9

GAMEBREAKERS

1941 – **Harry Shuman** pitches a three-hitter for his 14th straight victory and 21st of the season as the Harrisburg Senators defeat the Trenton Packers 1-0 in the first game of the Inter-State League playoffs.

1953 – **Al Rosen's** 40th homer – a two-run shot in the eighth inning – gives the Cleveland Indians a 2-1 victory over the Boston Red Sox.

1965 – **Sandy Koufax** pitches his fourth no-hitter in as many years, throwing the ninth perfect game in history and striking out 14 in a 1-0 win over the Cubs. Chicago pitcher Bob Hendley allows only one hit, a fifth-inning double by outfielder Lou Johnson.

STRONG IN DEFEAT

2002 – Linebacker **Ben Mahdavi** recovers a fumbled punt in the end zone for Washington's first touchdown of the season, but the Huskies lose 35-28 to Brigham Young.

MAZEL TOUGH

1888 – **Victor Schifferstein** runs 100 yards in 9.8 seconds at the Western National Association of Amateur Athletics meet in St. Louis, apparently breaking the world record of 10.0. The newly formed Amateur Athletic Union, a competing organization, refuses to acknowledge the time as a world mark.

1937 – **Maxie Berger** wins a 12-round decision over Dave Castilloux in Montreal to capture the Canadian lightweight title.

1951 – **Robert Cohen**, a bantamweight from Algeria, scores a second-round TKO over Lucien Gauche in his pro boxing debut in France.

1972 – **Sandor Erdos** wins an Olympic gold medal in team epee when Hungary beats Italy in the final at Munich. **Faina Melnik** of the Soviet Union wins the women's discus. **Don Cohan** of the United States wins a bronze in yachting's Dragon class.

1979 – **Jody Scheckter** of South Africa earns his last of 10 Formula One auto racing victories, beating Ferrari teammate Gilles Villenueve at the Grand Prix of Italy at Monza. His victory gives him an insurmountable 51 points, clinching the season drivers' championship with two races remaining.

1981 – George Mason University soccer goalkeeper **Ken Bernstein** begins a streak of 748 minutes, 7 seconds without allowing a goal.

1984 – **Amy Alcott** wins her 20th LPGA tournament, finishing three strokes ahead of runner-up Kathy Guadagnino in the Portland Ping Championship in Oregon.

2001 – **Irina Slutskaya** of Russia wins the gold medal in figure skating at the Goodwill Games in Brisbane, Australia.

2005 – **Morgan Pressel** defeats Maru Martinez 9-and-8 to win the U.S. Women's Amateur Golf Championship in Roswell, Ga.

TRANSITIONS

1895 – **Louis Stein** and **Samuel Karpf** help lay the foundation for what will become the American Bowling Congress at a meeting at Beethoven Hall in New York. Karpf becomes the new organization's secretary. Stein recommends that a perfect game be scored at 300, rather than 200, which was popular at the time, and sets the weight limit for a bowling ball at 16 pounds.

JEWS ON FIRST

1988 – Magyar Testnevelok Kore (MTK), a Jewish sports club, is formed out of the gymnastics-oriented NTE in Hungary.

1936 – **Fred Sington** of the Washington Senators hits his first of seven career home runs in an 11-4 victory over the Detroit Tigers.

A STAR IS BORN

1953 – **Steve Ratzer** (Montreal Expos pitcher)
1964 – **Skip Kendall** (golf)

SEPTEMBER 10

GAMEBREAKERS

1904 – **Barney Pelty** of the St. Louis Browns shuts out the Detroit Tigers 1-0.

1967 – **Joe Horlen** of the Chicago White Sox, who later converts to Judaism, pitches a no-hitter, beating the Detroit Tigers 6-0.

2002 – Florida Marlins pitcher **Justin Wayne** allows two hits and no runs over 6 1/3 innings, striking out four, as he earns his first major-league victory in a 2-1 win over the Philadelphia Phillies.

MAZEL TOUGH

1928 – **Benny Bass** knocks out **Harry Blitman** in the sixth round in Philadelphia to win the Pennsylvania featherweight title.

1928 – **Morton Solomon** wins the NRA indoor metallic sights and kneeling rifle titles.

1936 – **Lionel Van Praag** of Australia beats Eric Langton after 20 heats to win the first world speedway championship for motorcycle racing in Wembley, England.

1960 – Brazil beats Italy 78-75 for third place in the Olympic men's basketball competition, earning a bronze medal for **Moyses Blas.**

1972 – **Gyorgy Gedo** of Hungary wins an Olympic boxing gold medal in the light flyweight division in Munich.

RECORD SETTERS

1969 – **Mark Spitz** improves his world record in the 200 freestyle to 1:53.5 in Minsk. He also swims the first leg on a U.S. 4×200 relay team that sets a world record of 7:43.3.

TRANSITIONS

1998 – The NBA cancels a game because of a labor dispute for the first time in league history. The Oct. 12 exhibition in Tel Aviv between the Miami Heat and Maccabi Elite is canceled because of a lockout imposed by the league's owners.

Barney Pelty
(Jewish Major Leaguers)

A STAR IS BORN

1880 – **Barney Pelty** (St. Louis Browns, Washington Senators pitcher)
1898 – **Abe Goldstein** (bantamweight boxer)
1970 – **Yossi Abuksis** (Israeli soccer)
1973 – **Mike Saipe** (Colorado Rockies pitcher)

SEPTEMBER 11

GAMEBREAKERS

1938 – En route to finishing the season with 58 home runs, **Hank Greenberg** hits nos. 48 and 49 as Detroit beats the Chicago White Sox 10-1.

1959 – Relief ace **Larry Sherry** of the Dodgers pitches a six-hitter for his only career shutout as Los Angeles beats the Pittsburgh Pirates 4-0.

1966 – **Sandy Koufax** pitches a six-hitter as the Dodgers beat the Houston Astros 4-0 in the first game of a doubleheader and move into first place. Koufax's 40th shutout is the final one of his career.

1999 – **Vitaly Pisetsky** of Wisconsin kicks a 53-yard field goal in a 50-10 victory over Ball State.

STRONG IN DEFEAT

1959 – **Barry Latman** of the Chicago White Sox pitches 9 1/3 innings of five-hit ball, retiring 21 batters in a row at one point, but leaves with a no-decision in a 1-0 loss to the Baltimore Orioles.

MAZEL TOUGH

1930 – **Kingfish Levinsky** knocks **Leo Lomski** down six times in the first round, three times in the second, and three times in the fifth before the light heavyweight fight in Chicago is stopped.

1933 – **Jackie Brown** wins a 15-round decision over Valentin Angelmann in Manchester, England, to retain his NBA flyweight title.

1934 – **Bobby Jacobson**, a 16-year-old golfer from Deal, N.J., upsets U.S. Open champion Johnny Goodman on the 19th hole of match play in the third round of the U.S. Amateur Championship in Brookline, Mass.

1955 – **Henry Laskau** retains his National AAU 20-kilometer racewalking title in Pittsburgh.

1966 – **Barry Asher** finishes 191 pins ahead of runner-up Jim Godman to win the PBA Crescent City Open in New Orleans.

1966 – **Donald Spero** gives the United States its first-ever gold medal in a world rowing championship when he wins the single sculls by 1½ lengths in Bled, Yugoslavia.

1972 – **Neal Shapiro** of the United States wins an Olympic silver medal in equestrian for team jumping in Munich.

2004 – **Shaun Diner** catches a 20-yard touchdown pass as New Hampshire upsets Rutgers 35-24.

A STAR IS BORN

1900 – **Jimmy Duffy** (welterweight boxer)

1916 – **Ed Sabol** (swimming)

1919 – **Leo Center** (light heavyweight boxer)

1921 – **Robert "Buck" Friedman** (Washington football, Philadelphia Eagles)

1946 – **Dave Newmark** (Columbia basketball, Chicago Bulls, Atlanta Hawks, ABA Carolina Cougars)

Dan Spero *(U.S. Olympic Committee)*

SEPTEMBER 12

GAMEBREAKERS

1938 – **Hank Greenberg** hits his 50th home run of the season in a 4-3 win over the Chicago White Sox.

1947 – **Cy Block's** fourth single of the game in the bottom of the ninth – a line drive off the screen in right field – gives Nashville a 14-13 victory over New Orleans in Game 3 of the Southern Association semifinal playoff series. Block's other three hits were bunt singles.

1956 – **Nahum Stelmach** scores two goals as Israel defeats South Vietnam 2-1 in the Asian Nations Cup soccer tournament.

MAZEL TOUGH

1914 – **Abel Kiviat** wins the 1,500 at the AAU Outdoor Track and Field Championships in Baltimore.

1927 – **Benny Bass** wins a 10-round decision over **Red Chapman** to capture the NBA world featherweight championship at Municipal Stadium in Philadelphia.

1933 – **Barney Ross** beats Tony Canzoneri in a 15-round rematch at the Polo Grounds in New York to retain his world lightweight and junior lightweight titles. After the fight, Ross relinquishes his lightweight title because of the difficulty of making weight.

1959 – **Rafi Levi** scores a hat trick as Israel beats India 3-1 in an Asian Nations Cup soccer match.

1965 – **Kathy Harter** defeats Gail Sherriff 6-3, 6-1 to win the Heart of America tennis tournament in Kansas City, Mo.

1970 – In only his third professional boxing match, **Henry Nissen** wins a 15-round decision over Harry Hayes in Melbourne to win the Australian flyweight title.

1999 – **Adriana Behar** and Brazilian teammate Shelda Bede win the Bank of America U.S. Olympic Cup women's beach volleyball championship in San Diego.

2003 – **Daniela Krukower** of Argentina defeats Driulis Gonzalez of Cuba in the final to win the women's under-63 kilogram title at the World Judo Championships in Osaka, Japan.

RECORD SETTERS

1959 – **Maria Itkina** of the Soviet Union sets a world record of 53.4 seconds in the 200 meters.

TRANSITIONS

1965 – **Sid Luckman** is enshrined in the Pro Football Hall of Fame.

A STAR IS BORN

1900 – **S. Mortimer Auerbach** (speedboat racing)

1913 – **Al Roth** (featherweight boxer)

1916 – **Henry Laskau** (track and field)

1955 – **Neil Cohen** (soccer)

SEPTEMBER 13

GAMEBREAKERS

1936 – **Dave Smukler** throws a 55-yard touchdown pass as the Philadelphia Eagles defeat the New York Giants 10-7.

STRONG IN DEFEAT

2004 – **Shawn Green** hits a pair of solo homers – his 24th and 25th of the season – in the Los Angeles Dodgers' 9-7 loss to the San Diego Padres.

MAZEL TOUGH

1903 – **Myer Prinstein** of the United States wins his first of four consecutive long jump titles at the Canadian National Track and Field Championships in Montreal.

1909 – **Johnny Sharpe** beats future world champion **Ted "Kid" Lewis** in six rounds in London in Lewis's pro boxing debut.

1919 – **Bernard Lichtman** wins the pentathlon and **Charles Pores** captures the 5-mile run at the AAU Outdoor Track and Field Championships.

1947 – **Roy Romain** of Great Britain wins the 200-meter breaststroke in 2:40.1 at the European Swimming Championships.

1992 – **Brian Dunn** of Brandon, Fla., beats **Noam Behr** of Israel 7-5, 6-2 to win the U.S. Open Junior Boys tennis championship.

RECORD SETTERS

1971 – **Barry Asher** wins a pro bowling tournament in South Bend, Ind., with the highest-scoring finals in PBA history – a 247 average for 42 games.

TRANSITIONS

1947 – **Si Rosenthal** Night at Fenway Park raises $25,000 for the former Red Sox outfielder who was paralyzed when his ship was hit by a torpedo during World War II.

1960 – **Sid Luckman** of Columbia is elected to the National Football Foundation College Hall of Fame.

1970 – **Fred Lebow** co-directs the first New York City Marathon, with 127 runners competing over 26 miles entirely within Central Park. In 1976, Lebow will expand the race to include all five boroughs of New York.

A STAR IS BORN

1838 – **Jacob Pincus** (horse racing)
1906 – **Jim Levey** (St. Louis Browns baseball, Pittsburgh Pirates football)
1963 – **Stacy Winsberg** (UCLA softball)

Barry Asher
(Professional Bowlers Association)

SEPTEMBER 14

GAMEBREAKERS

1946 – **Hank Greenberg** drives in all seven Detroit runs with two homers and a three-run double as the Tigers beat the New York Yankees 7-4.

1952 – White Sox pitcher **Saul Rogovin** strikes out 14 Red Sox batters in 16 innings, but leaves without a decision. Chicago wins 4-3.

1963 – **Larry Yellen** pitches a two-hitter and strikes out nine batters as San Antonio defeats El Paso 2-0 to clinch the Texas League best-of-five semifinal playoff series three games to two.

1993 – **Jose Bautista** allows five hits, strikes out five and collects his only career RBI as the Chicago Cubs beat the San Francisco Giants 8-1.

STRONG IN DEFEAT

1969 – **Mike Epstein** hits a grand slam homer in the eighth inning to give the Senators a 4-2 lead, but Washington loses 7-4 to the Detroit Tigers in 12 innings.

MAZEL TOUGH

1960 – **Walter Blum** rides five winners at Atlantic City Race Course, including the feature King Neptune Handicap aboard Conestoga.

1971 – Baseball Hall of Famer **Hank Greenberg** wins the Dewars Cup celebrity tennis tournament.

1986 – **Martin Jaite** beats Jonas Svensson 7-5, 6-2 in the final of a clay-court tennis tournament in Stuttgart, Germany.

1926 – **Leo Lomski** knocks out Joe Roche in the fourth round in San Francisco to retain his Pacific Coast middleweight title.

2003 – **Tanya Kader** wins the Montreal International Marathon in 2 hours, 58 minutes, 54 seconds.

2003 – **Chanoch Nissany** of Israel clinches the overall Hungarian Formula 2000 auto racing championship with his second victory in two days.

RECORD SETTERS

1962 – **Maria Itkina** of the Soviet Union ties her world record of 53.4 seconds in the 200 meters at the European Championships in Belgrade.

1996 – **David Ettinger** ties his Hofstra school record with a 54-yard field goal in a 28-13 loss to Southwest Texas State.

JEWS ON FIRST

1919 – **Jesse Baker (Michael Myron Silverman)** plays in his only major-league game, starting at shortstop for the Washington Senators. In the second inning of a 9-4 Tigers victory, he is spiked by a sliding Ty Cobb at second base and is forced to leave the game without ever coming to bat.

TRANSITIONS

2002 – **Andrew Sznajder**, a five-time national champion, is inducted into the Canadian tennis hall of fame.

A STAR IS BORN

1886 – **Phil Cooney** (New York Highlanders baseball)

1940 – **Larry Brown** (North Carolina basketball, ABA player, pro and college coach)

1967 – **Alon Hazan** (Israeli soccer)

1974 – **Lindsay Durlacher** (Greco-Roman wrestling)

SEPTEMBER 15

GAMEBREAKERS

1928 – **Andy Cohen** scores the tying run in the ninth, then singles home the winning run with the bases loaded in the 13th inning as the New York Giants beat the Brooklyn Robins 9-4.

1950 – **Hy Cohen** holds regular-season champion Flint to eight hits as Grand Rapids wins 10-0 to tie the Central League best-of-five championship series at one game apiece. Flint goes on to win the series 3-1.

MAZEL TOUGH

1819 – **Israel Belasco** defeats Kit Barber in a 41-round fight at Tarbury Common, England.

1964 – **Roger Ginsberg** shoots 137 over 36 holes to win the Port Jefferson Open golf tournament on Long Island.

1968 – **Julie Heldman** defeats Laura Roussow 4-6, 6-2, 7-5 in the final of the Heart of America tennis tournament in Kansas City, Mo.

1974 – U.S. team captain **Julie Heldman** beats Evonne Goolagong 6-3, 6-1 to wrap up the Americans' victory over Australia in the best-of-nine Bonne Bell Cup team tennis tournament in Cleveland.

1991 – **Fabrice Benichou** knocks out Vicenzo Limatola in the 10th round in Nimes, France, to retain his European featherweight title.

2001 – Former Virginia star **Bonnie Rosen** helps the United States come from behind to beat Australia 14-8 in High Wycombe, England, for its fourth consecutive Lacrosse World Cup title.

2002 – **Anna Smashnova** of Israel beats Anna Kournikova 6-2, 6-3 to win the Shanghai Open, her fourth WTA tennis tournament championship of the year and sixth of her career.

Bruce Fleisher *(The Express-Times)*

RECORD SETTERS

1961 – **Sandy Koufax** strikes out 10 in an 11-2 win over the Braves, setting a National League season record of 243 for a left-hander.

2002 – **Bruce Fleisher** shoots a PGA Seniors Tour 54-hole record 19-under-par 191 to win the RJR Championship in Clemmons, N.C., by five strokes over Hale Irwin. The victory ends Fleisher's 38-tournament winless streak.

A STAR IS BORN

1893 – **Eddie Gottlieb** (NBA founder)
1906 – **Irving Jaffee** (speed skating)
1951 – **Johan Neeskens** (Netherlands soccer)
1959 – **Doug Shapiro** (cycling)

SEPTEMBER 16

GAMEBREAKERS

1913 – **Erskine Mayer** of the Philadelphia Phillies shuts out the Cincinnati Reds 4-0.

1923 – **Moritz Haeusler** scores in the 80th minute to give Hakoah Vienna a 1-0 soccer victory over Wacker Vienna.

1961 – **Barry Latman** pitches a four-hitter as the Cleveland Indians beat the Minnesota Twins 2-0.

STRONG IN DEFEAT

1970 – **Art Shamsky** hits two home runs in the New York Mets' 4-2 loss to the Montreal Expos.

1978 – **Dave Jacobs** of Syracuse kicks four field goals in a 27-19 loss to North Carolina State.

MAZEL TOUGH

1973 – **Tom Okker** beats John Alexander 7-5, 6-4 to win the Rainier International Classic tennis tournament in Seattle.

1977 – **Harold Solomon** beats Ken Rosewall in the Tournament of Champions tennis final in New York, winning the fifth game 6-3.

1978 – **Elliot Teltscher** beats John Alexander 6-3, 4-6, 6-2 in the final of a hard-court tennis tournament in Atlanta.

1984 – **Aaron Krickstein** beats **Shahar Perkiss** of Israel 6-4, 6-1 in the final of a hard-court tennis tournament in Tel Aviv.

RECORD SETTERS

1882 – **Lon Myers** sets an American record of 1:44.25 in the 800-yard run in Williamsburg, N.Y.

1921 – **Gerard Blitz** of Belgium sets a world record of 5:59.2 in the 400 backstroke. The record will stand for six years.

1995 – **David Ettinger** of Hofstra kicks a school-record 54-yard field goal in a 26-0 victory over Lafayette.

2000 – **Dara Torres**, at 33 the oldest swimmer on the U.S. Olympic team in Sydney, Australia, swims the third leg of a world-record 3:36.61 in the women's 400-meter freestyle relay.

TRANSITIONS

1903 – Pittsburgh Pirates owner **Barney Dreyfuss** and Boston Pilgrims owner Henry Killilea agree to a post-season championship between the pennant winners, a best-of-nine World Series. Boston wins in eight games.

A STAR IS BORN

1886 – **Harry Lewis** (welterweight boxer)

1918 – **Benjamin Sohn** (Southern Cal football)

1969 – **Andrew Borodow** (Canadian wrestler)

1975 – **Gal Fridman** (Israeli yachting)

Dara Torres
(U.S. Olympic Committee)

SEPTEMBER 17

GAMEBREAKERS

1930 – **Jim Levey** makes his major-league debut at shortstop for the St. Louis Browns and smacks two hits, including a two-run double, in a 9-8 win over the New York Yankees.

1938 – **Hank Greenberg** hits home runs nos. 52 and 53, moving two games ahead of Babe Ruth's record pace for 60, as the Tigers beat the Yankees 7-3.

1942 – **Harry Feldman** pitches a five-hitter as the New York Giants beat the Cincinnati Reds 11-1.

1946 – **Hank Greenberg** hits his 300th career home run and drives in four runs as the Detroit Tigers beat the Washington Senators 6-4.

1983 – Ohio State tight end **John Frank** catches seven passes for 108 yards and two touchdowns in a 24-14 win over Oklahoma.

2006 – **Kevin Youkilis's** three-run double in the seventh inning assures the Boston Red Sox of a 6-3 victory over the New York Yankees.

MAZEL TOUGH

1937 – **Herman Barron** wins the Metropolitan PGA golf tournament in White Plains, N.Y., by six strokes.

1966 – Squash specialist **Vic Niederhoffer** defeats handball champion **Howie Eisenberg** to win the U.S. Paddleball championship at Coney Island in Brooklyn.

1989 – **Martin Jaite** beats Jordi Arrese 6-3, 6-2 in the final of a clay-court tennis tournament in Madrid.

RECORD SETTERS

1958 – **Isaac Berger** sets world weight lifting records of 147.5 kg in the clean and jerk and 372.5 kg overall at the world championships in Stockholm.

1963 – **Sandy Koufax** blanks St. Louis 4-0 on four hits for his 11th shutout, breaking Carl Hubbell's modern record for a left-hander set in 1933. His eight strikeouts give him a National League-record 306.

Norm Miller *(Atlanta Braves)*

JEWS ON FIRST

1966 – **Norm Miller** of the Houston Astros hits his first of 24 career home runs off John Morris in an 11-2 victory over the Philadelphia Phillies.

TRANSITIONS

2004 – **Jose Nestor Pekerman,** three-time world youth championship manager, is named Argentina's national soccer coach.

A STAR IS BORN

1908 – **Lionel Van Praag** (motorcycle racing)
1909 – **Bernard Bienstock** (CCNY football)
1922 – **Frank Spellman** (weight lifting)
1952 – **Harold Solomon** (tennis)

SEPTEMBER 18

GAMEBREAKERS

1940 – **Hank Greenberg** hits three home runs, including a grand slam, as Detroit splits a doubleheader with the Philadelphia A's. Detroit wins the opener 14-0 before the A's rally for nine runs in the ninth and win the nightcap 13-6.

1965 – **Sandy Koufax** pitches his third straight 1-0 shutout, stopping the St. Louis Cardinals on four hits.

MAZEL TOUGH

1924 – Welterweight boxer **Jackie Fields** makes his pro debut with a four-round decision over Joe Salas, the same boxer he beat for the Olympic gold medal a few months earlier.

1933 – **Kingfish Levinsky** knocks former heavyweight champion Jack Sharkey down for a seven-count in the first round and goes on to take a 10-round decision at Comiskey Park in Chicago.

1958 – **Robert Mosbacher** wins the North American Sailing championship in Rye, N.Y.

1967 – **Bus Mosbacher** skippers Intrepid to a 4-0 sweep of Dame Pettie of Australia to win his second America's Cup yachting trophy.

2000 – **Lenny Krayzelburg** wins the 100-meter backstroke for his first of three swimming gold medals at the Olympics in Sydney, Australia.

2005 – **Justin Gimelstob** teams with Nathan Healy to win the China Open tennis tournament doubles title in Beijing.

RECORD SETTERS

1880 – **Lon Myers** ties the world amateur record of 10.0 seconds in the 100-yard dash.

2005 – **Deena Kastor** breaks Joan Benoit's 1984 American women's record in the half marathon (13.1 miles) in winning the Philadelphia Distance Run in 1 hour, 7 minutes, 53 seconds.

TRANSITIONS

1934 – In the middle of a pennant race, the Detroit Tigers beat the New York Yankees 2-0, even though **Hank Greenberg** takes the day off for Yom Kippur.

1934 – Binghamton Triplets first baseman **Sol Mishkin** and Williamsport Grays outfielder **Joe Bonowitz** both miss Game 6 of the New York-Penn League championship series because of Yom Kippur. Williamsport wins 7-2 to clinch the series 4-2.

1997 – **Marshall Goldberg's** No. 42 jersey is retired during a ceremony at halftime of the University of Pittsburgh's football game against Miami.

A STAR IS BORN

1918 – **Henry Wittenberg** (wrestling)

1918 – **Judith Deutsch** (Austrian swimming)

1926 – **Solly Cantor** (Canadian lightweight boxer)

Deena Kastor (*U.S. Olympic Committee*)

SEPTEMBER 19

GAMEBREAKERS

1934 – **Jim Levey** smacks three doubles as the Hollywood Stars defeat the Portland Beavers 10-4 in a Pacific Coast League game.

1978 – **Ron Blomberg's** eighth-inning grand-slam homer gives the Chicago White Sox an 8-4 victory over the Oakland Athletics. **Steve Stone** is the winning pitcher with ninth-inning relief help from **Ross Baumgarten**.

1992 – **Jay Fiedler** throws five touchdown passes as Dartmouth beats Penn 36-17.

1998 – **Steve Birnbaum** of Washington State passes for 299 yards and two touchdowns in a 24-16 win over Idaho. **Todd Braverman** of Virginia kicks a 30-yard field goal with 49 seconds remaining to beat Clemson 20-18. **Adam Abrams** of Southern Cal kicks four field goals in a 40-20 win over Oregon State.

2004 – **Shawn Green** hits an 0-2 pitch with two out in the top of the ninth for a two-run homer over the center-field fence to give the first-place Los Angeles Dodgers a 7-6 victory over the Colorado Rockies.

MAZEL TOUGH

1888 – **Victor Schifferstein** wins the long jump at the AAU championships in Detroit.

1927 – **Benny Bass** wins a 10-round decision over **Red Chapman** to capture the world featherweight title.

1933 – **Al Foreman** wins a 10-round decision over Tommy Bland in Montreal to capture the Canadian lightweight title.

1954 – **Robert Cohen** of Algeria wins a 15-round decision over champion Chamrern Songkitrat in Bangkok to win the vacant world bantamweight title.

1977 – **Tom Okker** and Marty Riessen team to beat brothers Tim and Tom Gullickson 3-6, 6-3, 6-3, 4-6, 6-1 to win the U.S. Pro Doubles tennis championship in Houston.

1998 – **Tanya Dubnicoff** of Canada defeats Michelle Ferris of Australia in the final to win the gold medal in track cycling sprint competition at the Commonwealth Games in Kuala Lumpur, Malaysia.

Ross Baumgarten
(Chicago White Sox)

JEWS ON FIRST

1896 – In the first marathon run on U.S. soil, **Louis Liebgold** of the New Jersey Athletic Club wins a bronze medal in the 25-mile race from Samford, Conn., to Bronx, N.Y.

1937 – **Hank Greenberg** becomes the first player to hit a home run into the center-field stands at Yankee Stadium in the Tigers' 8-1 victory over New York.

A STAR IS BORN

1899 – **Joe Benjamin** (lightweight boxer)
1909 – **Richard Fishel** (Syracuse football, Brooklyn Dodgers football)

SEPTEMBER 20

GAMEBREAKERS

1925 – Reading Keys shortstop **Moe Berg** collects eight hits in eight at-bats in an International League doubleheader against Providence.

1932 – **Hank Greenberg's** seventh-inning homer gives the Beaumont Explorers of the Texas League a 1-0 victory over the Chattanooga Lookouts of the Southern League in the opening game of the Dixie Series. Chattanooga will rally to win the best-of-seven series in five games.

1933 – **Harry Newman** scores on a 5-yard run, throws a 37-yard touchdown pass, and kicks a 39-yard field goal as the New York Giants defeat the Pittsburgh Pirates 23-2.

1935 – **Dave Smukler** runs for three touchdowns and passes for two more as Temple routs St. Joseph's 51-0.

1953 – **Cal Abrams** of the Pirates hits a grand-slam homer to give Pittsburgh an 8-4 victory over the New York Giants.

1961 – **Norm Sherry** hits a leadoff homer in the eighth to tie the game, and the Dodgers go on to defeat the Chicago Cubs 3-2 in 13 innings on **Sandy Koufax's** complete-game seven-hitter. Sherry's homer is the last one ever hit in the Los Angeles Coliseum.

1981 – **Dave Jacobs** kicks a pair of field goals as the Cleveland Browns defeat the Cincinnati Bengals 20-17.

2001 – **Shawn Green's** fourth hit of the game, a solo home run in the bottom of the 13th inning, gives the Los Angeles Dodgers a 3-2 win over the first-place Arizona Diamondbacks.

STRONG IN DEFEAT

1946 – **Marshall Goldberg** makes a 7-yard touchdown reception in the Chicago Cardinals' 14-7 loss to the Pittsburgh Steelers.

1997 – **David Ettinger** of Hofstra kicks a school-record four field goals in a 35-31 loss to Connecticut.

2003 – Jockey **Matt Garcia** rides Vow to victory in the Slady Castle Handicap at Monmouth Park in New Jersey.

MAZEL TOUGH

1900 – **Jean Bloch** and the French soccer team win a silver medal at the Paris Olympics.

1913 – **Alvah Meyer** wins the 100 and 220 and **Abel Kiviat** captures the mile run at the Metropolitan Track and Field Championships on Travers Island, N.Y.

1931 – **Eva Bein** retains her AAU outdoor 1-mile freestyle swimming title.

TRANSITIONS

1923 – **Sidney Franklin** makes his debut as an American matador in Mexico.

A STAR IS BORN

1907 – **Harry Litwack** (basketball)
1917 – **Red Auerbach** (basketball)
1952 – **Randy Grossman** (Temple football, Pittsburgh Steelers tight end)
1970 – **David Nainkin** (tennis)

SEPTEMBER 21

GAMEBREAKERS

1941 – **Harry Feldman** earns his first major-league victory by shutting out the Boston Braves 4-0 on nine hits in the first game of a doubleheader. **Harry Danning** is his catcher, and **Morrie Arnovich** and **Sid Gordon** each collect a hit for New York as a major-league team starts four Jewish players for the first time.

1941 – **Marshall Goldberg** throws an 11-yard touchdown pass as the Chicago Cardinals play to a 14-14 tie with the Detroit Lions.

1968 – **Steve Tannen** returns a punt 64 yards for a touchdown as Florida beats Air Force 23-20 in Tampa, Fla.

1991 – **Danny Rebuck** scores a school-record 10 points on four goals and an assist as South Carolina-Spartanburg defeats Columbus State in soccer.

2003 – In just his third major-league appearance, Pittsburgh Pirates relief pitcher **John Grabow** strikes out five of the six batters he faces in a 4-1 victory over the Chicago Cubs.

STRONG IN DEFEAT

1996 – In his first start at quarterback for Michigan State, **Gus Ornstein** completes 21 of 37 passes for 237 yards and a touchdown, but the Spartans lose to Louisville 37-21.

MAZEL TOUGH

1916 – **Joe Burman** stops Kid McCarthy in a bantamweight fight in Brooklyn. It is Burman's fifth victory in 16 days – and fourth by first-round knockout.

1922 – **Jackie "Kid" Wolfe** wins a 15-round decision over Joe Lynch in a bout promoted as the first junior featherweight (122-pound) championship at Madison Square Garden.

1926 – **Mushy Callahan** decisions Pinkey Mitchell in 10 rounds in Vernon, Calif., to retain the world junior welterweight title.

1957 – **Armand Mouyal** of France wins the epee title at the World Fencing Championships.

1961 – **Isaac Berger** lifts 810 pounds to defeat Yevgeni Minaev and win the featherweight title at the World Weightlifting Championships in Vienna.

RECORD SETTERS

1918 – **Charles Pores** sets an American record of 24 minutes, 36.8 seconds in the five-mile run at the National AAU Championships at the Great Lakes Naval Training Station in Illinois. **David Politzer** wins the long jump.

1958 – **Isaac Berger** sets a world record of 821.2 pounds to win the World Weightlifting Championships featherweight title in Stockholm, Sweden.

2000 – **Lenny Krayzelburg** wins the 200-meter backstroke in an Olympic-record 1 minute, 56.76 seconds for his second gold medal in Sydney, Australia.

JEWS ON FIRST

2003 – **Lee Korsitz** wins the gold medal in the Mistral event at the World Sailing Championships in Cadiz, Spain, becoming the first Israeli woman to win a world championship in any sport.

TRANSITIONS

1964 – Boston Celtics coach **Red Auerbach** is given the additional titles of vice president and general manager in a front-office reshuffling following the death of team president Walter Brown.

SEPTEMBER 22

GAMEBREAKERS

1934 – **Hank Greenberg** collects five hits and four RBI's as the Detroit Tigers sweep a doubleheader from the St. Louis Browns, 8-3 and 15-1.

1942 – **Goody Rosen** gets four hits and two RBI's as the Syracuse Chiefs beat Jersey City 9-8 in 10 innings to clinch the International League playoff series 4-0.

1948 – **Al Richter** hits a three-run double and an RBI single to lead the Scranton Miners to a 6-2 victory over the Albany Senators in the third game of the Eastern League's Governor's Cup finals. Scranton completes the series sweep the next day.

1999 – **Shawn Green** collects four hits, including his 40th home run of the season, as the Toronto Blue Jays beat the Boston Red Sox 14-9.

MAZEL TOUGH

1906 – **Myer Prinstein** of the United States wins the long jump for the fourth consecutive year at the Canadian National track and field championships in Montreal.

1943 – **Herman Barron** shoots 144 to win the Westchester PGA tournament in White Plains, N.Y., by three strokes.

1955 – **Lew Lazar** wins a 12-round decision over Terrence Murphy to win the vacant British (Southern Area) middleweight title.

1991 – **Riccardo Patrese** of Italy wins the Formula One Portuguese Grand Prix.

1993 – **Gary Jacobs** knocks out Daniel Birc-chieray in the fifth round in London to retain his European welterweight title

2000 – **Anthony Ervin** and Gary Hall Jr. both finish the 50-meter freestyle in 21.98 seconds to share the gold medal at the Olympics in Sydney, Australia.

2004 – **Keren Leibovitch** of Israel wins a gold medal in the women's 100-meter backstroke, one day after **Itzhak Mamistalov** of Israel wins the men's 100 freestyle at the Paralympic Games in Athens. **Elaine Barrett** of England wins the 100 breaststroke for swimmers in the totally blind division.

JEWS ON FIRST

1904 – **Samuel Berger**, an American who weighs 180 pounds, wins the first Olympic heavyweight boxing gold medal when he knocks out 158-pound Charles Mayer in the third round. Mayer wins the middleweight gold medal the same day.

A STAR IS BORN

1913 – **Al Roth** (light welterweight boxer)
1922 – **Abraham Karnofsky** (Arizona and pro football)
1942 – **David Stern** (NBA commissioner)

Anthony Ervin (*U.S. Olympic Committee*)

266

SEPTEMBER 23

GAMEBREAKERS

1934 – In his first major-league game, Washington outfielder **Fred Sington** singles home **Buddy Myer** as the Senators beat the Philadephia Athletics 2-1 at Shibe Park.

1947 – **Sid Schacht** pitches a six-hitter with 12 strikeouts as Stamford, Conn., defeats New London 5-0 to capture the Colonial League's Governor's Cup best-of-five championship series 4-1.

1973 – **Ron Blomberg** hits a pair of home runs and drives in four runs as the New York Yankees beat the Cleveland Indians 9-1 in the first game of a doubleheader.

2001 – Quarterback **Jay Fiedler** caps a 10-play, 80-yard drive with a 2-yard run for the winning touchdown with five seconds remaining as the Miami Dolphins beat the Oakland Raiders 18-15 in their home opener. Fiedler also scores on a 2-yard run in the first half.

MAZEL TOUGH

1937 – **Barney Ross**, fighting despite a severely bruised left hand, hangs on to defeat Ceferino Garcia in a 15-round fight in New York and retain his world welterweight title.

1956 – **Herb Flam** beats Ken Rosewall in the final of the Pacific Southwest tennis tournament in Los Angeles.

1984 – **Amy Alcott** wins her fourth LPGA tournament in a single year for the third time in her career, capturing the San Jose Classic when she finishes two strokes ahead of four other golfers, including **Beverly Klass.**

1984 – **Aaron Krickstein** wins for the second week in a row, beating Henrik Sundstrom 6-7, 6-1, 6-4 in the final of a clay-court tennis tournament in Geneva, Switzerland.

2000 – **Lenny Krayzelburg** swims the backstroke leg of the men's 4×100-meter relay for his third gold medal at the Olympics in Sydney, Australia. **Dara Torres** swims the final leg of the women's 4×100 medley to win the gold medal in a world-record 3:58.30. Torres also wins the bronze in the 50 freestyle with an American-record 24.63 seconds.

2001 – **Kenny Bernstein** beats Larry Dixon in the Top Fuel final at the NHRA AutoZone Nationals in Millington, Tenn.

RECORD SETTERS

1938 – **Hank Greenberg** of the Tigers sets a major-league record by hitting two homers in one game for the 10th time in a season. The two homers in Detroit's 6-5 loss to Cleveland give him 56 for the year.

2000 – Pacific Palisades (Calif.) quarterback **David Koral** sets a national high school record by passing for 724 yards and seven touchdowns in a 48-30 victory over Van Nuys Grant.

TRANSITIONS

1967 – **Gladys Heldman** signs nine top women's tennis players to symbolic $1 contracts and organizes the breakaway Virginia Slims Tour in Houston.

A STAR IS BORN

1861 – **Louis Rubenstein** (Canadian figure skater)

SEPTEMBER 24

GAMEBREAKERS

1904 – **Barney Pelty** of the St. Louis Browns shuts out the Philadelphia A's 5-0.

1914 – **Erskine Mayer** of the Philadelphia Phillies beats the Chicago Cubs 6-2 for his 21st victory of the season.

1915 – Fullback **Manny Littauer** scores five touchdowns in a 57-0 rout of St. Lawrence in Columbia's first game after a 10-year hiatus of its football program.

1937 – **Marshall Goldberg** intercepts a pass and returns it 55 yards for a touchdown on the first play of the season as Pitt defeats Ohio Wesleyan 59-0.

1938 – **Marshall Goldberg** scores two touchdowns as Pitt beats West Virginia 19-0 in its season opener.

1939 – **Marshall Goldberg** runs four yards for a touchdown as the Chicago Cardinals defeat the Pittsburgh Pirates 10-0.

1946 – **Hank Greenberg** hits a ninth-inning homer to give the Tigers a 4-3 win over St. Louis, then homers twice in the second game as Detroit beats the Browns 10-1. The 35-year-old Greenberg winds up leading the American League with 44 homers and 127 RBI's.

1953 – **Al Rosen** gets four hits, including his 42nd and 43rd homers of the season, as the Cleveland Indians beat the Detroit Tigers 12-3.

STRONG IN DEFEAT

1944 – **Sid Luckman** throws three touchdown passes in the Chicago Bears' 42-28 loss to the Green Bay Packers.

1949 – **Herb Rich** rushes for 102 yards in Vanderbilt's 12-7 loss to Georgia Tech.

1970 – **Elliott Maddox** goes 4 for 4 in the Detroit Tigers' 7-4 loss to the Baltimore Orioles.

1978 – **Jeff Newman** of the Oakland Athletics hits a home run off Milwaukee Brewers pitcher Mike Caldwell – his third pinch-hit homer of the season. The Brewers win 5-2.

MAZEL TOUGH

1923 – **Maxie Rosenbloom** makes his pro boxing debut with a six-round decision over Nick Scanlon in New York City.

1960 – **Jackie Mekler** of South Africa takes the lead at the eight-mile mark and wins the 52-mile, 710-yard London-to-Brighton ultramarathon in 5 hours, 25 minutes, 26 seconds.

1961 – **Isaac Berger** wins his second world weight lifting championship, capturing the featherweight class in Vienna.

1989 – **Aaron Krickstein** beats Michael Chang 2-6, 6-4, 6-2 in the final of a hard-court tournament in Los Angeles.

1999 – **Sebastian Rothmann** stops Robert Norton in the eighth round to win the WBU cruiserweight title in Merthyr, Wales.

2000 – **Sergei Charikov** of Russia wins a fencing gold medal in team saber at the Olympics in Sydney, Australia.

TRANSITIONS

1961 – New Mexico assistant **Marty Feldman** is named head coach at Oakland two games into the AFL season when the Raiders fire Eddie Erdelatz. Feldman compiles a 2-13 record before being dismissed in the middle of the 1962 season.

A STAR IS BORN

1931 – **Mark Midler** (Soviet fencing)

SEPTEMBER 25

GAMEBREAKERS

1932 – **Jack Grossman** runs two yards for a touchdown in the fourth quarter and **Benny Friedman** kicks the extra point as the Brooklyn Dodgers defeat the Staten Island Stapletons 7-0.

1937 – **Louis Babrow** scores two tries and sets up a third as the South African Springboks become the first foreign team to beat the All Blacks rugby team in New Zealand, 17-6.

1945 – **Goody Rosen** hits a three-run homer with two out in the ninth to give the Brooklyn Dodgers a 7-4 victory over the New York Giants.

1948 – **Norman Klein** rushes for 106 yards, including a 70-yard touchdown, as Kentucky beats Xavier 48-7.

1968 – **Mordechai Spiegler** scores all four goals within a span of 18 minutes as Israel defeats the United States 4-0 in Philadelphia in its final soccer tune-up before the Olympic games.

1969 – **Greg Goosen** hits two homers and a double as the Seattle Pilots beat the Minnesota Twins 5-1.

1976 – Backup quarterback **Pete Woods** caps an 80-yard drive with a touchdown pass with 12 seconds left and runs for the two-point conversion as Missouri defeats Ohio State 22-21 and ends the Buckeyes' 25-game home unbeaten streak.

2005 – **Jonathan Bornstein** scores two goals and adds an assist as UCLA defeats UNLV 3-0 in soccer.

STRONG IN DEFEAT

1954 – **Lou Limmer** hits the final home run in Philadelphia Athletics franchise history in a 10-2 loss to the New York Yankees.

MAZEL TOUGH

1899 – **Joe Choynski** knocks out Jimmy Hall in the seventh round to retain his unofficial world light-heavyweight title in Louisville, Ky.

1937 – **Gretel Bergmann** wins the high jump and shot put titles, **Rose Auerbach** the javelin, and **Claire Isicson** the 50 and 100 meters at the National AAU women's track championships.

1962 – **Bus Mosbacher** skippers Weatherly to a 4-1 victory over Gretel of Australia as the United States retains yachting's America's Cup.

1966 – **Allen Fox** upsets Roy Emerson 6-3, 6-3 to win the 40th annual Pacific Southwest tennis title.

1988 – **Seth Bauer** of the United States wins an Olympic gold medal in rowing at the Olympics in Seoul in the eight-oared shell with coxswain class.

1998 – **Dana Rosenblatt** wins a 12-round decision over Terry Norris to capture the IBA middleweight title in Mashantucket, Conn.

RECORD SETTERS

1980 – **Carina Benninga** scores a school-record eight goals as Old Dominion defeats Richmond 8-1 in field hockey.

JEWS ON FIRST

1966 – In the first major-league game in which both starting pitchers are Jewish, Cubs rookie **Ken Holtzman** takes a no-hitter into the ninth inning and finishes with a two-hitter and eight strikeouts in the Chicago's 2-1 win over Los Angeles. **Sandy Koufax** goes the distance for the Dodgers and allows four hits.

A STAR IS BORN

1917 – **Solly Sherman** (Univ. of Chicago football, Chicago Bears)

1963 – **Lee Saltz** (Temple quarterback, Canadian Football League)

1965 – **Steve Wapnick** (Detroit Tigers, Chicago White Sox pitcher)

SEPTEMBER 26

GAMEBREAKERS

1926 – **John Alexander** recovers a Hartford fumble in the end zone as the New York Giants beat the Blues 21-0 in an NFL season opener.

1931 – **Nat Grossman** scores three touchdowns as NYU defeats Hobart 65-0. **Jack Grossman** scores twice as Rutgers beats Providence 19-0.

1933 – **David Shapiro** returns an interception 20 yards for a touchdown as Temple defeats South Carolina 26-6.

1934 – **Hank Greenberg** collects six hits and nine RBI's in a doubleheader as the Detroit Tigers sweep the Chicago White Sox 12-10 and 10-3.

1934 – **Albert Weiner** kicks a 17-yard field goal as the Philadelphia Eagles defeat the Pittsburgh Pirates 17-0

1936 – **Marshall Goldberg** scores two touchdowns – one on a 76-yard run – and rushes for 203 yards in Pitt's 57-0 victory over Ohio Wesleyan.

1937 – **Dave Smukler** throws a 31-yard touchdown pass in the fourth quarter to rally the Philadelphia Eagles to a 6-6 tie with the Chicago Cardinals.

1948 – Birmingham runner **Mickey Rutner** fractures his collarbone but breaks up a ninth-inning double play by colliding with Nashville second baseman Buster Boguskie, who tears several knee ligaments. Birmingham scores the winning run on the play and takes Game 4 of the Southern Association championship series 7-6. The Bulls go on to win the series four games to two.

1954 – **Lou Limmer**, pinch hitting for Vic Power in the ninth inning of a 6-5 victory over the New York Yankees, strokes the final hit in Philadelphia Athletics franchise history.

1958 – **Barry Latman** allows three singles and strikes out nine for his first major-league complete game as the Chicago White Sox beat the Kansas City A's 1-0.

1992 – Cleveland Indians catcher **Jesse Levis** goes 3 for 3, including his first career home run – a solo shot off Kurt Knudsen – in a 7-4 victory over the Detroit Tigers.

1999 – **Eric Himelfarb** of the Sarnia Sting scores a hat trick against the Oshawa Generals in an Ontario Hockey League game. **Cory Pecker** of the Erie Otters has three goals and an assist in another OHL game.

2004 – **Matt Bernstein**, a blocking fullback, moves to tailback in the second half when Wisconsin's starter is injured, and rushes 27 times for a career-high 123 yards in the Badgers' 16-3 victory over Penn State. Bernstein didn't arrive at the stadium until five minutes before the 4:45 P.M. kickoff, and had not eaten in the previous 24 hours because of Yom Kippur.

STRONG IN DEFEAT

1976 – **Randy Grossman** catches seven passes for 47 yards, including an 11-yard touchdown, in the Pittsburgh Steelers' 30-27 loss to the New England Patriots.

MAZEL TOUGH

1976 – **Brian Gottfried** beats Arthur Ashe 6-2, 6-2 to win an indoor tennis tournament in Los Angeles.

2002 – **Neville Sacks** and **Joe Siegman** win the U.S. Lawn Bowls pairs championship in Walnut Creek, Calif.

TRANSITIONS

2001 – Dodgers outfielder **Shawn Green** sits out against San Francisco because of Yom Kippur, ending the major leagues' longest active consecutive-game streak at 415. The Giants win 6-4.

A STAR IS BORN

1969 – **Joe Jacobi** (canoeing)

SEPTEMBER 27

GAMEBREAKERS

1905 – Philadelphia Phillies pitcher **Harry "Klondike" Kane** limits St. Louis to five hits in a 6-0 victory – his only major-league shutout.

1913 – **Frank Glick** scores a touchdown on a 60-yard run as Princeton defeats Rutgers 14-3.

1936 – **Charley Siegel** runs for a touchdown and passes for another as the New York Yankees beat the Syracuse Braves 13-6 in the American Football League.

1969 – In his first start at quarterback, sophomore **Gary Wichard** throws two touchdown passes as C.W. Post defeats Wagner 14-7.

STRONG IN DEFEAT

1953 – **Al Rosen** of the Indians is thrown out on a close play at first base on his final at-bat of the season. Mickey Vernon of the Washington Senators wins the American League batting title with a .337 average – .0011 higher than Rosen, who wins the home run and RBI titles. Cleveland loses 7-3 to Detroit as Rosen finishes with an infield hit, a ground-rule double, and a bunt single in four at-bats.

1988 – **Yoel Sela** and **Eldad Amir** finish fourth in the Olympic yachting Flying Dutchman competition in South Korea. They just miss winning Israel's first-ever Olympic medal after having to forfeit the second race because it was contested on Yom Kippur. A finish of 11th or better would have assured the duo of a medal.

MAZEL TOUGH

1789 – **Daniel Mendoza** declares himself heavyweight champion when he wins his second consecutive fight against Richard Humphries in Doncaster, England.

1915 – **Ted "Kid" Lewis** beats Jack Britton in 12 rounds in Boston to retain his world welterweight title.

1981 – In the final of an indoor tennis tournament in San Francisco, **Eliot Teltscher** beats **Brian Teacher** 6-3, 7-6.

1987 – **Martin Jaite** beats Mats Wilander 7-6, 6-4, 4-6, 0-6, 6-4 in the final of a clay-court tennis tournament in Barcelona.

1991 – **Riccardo Patrese** of Italy outraces Ayrton Senna to win the Formula One Portuguese Grand Prix.

RECORD SETTERS

1938 – **Hank Greenberg** hits two home runs in the same game for a record 11th time in one season. One of his homers is inside the park as the Detroit Tigers beat the St. Louis Browns 10-2 in a game called after five innings because of darkness. The homers are Greenberg's last of the season. He finishes with 58, the most by a right-handed hitter until Mark McGwire and Sammy Sosa surpass the total in 1998.

1961 – **Sandy Koufax** breaks the National League record of 267 strikeouts set by Christy Mathewson in 1903 as the Dodgers beat the Phillies 2-1. Koufax accomplishes the feat in 269 innings – 98 fewer than Mathewson.

A STAR IS BORN

1904 – **Sid Terris** (lightweight boxer)
1915 – **Harry Chozen (**Cincinnati Reds catcher)

SEPTEMBER 28

GAMEBREAKERS

1947 – **Allie Sherman** runs for a touchdown in the Philadelphia Eagles' 45-42 victory over the Washington Redskins.

1959 – Rookie **Larry Sherry** pitches 7 2/3 innings of four-hit, scoreless relief as the Dodgers beat the Milwaukee Braves 3-2 in the first game of the best-of-three National League playoff series.

1972 – **Johan Neeskens** scores the first goal as Ajax of Holland beats Independiente of Argentina 3-0 to capture the Intercontinental Club Cup soccer championship.

1974 – **Ron Blomberg** hits two homers and drives in four runs in the first game and smacks a pinch-hit two-run homer in the eighth inning of the nightcap as the New York Yankees sweep the Cleveland Indians 9-3 and 9-7.

2002 – UCLA tight end **Mike Seidman** catches six passes for 134 yards and breaks three tackles en route to a 64-yard touchdown as the Bruins defeat San Diego State 43-7.

2003 – **David Koral** passes for 463 yards and five touchdowns – including 85- and 55-yarders – as Santa Monica Junior College defeats Citrus College 46-21.

STRONG IN DEFEAT

1975 – **Randy Grossman** catches a 20-yard touchdown pass – his first of five career regular-season TDs – in the Pittsburgh Steelers' 30-23 loss to the Buffalo Bills.

MAZEL TOUGH

1912 – **Alvah Meyer** of the United States wins his second straight Canadian National track and field championships title in the 100 meters in Montreal. **Abel Kiviat** wins the 1,500 meters for the fourth straight year.

1917 – **Johnny Rosner** knocks out Young Zulu Kid in the seventh round to win the American flyweight title in Brooklyn, N.Y.

1952 – **Dick Savitt** captures the Pacific Coast tennis championship.

1976 – **Brian Gottfried** wins the Pacific Southwest Open indoor tennis tournament in Los Angeles with a 6-2, 6-2 victory over Arthur Ashe.

1988 – Pitcher **Mike Milchin** and the United States baseball team earn a gold medal at the Seoul Olympics with a 5-3 victory over Japan.

JEWS ON FIRST

1857 – **Young Barney Aaron** of England beats American lightweight champion Johnny Monenghan in 80 rounds in Providence, R.I., becoming the first Jewish boxer to win a championship in the United States.

TRANSITIONS

1936 – **Al Schacht** leaves his coaching job with the Boston Red Sox to begin barnstorming as the first "Clown Prince of Baseball."

1952 – **Sid Gordon** strikes out in the 12th inning of a 5-5 tie with the Brooklyn Dodgers, thus becoming the Braves' final batter before the franchise moves from Boston to Milwaukee.

A STAR IS BORN

1898 – **Lew Tendler** (lightweight boxer)
1918 – **Eddie Feinberg** (Philadelphia Phillies shortstop)
1975 – **Lenny Krayzelburg** (swimming)

SEPTEMBER 29

GAMEBREAKERS

1946 – **Allie Sherman** throws touchdown passes of 38 and 28 yards as the Philadelphia Eagles beat the Los Angeles Rams 25-14. **Sid Luckman** throws TD passes of 23 and 33 yards in the Chicago Bears' 30-7 victory over the Green Bay Packers.

1946 – **Emil Moscowitz** pitches a three-hitter as the semi-pro Bushwicks of Brooklyn defeat the Minor-League All-Stars 3-2 in Dexter Park, Long Island. **Herb Karpel** of the Newark Bears is the losing pitcher.

1965 – **Sandy Koufax** picks up his 25th victory of the season, stopping the Cincinnati Reds 5-0 on two hits and 13 strikeouts.

1966 – **Sandy Koufax** beats the St. Louis Cardinals 2-1 on four hits. He becomes the first major-league pitcher to strike out 300 in a season three years in a row since Amos Rusie in 1890-92.

1973 – **Randy Grossman** catches six passes for 100 yards as Temple beats Holy Cross 63-34.

1979 – **Elliott Maddox** ties a Mets record with three doubles as New York beats the St. Louis Cardinals 8-7.

1980 – **Steve Stone** pitches six innings of the Baltimore Orioles' 4-3 victory over the Boston Red Sox and finishes his Cy Young Award-winning season with a 25-7 record.

1999 – **Shawn Green** goes 4 for 4 with two doubles as the Toronto Blue Jays beat the Tampa Bay Devil Rays 6-2.

2001 – Purdue sophomore **Brandon Hance** passes for 308 yards and three touchdowns – including a 19-yarder in overtime as the Boilermakers beat Minnesota 35-28. He also rushes for 70 yards and catches a halfback-option pass for a 31-yard touchdown.

STRONG IN DEFEAT

1935 – **Buddy Myer** of the Washington Senators goes 4 for 5 in an 11-8 loss to the Philadelphia Athletics on the final day of the season to win the American League batting title with a .3495 average. Joe Vosmik of Cleveland, who begins the day with a .3489 average, elects to sit out the final game in an attempt to protect his lead.

MAZEL TOUGH

1963 – **Norm Meyers** defeats runner-up Billy Welu by 260 pins to win the Seattle Open, his only victory on the PBA tour.

2003 – **Nicolas Massu** of Chile beats Paul-Henri Mathieu of France 1-6, 6-2, 7-6 (7-0) to win the Palermo Open clay-court tennis tournament, his third final in three weeks. Meanwhile, **Jonathan Erlich** and **Andy Ram** of Israel win the doubles title at the Thailand Open.

2003 – **Kenny Bernstein** defeats Larry Dixon in the Top Fuel final at the NHRA Carquest Nationals in Joliet, Ill. The victory is Bernstein's 36th of his career in the division and first since coming out of retirement to replace his son Brandon, who was injured in a crash earlier in the season.

TRANSITIONS

1934 – **Syd Cohen** of the Washington Senators gives up Babe Ruth's final American League home run but also is the last to strike out the star in a Yankees uniform. Cohen and the Senators win 8-5.

A STAR IS BORN

1883 – **Georges Stern** (French jockey)
1898 – **Benny Valgar** (lightweight boxer)
1954 – **Marshall Holman** (bowling)

SEPTEMBER 30

GAMEBREAKERS

1923 – **Mose Solomon** drives in the winning run in his first of two major-league games, breaking a 3-3 tie with an RBI double in the bottom of the 10th inning as the New York Giants beat the Boston Braves.

1930 – **Benny Friedman** runs for a 10-yard touchdown and throws a 10-yard touchdown pass as the New York Giants beat the Newark Tornadoes 32-0.

1933 – **Izzy Weinstock** kicks a field goal with 3½ minutes remaining, then intercepts a pass to set up a touchdown as Pitt escapes with a 9-0 victory over Washington & Jefferson.

1945 – **Hank Greenberg's** grand slam on the final day of the season gives the Detroit Tigers a 6-3 victory over the St. Louis Browns and the American League pennant.

1973 – **Steve Stone** of the Chicago White Sox pitches a three-hitter and strikes out a career-high 12 batters in a 1-0 victory over the pennant-winning Oakland Athletics on the final day of the regular season.

2000 – **Yari Allnut** scores Rochester's second goal as the Raging Rhinos beat the Minnesota Thunder 3-1 to win the A-League soccer championship.

2004 – **Geoff Blumenfeld's** 30-yard field goal with four seconds remaining gives Navy a 24-21 victory over Air Force.

STRONG IN DEFEAT

1949 – **Phil Slosberg** scores on a 1-yard run in the New York Bulldogs' 38-14 loss to the New York Giants.

MAZEL TOUGH

1973 – **Tom Okker** beats John Newcombe 3-6, 7-6, 6-3 to win the Tam International Tennis Tournament in Chicago.

1988 – **Brad Gilbert** wins the bronze medal in men's tennis at the Seoul Olympics. **Carina Benninga** and the Netherlands defeat Great Britain 3-1 to win the bronze medal in women's field hockey.

1990 – **Brad Gilbert** beats **Aaron Krickstein** 6-3, 6-1 in the final of an indoor tournament in Brisbane, Australia, for his last of 20 singles victories on the men's tennis tour.

2001 – **Kenny Bernstein** beats Darrell Russell in the Top Fuel final of the NHRA Nationals at Route 66 Speedway in Joliet, Ill.

A STAR IS BORN

1910 – **Kingfish Levinsky** (heavyweight boxer)
1916 – **Sidney Roth** (football)
1922 – **Julie Bort** (lightweight boxer)
1937 – **Rose Weinstein** (bowling)
1987 – **Sam Abay** (Australian auto racer)

Steve Stone
(Baltimore Orioles)

274

OCTOBER 1

GAMEBREAKERS

1915 – **Erskine Mayer** of the Philadelphia Phillies beats the Boston Braves 9-2 to finish with 21 victories for the second straight season.

1921 – **Sammy Bohne** goes 4 for 4 as the Cincinnati Reds beat the Chicago Cubs 5-3.

1922 – Fullback **Lawrence Weltman** scores the game's first touchdown as the Rochester Jeffersons beat All-Syracuse 13-0 in their season opener against a non-NFL opponent.

1938 – Columbia senior quarterback **Sid Luckman** completes 10 of 17 passes – including two for more than 50 yards each – in a season-opening 27-14 victory over Yale. He also rushes 20 times for 103 yards, kicks two field goals, and three extra points, and is named the game's outstanding defensive player.

1950 – **Al Rosen** of Cleveland gets two hits on the final day of the season as the Indians beat the Detroit Tigers 7-5. Rosen also draws his 100th walk of the season and scores his 100th run while increasing his total-bases amount to 301.

1977 – **Dave Jacobs** of Syracuse kicks a 56-yard field goal in a 30-20 win over Illinois.

MAZEL TOUGH

1972 – **Sheldon Karlin** of the University of Maryland wins the third New York City Marathon in 2 hours, 27 minutes, 52 seconds – five minutes ahead of the runner-up finisher. The early NYC Marathons consisted of four loops around Central Park.

1974 – **Tom Okker** beats John Newcombe 6-3, 7-6, 6-3 to win the Tam Tennis Tournament in Chicago.

1982 – **Kenny Bernstein** defeats Frank Hawley in the Funny Car final of an NHRA event in Fremont, Calif.

1989 – **Brad Gilbert** beats Anders Jarryd 7-5, 6-2 in the final of an indoor tennis tournament in San Francisco.

2000 – **Michael Kalganov** finishes third in the 1,500-meter kayak race to capture Israel's only medal at the Olympics in Sydney, Australia.

2001 – **Danielle Sanderson** of England wins the 55-mile London-to-Brighton run in 7 hours, 7 minutes, 12 seconds.

2006 – **Jonathan Erlich** and **Andy Ram** of Israel win the doubles tennis title at the Bangkok Open with a third-sets tiebreaker victory over Andy and Jamie Murray of Britain.

2006 – **Aleksandra Wozniak** of Canada defeats Agnes Szavay 6-1, 7-6 (2) in the final of a USTA Challenger tennis tournament in Ashland, Ky.

RECORD SETTERS

1922 – **Lilli Henoch** of Germany breaks the women's world discus record with a toss of 24.90 meters in Berlin.

TRANSITIONS

1903 – The first World Series game is played in Boston. Pilgrims owner Henry Killilea makes Pittsburgh Pirates owner **Barney Dreyfuss** pay his way into the ballpark.

1922 – **John Alexander** of the Milwaukee Badgers, normally a defensive tackle, originates the outside linebacker position in a 3-0 loss to the Chicago Cardinals.

1964 – Original Celtics player and longtime CCNY coach **Nat Holman** is inducted into the Basketball Hall of Fame.

A STAR IS BORN

1904 – **Jimmie Reese** (New York Yankees, St. Louis Cardinals infielder, California Angels coach)

1974 – **Alex Averbukh** (Israeli pole vaulter)

OCTOBER 2

GAMEBREAKERS

1920 – In his first game at Iowa, **Max Kadesky** catches the winning touchdown pass in a 14-7 victory over Indiana. The Hawkeyes will go 19-2 in his three-year career.

1932 – Player-coach **Benny Friedman** throws two touchdown passes to **Jack Grossman** as the Brooklyn Dodgers beat the Boston Braves 14-0 in the first professional football game played in Boston.

1937 – **Bernard Bloom** throws a 52-yard touchdown pass as NYU defeats Carnegie Tech 18-14.

1938 – **Harry Eisenstat** of Detroit beats Cleveland 4-1 on the final day of the season, taking a no-hitter into the eighth inning. **Hank Greenberg** hits a two-run double off losing pitcher Bob Feller, who strikes out a record 18 batters.

1938 – **Sam Nahem** makes his major-league debut with the Brooklyn Dodgers. He gets two hits and pitches a complete game in a 7-3 win over the Phillies.

1959 – **Larry Sherry** pitches the final three innings, allowing one run and three hits, as the Los Angeles Dodgers beat the Chicago White Sox 4-3 to tie the World Series at one game apiece.

1965 – **Sandy Koufax,** pitching on two days' rest, allows four hits and strikes out 12 as the Dodgers clinch the National League pennant with a 3-1 victory over the Milwaukee Braves. Koufax finishes the season with 383 strikeouts, breaking Bob Feller's record of 348.

1966 – **Sandy Koufax,** an emergency starter after Los Angeles loses the first game of a doubleheader, beats the Phillies 6-3 as the Dodgers win the National League pennant. He takes a 6-0 lead into the ninth inning and strikes out 10 to earn his final major-league victory. Koufax sets Dodgers records of 27 wins and a 1.73 season earned run average.

STRONG IN DEFEAT

1950 – **Herb Rich** returns a punt 86 yards for a touchdown to give Baltimore a 13-7 lead, but the Colts lose 55-13 to the Chicago Cardinals.

MAZEL TOUGH

1938 – **Sammy Luftspring** knocks Frankie Genovese down five times, finally stopping him in the 13th round in Toronto to win the Canadian welterweight title.

1955 – **Henry Laskau** wins the AAU 15-kilometer racewalking title in Atlantic City, N.J.

1980 – **Saoul Mamby** wins a 15-round decision over Termite Watkins to retain his WBC junior welterweight title in Las Vegas.

RECORD SETTERS

1963 – **Sandy Koufax** fans the first five batters and finishes with a World Series-record 15 strikeouts in a 5-2 win over the Yankees in Game One.

TRANSITIONS

1948 – **Hank Greenberg** is released by the Pittsburgh Pirates for the purpose of his retirement. Greenberg played 13 seasons and missed three years because of military service.

A STAR IS BORN

1942 – **Karl Sweetan** (Texas A&M and Wake Forest quarterback, Detroit Lions).

1973 – **Scott Schoeneweis** (Anaheim Angels, Chicago White Sox, Toronto Blue Jays, Cincinnati Reds, New York Mets pitcher)

OCTOBER 3

GAMEBREAKERS

1920 – Fullback **John Barsha** scores the game's only touchdown as the Rochester Jeffersons beat All-Buffalo 10-0 in an American Professional Football Association game.

1925 – **Benny Friedman** runs 65 yards for a touchdown and throws two TD passes as Michigan beats Michigan State 39-0.

1931 – **Nat Grossman** scores two touchdowns and **Joe Lefft** adds one as NYU defeats West Virginia Wesleyan 54-0. **Jack Grossman** scores three touchdowns as Rutgers beats Drexel 27-6.

1936 – In his first college game, **Sid Luckman** runs 38 yards for a touchdown and throws a TD pass as Columbia defeats Maine 34-0.

1937 – **Bernard Bloom's** 58-yard touchdown pass in the final two minutes gives NYU an 18-14 win over Carnegie Tech.

1938 – **Sid White** scores four touchdowns as Brooklyn College beats Fort Hamilton 32-0.

1943 – **Sid Luckman** throws three touchdown passes as the Chicago Bears beat the Detroit Lions 27-21.

STRONG IN DEFEAT

1934 – **Hank Greenberg** hits a World Series home run, but the Detroit Tigers lose Game 1 to the St. Louis Cardinals 8-3.

MAZEL TOUGH

1914 – **Alvah Meyer** wins the 100 and 220 and **Abel Kiviat** captures the mile run at the Metropolitan Track and Field Championships at Celtic Park on Long Island, N.Y.

1937 – Detroit beats Cleveland 1-0 and **Hank Greenberg** ends the season with 183 RBI's, one short of the major-league record held by Lou Gehrig.

1964 – Gun Bow, ridden by **Walter Blum,** upsets horse of the year Kelso in a photo finish in the Woodward Stakes at Aqueduct.

1971 – **Francois Cevert** of France takes the lead from Jackie Stewart on lap 14 and wins the 59-lap United States Grand Prix at Watkins Glen, N.Y. It is the only Formula One victory of his career, though he finishes second 10 times.

RECORD SETTERS

1885 – **Lon Myers** matches his world record of 1:55.4 in the half mile in New York.

TRANSITIONS

2001 – Staten Island Yankees first baseman **Aaron Rifkin** is named most valuable player of the rookie New York-Penn League. Rifkin hits .322 with 10 homers and 49 RBI's in the short-season league.

A STAR IS BORN

1869 – **Alfred Flatow** (German gymnastics)
1943 – **Roby Young** (Israeli soccer)

OCTOBER 4

GAMEBREAKERS

1930 – **Samuel Behr** returns a punt 70 yards for a touchdown in Wisconsin's 53-6 rout of St. Lawrence. **Marchy Schwartz** of Notre Dame scores the winning touchdown in a 20-14 victory over SMU in the first game played at Notre Dame Stadium. **Jack Grossman** scores two touchdowns as Rutgers tops George Washington 20-6.

1941 – **David Millman** catches a 26-yard touchdown pass with 6:55 remaining to give NYU a 6-0 victory over Lafayette.

1945 – **Hank Greenberg's** three-run home run in the fifth inning gives the Detroit Tigers a 4-1 victory over the Chicago Cubs in Game 2 of the World Series.

1959 – Relief pitcher **Larry Sherry** gets the final six outs of Game 3 of the World Series as the Dodgers beat the White Sox 3-1.

1970 – **Karl Sweetan** throws a 20-yard touchdown pass – the 17th and last of his career – in the Los Angeles Rams' 37-10 victory over the San Diego Chargers.

1979 – **Gidi Damti** scores twice as Israel defeats The Netherlands 4-3 in an Olympic qualifying soccer match.

2003 – **Gocha Ziziashvilly** of Israel scores a 2-0 overtime victory over two-time world champion Aza Abrhamian of Sweden to win the 84-kilogram division at the Greco-Roman Wrestling Championships in Creteil, France.

2003 – **Lane Schwarzberg** kicks a 22-yard field goal as time expires to give Colgate a 27-24 victory over Cornell.

STRONG IN DEFEAT

1970 – Cornerback **Steve Tannen** returns a blocked punt 41 yards for his only NFL touchdown and gives the New York Jets a 7-0 lead. The Buffalo Bills score two late touchdowns to win 34-31.

1987 – Six years after last playing in the NFL, **Dave Jacobs** kicks a 27-yard field goal as a replacement player for the Philadelphia Eagles in a 35-3 loss to the Chicago Bears. Jacobs kicks a field goal in each of three games – all losses – before the league resumes play with its regular players.

MAZEL TOUGH

1937 – **Benny Caplan** wins a 15-round decision over Joe Brahams in London to retain his British featherweight title.

1987 – Winning his second tennis tournament in as many weeks, **Martin Jaite** beats Karel Novacek 7-6, 6-7, 6-4 in the final of a clay-court event in Palermo, Sicily.

1987 – **Margie Goldstein** rides Daydream to first place in the Grand Prix of Baltimore equestrian event.

1992 – **Monte Scheinblum**, the runner-up the previous year, hits a golf ball 329 yards, 13 inches into a 20-mph wind to win the National Long Driving Championship in Boca Raton, Fla.

2001 – **Olga Karmansky** of the United States wins the all-around title at the Pan American Gymnastics Union rhythmic championships in Cancun, Mexico.

RECORD SETTERS

1959 – **Rudolph Pluykfelder** of the Soviet Union sets a world record of 1,008 3/5 pounds in the middle-heavyweight division and 305 1/3 pounds in the snatch at the World Weightlifting Championships in Warsaw, Poland.

A STAR IS BORN

1920 – **Steve Seymour** (javelin)
1927 – **Dan Dworsky** (Michigan football, Los Angeles Dons 1949)

OCTOBER 5

GAMEBREAKERS

1928 – **Moe Berg** collects three hits as the Chicago White Sox beat the Chicago Cubs 13-11 in Game 3 of their Chicago City Series. The Cubs win the postseason exhibition series 4-3.

1930 – **Julius Yablok** throws a 16-yard touchdown pass as the Brooklyn Dodgers defeat the Staten Island Stapletons 20-0 in the NFL.

1933 – **Buddy Myer** has three hits including an RBI single and run-scoring double as the Washington Senators beat the New York Giants 4-0 in Game 3 of the World Series at Griffith Stadium. The Giants will win the series four games to one.

1941 – **Sid Luckman** throws a 65-yard touchdown pass to **Johnny Siegal** in the Chicago Bears' 48-21 win over the Cleveland Rams.

1951 – **Sid Goldfader** scores two touchdowns as Brandeis defeats Hofstra 24-13.

1952 – Maurice Richard scores the tying goal off an assist from New York Rangers defenseman **Hy Buller** at 1:36 of the third period as the NHL Second-Team All-Stars tie the First-Team All-Stars 1-1 in Detroit.

1957 – Michigan quarterback **Stan Noskin** scores two touchdowns in a 26-0 victory over Georgia.

1959 – **Larry Sherry** pitches two scoreless innings in relief and is the winning pitcher as the Dodgers beat the White Sox 5-4 to take a 3-1 lead in the World Series.

1985 – Temple quarterback **Lee Saltz** completes 14 of 20 passes for 307 yards and two touchdowns, including a 96-yarder to Keith Gloster, as the Owls beat Cincinnati 28-16.

2002 – UCLA tight end **Mike Seidman** catches eight passes for 138 yards including a 24-yard touchdown as the Bruins defeat Oregon State 43-35. Seven of his catches produce first downs.

2002 – **Lane Schwarzberg** kicks a 20-yard field goal in the fourth quarter to force overtime, then kicks a 23-yarder to give Colgate a 13-10 victory over Bucknell.

2005 – New team captain **Jeff Halpern** collects three assists as the Washington Capitals defeat the Columbus Blue Jackets 3-2 in an NHL season opener.

STRONG IN DEFEAT

1941 – **Marshall Goldberg** catches a 76-yard touchdown pass in the Chicago Cardinals' 14-13 loss to the GreenBay Packers.

MAZEL TOUGH

1915 – **Charley White** knocks out Matty Baldwin in the first round of a lightweight fight in Boston.

1937 – **Maurice Holtzer** of France decisions Phil Dolhem in 15 rounds in Algiers to retain his European featherweight title and capture the vacant IBU world featherweight crown.

1980 – **Eliot Teltscher** beats Tim Wilkison 7-6, 6-3 in the final of a hard-court tennis tournament in Maui.

1987 – **Gilad Bloom** of Israel defeats Mark Dickson 7-6, 6-3 to win the Estoril Challenger tennis tournament in Portugal.

TRANSITIONS

1945 – The New York State Athletic Commission suspends welterweight boxer **Harold Green** for one year and fines him $1,000 for provoking a "minor riot" after he was knocked out in the third round by Rocky Graziano on Sept. 28 in New York.

1950 – The New York Knicks acquire **Max Zaslofsky** from the defunct Chicago NBA franchise for $15,000.

A STAR IS BORN

1905 – **Ray Miller** (lightweight boxer)
1918 – **Vic Hershkowitz** (handball)

OCTOBER 6

GAMEBREAKERS

1934 – **Herman Bassman** returns an interception 45 yards for a touchdown and Ursinus, a Division III school, upsets Penn 7-6. **Nathan Machlowitz** scores twice and **Charley Siegel** adds one TD as NYU defeats Johns Hopkins 32-0.

1946 – **Sam Nahem** pitches a five-hitter as the Bushwicks of Brooklyn, one of the top semi-pro teams in the country, defeat an All-Star team of major- and minor-league players 5-1. **Herb Karpel** is the losing pitcher.

1946 – **Allie Sherman** throws a touchdown pass in the Philadelphia Eagles' 49-25 victory over the Boston Yanks.

1963 – **Sandy Koufax** beats the Yankees 2-1 to complete the Dodgers' four-game sweep of the World Series.

1974 – **Ken Holtzman** of Oakland pitches a five-hit, 5-0 shutout to tie the best-of-five American League playoff series with Baltimore at one game apiece.

2000 – **Cory Pecker** of Sault Ste. Marie has three goals and an assist in an 8-3 win over Sarnia in the Ontario Hockey League.

2002 – **Hayden Epstein** kicks field goals of 34 and 31 yards as the Jacksonville Jaguars upset the Philadelphia Eagles 34-31.

STRONG IN DEFEAT

1959 – **Sandy Koufax** allows only five hits, but the White Sox beat the Dodgers 1-0 in Game 5 of the World Series when they score on a double-play groundout by Sherman Lollar in the fourth inning.

MAZEL TOUGH

1905 – **Young Otto** (**Arthur Suskind**) scores his 17th consecutive first-round knockout by stopping Jack Nelson in a lightweight fight in New York. Otto will finish his career with a record 42 first-round KOs.

1913 – **Ted "Kid" Lewis** knocks out Alec Lambert in the 17th round in London to win the British featherweight championship

1931 – Former world lightweight champion **Benny Leonard** knocks out Pal Silvers in the second round in Long Island City, N.Y., ending a 6½-year absence from the ring. The 35-year-old Leonard goes 18-0-1 over the next two years before losing his final bout.

1942 – **Maxie Shapiro**, a 5-to-1 underdog, wins a 10-round decision over future lightweight champion Bob Montgomery in Philadelphia. Shapiro knocks Montgomery down three times in the third round.

1946 – **Bill Steiner** of the New York Maccabi Club runs 30 kilometers in 1 hour, 38 minutes, 2 seconds to win the national title in Baltimore.

RECORD SETTERS

1934 – **Hank Greenberg** ties a World Series record with four hits in Detroit's 10-4 win over the St. Louis Cardinals in Game 4.

TRANSITIONS

1965 – **Sandy Koufax** skips the opening game of the World Series to attend Yom Kippur services. Minnesota beats Don Drysdale and takes a 1-0 series lead on the Dodgers.

A STAR IS BORN

1819 – **John Brunswick** (billiards, bowling)
1973 – **Israel Ajose** (British heavyweight boxer)

OCTOBER 7

GAMEBREAKERS

1919 – Erskine Mayer pitches a scoreless ninth inning as the Chicago White Sox beat the Cincinnati Reds 5-4 in the sixth game of the World Series.

1923 – Ralph Horween runs for a touchdown and **Arnold Horween** kicks two extra points as the Chicago Cardinals beat the Rochester Jeffersons 60-0 at Normal Park in Chicago.

1934 – Harry Newman of the Giants returns a kickoff 93 yards for a touchdown as New York beats the Boston Redskins 16-13.

1945 – Allie Sherman throws a 26-yard touchdown pass as the Philadelphia Eagles beat the Chicago Cardinals 21-6.

2006 – Shawn Green goes 3 for 5 with a pair of doubles and drives in two runs as the New York Mets beat the Los Angeles Dodgers 9-5 to complete a sweep of their best-of-five National League playoff series.

MAZEL TOUGH

1882 – Lon Myers of the Manhattan Athletic Club wins the 440 yards in 52 seconds and the one-half mile run in 2:14 at the Fall Championship Meeting in Montreal.

1937 – Maxie Berger wins a 10-round decision over Orville Drouillard in Montreal to retain his Canadian lightweight title.

1956 – Henry Laskau wins the AAU 15-kilometer racewalking title in Atlantic City, N.J.

1984 – Eliot Teltscher beats Francisco Gonzalez 3-6, 6-3, 6-4 in the final of an indoor tennis tournament in Brisbane, Australia.

1989 – Fabrice Benichou wins a 12-round decision over Ramon Cruz in Bordeaux, France, to retain his IBF super bantamweight title.

2001 – Sasha Cohen wins the Finlandia Trophy women's figure skating championship in Helsinki.

RECORD SETTERS

1967 – Mark Spitz improves his world record in the 100 butterfly to 55.68 seconds in a swim meet between the United States and Germany in Berlin.

TRANSITIONS

1931 – Benny Leonard, 35 and overweight, is knocked out in the sixth round by Jimmy McLarnin in New York and announces his retirement for the second time.

1935 – Hank Greenberg sits out the sixth and final game of the World Series because of Yom Kippur, but the Detroit Tigers score with two out in the ninth inning to beat the Chicago Cubs 4-3.

1938 – Columbia quarterback **Sid Luckman** announces he is turning down invitations to all postseason all-star games and will quit football to begin a career in business after graduation. Luckman will be elected to the Pro Football Hall of Fame in 1965 after a long career with the Chicago Bears.

1971 – The California Angels fire **Harold "Lefty" Phillips** after three seasons as their manager. He compiles a 222-225 record with two third-place finishes and one fourth-place finish.

A STAR IS BORN

1873 – Phil Wolf (bowling)
1907 – Ruby Goldstein (middleweight boxer)
1913 – Archie Kameros (LIU basketball)
1928 – Ira Kaplan (track and field)
1928 – Herb Rich (Vanderbilt football, Baltimore Colts, Los Angeles Rams, New York Giants defensive back)

OCTOBER 8

GAMEBREAKERS

1932 – **Sammy Fishman's** 44-yard touchdown run in the third quarter gives Dartmouth a 6-0 victory over Lafayette. **Harry Newman** returns a punt 52 yards for a touchdown and kicks a field goal in Michigan's 15-6 win over Northwestern.

1938 – **Sid Luckman** scores the winning touchdown as Columbia rallies from an 18-6 halftime deficit and upsets Army 20-8. **Marshall Goldberg** throws two touchdown passes and runs for another score as Pitt beats Duquesne 27-0. **Marty Glickman** of Syracuse scores on runs of 80, 40 and 5 yards in a 53-0 victory over Maryland.

1944 – **Melvin Bleeker** scores on a 16-yard run as the Philadelphia Eagles play the Washington Redskins to a 21-21 tie.

1949 – **Herb Rich** catches three passes for 127 yards, including touchdown receptions of 40 and 66 yards, and rushes for 55 yards as Vanderbilt beats Mississippi 28-27.

1959 – **Larry Sherry** pitches 5 2/3 innings of scoreless relief as the Dodgers beat the White Sox 5-4 in Game 6 of the World Series. He allows four hits and is named the Series MVP with two saves and two victories.

1984 – San Francisco 49ers tight end **John Frank** scores on his first NFL reception, a 1-yard pass from Joe Montana, in a 31-10 win over the New York Giants in a Monday night game.

1989 – Vikings tight end **Brent Novoselsky** catches a 2-yard touchdown pass to cap Minnesota's 24-point second quarter in a 24-17 victory over the Detroit Lions.

STRONG IN DEFEAT

1933 – Quarterback **Harry Newman** rushes for 108 yards, including an 80-yard touchdown, and becomes the first New York Giants player to run for more than 100 yards in a game. The Giants lose to the Boston Redskins 21-20.

1938 – University of Chicago quarterback **Lew Hamity** throws an 80-yard touchdown pass in a 45-7 loss to Michigan.

MAZEL TOUGH

1989 – **Bruce Fleisher**, 41-year-old head pro at a golf course in North Miami Beach, Fla., wins the PGA Club Pro Championship in La Quinta, Calif., by three strokes over Jeff Thomsen. He finishes at 7-under-par 277.

RECORD SETTERS

1881 – **Lon Myers** sets world records of 1:55.6 in the 880 and 2:13 in the 1,000-yard run.

1939 – **Max Stein** rolls 29 consecutive strikes, tying a sanctioned match-play bowling record.

1967 – **Mark Spitz** improves his world record in the 200 butterfly to 2:05.7 in a meet between the United States and Germany in Berlin.

JEWS ON FIRST

1881 – Harvard beats All-Canada of Montreal 2-0 in **Lucius Littauer's** first game as the Crimson's first-ever head football coach.

1971 – **Mickey Berkowitz,** who will become Israel's all-time leading scorer in basketball, makes his debut with Maccabi Tel Aviv in a 107-75 victory over Kiriat Haim. Berkowitz scores two points.

TRANSITIONS

1999 – **Ron Rothstein,** former coach of the NBA's Miami Heat, is named coach of the WNBA-expansion Miami Sol.

A STAR IS BORN

1883 – **Oszkar Gerde** (fencing)

1925 – **Sid Tanenbaum** (NYU basketball, New York Knicks, Baltimore Bullets)

1939 – **Tanhum Cohen-Mintz** (Israeli basketball)

OCTOBER 9

GAMEBREAKERS

1926 – **Julius Raskin** runs for a touchdown, sets up two more scores with his passing and kicks two extra points as CCNY ends St. Lawrence's 10-game winning streak with a 20-7 victory,

1927 – **Joe Alexander** returns a fumble 35 yards for a touchdown as the New York Giants beat the Pottsville Maroons 19-0 at Minersville (Pa.) Park.

1937 – **Marshall Goldberg** runs 77 yards on a reverse on Pitt's first possession to give the Panthers a 6-0 victory over Duquesne.

1937 – **Harry Danning** has three hits, including an RBI single that starts a six-run uprising in the second inning, and the New York Giants beat the Yankees 7-3 at the Polo Grounds to stay alive in the World Series.

1960 – Oakland Raiders end **Alan Goldstein** scores twice in the third quarter on a 16-yard run and an 8-yard pass – his only two career American Football League touchdowns – in a 20-19 victory over the Dallas Texans.

1973 – **Ken Holtzman** pitches a three-hitter, and Oakland beats Baltimore 2-1 when Bert Campaneris homers, leading off the bottom of the 11th in Game 3 of the American League Championship Series.

1993 – C.W. Post quarterback **Perry Klein** passes for 520 yards in a 55-14 win over Gannon.

1999 – **Vitaly Pisetsky** of Wisconsin kicks a 36-yard field goal with 2:59 remaining to tie the game, then boots a 31-yarder in overtime as the Badgers beat Minnesota 20-17.

2004 – **Shawn Green** goes 3 for 4 with a pair of solo homers as the Los Angeles Dodgers defeat the St. Louis Cardinals 4-0 for their first postseason victory since the 1988 World Series.

2005 – Astros catcher **Brad Ausmus**, who hit only three home runs during the regular season, smacks a solo shot with two out in the ninth to tie the game at 6-6, and Houston goes on to beat the Atlanta Braves 7-6 in 18 innings to win their best-of-five National League Division Series 3-1.

STRONG IN DEFEAT

1937 – **Sid Luckman** of Columbia completes 18 of 34 passes for 202 yards and returns a kickoff 82 yards for a touchdown in a 21-18 loss to Army.

MAZEL TOUGH

1976 – **Ian Scheckter** of South Africa wraps up his first of six South African Formula Atlantic auto racing series titles.

1977 – **Amy Alcott** finishes three strokes in front of five runners-up and wins the LPGA Houston Exchange Clubs Classic in Crosby, Texas.

1977 – **Jody Scheckter** wins the Formula One Grand Prix of Canada at Mosport, outracing Patrick Depailler to the finish line.

2005 – **Deena Kastor,** running her sixth marathon, scores her first victory by finishing the Chicago Marathon in 2 hours, 21 minutes, 24 seconds – five seconds faster than defending champion Constantina Tomescu-Dita of Romania.

RECORD SETTERS

1999 – **Hayden Epstein** of Michigan kicks his first college field goal, a 56-yarder that ties the school record in a 34-31 loss to Michigan State.

A STAR IS BORN

1934 – **Michael Sommer** (George Washington football, Washington Redskins, Baltimore Colts, Dallas Cowboys, Oakland Raiders back)

1949 – **Shep Messing** (soccer goalie)

1964 – **Martin Jaite** (Argentina tennis)

OCTOBER 10

GAMEBREAKERS

1925 – **Benny Friedman** of Michigan throws five touchdown passes in a 63-0 victory over Indiana. He also runs 55 yards for another touchdown and kicks eight extra points.

1937 – **Harry Newman** accounts for all of Rochester's scoring with a touchdown pass, a punt return for a touchdown, a field goal, and two extra points as the Tigers beat the Cincinnati Bengals 17-14 in the American Football League.

1937 – **Dave Smukler** throws a 10-yard touchdown pass in the Philadelphia Eagles' 14-0 victory over the Washington Redskins.

1937 – **Marty Glickman** scores on runs of 73 and 58 yards as Syracuse defeats St. Lawrence 40-0.

1977 – With **Arnie Mausser** in goal, the United States men's soccer team defeats the People's Republic of China 1-0 in Atlanta.

MAZEL TOUGH

1983 – **Gilles Elbilia** of France wins a 12-round decision over Frankie Decaestecker in Paris to win the European welterweight title.

1999 – **Bruce Fleisher** shoots 17 under par to win the PGA Senior Tour's Transamerica in Napa, Calif., by one stroke over Allen Doyle.

1999 – **Robin Levine** and her partner, Kim Russell, win the U.S. Racquetball Association doubles championship in Baltimore with a 15-12, 15-8 victory in the final.

2004 – **Jonathan Erlich** and **Andy Ram** of Israel defeat Jonas Bjorkman and Radek Stepanek 7-6 (7-2), 6-2 to win the doubles title at a Grand Prix indoor tennis tournament in Lyon, France.

JEWS ON FIRST

1874 – Racewalker **Daniel M. Stern** becomes the first American amateur to cover the mile in less than seven minutes.

1998 – **Limor Mizrachi** plays for the New England Blizzard in an ABL preseason game against the Philadelphia Rage in New Haven, Conn. She becomes the first Israeli to play in a professional basketball game in the United States.

TRANSITIONS

2002 – Indiana University President **Myles Brand** is named the fourth president in the history of the National Collegiate Athletic Association.

2003 – **Max Labovitch**, 79-year-old former New York Rangers hockey player, is pulled over and warned by police for exceeding the 30-mph limit for in-line skating in Winnipeg's Kildonan Park. Labovitch admits he didn't know how fast he was going. "I don't go as fast as I used to," he says.

A STAR IS BORN

1897 – **Young Montreal** (bantamweight boxer)

1912 – **Red Sarachek** (basketball coach)

1915 – **Harry Eisenstat** (Detroit Tigers, Brooklyn Dodgers, Cleveland Indians pitcher)

1922 – **Mervin Pregulman** (Michigan football, Green Bay Packers, Detroit Lions, New York Bulldogs center)

1923 – **Saul Rogovin** (Chicago White Sox, Detroit Tigers, Baltimore Orioles, Philadelphia Phillies pitcher)

1974 – **Oded Katash** (Israeli basketball)

1979 – **Nicolas Massu** (Chile tennis)

OCTOBER 11

GAMEBREAKERS

1936 – **Sid Gillman** catches a touchdown pass to help the Cleveland Rams defeat the Syracuse Braves 26-0.

1942 – **Leo Cantor** runs six yards for a touchdown in the New York Giants' 35-17 victory over the Philadelphia Eagles.

1947 – **Al Hoisch** rushes 11 times for 109 yards as UCLA beats Oregon 24-7.

1965 – **Sandy Koufax** pitches a four-hit, 7-0 shutout as the Dodgers take a 3-2 lead on the Minnesota Twins in the World Series.

1995 – **Ronen Harazi** scores two goals as Israel defeats Azerbaijan 2-0 in a Euro Cup soccer qualifier.

2006 – Detroit Red Wings defenseman **Mathieu Schneider** scores his second career hat trick and adds an assist in a 9-2 victory over the Phoenix Coyotes.

MAZEL TOUGH

1976 – **Harold Solomon** defeats Robert Lutz 6-3, 5-7, 7-5 in the final of the Maui WCT hard-court tennis tournament.

1981 – **Stuart Mittleman** wins the New York Road Runners Club 50-mile race through Central Park in 5 hours, 24 minutes, 28 seconds. He also wins the race in 1987 and 1993.

1987 – **Brad Gilbert** beats **Eliot Teltscher** 6-2, 6-2 in the final of a hard-court tennis tournament in Tel Aviv.

TRANSITIONS

1924 – On the day the Montreal Maroons receive their NHL franchise, **Cecil Hart** is named the team's manager.

Mathieu Schneider
(U.S. Olympic Committee)

A STAR IS BORN

1926 – **Joe Ginsberg** (Cleveland Indians, Baltimore Orioles, Chicago White Sox, New York Mets, Boston Red Sox, Kansas City A's, Detroit Tigers catcher)

1933 – **Sauveur Benamou** (Algerian lightweight boxer)

1963 – **Ronnie Rosenthal** (Israeli soccer)

OCTOBER 12

GAMEBREAKERS

1941 – **Sid Luckman** runs for a touchdown and passes for two others – including a 45-yarder to **Johnny Siegal** – as the Chicago Bears rout the Chicago Cardinals 53-7.

1947 – **Sid Luckman** of the Chicago Bears passes for 314 yards in a 40-7 victory over the Philadelphia Eagles. His three TD passes cover 74, 70 and 24 yards.

1974 – **Ken Holtzman** of Oakland is the winning pitcher in a 3-2 victory over the Dodgers in the World Series opener.

1998 – **Aaron Brand** has a goal and four assists as the St. John Maple Leafs skate to a 6-6 tie with the Saint John Flames in an American Hockey League game.

STRONG IN DEFEAT

1996 – Linebacker **Mitch Marrow** makes 12 tackles including four sacks in Penn's 20-19 loss to Columbia.

MAZEL TOUGH

1928 – **Arthur Gavrin** wins the Port Chester (N.Y.) Marathon.

1952 – **Henry Laskau** retains his AAU 20,000-meter racewalk title with a time of 1:37:43.4 in Providence, R.I.

1974 – **Paulina Peled** beats Robyn Murphy of Australia to become the first Israeli in two decades to capture the women's title at the Israeli International Tennis Championships at Ramat Gan. **Toma Ovici** of Romania wins the men's title by beating Bernard Mitton of South Africa 6-2, 6-2, 6-4.

1980 – **Amy Alcott** beats Patty Hayes and Beth Daniel by four strokes and wins the Inamori Classic in San Jose, Calif. It is the second straight year she has won four tournaments on the LPGA Tour.

1980 – **Harold Solomon** wins his fourth tennis tournament of the year, beating **Shlomo Glickstein** of Israel 6-2, 6-3 in a hard-court final in Tel Aviv.

1982 – **Mark Roth** beats Tom Milton 216-205 in the PBA Regional Champions Classic in Limerick, Pa.

1986 – **Brad Gilbert** beats **Aaron Krickstein** 7-5, 6-2 in the final of a hard-court tennis tournament in Tel Aviv.

2003 – **Jonathan Ehrlich** and **Andy Ram** of Israel defeat a French team 6-1, 6-3 to win the doubles title at the ATP Lyons Grand Prix indoor tennis tournament.

2003 – **Kenny Bernstein** beats Scott Kalitta in the Top Fuel final at the O'Reilly Fall Nationals in Ennis, Texas, for his 67th career NHRA victory.

2003 – **Charlee Minkin** wins the women's 52-kg. class at the U.S. Open Judo Championships in Las Vegas.

RECORD SETTERS

1964 – **Isaac Berger** sets world and Olympic weight lifting records in the press (270.06) and jerk (336.2), but settles for a featherweight silver medal in Tokyo.

TRANSITIONS

1912 – The first official Jewish Basketball League game in Philadelphia is played at Legion Hall.

A STAR IS BORN

1886 – **Young Otto** (lightweight boxer)

1907 – **Phil Weintraub** (New York Giants, Philadelphia Phillies, Cincinnati Reds outfielder)

1915 – **Len Maidman** (NYU basketball)

1948 – **Gilbert Cohen** (Tunisian boxer)

OCTOBER 13

GAMEBREAKERS

1928 – CCNY quarterback **Bernard Bienstock** accounts for four touchdowns and **Ed Dubinsky** returns an interception for another score as CCNY defeats St. Lawrence 38-0. **Phil Liflander** scores on a 75-yard run to help Columbia defeat Wesleyan 31-7.

1929 – **Benny Friedman** throws touchdown passes of 15 and 20 yards, and the New York Giants rally from a 9-6 halftime deficit to beat the Staten Island Stapletons 19-9. The TD passes are Friedman's first two of an NFL-record 20 that season.

1934 – **Izzy Weinstock** scores the first touchdown as Pitt defeats Southern Cal 20-6.

1946 – **Sid Luckman** throws three touchdown passes in the Chicago Bears' 28-28 tie with the Los Angeles Rams.

1951 – **Hal Seidenberg** scores three touchdowns as Cornell routs Harvard 42-6.

1962 – **Frank Lankewicz** catches a 77-yard touchdown pass as Georgia beats Clemson 24-16.

1968 – **Yehoshua Faygenbaum** scores three goals as Israel defeats Ghana 5-3 in a preliminary-round soccer match at the Olympics in Mexico City.

1973 – **Ken Holtzman** is the winning pitcher as the Oakland Athletics beat the New York Mets 2-1 in Game 1 of the World Series.

1993 – **Reuven Attar** scores 2½ minutes into injury time as Israel shocks France 3-2 in a World Cup soccer qualifier. **Ronen Harazi** and **Eyal Berkovic** also score for the Israelis. The loss sends Bulgaria to the World Cup instead of France, which had not lost in more than a year.

2000 – **Jamie Sokolsky** of the Greensboro Generals scores a hat trick in a 5-0 win over the South Carolina Stingrays in the East Coast Hockey League.

2001 – **Marc Samuel** kicks four field goals, including the game-winner from 41 yards out with 3:04 remaining, as Georgetown defeats Davidson 26-24.

2006 – **Amanda Rupp's** goal in the second overtime period gives Pepperdine a 2-1 soccer victory over the University of San Diego.

MAZEL TOUGH

1905 – Lightweight boxer **Young Otto (Arthur Susskind)** stops Tom Brady in the second round in New York to post his 17th consecutive victory by knockout. The previous 16 came in the first round.

1975 – **Brian Gottfried** defeats **Harold Solomon** 6-2, 7-6, 6-1 in the Melbourne indoor tennis tournament final.

2000 – **Dana Rosenblatt** wins a 12-round split decision over Will McIntyre to win the IBA Continental Americas super middleweight title in Ledyard, Conn.

2002 – **Stephanie Cohen-Aloro** of France defeats Sandra Kleinova 6-1, 6-1 to win a hard-court tennis tournament in Cardiff, Wales.

RECORD SETTERS

1954 – **Harry Kane** sets a British record of 51.5 seconds in the 440-yard hurdles.

A STAR IS BORN

1922 – **Cy Sussman** (table tennis)
1975 – **Noam Behr** (Israeli tennis)
1976 – **Lennie Friedman** (Duke football, Denver Broncos, Washington Redskins, Chicago Bears, Cleveland Browns guard)

OCTOBER 14

GAMEBREAKERS

1923 – **Ave Kaplan** catches a 25-yard touchdown pass and kicks a 35-yard field goal as the Minnesota Marines beat Jim Thorpe's Oorang Indians 23-0 in the NFL.

1928 – **Benny Friedman** throws three touchdown passes, runs for another touchdown, and kicks five extra points as the Detroit Wolverines beat the New York Yankees 35-12.

1933 – **Barney Mintz** returns an interception 50 yards for a touchdown as Tulane defeats Maryland 20-0. **Charley Siegel** scores two touchdowns as NYU defeats Lafayette 13-12.

1939 – **Paul Wexler** throws a touchdown pass at the end of the second quarter to give Penn a 6-0 win over Yale.

1945 – **Leo Cantor** scores on a pair of 2-yard runs as the Chicago Cardinals end a 29-game NFL losing streak with a 16-7 victory over the Chicago Bears at Wrigley Field. **Sid Luckman** throws a 64-yard TD pass for the Bears.

1965 – **Sandy Koufax** pitches a three-hitter on two days' rest as the Dodgers clinch the World Series with a 2-0 seventh-game victory over the Minnesota Twins. Koufax is named Series MVP.

1972 – **Ken Holtzman** is the winning pitcher as the Oakland A's beat the Cincinnati Reds 3-2 in the first game of the World Series.

2000 – Texas-El Paso tight end **Brian Natkin** catches seven passes for 92 yards and two touchdowns in a 47-30 victory over San Jose State.

2002 – **Joel Shanker** scores a hat trick as the Philadelphia Kixx defeat the Cleveland Force 13-5 in a Major Indoor Soccer League match.

MAZEL TOUGH

1916 – **Battling Levinsky (Barney Lebrowitz)** wins a 12-round decision over Jack Dillon in Boston to claim the world light heavyweight championship.

1921 – **Ted "Kid" Lewis** stops Johnny Basham in the 12th round in London to win the European middleweight title and retain his British welterweight title.

1964 – **Irena Kirszenstein-Szewinska** wins the silver medal in the long jump at the Olympics in Tokyo.

1968 – **Irena Kirszenstein-Szewinska** of Poland ties her world record of 11.1 in the 100 meters in Mexico City.

1979 – **Amy Alcott** wins the LPGA United Virginia Bank Classic in Portsmouth, Va., by one stroke over runner-up Susie McAllister.

1979 – **Tom Okker** beats Per Hjertquist of Sweden 6-4, 6-3 in the final of a hard-court tennis tournament in Tel Aviv.

1980 – **Mark Roth** wins the Brunswick PBA Regional Champions Classic in Rochester, NY, with a 217-210 victory over Eddie Ressler in the final.

A STAR IS BORN

1941 – **Art Shamsky** (Cincinnati Reds, New York Mets, Chicago Cubs, Oakland A's outfielder)

1962 – **Shahar Perkiss** (Israeli tennis)

Ken Holtzman *(Chicago Cubs)*

OCTOBER 15

GAMEBREAKERS

1890 – The first time he touches the ball in a varsity game, **Phil King** runs 25 yards for a touchdown for Princeton. King scores twice as the Tigers beats Penn 18-0.

1922 – **Arnold Horween** scores two touchdowns as the Chicago Cardinals beat the Green Bay Packers 16-3 at Comiskey Park.

1927 – Future major-league infielder **Jonah Goldman** scores two touchdowns as Syracuse upsets Georgetown 19-6.

1930 – Marchy Schwartz scores four touchdowns to lead Notre Dame to a 35-19 victory over Pittsburgh.

1932 – **Izzy Weinstock** scores the winning touchdown in the third quarter as Pitt beats Army 18-13. **Harry Newman** throws two touchdown passes in Michigan's 14-0 victory over Ohio State.

1933 – **Buckets Goldenberg** scores on a 3-yard run and a 65-yard interception return as the Green Bay Packers beat Pittsburgh 47-0.

1949 – **Herb Rich's** 2-yard touchdown run erases a one-point deficit and gives Vanderbilt a 22-17 victory over Florida.

1955 – Making his first start, backup quarterback **Pete Neft** throws a touchdown pass and directs two other scoring drives as Pitt beats Nebraska 21-7.

MAZEL TOUGH

1964 – **Ildiko Rejto** of Hungary defeats Helga Mees of Germany 4-0 to win the Olympic gold medal in women's individual foil after a three-way fence-off for first place in Tokyo.

1968 – **Irena Kirszenstein-Szewinska** of Poland wins a bronze medal in the 100 at the Olympics in Mexico City.

1982 – **Riccardo Patrese** of Italy wins the Formula Open South African Grand Prix.

1988 – **Andrew Sznajder** of Canada defeats Doug Burke 6-1, 6-1 in the final of an indoor tennis tournament in Las Vegas.

1996 – **Marshall Holman** wins his first PBA title in eight years by beating Wayne Webb 246-235 in the final of the Ebonite Classic in Troy, Mich. It is his 22nd career title.

2000 – **Romans Vainsteins** becomes the first cyclist from Latvia to win the world pro road race championship in Plouay, France. He wins the 268.9-km in 6 hours, 15 minutes, 28 seconds and edges Zbigniew Spruch of Poland in a sprint to the finish.

2006 – **Paul Goldstein** defeats Rajeev Ram 7-6 (5), 4-6, 7-5 to win the USTA Swanston Challenge tennis tournament in Sacramento, Calif., then teams with Jeff Morrison to win the doubles title.

TRANSITIONS

1932 – New York Giants quarterback **Benny Friedman**, writing in Collier's magazine, accuses Chicago Bears lineman Bill Fleckenstein of being a "thug." Fleckenstein sues Friedman for libel and wins. The jury awards him six cents.

2001 – Hungarian gymnast **Agnes Keleti** is inducted into the International Women's Sports Hall of Fame.

A STAR IS BORN

1901 – **Louis "Kid" Kaplan** (featherweight boxer)

1909 – **Sam Balter** (UCLA basketball, broadcasting)

1921 – **Angelica Rozeanu** (Romanian table tennis)

OCTOBER 16

GAMEBREAKERS

1937 – **Sid White** of Brooklyn College scores six touchdowns and an extra point in a 50-0 win over Wagner College. Syracuse sophomore **Marty Glickman** scores two touchdowns – one on a 55-yard punt return – in a 14-6 upset victory over Cornell. **Sid Luckman** throws TD passes of 58 and 20 yards and runs for a third touchdown as Columbia beats Penn 26-6.

1930 – **Benny Friedman** runs for two touchdowns as the New York Giants beat the Chicago Cardinals 25-12.

1974 – Oakland Athletics pitcher **Ken Holtzman**, batting for the first time all season, hits a home run in the third inning en route to a 5-2 win over the Los Angeles Dodgers in Game 4 of the World Series. Oakland takes a 3-1 lead in the Series.

1988 – Chicago Blackhawks goalie **Mike Veisor** makes 34 saves as he shuts out the Buffalo Sabres 2-0.

1993 – **Tamir Linhart** of George Mason scores a hat trick in a soccer victory over William & Mary.

2000 – **Greg Gardner** makes 21 saves for his first of 12 shutouts during the hockey season as Niagara defeats Boston University 2-0.

MAZEL TOUGH

1964 – **Mark Midler** wins an Olympic fencing gold medal when the Soviet Union beats Poland 9-7 in the team foil final in Tokyo.

1968 – **Garry Garber** wins an eight-round decision over Virgilio Brown to win the North American bantamweight title in Roanoke, Va.

1983 – **Aaron Krickstein** beats Christoph Zipf 7-6, 6-3 to win a hard-court tennis tournament in Tel Aviv. At 16 years, 2 months, 14 days, he is the youngest American to win an ATP men's singles title.

1988 – **Brad Gilbert** beats **Aaron Krickstein** 4-6, 7-6, 6-2 in the final of a hard-court tennis tournament in Tel Aviv.

2005 – **Aleksandra Wozniak** of Canada defeats Olga Blahotova of the Czech Republic 6-4, 4-6, 7-6 (1) in the finals of a USTA Challenger tennis tournament in Mexico.

RECORD SETTERS

1966 – **Karl Sweetan** of the Detroit Lions ties an NFL record with a 99-yard touchdown pass to Pat Studstill in a 45-14 loss to the Baltimore Colts. The TD pass is the first of 17 in the NFL for the rookie quarterback.

TRANSITIONS

1952 – **Harry Litwack** is named basketball coach at Temple. He will retire after the 1973 season with a 373-193 record.

1960 – **Abe Saperstein** is elected commissioner of the new eight-team American Basketball League. The league will fold at the end of 1962.

2001 – **Jeff Agoos** of the San Jose Earthquakes is named Major Soccer League's Defensive Player of the Year.

A STAR IS BORN

1899 – **Sam Rothschild** (Montreal Maroons hockey)

1925 – **Armand Mouyal** (fencing)

1948 – **Bruce Fleisher** (golf)

1975 – **Jamila Wideman** (Stanford women's basketball)

OCTOBER 17

GAMEBREAKERS

1925 – In a 21-0 victory over Wisconsin, **Benny Friedman** of Michigan throws a touchdown pass on the first play of the game, returns a kickoff 85 yards, throws another touchdown pass, and kicks all three extra points.

1931 – **Nat Grossman** runs for a touchdown and passes for another as NYU defeats Rutgers 27-7. Nat's brother, **Jack Grossman**, scores for Rutgers on a fourth-and-four run late in the fourth quarter.

1943 – **Sid Luckman** throws three touchdown passes as the Chicago Bears beat the Philadelphia-Pittsburgh Steagles 48-21.

1964 – **Larry Brown** leads the United States with 14 points in an 86-53 win over Brazil in the Olympic basketball tournament.

1998 – **Amos Magee** assists on both goals and is named the game's MVP as the Minnesota Thunder beat the Rochester Raging Rhinos 2-1 in the A-League soccer championship game.

1999 – **Jay Fiedler** replaces injured Jacksonville starting quarterback Mark Brunell and rallies the Jaguars to 17 points in the final 1½ quarters for a 24-7 win over the Cleveland Browns. Fiedler completes 12 of 14 passes for 113 yards, including a 7-yarder to tight end Kyle Brady for his first of 69 career TD passes. He also rushes three times for 27 yards.

1999 – Tight end **Scott Slutzker** catches a 10-yard pass for his only NFL touchdown as the New Orleans Saints defeat the Tennessee Oilers 24-21. Slutzker catches four passes for 63 yards.

STRONG IN DEFEAT

1959 – For the second straight year, **Alan Goldstein** returns an interception for a touchdown against Maryland, going 40 yards in the Tar Heels' 14-7 loss to the Terrapins.

1986 – **Mike Hartman** scores his first of 43 career NHL goals to give Buffalo a 3-1 lead in the second period, but the Pittsburgh Penguins rally to defeat the Sabres 7-3.

MAZEL TOUGH

1989 – **Najib Daho** of Morocco wins a 12-round decision over John Kalbhenn in Oldham, England, to retain his British Empire lightweight title.

1996 – **Michelle Feldman** beats Lisa Wagner 245-195 in the Columbia 300 Delaware Open in Wilmington for her first title on the women's pro bowling tour.

RECORD SETTERS

1964 – **Marilyn Ramenofsky** of the United States sets an Olympic record of 4:47.7 in the 400-meter freestyle swimming heats in Tokyo. She earns the silver medal a day later.

1968 – **Mark Spitz** swims the third leg of a world-record setting 4×100 freestyle relay team that wins an Olympic gold medal in 3:31.7 in Mexico City. **Semyon Belits-Geiman** of the Soviet Union wins a bronze in the same event.

1992 – **Jay Fiedler** of Dartmouth passes for a school-record 419 yards and four touchdowns, completing 20 of 31 passes, in a 39-27 victory over Yale.

TRANSITIONS

1920 – With the Sacramento Senators holding a big lead in the eighth inning of the final Pacific Coast League game of the season, Los Angeles Angels manager Red Killifer inserts former batboy **Jimmie Reese** into the game at second base. The 14-year-old Reese handles his one fielding chance flawlessly.

A STAR IS BORN

1906 – **Hans Haas** (Austrian weight lifting)
1920 – **Arthur Spector** (Villanova basketball, Boston Celtics)
1921 – **Maria Gorokhovskaya** (Soviet Union gymnastics)
1958 – **James Espir** (British runner)

OCTOBER 18

GAMEBREAKERS

1924 – **David Rosenfeld** runs for touchdowns of 65 and 55 yards as Alabama beats Sewanee 14-0. **Al "Truck" Miller's** 60-yard touchdown run in the third quarter gives Harvard a 12-6 victory over Holy Cross.

1930 – **Jack Grossman** scores four touchdowns – one on a 60-yard run – in Rutgers' 33-0 win over Johns Hopkins.

1931 – **David Mishel** throws a 2-yard touchdown pass as the Cleveland Indians beat the Providence Steam Rollers 13-6 in the NFL.

1937 – **Sid Luckman** throws touchdown passes of 55 and 20 yards, runs one yard for another TD and sets up the final TD with a 15-yard punt return as Columbia beats Penn 26-6.

1941 – **Mervin Pregulman** returns an interception 65 yards for a touchdown as Michigan defeats Northwestern 14-7.

1958 – **Alan Goldstein** of North Carolina returns an interception 46 yards for a touchdown in a 27-0 victory over Maryland.

1986 – Penn tight end **Brent Novoselsky** catches three touchdown passes in a 30-26 win over Navy.

1997 – **Adam Abrams** kicks a 42-yard field goal to tie the game in the third quarter, then boots a 37-yarder with 1:05 remaining in the game to give Southern Cal a 20-17 win over Notre Dame, the Trojans' first victory in South Bend since 1981.

MAZEL TOUGH

1953 – **Henry Laskau** wins the national AAU 15,000-meter racewalking title with a time of 1:15.9 in Brooklyn, N.Y.

1983 – **Mark Roth** beats Ted Hannahs 212-189 in the PBA Northern Ohio Open in Rocky River, Ohio.

2001 – Top qualifier **Michelle Feldman** beats Tammy Turner 206-191 to win the PWBA Three Rivers Open bowling tournament in Pittsburgh.

RECORD SETTERS

1968 – **Walter Blum** rides six straight winners at Garden State Park, tying the New Jersey record set in 1965 by Jorge Velasquez.

1968 – **Irena Kirszenstein-Szewinska** of Poland breaks her world record in the 200 meters, running the distance in 22.5 seconds to win the Olympic gold medal in Mexico City.

A STAR IS BORN

1896 – **Nat Holman** (basketball, CCNY coach)

1909 – **Sammy Farber** (bantamweight boxer)

1911 – **Victor Young Perez** (Tunisian flyweight boxer)

1927 – **Marv Rotblatt** (Chicago White Sox pitcher)

OCTOBER 19

GAMEBREAKERS

1908 – Midfielder **Harold Bohr** scores two goals as Denmark beats the French B team in the first round of the Olympic soccer tournament in London.

1930 – **Benny Friedman** throws five touchdown passes – all between 20 and 60 yards – as the New York Giants beat the Frankford Yellow Jackets 53-0.

1935 – **Al Hessberg** scores on a 12-yard run as Yale beats Navy 7-6.

1940 – **Mort Landsberg's** 53-yard touchdown run highlights Cornell's 33-6 win over Syracuse.

1947 – **Sid Luckman** of the Chicago Bears passes for 342 yards and three touchdowns in a 33-24 victory over the Detroit Lions.

1957 – In a college football game attended by Queen Elizabeth and Prince Philip of England, **Phil Perlo** returns an interception 50 yards for a touchdown as Maryland upsets North Carolina 21-7.

1963 – Cornell quarterback **Gary Wood** runs 80 yards for a touchdown in a 13-10 win over Yale.

MAZEL TOUGH

1908 – **Young Joseph Aschel** wins a 15-round decision over Lt. Corporal Baker in London to win the British welterweight title.

1923 – **Abe Goldstein** wins a 12-round decision over **Joe Burman** to win the New York State Athletic Commission bantamweight title at Madison Square Garden.

1961 – Jockey **Walter Blum** rides six winners at Garden State Park in New Jersey.

1964 – **Grigori Kriss** of the Soviet Union wins the Olympic fencing gold medal in individual epee, beating Henryk Hoskyns of Great Britain in a fence-off for first place. **Irena Kirszenstein-Szewinska** of Poland wins a silver medal in the 200 meters.

1968 – **Mark Spitz** wins a bronze medal in the 100-meter freestyle at the Mexico City Olympics.

JEWS ON FIRST

1999 – **Jeff Halpern** of the Washington Capitals scores his first NHL goal in the third period of a 7-1 loss to the Anaheim Mighty Ducks.

A STAR IS BORN

1915 – **Sam Nahem** (St. Louis Cardinals, Brooklyn Dodgers, Philadelphia Phillies pitcher)

1958 – **Mark Laskin** (Canadian equestrian)

OCTOBER 20

GAMEBREAKERS

1928 – **Robert Halpern** blocks two kicks, both of which set up CCNY touchdowns in a 26-6 victory over Drexel.

1929 – **Benny Friedman** throws touchdown passes of 18, 43, and 25 yards in the second quarter as the New York Giants beat the Frankford Yellow Jackets 32-0.

1934 – **Nathan Machlowitz** scores on runs of 44 and 40 yards as NYU defeats Lafayette 12-7.

1940 – **Maurice Patt** catches a 38-yard touchdown pass as the Cleveland Rams defeat the Chicago Cardinals 26-14. **Solly Sherman** tosses a 15-yard touchdown pass to lead the Chicago Bears to a 16-7 victory over the Brooklyn Dodgers.

MAZEL TOUGH

1930 – **Al Foreman** of Canada knocks out George Rose in the sixth round in Manchester, England, to retain his British and British Empire lightweight titles.

1968 – **Boris Gurevitsch** of the Soviet Union wins an Olympic gold medal in middleweight freestyle wrestling in Mexico City.

1985 – **Brad Gilbert** beats **Amos Mansdorf** of Israel 6-3, 6-2 in the final in a hard-court tennis tournament in Tel Aviv.

RECORD SETTERS

1946 – **Grigori Novak** of the Soviet Union sets a light heavyweight world record of 286 pounds in the two-handed snatch at the World Weightlifting Championships in Paris. The world record is his seventh of the year.

JEWS ON FIRST

1998 – **Mathieu Schneider** scores his first goal for the New York Rangers, getting the game-winner in a 3-2 victory over the Edmonton Oilers on a third-period power play.

2001 – **Joel Shanker** of the Philadelphia Kixx scores the first goal of the new Major Indoor Soccer League at 4:20 of the first quarter against the Milwaukee Wave.

TRANSITIONS

1924 – **Sam Rothschild** signs with the Montreal Maroons, becoming the first Jewish player under contract in the National Hockey League.

1934 – Light-hitting catcher **Moe Berg** joins a group of major-league all-stars who leave on an exhibition tour to Hawaii, the Philippines, China, and Japan. Berg later claims that while in Japan, he secretly takes photos of the Tokyo skyline that become useful to the United States in World War II.

1935 – Detroit Tigers first baseman **Hank Greenberg** wins the American League MVP award over runner-up Wes Ferrell.

A STAR IS BORN

1965 – **Amos Mansdorf** (Israeli tennis)
1983 – **Yulia Beygelzimer** (Ukrainian tennis)

OCTOBER 21

GAMEBREAKERS

1973 – **Ken Holtzman** pitches just five innings but earns the victory as the Oakland Athletics beat the New York Mets 5-2 in Game 7 of the World Series.

STRONG IN DEFEAT

1995 – Iowa tight end **Scott Slutzker** catches eight passes for 167 yards in a 41-27 loss to Penn State.

2005 – **Sage Rosenfels** of the Miami Dolphins throws just one pass – a 71-yard touchdown strike to Chris Chambers – in a 30-20 loss to the Kansas City Chiefs.

MAZEL TOUGH

1929 – **Ruby Goldstein** knocks out Joe Reno in the third round at Madison Square Garden, where 20,000 fans contribute $100,000 to the Palestine Relief Fund. In other bouts decided by 10-round decisions, **Maxie Rosenbloom** beats Joe Sekyra, **Al Singer** defeats Dave Abad, **Jackie "Kid" Berg** beats Bruce Flowers, and **Yale Okun** bests Matt Adgie.

1964 – **James Bregman** of Arlington, Va., wins a bronze medal in the middleweight division of judo, a new Olympic sport at the Tokyo Games. **Tamas Gabor** earns a gold medal when Hungary beats Italy 8-3 in the team epee fencing final. **Yves Dreyfus** earns a bronze medal when France beats Japan 9-4 for third place. **Valentin Mankin** of the Soviet Union wins gold in yachting's Finn class.

1968 – **Mark Spitz** and the U.S. 800-meter freestyle relay team win an Olympic gold medal in Mexico City. Spitz also earns a silver in the 100 butterfly.

Semyon Belits-Geiman of the Soviet Union wins a bronze in the 800 freestyle relay.

1973 – **Tom Okker** beats Jaime Fillol of Chile 4-6, 6-3, 6-3, 7-5 to win the Trofeo Melia International tennis tournament in Madrid.

1979 – **Brian Gottfried** beats Johan Kriek 7-5, 6-1, 4-6, 6-3 in the final of an indoor tennis tournament in Basel, Switzerland.

RECORD SETTERS

1880 – **Lon Myers** sets a world record of 39.5 seconds in the 350-yard run at the Elizabeth AC track meet in New Jersey.

1964 – **Gerald Ashworth** of Dartmouth runs the second leg of the United States' 4×100 relay team's world-record time of 39.0 seconds en route to the gold medal at the Tokyo Olympics. **Irena Kirszenstein-Szewinska** runs the second leg of Poland's gold-medal 400-meter relay team, which sets a world and Olympic record of 43.6 seconds.

TRANSITIONS

1917 – **Nat Holman** is appointed instructor of hygiene and freshman basketball coach at CCNY, where he will continue to coach basketball until 1960.

A STAR IS BORN

1900 – **Eddie "Kid" Wagner** (lightweight boxer)

1921 – **Red Klotz** (Villanova basketball, Baltimore Bullets)

OCTOBER 22

GAMEBREAKERS

1932 – **Richard Fishel** and **Seymour Stark** score touchdowns for Syracuse, which defeats Penn State 12-6 when the game ends with the Nittany Lions inside the Orangemen's the 1-yard line.

1944 – **Melvin Bleeker** scores touchdowns on an 18-yard run and 75-yard pass reception as the Philadelphia Eagles beat the Boston Yankees 38-0.

1967 – **Karl Sweetan** throws touchdown passes of 25 and 10 yards in the fourth quarter as the Detroit Lions beat the Atlanta Falcons 24-3.

1980 – **Mike Veisor** posts his first NHL shutout in goal as the Hartford Whalers beat the Colorado Rockies 3-0.

1983 – Ohio State tight end **John Frank** catches five passes for 115 yards and a touchdown in a 21-11 win over Michigan State.

2002 – **Scott Schoeneweis** allows one hit in two innings of relief with two strikeouts, including the final batter in the ninth inning as the Anaheim Angels beat the San Francisco Giants 10-4 in Game 3 of the World Series.

MAZEL TOUGH

1927 – **Pinky Silverberg** is declared the winner when Ruby "Dark Cloud" Bradley is disqualified for a low blow in the seventh round of the NBA flyweight title fight in Bridgeport, Conn. A few days later, Silverberg is stripped of the title – one of three disputed versions.

1930 – **Maxie Rosenbloom** knocks out **Abie Bain** in the 11th round to retain his world lightweight championship in New York.

1968 – **Grigori Kriss** of the Soviet Union wins an Olympic fencing bronze medal in individual epee at Mexico City.

1978 – **Tom Okker** defeats Peter Feigl 6-7, 6-4, 6-2 in the final of a hard-court Challenger tennis tournament in Tel Aviv.

1989 – **Aaron Krickstein** beats Stefan Edberg 2-6, 7-6, 7-6 in the semifinals, then defeats Carl-Uwe Steeb 6-2, 6-2 in the final on the same day to win the Tokyo Indoor Tennis Tournament.

RECORD SETTERS

1881 – **Lon Myers** sets world records of 35 seconds at 330 yards and 43.75 seconds in the 400 in New York.

JEWS ON FIRST

1939 – **Leo Disend** and **Ed Merlin** of the Brooklyn Dodgers and **Dave Smukler** of the Philadelphia Eagles participate in the first televised pro football game. The Dodgers win 23-14 at Ebbets Field in Brooklyn.

1939 – **Sid Luckman** throws a 68-yard touchdown pass – his first of 137 in his NFL career – in the Chicago Bears' 16-13 loss to the New York Giants.

TRANSITIONS

1898 – The Bar Kochba athletic club, one of the first national Jewish sports organizations in central Europe, is created in Berlin.

A STAR IS BORN

1896 – **Sammy Bohne** (St. Louis Cardinals, Cincinnati Reds, Brooklyn Dodgers infielder)

1906 – **Armand Emanuel** (middleweight, light heavyweight boxer)

OCTOBER 23

GAMEBREAKERS

1921 – **Leonard Sachs** catches a touchdown pass and **Ralph Horween** kicks a field goal as the Chicago Cardinals beat the Columbus Panhandlers 17-6 in an American Professional Football Association game in Chicago.

1937 – **Marshall Goldberg** scores twice, including a 63-yard run, as Pitt defeats Wisconsin 21-0. **Sid White** runs for two touchdowns and throws a 10-yard TD pass as Brooklyn College defeats Lowell Textile 19-0.

1948 – **Herb Rich** rushes for 131 yards as Vanderbilt defeats Yale 35-0.

1971 – **Gary Wichard** passes for 289 yards and runs for two touchdowns as C.W. Post defeats Maine 42-21.

1976 – **Pete Woods** throws a 98-yard touchdown pass to Joe Stewart – the longest in Missouri history – as the Tigers beat Nebraska 34-24.

1978 – Pittsburgh Steelers tight end **Randy Grossman** has nine catches for 116 yards – both career highs – in a 27-10 Monday night victory over the Houston Oilers.

1999 – **Vitaly Pisetsky** of Wisconsin kicks four field goals in a 40-14 rout of Michigan State.

STRONG IN DEFEAT

1966 – **Karl Sweetan** throws touchdown passes of 73 and three yards within a span of 51 seconds to give Detroit the lead, but the San Francisco 49ers rally and score with three seconds left to beat the Lions 27-24. Sweetan completes 19 of 34 passes for 227 yards in his first start in place of injured Milt Plum.

MAZEL TOUGH

1926 – Brown's 11 starters – including guard **Lou Farber**, halfback **Dave Mishel**, and fullback **Albert Cornsweet** – play the entire game in a 7-0 victory over Yale.

1964 – **Larry Brown** scores six points as the United States defeats the Soviet Union 73-59 to win the basketball gold medal at the Olympics in Tokyo. Brown averages 4.1 points per game in the nine-game event. **Arpad Orban** of Hungary wins a men's soccer gold medal, **Mark Rakita** of the Soviet Union claims a fencing gold medal in team saber, and **Nelly Abramova** of the Soviet Union earns a silver medal in women's volleyball.

1979 – **Mark Roth** beats Joe Berardi 226-200 to win the Kessler Classic in Greenwood, Ind. Roth becomes the first pro bowler to win $100,000 in three separate years.

1983 – **Eliot Teltscher** beats Andres Gomez 7-5, 3-6, 6-1 in the final of the Japan Open hard-court tournament in Tokyo, and **Brian Gottfried** wins his third championship in Vienna by beating Mel Purcell 6-2, 6-3, 7-5. Gottfried's victory is his 16th and last on the men's tennis tour.

TRANSITIONS

1967 – The expansion Philadelphia Flyers purchase the contract of **Larry Zeidel** from the Cleveland Barons of the American Hockey League. Zeidel returns to the NHL for the first time since playing for the Chicago Black Hawks in 1953-54.

2000 – One hundred years after setting the world long jump record and winning the Olympic triple jump gold medal, **Meyer Prinstein** is elected to the National Track and Field Hall of Fame in Indianapolis.

A STAR IS BORN

1894 – **Al McCoy** (middleweight boxer)
1902 – **Izzy Schwartz** (flyweight boxer)
1924 – **Claude Netter** (French fencer)
1930 – **Abe Segal** (South African tennis)

OCTOBER 24

GAMEBREAKERS

1925 – **Benny Friedman** kicks a 15-yard field goal near the end of the second quarter as Michigan beats Red Grange's Illinois team 3-0 before 67,000 fans.

1934 – **David Smukler** runs 26 yards for a touchdown and kicks a 22-yard field goal as Temple beats Villanova 22-0.

1936 – **Marshall Goldberg** of Pitt rushes 22 times for 117 yards and a touchdown and passes for another touchdown in a 26-0 win over Notre Dame.

1937 – **Biff Schneidman** catches a 12-yard touchdown pass as the Green Bay Packers defeat the Cleveland Rams 35-7.

1990 – **Mike Kelfer** scores 5:36 into overtime as the Kansas City Blades win their first game in franchise history, beating the Salt Lake Golden Eagles in an International Hockey League game.

2004 – **Jay Fiedler** throws touchdown passes of 42 and 71 yards as the Miami Dolphins, winless in their first six games, defeat the St. Louis Rams 31-14. Fiedler completes 13 of 17 passes for 203 yards.

STRONG IN DEFEAT

1967 – **Steve Chubin** of the Anaheim Amigos scores 42 points in the franchise's third game in the fledgling American Basketball Association, a 128-127 loss to the Kentucky Colonels who are playing their first home game in Louisville.

MAZEL TOUGH

1908 – **Harold Bohr** and **Charles Buchwald** earn silver medals when Denmark loses to Britain 2-0 in the Olympics soccer final.

1910 – **Abe Attell** wins a 10-round decision over Johnny Kilbane in Kansas City to retain his world featherweight title.

1916 – **Battling Levinsky** wins a 12-round decision over champion Jack Dillon in Boston in his third try and begins a four-year reign as light heavyweight champion.

1982 – **Brian Gottfried** beats Bill Scanlon 6-1, 6-4, 6-0 in the final of an indoor tournament in Vienna.

1999 – **Bruce Fleisher** wins the Kaanapali Classic in Maui by one stroke over Allen Doyle. His seventh victory of the season wraps up the leading money-winner title in his first year on the PGA Senior Tour.

RECORD SETTERS

1936 – **Barney Marcus** of Bates returns an interception a school-record 102 yards in a 21-19 loss to Maine.

1975 – **Wendy Weinberg** shaves nearly 10 seconds off the Pan American Games record in winning the 800 freestyle gold medal in 9:05.47 in Mexico City.

1992 – Dartmouth linebacker **Josh Bloom** makes a school-record 26 tackles in a 26-16 loss to Cornell.

TRANSITIONS

1938 – After leading Columbia to upset victories over Yale and Army, **Sid Luckman** becomes just the second athlete to appear on the cover of Life magazine. Football player Chuck Williams appeared on the cover one year earlier.

1955 – **Benny Leonard** and **Barney Ross** are inducted into the Boxing Hall of Fame.

1963 – **Sandy Koufax** is unanimously named the winner of the major-league Cy Young Award.

A STAR IS BORN

1893 – **Ted "Kid" Lewis** (British welterweight boxer)

1894 – **Phil Bloom** (lightweight boxer)

1917 – **Marshall Goldberg** (Pitt football, Chicago Cardinals)

1924 – **Harold Green** (middleweight boxer)

1974 – **Michael Kalganov** (kayaking)

OCTOBER 25

GAMEBREAKERS

1924 – In his first game as a starter at Michigan, **Benny Friedman** throws a 62-yard TD pass from his right halfback position and runs 26 yards for another touchdown as the Wolverines beat Wisconsin 21-0.

1930 – **Marchy Schwartz** scores four touchdowns as Notre Dame beats Pitt 35-19. **Jack Grossman** scores twice in Rutgers' 40-0 win over Delaware. Sophomore **Harry Newman** throws two touchdown passes in his first start as Michigan beats Illinois 15-7.

1936 – **Walt Singer** returns a fumble three yards for a touchdown to help the New York Giants defeat the Philadelphia Eagles 21-17. **Dave Smukler** throws two touchdown passes and kicks a 37-yard field goal for Philadelphia.

1941 – **Sid Luckman** throws touchdown passes of 37 and 56 yards as the Chicago Bears beat the Pittsburgh Steelers 34-7.

1975 – **Dave Jacobs** of Syracuse kicks a 58-yard field goal in a 22-14 win over Boston College.

STRONG IN DEFEAT

1942 – **Leo Cantor's** 1-yard touchdown run gives New York the lead, but the Brooklyn Dodgers rally for a 17-7 victory over the Giants.

MAZEL TOUGH

1953 – **Henry Laskau** wins the AAU 10-kilometer racewalking title in Buffalo, N.Y.

1960 – **Alphonse Halimi** beats Freddie Gilroy in a 15-round decision in London to win the European Boxing Union bantamweight title.

1968 – **Yosef Vitebsky** and **Grigori Kriss** of the Soviet Union win Olympic silver medals in fencing in team epee in Mexico City.

1992 – **Riccardo Patrese** of Italy earns his last of six Formula One racing victories, easily beating Gerhard Berger to the finish in the Grand Prix of Japan.

1992 – **Jim Grabb** beats Jamie Morgan 6-3, 6-3 in the final of an indoor tennis tournament in Taipei, Taiwan.

2003 – **Sasha Cohen** wins Skate America, her third career Grand Prix figure skating title, in Reading, Pa.

A STAR IS BORN

1895 – **Manny Littauer** (Columbia football)

1904 – **Andy Cohen** (New York Giants baseball second baseman, Alabama football)

1973 – **Darin Shapiro** (wakeboarding)

OCTOBER 26

GAMEBREAKERS

1913 – **Vilmos Kertesz** scores two goals to lead Hungary to a 4-3 victory over Austria in international soccer.

1929 – **Bernard Bienstock** scores three times and **Morris Goldhammer** adds two touchdowns as CCNY defeats George Washington 45-0.

1930 – **Benny Friedman** throws three touchdown passes as the New York Giants beat the Providence Steam Rollers 25-0.

1935 – **Nathan Machlowitz** returns a punt 46 yards for a touchdown as NYU defeats Georgetown 7-6.

1938 – **Dave Smukler** throws a 5-yard touchdown pass in the second quarter to give the Philadelphia Eagles a 7-0 victory over the Chicago Cardinals.

1947 – **Sid Luckman** throws three touchdown passes in the Chicago Bears' 56-20 win over the Washington Redskins.

1967 – **Art Heyman** scores 30 points as the New Jersey Americans beat the Kentucky Colonels 134-131 in the American Basketball Association.

1979 – Goalie **Arnie Mausser** posts the shutout as the United States men's soccer team defeats Hungary 2-0 in Budapest.

1985 – Temple quarterback **Lee Saltz** completes 11 of 21 passes for 281 yards and two touchdowns, including a 75-yarder to Willie Marshall, in the Owls' 29-14 loss to Syracuse.

1996 – **Eyal Berkovic** of Israel scores two goals to help Southampton beat Manchester United 6-3 in English Premier League soccer.

2002 – **Lane Schwarzberg's** third field goal of the day, a 39-yarder with one second remaining, gives Colgate a 9-7 victory over Towson.

STRONG IN DEFEAT

1929 – **Arthur Davidowitz** of Lehigh returns a punt 65 yards for a touchdown in a 10-7 loss to Penn.

2002 – **Jared Siegel** kicks four field goals and three extra points in Oregon's 44-33 loss to Southern Cal.

MAZEL TOUGH

1908 – **Bert Solomon** and **John "Barney" Solomon** of Ireland win silver medals as Great Britain finishes second in the London Olympics rugby competition. Bert Solomon scores all three points for Britain in a 32-3 loss to Australia in the finals.

1915 – **Ted "Kid" Lewis** wins a 12-round decision over Joe Mandot in Boston to retain his world welterweight title.

1931 – **Victor "Young" Perez** of Tunisia wins the International Boxing Union version of the world flyweight title by knocking out champion Frankie Genaro in the second round in Paris.

1980 – **Brian Gottfried** beats Trey Waltke 6-2, 6-4, 6-3 in the final of an indoor tennis tournament in Vienna.

1986 – **Brad Gilbert** beats Karel Novacek 3-6, 6-3, 7-6, 6-0 in the final of a hard-court tennis tournament in Vienna.

2002 – **Sebastian Rothmann** knocks out Anthony Bigeni in the fifth round to win the vacant IBO cruiserweight title in Brakpan, South Africa.

TRANSITIONS

1940 – Detroit Tigers outfielder **Hank Greenberg** outpolls Bob Feller to win his second American League MVP award. He won in 1935 as a first baseman.

A STAR IS BORN

1899 – **Lilli Henoch** (German track and field)

1911 – **Sid Gillman** (Ohio State football, AFL coach)

1984 – **Sasha Cohen** (figure skating)

OCTOBER 27

GAMEBREAKERS

1928 – **Sam Behr** throws a touchdown pass as Wisconsin beats Michigan 7-0, the Badgers' first victory over the Wolverines in 29 years. **Albert Cornsweet** runs 72 yards for a touchdown with five minutes remaining to give Brown a 19-13 win over Tufts. **Phil Liflander** catches two touchdown passes as Columbia beats Williams 20-6.

1962 – **Gary Wood** passes for 212 yards as Cornell beats Princeton 35-34.

STRONG IN DEFEAT

1962 – **Mike Basset** throws an 82-yard touchdown pass, but Harvard loses to Dartmouth 24-6.

MAZEL TOUGH

1918 – **Charles Pores** wins the 10-mile run at the AAU Track and Field Championships in 54 minutes, 17.6 seconds. He also wins the 5-mile run in 24:36.8. **David Politzer** finishes first in the long jump.

1981 – **Mark Roth** beats Gil Sliker 200-192 in the final of the PBA Lansing Open in Michigan. Roth rolls a "Dutch 200," alternating strikes and spares in the final.

1995 – **Dana Rosenblatt** wins a 12-round decision over Floyd Williams to retain his WBC Continental Americas middleweight title.

2001 – **Galit Chait** and **Sergei Sakhnovsky** of Israel win the ice dancing silver medal at SkateAmerica in Colorado Springs.

A STAR IS BORN

1903 – **Leo Lomski** (light-heavyweight boxer)
1904 – **Erno Schwarcz** (Hungarian soccer)
1912 – **Abe Feldman** (heavyweight boxer)
1946 – **Kathy Harter** (tennis)

Mark Roth
(Professional Bowlers Association)

OCTOBER 28

GAMEBREAKERS

1923 – **Jozsef Eisenhoffer** scores both goals in Hungary's 2-1 soccer victory over Sweden.

1933 – **Sid Gilman** runs 43 yards for a touchdown and also scores on a 57-yard fumble return as Ohio State beats Northwestern 12-0. **Harry Newman** returns a punt 70 yards for a touchdown as Michigan beats Chicago 28-0.

1934 – **Jack Grossman** scores on a 72-yard punt return and a 26-yard pass reception as the Brooklyn Dodgers beat the Pittsburgh Pirates 21-3 in the NFL.

1950 – **Yehoshua Glazer** scores a hat trick as Israel beats Turkey 5-1 in soccer.

1981 – **Beni Tabak** scores three goals as Israel beats Portugal 4-1 in a World Cup soccer qualifier.

MAZEL TOUGH

1901 – **Abe Attell** wins a 15-round decision over George Dixon in St. Louis.

1934 – **Morrie Bodenger** and the Detroit Lions' defense posts its seventh straight shutout at the start of the NFL season in a 38-0 victory over the Cincinnati Reds in Portsmouth, Ohio. The streak will end a week later in a 40-7 victory over Pittsburgh, which scores on a 62-yard pass off a fake punt.

1990 – **Robbie Weiss** beats Jaime Ygaza 3-6, 7-6, 6-3 in the final of an indoor tournament in Sao Paulo, Brazil, for his only victory on the men's tennis tour.

TRANSITIONS

1958 – **Marshall Goldberg** of Pittsburgh is inducted into the National Football Foundation college Hall of Fame.

A STAR IS BORN

1981 – **Adam Duvendeck** (cycling)

Marshall Goldberg
(University of Pittsburgh)

OCTOBER 29

GAMEBREAKERS

1890 – **Phil King** scores 11 touchdowns – worth four points each – as Princeton defeats Columbia 60-0.

1932 – **Harry Newman's** 12-yard touchdown pass gives unbeaten Michigan a come-from-behind 14-7 victory over Princeton. **Jack Diamond** scores two touchdowns as CCNY beats Brooklyn College 18-7.

1933 – **Charles "Buckets" Goldenberg** scores three times – on a short run, an 8-yard pass and a 30-yard punt return – in the Green Bay Packers' 35-9 victory over the Philadelphia Eagles. Goldenberg will score 10 career NFL touchdowns before being switched to offensive guard.

1933 – **Benny Friedman** throws a 9-yard touchdown pass in the second quarter to give the Brooklyn Dodgers a 7-0 victory over the Chicago Cardinals.

1938 – **Marshall Goldberg** scores two fourth-quarter touchdowns as Pitt rallies to extend its unbeaten streak to 22 games with a 24-13 win over Fordham.

1967 – **Karl Sweetan** throws a 19-yard touchdown pass and runs five yards for another score as the Detroit Lions defeat the San Francisco 49ers 45-3.

STRONG IN DEFEAT

2006 – **Sage Rosenfels** throws three touchdown passes, but the Houston Texans lose 28-22 to the Tennessee Titans.

MAZEL TOUGH

1907 – **Abe Attell** knocks out Freddie Weeks in four rounds in Los Angeles to retain his world featherweight title.

1934 – **Jackie "Kid" Berg** knocks out **Harry Mizler** in the 10th round in London to capture Mizler's British lightweight title.

1994 – **Andrew Seras** wins a gold medal in Greco-Roman wrestling at the World Cup in Kecskemet, Hungary.

RECORD SETTERS

1949 – **Stanford Lavine** throws a school-record 92-yard touchdown pass as Maryland beats South Carolina 44-7.

2000 – **Jay Fiedler** begins a streak of 92 consecutive passes without an interception, spanning five full games – a Miami Dolphins team record.

A STAR IS BORN

1892 – **Jeno Fuchs** (fencing)
1922 – **Ernie Silverman** (minor-league baseball)
1928 – **Sherwin Raiken** (Villanova basketball)
1938 – **Michael Long** (Brandeis football, Boston Patriots)
1973 – **Adam Bacher** (South African cricket)

OCTOBER 30

GAMEBREAKERS

1927 – **Benny Friedman** runs 4 yards for a touchdown and throws a 70-yard touchdown pass as the Cleveland Bulldogs beat the Duluth Eskimos 21-20 at Luna Park in Cleveland. Ernie Nevers scores all 20 points for Duluth.

1937 – **Harry Shorten** scores on a 59-yard pass reception in the fourth quarter to give NYU a 14-7 win over Colgate.

1939 – Five years after playing his final NFL game, **Benny Friedman** comes out of retirement to play for the semi-pro Cedarhust Wolverines of Long Island, N.Y. Friedman throws three touchdown passes and kicks three field goals and an extra point as the Wolverines beat the all-black Brown Bombers 35-6.

1996 – **Chad Levitt** of Cornell rushes for 218 yards in a 28-20 win over Yale.

STRONG IN DEFEAT

1932 – **Jack Grossman's** 20-yard touchdown run helps the Brooklyn Dodgers avoid a shutout in a 27-7 loss to the Chicago Cardinals.

1976 – **Dave Jacobs** of Syracuse kicks a 55-yard field goal in a 23-13 loss to Pitt.

1999 – **Jason Feinberg** ties a Penn school record by kicking four field goals in a 23-19 loss to Yale.

MAZEL TOUGH

1906 – **Abe Attell** wins a 20-round decision over Henry Baker in Los Angeles to retain his world featherweight title.

1982 – **Gilles Elbilia** wins a 12-round decision over Claude Lancastre in Paris to win the French welterweight boxing title.

1988 – **Amos Mansdorf** beats **Brad Gilbert** 6-3, 6-2, 6-3 in the final of an indoor tennis tournament in Paris.

2005 – Top-seeded **Justin Gimelstob** defeats Amer Delic 7-6 (5), 6-2 to win the USTA Home Depot Challenger tennis tournament in Carson, Calif.

RECORD SETTERS

1948 – **Hal Moffie** scores on a school-record 89-yard punt return and sets another Harvard record with 137 yards in punt returns in a 20-13 victory over Holy Cross.

1978 – **Mark Roth** beats David Ozio by 287 pins to win the Brunswick Regional Champions Classic in Rochester, N.Y. The victory is his eighth of the year, a PBA record.

1994 – **Kenny Bernstein** becomes the first NHRA Top Fuel driver to top 310 mph when he registers 311.85 in the preliminaries at Pomona, Calif.

JEWS ON FIRST

1871 – Longtime amateur player **Nate Berkenstock**, in his only major-league game, makes the final putout in right field as the Philadelphia Athletics win the National Association title with a 4-1 victory over the Chicago White Stockings in Brooklyn, N.Y. Berkenstock strikes out three times in four plate appearances, and at age 40 is the oldest player to appear in a National Association game.

TRANSITIONS

1953 – **Red Holzman** makes his NBA coaching debut with the Milwaukee Hawks in a 69-59 victory over the Minneapolis Lakers.

1963 – **Sandy Koufax** wins the National League MVP Award, outpolling Pittsburgh's Dick Groat 237-190.

A STAR IS BORN

1916 – **Herb Gershon** (basketball)

1926 – **Phil Slosberg** (Temple and pro football back)

OCTOBER 31

GAMEBREAKERS

1903 – **Sigmund Harris's** 40-yard kickoff return sets up Minnesota's tying touchdown as the Gophers play unbeaten Michigan to a 6-6 tie in the game that launches the Little Brown Jug series.

1937 – **Edwin Kahn** returns a fumble 10 yards for a touchdown as the Washington Redskins defeat the Brooklyn Dodgers 21-0.

1943 – **Sid Luckman's** three touchdown passes lead the Chicago Bears to a 35-14 victory over the Detroit Lions.

1947 – **Norm Rosen** scores 16 points as the New Orleans Hurricanes defeat the Chattanooga Majors 75-57 in a Professional Basketball League of America game.

1949 – **Mervin Pregulman** kicks a 27-yard field goal and three extra points as the Detroit Lions beat the Green Bay Packers 24-20.

2003 – New Hampshire freshman **Jacob Micflikier** scores four goals and adds an assist in a 9-2 win over Union College. Micflikier wraps up the Hockey East Player of the Month award.

MAZEL TOUGH

1921 – Former bantamweight champion **Joe Fox** wins a 20-round decision over Mike Honeyman in London to win the British featherweight title.

1932 – **Jackie Brown** of England beats **Victor "Young" Perez** of Tunisia in the 13th round to capture Perez's International Boxing Union world flyweight title in Manchester, England.

1936 – **Stanley Amos** rides Moonlit to victory in the prestigious Metropolitan Handicap in South Africa.

1979 – **Mark Roth** beats Paul Moser 258-257 in the final of the PBA Lawsons Open in Fairview Park, Ohio, when Moser leaves the 7-pin in the final frame.

2006 – **Jonathan Bornstein** of Chivas USA is named Major League Soccer Rookie of the Year after scoring six goals and adding four assists during the season.

RECORD SETTERS

1926 – **Lillian Copeland** sets a world record of 35.26 meters in the javelin.

Lillian Copeland
(U.S. Olympic Committee)

JEWS ON FIRST

1920 – **Leonard Sachs**, a future Basketball Hall of Famer, scores the first points in Chicago Cardinals football history in a 21-0 victory over the Detroit Heralds. All three Chicago TDS are scored on blocked punts.

1985 – **Brian Wilks** scores his first of four career NHL goals in the Los Angeles Kings' 7-4 loss to the Boston Bruins.

A STAR IS BORN

1913 – **Milton Green** (track and field)

1931 – **Jack Molinas** (Columbia basketball, Fort Wayne Pistons).

1964 – **Steve Rosenberg** (Chicago White Sox, San Diego Padres pitcher)

NOVEMBER 1

GAMEBREAKERS

1889 – **Phil King** scores seven touchdowns as Princeton beats Virginia 115-0.

1947 – **Norm Rosen** scores a game-high 15 points as the New Orleans Hurricanes beat the Louisville Colonels 51-49 in a Professional Basketball League of America game.

1972 – **Johan Neeskens** scores three of the first four goals and The Netherlands defeats Norway 9-0 in a World Cup soccer qualifying match.

1987 – **John Frank** catches a 2-yard touchdown pass as the San Francisco 49ers defeat the Los Angeles Rams 31-10.

STRONG IN DEFEAT

1942 – **Marshall Goldberg** returns a kickoff 95 yards for a touchdown in the Chicago Cardinals' 55-24 loss to the Green Bay Packers.

MAZEL TOUGH

1938 – In his 91st professional bout, **Solly Krieger** knocks out champion Al Hostak in the fourth round in Seattle to capture the National Boxing Association middleweight title.

1947 – In his only Ryder Cup golf appearance, **Herman Barron** and Byron Nelson team up to defeat Dai Rees and Sam King 2 and 1, helping the United States defeat Great Britain 11-1 in Portland, Ore.

1975 – **Harold Solomon** defeats Alan Mayer 6-2, 7-6, 7-5 to win a hard-court tennis tournament in Perth, Australia.

1976 – **Mark Roth** finishes 99 pins ahead of runner-up Paul Colwell to win the PBA Northern Ohio Open in Fairview Park, Ohio.

1987 – **Eliot Teltscher** beats John Fitzgerald 6-7, 3-6, 6-1, 6-2, 7-5 in the final of a hard-court tennis tournament in Hong Kong.

2003 – **Sasha Cohen** wins Skate Canada in Mississauga, Ontario, her second straight Grand Prix figure skating title.

RECORD SETTERS

1880 – **Lon Myers** sets an American record of 61 5/8 seconds in the 440-yard low hurdles.

JEWS ON FIRST

1946 – **Ossie Schechtman** of the Knickerbockers scores the first basket in the history of the Basketball Association of America, the forerunner of the NBA, as New York beats the host Toronto Huskies 68-66. **Leo Gottlieb** leads the Knicks with 14 points and Schechtman adds 11. Also contributing for New York are **Ralph Kaplowitz** with seven, **Nat Militzok** and **Hank Rosenstein** with five each and **Sonny Hertzberg** with two.

TRANSITIONS

1966 – **Sandy Koufax** becomes the first three-time Cy Young Award winner, capturing the award unanimously for the second straight year.

2002 – **Dave Sarachan**, assistant coach of the U.S. National Team, is named head coach of the Chicago Fire of the Major Indoor Soccer League.

A STAR IS BORN

1891 – **Arthur Bluethenthal** (Princeton football)

1910 – **Jack Grossman** (Rutgers and pro football)

NOVEMBER 2

GAMEBREAKERS

1902 – **Paul "Twister" Steinberg** scores the game's first touchdown as the Philadelphia Athletics' pro football team defeats the Pennsylvania Railroad YMCA 40-0.

1929 – **Benny Lom** of California runs 85 yards for a touchdown off a fake punt in a 15-7 win over Rose Bowl-bound Southern Cal.

1935 – **Barney Mintz** returns an interception 85 yards for a touchdown as Tulane beats Colgate 14-6. **Irwin Klein** scores on a 17-yard pass and **Joseph Mandel** runs 17 yards for another TD as NYU defeats Bucknell 14-0.

1946 – **Max Zaslofsky** scores a game-high 18 points in the Chicago Stags' first game, a 63-47 victory over the New York Knicks. **Leo Gottlieb** leads the Knicks with 12 points.

1947 – **Sid Luckman** throws four touchdown passes, including two during a fourth-quarter rally, as the Chicago Bears beat the Boston Yanks 28-24.

1949 – **Hank Rosenstein** scores 14 points as the Scranton Miners defeat the Harlem Yankees 61-54 in the American Basketball League.

1952 – **Herb Rich** of the Los Angeles Rams returns an interception 97 yards for a touchdown in a 42-20 victory over the Dallas Texans.

1991 – **Gilad Landau** of Israel kicks a 37-yard field goal as time expires to give Grambling a 30-27 victory over Texas Southern.

2000 – **Stacey Britstone** scores three goals as the Plymouth Whalers defeat the North Bay Centennials 8-0 in an Ontario Hockey League game.

2002 – **Greg Gardner** makes 52 saves in goal as the Mississippi Seawolves beat Pensacola 3-1 in the East Coast Hockey League.

2005 – **Lior Eliyahu** scores 27 points on 12-for-13 shooting to lead Galil Elyon to a 98-80 victory over Gravelines of France in a Euro Cup League basketball game.

MAZEL TOUGH

1915 – **Ted "Kid" Lewis** beats Milburn Saylor in 12 rounds in Boston to retain his world welterweight title.

1952 – **Dave Hilton** knocks out Buddy Daye in the first round to retain his Canadian featherweight title in Quebec City.

1975 – **Tom Okker** defeats Arthur Ashe 6-3, 2-6, 6-3, 3-6, 6-4 in the final of the Paris Indoor tennis tournament.

1980 – **Brian Gottfried** wins his fourth tennis tournament of the year, beating Adriano Panatta 4-6, 6-3, 6-1, 7-6 in the final of an indoor event in Paris.

1985 – **Marshall Holman** beats Amleto Monacelli 266-217 in the final of the Kodak Invitational in Rochester, N.Y. His 19th career PBA victory comes after he leads the qualifying field by 389 pins.

2002 – **Sasha Cohen** wins Skate Canada International in Quebec City, her first Grand Prix figure skating championship.

RECORD SETTERS

1982 – **Mike Veisor** makes a Hartford Whalers franchise-record 52 saves in a 7-6 loss to the Minnesota North Stars.

JEWS ON FIRST

1946 – **Red Auerbach** makes his pro coaching debut with the Washington Capitals of the Basketball Association of America. Washington defeats the Detroit Falcons 50-33.

A STAR IS BORN

1869 – **Phil Wolf** (bowling)
1972 – **Phoebe Mills** (gymnastics)

NOVEMBER 3

GAMEBREAKERS

1937 – **Moe Frankel** scores 14 points to lead the Jersey Reds to a 29-26 victory over the Kingston Colonials in the ABL season opener. **Phil Rabin** scores 17 for Kingston.

1946 – **Leonard "Butch" Levy** recovers a blocked punt in the end zone for a touchdown as the Los Angeles Rams beat the Detroit Lions 41-20.

1948 – **Irv Rothenberg** scores a game-high 17 points to lead the New York Knicks past the Fort Wayne Pistons 80-76 in the Basketball Association of America season opener.

2004 – **Baruch Dago** scores twice in the second half as Maccabi Tel Aviv defeats Ajax of the Netherlands 2-1 for its first victory in UEFA Champions League soccer.

STRONG IN DEFEAT

1949 – **Ralph Kaplowitz** scores 17 points in the Hartford Hurricanes' 88-68 loss to the Wilkes-Barre Barons in the ABL.

2001 – **Hayden Epstein** of Michigan kicks a 57-yard field goal in the Wolverines' 26-24 loss to Michigan State.

MAZEL TOUGH

1932 – Heavyweight boxer **Lew Lazar** wins a 10-round decision over **Abie Bain** in Paterson, N.J., to improve his record to 26-0-1.

1933 – **Maxie Rosenbloom** wins a 15-round decision over Mickey Walker in New York to retain his world light heavyweight title.

1973 – **Willie Harmatz** rides Speak Action to a 15-length victory in the Smithville Stakes at Atlantic City Race Track.

1974 – **Julie Heldman** defeats Glynis Coles 6-4, 6-2 to win the Dewar Cup tennis tournament in Cardiff, Wales. The victory is her last of 25 career singles titles.

1979 – **Amy Alcott** beats Sandra Post by one stroke to win the Mizuno Japan Classic in Osaka, her fourth LPGA tournament victory of the year.

1981 – **Mark Roth** beats Boysie Huber 206-188 in the final of the Columbia 300 Open in Fairview Park, Ohio. The victory is his 26th on the PBA Tour and marks the fourth time he has won tournaments back-to-back.

1991 – **Brenda Levy** finishes first in the wheelchair division at the Marine Corps Marathon in Arlington, Va.

2002 – Unseeded **Paul Goldstein** beats top-seeded Mardy Fish 6-7 (4-7), 6-4, 6-3 to win the Azalea Challenger tennis tournament in Tyler, Texas.

TRANSITIONS

1965 – **Sandy Koufax** is a unanimous choice as Cy Young Award winner.

1986 – Former Kansas City Chiefs coach **Marv Levy** is named head coach of the Buffalo Bills, replacing Hank Bullough.

A STAR IS BORN

1904 – **Al Foreman** (Canadian lightweight boxer)

1905 – **Mushy Callahan** (junior welterweight boxer)

1913 – **Nat Frankel** (Brooklyn College basketball)

1945 – **Ken Holtzman** (Chicago Cubs, Oakland A's, New York Yankees, Baltimore Orioles pitcher)

1969 – **George Weissfisch** (taekwondo)

1986 – **Yael Averbuch** (soccer)

NOVEMBER 4

GAMEBREAKERS

1890 – **Phil King** scores 11 touchdowns as Princeton defeats Columbia 85-0.

1923 – **Ave Kaplan** throws touchdown passes of 35 and 40 yards and kicks an extra point as the Minnesota Marines beat the Racine Legion 13-6 in the NFL.

1939 – **Arthur Gottlieb** scores two touchdowns as Rutgers defeats New Hampshire 32-13.

1945 – **Melvin Bleeker** runs 14 yards for a touchdown and **Abe Karnofsky** scores on a 19-yarder as the Philadelphia Eagles beat the Pittsburgh Steelers 45-3.

1979 – **Randy Grossman** catches a 4-yard touchdown pass as the Pittsburgh Steelers defeat the Washington Redskins 38-7.

2000 – **Josh Frankel** of Oregon kicks a career-long 47-yard field goal to beat Washington State 27-24 in overtime. **Jason Feinberg** kicks four field goals and four extra points as Penn defeats Princeton 40-24.

STRONG IN DEFEAT

1945 – **Leo Cantor** runs three yards for a touchdown in the Chicago Cardinals' 24-21 loss to the Washington Redskins.

MAZEL TOUGH

1938 – **Herman Barron** shoots 142 over two rounds to win the Westchester PGA Championship in White Plains, N.Y.

1979 – **Harold Solomon** beats Corrado Barazzutti of Italy 6-3, 2-6, 6-3, 6-4 in the final of an indoor tennis tournament in Paris.

1984 – **Brad Gilbert** beats Wally Masur 6-3, 6-3 in the final of an indoor tennis tournament in Taipei.

2001 – **Deena Drossin** wins the U.S. women's national marathon championship as the first American to finish the New York City Marathon and the seventh woman overall. Running her first marathon, Drossin finishes in 2 hours, 26 minutes, 58 seconds, the fourth-fastest time in history for an American woman.

2006 – **Roman Greenberg** stops Alexei Varakin in the sixth round to retain his IBO Intercontinental heavyweight title in Monte Carlo, Monaco.

JEWS ON FIRST

1951 – Rangers defenseman **Hy Buller** scores his first of 22 career goals at 10:12 of the second period to give New York a 2-1 lead, but the Detroit Red Wings rally for a 4-2 victory.

A STAR IS BORN

1897 – **Dolly Stark** (baseball umpire, Dartmouth basketball coach)

1974 – **Gaston Etlis** (Argentina tennis)

1978 – **John Grabow** (Pittsburgh Pirates pitcher)

Hy Buller *(Cleveland Barons)*

NOVEMBER 5

GAMEBREAKERS

1892 – **Phil King** scores his 21st touchdown of the season and Princeton beats Penn 6-4 in Manheim, Pa., for its first victory over the Quakers.

1922 – **Arnold Horween** runs for a touchdown and drop kicks a game-winning 31-yard field goal as the Chicago Cardinals beat the Buffalo All-Americans 9-7.

1926 – **Davey Banks** scores 17 points to lead the New York Original Celtics to a 35-34 victory over the Jersey City-Newburgh Skeeters in the National Basketball League.

1929 – **Benny Friedman** throws two touchdown passes as the New York Giants beat the Buffalo Bisons 45-6.

1932 – **Harry Newman** scores the game's only touchdown on a one-yard run in the third quarter as Michigan defeats Indiana 7-0. Backup quarterback **Len Tarcher** drop kicks the extra point to give Rutgers a 7-6 win over Lafayette.

1938 – In the Rutgers Stadium dedication game, **Arthur Gottlieb** throws a fourth-down touchdown pass with five minutes remaining as Rutgers rallies to beat Princeton 20-18. The victory is the first for the Scarlet Knights over the Tigers since the first collegiate football game in 1869.

1944 – **Melvin Bleeker** catches a 57-yard touchdown pass as the Philadelphia Eagles beat the Brooklyn Tigers 21-7. **Sid Luckman** runs for a touchdown and passes for two as the Chicago Bears beat the Green Bay Packers 21-0.

1950 – **Herb Rich** returns an interception 45 yards for a touchdown in the Baltimore Colts' 41-21 victory over the Green Bay Packers.

2003 – **Sara DeCosta** makes 16 saves as the United States women's hockey team beats Finland 8-0 on its way to the gold medal in the Four Nations Cup Tournament in Sweden.

MAZEL TOUGH

1999 – **Dana Rosenblatt** wins a 12-round split decision over Vinny Pazienza to capture the IBO super middleweight championship in Ledyard, Conn.

2002 – **Paul Goldstein** defeats Mardy Fish 6-7 (4-6), 6-4, 6-3 in the final of a USTA Challenger tennis tournament in Tyler, Texas.

2004 – **Maxim Staviyski** and his partner Albena Denkova of Bulgaria win the ice dancing at the NHK Trophy figure skating championships in Nagoya, Japan.

2004 – **Boyd Melson** of the United States decisions Elshod Rasulov of Uzbekistan to win the 69-kg. title at the World Military Boxing Championships at Fort Huachuca, Ariz.

TRANSITIONS

1870 – **Moses Henry Epstein,** one of two Jews attending Columbia, plays for the Lions against Rutgers in the third college football game ever played. Rutgers wins 6-3.

1940 – The Baseball Writers Association names **Hank Greenberg** of the Detroit Tigers the American League MVP. Greenberg, who also won the award in 1935, finishes with 41 homers, 150 RBI's and a .340 batting average.

2005 – Long-time minor-league goalie **Moe Roberts** is inducted into the United States Hockey Hall of Fame.

A STAR IS BORN

1879 – **Otto Wahle** (swimming)

1899 – **Jack Bernstein** (junior lightweight boxer)

1906 – **Endre Kabos** (Hungary fencing)

1908 – **Lew Feldman** (lightweight boxer)

1942 – **Richie Scheinblum** (Kansas City Royals, Cleveland Indians, Cincinnati Reds, St. Louis Cardinals, California Angels, Washington Senators outfielder)

NOVEMBER 6

GAMEBREAKERS

1921 – In his only professional football game, **Nathan Abrams** returns an interception for a touchdown as the Green Bay Packers beat the Evansville Crimson Giants 43-6 in the American Professional Football Association – which becomes the NFL a year later.

1927 – **Benny Friedman** throws two touchdown passes to Oscar Wiberg as the Cleveland Bulldogs beat the New York Yankees 15-0.

1934 – **Albert "Red" Weiner** throws two touchdown passes and kicks two extra points as the Philadelphia Eagles set a league scoring record with a 64-0 victory over the Cincinnati Reds. Weiner completes just three of six career passes in the NFL.

1937 – **Bernard Bloom** throws a 55-yard touchdown pass to **Harry Shorten** as NYU beats Lehigh 13-0.

1947 – **Moe Becker** scores 11 points to help the Atlanta Crackers defeat the Springfield Squires 56-46 in a Professional Basketball League of America game.

1971 – **Gary Wichard** throws three touchdown passes in C.W. Post's 62-0 rout of Ithaca.

STRONG IN DEFEAT

1937 – **Solly Sherman** throws two touchdown passes to give the University of Chicago a 12-0 lead, but Michigan rallies with one minute left in the fourth quarter to win 13-12.

1946 – Sugar Ray Robinson is knocked down by **Artie Levine** in the fifth round, but is able to continue after a disputed "long count." Robinson stops Levine in the 10th round in Cleveland to retain his world welterweight title. Robinson says it is the hardest he is ever hit in a fight.

MAZEL TOUGH

1922 – **Benny Schwartz** wins a 10-round decision over Little Jeff to win the Southern flyweight title in Baltimore.

1953 – **Robert Cohen** wins a 15-round decision over Maurice Sandeyron in Paris to win the French bantamweight title.

1957 – **Alphonse Halimi** wins a 15-round decision over Raul "Little Mouse" Macias of Mexico in Los Angeles to win the unified world bantamweight title.

1988 – **Jay Berger** beats Horacio de la Pena 6-4, 6-4 in the final of a hard-court tennis tournament in Sao Paulo, Brazil. Berger also teams with De la Pena to capture his only career doubles title.

2005 – **Paul Goldstein** defeats Frank Dancevic 5-7, 7-5, 6-3 to win the USTA Adtech Challenger tennis tournament in Sudbury, Mass.

2006 – **Sergio Roitman** of Argentina wins the Petrobus Cup challenger tennis tournament in Aracaju, Brazil, defeating Boris Pashanski 6-1, 6-3.

RECORD SETTERS

1993 – C.W. Post quarterback **Perry Klein** passes for seven touchdowns and an NCAA Division II record 614 yards in a 58-18 victory over Salisbury State.

Perry Klein *(Atlanta Falcons)*

NOVEMBER 7

GAMEBREAKERS

1915 – **Alfred "Spezi" Schaffer** scores a hat trick in his international soccer debut as Hungary defeats Austria 6-2 in Budapest.

1926 – Player-coach **Joe "Doc" Alexander** intercepts a pass inside the 1-yard line and scores as the New York Giants beat the Chicago Cardinals 20-0 at the Polo Grounds.

1937 – **Dave Smukler** runs for a touchdown and passes for another to give the Philadelphia Eagles a 14-10 victory over the Brooklyn Dodgers.

1943 – **Sid Luckman** runs for a touchdown and throws for two more as the Chicago Bears beat the Detroit Lions 35-14.

1946 – **Ossie Schechtman** scores 12 points and **Sonny Hertzberg** adds 11 as the New York Knicks beat the St. Louis Bombers 68-63.

1999 – **Eyal Berkovic** of Israel scores two goals to help the Rangers defeat Celtic 4-2 in Scottish Premier League soccer.

MAZEL TOUGH

1923 – **Morrie Schlaiffer** knocks out Harvey Summers in the first round of a welterweight fight in his hometown of Omaha, Neb.

1980 – **Mark Laskin** of Canada rides Damuraz to victory in the World Cup Class at the National Horse Show at Madison Square Garden.

TRANSITIONS

1946 – The Philadelphia Warriors make their debut in the BAA by defeating the Pittsburgh Ironmen 81-75. The teams end up playing 4 on 4 after five Pittsburgh players foul out and the Ironmen reject Warriors coach **Eddie Gottlieb's** offer to allow a disqualified player to return. **Moe Becker** leads Pittsburgh with 20 points.

A STAR IS BORN

1877 – **Joe Bernstein** (featherweight boxer)

1885 – **Eddie Mensor** (Pittsburgh Pirates outfielder)

1915 – **Leo Disend** (Albright, Brooklyn Dodgers football, Green Bay Packers)

1928 – **Herb Flam** (tennis)

1969 – **Tanya Dubnicoff** (Canadian cycling)

1984 – **Jonathan Bornstein** (soccer)

NOVEMBER 8

GAMEBREAKERS

1925 – **Joe Alexander** returns an interception 50 yards for a touchdown on the final play of the game as the New York Giants beat the Columbus Tigers 19-0 at the Polo Grounds.

1930 – **Harry Newman's** 18-yard touchdown pass in the fourth quarter gives Michigan a 6-3 win over Harvard.

1958 – **Alan Goldstein** of North Carolina catches a 68-yard touchdown pass in a 42-0 win over Virginia.

1970 – One week before a plane crash that kills the entire Marshall football team, **Marcelo Lajterman** kicks field goals of 26 and 30 yards to give the Thundering Herd a 20-17 victory over Kent State.

1997 – Linebacker **Mitch Marrow** makes six tackles, including three sacks, and forces a fumble as Penn beats Princeton 20-17.

2003 – **Scott Goldberg** returns a kickoff 98 yards for a touchdown as Southeastern Louisiana defeats Jacksonville 43-23.

STRONG IN DEFEAT

1925 – **George Abramson** kicks field goals of 30 and 35 yards to give Green Bay a 6-0 lead in the fourth quarter, but the Chicago Cardinals rally to defeat the Packers 9-6.

1930 – **Jack Grossman** of Rutgers throws a 58-yard touchdown pass – the longest in college football that season – in a 31-26 loss to Lafayette.

1936 – Despite two touchdown passes and two extra points by **Harry Newman**, the Brooklyn Tigers lose 15-14 to the Cleveland Rams on a fourth-quarter field goal.

MAZEL TOUGH

1960 – **Donald Shapiro** rides Rivera Wonder to the open jumper title at the National Horse Show in Madison Square Garden.

1969 – **Julie Heldman** defeats Virginia Wade 4-6, 8-6, 6-3 to win the Dewar's Cup tennis tournament in Torquay, England.

1998 – South African jockey **Basil Marcus** rides the filly Visual Displays from last place to first in winning the Great Western 1400 before 100,000-plus spectators in Melbourne, Australia.

A STAR IS BORN

1868 – **Joe Choynski** (heavyweight boxer)
1895 – **Cyril Haas** (Princeton basketball)
1956 – **Beverly Klass** (golf)

Alan Goldstein
*(University of North Carolina
Athletic Communications)*

NOVEMBER 9

GAMEBREAKERS

1930 – **Sammy Stein** catches a 10-yard touchdown pass as the Staten Island Stapletons play to a 13-13 tie with the Portsmouth Spartans in the NFL.

1936 – **Phil Rabin** scores 19 points as the Kingston Colonials defeat the New York Jewels 27-19 in the ABL. **Mac Kinsbrunner** scores 12 for New York.

1940 – **Mort Landsberg** scores two touchdowns, including a 37-yarder, as Cornell defeats Yale 21-0.

2003 – Playing her first varsity basketball game, Maryland freshman guard **Shay Doron** of Israel scores a game-high 19 points – including her team's final six – as the Terrapins defeat the Turkish National Team 58-56 in an exhibition.

STRONG IN DEFEAT

1985 – Temple quarterback **Lee Saltz** completes 16 of 27 passes for 250 yards, including a 79-yard non-scoring pass to Willie Marshall, in the Owls' 21-17 loss to Pitt.

2003 – Third-string quarterback **Sage Rosenfels** throws his first NFL touchdown pass, a 21-yarder in the fourth quarter of the Miami Dolphins' 31-7 loss to the Tennessee Titans.

MAZEL TOUGH

1978 – **Eliot Teltscher** beats Pat Dupre 6-4, 6-3, 6-2 in the final of a hard-court tennis tournament in Hong Kong.

2003 – **Kenny Bernstein** defeats Scott Kalitta in the Top Fuel final at the Auto Club Championships in Pomona, Calif., for his 69th career NHRA victory.

Kenny Bernstein
(Quaker State/King Racing)

TRANSITIONS

1975 – **Mendy Rudolph** referees his last of a record 2,113 NBA games in a 23-year career.

NOVEMBER 10

GAMEBREAKERS

1877 – **Lucius Littauer** scores a touchdown to give Harvard a 1-0 victory over McGill University in Montreal. Littauer becomes Harvard's first football coach in 1881 and leads the team to a 6-1-1 record in his only season.

1928 – **Morris Goldhammer** scores two touchdowns – one after an 80-yard run to the 1-yard line – as CCNY defeats Norwich 19-0. **Phil Liflander** scores two touchdowns and kicks both extra points to give Columbia a 14-13 win over Johns Hopkins. **Howard Caplan** scores both touchdowns for Johns Hopkins – one on a 95-yard kickoff return.

1934 – **Joseph Mandel** returns an interception 45 yards for a touchdown and **Nathan Machlowitz** also scores as NYU defeats CCNY 38-13.

1935 – **Jim Levey** runs for a touchdown and catches a 34-yard pass for another as the Pittsburgh Pirates defeat the Brooklyn Dodgers 16-7 in the NFL. **Jack Grossman** scores on a 5-yard run for Brooklyn.

1946 – **Sid Luckman** throws three touchdown passes as the Chicago Bears beat the Los Angeles Rams 27-21.

1951 – **Hal Seidenberg's** touchdown run with 5:54 remaining seals Cornell's 20-7 victory over defending Big Ten Conference champion Michigan. The teams were meeting for the first time since 1933.

MAZEL TOUGH

1914 – **Al McCoy** retains his world middleweight title by fighting to a 10-round no-decision with **Soldier Bartfield** in Brooklyn, N.Y.

1984 – **Mark Roth** becomes bowling's second millionaire when he beats Pete Weber 243-153 in the final of the Greater Detroit Open in Dearborn, Mich., for his 31st career title.

2000 – **Shawn Mamane** scores three goals to give the Peoria Rivermen a 6-3 victory over the Birmingham Bulls in the East Coast Hockey League.

2001 – **Sarah Abitbol** of France and her partner Stephen Benadis win the pairs competition at the Golden Skate Championships in Zagreb, Croatia.

JEWS ON FIRST

2001 – **Bubba Berenzweig** scores his first NHL goal but the Nashville Predators lose 3-2 to the Ottawa Senators. Meanwhile, **Jeff Halpern** gets the game-winning goal and an assist as the Washington Capitals beat the Atlanta Thrashers 3-0.

TRANSITIONS

1950 – **Red Auerbach**, who coached the Washington Capitols the previous three seasons, is named head coach of professional basketball's Tri-City Blackhawks. He will take over as coach of the Boston Celtics one year later.

1978 – **Red Holzman** comes out of retirement to coach the New York Knicks for the second time.

A STAR IS BORN

1910 – **Abraham Eliowitz** (Michigan State and CFL football)

1916 – **Sam Goldman** (Howard U. and pro football)

1919 – **Harry Feldman** (New York Giants pitcher)

1942 – **Barry Kramer** (NYU basketball, Golden State Warriors, New York Knicks)

1972 – **Shawn Green** (Toronto Blue Jays, Los Angeles Dodgers, Arizona Diamondbacks, New York Mets outfielder)

NOVEMBER 11

GAMEBREAKERS

1916 – **Ralph Horween** kicks a 35-yard field goal as Harvard beats previously unbeaten Princeton 3-0.

1923 – **Ave Kaplan** drop-kicks field goals of 45 and 50 yards as the Minnesota Marines tie the Rock Island Independents 6-6 in an NFL game. **Max Kadesky** sets up Rock Island's tying touchdown by returning a blocked field-goal attempt 40 yards to the Marines' 25-yard line.

1926 – **Corporal Jim Levey** scores touchdowns on runs of 65 and 70 yards as the Quantico Marines beat Temple University 41-12 in Philadelphia.

1933 – **Izzy Weinstock's** 3-yard touchdown run and extra point in the third quarter give Pittsburgh a 7-0 victory over Duquesne.

1934 – **Harry Newman** rushes an NFL-record 39 times for 114 yards and two touchdowns as the New York Giants beat the Green Bay Packers 17-3. **Jack Grossman** throws a 47-yard touchdown pass as the Brooklyn Dodgers defeat the Philadelphia Eagles 10-7.

1946 – **Marv Rottner** scores 20 points to lead the Chicago Stags to a 78-68 overtime victory over New York in the Knicks' home opener in their first Basketball Association of America season. **Sonny Hertzberg** leads New York with 14 points.

2000 – **Jason Feinberg** of Penn boots three field goals and three extra points in a 36-35 victory over Harvard to become the Ivy League's all-time scorer among kickers. **Brian Natkin** catches eight passes for 110 yards as UTEP captures its first Western Athletic Conference title with a 38-21 victory over Rice.

2001 – **Jay Fiedler** passes for 259 yards and two touchdowns – including a 74-yarder – as the Miami Dolphins beat the Indianapolis Colts 27-24.

STRONG IN DEFEAT

1938 – **Dave Smukler** of the Eagles returns a kickoff 101 yards for a touchdown, but Philadelphia loses to the Brooklyn Dodgers 32-14.

1945 – **Sid Luckman** throws four touchdown passes in the Chicago Bears' 35-28 loss to the Detroit Lions.

RECORD SETTERS

1908 – **Otto Scheff** of Austria sets a world record of 2:31.6 in the 200 freestyle in Vienna.

1996 – Soccer goalie **Adam Spitzer** posts his fifth straight shutout, 1-0 over Syracuse, to finish with a school-record 25 for his career at the University of Pittsburgh.

TRANSITIONS

1998 – Former Olympian **Carina Benninga** of the Netherlands is named interim head coach of the United States field hockey team.

A STAR IS BORN

1892 – **Al Schacht** (Washington Senators pitcher)

1918 – **Georgie Abrams** (middleweight boxer)

1937 – **Rudy LaRusso** (Dartmouth basketball, LA Lakers, San Francisco Warriors)

1954 – **David Edge** (Canadian marathoner)

NOVEMBER 12

GAMEBREAKERS

1922 – **Arnold Horween** throws a 60-yard touchdown pass to Paddy Driscoll in the second quarter to give the Chicago Cardinals a 7-0 victory over the Akron Indians.

1932 – **Harry Newman** returns a punt 78 yards for a touchdown and also scores on a 25-yard run as Michigan beats the University of Chicago 12-0.

1933 – **Harry Newman's** 15-yard touchdown pass in the second quarter gives the New York Giants a 7-0 victory over the Boston Redskins. **Richard Fishel** runs seven yards for a touchdown as the Brooklyn Dodgers defeat the Pittsburgh Pirates 32-0.

1944 – **Melvin Bleeker** catches two touchdown passes as the Philadelphia Eagles play to a 21-21 tie with the New York Giants. **Sid Luckman** throws three touchdown passes in the Chicago Bears' 21-7 victory over the Boston Yanks.

1946 – In the first pro basketball game at Madison Square Garden since 1929, **Marvin Rottner** scores 20 points and **Max Zaslofsky** adds nine to help the Chicago Stags beat the New York Knickerbockers 78-68 in overtime. For New York, **Sonny Hertzberg** scores 18, **Leo Gottlieb** and **Nat Militzok** add 10 each, and **Ossie Schechtman** – who sent the game into overtime with a last-second shot – contributes eight points.

1947 – **Jules Kasner** of the Chattanooga Majors scores a game-high 18 points in a 48-46 victory over the Atlanta Crackers in the final game of the Professional Basketball League of America. The league disbands the next day.

2005 – **Ryan Heller** has nine catches for 134 yards, including a 15-yard touchdown pass with 2.3 seconds remaining, as C.W. Post defeats West Chester 24-20 in an NCAA Division II playoff game.

STRONG IN DEFEAT

1997 – **Leeor Shtrom** makes 47 saves in goal, but Union College loses 3-2 to RPI in hockey.

MAZEL TOUGH

1792 – **Daniel Mendoza** wins a 15-minute heavyweight fight against Bill Warr in Bexley Commons, England.

1931 – **Erich Seelig** wins a 12-round decision over Hans Siefried in Berlin to capture the German middleweight title.

1967 – **Ben Gurevitch** of the Soviet Union wins the 87-kg. freestyle wrestling title at the World Championships in New Delhi, India.

1989 – **Martin Jaite** beats Javier Sanchez 7-6, 6-3 in the final of an indoor tennis tournament in Sao Paulo, Brazil.

2000 – **Charlee Minkin** wins the women's 52-kg. division at the Pan American Judo Union Championships in Orlando, Fla.

2001 – **Kenny Bernstein** defeats Mike Dunn in the Top Fuel final at the NHRA Auto Club of Southern California event.

2006 – **Aleksandra Wozniak** of Canada captures a USTA tennis tournament title in Pittsburgh when Vioktoria Azarenka retires after losing the first set 6-2.

JEWS ON FIRST

1937 – Lightweight **Allie Stolz** makes his pro-boxing debut with a second-round knockout of Ricardo Nunez at the Hippodrome in New York.

TRANSITIONS

1980 – Baltimore Orioles pitcher **Steve Stone** outpolls Mike Norris of the Oakland A's to win the American League Cy Young award after going 25-7.

A STAR IS BORN

1904 – **Archie Bell** (bantamweight boxing)
1975 – **Jason Lezak** (swimming)

NOVEMBER 13

GAMEBREAKERS

1909 – **Joe Magidsohn** scores both Michigan touchdowns, including one on a 33-yard run, as the Wolverines end Penn's 23-game winning streak, 12-6.

1921 – **Moritz Haeusler** scores a pair of goals as Hakoah Vienna defeats WR Association 5-3 in Austrian soccer.

1926 – **Benny Friedman** throws two touchdown passes and kicks a game-winning 43-yard field goal as Michigan tops previously unbeaten Ohio State 17-16.

1927 – **Benny Friedman** scores on a 30-yard run, throws a touchdown pass and kicks five extra points as the Cleveland Bulldogs beat the Frankford Yellow Jackets 37-0.

1932 – **Benny Friedman's** field goal gives the Brooklyn Dodgers a 3-0 victory over the Chicago Cardinals.

1937 – **Moe Goldman** scores 24 points, **Inky Lautman** 14 and **Reds Rosan** 13 as the Philadelphia Sphas defeat the New York Celtics 64-46 in the ABL.

1938 – **Moe Frankel** scores 17 points as the Troy Haymakers defeat the Jersey Reds 37-32 in the ABL.

1971 – **Gary Wichard** throws for 232 yards and three touchdowns as C.W. Post beats Kings Point 47-0.

1983 – **Larry Ginsberg** makes nine saves in goal as North Carolina upsets top-ranked Duke 2-1 in the Tar Heels' regular-season soccer finale.

MAZEL TOUGH

1905 – **Cockney Cohen** wins a six-round decision over former world bantamweight champion Thomas "Pedlar" Palmer in London.

1910 – **Abe Attell** decisions Frankie Conley in 15 rounds in McDonoughville, La., to retain his world featherweight title.

1918 – **Ted "Kid" Lewis** knocks out Johnny McCarthy in the fourth round in San Francisco to retain his world welterweight title.

1964 – **Walter Blum,** the track's 1963 champion jockey, rides four winners on opening day at Pimlico.

1978 – **Marshall Holman** wins the PBA Northern Ohio Open in Fairview Park, Ohio. **Mark Roth** rolls a 300 game to finish second.

2004 – **Irina Slutskaya** of Russia, returning to skating after an extended break because of illness, wins the Cup of China competition in Beijing.

2004 – **Justin Gimelstob** defeats Amer Delic 7-6 (7-3), 7-6 (7-4) in the final of the USTA Music City Challenger indoor tennis tournament in Nashville, Tenn.

2005 – **Olga Karmansky** of the United States wins the all-around title at the Pan American Rhythmic Gymnastics Championships in Vitoria, Brazil.

2005 – **Aleksandra Wozniak** of Canada wins her third USTA Challenger tennis tournament of the year, defeating Olena Antypina of Ukraine 6-4, 6-3.

A STAR IS BORN

1900 – **Victor Ross** (Syracuse lacrosse)
1903 – **Si Rosenthal** (Boston Red Sox outfielder)
1981 – **Charlee Minkin** (judo)

NOVEMBER 14

GAMEBREAKERS

1931 – **Sid Eisenberg** scores on a lateral from **Hy Kaplowitz** and throws a long pass to set up a second touchdown as CCNY defeats Haverford 14-0. **Jack Grossman** scores on runs of 2, 10 and 60 yards in his final game as Rutgers defeats Lehigh 26-12. He also returns an 84-yard kickoff to the 11-yard line.

1937 – **Buckets Goldenberg** returns an interception 27 yards for a touchdown as the Green Bay Packers defeat the Philadelphia Eagles 37-7.

1937 – **Moe Goldman** scores 13 points in the Philadelphia Sphas' 41-38 victory over the Kingston Colonials in the ABL.

1939 – **Sammy Kaplan** scores 15 points to lead the Kingston Colonials to a 39-32 victory over the New York Jewels in the ABL.

MAZEL TOUGH

1888 – In his first professional fight, heavyweight **Joe Choynski** knocks out George Bush in the second round in San Francisco.

1982 – **Brad Gilbert** beats Craig Wittus 6-1, 6-4 in the final of an indoor tournament in Taipei for his first of 20 career singles victories.

RECORD SETTERS

1943 – **Sid Luckman** of the Chicago Bears becomes the first pro quarterback to pass for more than 400 yards in a game, completing 23 of 30 passes for 433 yards and a record seven touchdowns in a 56-7 win over the New York Giants. Luckman's scoring throws cover 4, 31, 27, 62, 15, 3, and 40 yards.

TRANSITIONS

1946 – **Jake Pitler** is named manager of the Binghamton Triplets of the Eastern League.

NOVEMBER 15

GAMEBREAKERS

1919 – Syracuse guard **Joe Alexander** makes tackles on 11 consecutive plays against Colgate in a 13-7 victory.

1930 – **Jack Grossman** scores both Rutgers touchdowns in a 14-13 win over Lehigh.

1942 – **Sid Luckman** returns an interception 54 yards for a touchdown as the Chicago Bears beat the Green Bay Packers 38-7.

1947 – **Herb Rich** catches a 60-yard touchdown pass as Vanderbilt beats Miami 33-7.

1981 – **Randy Grossman** catches a 14-yard touchdown pass as the Pittsburgh Steelers beat the Atlanta Falcons 34-30.

1997 – **Ronnie Rosenthal** scores both goals for Watford in a 2-1 victory over Barnet in the first round of the English FA Cup soccer tournament.

1997 – **David Ettinger** of Hofstra kicks a 52-yard field goal in a 40-27 victory over Liberty University.

STRONG IN DEFEAT

1958 – **Alan Goldstein** of North Carolina catches four passes for 101 yards in a 34-24 loss to Notre Dame.

MAZEL TOUGH

2003 – **Sasha Cohen** wins the Lalique Trophy in Paris, her third consecutive Grand Prix figure skating title.

A STAR IS BORN

1908 – **Oscar Goldman** (featherweight boxer)

1924 – **Lionel Malamed** (CCNY basketball)

1930 – **Robert Cohen** (Algerian bantamweight boxer)

1941 – **Sydney Nomis** (South African rugby)

Sasha Cohen
(U.S. Olympic Committee)

NOVEMBER 16

GAMEBREAKERS

1935 – **Joseph Mandel** catches two touchdown passes and **Nathan Machlowitz** runs for one TD and passes for another as NYU defeats Rutgers 48-0.

1939 – **Moe Goldman** scores 17 points, **Inky Lautman** 13, and **Petey Rosenberg** 10 as the Philadelphia Sphas defeat the Wilkes-Barre Barons 59-48 in the ABL.

1946 – **Al Hoisch** scores on an 87-yard run as UCLA beats Montana 61-7.

1949 – **Marty Zippel** scores 15 points as the Wilkes-Barre Barons defeat the Schenectady Packers 108-69 in the ABL.

1946 – **Irv Mondschein** catches touchdown passes of 68 and 53 yards as NYU defeats Fordham 33-28.

1947 – **Sid Luckman** throws three touchdown passes in the Chicago Bears' 41-21 victory over the Los Angeles Rams.

1948 – **Al Hoisch** scores on an 87-yard run as UCLA beats Montana 61-7.

1987 – **Doron Jamchi** scores 34 points and **Mickey Berkowitz** makes both ends of a one-and-one with 13 seconds remaining as Maccabi Tel Aviv defeats Barcelona 109-107.

STRONG IN DEFEAT

1941 – **Maurice Patt** catches a 2-yard touchdown pass – his second of two career NFL touchdowns – in the Cleveland Rams' 49-14 loss to the New York Giants.

MAZEL TOUGH

1906 – **Abe Attell** wins a 15-round decision over Billy DeCoursey in San Diego to retain his world featherweight title.

1916 – **Charley White** knocks out Milburn Saylor in the first round of a lightweight fight in Boston. White will fight Saylor six months later in Cincinnati – and knock him out in the first round again.

1932 – **Maxie Rosenbloom** wins a 10-round decision over John Henry Lewis in San Francisco.

1934 – **Bob Olin** takes the world light heavyweight title from **Maxie Rosenbloom** in a 15-round decision in New York.

1986 – **Jay Berger** wins his first of three tournaments on the men's tennis tour, beating Franco Davin of Argentina 6-3, 6-3 in the final of a clay-court event in Buenos Aires.

2002 – **Sasha Cohen** skates past leader Yoshie Onda of Japan on the final day of competition to capture the Lalique Trophy figure skating title in Paris, her second Grand Prix title of the year.

2003 – **Paul Goldstein** defeats Robert Kendrick 6-3, 6-4 to win a USTA Challenger hard-court tennis tournament in Austin, Texas.

JEWS ON FIRST

2002 – **Mike Cammalleri** of the Los Angeles Kings breaks a 1-1 tie with his first career NHL goal in a 5-1 victory over the Edmonton Oilers.

A STAR IS BORN

1909 – **Art Lasky** (heavyweight boxer)

1910 – **Morrie Arnovich** (New York Giants, Philadelphia Phillies, Cincinnati Reds outfielder)

1936 – **Isaac Berger** (weight lifting)

1977 – **Maxim Staviyski** (Bulgarian ice dancer)

1980 – **Hayden Epstein** (Michigan football placekicker)

NOVEMBER 17

GAMEBREAKERS

1929 – **Benny Friedman** throws touchdown passes covering 37, 6, 15, and 20 yards as the New York Giants beat the Chicago Bears 34-0. Friedman also completes non-scoring passes of 35, 35, and 40 yards.

1962 – **Mike Basset** throws a 76-yard touchdown pass as Harvard beats Brown 31-19.

1973 – **Randy Grossman** catches seven passes for 126 yards as Temple beats Drake 35-10.

2001 – **Hayden Epstein's** 31-yard field goal with 10 seconds remaining gives Michigan a 20-17 win over Wisconsin. The winning kick is set up after a Wisconsin player inadvertently touches Epstein's punt and Michigan recovers.

2002 – **Lane Schwarzberg** kicks a 33-yard field goal with 2:53 remaining to give Colgate a 15-13 victory over Bucknell.

2002 – **Guy Melamed** scores in overtime as Boston College defeats Connecticut 3-2 for the Big East Conference soccer championship.

MAZEL TOUGH

1933 – **Barney Ross** wins a 10-round decision over Sammy Fuller in Chicago to retain his world junior welterweight title.

1973 – **Tom Okker** beats Ilie Nastase 6-3, 6-4 to win the Dewar Cup Grand Prix tennis final in London.

1979 – **Marshall Holman** becomes the third bowler to win $100,000 in one season by winning the Brunswick Memorial World Open in Deerfield, Ill. Holman beats Jim Plessinger 204-203 in the semifinals and Steve Martin 246-191 in the final.

JEWS ON FIRST

1928 – In the first event ever held at the new Boston Garden, lightweight **Arthur "Hy" Diamond** wins a four-round decision over George Flate in an undercard bout.

TRANSITIONS

1973 – **Brian Gottfried** is named rookie of the year by Tennis magazine.

2003 – **Stan Kasten**, the first person to serve simultaneously as head of three major sports teams, resigns as president of baseball's Atlanta Braves, basketball's Atlanta Hawks, and hockey's Atlanta Thrashers.

A STAR IS BORN

1941 – **James Bregman** (judo)

1976 – **Tamara Levinson** (rhythmic gymnastics)

1983 – **Ryan Braun** (Milwaukee Brewers third baseman)

Tom Okker
(Association of Tennis Professionals)

NOVEMBER 18

GAMEBREAKERS

1911 – Minnesota defensive lineman **Leonard Frank** pushes Wisconsin quarterback Keekie Moll out-of-bounds at the 1-yard line on the game's final play to preserve a 6-6 tie. Minnesota finishes the season 6-0-1.

1933 – **Albert "Red" Weiner** scores all 10 points on a touchdown, extra point, and field goal as Muhlenberg defeats Lehigh 10-0.

1933 – **Cy Kaselman** scores 16 points as the Philadelphia Sphas defeat the Hoboken Thourots 34-20 in the ABL.

1936 – **Moe Spahn** scores 17 points to lead the Jersey Reds to a 46-34 victory over the Atlantic City Snipers in the ABL.

1945 – **Sam Fox** catches a 23-yard touchdown pass as the New York Giants beat the Detroit Lions 35-14. **Abe Karnofsky** runs 12 yards for a touchdown as the Philadelphia Eagles beat the Pittsburgh Steelers 30-6.

1950 – **Max Zaslofsky** scores 21 points to lead the New York Knicks to a 93-87 win over the Philadelphia Warriors.

1987 – **Danny Schayes** of the Denver Nuggets grabs 19 rebounds against the Indiana Pacers.

STRONG IN DEFEAT

1945 – **Sid Luckman** throws three touchdown passes in the Chicago Bears' 28-21 loss to the Washington Redskins.

MAZEL TOUGH

1945 – The Philadelphia Sphas beat the **Barney Sedran**-coached New York Gothams 68-65 in the ABL season opener.

TRANSITIONS

1934 – **Al Schacht** leaves the Washington Senators to join the Boston Red Sox as a coach, breaking up the clown act he performed with teammate Nick Altrock.

1950 – Guard **Bernie Lemonick** is named Lineman of the Week by a national wire service after Penn beats Wisconsin 20-0.

1966 – **Sandy Koufax** announces his retirement from baseball because of pain in his arthritic elbow.

2000 – Freshman guard **Tamir Goodman**, an Orthodox Jew who draws national attention while a prep athlete at a Jewish day school in Baltimore, makes his collegiate basketball debut, scoring two points and handing out four assists in 49 minutes of play in Towson's 87-76 loss to Maryland-Baltimore County.

RECORD SETTERS

2000 – **Jason Feinberg** breaks the school record of 210 career points as Penn defeats Cornell 45-15. Feinberg ends his career with 218 points on 41 field goals and 56 points-after-touchdown.

A STAR IS BORN

1880 – **Harry Harris** (bantamweight boxer)
1911 – **Benny Sohn** (Washington and pro football)
1930 – **Irving Bemoras** (Illinois basketball)

NOVEMBER 19

GAMEBREAKERS

1927 – **Herbert Fleishhacker** throws the winning touchdown pass as Stanford defeats California 13-6.

1932 – **Harry Newman** kicks a 15-yard field goal as Michigan beats Minnesota 3-0 and clinches the Big Ten Conference and national championships.

1935 – **Jack Grossman's** 19-yard touchdown run helps the Brooklyn Dodgers defeat the Chicago Cardinals 14-12.

1939 – **Reds Rosan** scores 14 points and **Inky Lautman** and **Phil Rabin** add 13 each as the Philadelphia Sphas defeat the Jersey Reds 46-44 in the ABL. **Moe Spahn** scores 12 and **Ace Goldstein** 11 for Jersey.

1944 – **Melvin Bleeker's** 9-yard touchdown run helps the Philadelphia Eagles beat the Washington Redskins 37-7.

1947 – **Max Zaslofsky's** 26 points help the Chicago Stags defeat the New York Knicks 81-63.

2004 – **Michael Cammalleri** scores three power-play goals as the Manchester Monarchs defeat the Lowell Lock Monsters 5-4 in the American Hockey League.

2005 – **Ryan Heller** catches four passes for 85 yards and two touchdowns (58 and 5 yards) as C.W. Post defeats Shepherd 28-21 in an NCAA Division II playoff game.

STRONG IN DEFEAT

1983 – Ohio State tight end **John Frank** catches 10 passes for 123 yards in a 24-21 loss to Michigan.

2005 – **Dan Grunfeld** scores 29 points and grabs nine rebounds in Stanford's 79-63 loss to Cal-Irvine.

MAZEL TOUGH

1910 – **Young Joseph Aschel** wins a 20-round decision over Battling LaCroix in Paris to retain his European welterweight title.

1920 – **Ted "Kid" Lewis** knocks out Johnny Basham in the 19th round in London to retain his European welterweight title. He relinquishes the title a few weeks later.

1925 – **Harry Mason** wins a 20-round decision over Hamilton Johnny Brown in London to win the British welterweight title.

1977 – **Marshall Holman** wins the Brunswick World Open bowling tournament in Glendale Heights, Ill., beating top qualifier **Mark Roth** 277-250 in the final.

1978 – **Brian Teacher** posts his first of seven pro tennis victories by beating Tom Gorman 6-3, 6-3, 6-3 at the Cathay Trust Open indoor tournament in Taipei, Taiwan. **Eliot Teltscher** wins his first of 10 singles titles by beating Pat Dupre 6-4, 6-3, 6-2 in Hong Kong.

1995 – The Baltimore Stallions, with punter **Josh Miller**, defeat the Calgary Stampeders 37-20 to become the first U.S.-based team to win the Gray Cup in the Canadian Football League's 83-year history.

2006 – **Sergio Roitman** of Argentina defeats countryman Mariano Zabaleta 6-3, 4-6, 6-1 to win a clay-court challenger tennis tournament in Guayaquil, Ecuador.

A STAR IS BORN

1888 – **Sam Melitzer** (Columbia basketball, gymnastics)

1901 – **Morris Blumenthal** (Northwestern football, Chicago Cardinals)

1977 – **Kerri Strug** (gymnastics)

NOVEMBER 20

GAMEBREAKERS

1909 – **Joe Magidsohn** scores two touchdowns – one on a 35-yard interception return – as Michigan beats Minnesota 15-6.

1920 – **Ralph Horween** kicks a 42-yard field goal as Harvard beats Yale 9-0 to finish 8-0-1. **Joe Alexander** of Syracuse makes three straight tackles, then intercepts the ball on fourth down to preserve a 14-0 victory after Colgate faces first-and-goal from the 1-yard line.

1926 – **Harry Herbert's** field goal gives Boston University a 3-0 victory over Holy Cross, which loses its first game at home since 1921.

1936 – **Moe Goldman's** 13 points lead the Philadelphia Sphas to a 39-31 victory over the Brooklyn Visitations.

1937 – **Inky Lautman** and **Shikey Gotthoffer** score 16 points apiece as the Philadelphia Sphas defeat the Kingston Colonials 47-37 in the ABL. **Phil Rabin** and **Allie Schuckman** score 12 points apiece for Kingston.

1938 – **Dave Smukler** throws two touchdown passes and kicks an extra point as the Philadelphia Eagles beat the Pittsburgh Pirates 14-7 in Charleston, w.va.

1946 – **Sonny Hertzberg** scores 19 points as the New York Knicks beat the Chicago Stags 72-69.

1948 – **Harold Moffie** of Harvard runs 80 yards for a touchdown on the first play of the game in a 20-7 win over Yale.

STRONG IN DEFEAT

1999 – **David Nemirovsky** scores all three goals for the St. John Maple Leafs in a 5-3 loss to the Hamilton Bulldogs of the American Hockey League.

MAZEL TOUGH

1922 – **Ted "Kid" Lewis** wins a 20-round decision over Roland Todd in London to retain his European, British Empire, and British middleweight titles.

1977 – **Marshall Holman** rolls nine strikes in a row before leaving the No. 4 pin in the 10th frame, and defeats **Mark Roth** 277-250 in the PBA World Open in Glendale Heights, Ill.

TRANSITIONS

1933 – Nineteen colleges join the American Jewish Congress in requesting the Amateur Athletic Union refuse to name an Olympic team for 1936 if the games are held in Germany.

1966 – **George Morton Levy**, who founded New York's Roosevelt Raceway in 1948 and popularized night racing, is elected to the U.S. Harness Racing Hall of Fame.

A STAR IS BORN

1917 – **Mike Schemer** (New York Giants first baseman)

1922 – **Marty Goldstein** (NYU basketball)

1981 – **Sam Fuld** (Chicago Cubs outfielder)

NOVEMBER 21

GAMEBREAKERS

1902 – **Paul "Twister" Steinberg** runs 50 yards to the 4-yard line with 30 seconds remaining, setting up the Philadelphia Athletics' 12-6 victory over Pittsburgh for the pro football championship.

1933 – **Irwin Klein** scores on a 44-yard reception of a tipped pass as NYU ties Rutgers 6-6.

1936 – **Cy Kaselman** scores 15 points and **Reds Rosan** adds 14 as the Philadelphia Sphas defeat the Atlantic City Sandpipers 45-38 in the ABL.

1948 – **Mervin Pregulman** kicks a 33-yard field goal as the Detroit Lions beat the Pittsburgh Steelers 17-14. **Sid Luckman** throws two touchdown passes in the Chicago Bears' 51-17 victory over the Boston Yanks.

2003 – Maryland freshman **Shay Doron** scores 25 points, including 23 for 27 from the free-throw line as the Terrapins open their season with a 79-64 victory over Coppin State. Doron's 23 free throws tie an NCAA women's record.

2004 – **Liad Suez** scores 20 points to lead Villanova past Penn State 73-65 in women's basketball. **Shay Doron** scores a game-high 21 points and adds career highs of 7 assists and 5 steals as Maryland defeats Siena 73-52.

MAZEL TOUGH

1923 – **Harry Mason** wins a 20-round decision over Ernie Rice in London to retain his British and European lightweight titles.

1933 – **Ben Jeby** wins a 15-round decision over Chick Devlin to win the New York version of the world middleweight title.

1978 – **Gilbert Cohen** of France stops Jimmy Batten in the third round in Paris to win the vacant European light middleweight title.

1982 – **Brian Teacher** beats Wojtek Fibak 6-7, 6-4, 6-4, 2-6, 6-4 in a WCT indoor tennis tournament final in Dortmund, Germany.

1999 – **Danny Chocron** of Venezuela wins the 25-kilometer International Open Water Pre-World swimming championship in Waikiki Beach, Hawaii.

TRANSITIONS

1949 – **Hank Greenberg** becomes the Cleveland Indians' general manager.

A STAR IS BORN

1800 – **Barney Aaron** (British bare-knuckle boxer)

1907 – **Ben Jeby** (middleweight boxer)

1916 – **Sid Luckman** (Columbia football, Chicago Bears quarterback)

1950 – **Gennadi Karponosov** (figure skating)

1972 – **Eyal Ran** (Israeli tennis)

1975 – **Chad Levitt** (Cornell football, Oakland Raiders running back)

NOVEMBER 22

GAMEBREAKERS

1925 – **Sol Mishkin** scores a touchdown in the closing minutes to give Occidental a 6-3 victory over Pomona and the Southern California Conference football championship.

1936 – **Herman "Biff" Schneidman** catches a 46-yard touchdown pass as the Green Bay Packers defeat the New York Giants 26-14.

1942 – **Sid Luckman** throws two touchdown passes and **Johnny Siegal** catches a 28-yarder from the Bears' backup quarterback as Chicago beats the Detroit Lions 42-0.

1953 – **Herb Rich** returns an interception 53 yards late in the fourth quarter to secure the Los Angeles Rams' 21-13 victory over the Baltimore Colts.

1996 – **Doron Sheffer** scores 30 points and **Oded Katash** adds 20 as Maccabi Tel Aviv beats Stefanel Milan 88-84 in Italy.

1997 – Boston College tight end **Todd Pollack** catches an 8-yard touchdown pass midway through the fourth quarter to give the Eagles a 24-20 victory over Army.

2006 – **Jeff Halpern** scores at 4:11 of the third period to give the Dallas Stars a 1-0 NHL victory over the Nashville Predators.

STRONG IN DEFEAT

1987 – North Carolina defeats Massachusetts 1-0 in the NCAA women's soccer final in Amherst, Mass., but All-American defender **Debbie Belkin** of UMass is named most valuable defensive player of the Final Four.

MAZEL TOUGH

1915 – **Joe Fox** knocks out Jim Berry in the 16th round in London to win the vacant British bantamweight title.

1927 – **Moise Bouquillon** scores a 10-round decision over Fernand Delarge to win the French light heavyweight title in Paris.

1998 – **Sarah Abitbol** of France and her partner Stephane Bernadis win the senior pairs at the Troplee Lalique figure skating championships in Paris.

Doron Sheffer
(University of Connecticut)

TRANSITIONS

2003 – First-year coach **Dave Sarachan** of the Chicago Fire is named Coach of the Year in Major League Soccer after leading his team to the best regular-season record.

A STAR IS BORN

1900 – **Danny Kramer** (featherweight boxer)

1913 – **Herman "Biff" Schneidman** (Iowa and pro football)

1929 – **Ben Helfgott** (Polish weight lifter)

1941 – **Gerald Greenspan** (Maryland basketball)

NOVEMBER 23

GAMEBREAKERS

1918 – Syracuse lineman **Joe Alexander** intercepts two passes and returns a kick 75 yards for a touchdown in a 21-0 win over Rutgers.

1935 – **Moe Goldman** scores 12 points to lead the Philadelphia Sphas to a 29-25 victory over the Brooklyn Visitations in the ABL.

1939 – **Bernie Fliegel** scores 11 points as the Kingston Colonials defeat the Jersey Reds 27-26 in the ABL.

1939 – **Izzy "Spook" Specter** scores two touchdowns as Utah defeats Utah State 27-0.

2002 – **Evan Wax** scores four goals as Yale defeats Vermont 5-4 in hockey.

2003 – **Greg Gardner** stops 32 shots for his sixth shutout of the season as the Mississippi Sea Wolves defeat the Texas Wildcatters 4-0 in the East Coast Hockey League.

2003 – **Jay Fiedler**, out with a sprained left knee since Oct. 19, returns late in the third quarter and rallies Miami from a 13-point deficit in the Dolphins' 24-23 victory over the Washington Redskins. Fiedler's first play is a 31-yard pass that sets up a 71-yard touchdown drive.

2004 – **Dan Grunfeld** scores a game-high 20 points, including eight in an 11-0 run to open the second half as Stanford defeats Brigham Young 62-53 in the Maui Invitational.

STRONG IN DEFEAT

2005 – **Jordan Farmar** scores 28 points, but UCLA loses to Memphis 88-80.

MAZEL TOUGH

1915 – **Ted "Kid" Lewis** knocks out **Jimmy Duffy** in the first round in Boston to retain his world welterweight title.

1921 – **Fred J. Meyer** wins the 174-pound and heavyweight freestyle titles at the AAU Wrestling Championships.

1956 – **Isaac Berger** wins the weight lifting gold medal in the 60-kg. (featherweight) class at the Olympics in Melbourne with a total lift of 776.5 pounds.

1986 – Unseeded **Amos Mansdorf** of Israel beats Matt Anger 6-3, 3-6, 6-2, 7-5 in the final of the South African Open hard-court tennis tournament in Johannesburg.

1998 – **Adam Goucher** of Colorado wins the NCAA Cross Country championship in 29 minutes, 26.9 seconds in Lawrence, Kan.

A STAR IS BORN

1893 – **Joseph Bernstein** (LSU, Tulsa and pro football)

Isaac Berger

NOVEMBER 24

GAMEBREAKERS

1929 – **Jack Shapiro**, the shortest player in the history of pro football at 5 feet,½ inch, plays in his only pro game. Shapiro, a blocking back, rushes five times for seven yards and returns a punt 12 yards in the Staten Island Stapletons' 34-0 victory over the Minneapolis Redjackets. **Sammy Stein** catches a 50-yard touchdown pass.

1934 – **Dave Smukler** rushes 29 times for 152 yards and scores 10 points as Temple defeats Villanova 22-0.

1940 – **Johnny Siegal** returns a fumble two yards for a touchdown and **Sid Luckman** throws a 74-yard touchdown pass as the Chicago Bears defeat the Cleveland Rams 47-25.

1946 – **Abe Karnofsky** returns the opening kickoff 97 yards for a touchdown as the Boston Yanks defeat the Los Angeles Rams 40-21.

1951 – Chicago Black Hawks assistant trainer **Moe Roberts**, retired as a player since 1942, suits up in an emergency because of injuries to starting goalie Harry Lumley. The 46-year-old plays the third period and shuts out the Detroit Red Wings as Chicago wins 6-2.

1973 – **Randy Grossman** catches five passes for 109 yards and a touchdown in Temple's 34-0 win over Villanova.

1995 – Boston College tight end **Todd Pollack** catches two touchdown passes, including the game-winner, in a 41-38 victory over Rutgers.

2002 – **Haim Shimonovich** is named Hawaiian Airlines Tip-Off Tournament MVP as he scores 18 points in Hawaii's 100-81 victory over Texas A&M-Corpus Christie. The Israeli also scored 18 points in an 81-65 first-round victory over Arkansas-Little Rock.

STRONG IN DEFEAT

1935 – **Jim Levey** catches a 13-yard touchdown pass and runs three yards for another score, but the Pittsburgh Pirates lose to the Green Bay Packers 34-14.

MAZEL TOUGH

1906 – **Walter Miller** rides winners in all five races at Benning racetrack near Washington, D.C.

1949 – **Henry Laskau** wins the 10.5-mile Walker's Club of America race from New York's City Hall to Coney Island in 1 hour, 23 minutes, 3 seconds.

1964 – **Claude Netter** of France wins a fencing silver medal for team foil when Italy defeats France 9-7 in the final at the Melbourne Olympics.

1974 – The Montreal Alouettes, coached by **Marv Levy**, beat the Edmonton Eskimos 20-7 to win the Canadian Football League's Grey Cup championship in Vancouver.

1975 – **Harold Solomon** beats **Brian Gottfried** 6-3, 6-2, 5-7, 6-2 to win the Johannesburg hard-court tennis tournament in South Africa.

RECORD SETTERS

1962 – Cornell quarterback **Gary Wood** sets an Ivy League total offense record with 387 yards in a 29-22 win over Penn. He rushes for 207 yards and throws for 160.

TRANSITIONS

1966 – **Syd Halter**, first commissioner of the Canadian Football League, is elected to the CFL Hall of Fame in the builder's category.

A STAR IS BORN

1906 – **Anna Dresden-Polak** (Dutch gymnast)

1914 – **Andre Jesserun** (French Guiana welterweight boxer)

1939 – **Eugene Glazer** (fencing)

1966 – **Robert Burakovsky** (Ottawa Senators hockey)

NOVEMBER 25

GAMEBREAKERS

1905 – **Dutch Levine's** touchdown gives Yale a 6-0 victory over Harvard to finish off a 10-0 season.

1926 – Player-coach **Joe "Doc" Alexander** returns a fumble 52 yards for a touchdown as the New York Giants beat the Brooklyn Lions 17-0.

1928 – **Benny Friedman** runs for two touchdowns to rally the Detroit Wolverines to a 14-7 victory over the Chicago Bears.

1933 – Muhlenberg captain **Albert "Red" Weiner** ends his college football career by scoring on a 4-yard run, kicking the extra point, and returning an interception 48 yards in the Mules' 7-0 victory over Dickinson. **Charley Siegel** scores on a 33-yard pass reception in the second quarter to give NYU a 7-0 victory over Carnegie Tech.

1951 – Defenseman **Larry Zeidel** collects a goal and two assists as the Indianapolis Caps defeat Providence 6-5 in an American Hockey League game.

2001 – **Jay Fiedler** passes for 262 yards and three touchdowns, including a 32-yarder with 48 seconds remaining, as the Miami Dolphins rally to beat the Buffalo Bills 34-27.

2006 – **Shay Doron** has 23 points and seven assists and is named tournament MVP as top-ranked Maryland defeats Mississippi 110-79 in the Junkanoo Jam women's basketball final in Freeport, Bahamas.

MAZEL TOUGH

1911 – **Sid Smith** wins a 20-round decision over Stoker Hoskyne in London to claim the British flyweight title.

1938 – **Abe Denner** earns a 10-round decision over Tony Dupre in Boston to win the New England featherweight title.

1974 – **Julie Heldman** beats Fiorella Bonicelli of Uruguay 6-3, 6-1 to win the Argentine Open tennis tournament. **Ilana Kloss** teams with Kerry Melville to win the doubles at the South African Open in Johannesburg.

1984 – **Eliot Teltscher** beats Vitas Gerulaitis 6-3, 6-1, 7-6 in the final of a hard-court tennis tournament in Johannesburg, South Africa.

1989 – **Martin Jaite** defeats **Jay Berger** 6-4, 6-4 in the final of a hard-court tennis tournament in Itaparica, Brazil.

2001 – **Galit Chait** and **Sergei Sakhnovsky** of Israel, performing to a medley of Jewish folk music, win the silver medal in ice dancing at the Cup of Russia championships in St. Petersburg.

2006 – **Hagar Shmoulefeld** knocks out Judith Palacian of Hungary in the third round to retain her WIBF Intercontinental super flyweight title in Hasharon, Raanana, Israel.

2006 – **Ben Agosto** teams with Tanith Belbin to win the ice dancing competition at the Cup of Russia championships in Moscow.

TRANSITIONS

1997 – Toronto Maple Leafs defenseman **Mathieu Schneider** plays in his 500th career NHL game and registers his 200th assist in a 3-1 victory over the San Jose Sharks.

2002 – **Theo Epstein** is named general manager of the Boston Red Sox. At 28, he is the youngest GM in Major League Baseball history.

A STAR IS BORN

1904 – **Lillian Copeland** (track and field)

NOVEMBER 26

GAMEBREAKERS

1920 – **Nat Holman** scores 16 points and sets an Eastern Basketball League record with six assists as the Germantown Germs beat the Philadelphia Phillies.

1933 – **Cy Kaselman** scores 13 points and **Shikey Gotthoffer** adds 10 as the Philadelphia Sphas defeat the Bronx Americans 34-23 in the ABL.

1933 – **Moe Goldman** and **Pete Berenson** score eight points apiece to lead NYU to a 39-17 victory over St. Francis (N.Y.).

1936 – Pitt sophomore **Marshall Goldberg** scores three touchdowns, one on an 87-yard kickoff return, as the Panthers defeat Carnegie Tech 31-14.

1936 – **Moe Spahn** scores 10 points, including the game-winning basket in the final minute, as the Jersey Reds defeat the Brooklyn Jewels 33-31 in the ABL. **Allie Schuckman** leads the Jewels with seven points. **Phil Rabin** scores 13 points as the Kingston Colonials defeat the Atlantic City Sandpipers 27-16.

1939 – **Sid Luckman** throws two touchdown passes – one to **Johnny Siegal** – and returns an interception 33 yards for another score as the Chicago Bears defeat the Chicago Cardinals 48-7. **Solly Sherman** scores on a 68-yard interception return for the Bears.

1951 – **Boris Nachamkin** scores 23 points as NYU beats Fairleigh Dickinson 82-69.

2005 – Defenseman **Mathieu Schneider** scores three goals and adds an assist as the Detroit Red Wings defeat the San Jose Sharks 7-6. The hat trick is the first for Schneider in 17 years in the NHL.

2005 – **Julian Rauch** kicks field goals of 39 and 27 yards and adds four extra points as Appalachian State rallies to defeat Lafayette 34-23 in the first round of the NCAA Division I-AA football playoffs.

MAZEL TOUGH

1920 – Lightweight champion **Benny Leonard** knocks out Joe Welling in the 14th round in New York.

1949 – The Montreal Alouettes, coached by **Lew Hayman**, beat the Calgary Stampeders 28-15 to win their first Canadian Football League Grey Cup championship.

1994 – Goaltender **Larry Bercutt** makes six saves as Stanford beats Southern Cal 11-9 for the NCAA water polo championship. Bercutt and Southern Cal's **Uzi Hadar**, an Israeli national team member, are named tournament CO-MVPs.

2005 – **Irina Slutskaya** wins the Cup of Russia figure skating competition in St. Petersburg.

RECORD SETTERS

1944 – **Sid Luckman** throws a touchdown pass in his 19th consecutive game – still a Bears record – as Chicago beats the Philadelphia Eagles 28-7.

1999 – **Dan Hadenfeldt** of Nebraska punts seven times for 403 yards, a single-game school-record 57.6-yard average, as the Cornhuskers defeat Colorado 33-30 in overtime.

TRANSITIONS

1960 – **Red Auerbach** posts his 600th career NBA coaching victory as the Boston Celtics beat the Syracuse Nationals 129-110.

2002 – Philadelphia 76ers coach **Larry Brown** is named head coach of the U.S. basketball team that will compete in the 2004 Olympics in Athens.

A STAR IS BORN

1966 – **Jay Berger** (tennis)

NOVEMBER 27

GAMEBREAKERS

1921 – **Alec Fishman** scores his lone career touchdown on a 5-yard run as the Evansville Crimson Giants beat the Cincinnati Celts 48-0 in an American Professional Football League game.

1921 – **Moritz Haeusler** scores two goals as Hakoah Vienna's soccer team defeats Amateure Vienna 6-4.

1937 – **Moe Goldman** scores 12 points to lead the Philadelphia Sphas to a 35-31 victory over the Jersey Reds in the ABL.

1960 – **Shlomo Levi** scores a hat trick as Israel beats Cyprus 6-1 in a World Cup soccer qualifier.

2006 – **Mathieu Schneider** scores a short-handed goal with 7:47 remaining to give the Detroit Red Wings a 2-1 victory over the Dallas Stars.

STRONG IN DEFEAT

1924 – **Dutch Strauss** of the Kansas City Blues runs nine yards for his lone NFL touchdown in the closing minutes of a 17-6 loss to the Green Bay Packers at Muehlebach Field in Kansas City.

MAZEL TOUGH

1936 – **Barney Ross** beats Izzy Janazzo in 15 rounds in New York to retain his world welterweight title.

1976 – **Amy Alcott** beats Donna Caponi by one stroke and wins the LPGA Colgate-Far East Championship in Manilla.

1977 – The Montreal Alouettes, coached by **Marv Levy**, beat the Edmonton Eskimos 41-6 in Montreal to win the Canadian Football League's Grey Cup. It is Levy's second CFL title.

1978 – **Morris Wainstein** of South Africa wins a 10-round decision over Hansie van Rooyen in Johannesburg to capture the Transvaal featherweight title.

RECORD SETTERS

1997 – **David Nemirovsky** scores a Carolina Monarchs franchise-record five goals and adds one assist in a 12-1 victory over the Baltimore Bandits in an American Hockey League game. He scores another goal the next night against the Hershey Bears and earns a call-up to the NHL's Florida Panthers.

TRANSITIONS

1945 – Pitcher **Saul Rogovin** spends the night in jail after Oscar Yanes, head of his Caracus Winter League club, accuses him of walking too many batters. Rogovin is released without charge when team directors overrule Yanes.

1953 – **Al Rosen** of the Cleveland Indians is a unanimous selection as American League MVP, receiving a record 336 votes to easily outdistance runner-up Yogi Berra.

A STAR IS BORN

1892 – **Norman Cahn** (football)
1935 – **Lewis Stieglitz** (track and field)

David Nemirovsky
(Florida Panthers)

332

NOVEMBER 28

GAMEBREAKERS

1918 – Syracuse guard **Joe Alexander** scores on a 75-yard kick return and intercepts two passes as the Orangemen defeat Rutgers 21-0 at the Polo Grounds in New York.

1929 – **Benny Friedman** throws two touchdown passes, including a 20-yarder off a fake field-goal attempt, as the New York Giants beat the Staten Island Stapletons 21-7 on Thanksgiving Day.

1936 – **Moe Spahn** scores 12 and 15 points, respectively, as the Jersey Reds defeat both the Philadelphia Sphas 38-36 and the Brooklyn Visitations 37-35 to run their ABL record to 7-0.

1941 – **Jack "Dutch" Garfinkel** of St. John's is named MVP of the College All-Star basketball game in Chicago.

1943 – **Sid Luckman** throws four touchdown passes to lead the Chicago Bears to a 35-24 victory over the Chicago Cardinals.

1946 – **Abe Karnofsky** runs 35 yards for a touchdown as the Boston Yanks beat the Detroit Lions 34-10.

2003 – **Jay Fiedler** runs for a touchdown and throws for 239 yards including three TD passes to Chris Chambers as the Miami Dolphins beat the Dallas Cowboys 41-20 on Thanksgiving Day. Fiedler's 10th rushing touchdown is the most by a quarterback in Dolphins history.

2003 – **Shay Doron** is named to the all-tournament team and scores 15 points as Maryland defeats Maryland-Eastern Shore 97-65 in the Terrapin Classic final. The previous night, she scored a game-high 22 points as the Terps beat Sacred Heart 90-49.

STRONG IN DEFEAT

1967 – **Barry Leibowitz** scores 28 points, but the Pittsburgh Condors lose to the New Orleans Buccaneers 106-99 in the American Basketball Association.

MAZEL TOUGH

1927 – **Leo Lomski** wins a 12-round decision over Tony Marullo and **Battling Levinsky** decisions Joe Lohman in 10 rounds in New York. **Joey Medill** wins an eight-round decision over Ralph Mendoza in Chicago and **Willie Harmon** knocks out Young Sailor in eight rounds in Pittsburgh.

2001 – One day after winning the 100 freestyle in 47.67 seconds, **Jason Lezak** captures the 50 freestyle in 21.86 seconds at the FINA World Cup Swimming Championships in East Meadow, N.Y.

TRANSITIONS

1969 – **Abe Eliowitz**, a fullback and halfback for the Ottawa Rough Riders and Montreal Alouettes, is elected to the Canadian Football League Hall of Fame.

2006 – Former Rice and Duke coach **Fred Goldsmith** is named head football coach at Lenoir-Rhyne.

A STAR IS BORN

1883 – **Cecil Hart** (Montreal Canadiens coach)

1920 – **Leo Gottlieb** (New York Knicks)

NOVEMBER 29

GAMEBREAKERS

1925 – **Jozsef Eisenhoffer** scores three goals as Hakoah Vienna defeats S.C. Rudolfshugel 4-0 in Austrian soccer.

1928 – **Benny Friedman** throws two touchdown passes and runs six yards for another TD as the Detroit Wolverines beat the Dayton Triangles 33-0.

1942 – **Sid Luckman** throws two touchdown passes, including a 24-yarder to **Johnny Siegal**, as the Chicago Bears beat the Cleveland Rams 47-0.

1959 – **Mike Sommer** scores his first of two NFL touchdowns on a three-yard run to help the Baltimore Colts beat the Los Angeles Rams 35-21.

1997 – **Todd Simon** scores a hat trick as the Cincinnati Cyclones beat the Cleveland Lumberjacks 5-2 in an International Hockey League game. His empty-net goal with 15.6 seconds remaining is his 12th goal of the season.

2003 – **Mike Cammalleri** scores two goals as the Los Angeles Kings defeat the Chicago Blackhawks 3-1.

2003 – **Liad Suez** of Israel scores 16 points and is named tournament MVP as Villanova defeats New Mexico 70-57 in the championship game of the Lobo Invitational women's basketball tournament. **Amy Argetsinger** scores 26 points and grabs 11 rebounds as DePauw defeats Maryville 77-65 in the Maryville (Tenn.) Thanksgiving Classic championship game.

MAZEL TOUGH

1887 – **Joe Choynski** defeats William Kenneally to win the Pacific Coast amateur boxing heavyweight championship in San Francisco.

1950 – Jockey **Sidney Cole** rides his first career winner aboard Cassina at the Fair Grounds in New Orleans.

1956 – **Yves Dreyfus** and **Armand Mouyal** win fencing bronze medals for team epee at the Melbourne Olympics when France loses to Hungary 9-7 and gold-medallist Italy 15-1.

1962 – **Ralph Cooperman** wins the gold medal in individual saber at the Commonwealth Games fencing competition in Perth, Australia. Cooperman also wins gold in team saber and team foil.

1976 – **Harold Solomon** beats **Brian Gottfried** 6-2, 6-7, 6-2, 6-4 to win the South African Open tennis tournament.

1988 – **Gary Jacobs** knocks out Richard Rova in the fourth round in London to retain his British Commonwealth welterweight title.

RECORD SETTERS

1930 – **Marchy Schwartz** sets a Notre Dame school record by punting 15 times and scores the Fighting Irish's only touchdown on a 54-yard run in a 7-6 victory over previously unbeaten Army at Soldier Field in Chicago.

TRANSITIONS

1969 – Former Cheney State (Pa.) coach **Hal Blitman** takes over as head coach of the ABA's Miami Floridians after the team gets off to a 5-15 start.

1978 – Chicago White Sox pitcher **Steve Stone** signs a four-year guaranteed contract with the Baltimore Orioles and becomes the first player to go through the free-agent re-entry draft twice.

A STAR IS BORN

1931 – **Allen Rosenberg** (rowing)
1972 – **Carrie Sheinberg** (skiing)

NOVEMBER 30

GAMEBREAKERS

1918 – **Joe Alexander** picks up a fumble and returns it 75 yards for a touchdown as Syracuse defeats Rutgers 21-0.

1929 – **Lou Spindell** scores a game-high eight points and **Milt Trupin** adds seven as CCNY defeats St. John's 25-21.

1941 – **Johnny Siegal** catches a 59-yard touchdown pass and **Sid Luckman** throws for two touchdowns as the Chicago Bears beat the Philadelphia Eagles 49-14.

1967 – **Larry Brown** scores a game-high 24 points as the New Orleans Buccaneers beat the Oakland Oaks 141-119 in the American Basketball Association.

MAZEL TOUGH

1897 – **Joe Choynski,** weighing 168 pounds, fights to a 20-round draw with future heavyweight champion Jim Jeffries, who weighs 220.

1928 – **Ray Miller** stops future welterweight champion Jimmy McLarnin at the start of the eighth round in Detroit – the only knockout of McLarnin's career.

1956 – **Laszlo Fabian** of Hungary wins the 10,000-meter pairs kayak gold medal in 43:37 at the Olympics in Melbourne. **Leon Rottman** of Romania wins a gold medal in 10,000-meter Canadian singles canoe when he finishes in 56 minutes, 41 seconds – 30 seconds ahead of the silver medalist. **Imre Farkas** of Hungary captures a bronze in 10,000-meter Canadian pairs canoeing. **Eva Szekely** of Hungary wins a swimming silver medal in the 200 breaststroke.

1989 – **Margie Goldstein** rides Saluut II to victory in the speed competition portion of the North American Grand Prix equestrian event.

1991 – Defender **Debbie Belkin** and the United States women's soccer team beat Norway 2-1 in China to capture the first FIFA Women's World Cup.

1996 – **Gordie Sheer** teams with Chris Thorpe to win a World Cup luge event at Sigulda, Latvia.

1990 – Heavyweight **Tim Puller** makes his pro boxing debut with a second-round knockout of Pedro Garza.

2003 – **Jason Lezak** wins the 50 freestyle in 21.68 seconds at the World Cup Short-Course Swimming Championships in Melbourne, Australia.

A STAR IS BORN

1899 – **Reuben Ewing** (St. Louis Cardinals pitcher)

1931 – **Ed Mayer** (Chicago Cubs pitcher)

1943 – **Steve Kolinsky** (minor-league baseball)

1955 – **Joel Kramer** (San Diego State basketball, Phoenix Suns)

1979 – **Antonio Garay** (Boston College, Cleveland Browns defensive tackle)

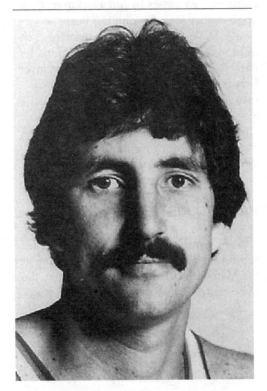

Joel Kramer *(Phoenix Suns)*

DECEMBER 1

GAMEBREAKERS

1924 – Rochester center **Joe Alexander** scores the tying touchdown, and the Jeffersons go on to beat the previously unbeaten Pottsville Maroons of the Anthracite Football Association 10-7.

1929 – **Benny Friedman** throws touchdown passes of 12 and 21 yards – extending his streak to seven consecutive games with at least one TD pass – as the New York Giants beat the Chicago Cardinals 24-21.

1935 – **Walt Singer** catches a 7-yard touchdown pass as the New York Giants defeat the Philadelphia Eagles 21-14.

1938 – **Phil Rabin** scores 31 points as the Jersey Reds defeat the Washington Brewers 39-34 in the ABL.

1946 – **Marshall Goldberg** runs 32 yards for a touchdown as the Chicago Cardinals overcome two TD passes by **Sid Luckman** for a 35-28 victory over the Chicago Bears.

1954 – **Dave Gotkin** scores a team-high 23 points as North Carolina State opens its basketball season with a 100-74 victory over Furman.

1956 – **Syd Levy** scores 25 points in CCNY's 82-74 victory over Hunter.

1962 – **Art Heyman** scores 31 points in Duke's 80-58 victory over Florida.

1967 – **Neal Walk** scores 37 points as Florida defeats Jacksonville 109-73.

MAZEL TOUGH

1956 – **Leon Rottman** of Romania wins his second Olympic gold medal for canoeing at the Melbourne Games when he captures the 1,000-meter Canadian singles event in 5:05.3.

1984 – **Mark Roth** beats **Marshall Holman** 194-177 in the final of the PBA Angle Tournament Players Championship in Charlotte, N.C.

2001 – **Maxim Podoprigora** of Austria wins the 200 breaststroke in 2:11.59 at a FINA World Cup swim meet in Shanghai, China.

2002 – **Tzipi Obziler** of Israel, who recently came out of retirement, defeats Adriana Barna of Germany 6-2, 6-2 to win her 10th career ITF Challenger Series tennis tournament in Mumbai, India.

2002 – **Stephanie Cohen-Aloro** of France defeats Melinda Czink 6-4, 6-2 in the finals of a tennis tournament in Mount Gambier, Australia.

RECORD SETTERS

1998 – **Doug Gottlieb** sets an Oklahoma State basketball record with 18 assists in an 83-81 loss to Florida Atlantic.

JEWS ON FIRST

1924 – **Sam Rothschild** becomes the first Jewish skater to appear in an NHL game when he comes off the bench in the Montreal Maroons' 2-1 loss to the Boston Bruins.

A STAR IS BORN

1889 – **Leonard Frank** (Minnesota football)
1928 – **Stanley Lampert** (track and field)
1932 – **Sid Youngelman** (Alabama football, San Francisco 49ers, Philadelphia Eagles, Cleveland Browns, New York Titans, Buffalo Bills lineman)
1942 – **Gary Gubner** (track and field, weight lifting)

DECEMBER 2

GAMEBREAKERS

1923 – **Ralph Horween** runs for a touchdown and his brother **Arnold Horween** kicks a 35-yard field goal as the Chicago Cardinals beat the Oorang Indians 22-19.

1923 – **Alexander Nemes-Neufeld** scores all three goals for Hakoah Vienna in a 3-1 soccer victory over WR Association FC.

1933 – **Allie Schuckman** scores 17 points and **Mac Kinsbrunner** adds 12 as the Brooklyn Jewels defeat the Philadelphia Sphas 36-26 in the ABL.

1937 – **Moe Frankel** scores 15 points to lead the Jersey Reds to a 34-22 victory over the Philadelphia Sphas in the ABL.

1938 – **Allie Schuckman** scores 13 points as the Wilkes-Barre Barons defeat the Brooklyn Visitations 33-31 in the ABL.

1945 – With the ball two inches from the goal line, **Sam Fox** of the Giants catches one of the shortest touchdown passes in NFL history on fourth down to give New York a 28-21 victory over the Philadelphia Eagles. **Sid Luckman** throws for two touchdowns as the Chicago Bears overcome two TD runs by **Leo Cantor** for a 28-20 victory over the Chicago Cardinals.

1979 – **Dave Jacobs** kicks his first three field goals in the NFL, covering 27, 28, and 42 yards, as the New York Jets defeat the Baltimore Colts 30-17.

2001 – **Jeff Halpern** of Washington scores with 1:36 left in overtime to give the Capitals a 4-3 victory over the Carolina Hurricanes in Raleigh, N.C.

MAZEL TOUGH

1919 – Featherweight **Benny Bass** makes his pro boxing debut with a first-round knockout of Jack Martin in Philadelphia.

TRANSITIONS

1933 – Former Pittsburgh Pirates infielder **Jake Pitler** is named manager of the Scranton Miners of the New York-Penn League. Pitler managed at Springfield, Ohio, Elmira, N.Y., and Hazleton, Pa., before taking the Scranton job.

1967 – The New Jersey Americans trade **Art Heyman** to the 11-12 Pittsburgh Condors for **Barry Leibowitz**. Heyman averages 20.9 points as Pittsburgh wins its next 15 games. The Condors finish 54-24 and go on to win the American Basketball Association title.

1967 – **Dov Markus** of Long Island University is named the first winner of the Hermann Trophy, awarded to the top college soccer player.

DECEMBER 3

GAMEBREAKERS

1933 – **Harry Newman** throws two touchdown passes in the New York Giants' 27-3 victory over the Pittsburgh Pirates.

1944 – **Allie Sherman** scores on a 3-yard run as the Philadelphia Eagles beat the Brooklyn Tigers 34-0.

1957 – **Murray Guttman** scores 37 points, including a game-winning 40-foot shot, as Toledo defeats ninth-ranked Niagara 91-89 in overtime. Guttman makes a school-record 17 field goals.

1959 – **Harvey Salz** scores 18 points, including 14-of-18 from the foul line, as North Carolina beats South Carolina 93-56 in the basketball season opener.

1964 – **Jeff Neuman** scores 21 points to help Penn defeat Rutgers 100-75.

2000 – **Jay Fiedler** throws for 214 yards and three touchdowns as the Miami Dolphins beat the Buffalo Bills 33-6.

2006 – **Brian Bacharach** scores two goals as California defeats Southern Cal 7-6 to win the NCAA water polo championship in Los Angeles.

MAZEL TOUGH

1907 – **Harry P. Cline** defeats John Daly 50-41 to win a playoff for the National Three-Cushion billiards championship in St. Louis.

1967 – In his first golf tournament since turning professional, **Marty Fleckman** sinks a 30-foot birdie putt to beat Jack Montgomery in a one-hole playoff to win the PGA Cajun Classic in Lafayette, La. Both golfers finish 72 holes at 13-under-par 275.

RECORD SETTERS

1956 – **Lenny Rosenbluth** of North Carolina scores a school-record 47 points in a season-opening 94-66 win over Furman.

JEWS ON FIRST

1998 – **Cliff Bayer** becomes the first American men's foil fencer to win a gold medal at a World Cup event, winning the Junior A division at Aix-En-Provence, France.

TRANSITIONS

1999 – The Minnesota Timberwolves release 18-year veteran **Danny Schayes,** leaving the NBA without a Jewish player for the first time in the league's history.

2003 – **Rudi Ball**, who played on eight German national championship teams in the 1920s and 1930s, is elected to the International Ice Hockey Federation Hall of Fame.

A STAR IS BORN

1887 – **Abe Hollandersky** (welterweight boxer)

Cliff Bayer
(U.S. Olympic Committee)

DECEMBER 4

GAMEBREAKERS

1937 – **Cy Kaselman** scores 15 points to lead the Philadelphia Sphas over the New York Jewels 44-36. **Shikey Gotthoffer** adds 13 points and **Moe Goldman** contributes 11.

1938 – Running back **Dave Smukler** throws three touchdown passes and kicks all three extra points as the Philadelphia Eagles beat the Detroit Lions 21-7 in the season finale.

1948 – **Herb Rich** catches a 50-yard touchdown pass in Vanderbilt's 33-6 win over Miami.

1962 – **Neil Farber** scores 22 points as Columbia defeats CCNY 67-42 in its basketball season opener.

1966 – **Gary Wood** throws a 33-yard touchdown pass and runs for TDs of 5 and 16 yards in the New York Giants' 49-40 loss to the Cleveland Browns.

2005 – **Sage Rosenfels** enters the game in the third quarter and passes for 272 yards and two touchdowns, including a 4-yarder to Chris Chambers with six seconds left as the Miami Dolphins rally past the Buffalo Bills 24-23. He directs scoring drives of 70, 49, and 73 yards in the fourth quarter.

STRONG IN DEFEAT

1967 – **Neal Walk** of Florida has 24 points and 29 rebounds in the Gators' 99-76 loss to Kentucky.

MAZEL TOUGH

1940 – Spokane Bombers goalie **Sam "Porky" Levine** is hit in the throat by a puck and knocked unconscious in a Pacific Coast Hockey League game against the Portland Buckaroos. Against doctor's orders, Levine returns to the ice, plays with a towel wrapped around his neck for protection, and leads Spokane to a 3-2 victory. After the game, Levine undergoes emergency surgery.

1956 – **David Tyschler** of the Soviet Union wins an Olympic fencing bronze medal in team saber when the Russians beat France 9-7 for third place in Melbourne.

2000 – **George Weissfisch** of the United States defeats opponents from Canada, Brazil, and the Dominican Republic in winning the taekwondo heavyweight gold medal at the Pan American Games in Oranjestad, Aruba.

JEWS ON FIRST

1929 – The St. John's "Wonder Five" – returning starters **Mac Kinsbrunner**, **Max Posnack**, **Allie Schuckman**, **Rip Gerson**, and newcomer Matt Begovich – play together for the first time and defeat the Columbus Council K of C 32-29 as Gerson scores three points in overtime. The Wonder Five will compile a two-year record of 44-2.

TRANSITIONS

1950 – **Nat Holman**, basketball coach of national champion CCNY, makes the cover of Newsweek.

1997 – **Henry Laskau**, winner of 42 national race walks, is inducted into the National Track and Field Hall of Fame.

A STAR IS BORN

1917 – **Daniel Bukantz** (fencing)

1936 – **Don Rogers** (South Carolina football, San Diego Chargers offensive lineman)

DECEMBER 5

GAMEBREAKERS

1908 – **Ira Streusand** scores 14 points and **Max Kaplan** adds 10 as CCNY opens its basketball season with a 32-16 victory over Yale.

1931 – **Lou Wishnewitz** scores 10 points and **Moe Goldman** adds seven as CCNY defeats St. Joseph's 39-18.

1936 – **Inky Lautman** scores 13 points as the Philadelphia Sphas defeat the Jersey Reds 42-30 in the ABL.

1948 – **Sid Luckman** throws three touchdown passes in the Chicago Bears' 42-14 victory over the Detroit Lions.

1997 – **Sara Whalen** scores twice as Connecticut upsets Notre Dame 2-1 in the NCAA women's soccer semifinals. Despite a 2-0 loss to North Carolina two days later in the final, Whalen is named Most Outstanding Defensive Player of the Final Four.

1998 – **Gus Ornstein** passes for 332 yards and two touchdowns as Rowan beats Wisconsin-Eau Claire 22-19 in the NCAA Division III semifinals.

MAZEL TOUGH

1942 – The Toronto Argonauts of the Canadian Football League, coached by **Lew Hayman**, beat the Winnipeg Blue Bombers 8-5 for the Grey Cup championship.

1956 – **Agnes Keleti** of Hungary wins gymnastics gold medals in floor exercise and balance beam and a silver medal in all-around at the Olympics in Melbourne.

TRANSITIONS

2003 – Distance runner **Deena Drossin** is presented the Jesse Owens Award as the year's top female track and field athlete in the United States.

Sara Whalen
(U.S. Olympic Committee)

A STAR IS BORN

1837 – **Philo Jacoby** (shooting)
1938 – **Mark Lazarus** (English soccer)
1947 – **Yehoshua Feigenbaum** (Israeli soccer)
1950 – **Steve Furness** (Rhode Island football, Pittsburgh Steelers, Detroit Lions defensive lineman)

DECEMBER 6

GAMEBREAKERS

1924 – **Leo Palitz** scores 14 points to lead CCNY to a 27-18 victory over Manhattan.

1931 – **Benny Friedman** throws for two touchdowns as the New York Giants beat the Brooklyn Dodgers 19-6 at Ebbets Field.

1936 – **Inky Lautman** scores 13 points and **Reds Rosan** adds nine as the Philadelphia Sphas end the Jersey Reds' eight-game winning streak at the start of the ABL season with a 42-30 victory. The Reds play without star **Moe Spahn**, who is coaching CCNY against Brooklyn College while **Nat Holman** stays with his ill father.

1970 – **Dave Newmark** comes off the bench in the fourth quarter and scores 10 points to help the Carolina Cougars beat the New York Nets 94-90 in the American Basketball Association.

1977 – **Bobby Gross** scores 27 points to lead the Portland Trail Blazers past the Cleveland Cavaliers 116-94.

1990 – Toronto Maple Leafs goalie **Peter Ing** stops 29 of 30 shots in a 2-1 overtime victory over the Minnesota North Stars.

MAZEL TOUGH

1926 – **Mortimer Lindsey** rolls 1,761 over eight games to win the Dwyer's Individual Sweepstakes bowling tournament in New York.

1928 – **Jackie "Kid" Berg** wins a 15-round decision over champion Alf Mancini in London to capture the British lightweight title.

1956 – **Agnes Keleti** of Hungary wins a gymnastics gold medal on the bars at the Olympics in Melbourne.

1959 – **Sauveur Benamou** of Algeria wins a 15-round decision over Fernand Nollet in Olan, Algeria, to capture the French lightweight title.

2002 – **Lenny Krayzelburg** wins the 100 backstroke in 55.09 seconds at the U.S. Open Long Course Indoor Swimming Championships in Minneapolis.

JEWS ON FIRST

1925 – **Nat Holman** scores three points to help the Original Celtics beat the Palace Club of Washington, D.C., 35-33 in the first pro basketball game at the new Madison Square Garden. Both teams' captains are served with a summons for violating the Sabbath law.

A STAR IS BORN

1905 – **Joey Kaufman** (lightweight boxer)

1927 – **James Emanuel Fuchs** (track and field)

1933 – **Boris Nachamkin** (NYU basketball, Rochester Royals)

1935 – **Phil Perlo** (Maryland football, Houston Oilers linebacker)

Lenny Krayzelburg
(U.S. Olympic Committee)

DECEMBER 7

GAMEBREAKERS

1929 – **Benny Friedman** returns an interception 23 yards for a touchdown as the New York Giants beat the Frankford Yellow Jackets 12-0.

1936 – **Moe Spahn** scores 15 points as the Jersey Reds defeat the Atlantic City Snipers 37-28 in the ABL. **Sam Winograd** leads Atlantic City with 10 points.

1938 – **Si Boardman** scores 13 points as the Wilkes-Barre Barons defeat the Troy Haymakers 32-21, and **Bernie Fliegel** scores 11 points in the Kingston Colonials' 29-17 victory over the Brooklyn Visitations in the ABL.

1939 – **Mike Bloom** scores 13 points to lead the Washington Brewers to a 31-20 victory over the Wilkes-Barre Barons in the ABL.

1962 – **Neil Farber's** 23 points lead Columbia to a 78-67 win over Colgate. **Barry Kramer** scores a career-high 42 points as NYU defeats Georgetown 85-65.

1967 – **Neal Walk** collects 30 points and 27 rebounds in Florida's 95-87 victory over Florida State.

1968 – **Neal Walk** scores 31 points as Florida beats Miami 111-62.

2002 – **Shiri Sharon** of Duquesne scores a game-high 18 points as the Dukes defeat Towson State 41-38 in women's basketball.

STRONG IN DEFEAT

1957 – **Mel Brodsky** of Temple scores 24 points, but the Owls lose to Kentucky 85-83 in three overtimes.

MAZEL TOUGH

1906 – **Abe Attell** beats Jimmy Walsh with an eighth-round knockout to reclaim the world featherweight title he previously held from 1903-04.

1926 – **Leo Lomski** knocks out Harry Dillon in the seventh round in Portland, Ore., to win the Pacific Coast light heavyweight title.

1956 – **Agnes Keleti** and **Aliz Kertesz** win Olympic gold medals in Melbourne for gymnastics team exercise with portable apparatus. They also earn silver medals in team combined exercises.

1987 – **Cindy Bortz** of the United States wins the girls championship at the World Juniors Ice Skating Championships in Kitchener, Ontario.

RECORD SETTERS

1962 – **Barry Kramer** scores a school-record 42 points, breaking the old mark of 40, as NYU defeats Georgetown 85-65. Kramer also breaks the single-game school record of 18 free throws.

TRANSITIONS

1914 – **Charlotte Epstein** forms the National Women's Life Saving League in New York, which becomes the New York Women's Swimming Association. Epstein eventually lobbies the national Amateur Athletic Union to permit women to compete in swimming events.

1965 – **Red Auerbach** wins his 900th game as an NBA coach when the Boston Celtics beat the St. Louis Hawks 112-96.

2006 – **Young Barney Aaron**, a nineteenth-century British lightweight, is elected to the International Boxing Hall of Fame.

A STAR IS BORN

1905 – **Jackie Cohen** (featherweight boxer)

1925 – **Max Zaslofsky** (St. John's basketball, New York Knicks, Chicago Stags, Baltimore Bullets, Milwaukee Hawks, Fort Wayne Pistons)

1942 – **Rick Kaminsky** (Yale basketball)

DECEMBER 8

GAMEBREAKERS

1940 – **Sid Luckman** throws a 30-yard touchdown pass and runs one yard for another touchdown as the Chicago Bears crush the Washington Redskins 73-0 for the NFL championship. Luckman completes 4 of 6 passes for 102 yards and sits out the second half of the biggest rout in championship game history. **Solly Sherman** passes for one point after touchdown conversion.

1946 – **Abe Karnofsky** catches a 56-yard touchdown pass in the Boston Yanks' 40-14 loss to the Philadelphia Eagles.

1958 – **Sid Cohen** of Kentucky comes off the bench seven minutes into the game and scores a game-high 19 points to lead the Wildcats past Duke 78-64.

1962 – **Art Heyman** scores 33 points as Duke beats Louisville 86-56.

MAZEL TOUGH

1956 – **Boris Razinsky** of the Soviet Union wins an Olympic gold medal in Melbourne when Russia defeats Yugoslavia 1-0 in soccer.

2002 – **Tzipi Obziler** of Israel wins her second straight ITF Challenger Series tennis tournament, beating Ivana Abramovic 6-4, 6-4 in Nonthaburi, Thailand.

TRANSITIONS

1935 – The Amateur Athletic Union defeats a proposal to boycott the 1936 Olympics in Germany by 2½ votes.

A STAR IS BORN

1816 – **August Belmont** (horse racing)
1900 – **Mose Solomon** (New York Giants outfielder)
1907 – **Robert Fein** (Austrian weight lifter)
1923 – **Stanley Landes** (National League umpire)
1931 – **Bob Arum** (boxing promoter)
1945 – **Julie Heldman** (tennis)
1950 – **Bill Ellenbogen** (Virginia Tech, New York Giants offensive lineman)

DECEMBER 9

GAMEBREAKERS

1928 – **Benny Friedman** runs 15 yards for a touchdown and throws TD passes of 50, 49, and 5 yards as the Detroit Wolverines beat the New York Yankees 34-6 at Yankee Stadium.

1936 – **Phil Rabin** scores 18 points to lead the Kingston Colonials to a 44-27 victory over the Brooklyn Jewels.

1938 – **Inky Lautman** scores 16 points as the Philadelphia Sphas defeat the Washington Brewers 43-34 in the ABL.

1939 – **Petey Rosenberg** scores 16 points and **Phil Rabin** adds 11 as the Philadelphia Sphas' 59-45 victory over the Troy Haymakers in the ABL.

1945 – **Allie Sherman** runs for a touchdown in the Philadelphia Eagles' 35-7 victory over the Boston Yanks.

1957 – Behind 19 points by **Alan Seiden**, St. John's defeats Bridgeport 78-66.

1967 – **Neal Walk** of Florida scores 31 points and grabs 23 rebounds in the Gators' 82-72 victory over West Virginia.

1979 – **Dave Jacobs** kicks a pair of field goals, including a 25-yarder in the fourth quarter as the New York Jets hold off the New England Patriots 27-26.

1989 – **Nadav Henefeld** has 12 points and 11 rebounds as Connecticut defeats Maine 95-55.

2000 – **Shawn Mamane** scores two goals as the Worcester IceCats beat the Portland Pirates 6-2 in the American Hockey League.

2000 – **Jeff Halpern** of the Washington Capitals scores the game-winning goal in the first period of a 3-2 victory over the New Jersey Devils.

2003 – **Liad Suez** scores 26 points including two free throws with seven seconds left to seal Villanova's 72-68 victory over St. Joseph's in women's basketball.

2006 – **Mike Cammalleri** scores his 11th and 12th goals of the season as the Los Angeles Kings defeat the Colorado Avalanche 5-4.

2006 – Freshman guard **Jon Scheyer** scores 18 points to help Duke defeat George Mason 69-53.

MAZEL TOUGH

2001 – **Stephanie Cohen-Aloro** of France defeats Marina Caiazzo 6-4, 7-5 in the final of a satellite tennis tour hard-court tournament in Nonthabori, Thailand.

2004 – **Sarah Poewe** of Germany wins the 50 breaststroke in 31.09 seconds at the European Short-Course swimming championships in Vienna.

RECORD SETTERS

1947 – **Grigori Novak** of Ukraine sets one of his 55 world weight lifting records in the light heavyweight division.

TRANSITIONS

1938 – The Pittsburgh Steelers make Columbia quarterback **Sid Luckman** their No. 1 pick, and the second player chosen overall in the NFL draft. By prior arrangement, he is traded to the Chicago Bears. With the 12th pick overall, the Chicago Cardinals select University of Pittsburgh running back **Marshall Goldberg**.

A STAR IS BORN

1905 – **Leo Palitz** (CCNY basketball)
1936 – **Eleazar Davidman** (Israeli tennis)

DECEMBER 10

GAMEBREAKERS

1933 – **Harry Newman** throws a touchdown pass and catches a pass for a touchdown in the New York Giants' 20-14 victory over the Philadelphia Eagles.

1938 – **Inky Lautman** scores 13 points and **Petey Rosenberg** adds 12 as the Philadelphia Sphas defeat the Jersey Reds 44-34 in the ABL.

1967 – **Art Heyman** scores 31 points as Pittsburgh beats Minnesota 114-94 in the American Basketball Association.

1967 – **Karl Sweetan** throws three touchdown passes in the first half and finishes with 216 yards passing as the Detroit Lions beat the New York Giants 30-7.

1978 – **Randy Grossman** catches a 12-yard touchdown pass as the Pittsburgh Steelers defeat the Baltimore Colts 35-13.

2001 – Miami Dolphins quarterback **Jay Fiedler** throws three touchdown passes and runs nine yards for another TD in a 41-6 rout of the Indianapolis Colts in a Monday Night Football game.

MAZEL TOUGH

1933 – **Viktor Barna** beats **Laszlo Bellak** 12-21, 21-14, 15-21, 21-5, 21-14 to win the world table tennis championship in Paris.

1933 – **Morris Fleischer** wins the 25,000-meter walk at the AAU championships, finishing in 2:17:17, nearly a minute in front of runner-up **Morris Davis**.

1934 – **Barney Ross** wins a 12-round decision over Bobby Pacho in Cleveland to retain his world super lightweight title.

1938 – The Toronto Argonauts, coached by **Lew Hayman**, beat the Winnipeg Blue Bombers 30-7 for the Canadian Football League's Grey Cup championship. Hayman's teams win five titles – four with Toronto and one with Montreal.

1973 – **Julie Heldman** beats Fiorella Bonicelli of Peru 6-1, 6-2 to win the Brazilian International tennis tournament in Sao Paulo.

2000 – **Jonathan Tiomkin** wins the men's foil at the North American Cup Open Fencing Championships in Palm Springs, Calif.

JEWS ON FIRST

1933 – **Max Kaminsky** scores unassisted for the game's first goal, leading the Ottawa Senators to a 5-2 victory over the New York Americans. The goal is Kaminsky's first of 22 in the NHL.

A STAR IS BORN

1912 – **Henry Prusoff** (tennis)
1945 – **Mickey Abarbanel** (minor-league baseball)
1965 – **Gary Jacobs** (Scottish welterweight boxer)

Jay Fiedler *(The Express-Times)*

DECEMBER 11

GAMEBREAKERS

1929 – **Allie Schuckman** scores 12 points to lead St. John's to a 47-23 victory over Cathedral College.

1937 – **Willie Rubenstein** scores 10 points to lead the New York Jewels to a 44-40 victory over the Philadelphia Sphas. **Reds Rosan** and **Cy Kaselman** score 10 points each for the Sphas.

1947 – **Dolph Schayes** scores 25 points in NYU's 85-62 win over Arkansas.

2004 – **Jordan Farmar** scores 25 points as UCLA defeats Pepperdine 85-83.

MAZEL TOUGH

1933 – **Jackie Brown** wins a 15-round decision over Ginger Foran in Manchester, England, to retain his NBA world flyweight title.

1947 – **Dave Katzen** wins a 12-round decision over Jackie Solomons to win the South African lightweight title in Durban, South Africa.

1975 – **Marshall Holman** beats Carmen Salvaggio 208-203 in the final of the PBA Hawaiian Invitational.

JEWS ON FIRST

1959 – **Sylvia Wene Martin** bowls her second career 300 game in the World Invitational Match Game Tournament in Chicago. It is the first perfect game bowled by a woman in national competition.

TRANSITIONS

1963 – **Marv Levy** resigns as head football coach at the University of California to take the same position at William & Mary, where he is named Southern Conference coach of the year in 1964 and 1965.

1978 – The New York Knicks fire coach Willis Reed and hire **Red Holzman** to coach the team for the third time. Holzman previously coached the Knicks in 1969-70 and 1972-73.

1992 – **Gary Bettman,** the NBA's senior vice president and general counsel, is named the National Hockey League's first commissioner.

A STAR IS BORN

1959 – **Steve Richmond** (Michigan hockey, New Jersey Devils, New York Rangers)

Marv Levy
(The Express-Times)

DECEMBER 12

GAMEBREAKERS

1936 – **Phil Rabin** scores an American Basketball League-record 25 points as the Kingston Colonials defeat the Philadelphia Sphas 49-43. **Reds Rosan** scores 15 for the Sphas.

1953 – **Boris Nachamkin** scores 27 points in NYU's 78-73 victory over Syracuse.

1959 – With his team trailing 10-0, **Mike Sommer** runs 53 yards for a touchdown to help rally the Baltimore Colts to a 45-26 victory over the Los Angeles Rams. The Colts clinch the Western Division title with the win. Before the game, **Sid Gilman** announces his resignation after five years as Rams head coach.

1959 – **Harvey Salz** scores 17 points to help North Carolina beat Kansas State 68-52.

1977 – **Nancy Lieberman** scores a career-high 40 points as Old Dominion defeats Norfolk State 111-56.

2003 – **Cory Pecker** scores two goals, including the game-winner with 6:17 remaining, as the Cincinnati Mighty Ducks defeat the San Antonio Rampage 4-3 in the American Hockey League.

2004 – **Todd Simon** scores twice in the final seven minutes – including the tying goal with 13 seconds left – and Wolfsburg goes on to defeat Krefeld 5-4 in a penalty shootout in the German Elite Hockey League.

MAZEL TOUGH

1927 – **Izzy Schwartz** wins a 15-round decision over **Newsboy Brown** in New York to capture the New York State version of the world flyweight title.

1938 – **Sammy Luftspring** wins a 10-round decision over Tommy Bland in Toronto to retain his Canadian welterweight title.

1996 – **Andy Borodow** of Canada finishes second in the Sumo wrestling world championships in Tokyo.

RECORD SETTERS

1882 – **Lon Myers** sets an American record of 6.25 seconds in the 60-yard run in New York.

TRANSITIONS

1944 – Lt. Commander **Benny Leonard**, former lightweight champion, is awarded the Edward J. Neil Memorial Plaque by the Boxing Writers Association of New York.

1962 – **Allie Sherman** of the New York Giants is named NFL Coach of the Year for the second straight season by the Associated Press.

1974 – Formula One driver **Jody Scheckter** of South Africa is voted driver of the year by the British Guild of Motoring Writers.

2006 – Boston outfielder **Gabe Kapler** announces his retirement as a player and is named manager at Greenville, S.C., the Red Sox's Class A South Atlantic League affiliate.

A STAR IS BORN

1889 – **Otto Scheff** (swimming and water polo)

1898 – **Joe Burman** (bantamweight boxer)

DECEMBER 13

GAMEBREAKERS

1924 – **Pincus Match** scores nine points and **Leo Palitz** adds seven as CCNY beats Dickinson 27-23. **Jacob Goldberg** scores eight to lead Dickinson, which will finish with a 17-2 record.

1929 – Brothers **Rudi Ball**, **Gerhard Ball**, and **Heinz Ball** of Germany play hockey together in an international game for the first time as Berliner SC defeats Oxford 6-0. Rudi scores two goals and goaltender Gerhard posts the shutout.

1935 – **Java Gotkin** scores 17 points – a season high for St. John's – in a 48-12 victory over Savage School for Physical Education.

1936 – **Lou Gordon's** fumble recovery at the 48-yard line sets up Green Bay's first touchdown three plays later, and the Packers go on to beat the Boston Redskins 21-6 in the NFL championship game at the Polo Grounds in New York.

1962 – **Art Heyman** scores 39 points, including 26 in the final 12 minutes, as Duke beats South Carolina 76-69.

1974 – **Lou Silver** scores 38 points as Harvard beats Cincinnati 77-76 in the first round of the Volunteer Classic in Knoxville, Tenn.

STRONG IN DEFEAT

1983 – **Danny Schayes** of the Nuggets contributes 11 points – all on foul shots – but Denver loses 186-184 to the Detroit Pistons in the highest-scoring game in NBA history.

MAZEL TOUGH

1925 – **Louis "Kid" Kaplan** defeats Babe Herman in 15 rounds to retain his world featherweight title in New York City.

1926 – **Meyer Cohen** decisions George "Kid" Lee in 12 rounds to win the New England welterweight title in Holyoke, Mass.

1934 – **Maurice Holtzer** wins a 12-round decision over Francois Augier in Paris to win the French featherweight title.

Moe Roberts
(Cleveland Barons)

TRANSITIONS

1926 – **Al Friedman** knocks out Charles Peguilhan in the eighth round of a heavyweight fight in Hartford, Conn. Peguilhan, a Frenchman making his U.S. debut as a late replacement for George Lamson, dies the next day of a fractured skull. Friedman is charged with manslaughter, but the charges are dropped when the death is ruled "accidental."

1996 – Indiana Pacers coach **Larry Brown** earns his 1,000th career victory on the college and pro levels with a 97-94 win over the Boston Celtics.

A STAR IS BORN

1907 – **Moe Roberts** (Chicago Black Hawks hockey goalie)

DECEMBER 14

GAMEBREAKERS

1935 – **Mac Kinsbrunner** scores 15 points and **Allie Schuckman** adds 12 as the New York Jewels defeat the Philadelphia Sphas 40-28 in the ABL. **Cy Kaselman** scores 11 and **Shikey Gotthoffer** 10 for the Sphas.

1938 – **Moe Goldman** scores 14 points as the Philadelphia Sphas defeat the Troy Haymakers 43-33 in the ABL.

1939 – **Ralph Kaplowitz** scores 17 points and **Robert Lewis** adds 15 as NYU beats Hofstra 70-27.

1947 – **Melvin Bleeker** returns a fumble 35 yards for a touchdown as the Los Angeles Rams beat the New York Giants 34-10.

1955 – **Lenny Rosenbluth** scores 17 of his 29 points in the first half as North Carolina beats fifth-ranked Alabama 99-77. The victory improves the Tar Heels to 15-0 and enables them to take over the No. 1 spot in the polls from Kansas.

1960 – **Howie Carl** scores two baskets in a span of 12 seconds during the final minute to rally DePaul past Bowling Green 62-60.

2002 – **Laine Selwyn** ties the game with two free throws with one second remaining in regulation, and finishes with 26 points as Pittsburgh defeats No. 11 Penn State 92-88 in overtime for the Panthers' first victory over a ranked women's basketball team in two years.

MAZEL TOUGH

1927 – Light heavyweight champion **Moise Bouquillon** knocks out Francois Charles in the second round in Paris to win the French heavyweight title.

1934 – **Maurice Holtzer** wins a 12-round decision over Francois Augier in Paris to capture the French featherweight title.

1994 – **Dana Rosenblatt** wins an eighth-round knockout of Frank Savannah to capture the WBC Continental Americas middleweight title in Boston.

2003 – **Sarah Poewe**, a South African swimming for Germany, wins the 100 breaststroke in 1:06.31 at the European Short Course Championships in Dublin, Ireland. A day earlier, she won the 50 breaststroke.

TRANSITIONS

1954 – Rookie **Sandy Koufax** signs a two-year contract worth $6,000 with the Brooklyn Dodgers. He receives a $14,000 signing bonus.

A STAR IS BORN

1879 – **Michael Spring** (distance running)
1886 – **Matt Wells** (British lightweight boxer)
1904 – **Attila Petschauer** (Hungarian fencer)

DECEMBER 15

GAMEBREAKERS

1928 – **Max Wortmann** scores two goals as New York Hakoah defeats the I.R.T. Rangers 5-1 in the Eastern Soccer League.

1929 – **Benny Friedman** throws his 20th touchdown pass of the season, a 27-yarder early in the fourth quarter, to rally the New York Giants to a 14-9 victory over the Chicago Bears.

1946 – **Sid Luckman** throws a 21-yard touchdown pass, then goes 19 yards for the winning touchdown on his only running play of the season as the Chicago Bears beat the New York Giants 24-14 for the NFL championship. The game is played in front of an NFL-record crowd of 58,346 at the Polo Grounds.

1954 – **Jerry Domershick** scores 29 points to lead CCNY to an 85-74 win over Mitchel Air Force Base.

1966 – **Bruce Kaplan** scores 28 points, shooting 10-for-12 in the second half, as NYU rallies to defeat Denver 76-70.

2002 – Defenseman **Mathieu Schneider** scores with 37.4 seconds remaining in overtime as the Los Angeles Kings defeat the Pittsburgh Penguins 3-2.

STRONG IN DEFEAT

1962 – **Richie Richman** plays quarterback for Villanova in a 6-0 loss to Oregon in the Liberty Bowl in Philadelphia, then plays with the Wildcats' basketball team in a 73-71 loss to Niagara later in the day. Richman, who also plays baseball, is one of the last three-sport athletes in Division I.

MAZEL TOUGH

1931 – **Al "Bummy" Davis** knocks out future world junior lightweight champion Tippy Larkin and raises his professional record to 35-0-2.

1964 – **Bernie Lefkofker**, the Metropolitan AAU champion, beats Ernie Cates at heavyweight and earns the award for most outstanding black-belt performer at the annual North-South Judo All-Star match at the New York Athletic Club.

1996 – **Gordie Sheer** teams with Chris Thorpe to win a World Cup luge race in Altenberg, Germany.

2002 – **Gal Fridman** wins four of 11 races and becomes the first Israeli to win a gold medal at the World Mistral Sailboarding Championships in Pattaya, Thailand.

JEWS ON FIRST

1931 – Toronto defenseman **Alex Levinsky** scores his first of 19 career NHL goals to help the Maple Leafs rally from a 2-0 deficit for a 2-2 tie with the New York Americans. Levinsky's disputed goal at 4:35 of the second period leads to a bench-clearing brawl that is broken up by police.

TRANSITIONS

1928 – After eight days of negotiations, the Boston Red Sox trade third baseman **Buddy Myer** back to the Washington Senators for two pitchers, two infielders, and an outfielder. Myer, who hit .313 and led the American League in stolen bases the previous season, was obtained by Boston from Washington in 1927 in a one-for-one trade with Tupper Rigney, who soon disappeared from the major leagues. "I need ballplayers more than I need cash," Red Sox President Bob Quinn says about the five-player deal.

A STAR IS BORN

1899 – **Harold Abrahams** (British track and field)
1904 – **Benny Bass** (featherweight boxer)
1918 – **Bobby Jacobson** (golf)
1958 – **Marty Roth** (auto racing)

DECEMBER 16

GAMEBREAKERS

1926 – **Davey Banks** scores 15 points and **Nat Holman** adds 13 as the New York Celtics set an American Basketball League scoring record with a 59-46 victory over the Detroit Lions.

1933 – **Moe Goldman** scores 11 points to lead CCNY past Westminster 25-13.

1936 – **Phil Rabin's** 17 points helps the Kingston Colonials defeat the Brooklyn Visitations 40-36 in the ABL.

1943 – **Max Labovitch** scores a hat trick as the New York Rovers beat the Brooklyn Crescents 12-5 in the Eastern Hockey League.

1957 – **Rudy LaRusso** scores 21 points in Dartmouth's 81-54 victory over Colby.

1967 – **Art Heyman** scores 36 points as Pittsburgh beats the Indiana Pacers 122-117 in the American Basketball Association.

1968 – North Carolina beats Clemson 90-69 as **Eddie Fogler** scores 10 points and hands out 10 assists.

1982 – **Mickey Berkowitz** scores 30 points, including six in the final minute, as Maccabi Tel Aviv defeats Real Madrid 99-93.

STRONG IN DEFEAT

1953 – **Max Zaslofsky** scores a game-high 22 points, but the NBA's Milwaukee Hawks lose 69-63 in overtime to the first-place Minneapolis Lakers. A week later, Zaslofsky is traded to the Fort Wayne Pistons.

MAZEL TOUGH

1913 – **Abel Kiviat** wins the 6-mile AAU Premiership national cross-country championship in 33 minutes, 52 seconds.

1927 – **Izzy Schwartz** wins a 15-round decision over **Newsboy Brown** to capture the New York State version of the world flyweight championship.

1937 – **Solly Krieger** upsets Billy Conn in a 12-round decision in Pittsburgh. A year later, Conn will take away Krieger's world middleweight title.

1974 – **Nessim Max Cohen** of Morocco knocks out Jean-Claude Bouttier in the 11th round to recapture the French middleweight title in Paris.

1993 – **Dana Rosenblatt** knocks out Sean Fitzgerald in the first round to win the New England middleweight title in Ledyard, Conn.

2001 – **Irina Slutskaya** of Russia beats Michelle Kwan of the United States for the third straight year in the Grand Prix of Figure Skating championships in Kitchener, Ontario.

A STAR IS BORN

1888 – **Ivan Osiier** (Danish fencer)
1908 – **Lou Spindell** (CCNY basketball)

Nat Holman
(Naismith Memorial Basketball Hall of Fame)

DECEMBER 17

GAMEBREAKERS

1928 – **Milton Cohen** scores 10 points to lead Pitt to a 34-26 victory over Ohio State.

1929 – **Allie Schuckman** scores 10 points to lead St. John's to a 41-26 victory over the Savage School of Physical Education.

1939 – **Ace Goldstein** scores 12 points as the Jersey Reds defeat the Wikes-Barre Barons 35-33 in the ABL.

1944 – Right guard **Charles "Buckets" Goldenberg** opens a hole on fourth-and-one as Packers fullback Ted Fritsch scores in the second quarter to give Green Bay a 7-0 lead. The Packers go on to beat the New York Giants 14-7 for their third NFL championship.

1962 – **Larry Brown** scores a game-high 19 points as North Carolina edges Kentucky 68-66.

1967 – **Art Heyman** scores 31 points as the Pittsburgh Pipers win their eighth straight American Basketball Association game, 121-116 over the Minnesota Muskies.

STRONG IN DEFEAT

1933 – **Harry Newman** of the Giants passes for 201 yards and two touchdowns and completes 13 consecutive passes, but the Chicago Bears beat New York 23-21 to win the first NFL championship game.

1965 – **Dave Newmark** scores 26 points in Columbia's 97-79 loss to Georgetown.

MAZEL TOUGH

1909 – **Monte Attell** fights Danny Webster to a 20-round draw in San Francisco and retains his world bantamweight title.

1925 – **Armand Magyar** of Hungary wins the 58-kg. Greco-Roman title at the European Wrestling Championships in Milan, Italy.

1966 – **Taffy Pergament** wins the Senior Women's title at the North American Figure Skating Championships in Lake Placid, N.Y.

JEWS ON FIRST

1982 – **Mike Veisor** becomes the first goalie in Hartford Whalers franchise history to post a shutout on the road, beating the Winnipeg Jets 2-0.

A STAR IS BORN

1915 – **Leah Thal Neuberger** (table tennis)
1916 – **Morton Goldberg** (billiards)

Mike Veisor
(Hartford Whalers)

DECEMBER 18

GAMEBREAKERS

1926 – **Max Rubenstein** scores eight points to lead CCNY past Union College 21-13.

1928 – **Ed Wineapple,** the only Jewish student at Providence, scores 15 points to lead the Friars to a 32-30 victory over St. John's.

1934 – **Java Gotkin** scores 16 points as St. John's beats Providence 40-37.

1935 – **Rip Kaplinsky** scores 15 points to lead St. John's to a 35-26 victory over Westminster.

1943 – **Max Labovitch** scores three goals as the New York Rovers defeat the Brooklyn Crescents 12-5 in the Eastern Hockey League.

1949 – **Nat Militzok** scores 18 points and **Hank Rosenstein** adds 14 as the Scranton Miners defeat the Wilkes-Barre Barons 70-54 in the ABL.

1963 – **Steve Chubin** scores 27 points as Rhode Island defeats St. John's 74-65.

1982 – **Danny Schayes** scores 18 points and grabs an NBA career-high 24 rebounds as the Utah Jazz beat the Houston Rockets 114-97.

2005 – **Cory Pecker** scores twice, including the game-winner with 6:15 remaining, as the Binghamton Senators defeat the Rochester Americans in the American Hockey League.

STRONG IN DEFEAT

1968 – **Neal Walk** scores 34 points, but Florida loses to LSU 93-89 in overtime.

MAZEL TOUGH

1925 – **Louis "Kid" Kaplan** wins a 15-round decision over Babe Herman in New York to retain his world flyweight title.

1933 – **Art Laskey** knocks out Andy Mitchell in the first round of a heavyweight fight in Hollywood, Calif.

1939 – **Georgie Abrams** knocks out Joe Duca in eight rounds in a middleweight fight in Washington, D.C.

1998 – **Oleg Veretelnikov** of Uzbekistan finishes first in the discus and 1,500-meter run to win the decathlon at the Asian Games in Bangkok with 8,278 points.

2005 – The U.S. four-man bobsled team, including brakeman **Steve Mesler**, wins a World Cup race in Cortina D'Ampezzo, Italy.

TRANSITIONS

1949 – **Abraham Watner** is named Baltimore Colts team president as the All-America Football Conference merges with the National Football League.

1963 – **Al Davis** of the Oakland Raiders is named American Football League Coach of the Year by the Associated Press.

A STAR IS BORN

1888 – **Robert Moses** (Yale swimming)

1897 – **Nathan Abrams** (Green Bay Packers end)

1924 – **Herb Gorman** (St. Louis Cardinals outfielder)

1951 – **Bernie Wolfe** (Washington Capitals goalie)

1973 – **Ilya Averbuck** (Russian ice dancer)

DECEMBER 19

GAMEBREAKERS

1931 – **Nat Lazar** scores nine points to lead St. John's to a 33-25 victory over Providence. **Joe Davidoff** and **Moe Spahn** each score 11 points as CCNY ends Dartmouth's six-game winning streak 37-18.

1933 – **Rip Kaplinsky** scores 12 points to lead St. John's to a 43-31 victory over Providence.

1936 – **Reds Rosan** scores 15 points and **Red Wolfe** adds 12 as the Philadelphia Sphas defeat the New York Jewels 52-38 in the ABL. **Mac Kinsbrunner** scores 18 for New York.

1937 – **Sammy Kaplan's** 13 points lead the Jersey Reds to a 39-32 ABL victory over the New York Celtics. **Willie Rubenstein** scores 15 points and **Mac Kinsbrunner** adds 10 as the New York Jewels defeat the Kingston Colonials 49-32.

1943 – **Hy Buller** scores the winning goal, giving the Indianapolis Capitals a 3-1 victory over the Cleveland Barons in an American Hockey League game.

1950 – **Abe Becker** has 20 points and nine rebounds and **Mel Seeman** adds 18 points as NYU defeats Yale 82-64.

1964 – **Tal Brody** scores 25 points as unranked Illinois defeats No. 8 Kentucky 91-86 for the Kentucky Invitational Tournament championship.

2003 – **Max Birbraer** gets two goals and an assist as the Laredo Bucks defeat the Corpus Christi Rayz 7-2 in the Central Hockey League.

MAZEL TOUGH

1929 – **Benny Bass** moves up a weight class and knocks out champion Tod Morgan in the second round to claim the world junior lightweight title.

JEWS ON FIRST

1917 – The Montreal Wanderers, owned by **Samuel Lichtenhein,** beat the Toronto Arenas 10-9 in the first National Hockey League game.

TRANSITIONS

1957 – **Andy Cohen**, manager at Double-A Indianapolis, is named manager at Denver, the Yankees' top farm club.

A STAR IS BORN

1880 – **Caesar Attell** (lightweight boxer)

Tal Brody
(University of Illinois)

DECEMBER 20

GAMEBREAKERS

1924 – **Leo Palitz** scores 18 points and **Pincus Match** adds 12 in CCNY's 25-17 victory over St. John's.

1936 – **Moe Spahn** scores 19 points to lead the Jersey Reds to a 36-34 ABL victory over the Kingston Colonials. **Phil Rabin** leads Kingston with 15 points.

1933 – **Willie Rubenstein** scores 10 points to lead NYU to a 28-18 victory over St. Francis of Brooklyn in the Violets' season opener.

1941 – **Leo Cantor** rushes 18 times for 117 yards as UCLA beats Florida 30-27 in Jacksonville, Fla.

1947 – **Ed Lerner** scores 22 points and **Nelson "Nitzi" Bobb** adds nine, including the winning basket with 90 seconds remaining as Temple defeats Kentucky 60-59. Kentucky will lose only one other regular-season game and win both the NCAA championship and Olympic gold medal.

1958 – **Sid Cohen** scores 23 points as Kentucky overcomes 36 points by Jerry West for a 97-91 victory over West Virginia in the Kentucky Invitational Tournament final. **Alan Seiden** scores 22 points as St. John's defeats Virginia 90-71.

1969 – Chiefs linebacker **Bob Stein** recovers a fumbled punt by the Jets' Mike Battle in the final minute to preserve Kansas City's 13-6 win over New York in the American Football League playoff semifinals.

1995 – **Danny Schayes** of the Miami Heat has 17 points and 16 rebounds in a 112-104 win over the New Jersey Nets.

2005 – **Jordan Farmar** scores 24 points in UCLA's 67-56 victory over Nevada.

MAZEL TOUGH

1921 – **Benny Leonard** knocks out Tim Droney in the eighth round in Philadelphia to retain his world lightweight title.

1981 – **Saoul Mamby** wins a 15-round decision over Obisia Nwankpa in Lagos, Nigeria, to retain his WBC super lightweight title.

JEWS ON FIRST

1920 – With former Penn standout **Michael A. Saxe** serving as Villanova's first head coach, the Wildcats win their first basketball game 43-40 over Catholic University. Saxe compiles a 64-30 record in six seasons.

TRANSITIONS

1942 – Former champion **Barney Ross**, a Marine corporal who killed 10 Japanese soldiers while protecting three wounded men at Guadalcanal, is voted the Edward J. Neil Memorial Plaque by the Boxing Writers Association.

1977 – The Kansas City Chiefs name **Marv Levy** head coach.

1985 – **Howard Cosell** retires from broadcasting television sports after 20 years with ABC.

A STAR IS BORN

1888 – **Mortimer Lindsey** (bowling)
1888 – **Joseph Magidsohn** (Michigan football)
1972 – **Scott Slutzker** (Iowa football, Indianapolis Colts, New Orleans Saints tight end)

DECEMBER 21

GAMEBREAKERS

1926 – **Nat Holman** scores 14 points to lead the New York Celtics to a 27-25 win over the Fort Wayne Hoosiers in the American Basketball League.

1935 – **Shikey Gotthoffer** scores nine points to lead the Philadelphia Sphas to a 41-30 victory over the Trenton Bengals in the ABL. **Phil Rabin** scores 16 for Trenton.

1955 – **Syd Levy** scores 26 points to lead CCNY to a 79-67 win over Queens.

2003 – Mississippi Sea Wolves goalie **Greg Gardner** makes 34 saves in a 4-0 victory over the Columbus Cottonmouths in an East Coast Hockey League game.

2005 – **Mike Cammalleri** scores two goals as the Los Angeles Kings beat the Calgary Flames 5-2.

2006 – Arizona State freshman **Derek Glasser** scores 13 of his 16 points in the second half as the Sun Devils defeat North Carolina A&T 71-66 in the first round of the ASU Classic.

MAZEL TOUGH

1955 – **Victor Elmaleh** defeats **James Prigoff** in the final of the Squash Handicap Tournament in New York.

1986 – **Amy Alcott** birdies the first playoff hole and combines with Bob Charles of Australia to win the 11-team Mazda Invitational Championship in Montego Bay, Jamaica. They earn $500,000 for their victory in the best-ball format matching players from the PGA and LPGA tours.

RECORD SETTERS

1961 – **Rudolph Pluykfelder** sets a world weight lifting record of 1,019¼ pounds in the light-heavyweight division at the Soviet National Championships in Ukraine. He also improves his record in the snatch to 313 pounds.

A STAR IS BORN

1851 – **Edward Lawrence Levy** (English weight lifter)

1907 – **Albert Schwartz** (swimming)

1921 – **Benny Goldberg** (bantamweight boxer)

1976 – **Tony Cogan** (Kansas City Royals pitcher)

Amy Alcott
(The Express-Times)

DECEMBER 22

GAMEBREAKERS

1933 – **Harry Litwack** and **Inky Lautman** score nine points apiece to lead the Philadelphia Sphas to a 38-29 victory over the Newark Bears in the ABL. **Moe Spahn** leads Newark with 12 points.

1934 – **Sam Winograd** scores a game-high 10 points as CCNY defeats Dartmouth 26-22.

1937 – **Jules Rivlin** scores 18 points to lead Marshall College to a 64-47 win over the Prospect Park YMCA.

1945 – **Harry Boykoff** scores 21 points as St. John's defeats Ohio U. 67-33 after leading 42-8 at halftime.

1947 – In a doubleheader at Madison Square Garden, **Lionel Malamed** scores 13 points to lead CCNY past Utah 82-46 and **Lou Lipman** scores 22 in LIU's 49-47 win over Oregon.

1954 – **Harvey Babetch** of Bradley scores a career-high 31 points in an 82-73 basketball victory over SMU.

2002 – **Michal Epstein** scores 25 points as Providence defeats Rhode Island 63-55 in women's basketball.

2003 – **Dan Grunfeld** scores 22 points in Stanford's 67-37 victory over Southern Utah State.

MAZEL TOUGH

1914 – **Al McCoy** fights **Soldier Bartfield** to a 10-round no-decision in Brooklyn, N.Y., for the second time in a little more than a month, retaining his world middleweight title.

1933 – **Sol Schiff** defeats **Abe Berenbaum** 21-17, 21-19, 21-18 to win the Manhattan table tennis championship. Schiff also wins the doubles title with **Seymour Solomon**.

1944 – For the second time in two months, **Harold Green** wins a 10-round decision over future world middleweight champion Rocky Graziano in New York.

1973 – **Ilana Kloss** of South Arica beats Brenda Kirk 6-4, 6-3 to win the Western Province Sugar Circuit tennis tournament in Capetown.

1996 – **Gordie Sheer** teams with Chris Thorpe to win a World Cup luge event in Kuenigree, Germany.

Gordie Sheer
(U.S. Olympic Committee)

TRANSITIONS

1912 – **Hugo Meisl** is named head coach of the Austrian national soccer team. He coaches Austria to 78 international victories through 1937, including the "Wunderteam" of the 1930s that won 14 straight matches.

A STAR IS BORN

1887 – **Charley Goldman** (bantamweight boxer, trainer)

1909 – **Julius Seligson** (tennis)

DECEMBER 23

GAMEBREAKERS

1933 – **Sam Winograd** and **Moe Goldman** share game-high honors with eight points apiece as CCNY defeats Dartmouth 42-26.

1947 – **Don Forman** scores 20 points and **Dolph Schayes** adds 15 as NYU defeats Cornell 61-48.

1973 – With Chicago's Tony Esposito getting the night off, **Mike Veisor** makes 37 saves in his first NHL start in goal as the Blackhawks beat the Vancouver Canucks 6-2. Chicago leads 6-0 before Vancouver scores late in the second period.

2004 – **Dan Grunfeld** scores a game-high 18 points as Stanford defeats Montana 84-66.

STRONG IN DEFEAT

1952 – Despite 23 points by **Boris Nachamkin**, NYU loses to Seattle University 102-101, the highest-scoring college game in Madison Square Garden history.

MAZEL TOUGH

1959 – **Walter Blum** rides three winners at Tropical Park in Coral Gables, Fla.

2001 – **Shahar Peer** of Israel defeats Jenny Heiser of the United States 6-3, 7-5 to win the under-14 girls title at the Orange Bowl International in Miami, the unofficial world tennis championships for junior players.

RECORD SETTERS

1960 – **Howie Carl** of DePaul scores a school-record 43 points in an 81-78 overtime win over Marquette.

1963 – **Rick Kaminsky** ties a Yale school record for points in an away game by scoring 36 in a 97-85 victory over Tulane.

Tamir Bloom
(U.S. Olympic Committee)

A STAR IS BORN

1902 – **Max Rosenfeld** (Brooklyn Dodgers outfielder)

1909 – **Herman Barron** (golf)

1909 – **Miki Gelb** (Hungarian featherweight boxer)

1909 – **Barney Ross** (lightweight, welterweight boxer)

1936 – **Myron Franks** (tennis)

1954 – **Brian Teacher** (tennis)

1964 – **Andy Gabel** (speed skating)

1971 – **Tamir Bloom** (fencing)

1983 – **Jamie Silverstein** (figure skating)

DECEMBER 24

GAMEBREAKERS

1938 – **Petey Rosenberg** scores 15 points as the Philadelphia Sphas defeat the Brooklyn Visitations 50-38 in the ABL.

2000 – **Jay Fiedler** completes 30 of 45 passes for a season-high 264 yards and one touchdown as the Miami Dolphins clinch their first AFC East title since 1994 with a 27-24 victory over the New England Patriots. Fiedler rallies the Dolphins from a 24-17 deficit in the fourth quarter, completing 11 of 14 passes for 100 yards.

MAZEL TOUGH

1911 – **Ted "Kid" Lewis** wins a six-round decision over Frankie Fay in a welterweight bout in London.

1971 – **Ilana Kloss** defeats Linda Tuero 6-3, 6-2 to win the Border Championships tennis tournament in East London, South Africa.

RECORD SETTERS

1945 – **Grigori Novak** of the Soviet Union sets a world weight lifting record of 127 kilos (approximately 279 pounds) in Leningrad.

A STAR IS BORN

1893 – **George Ashe** (middleweight boxer)
1940 – **Grigori Kriss** (Soviet fencer)

Grigori Novak

DECEMBER 25

GAMEBREAKERS

1936 – **Phil Rabin** scores 19 points as the Kingston Colonials defeat the Philadelphia Sphas 47-30 in the ABL. **Reds Rosan** scores 12 for the Sphas.

1937 – **Inky Lautman** scores 12 points and **Shikey Gotthoffer** adds 11 as the Philadelphia Sphas defeat the New York Yankees 46-40 in the ABL.

1939 – **Shikey Gotthoffer** scores 16 points as the Philadelphia Sphas defeat the Jersey Reds 40-31 in the ABL.

1945 – **Jackie Goldsmith** scores 18 points and **Stan Waxman** adds 11 as LIU defeats Tennessee 45-43.

1951 – **Max Zaslofsky** scores a game-high 23 points to lead the New York Knicks over the Fort Wayne Pistons 72-65.

1955 – **Larry Friend** scores 20 points to lead California over Dartmouth 78-59.

1957 – **Dolph Schayes** scores 33 points as the Syracuse Nationals beat the New York Knicks 134-130.

1968 – **Art Heyman** scores 26 points as the Minnesota Pipers beat the Kentucky Colonels 129-118 in the American Basketball Association.

1989 – Vikings tight end **Brent Novoselsky** catches a 1-yard touchdown pass with 4:17 remaining to secure Minnesota's 29-21 victory over the Cincinnati Bengals in a Monday Night Football game. The victory on the final day of the season clinches a playoff berth for the Vikings.

Brent Novoselsky
(Minnesota Vikings)

MAZEL TOUGH

1924 – **Lew Tendler** wins a 10-round decision over **Joe Tiplitz** in Philadelphia.

A STAR IS BORN

1884 – **Samuel Berger** (heavyweight boxer)
1907 – **Sam Cozen (**Temple basketball)
1907 – **Joey Medill** (welterweight boxer)
1908 – **Alta Cohen** (Brooklyn Dodgers, Philadelphia Phillies outfielder)
1915 – **Benjamin "Baby Yack" Yakubowitz** (Canadian bantamweight boxer)

DECEMBER 26

GAMEBREAKERS

1911 – **Albert Rosenfeld** of Huddersfield scores eight tries against Wakefield Trinity in the Northern Rugby Football League of England.

1936 – **Reds Rosan** scores 15 points to lead the Philadelphia Sphas to a 40-34 victory over the Brooklyn Visitations in the ABL.

1937 – **Shikey Gotthoffer** scores 11 points in the Philadelphia Sphas' 29-25 victory over the Brooklyn Visitations. **Nat Frankel** leads Brooklyn with 10. **Mac Kinsbrunner** scores 15 points as the New York Jewels defeat the New York Celtics 49-33.

1943 – **Sid Luckman** completes 15 of 26 passes for 285 yards and five touchdowns and rushes eight times for 64 yards as the Chicago Bears beat the Washington Redskins 41-21 for the NFL championship.

1950 – **Abe Becker** scores 35 points as NYU hands Stanford its first loss of the season, 84-70.

1963 – **Jack Hirsch** scores 13 points to help UCLA defeat Yale 95-65 in the first round of the Los Angeles Basketball Classic. **Rick Kaminsky** scores 26 points for Yale and holds UCLA star Walt Hazzard to seven points.

1964 – Georgia fullback **Frank Lankewicz** scores on a 2-yard run in the second quarter to give the Bulldogs a 7-0 victory over Texas Tech in the Sun Bowl in El Paso, Texas.

MAZEL TOUGH

1911 – **Abel Kiviat** wins the 600 and 1,000 and **Alvah Meyer** wins the 60-, 75- and 150-yard runs at the two-day AAU Indoor Track and Field Championships in New York.

1927 – **Viktor Barna** wins the Hungarian Junior National Championship, his first of 16 world table tennis titles.

1927 – **Corporal Izzy Schwartz** wins a 15-round decision over **Newsboy Brown** for the vacant world flyweight championship in New York.

1947 – **Sidney Schwartz** defeats **Daniel Rivkin** 6-3, 6-0, 6-0 for his third consecutive Eastern Junior tennis championship title.

TRANSITIONS

1962 – **Allie Sherman** of the New York Giants beats out Bill McPeak of the Washington Redskins to win his second straight NFL Coach of the Year award.

A STAR IS BORN

1895 – **Willy Meisl** (Austrian soccer)
1973 – **Eric Gingold** (Williams College basketball)

DECEMBER 27

GAMEBREAKERS

1929 – **Allie Schuckman** scores 14 points as St. John's defeats the New York Athletic Club 35-22.

1935 – **Rip Kaplinsky** scores a game-high 14 points to lead St. John's to a 27-18 victory over Brooklyn College.

1936 – **Moe Spahn** scores 13 and 10 points, respectively, as the Jersey Reds sweep an ABL doubleheader against the Brooklyn Jewels, 37-33 and 37-27. **Max Kinsbrunner** leads the Jewels with 11 points in the opener, and **Sam Winograd** scores nine in the nightcap.

1939 – **Sammy Kaplan** scores 13 points in the Troy Haymakers' 37-33 ABL victory over the Jersey Reds.

1947 – **Max Zaslofsky** scores 24 points to lead the Chicago Stags past the New York Knicks 79-70.

1947 – **Don Forman** scores 18 points to lead NYU to a 70-63 win over Missouri. **Nelson Bobb** scores 24 points as Temple defeats Dartmouth 73-54.

1952 – **Jerry Domershick** scores 27 points as CCNY beats Tufts 81-58.

1957 – **Rudy LaRusso's** 23 points help Dartmouth run its record to 8-0 with an 84-65 win over Colgate.

1987 – **John Frank** catches an 11-yard touchdown pass as the San Francisco 49ers defeat the Los Angeles Rams 48-0.

1991 – **Scott Drevitch** scores 1:06 into overtime to give the Richmond Renegades a 4-3 victory over the Nashville Knights in the East Coast Hockey League.

2002 – **Haim Shimonovich** totals 20 points and nine rebounds as Hawaii defeats Bradley 90-69.

STRONG IN DEFEAT

1967 – **Neal Walk** scores 32 points, but Florida loses to St. Joseph's 89-69 in the Gator Bowl Classic basketball tournament in Jacksonville.

RECORD SETTERS

1996 – **David Nemirovsky** sets a Carolina Monarchs franchise record by scoring five goals in a 12-1 victory over the Baltimore Bandits in the American Hockey League. He also adds an assist, tying the club single-game points record with six.

TRANSITIONS

1961 – **Dolph Schayes** of the Syracuse Nationals suffers a shattered cheekbone against the Los Angeles Lakers in a game played in Philadelphia, ending his NBA-record streak of 764 straight game appearances (including playoffs) dating to 1952.

1967 – **Red Holzman,** a scout and assistant coach for the past 10 seasons with the New York Knicks, is promoted to head coach, replacing Dick McGuire.

A STAR IS BORN

1911 – **Roy Lazer** (heavyweight boxer)

1917 – **Herb Karpel** (New York Yankees pitcher)

1942 – **Ron Rothstein** (Rhode Island basketball, Miami Heat coach)

1959 – **Andre Tippett** (Iowa football, New England Patriots linebacker)

1966 – **Bill Goldberg** (Georgia football, Atlanta Falcons defensive tackle, pro wrestling)

DECEMBER 28

GAMEBREAKERS

1929 – **Herbert Fleishhacker** scores two touchdowns as Stanford defeats Army 34-13.

1929 – **Milton Trupin** scores 10 points to lead CCNY to a 32-18 victory over Davis & Elkins.

1947 – **Max Zaslofsky** scores 24 points as the Chicago Stags beat the New York Knicks 79-70 in a matchup of Basketball Association of America division leaders.

1977 – Chicago Blackhawks goalie **Mike Veisor** makes 31 saves as he shuts out the Toronto Maple Leafs 4-0.

1996 – Stanford point guard **Jamila Wideman** makes seven steals in a 64-48 victory over Colorado.

2000 – **Sage Rosenfels** completes 23 of 34 passes for 308 yards and two touchdowns as Iowa State records its first-ever bowl victory, 37-29 over Pittsburgh in the Insight.com Bowl in Phoenix. Rosenfels is named Offensive Player of the Game.

2003 – **Jay Fiedler** completes 21 of 29 passes for a career-high 328 yards and one touchdown as the Miami Dolphins rally in the fourth quarter to defeat the New York Jets 23-21.

STRONG IN DEFEAT

1925 – **William Fleishman** scores 18 points to lead Western Reserve in a 47-41 loss to West Virginia.

1962 – **Barry Kramer** matches his career high with 42 points in NYU's 91-84 loss to Illinois.

2003 – Steelers punter **Josh Miller** throws an 81-yard touchdown pass in Pittsburgh's 13-10 overtime loss to the Baltimore Ravens.

2005 – **Jon Scheyer** of Glenbrook North High School in Northbrook, Ill., scores 21 points in the final 75 seconds of an 85-79 loss to Proviso West. Scheyer finishes with 52 points before fouling out with six seconds remaining.

MAZEL TOUGH

1946 – **Estelle Osher** of Hunter College wins 16 of 17 bouts to capture the Holiday Intercollegiate Fencing Tournament title in East Orange, N.J.

1980 – **Brian Teacher** captures the Australian Open tennis title by beating Kim Warwick 7-5, 7-6, 6-2 in the final in Melbourne. Teacher defeats Tim Mayotte, Ulrich Marten, John Austin, Paul McNamee, and Peter McNamara on his way to the final of the grass-court Grand Slam tournament.

RECORD SETTERS

1950 – **Dolph Schayes** of the Syracuse Nationals grabs an NBA-record 35 rebounds in a 91-88 loss to the Philadelphia Warriors.

JEWS ON FIRST

1902 – **Paul "Twister" Steinberg** and **Dave Freeman** of the Syracuse Athletic Club participate in the first indoor football game as Syracuse defeats New York 5-0 at Madison Square Garden.

A STAR IS BORN

1903 – **Bobbie Rosenfeld** (Canada track and field, basketball)

1912 – **Willie Rubenstein** (NYU basketball)

DECEMBER 29

GAMEBREAKERS

1933 – **Harry Litwack** scores 11 points to lead the Philadelphia Sphas to a 42-21 victory over the Bronx Americans in the ABL.

1934 – Before 16,188 fans at Madison Square Garden, Jewish players account for all of NYU's points in a 25-18 victory over Notre Dame. **Milt Schulman** scores seven, **Len Maidman** six, **Sid Gross** and **Willie Rubenstein** five each, and **Irwin Klein** two as NYU wins its 19th straight game.

1939 – **Allie Schuckman** scores 15 points as the Wilkes-Barre Barons defeat the Washington Wizards 33-29.

1940 – **Sid Luckman** throws touchdown passes of 48 and 65 yards and runs one yard for the go-ahead TD as the Chicago Bears beat the NFL All-Stars 28-14 in Los Angeles.

1945 – **Harry Boykoff** scores a game-high 27 points as St. John's beats Kentucky 73-59 at Madison Square Garden.

1955 – **Mark Binstein** scores 50 points as Army beats Rhode Island 99-74 in the semifinals of a holiday basketball tournament in Richmond, Va.

1959 – **Howie Carl** scores 21 points to lead unbeaten DePaul to its seventh victory, 75-55 over Marquette.

1963 – **Roby Young** scores to give Israel a 1-0 victory over South Vietnam in an Olympic qualifying soccer match.

1966 – **Neal Walk** grabs 22 rebounds as Florida defeats Virginia Tech 92-73.

1969 – Florida defensive back **Steve Tannen** blocks a punt that teammate Mike Kelley returns for the game's first touchdown, and the Gators go on to upset Tennessee 14-13 in the Gator Bowl in Jacksonville, Fla.

1975 – A day after scoring 36 points in a 77-70 victory over Penn, **Ernie Grunfeld** scores 36 more as 12th-ranked Tennessee beats Tulane 97-73 in the championship game of the Sugar Bowl Classic in New Orleans. Grunfeld is named tournament MVP.

1991 – Freshman **Anita Kaplan** scores 21 points and grabs 10 rebounds as second-ranked Stanford defeats San Diego 103-68.

1998 – **David Nemirovsky** collects three goals and an assist as the Fort Wayne Comets defeat the Indianapolis Ice 9-5 in the International Hockey League.

2001 – **Bubba Berenzweig** scores the game-winning goal at 2:20 of overtime and assists on both Nashville goals in the final 4:20 of regulation as the Predators beat the Detroit Red Wings 3-2.

MAZEL TOUGH

1915 – **"Oakland" Jimmy Duffy** wins a four-round decision over Johnny Conde in Oakland to win the Pacific Coast bantamweight title.

1925 – **Sammy Dorfman** knocks out Pepe Revere in the first round of a featherweight fight in New York City.

TRANSITIONS

1929 – Retired lightweight boxing champion **Benny Leonard** announces plans to start a four-team pro hockey league with teams in Dallas, Fort Worth, Tulsa, and Oklahoma City.

1958 – The Boston Celtics beat the Syracuse Nationals 107-105 to give **Red Auerbach** his 500th coaching victory in the NBA.

1964 – Jockey of the Year **Walter Blum** fractures a vertebra, breaks two ribs, and suffers a concussion in a two-horse collision at Santa Anita.

A STAR IS BORN

1871 – **Jay Fiedler** (Dartmouth football)

DECEMBER 30

GAMEBREAKERS

1938 – **Jack Garfinkel** scores 10 points to lead St. John's to a 39-37 victory over Colorado.

1947 – **Don Forman** scores 16 points and **Do.'ph Schayes** adds 14 as NYU defeats Temple 64-41.

1948 – **Louis Lehman** scores a team-high 12 points as St. Louis University hands Kentucky its only loss of the season, 42-40 in the Sugar Bowl Basketball Tournament final in New Orleans. Lehman scores a majority of his points in the second half as the Billikens rally from a 27-18 deficit.

1958 – **Sid Cohen** scores a game-high 23 points, including 13 of 14 from the foul line, and grabs nine rebounds as top-ranked Kentucky defeats unranked Illinois 76-75.

1962 – **Art Heyman** scores 30 points as Duke beats Wake Forest 75-73.

1995 – **Doron Sheffer** achieves the second triple-double in UConn basketball history, scoring 10 points, grabbing 10 rebounds, and handing out 11 assists in a 102-63 victory over Hartford.

2002 – **Wendy Gabbe** scores 26 points to lead Cal-Irvine to an 86-64 women's basketball victory over Portland State.

2004 – **Shay Doron** scores 21 of her 26 points in the second half as Maryland defeats Marshall 83-68 in the Terrapin Classic women's basketball final.

MAZEL TOUGH

1934 – **Paul Friesel,** the junior national 200-meter champion, wins the 100-yard breaststroke in the Senior Open AAU meet.

1961 – **Mike Belkin** beats Geoffrey Pollard in three sets to win the Orange Bowl juniors tennis title in Miami Beach.

1973 – **Harold Solomon** beats Clark Graebner 3-6, 6-4, 6-3 in the final of the Bluebonnet Invitational tennis tournament in Houston.

JEWS ON FIRST

1976 – In the first NBA matchup of teams coached by brothers, **Larry Brown's** Denver Nuggets defeat **Herb Brown's** Detroit Pistons 123-196 in Denver. Larry will finish with a 4-2 advantage over Herb in head-to-head matchups between 1976 and 1978.

TRANSITIONS

1950 – **Marchy Schwartz** resigns as football coach at Stanford. He has a 28-28-4 record in six seasons.

A STAR IS BORN

1933 – **Norm Meyers** (bowling)

1935 – **Sandy Koufax** (Brooklyn/Los Angeles Dodgers pitcher)

1937 – **Barbara Breit** (tennis)

DECEMBER 31

GAMEBREAKERS

1927 – **Irving "Brick" Marcus** scores two touchdowns – one on a 55-yard run – as California beats Penn 27-13.

1931 – **Joe Davidoff** scores a game-high six points as CCNY beats Fordham 23-11 as part of a charity tripleheader at Madison Square Garden.

1951 – **Max Zaslofsky** scores 30 points as the New York Knicks beat the Boston Celtics 87-86 in overtime.

1951 – **Jerry Domershick** scores 25 points and **Sy Cohen** adds 18 as CCNY defeats the University of Puerto Rico 72-54.

1967 – Defenseman **Larry Zeidel** scores his last of three career NHL goals at 6:29 of the second period and also adds an assist in the Philadelphia Flyers' 9-1 victory over the Los Angeles Kings. It is his first goal since the 1953-54 season with Chicago.

1991 – With **David Littman** in goal, the Rochester Americans end the Hershey Bears' six-game winning streak, 3-0 in the American Hockey League.

MAZEL TOUGH

1924 – Lightweight **Ruby Goldstein** makes his pro boxing debut with a first-round knockout of Al Vano at the Pioneer Club in New York.

1945 – **Dick Savitt** and **Leonard Steiner** beat **Sidney Schwartz** and Alex Hetzell 14-12, 6-4, 6-4 to win the boys doubles title at the U.S. Junior National Indoor tennis championships in New York.

1973 – Rutgers' women's crew, led by coxswain **Susy Weinstein**, wins the 8-oared race at the New Year's Eve Regatta in the Bronx, N.Y.

1950 – **Albert Yvel** of France knocks out Paco Bueno in the eighth round in Algiers to retain his European light heavyweight title.

TRANSITIONS

1929 – The New York State Athletic Commission abolishes boxing's junior lightweight class, eliminating the world title **Benny Bass** won a month earlier with a second-round knockout of Tod Morgan.

1997 – **Marv Levy** retires after 11 seasons as head coach of the Buffalo Bills. He was 112-70 in regular-season games and 11-8 in playoffs.

A STAR IS BORN

1902 – **Louis Farber** (CCNY and Columbia basketball)

1921 – **Irv Rothenberg** (LIU basketball)

1944 – **Michael London** (Wisconsin football, San Diego Chargers linebacker)

Larry Zeidel
(Detroit Red Wings)

APPENDIX

JEWISH ATHLETES FEATURED ON WHEATIES BOXES
Red Auerbach – basketball
Morrie Arnovich – baseball
Harry Danning – baseball
Benny Friedman – football
Hank Greenberg – baseball
Nat Holman – basketball
Sarah Hughes – figure skating
Irving Jaffe – speed skating
Al Rosen – baseball
Kerri Strug – gymnastics

NBA FIRST-ROUND DRAFT PICKS
1948 – Dolph Schayes, NYU (New York Knicks)
1948 – Phil Farbman, CCNY (Philadelphia Warriors)
1950 – Irwin Dambrot, CCNY (New York Knicks)
1953 – Jack Molinas, Columbia (Fort Wayne Pistons)
1957 – Lenny Rosenbluth, North Carolina (Philadelphia Warriors)
1963 – Art Heyman, Duke (New York Knicks)
1964 – Barry Kramer, NYU (San Francisco Warriors)
1969 – Neal Walk, Florida (Phoenix Suns)
1977 – Ernie Grunfeld, Tennessee (Milwaukee Bucks)
1981 – Danny Schayes, Syracuse (Utah Jazz)
2006 – Jordan Farmar, UCLA (Los Angeles Lakers)

JEWISH ATHLETES ON TIME MAGAZINE COVERS
Dick Savitt, tennis – Aug. 27, 1951
Mark Spitz, swimming – Sept. 11, 1972
Sarah Hughes, figure skating – Feb. 11, 2002

JEWISH WOMEN ON SPORTS ILLUSTRATED COVERS
Suzy Weiner (with husband Mark Spitz) – May 14, 1973
Jamila Wideman, basketball – March 17, 1997
Sarah Hughes, figure skating – March 4, 2002

WINNING JOCKEYS IN TRIPLE CROWN RACES
1906 Preakness – Walter Miller (Whimsical)
1959 Preakness – Willie Harmatz (Royal Orbit)
1971 Belmont – Walter Blum (Pass Catcher)

TALLEST JEWS IN THE NBA
7-0 – Dave Newmark
6-11 – Danny Schayes
6-10 – Neal Walk
6-9 1/2 – Harry Boykoff
6-8 – Rudy LaRusso, Ed Miller, Dolph Schayes
NOTE: 7-4 Eric Gingold was in the Chicago Bulls' training camp in 1996 and 1997 but failed to make the team.

LONGEST CONSECUTIVE-GAME HITTING STREAKS
28 – Shawn Green, Toronto Blue Jays, 1999
28 – Gabe Kapler, Texas Rangers, 2000
23 – Buddy Myer, Boston Red Sox, 1928
23 – Kevin Youkilis, Boston Red Sox, 2007
21 – Buddy Myer, Washington Senators, 1935
20 – Al Rosen, Cleveland Indians, 1953

FINAL OUTS OF SANDY KOUFAX'S NO-HITTERS
1962 – Felix Mantilla, Mets, grounded into forceout, shortstop to second.
1963 – Harvey Kuenn, Giants, grounded out pitcher to first.
1964 – Bobby Wine, Phillies, struck out swinging.
1965 – Harvey Kuenn, Cubs, struck out swinging.

FINAL OUTS OF KEN HOLTZMAN'S NO-HITTERS
1969 – Hank Aaron, Braves, grounded out second to first.
1971 – Lee May, Reds, struck out.

NFL FIRST-ROUND DRAFT PICKS
1939 – Sid Luckman, Columbia (Chicago Bears)
1944 – Merv Pregulman, Michigan (Green Bay Packers)
1948 – Dan Dworsky, Michigan (Los Angeles Dons)
1958 – Mike Sommer, George Washington (Washington Redskins)
1989 – Harris Barton, North Carolina (San Francisco 49ers)
1960 – Ron Mix, Southern Cal (Baltimore Colts)
1970 – Steve Tannen, Florida (New York Jets)

FOREIGN-BORN MAJOR-LEAGUE PLAYERS
Duke Markell – Paris
Goody Rosen – Toronto
Reuben Ewing – Odessa, Russia
Bill Cristall – Odessa, Russia
Jose Bautista – Bani, Dominican Republic

20-GAME WINNERS
27 – Sandy Koufax, Dodgers, 1966
26 – Sandy Koufax, Dodgers, 1965
25 – Sandy Koufax, Dodgers, 1963
25 – Steve Stone, Orioles, 1980
21 – Erskine Mayer, Phillies, 1914
21 – Erskine Mayer, Phillies, 1915
21 – Ken Holtzman, A's, 1973

PLAYERS ON STANLEY CUP-WINNING TEAMS
Sam Rothschild – 1926 Montreal Maroons
Alex Levinsky – 1932 Toronto Maple Leafs, 1938 Chicago Black Hawks
Larry Zeidel – 1952 Detroit Red Wings
Mathieu Schneider – 1993 Montreal Canadiens
Mike Hartman – 1994 New York Rangers

MAJOR SPORTS LEAGUE TEAMS' PRINCIPAL OWNERS
NBA
David Stern, Commissioner
Leslie Alexander – Houston Rockets
Micky Arison – Miami Heat
Mark Cuban – Dallas Mavericks
William Davidson – Detroit Pistons
Dan Gilbert – Cleveland Cavaliers
Herb Kohl – Milwaukee Bucks
Abe Pollin – Washington Wizards
Bruce Ratner – New Jersey Nets
Jerry Reinsdorf – Chicago Bulls
Howard Schultz – Seattle SuperSonics
Ed Snider – Philadelphia 76ers
Donald Sterling – Los Angeles Clippers
Larry Tanenbaum – Toronto Raptors
WNBA
William Davidson – Detroit Shock
NHL
Gary Bettmann, Commissioner
Steve Belkin – Atlanta Thrashers
William Davidson – Tampa Bay Lightning
Steve Ellman – Phoenix Coyotes
Henry and Susan Samueli – Anaheim Ducks
Ed Snider – Philadelphia Flyers
Larry Tanenbaum – Toronto Maple Leafs
NFL
Arthur Blank – Atlanta Falcons
Al Davis – Oakland Raiders

Malcom Glazer – Tampa Bay Buccaneers
Bob Kraft – New England Patriots
Randy Lerner – Cleveland Browns
Jeff Lurie – Philadelpha Eagles
Dan Snyder – Washington Redskins
Zigy Wilf – Minnesota Vikings
MLB
Bud Selig, Commissioner
John Fisher and Lewis Wolff – Oakland Athletics
Jeffrey Loria – Florida Marlins
Jamie Luskin McCourt – Los Angeles Dodgers
Jerry Reinsdorf – Chicago White Sox
Stuart Sternberg and Randy Frankel – Tampa Bay Devil Rays
Fred Wilpon – New York Mets

QUIZ QUESTIONS

1. When outfielder Art Shamsky became the third Jewish player to join the 1972 Oakland A's roster, who did Oakland pitcher Ken Holtzman suggest the team sign to play shortstop?

2. Who was the first batter in the first major-league game played at Fenway Park in Boston?

3. Who was the only Yeshiva University basketball player drafted by an NBA team?

4. Pitcher Barry Latman regularly exchanged correspondence with which former baseball Hall of Famer?
   a) Bob Feller
   b) Carl Hubbell
   c) Ty Cobb
   d) Jimmy Foxx

5. In 1951, Dick Savitt became the only Jewish tennis player to win a Wimbledon singles title. Which Jewish player did he defeat in the semifinals?

6. Alphonse Halimi and Robert Cohen both held world bantamweight boxing titles in the 1950s. What was their native country?

7. In 1955, Sheila Van Damm became the first British woman in 23 years to win which event?
   a) Irish Derby as a jockey
   b) Monte Carlo rally as a race car driver
   c) Boston Marathon
   d) South African Open golf tournament

8. Tal Brody, captain of the Maccabi Tel Aviv team that captured the 1977 European basketball championship, was an All-American at which American university?

9. Pittsburgh Steelers and New England Patriots punter Josh Miller was a 1994 Canadian Football League all-star for which team?

   a) Baltimore
   b) Sacramento
   c) Shreveport
   d) British Columbia

10. What was the first major-league baseball stadium with a kosher food concession?
    a) Ebbets Field
    b) Tiger Stadium
    c) Camden Yards
    d) Shea Stadium

11. Where was 1920s bantamweight boxer Young Montreal born?

12. Which Israeli basketball player for the University of Connecticut in 1989 was nicknamed "The Gaza Strip" because of his defensive prowess?

13. In 1938, which Jewish college football players finished second and third in the Heisman Trophy voting?

14. Charlotte Epstein successfully lobbied to include events for women in which sport in the 1920 Olympics?
    a) archery
    b) swimming
    c) skiing
    d) figure skating

15. Who was the first golfer to win the first PGA tournament he entered as a pro?

16. Julius Seligson became the first Jewish tennis player to win an NCAA championship in 1928. What college did he attend?
    a) Lafayette
    b) Lehigh
    c) Bucknell
    d) Colgate

17. Which one of these major leaguers from the early part of the 20th Century did not change his last name from Cohen?

a) Harry "Klondike" Kane
b) Phil Cooney
c) Reuben Ewing
d) Jesse Baker

18. In one of Jack Bernstein's first pro fights in 1914, the promoter did not make enough from the gate to pay the fighters. What did Bernstein receive as compensation?

19. In 1939, Harold "Bunny" Levitt set a record for consecutive free throws during a shooting exhibition. How many did he make in a row?
a) 399
b) 499
c) 501
d) 701

20. Who was the first Jewish player selected in the inaugural American Basketball Association draft in 1967?

21. Who was the first Jewish player to score a Super Bowl touchdown?

22. In 1929, Ed Wineapple became the first Jewish All-American basketball player. At which college was he the only Jewish student?
a) Villanova
b) Notre Dame
c) St. Bonaventure
d) Providence

23. Who among these ballplayers has not hit home runs in four consecutive at-bats?
a) Mike Epstein
b) Shawn Green
c) Hank Greenberg
d) Art Shamsky

24. Who is the boxer who claims to have been knocked out on every continent except Antarctica?

25. How many of the starters on St. John's University's 1931 "Wonder Five" basketball team that went 21-1 were Jewish?

26. Who was the first Jewish major-leaguer to catch a no-hitter?
a) Joe Ginsberg
b) Harry Danning
c) Norm Sherry
d) Jesse Levis

27. From 1950 to 1955, Angelica Rozeanu of Romania won consecutive world titles in which sport?
a) gymnastics
b) table tennis
c) fencing
d) rowing

28. Who threw the first touchdown pass in the first NFL championship game in 1933?

29. Harry Hartman, who originated the home run call of "going, going, gone," began in 1931 as a radio broadcaster for which major-league team?
a) Detroit Tigers
b) St. Louis Browns
c) Cincinnati Reds
d) Cleveland Indians

30. Who was the first goaltender to win the Most Valuable Player award in the Major Indoor Soccer League?

31. Who was the first Jewish player to appear in a Super Bowl?

32. After retiring as a lightweight fighter, Ruby Goldstein continued with boxing in what capacity?
a) referee
b) ring announcer
c) journalist
d) promoter

33. In how many consecutive years was Dolph Schayes selected to the NBA All-Star Game?

34. Who published the first book of rules for women's basketball in 1901?

35. Who is the winningest Jewish major-league baseball manager?

36. Which early 18th Century boxer is reputed to have invented the uppercut?

37. In what country was NBA player and executive Ernie Grunfeld born?

38. Name the player who was a member of both the NFL's Pittsburgh Pirates and major-league baseball's St. Louis Browns in the 1930s.

39. How many gold medals were won by Jewish athletes at the first modern Olympics in Athens in 1896?
   a) 1
   b) 3
   c) 6
   d) 8

40. What former University of Nevada-Las Vegas basketball player is the all-time leading scorer for Maccabi Tel Aviv?

41. Ed Newman, a four-time All-Pro guard for the Miami Dolphins in the 1980s, was the Atlantic Coast Conference heavyweight wrestling champion at what college?
   a) Duke
   b) Wake Forest
   c) North Carolina State
   d) Maryland

42. Who was the only Jewish woman tennis player ever to reach the final of a Wimbledon singles event?
   a) Andrea Leand
   b) Julie Heldman

c) Elise Burgin
d) Angela Buxton

43. Who hit the final home run in the history of the Philadelphia Athletics?

44. Which one of these world title boxing matches did not pair two Jewish fighters?
   a) Benny Leonard vs. Charlie White, July 5, 1920
   b) Benny Bass vs. Red Chapman, Sept. 12, 1927
   c) Mushy Callahan vs. Jackie Berg, Feb. 18, 1930
   d) Al Singer vs. Sammy Mandell, July 17, 1930

45. Herb Rich had 29 career interceptions, the most by a Jewish NFL player. At what university was he an all-Southeastern Conference running back in 1948 and 1949?

46. Who was the first Jewish head coach of the Oakland Raiders?

47. Who scored the first basket in the history of the Basketball Association of America, forerunner of the NBA?
   a) Ossie Schechtman
   b) Philip Farbman
   c) Norm Greckin
   d) Art Spector

48. Who played shortstop for Columbia University in the first national telecast of a sporting event in 1939?

49. Which college star was the 1997 first draft pick of the Los Angeles Sparks of the WNBA?
   a) Anita Kaplan, Stanford
   b) Jamila Wideman, Stanford
   c) Orly Grossman, Connecticut
   d) Limor Mizrachi, Maryland

50. Who was the only Jewish athlete to light

the torch at an Olympics opening ceremony?

51. Who was the first Jewish switch-hitter to play in the major leagues?

52. Which one of these baseball players with a Biblical last name was Jewish?
   a) Wally Moses
   b) Mose Solomon
   c) Mike Mordecai
   d) Babe Ruth

53. Middleweight champion Al McCoy began his boxing career with the second-longest unbeaten streak in history. How many fights did he win before suffering his first defeat?
   a) 67
   b) 89
   c) 139
   d) 152

54. What was the first year in which the opposing basketball coaches in the National Invitation Tournament final were both Jewish?
   a) 1949
   b) 1951
   c) 1987
   d) 1999

55. Who was the first Israeli to qualify for an Olympic track and field event final?

56. Who was the first Jewish major-leaguer to play baseball in Japan?
   a) Norm Miller
   b) Richie Scheinblum
   c) Don Taussig
   d) Gabe Kapler

57. Who is the only Jewish boxer to fight for the world heavyweight title in the modern era?

58. In 1931, Baroness Maud Rosenbaum

achieved a No. 2 national ranking in Italy in what sport or event?
   a) tennis
   b) golf
   c) 400-meter run
   d) 100-meter backstroke

59. Name the coach who led LSU to NCAA baseball championships in 1991, 1993, 1996 and 1997.

60. Barney Dreyfuss arranged to have his team face the Boston Pilgrims in the first World Series in 1903. What team did Dreyfuss own?

61. Who was the former Olympic champion who served as chief timekeeper when Roger Bannister ran the first sub-4-minute mile on May 6, 1954?

62. Who was the first Jewish boxer to win a world title under modern rules?

63. Henry Laskau won 42 national championships, the most ever by an American athlete. What event was his specialty?

64. Who was the first figure skater to complete a free-skate program while accompanied by music?

65. Which one of these major-league pitchers played in the Mexican League under the name Pablo Garcia?
   a) Izzy Goldstein
   b) Syd Cohen
   c) Moe Savransky
   d) Cy Malis

66. Sam Balter and four of his college teammates were among the United States participants in the first Olympic basketball competition at the 1936 Games in Berlin. What college did Balter attend?

67. In which sport was Sylvia Wene selected Professional of the Year in 1956 and 1960?

68. What member of the 1960 World Champion Pittsburgh Pirates' coaching staff only participated in home games?

69. What Jewish boxer appeared in the film "Abbott and Costello Meet the Keystone Cops"?

70. Albert "Dolly" Stark, who coached basketball at Dartmouth from 1929–36 and 1945–46, was better known as:
   a) NBA team owner
   b) tennis pro
   c) fight promoter
   d) baseball umpire

71. Nathan Abrams of the Green Bay Packers scored a touchdown in his only professional game in 1921. How did he score?
   a) rushing
   b) receiving
   c) punt return
   d) interception return

72. Who was the first winner of baseball's Most Valuable Player award to be selected unanimously?

73. Who was the first Israeli to earn an Olympic medal?

74. Paul "Twister" Steinberg of Syracuse became the first Jewish professional basketball player in 1900. At what college did he coach from 1910-12?
   a) Columbia
   b) Brown
   c) Cornell
   d) Syracuse

75. Name the NFL quarterback with a Jewish mother and Native American father who appeared in the film "Paper Lion."

76. Which one of these baseball players has not had his uniform number retired?
   a) Hank Greenberg (5), Tigers
   b) Sandy Koufax (32), Dodgers
   c) Sid Gordon (20), Giants
   d) Jimmie Reese (50), Angels

77. Faina Melnik of the Soviet Union, Lili Henoch of Germany and Lilian Copeland of the United States each held world records in which track and field event?
   a) high jump
   b) discus
   c) 800 meters
   d) 400-meter hurdles

78. Who was the first Jewish player in the National Hockey League?

79. Name the boxer who participated in 1,309 fights, the most professional bouts in history by one fighter.

80. After the Milwaukee Bucks won a coin flip for rights to the first draft pick in 1969 and selected Lew Alcindor (Kareem Abdul-Jabbar), who did the Phoenix Suns take with the second pick?

81. Who is the only Jewish player to appear in a game with the Montreal Expos?

82. Who was the first Jewish player to appear in a college football game?

83. Merv Pregulman, the Green Bay Packers' first-round draft pick in 1944, played for which Big Ten Conference college?
   a) Wisconsin
   b) Michigan
   c) Illinois
   d) Minnesota

84. Who was the first Jewish coach to lead a team to an NBA title?
   a) Red Holzman

b) Red Auerbach
c) Lester Harrison
d) Eddie Gottlieb

85. Gerard Blitz, son and nephew of Olympic swimming and water polo medalists Maurice and Gerard Blitz of Belgium, founded what chain of resorts in 1950 in Mallorca, Spain?

86. What was the first year in which Israel was represented at the Winter Olympics?
  a) 1952
  b) 1956
  c) 1984
  d) 1994

87. Who was the only Jewish winner of the Boston Marathon?

88. Who was the shortest player in the history of professional football?

89. Who is the shortest member of the National Basketball Hall of Fame?

90. Who was the shortest player in the history of the American Basketball Association?

91. Fred Oberlander won national titles representing four different countries in what sport?

92. What former Wolverines football player designed Michigan Stadium's yellow "Block M" and the school's basketball arena?

93. Which one of these major-league baseball players did not attend the University of Alabama?
  a) Max Rosenfeld
  b) Fred Sington
  c) Alan Koch
  d) Andy Cohen

94. What five-man United States team that finished fourth in the 1956 Olympics in Melbourne was comprised entirely of Jewish athletes?

95. Marty Hogan became the first millionaire in what sport?
  a) bowling
  b) racquetball
  c) billiards
  d) squash

96. Abe Saperstein, owner of the Harlem Globetrotters basketball team, was a scout for which major-league baseball team?
  a) Chicago Cubs
  b) Cleveland Indians
  c) Chicago White Sox
  d) St. Louis Cardinals

97. Who was the first winner of the Hermann Trophy, presented to the nation's outstanding college soccer player?

98. The Gladys Heldman Award is presented annually to the top college senior in which women's sport?

99. Who is the only Jewish switch-hitter to bat .300 for an entire season?

100. Name the player who holds the Rose Bowl record for longest punt return.

101. Who had the last hit in the final baseball game at Philadelphia's Baker Bowl?

102. Between 1957 and 1976, Maria Itkina of the Soviet Union set six world records in which track and field event?
  a) 110 high hurdles
  b) 400 meters
  c) heptathlon
  d) javelin

103. Ken Holtzman posted a 9-0 record in 1967 while pitching in just 12 games for the

Chicago Cubs. Why did Holtzman only pitch on weekends?
- a) He was a full-time college student
- b) He was on active military duty
- c) He was a Canadian citizen who had a restricted work visa
- d) The Cubs experimented with a seven-man pitching rotation

104. What religious object did junior welterweight Jackie "Kid" Berg hang on the ring post before each fight?

105. Which country was the first to be represented by an all-Jewish squad in an Olympic team sport?
- a) Canada
- b) Israel
- c) Hungary
- d) Austria

106. Who is the only Jewish athlete to carry the United States flag during the parade of nations at an Olympic Games opening ceremony?

107. Who is the only Jewish college basketball player to appear in an NCAA Final Four game and coach a team in the NCAA tournament?

108. Tennis players Brad Gilbert, Robbie Weiss and Andrew Sznajder all earned All-America status while being coached by Alan Fox at which university?
- a) UCLA
- b) Stanford
- c) Pepperdine
- d) Georgia

109. The Cy Kaselman Trophy is presented annually to basketball's most accurate free-throw shooter among Division I colleges in what city?
- a) New York
- b) Chicago
- c) Cincinnati

d) Philadelphia

110. What Hall of Famer gave up nine career home runs to Hank Greenberg, the most of any pitcher?

111. Who scored the first penalty-shot goal in a World Cup soccer final

112. Alex Schoenbaum, a former Ohio State football player, opened the first of what restaurant chain in Charleston, w.va., in 1947?

113. What major U.S. horse racetrack is named after its Jewish founder?

114. Between 1965 and 1973, gymnasts Mike Jacobson, Steve Cohen (twice) and Marshall Avener each won all-around NCAA gymnastics championships. For which college did they compete?
- a) Illinois
- b) UCLA
- c) Penn State
- d) Springfield

115. Larry Zeidel was sent to the minor leagues after playing for the Chicago Black Hawks during the 1953–54 season. How many seasons did it take for Zeidel to return to the NHL?
- a) 9
- b) 11
- c) 12
- d)13

116. What American Basketball Association team used a Jewish Community Center for its practice court?

117. Hugo Friend, the judge at the trial in which the Chicago Black Sox players were acquitted of fixing the World Series in 1919, won an Olympic bronze medal for the United States in 1906 in which sport?
- a) epee fencing

b) long jump
c) 800-meter freestyle swimming
d) team gymnastics

118. In the 1930s, swimmer Paul Friesel popularized a new stroke that is now included in Olympic events. Which stroke?
a) freestyle
b) backstroke
c) breaststroke
d) butterfly

119. Which of these NBA awards is not named after a Jew?
a) Most Valuable Player
b) Coach of the Year
c) Rookie of the Year
d) Sixth-Man Award

120. Louis Wolfson owned which Triple Crown-winning horse?
a) Gallant Fox
b) Whirlaway
c) Secretariat
d) Affirmed

121. Jabez "Jappy" Wolffe of Great Britain holds the record for the most unsuccessful attempts to swim the English Channel. How many times did he fail to reach France?
a) 14
b) 17
c) 21
d) 27

122. Jimmy Jacobs, a boxing manager and member of the International Boxing Hall of Fame, won every match he played between 1955 and 1969 in what sport?

123. Name the Danish fencer who holds the longest Olympic Games career – 40 years between his first and last Olympic participation.

124. Ron Rothstein, first coach of the NBA's Miami Heat, played at what college?
a) Rhode Island
b) Vermont
c) Northeastern
d) Maine

125. In 1963, Jewish coaches led their teams to both the National Football League and American Football League championship games. Name the coaches.

126. Which Jewish player hit home runs while pinch-hitting for both Frank Robinson (586 career home runs) and Tony Perez (379 career home runs)?

127. The Bobbie Rosenfeld Trophy is presented annually to the top female athlete in which country?
a) Australia
b) Canada
c) Israel
d) South Africa

128. Who was the first Jewish player to lead the Dodgers in single-season home runs?
a) Shawn Green
b) Cal Abrams
c) Goody Rosen
d) Steve Yeager

129. Who was the first Olympic athlete to win medals in two different sports?

130. When was the first season in which there were no Jewish players in the NBA?
a) 1954–55
b) 1967–68
c) 1974–75
d) 2000–01

131. Name the college basketball player who led the nation in assists in 1998–99.

132. Rosenblatt Stadium in Omaha, Neb.,

named after former mayor Johnny Rosenblatt, hosts what annual event?

133. Name the catcher who holds the Southern Association record of hitting in 49 consecutive games at Mobile in 1945.

134. Bluethenthal Field, the airport in Wilmington, N.C., is named after Arthur Bluethenthal. At what college did the All-American center play football?
   a) Duke
   b) Penn
   c) North Carolina
   d) Princeton

135. Barney Pelty pitched 22 career shutouts for the St. Louis Browns. How many times was he on the losing end of a 1-0 game?
   a) 7
   b) 9
   c) 11
   d) 18

136. Name the deaf fencer who won medals in five straight Olympics, including gold in 1964.

137. Saul Rogovin led the American League with a 2.78 earned run average despite pitching for two different teams in 1951. Name the teams.
   a) Tigers and Browns
   b) Indians and Tigers
   c) Tigers and White Sox
   d) Indians and White Sox

138. Who participated in the first College Football All-Star Game against the NFL in 1934 as a player and in the last game in 1976 as an assistant coach?

139. Name the University of Rhode Island's all-time scoring leader who twice played for four different American Basketball Association teams in one season.

140. How many Jewish major-league baseball players attended Fairfax High School in Los Angeles?

141. Who was the first Division I college basketball player to shoot better than 90 percent from the foul line over an entire season?

142. Tennis player Ilona Kloss won the 1976 U.S. Open women's doubles and the 1976 French Open mixed doubles titles. What country is she from?

143. Who was the New York Mets' starting catcher in their first-ever home game?

144. Which one of these boxers never held a European professional title?
   a) Ted "Kid" Lewis
   b) Harry Mizler
   c) Bob Olin
   d) Al Phillips

145. Who led the International League with a 2.41 earned run average with Newark in 1946, the same year he pitched in his only two major-league games with the New York Yankees?

146. Joe Magidsohn, an All-American halfback in 1909 and 1910, was the first Jewish athlete to win a varsity letter at which Big Ten college?
   a) Wisconsin
   b) University of Chicago
   c) Purdue
   d) Michigan

147. Who is the only Jewish player to return a blocked punt for a touchdown in the NFL?

148. Who has the most NFL career touchdown catches among Jewish receivers?

149. Shaun Tomson appeared in the films North Shore (1987), Endless Summer 2

(1994) and In God's Hands (1998). In what sport was Tomson a world champion?
   a) sailing
   b) cliff diving
   c) surfing
   d) sea kayaking

150. In 1991, Syracuse pitcher Steve Wapnick led the International League with 20 in what category?
   a) wins
   b) saves
   c) hit batters
   d) balks

151. Who is the only Jewish athlete to carry the flag of an Arab country at an Olympics opening ceremony?

152. In 1995, Jill Gelfenbien of Connecticut was a member of NCAA Final Four teams in two different sports. Which ones?
   a) lacrosse and field hockey
   b) softball and soccer
   c) basketball and soccer
   d) basketball and lacrosse

153. How many years elapsed between Herman Barron's first and last major golf victories?

154. Who has the most career victories for France in Davis Cup tennis play?

155. Name the player for Rochester of the International League who was named Minor League Player of the Year in 1966.

156. The Hart Trophy, presented to the National Hockey League MVP, is named after Dr. David Hart. His son Cecil was head coach of which team?
   a) Toronto Maple Leafs
   b) Victoria Cougars
   c) Detroit Red Wings
   d) Montreal Canadiens

157. Who holds the Pro Bowlers Association record for most tournament titles in one year with eight?

158. Who was the first tennis player to play for four straight NCAA team champions?

159. Name the player who led all of organized baseball with a .439 batting average in 1938.

160. Who was the first coach of the NBA team that eventually became the Atlanta Hawks?

QUIZ ANSWERS

1. Golda Meir.
2. Guy Zinn of the New York Highlanders on April 20, 1912. He walked and later scored the first run.
3. Dave Kufeld, in the 10th round by the Portland Trail Blazers in 1980.
4. Ty Cobb.
5. Herb Flam.
6. Algeria.
7. Monte Carlo Rally.
8. Illinois.
9. Baltimore Stallions.
10. Camden Yards, Baltimore.
11. Russia. His real name was Morris Billingkoff.
12. Nadiv Henefeld.
13. Marshall Goldberg of Pittsburgh and Sid Luckman of Columbia.
14. Swimming.
15. Marty Fleckman, 1967
16. Lehigh.
17. Jesse Baker was born Michael Myron Silverman.
18. Half a salami.
19. 499.
20. Barry Leibowitz, Long Island University, by the Pittsburgh Pipers.
21. Randy Grossman, Pittsburgh Steelers, 7-yard pass reception in Super Bowl x vs. Dallas.
22. Providence
23. Shawn Green.
24. Bruce "Mouse" Strauss.
25. Four – Max Posnack, Max Kinsbrunner, Allie Shuckman, and Jack Gerson.
26. Joe Ginsberg of Detroit caught Virgil Trucks' 1-0 no-hitter against Washington on May 15, 1952.
27. Table tennis.
28. Harry Newman, New York Giants vs. Chicago Bears.
29. Cincinnati Reds
30. Alan Mayer, San Diego Sockers, 1982-83 season.
31. Bob Stein, Kansas City Chiefs linebacker, Super Bowl iv.

32. Referee.
33. 12.
34. Senda Berenson Abbott
35. Harold "Lefty" Phillips, 1969-71 California Angels (222 wins, 225 losses).
36. Dutch Sam (Samuel Elias).
37. Romania.
38. Jim Levey.
39. Eight – Alfred Flatow of Germany won three gold medals and Felix Flatow of Germany won two in gymnastics. Alfred Hajos-Guttman of Hungary won two and Dr. Paul Neumann of Austria captured one in swimming.
40. Mickey Berkowitz.
41. Duke.
42. Angela Buxton, 1956.
43. Lou Limmer.
44. Al Singer vs. Sammy Mandell. Mandell was not Jewish.
45. Vanderbilt.
46. Marty Feldman, 1961.
47. Ossie Schechtman, New York Knicks, 1946.
48. Sid Luckman.
49. Jamila Wideman.
50. Alain Calmat, French figure skater, Grenoble, 1964.
51. Ed Mensor, Pittsburgh Pirates, 1912
52. Mose Solomon, who appeared in two games for the 1923 New York Giants.
53. 139.
54. 1999. Ben Braun's California Golden Bears defeated Larry Shyatt's Clemson Tigers 61–60.
55. Esther Rot, who finished sixth in the 100-meter hurdles in 1976.
56. Richie Scheinblum, 1975–76
57. Abe Simon, who lost in six rounds to Joe Louis in 1941 and in 13 rounds to Louis in 1942.
58. Tennis.
59. Skip Bertman.
60. Pittsburgh Pirates.
61. Harold Abrahams.

62. Harry Harris won the bantamweight title in 1901.

63. Race walking.

64. Lili Kronberger of Hungary, 1911.

65. Syd Cohen – an El Paso, Texas, native who spoke fluent Spanish.

66. UCLA.

67. Bowling.

68. Len Levy. Travel interfered with his automobile dealership a block from Forbes Field.

69. "Slapsy" Maxie Rosenbloom.

70. National League umpire.

71. Interception return.

72. Al Rosen, Cleveland Indians, 1953.

73. Yael Arad won a silver medal in women's judo in 1992.

74. Cornell

75. Karl Sweetan

76. Sid Gordon.

77. Discus.

78. Samuel Rothschild, Montreal Maroons, 1924

79. Abe "Newsboy" Hollandersky.

80. Neal Walk, University of Florida.

81. Steve Ratzer, who pitched in 13 games during 1981 and 1982.

82. Moses Henry Epstein, for Columbia against Rutgers on Nov. 12, 1870.

83. Michigan.

84. Eddie Gottlieb, Philadelphia Warriors, 1947.

85. Club Med.

86. Figure skater Misha Shmerkin was Israel's first Winter Olympian in 1994.

87. Michael Spring, 1904

88. Jack Shapiro, 5-foot-1, 119 pounds, who appeared in one game for the Staten Island Stapletons in 1929.

89. Barney Sedran, 5-foot-4.

90. Larry Brown, 5-foot-9.

91. Oberlander won heavyweight freestyle wrestling titles for Austria, France, Great Britain, and Canada.

92. Dan Dworsky.

93. Alan Koch pitched for Auburn.

94. Fencing, men's team foil (Albert Axelrod, Byron Krieger, Nathaniel Lubell, Daniel Bukantz, and Harold Goldsmith).

95. Racquetball.

96. Cleveland Indians.

97. Dov Markus, Long Island University, 1967.

98. Tennis.

99. Richie Scheinblum, who batted .300 in 450 at-bats for the Kansas City Royals in 1972.

100. Al Hoisch, UCLA, 103 yards against Illinois in 1947.

101. Phil Weintraub.

102. 400 meters.

103. Holtzman was on active military duty.

104. A tallis

105. Six members of the Montreal YMHA and coach Moe Abromowitz comprised the Canadian men's basketball team in 1948.

106. Norman Armitage, fencer, 1952 and 1956.

107. Eddie Fogler played for North Carolina when it finished second in 1968 and fourth in 1969. He has coached Wichita State, Vanderbilt, and South Carolina in the tournament.

108. Pepperdine.

109. Philadelphia.

110. Lefty Grove

111. Johan Neeskins, Netherlands vs. West Germany, 1974.

112. Shoney's Big Boy.

113. Belmont Park, named after August Belmont Sr.

114. Penn State.

115. 13. Zeidel played for the expansion Philadelphia Flyers in 1967-68.

116. The Virginia Squires practiced at the Norfolk JCC.

117. Long jump (Myer Prinstein won the gold medal).

118. Butterfly.

119. Sixth-Man Award. (MVP – Maurice Podoloff Trophy; Coach – Red Auerbach Trophy; Rookie – Eddie Gottlieb Trophy.)

120. Affirmed won the Kentucky Derby, Preakness and Belmont in 1978.

121. 21. In 1908 he was within 300 yards of shore, and came within a quarter mile of his goal in 1919.

122. Handball.

123. Ivan Osiier, 1908 to 1948.

124. Rhode Island.

125. Allie Sherman, whose New York Giants beat the Chicago Bears 14-10 in the NFL championship game, and Sid Gilman, whose San Diego Chargers lost to the Boston Patriots 51-10 in the AFL title game.

126. Art Shamsky of the Cincinnati Reds, batting for Robinson against the Mets on May 2, 1965 and batting for Perez against the Cubs on Aug. 31, 1966.

127. Canada.

128. Goody Rosen, 12 home runs in 1945.

129. Otto Herschman of Austria won a bronze in swimming in 1896 and a silver in fencing in 1912.

130. 2000–01. Danny Schayes retired after being released by the Minnesota Timberwolves.

131. Doug Gottlieb, Oklahoma State.

132. College World Series.

133. Harry Chozen. In two games during the streak he had pinch hits, and on two other occasions he only had one at-bat in a game.

134. Princeton, 1910–12.

135. Nine.

136. Ildiko Rejto of Hungary.

137. Tigers and White Sox.

138. Sid Gilman.

139. Steve Chubin, 1968–69 (Los Angeles Stars, Minnesota Pipers, Indiana Pacers, and New York Nets) and 1969–70 (New York Nets, Pittsburgh Condors, Indiana Pacers, and Kentucky Colonels).

140. Five. (Larry Sherry, Norm Sherry, Al Silvera, Barry Latman, and Mike Epstein)

141. Steve Nisenson, Hofstra, 1964. He shot 91.6 percent.

142. South Africa.

143. Joe Ginsberg.

144. Bob Olin was from the United States.

145. Herb Karpel.

146. Michigan

147. Steve Tannen, New York Jets vs. Buffalo Bills, 1970.

148. San Francisco 49ers tight end John Frank, 10.

149. Surfing.

150. Saves.

151. Raoul Meir Barouch, Tunisian fencer, 1960 Olympics in Rome.

152. Basketball and soccer.

153. 29 years. Barron won the 1934 Philadelphia Open and the 1963 World Series of Golf.

154. Pierre Darmon, 44.

155. Mike Epstein.

156. Montreal Canadiens.

157. Mark Roth, 1978.

158. Paul Goldstein, Stanford.

159. Murray Franklin, at Beckley of the Mountain State League.

160. Red Auerbach, Tri-City Blackhawks, 1949–50.

Index

Founded in 1892, the American Jewish Historical Society fosters aware-
ness and appreciation of Jewish heritage in the United States and serves as a
leading scholarly research resource by collecting, preserving and disseminat-
ing materials documenting American Jewish history. The Society's library,
archives, photograph, and art and artifacts collections cover virtually every
aspect of the American Jewish experience from the 1500s to the present.

AJHS collections include a wide variety of materials on Jews
in American sports. The Society's website, www.ajhs.org, con-
tains useful information on the topic and links to the Soci-
ety-sponsored Jewish sports site, www.jewsinsports.org.

For more than a century, the American Jewish Historical Society has been
and remains "responsible for the future of the American Jewish past."